Black American Witness

Reports From The Front

By Earl Caldwell

Published by

Lion House Publishing
1119 Staples St., N.E.,
Washington, D.C., 20002

Editors: Lurma Rackley
Kenneth Walker

LIBRARY OF CONGRESS CATALOG NUMBER
94-73095

ISBN
1-886446-10-5

Introduction

Earl Caldwell has been a leading journalist for over 30 years.

As a journalist, Caldwell has covered some of the most important events in contemporary American history. There were a number of occasions, such as the assassination of Dr. Martin Luther King Jr., when he was the only journalist present.

So unique was his reporting on the Black Panther Party in the 1960s, that J. Edgar Hoover's FBI, requested, then insisted, that Earl Caldwell serve as a bureau spy on Panther activities. When he refused, the FBI then set about destroying Caldwell's relationship with the Panthers by publicly demanding that he honor a grand jury subpoena to question him about the leaders of the Panthers.

This refusal led to a landmark First Amendment case that, eventually, was decided by the U.S. Supreme Court. His stand also led to the enactment throughout the United States of "shield laws," designed as legal cover for reporters' rights to protect confidential sources.

He began writing a column at *The Washington Star* in the 1970s and continued it at The New York Daily News from 1979 until 1994. One of the city's most prolific columnists, Caldwell wrote three times a week.

Before joining The News, Mr. Caldwell was a national correspondent on the staff of The New York Times. Before joining the national staff there, Mr. Caldwell worked as a local reporter, covering a wide variety of stories in the city.

Earl Caldwell is a product of a small town, who made his name in big-city journalism. He is a native of Clearfield, a town of 10,000 in the mountains of Pennsylvania. He attended public schools there, and later the University of Buffalo. His first job was with his hometown paper, *The Clearfield Progress.* He moved to *The Intelligencer Journal* in Lancaster, Pa.

Earl Caldwell got his start in big-city journalism when Al Neuharth, who went on to found *USA Today*, hired him as a reporter for the Democrat and Chronicle in Rochester, N.Y. He left Rochester in 1966 to join *The New York Herald Tribune.* After a brief stint with *The New York Post,* Mr. Caldwell joined *The New York Times.*

Mr. Caldwell was a founding director of the Institute for Journalism Education. The Institute has been the largest single supplier of minority talent to daily newspapers. Mr. Caldwell also is a director of the Reporters Committee for Freedom of the Press.

In his columns, Earl Caldwell continued the reporter's tradition. Rather than merely offer his views on the events of the day, Earl Caldwell continued to report them -- from the front.

His columns illuminated events in the lives of people both ordinary and famous. They constitute the most comprehensive record available of how American cities, children, unions, health care, police and race relations, got to where they are today.

He genuinely is a Black American Witness.

Table of Contents

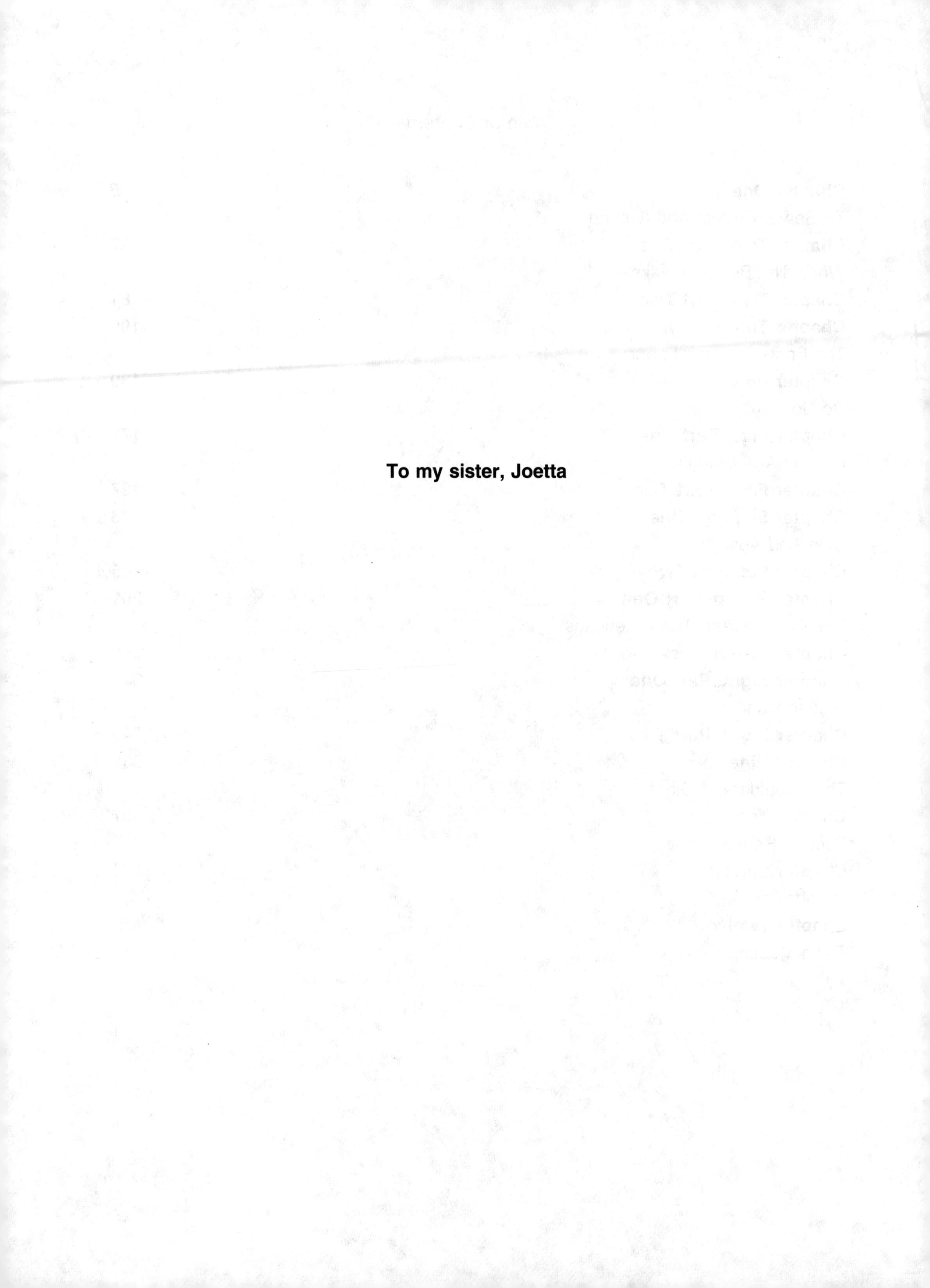

To my sister, Joetta

Chapter One

TO SERVE, PROTECT AND DEFEND

Editor's Note

No institution in American society has a more wide-spread, ongoing, bloody conflict with African Americans and other minorities than urban police departments. From Watts to Rodney King, urban communities throughout the nation have had to pay a heavy price -- in blood, justice, stability and economic development. This chapter contains some of Earl Caldwell's writings on the prevailing experience of African Americans and others -- not only with police departments -- but with various aspects of the criminal justice system. According to a number of studies in the early 1990s, one in four African American males in major urban areas were said to be under some jurisdiction of the criminal justice system.

Given the virtual state of war that exists between police departments and many African American communities, there is nothing surprising about these surveys.

1979

EVEN BEFORE THE DEMONSTRATION was to begin, the crowd began to gather on the sidewalk across from the Criminal Courts Building.

There were teenagers, men and women of all ages. They came with slogans they would later shout, and signs made by hand. As the noon hour approached, their numbers began to swell. The police, who had stood off at a distance, moved closer. Soon, they began to take lumber that was painted blue and they used it to build barricades.

The demonstration was a show of support for Bruce Wright, the judge, and an endorsement of his decision to free, without bail, a young man who was accused of knifing a decoy policeman posing as a derelict.

What came together on the city streets, down the canyon from City hall, was much more than that. It was a clear signal of the kind of anger and frustration that is building up now in the City of New York.

It was aimed as much at the mayor as it was at the Police Department. It was as much about the lack of jobs and housing as it was about high bail. And it is growing.

Late in the morning, while the demonstration built, Judge Wright sat in a courtroom on the second floor.

In his black robe, he looked out from behind dark-rimmed glasses. There was a matter before him involving two youths who were Black. They stood back, behind the lawyers who were at the bench in discussions with Judge Wright.

It was a big courtroom, but most of the seats were empty. There were 34 people in the spectator section. Except for one, all the cops were White.

It is that way, almost every day, in every criminal courtroom in the city. It is that way in the prisons too. That was a part of what yesterday's demonstration was all about.

A young Black woman from Brooklyn, a law student at Hofstra, sat on the bench next to Judge Wright and watched him work.

Judge Wright has made us stop now and look at the judicial system. It has forced us to take a hard look at what is happening in the city. Something too important to be ignored was building.

Now the discussion is bail. One morning last week, Judge Wright was in his office, talking about a speech he had made in a neighborhood out in Queens.

It was a speech about bail. When he finished, Wright said, another judge who was in the audience got up.

"You know what he said," Judge Wright was saying. "He said that in his courtroom, any time anyone who is charged with armed robbery is brought before him, the bail starts at $10,000."

Now in telling the story, he paused. "Nobody says anything about that," Judge Wright said. "It's against the law to use bail as preventive detention. These are the kind of judges, who should be investigated."

As the rally came together, a few blocks away on the steps of City Hall a minister stood with a woman whose name was Betty Shephard.

It was her brother, Jerome Singleton, who was arrested and charged with knifing the cop. She went to City Hall with the minister, the Rev. Al Sharpton, to ask that the case be transferred out of New York.

"I want my brother to get a fair trial," she said. "He deserves a fair trial." She would not say anything else.

But the Rev. Sharpton did. He accused the mayor and the news media of interfering, of prejudicing public opinion against Singleton. He said that it is impossible now for Singleton to get a fair trial in New York.

"Where do you want the trail held?" he was asked.

"Anywhere but here," he said. "The further away, the better."

The rally got under way. The demonstration used up the entire block in front of the Criminal Courts Building. It was a noisy gathering and the chant now was "Bruce is right, Koch is bizarre."

The demonstration was organized by the Black United Front, out of Brooklyn. Rev. Herbert Daughtry, head of the BUF, was the first to speak.

All that he said drew loud applause, especially when he called for a federal investigation of the city's Police Department, the Manhattan district attorney's office, and the entire criminal justice system. Of the mayor, Daughtry said: "He can't back away now. His position is already out there."

Once it had been lonely for the Rev. Daughtry. Once he was out there pretty much alone, saying that bail was being misused, that the Police Department should be investigated, and that the mayor was the center of the problems that are with us now.

But the Rev. Daughtry is not alone now. It is no longer just a few. Now there are many voices. That was evident yesterday on the streets of New York. It would be good if the mayor began to listen.

1979

NOW, THERE ARE ONLY the photographs. It is all they have left.

Grace Rodriguez carries hers in a large brown envelope. They are big color photographs stuffed inside a brown envelope. When Grace Rodriguez tries to explain what happened to her husband, tears well in her eyes. The words stick in her throat. She takes the envelope, thrusts it out and says, "Here, you look and then you'll know what I'm talking about."

It is the same with the other woman, Grace Funches. She sits in the living room of her apartment, which is on the ground floor of a rotting old tenement in Harlem. When the words give out, she mentions the photographs.

"You look at the pictures," Grace Funches says. "The pictures don't lie. You just look at 'em and you'll see."

The photographs that the women carry are pictures of dead men -- dead men who were their husbands. Both men were in the hands of the police when they died. The two women are certain that their husbands were murdered.

They are the worst kind of photographs. They are pictures of bodies that are covered with scars, cuts and bruises. It is impossible to look at the photographs, and not understand why the women believe that their husbands were beaten to death.

Peter Funches died last June. It was on a Sunday, Father's Day. The police said that his death was the result of an automobile accident. Late Saturday night, Funches was seen by the police driving the wrong way on a one-way street. A chase ensued. It ended up in the Bronx. The police said the car that Funches was driving slammed into a wall. They said the car hit the wall with such force that the injuries he suffered were fatal.

Then the police go on to claim, that despite these fatal car injuries, that Funches resisted arrest, that he came at them with a knife. To arrest him, they say, force had to be used. Funches died. He was dead when the police from the 46th Precinct delivered him to the Bronx-Lebanon Hospital.

It was Sunday morning when the chase involving Peter Funches and the police came through the quiet block of W. 180th St., in the block just before Andrews Ave. There was a commotion. The people who live there were aroused by it. They went to their windows. Those who looked out were frightened by what they saw.

The witnesses said the police dragged Peter Funches from his car. They said the police pulled him out onto the ground, and repeatedly kicked him. When they finally dragged him away, witnesses say, he appeared to be unconscious.

The witnesses who saw what happened talked about it. They spoke to reporters. Some called Mrs. Funches. Soon a protest mounted. There was an investigation. Finally, the issue was put before the grand jury in the Bronx.

In the Bronx, a young assistant district attorney, Nicholas Iacovetta was assigned to handle the case. For weeks, he tried to piece together what had happened. When he was ready, the case was presented to the grand jury. In all, he called 47 witnesses. After the grand jury heard them, the grand jury decided that there was no cause for charges to be brought against the policemen involved.

It didn't end there. Maybe it was the photographs.

Mrs. Funches put the photographs of her husband's body in the hands of the Rev. Herbert Daughtry. She knew that he had been protesting what he believed to be abuses by the police. She asked him to help and Daughtry brought in his organization, the Black United Front.

Last week, during the lunch hour on Wednesday, Daughtry and his people were in Foley Square outside the Federal Courthouse. They had the pictures of Peter Funches's brutalized body there with them. After their protest, they went to the office of the U.S. Attorney.

Dennison Young, the chief of the civil rights division, told them, yes, there were questions about the death of Peter Funches. He said that his office was looking into the death.

"What we really want," the Rev. Daughtry said, "is an investigation of the entire police department. We need the kind of investigation here that the Justice Department is conducting in Philadelphia. There have been too many of these kinds of killings. Somebody has got to put a stop to it."

Late in the afternoon yesterday, Grace Funches was in the living room of her apartment. "Nothing will happen," she said. "They didn't murder my husband. I say they executed him."

She sat on a wine-colored couch with a knit sweater across her lap. Her daughter Thomasina, who is 17, sat next to her. Grace Funches has six children. All except Thomasina are boys.

"The death certificate said that he died at the hospital," she said of her husband. "He didn't die at no hospital. They told me that. They beat him with crowbars. They didn't use no blackjacks. I can tell they used crowbars by the hole in his head. It was bigger than my two fists."

Her husband was a veteran. He had served in Vietnam. When he came home he was sick. "A mental disorder," the wife said. "But he never bothered anyone. Nobody can say a bad word about him because he never bothered anybody."

She talked about the night he died. "I called the police," she said. "Peter was sick. When he went out, I was worried about him. He shouldn't have been driving. That's why I called the police. I didn't know they would murder him."

Grace Rodriguez's husband, whose name was Louis also died in the 46th Precinct in the Bronx. He had been involved in a disturbance at a grocery store. The police were called. The reports say he resisted arrest. It happened on the 14th of July, the day after his 37th birthday. He died while in the custody of the police.

Grace Rodriguez lives in a small apartment over a delicatessen in Throgs Neck, Bronx. She keeps the photographs in a small pouch that she uses to keep any information she can find about her husband's death.

She sat on a chair, and fingered a yellow piece of paper that was the death certificate. She had been separated from her husband for three years. Her daughter, who is 6, was at school. In the afternoon, when she was alone, it was alright for her to cry.

"Every time they arrested him, they beat him up," she said. "The last time, they stole his pay check. You looked at him, and you saw a man. He wasn't the type to take anything. They killed him. I know it."

Up in the Bronx, Nicholas Iacovetta, the assistant district attorney, was busy digging into the killing of Louis Rodriguez. Now, he will put that case before the grand jury.

The two women keep going around with the photographs -- pictures which are powerful evidence. It is said that a picture is worth a thousand words. In any language, the pictures of the bodies of Peter Funches and Louis Rodriguez, make it crystal clear that something is wrong in the 46th Precinct.

1979

OUTSIDE THE PRECINCT, the cops were everywhere. They had put wooden barricades on the sidewalk. Behind them, all through the block, there was nothing but police, dressed in riot gear.

They had on dark-blue helmets. With their guns, they carried sticks the size of baseball bats. They were on the roof, across from the precinct, huddled in doorways. There were others in cars, trucks and other police vehicles that were doubled-parked on the side street.

All of it was out of the '60s, out of that time of turmoil. Now, as the darkness of Monday night closed in, it was here again in Brooklyn, in the City of York.

In a park down from the 79th Precinct station, there was a crowd that numbered more than a thousand, and the cops, although a block away, could hear the shouts that rose in the night.

Again at the center of the rising anger was a killing.

The victim who brought the crowd into the park was Luis Baez. He was 29, a Puerto Rican. He was shot to death outside a tenement where he lived with his mother.

Twenty-one police bullets left him dead on the sidewalk.

It is only a short distance from the station to the tenement where Baez was killed. All of it is a part of that section of Brooklyn known as Bedford-Stuyvesant.

On Monday night, while the emotion of the rally in the park grew across from the tenement where Baez was killed, a group of men stood in the evening outside the Mid-Clif auto body shop and talked.

There is no dispute as to what brought the police to Clifton Place last Wednesday night. Luis Baez'smother called the cops. He had been under psychiatric care at Kings County Hospital. He had been hospitalized for three months, and was released last May. On this night, his mother said that her son was slashing the tile on the kitchen floor. When she could not get him to stop, she called the police to ask for help.

Two officers responded. When the cops came, Baez ran out onto the fire escape. He had a pair of scissors. The police called for backup support.

Two officers went into the building and came out a window to try to talk Baez off the fire escape. Two others, the backup team, waited below, and tried to force him down. Neither Baez nor his mother speaks English. More police were called.

"There were about 12 or 14 of 'em here," a man in a blue T-shirt who stood in front of the auto shop said. "The two at the top, they pulled the fire escape up, and it released the safety, and it dropped, and (Baez) fell off."

The man pointed across the street: "He was standing right over there." The fire escape, when lowered, drops into a fenced area. It is an old, iron fence, partly broken, with much of the green paint chipped away by time and neglect.

"The mother tried to get him," the man said, "but they (the police) pushed her aside. He jumped over the fence. He dropped the scissors. But when he made his first step, that was it."

"What happened?"

"This one officer, he started to shoot. When his gun went off, it sounded like firecrackers. All of them started shooting."

The man shook his head. He had been there. On this night, the killing of Luis Baez was the action on the block. In the summertime in the city the streets are full and there are many witnesses. This did not bother the police.

"The way it happened," the man said, "it shouldn't have happened like that. When they got out of their cars, they had their guns out. They claim that he was attacking them. I was there. He wasn't attacking them. The way it happened, it's bad. They should have never done anything like that."

Around the corner in the housing projects, there was a young fellow in his 20s who was among those who stood on Clifton Place and saw Luis Baez die.

"Two gunshots could have done it. They could have shot him in the arm. You could tell he was scared. He was backing up. It was just like the paper said, it was unnecessary force. I can vouch for it. I was there.

Afterwards, the fellow said that he approached one of the cops, an officer who was Black. "He asked me if I knew anything about guns. I was in the army. I slept with guns. I was in artillery. They had clubs. They could have knocked him out."

After the killing was done, witnesses said the cops laughed.

"They were steady giggling," the fellow at the project said. "Like it was a big joke and everything. It was like a firing squad. They should of put a blindfold on him and a cigarette in his mouth. Then, it would have been right." He said that he didn't believe the cops would shoot. "They were all around him, standing with their guns pointed at him but they just blew him away. And I don't go against the police," he said. "I've got three uncles on the police force."

Now, as the police waited outside the precinct, on the roof, and in the cars and vans they use, lightning flashed in the sky. Rain began to fall.

On the speaker's platform in the park, Baez's father was talking. His words were in Spanish, but many understood because the crowd was a mixture of Black and Puerto Rican.

Next, the Rev. Herbert Daughtry took the microphone. He has been involved in many issues in the last year, but nothing has taken more of his time than protests against police killings.

He said the police had bottles, that others were waiting outside the park to start trouble. He questioned the wisdom of confronting the police. Others, young and angry, did not want to listen. Some of them began to leave the rally. They moved towards the precinct.

The rain began to come with force. Soon, the rally broke up, and there were a thousand marchers in the street. Police barricades were at the corner so the marchers sought another way to the station. They met more barricades so they looked for still another route, ignoring the rain. Somewhere the march dissolved, but there were too many youths on the street. They were aroused now. Soon the battle began. For hours, deep into the night, it was hit and run. There were victims. They staggered on the street, beaten and bloody.

Police commissioner Robert McGuire was saying that the killing of Baez was unfortunate and tragic, but it was too late for words. The use of police guns is out of control in the city of New York. There is something taking place within the Police Department that sorely needs looking into. There is the killing of Peter Funches in the Bronx that is in need of investigation. The same is true of the Rodriguez death that also occurred at the 46th Precinct in the Bronx.

Yesterday, out in Brooklyn, the district attorney was looking into the Baez killing. From Washington, the Attorney General said that he, too, will investigate. But it is not enough. There is a need now in New York for the kind of federal investigation of the police that is taking place in Philadelphia. Otherwise, the trouble that is in the streets may grow.

The battles in the streets in Brooklyn lasted through the night. But when you crossed the bridge, and came into Manhattan -- the New York of the haves -- it was another world. The streets were crowded. The night was filled with neon lights and laughter. Manhattan is the Big Apple. Out at the 79th Precinct, where the cops pushed aside their commander to get at the crowd, people on the streets were saying that it was worse than Mississippi.

1980

NOBODY CONNECTED WITH THE FBI had much to say. Not even Joseph J. McFarlane, the special agent who led the raid.

"What charges?" McFarlane said yesterday. "There were no charges. Nor have I been advised of any charges; not to this date I haven't."

"You haven't heard anything?" he was asked.

"I've heard the innuendo, the rumors going around that's all."

"And you're saying the FBI acted properly?"

"That's right. That's what I'm saying."

Uptown, in the building where it happened, Douglas Harris spent the gloomy morning that was yesterday in his study, in the rear of his apartment. His 2-year-old son, Toure, was nearby on the floor, busy with some pictures he was making with magic markers.

"There was no question that they were out of control," Harris said. "That's why I'm so proud of the way everyone here reacted; how calm everyone was. If the people here hadn't been so calm, somebody would have gotten hurt. There's no doubt about that."

The Harlem building where Douglas Harris lives is on Morningside Ave. Like a lot of buildings in Harlem, it has a rich past and some promise for the future. But right now, it is in the midst of hard times. It is another of the buildings in Harlem sorely in need.

In the early morning hours, nine days ago, the building was the scene of a raid conducted by the FBI that has become one of the hottest controversies in Harlem. The tenants say the FBI came in the middle of the night, armed with shotguns, pistols and machine guns, in a raid that Congressman Charles Rangel was later to say was, if all the reports he received were correct, "Gestapo-like."

In detail, Douglas Harris described the raid. First, he was shocked. Then he got scared. When it was over, he was so embarrassed that he did not want to tell anyone what happened. By yesterday, he had changed his mind. "Right now," he said, "I'm glad. I'm glad that it happened here in our building, because we know what to do. We don't have to take this kind of treatment. Nobody does, and we're doing something about it."

Douglas Harris, an independent film maker, talked as he kept going around the room, picking up first one piece of paper, then another.

"This is just some of what we're doing," he said, holding up the papers. They've already started on the investigation. But we have our own lawyers now. We intend to push this. We've got the American civil Liberties Union and the National Conference of Black Lawyers, the community, the churches -- everyone, They're really supporting us."

The tenants didn't organize to fight the FBI. They came together years ago, organizing themselves the way many people in New York do, to fight their landlord. "We couldn't get anything done in the building," Douglas Harris said. "Finally, we just had to get together -- organize against the landlord."

The machinery was in place. After the shock, the fear and embarrassment had worn off, the tenants used the organization they have to go against the FBI.

Early in the afternoon yesterday, Richard Emery, who is an ACLU lawyer, talked about the raid.

"What is absolutely clear," he said, "is that the nature of the search went beyond any search for a person. They (the FBI) went through papers and drawers in apartments, and two places, they were just ransacked.

"One fellow was hit with the butt of a gun, and another fellow was dragged down the stairs. These things, they cannot be justified."

"What do you plan to do?" he was asked.

"We're filing a lawsuit," he said. "That's what we're working on right now."

Why did the FBI raid? Why did a party of agents, estimated to be 50 in number, come into the building in the wee hours, smashing down some doors and threatening to dismantle others?

"We had a warrant," Quentin Ertell, a spokesman for the FBI said. "We had reason to believe that Joanne Chesimard was there. But right now, we're really not discussing the incident as to what went on inside the building."

Joanne Chesimard is the Black woman who was convicted of the 1979 slaying of a state trooper in New Jersey, then escaped from a prison in Clinton, N.J., where she had been serving a life sentence.

"They said they had information that Joanne Chesimard was here," Douglas Harris said. "I don't believe it. If that's true, then why were they making women in the building show their thighs, looking for a mark to identify Joanne Chesimard. At least you would think that they know what she looks like."

The target of the FBI raid was a third floor apartment of Ebun Adelona, a Black woman who holds two degrees in nursing and who is now a candidate for a doctoral degree in anthropology at Columbia University.

Her door was shattered in the raid. She says that she and her 5-year-old daughter were confronted in the middle of the night by agents aiming shotguns, pistols and machine guns.

"If they had been investigating, if they had any real surveillance, then they should have know that Ms. Adelona had been living in this building for the past 12 years," Harris said. "They would have seen her going out every morning with her daughter."

"Did the FBI have a warrant?"

"There was a warrant," Quentin Ertell, the FBI spokesman, said. He said that the warrant that the FBI used was one issued just after Joanne Chesimard's escape, the fugitive warrant for her arrest.

"That was no good," Richard Emery, the ACLU attorney, said. "It was nothing but an arrest warrant. They needed a search warrant. When you are searching for an escapee, and looking in the house of another person, you need a search warrant."

"Is the FBI conducting the investigation into what happened?"

"Yes," Quentin Ertell said. "A team of inspectors came up from Washington, but that inquiry is still being conducted. The inspectors are still here."

The investigation into the FBI's conduct came after Congressman Rangel filed a complaint with Attorney General Benjamin Civiletti. It was the tenants who brought Rangel into the controversy. They have made all of the moves. They were ready. It is a lesson in the importance of being organized.

"That's why I say that I'm glad that they busted into our building," Douglas Harris said. "This building is organized. The people here, they know what to do when something happens." Yesterday, that is precisely what the FBI was finding out.

1980

THE POLICE OFFICER IS WHITE. The two men he is accused of killing are Puerto Ricans. Neither of the victims was armed. Neither had previously committed any crime.

The killings go back to a night late in February 1979. The two men were shot to death. It happened in a little corner bar called Mr. G's, a place known as a hangout for cops just across from the 46th Precinct stationhouse in the Bronx.

The police officer accused in the killings is Kevin Durkin, who is 29, and lives in the Westchester County community of Eastchester.

Durkin was a hero cop. In eight years on the force, he received 16 special commendations. His work was considered so outstanding, that, in time, it won him assignment to an elite police unit that fought street crime.

On the night of the killings, Durkin sat drinking at Mr. G's. He was off duty and exactly what happened in the bar is still not known.

Witnesses said that Durkin, and the two men who were to become victims were together. One minute they were talking, the next Durkin was shooting.

Two days after the shooting, Domingo Morales, who was 25 and lived in the Bronx, died in the hospital of gunshot wounds.

Two days later, Manuel Martinez, another Bronx resident who was 40, also died from gunshot wounds. Durkin was suspended without pay, then arrested and charged with murder before being freed on $100,000 bail.

But the wheels turn slowly, and more than a year passed. Finally, late last month, in state Supreme Court in the Bronx, the case of Police Officer Kevin Durkin was called for trial.

The killing of Morales and Martinez never attracted much attention. It did not become a cause even though one morning just after the killings the wives of the two men did call a press conference, and complained about how quickly Durkin had been freed on bail. But that was it.

Then, late Tuesday, Mario Merola did something that has never been done in the eight years he has been Bronx district attorney. On Tuesday, Merola went before the Appellate Division and asked that Judge John J. Walsh be prohibited from conducting any further proceedings in the case. Merola was blunt.

He said that Justice Walsh was so biased, so partial, in favor of Durkin, the cop, that with him presiding over the trial, justice would not be done. Merola's action is certain now to bring both attention and controversy to the case involving Police Officer Durkin.

The issue that so riled Merola involved selection of jurors who will hear and then eventually make the decision in the Durkin case.

Jury selection in the trial had been going on for more than two weeks. Ten jurors had been seated when Merola acted. Merola said that Justice Walsh showed his bias in favor of Durkin by refusing to dismiss, with cause, prospective jurors who displayed what he called "clear and certain bias" against the prosecution.

Justice Walsh, a former assemblyman from Washington Heights, was in the Bronx County Courthouse. He refused to talk to reporters. A spokesman said that he would not comment as long as the matter is in the courts.

Merola did not argue before the Appellate Division. He sent an assistant to do that. But the arguments that were submitted carried his name. In papers filed with the court, he detailed a long series of examples of what he said proved his charges that Walsh was not impartial.

Merola said that Walsh erred in refusing to dismiss, for cause, a woman who volunteered in the courtroom that she felt "so sorry for that poor, young boy over there," when referring to Durkin.

He mentioned also a former cop who, when questioned, admitted that he would be biased, but was not dismissed for cause. Another example was a man who said he would have a problem convicting Durkin, even if the prosecution established his guilt beyond reasonable doubt. There was a long list of other examples.

In any trial the jury is key. It is sometimes said that the most important phase of any criminal trial is the selection of the jury; tamper with the selection of the jury and you tamper with the ability to conduct a fair trial.

That was the guts of the argument that Merola put before the Appellate Division on Tuesday. In the formal language of the court, he accused Justice Walsh of tampering with the selection of the jury.

He said that the judge, by refusing to dismiss biased prospective jurors for cause, was forcing the prosecution to use up its allotted challenges to do that, and was, thus, leaving the state in the vulnerable position of having to accept any jury seated. Merola cried foul.

Nowhere in the papers that were filed with the Appellate Division on Tuesday did Merola mention Miami and the case there that triggered a recent outbreak of rioting by Blacks.

The case in Miami involves cops who were White and were charged with beating to death a man who was Black. Rioting erupted when the jury in the case delivered a verdict that was perceived as being unjust.

Merola did not mention Miami, but he did warn that because the cop on trial in the Bronx (Kevin Durkin) is White and the victims were members of a minority, there will be close public scrutiny of the proceedings.

"If the judicial system is to succeed under these most trying of circumstances," Merola said to the court, "what must result is a verdict that is impartial and just."

The Appellate Division said it had no authority to remove Justice Walsh from the Durkin case. It said that the issue should be taken to the Court of Appeals. But the Appellate Division said also that, if it had the power to do so, it would have granted Merola's request.

It suggested that "in the interests of both propriety and justice" Justice Walsh ought to remove himself and allow jury selection to proceed before another judge. The Appellate Division stayed the trial until next Wednesday, and now the issue goes before the Court of Appeals.

The trial has not gone entirely unnoticed. Each day of jury selection, the two wives of the victims -- Zaria Morales and Carmen Martinez -- were in the courtroom. The two women are widows now. Nothing will bring their husbands back. Still they go to the courtroom. It is about justice. It is all they have left.

1981

AT FIRST, HE WAS CAREFUL with his answers. He kept the anger hidden that way.

"God blessed me," he said.

"I'm glad to be out, glad to be alive."

For a moment, it seemed that for Reginald Carthens, the whole nightmare was buried in the past. He lit another cigarette. The words kept coming. Emotion crept into his voice.

"Jail ain't no place for anybody," he said. "You go into jail and you're walking into death. You worry and worry so much, but something told me, you hold your head. Don't you lose your mind. A lot of people in there, they lose their mind. A lot of people in there, they lose their minds, and they end up killing themselves."

Reginald Carthens, who had just done 10 months in the Brooklyn House of Detention, was in his lawyer's office. The lawyer, Joseph Giannini, was at his desk and right in front of the desk was a chair for Carthens. Over on the side of the room, on a blue couch, was Leroy Callender.

It was supposed to be a celebration. The three of them were supposed to be hollering, shouting, perhaps even drinking a little champagne. There was a reason for them to do it. They had won their case, the toughest kind to win.

Reginald Carthens, 22, was arrested on an April night in Brooklyn. He was charged with murder. He said over and over again that he did not do it. But he was identified by a witness, and the system began to move against him. The days turned to weeks, the weeks to months.

"Once they make an arrest," Joseph Giannini, the lawyer, said, "its like turning around a freight train."

Giannini was a court-appointed lawyer. The first time he met with his client, he remembers Carthens telling him that he was innocent. When the lawyer said that he believed him, his client said, "I'm not going to be here long, am I?"

"I told him then, even if there wasn't a trial, that it would be eight to 10 months, maybe more."

It then became Carthens's job to tough it out in jail. Giannini dug into the evidence. One of the first things he knew was that he needed an investigator. He asked the court, but the answer came back no. Later, he improved his argument, asked again, and this time he got the investigator. He also got a break. Leroy Callender was assigned to the case.

It was in October when Callender entered the case. All of them went to work. Carthens worked at staying alive in the jail. His lawyer and the investigator worked at getting him out.

It is a story of hard work, and heroes.

The lawyer, Giannini, and the investigator, Leroy Callender, believed their client innocent of the murder charge. To prove it, they did what a good cop or a good reporter does. They conducted an investigation; went at it with abandon. They were determined to turn up every witness, explore every lead. They found what they were after.

"Why didn't the cops find the same witnesses that you found?" they were asked. "They didn't do a proper job," came the answer.

Carthens, the client, is Black. He was born at Kings County Hospital in Brooklyn. Before the April night of his arrest, he was kicking around to make ends meet with odd jobs. But he was not getting into any trouble. His father died when he was 9. He lived with his mother, and she kept after him. She understood the pitfalls and tried as best she could to keep a tight rein on her son.

On the night he was arrested, he had been out drinking. It was late and he was walking home. There had been an attempted robbery. The police had a witness, who described the robber as a male, Black, about 5-feet 11 and 155 pounds. "A slightly built man," the witness said. The witness also said that the man was wearing a green Army jacket.

"You've heard that we all look alike," Callender said. "They (the police) could have gotten the same results, but there were a lot of loopholes that they didn't follow up on," Callender said.

Callender is a tall, husky, Black man. He has been a private investigator for 21 years. He knows his business. For 12 years, Callender worked as a federal investigator. In the last nine years he has worked for himself. The court-appointed him to the Carthens case.

"We did everything," he said. "We went to the scene, to bars, to rooftops. We made over 100 photographs and got polygraph tests. We did everything."

"On many occasions we went out together," Giannini said.

"What about the stories of the court-appointed lawyers who take the money and run?" he was asked.

"In any profession there is the good, the bad and the ugly," he said. "Unfortunately, the bad ones get more attention than the good ones. But we try to do a good job. We don't compromise ourselves or our clients."

Giannini is White. He also is Brooklyn-born. He grew up in Canarsie, earned his degree at Brooklyn Law, and has been practicing for seven years. "Since Vietnam," the former marine says.

Despite all the hard work by the attorney and the investigator, Reggie Carthens drew the toughest assignment -- staying alive and sane in jail.

"One day I thought I was going to get hurt up real bad," he said. "You had to fight," he said. "There was no choice."

He tried to talk about the way it was for him, the nightmare that he had to live for no reason. He was there because of a mistake. Because of sloppy police work. When he says that jail is no place to be, his voice is strained.

"I been through hell, man," he says. "I was lucky to get out of there alive."

It isn't over.

"The final chapter has yet to be written," the lawyer said. "He was wrongfully arrested, wrongfully charged, and he has been scarred for life. Justice has been done, but I don't think the scales have been balanced out."

Giannini stood behind his desk, and toyed with the light blue tie he wore with his dark blue suit.

"He was lucky," Giannini said of his client. "His chances of getting the right people -- the right lawyer, the right investigator and everything -- I'd say it was about 500 or a thousand to one. There are others like him in the system. It happens more often than people believe. It's frightening, really frightening."

Reggie Carthens walks away. But the thought that would not go away was of capital punishment. Always, one of the major arguments against capital punishment has been: What if the wrong man is killed?

"That's one of the disturbing things about this," Joseph Giannini, the lawyer, said. "If they ever bring capital punishment back, there should be some independent group that makes its own investigation of every case, some group that just tries to make certain that something like this doesn't happen."

It was an idea. But it seemed that the important lesson in the Reggie Carthens case was that the police do make mistakes. When that happens, it is like Giannini said: it is like trying to turn a freight train around.

1981

NOT A DAY PASSES that the mail does not bring at least one of the letters but most often there are two, three, sometimes as many as half a dozen. They are all the same.

These are letters that come out of New York prisons. All of them say how bad it is inside. They mention beatings. They write about the drug traffic that goes on behind bars. They explain how dangerous it can be just trying to use a telephone.

If only a small part of what the inmates who write the letters say is true, then they are horrible places. Prisons are not supposed to be nice. They are places for punishment. But the inmates tell stories of torture.

It is a part of the reason why it was not surprising in the morning yesterday that, when Abbie Hoffman stood for sentencing, he said openly that he was afraid of imprisonment. In the 60s, Hoffman was one of the young Whites who dropped out. He became something of a legendary figure. He and Jerry Rubin founded what they called the Yippie Party. The two of them espoused revolution. But that was the 60s. Rubin has since dropped back in. He is now a stockbroker on Wall Street. He says the 80s are about making money. Hoffman was in court yesterday for sentencing. He had already pleaded guilty to selling cocaine to an undercover agent.

In return for his guilty pleas, the "A" felony that he was charged with was lowered to a "C" offense. It meant that instead of facing 15 years to life, the most he could get was five.

After discussion and some deliberation, what Acting Justice Brenda Soloff decided on in State Supreme Court in Manhattan was a prison term of up to three years. However, after a year, Hoffman is eligible for parole.

Gerald Lefcourt, Hoffman's lawyer, argued for probation, saying his client would work in a heroin treatment center. But the judge did not buy it. To cut the ground out from under Lefcourt's argument, she brought up a case involving a 16-year-old. This was a youth the judge identified as a ghetto child. Her point was that he was charged with selling a substantial amount of heroin, and that in his case the prosecutor wanted a sentence of from six years to life. The ghetto child had not been able to make the kind of deal that Abbie Hoffman was able to make. One reason may have been the impressive list of persons who came forward in Hoffman's behalf.

In the courtroom, that was what a lot of yesterday came down to in hard terms. It was another round of proof that it does make a difference who it is that stands in front of the judge. Hoffman had been on the run for six years. It is a hard time that he is going to have now, but still he was able to make a better deal than the ghetto child could make. There are some who can drop out and when they are ready, they have the option of dropping back in. But the system does not work that way for all people.

Abbie Hoffman, though, was not the real example. The real example was in another courtroom, next door in Foley Square in Federal Court, where the judge was Leonard B. Sand. The defendant was John Phillips, famous in the 60s as the leader of the musical group, The Mamas and the Papas.

Phillips's offense also involved drugs. He pleaded guilty and faced up to 15 years in prison and a fine of $25,000.

Phillips is 44. He was arrested last July out in Southampton. He pleaded guilty to involvement in a conspiracy that was engaged in selling "tens of thousands" of pills classified as being dangerous. This included Quaaludes, Dexadrine and Tylenol and another called Dialudid, a synthetic morphine known in certain circles as "hospital heroin."

According to Mark Pomerantz, the assistant U.S. attorney who was before Judge Sand to argue for the people, Phillips was involved in an illegal scheme with a Madison Ave. drug store. With the use of phony prescriptions, the drug store diverted thousands of pills to Phillips on a regular basis. In turn, Phillips, an addict himself, kept the hospital heroin for his own use and sold the others to street pushers who paid him cash or supplied him with cocaine.

The racket operated from 1977 until 1980. It involved hundreds of thousands of dollars. When caught, Phillips became a government witness and fingered the others. But yesterday the U.S. attorney said Phillips's help "did not enable the government to undertake any major prosecutions."

But Phillips had been helpful. As for himself, he entered a drug treatment center in New Jersey and then proceeded to speak out nationally against the use of drugs. He announced to the court that he and his whole family were "free of drugs."

"I am sincerely sorry about what has happened and hope to make amends," he said.

The judge sentenced him to 30 days.

Phillips's lawyer promptly proceeded to ask if the time could be served on weekends. When the judge said no, Phillips's lawyer then asked if he could have another 30 days to get ready to serve his 30-day sentence. That request also was too much for the judge. He gave him two weeks to get ready.

The formal sentence was eight years in jail but all of the time was suspended except the 30 days. The judge also said that Phillips would also have to do 250 hours of community service work. Using a 40-hour week, that comes to six weeks and a day.

The judge did not say what would have happened had Phillips been a ghetto child. It was mentioned, though, that Phillips might serve the 30 days at the Metropolitan Correctional Center, a place known among some prison people as "The Hilton."

1981

"THE DIRTIEST TRIAL I EVER SAW," is what Conrad Lynn, the lawyer, said. "I've seen some rough stuff in my time," he went on, "but never anything like this."

The judge, Stephen Zardine, talked about it being time to get tough and the need to make examples. He then used those words as the basis for slapping Amiri Baraka with a 90-day sentence.

It was no bluff. There are no bluffs any more. They were prompt in taking Baraka to Rikers Island, where he stayed until another judge came on. There was a hasty reversal and Baraka was released without bail while his lawyers appealed.

The appeals were lost. There were moves to suspend the sentence. Those also were unsuccessful. There were arguments for a new trial and charges of misconduct. Nothing came from any of those hearings either. Today, at 9:30 this morning, Amiri Baraka, the former Leroi Jones, is to go into court and surrender himself to begin a prison sentence on Rikers Island.

The proceedings in the courtroom where Baraka stands this morning just might be among the most important pieces of business conducted today in the City of New York. It is not because this is a man out of "Who's Who," even though that is part of it. He is a distinguished artist. As a playwright, poet, author and teacher, he has drawn international acclaim. When you talk of Amiri Baraka, start with the word activist, because here is a man so committed to what he believes that he never backs up or slacks off or lies down. He stays steady on the case. He always has.

What makes this case important is that it brings us back to the issue of equal treatment under the law. Baraka is a poet, author and teacher, but he is also Black. In this case, although the argument is that race is irrelevant, that might not necessarily be the case. It would be best if race could be discounted, but it is not that easy.

Keep in mind what is involved: The charge against Baraka was resisting arrest. It goes back to a June night in Greenwich Village. There are, of course, two versions. The police say Baraka was beating his wife and that they went to her rescue. When they did, they say, he turned on them, injuring two officers. Baraka tells it another way. He says that he and his wife were sitting in a car in front of a theater. There was an argument, and then, bam, he was being grabbed and beaten by the cops.

It comes down to some kind of family matter. He didn't rob anybody. He wasn't mugging people on the subway. He wasn't in the street with a gun. This is a city that has so much crime now it doesn't know which way to turn. Real crime. That should be what the courts are concerned with. But they are not. It's something they believe is so important that they have hounded Baraka for more than two years. We're talking about a family man with no record. Even the probation department has said to the court it doesn't believe he should be going to jail.

"What do you mean?" Conrad Lynn was asked. "What do you mean when you say Baraka's was the dirtiest trial ever?"

"Do you know what they did?" he said. "I'll tell you what: They tried him on one charge, then convicted him on another. Oh, that trial was something. I mean I've seen some rough stuff but...."

Baraka was charged with assault on the cops, possession of a weapon and resisting arrest. All of these charges except resisting were thrown out by the grand jury. The trial jury was out 20 minutes. Lynn had thought he would win the case on appeal. His argument was that since there was no basis for a legal arrest, there could be no charge of resisting.

At best, the case is borderline. It is one of those cases where, after two years, it figures that the sentence would be suspended, or that some accommodation be made. But that is not the case. With Baraka, the authorities have moved to press for imprisonment. They want Baraka in jail. Is it another signal? It is hard time that they are demanding for Baraka, and the question is why?

When sentence is passed today, right away the name David Ross is going to come up. He was the 23-year-old college student Criminal Court Judge Stanley Gartenstein said richly deserved jail because he attacked a cop. But then, instead of a sentence, he was ordered to write an essay and do community work because the judge said, "With his color (White) and ethnic background, he wouldn't last 10 minutes on Rikers Island."

It is something like Abbie Hoffman. He admitted selling cocaine to undercover officers but didn't believe he should go to jail. Too dangerous. Hoffman worried about homosexual attack. He feared for his life. Although he did go into prison with a lot of fanfare, no time was wasted quickly altering the terms of his punishment so that most of his time is being done at home.

Now it is Amiri Baraka, 46, one of country's distinguished artists and political activists, who stands before the court today. Last weekend, a rally was held across from the Harlem State Building to muster support for Baraka. Leaflets were passed out asking supporters to go to the courtroom today, and there were speeches. At the end, the words were those of Baraka.

"It's only 90 days," a passerby said to one of the demonstrators. It touched off a storm. That is precisely the point. What is there that says Amiri Baraka is any safer in Rikers than Ross or Hoffman? How many cases have there been where the sentence that was passed by the court was short but then, jails being what they are, the time served was long. Prisons are dangerous places. Nobody wants to do hard time, regardless of race.

Late in the afternoon on Saturday, at the street corner rally in Harlem, Baraka took the bullhorn. His voice was raspy, but he shouted his words. All of them encouraged struggle.

"Unity," he said, "we must have unity. The only weapon we have is to organize. We must be organized now."

1982

IT HAD BEEN DIFFERENT WITH MALCOLM Brown, who was the first member of the Guardian Angels to die. He was shot and killed last summer on a street in the Brownsville section of Brooklyn.

He died while trying to stop a mugging. His was a hero's death.

Now, another of the Guardian Angels has been killed. This time the victim was 26-year-old Frank Melvin.

There are different accounts of what exactly happened. The police tell one story, the Guardian Angels tell another. Both agree that it was a cop who shot and killed Frank Melvin.

Yesterday Angels leader Curtis Sliwa stood on the steps of City Hall here and said that Melvin was "gunned down in a cold-blooded murder."

The Guardian Angels are not just in New York City any more. They are in 33 cities across the country and are growing.

In New York, Boston and Los Angeles there are official relationships between the Angels and the police.

This is one of the cities where the Angels were given no official welcome. The director of the Police Department didn't want them. The mayor didn't want them.

But the Guardian Angels are volunteers who do not wait to be invited. They believed they could serve a useful purpose in Newark. A year ago, without any official blessing, safety patrols were started.

"When they ask me what we are going to do, I tell them we're going to patrol the projects," Sliwa said. "I don't even have to see them, but I know that everywhere, the people in the projects have trouble, and they always welcome the Guardian Angels."

In Newark, the Guardian Angels were patrolling the senior citizens wing of the Dayton St. projects, officially known as the Otto Kretchner Houses.

It was Frank Melvin's patrol. He lived in Kretchner Houses with his wife and two sons, 5 and 1.

The way the Angels tell it, the patrol heard a loud crash outside and went to investigate. They saw a police car, and headed toward it when they were interrupted by a cop.

"They (the Angels) were clearly identifiable," Sliwa said. "Frank opened his jacket to expose his shirt. There was no need to shoot him. He wasn't armed. He had said, 'I'm a Guardian Angel.' But the cop, he just clicked off one shot...that was it, only one shot was fired."

The police typed their version on two sheets of paper and handed it to reporters. It told of police receiving a report of a burglary in progress, just across from the projects. Officers Milton Medina and Angel Ramos responded.

The police say Medina climbed onto the roof of a nearby building and saw a group of men he thought were advancing on his partner. He fired one shot from the roof. The shot killed Frank Melvin.

Sliwa was accompanied to City Hall by a large group of Angels in their T-shirts and red berets. They stood on the steps just beneath Mayor Kenneth Gibson's office. The street in front of them was lined with cops.

"What is your proof?" reporters asked Sliwa. He pointed to 20-year-old George McGaherton, one of the Angels on the patrol with Frank Melvin when he was shot.

"Without saying stop or freeze or anything, he (the cop) just shot," McGaherton said.

"I said don't shoot, I'm a Guardian Angel. You could look at his face and see he was a little wary of what he had done."

"How can you be sure?" he was asked.

"Because I saw him," McGaherton said. "He was a sergeant and his badge number was 891."

"Have the police questioned you?" he was asked.

"Yes," he said.

"Did you see an officer on the roof?"

"I saw an officer on the roof. He had a shotgun."

There is that much difference in the stories they tell.

"We're going to ask the state's attorney general to investigate," Sliwa said. "We don't trust the Newark police."

Sliwa said after the shooting the police would not let any of the Angels try to aid Frank Melvin. "They just left him lying there to bleed to death." he said. Bruce McGaherton agreed.

An aide to the mayor came out of City Hall and asked the reporters to come inside, to talk with Kenneth Gibson.

"I've talked with the police director," Gibson said. "It's not appropriate for us to sit and try to prejudge this. We have a professional Police Department. Therefore, there is no need for me to give any special directions. They will investigate."

The police headquarters sits in an old building just behind City Hall. The police director, Hubert Williams, sent word from his fourth-floor office that he would not see any reporters.

A detective whose name was Ernest Newby said he could not identify the badge number quoted by the Guardian Angels. "But sergeants don't have numbers that go that high," he said.

"What about the discrepancy of where the shot was fired from?" he was asked.

"Our reports say it came from the roof," he said.

Detective Newby said that an autopsy would answer the questions. He said Medina had fired the shot and that he had been transferred.

"The true blame does not lie with the cop," Curtis Sliwa said. "It's Williams and Gibson (the mayor). They refused to meet with us. Time and time again we tried to see them, but they would not allow anyone to speak with us.

"They think we're trying to take away their jobs. We keep telling them, we're just here to augment the police because of the cutbacks."

In Newark, in addition to their T-shirts and berets, the Guardian Angels also wear bright red nylon jackets. "The people at the projects raised the money and bought them," Sliwa said. "That tells you something about how they feel about the Guardian Angels."

"Will the patrols continue to operate here?" he was asked.

"The patrols will continue to operate and continue to grow," he said. Then Sliwa was asked about the police. "Why don't they just lay off our case," he said. "There are too many criminals out there for them to deal with."

1982

THE PARTY WAS A SURPRISE, which meant they couldn't begin to paste the pink and yellow streamers or the baby-blue balloons on the walls until Elizabeth, the one who is having the baby, was out of the apartment.

PJ's mother had hurried down to the store. Elizabeth's mother was so busy that she still hadn't had time to take the curlers out of her hair.

Her oldest daughter, Robin, who is 29, was dressed in a dark pants suit and she worked with the kids who were there hanging the crepe paper streamers. Another older woman brought trays of potato chips, pretzels and peanuts from the kitchen and placed them on a big table.

PJ, who watched from a corner, seemed nervous. "Excited," he said. "I've been with my lady 7 1/2 years."

The baby is due in October. PJ, the father to be, is 20. Elizabeth, his lady, is 18. The surprise was a baby shower that Elizabeth's mother, Willetta Small, had in her apartment in Harlem.

The intrusion was the trouble that PJ had with the police. "Tell him what happened," Willetta Small said.

PJ sat on an arm of a fluffy brown chair and took two pieces of paper out of his pocket. One of the papers was white. It had burn marks on both sides. His name was written on the top of the paper. It said that he had "satisfactorily completed a parental training course."

"That's so I can go with her inside the delivery room," he said.

"It's a shame what they're doing to these kids," Willetta Small interrupted.

The other piece of paper that PJ took from his pocket was pink and crumpled and hard to read.

"That's the summons the cop gave me," PJ said.

He had been working in midtown. "Car washing," he calls it, but PJ is one of the young people you see on the corners at busy intersections, the ones who dash out with short squeegie sticks dripping soapy water. They make their money washing car windows.

He said the cop grabbed him at the fish market. "I was cashing in my change," he said. "He (the cop) had one of my friends already. I wasn't even washing (car windows), but he saw my stick."

PJ said the cop took him and his buddy into a hallway at the Port Authority. "He started searching us. He took the squeegie and started putting it all over my face and my neck." The cop let the two of them go, but PJ went upstairs to the police station there to make a complaint.

He said he was at the desk, telling his story to the sergeant on duty, when the cop came in. "He grabbed me by the neck, in front of the sergeant, and took me into another room. He said that's the wrong thing to do, to come up and complain after he had let me go. Then he gave me a summons. He said the next time it's going to be six days in jail."

"Why did you try and make a complaint?" PJ was asked.

"What he (the cop) did was wrong. He had let me go, but he started to hit me in the face with the stick. I didn't even get to tell the sergeant. He took us into a room and told us to get outta there, and then he broke our sticks."

"Did the sergeant do anything?" he was asked.

"No."

He took the piece of paper with the burn marks. "That happened on 40th St. and Eighth Ave. I was on my way uptown. I had that stick in my hands. My friends cut out. I didn't have time to run. He (the cop) searched me in public and everything and burned that (his document) and my money. He put a match to it and then stomped it out. He said he was setting an example and told me to tell my friends (that this will happen) if they got caught with sticks."

"Have you been back washing car windows?"

"Yes, of course. I got to go back until I get a job. I been accepted to a school for training to get my GED (high school equivalency)."

He took a card out of his wallet. The top of the card said Jobs for Youths, Inc., and underneath was the name of vocational counselor Barbara Raffell. "They find you a job. You go to school in the morning and work at night," he said.

PJ's mother, who had returned from the store, came into the room.

"I was going to take this to court," she said. "Why do they pick on him?" she asked. "He's down there trying to make a dollar for his family. I'd rather he washed car windows than hold up somebody." ."

"Here's a young boy who wants to get in the service," Willetta Small interrupted. "You have to pass a test to get in the Army."

PJ was turned down when he tried to enlist. He had not finished high school. He quit after the 10th grade to join the Job Corps, but that didn't work out when he was sent to Utah.

"It's a terrible thing," Willetta Small said. "I see boys who are White down there shining shoes. They (the cops) don't say nothing to them. Since Ronald Reagan been in the White House, they're just showing their prejudice. I say, let them go in the Army, or give them jobs.

"Here's a boy who wants to take care of his family. He's been there working to buy a crib. As long as he's not robbing or stealing, I don't see no harm in washing a few cars. He could get on welfare, but who wants that?"

PJ said the summons he got was either his fifth or sixth.

"If the judge sees his face too much, he'll give him six months," his mother said.

"The only thing on my record is this," PJ said.

"That's why the prisons are so full," Robin, the sister of PJ's girlfriend, said.

"Ronald Reagan has got this country down to a frazzle," Willetta Small said. "It's a terrible, terrible shame if you don't have a job."

PJ wore a blue wind-breaker over a red T-shirt. He is small and dark-skinned and his hair was cut short. He fingered the pink piece of paper that was the summons "The cop gave me this. Who do I think the judge is going to believe, me or him? But I got to go back (to washing car windows) until I get a job."

Now, the noise that came into the room was the buzzer from the door downstairs. The guests were beginning to arrive. They were coming for the party, the shower for the baby PJ and Elizabeth are going to have in October.

1983

HE HAD THE NAMES OF THE TWO officers and all of the details of the horrible story that he kept repeating yesterday were locked in the front of his mind.

"One of the officers was named Messina," he said, "and the other one was named Teller. I'll never forget Teller. He was just filled, so filled with hate. He just kept calling me nigger, nigger, nigger."

He said it was the policeman Teller who did most of the beating.

"The other cop, Messina, he had me by the throat and Teller, he was the one who did most of the beating. He kept saying: 'Nigger, we're going to teach you a lesson you won't forget,' and I don't know how many times he hit me."

He said that one cop held him, and that the other beat him. He said that this happened in a stairwell inside the 28th Precinct stationhouse in Harlem. That was not all.

"Then, they put me in a cell and Teller, he stayed there and began to kick me, he just kept kicking." He leaned over and pulled up the leg of the trousers he was wearing and just beneath his kneecap, the scars and scabs were there.

"This officer, Teller, he told me, 'Nigger, you are going to learn that from now on, when you open your mouth, you better say, sir, first.'"

The details of the horrible story were repeated again and again yesterday. They came from the Rev. Lee Johnson, a student at the Union Theological Seminary and an assistant minister at the Concord Baptist Church in Brooklyn.

Yesterday morning, Johnson stood with a crowd of ministers and the president of the seminary at the Abyssinian Baptist Church in Harlem. He told his horrible story there.

In the afternoon, he sat alongside a lawyer in an office downtown on Broadway and he repeated the story. It goes back to Harlem, early in the evening last Saturday.

The way that Johnson tells the story, it was a clear cut case of police brutality. He said he was with two friends who had been classmates when he was a student at the University of California at Los Angeles. He said that the three of them were riding in a car he was driving in Harlem when he noticed flashing lights from a police van behind him.

"I saw the lights, and I pulled over to the curb," he said. He said that one of the officers, Messina, asked for his license. He said he told the officer he needed to get out of the car because he was too cramped in the bucket seat to reach his wallet.

"The cop said no," Johnson said.

He said he asked the officer why he should not get out of the car? He said the policemen swore at him and said he should do as he was told.

"I told him that obviously he must be new on the force because he didn't know how to approach citizens. It must have touched off something because he opened the door, came in, and tried to punch me. I moved over and then be began to beat me on the leg with a flashlight."

Johnson is 32 years old. He is short and his afro hair recedes from his forehead. Yesterday, as he told his story, his voice was soft and he measured his words. He said the cop pulled him from the car. He was then thrown into the police van.

All of it was happening on the street in front of Sylvia's, which is one of Harlem's most popular restaurants. It did not take long for a crowd to gather.

"One of the cops pulled a gun," the young minister said.

He said that when he was put in the van, "I told him (the cop), your conscience is going to kill you because you hit the wrong person for the wrong reason." He said that got him another beating inside the vehicle.

At the precinct, he said that the desk officer took a cross that was on the top of a pen, and shoved it in his face. He said the cop told him: "I don't believe in that anyway, Reverend."

From the desk, he said, he was taken to the stairwell where he said he was beaten, and from there, to the cell. He said the beating had been so severe that once he was free, he had to go to St. Luke's Hospital for treatment.

At the 28th Precinct yesterday, a lieutenant told the story another way. He said that the minister was arrested because he became abusive. He said that officers used force because the minister resisted arrest and was inciting the crowd on the street.

"Was he beaten in the stationhouse?" the lieutenant was asked.

"We don't do that," he said.

The lieutenant said that the two officers involved were not assigned to the 28th. "They were from a tactical patrol unit," he said.

C. Vernon Mason, the lawyer who sat beside Lee Johnson in the afternoon yesterday, said that this case is different. "Because we have witnesses," he said. "We have good witnesses, people from Sylvia's, and they saw what happened and they are coming forward."

Mason did not stop there. "Imagine," he said, "this is a minister from Concord Baptist Church. From one of the largest, most prestigious churches in the city, and this happens to him. Can you imagine this happening to a Jewish rabbi or a Catholic priest downtown on Fifth Ave? Can you imagine what the crowd there would have done?"

In the morning yesterday, Donald Shriver, president of the Union Theological Seminary, was at the Abyssinian Baptist Church. He stood with the Rev. Calvin Butts, associate minister at Abyssinian, and a number of other ministers. They called for the immediate suspension of the officers who were involved.

"This really worries me," Butts said. "Not just the fact that he (Johnson) was Black and a minister, but what worries me, too, is this officer holding up the cross and cursing. It worries me because that's fascism, and the Fascists have no regard for religion. If this slips by, it gives even more of a license for the police to continue these attacks."

Butts in Harlem and the lawyer, Mason, who was downtown, spoke again of the dangerous atmosphere that is rising in the city. "And nobody is speaking out. Nobody is saying that we are not going to tolerate this kind behavior in New York," Mason said.

"I'm from Arkansas, from Little Rock, and this is the kind of thing that we had in the worst days of the old South, and now it's happening here in New York."

"The top," Butts said. "The tone is set by the leadership at the top. It's a bad scene. The ministers are very angry about it. We've gone to (Police Commissioner Robert) McGuire about this before, but nothing happens. Nothing. At the top, nobody is saying anything."

"If we had a mayor who was sensitive to all of the people it would be different," Mason said. "But there is never any official response . . ." It keeps coming back to the mayor, who is the one at the top. The horrible story that the Rev. Lee Johnson told became one more part of the issue of 1985, which is the election year.

1983

HE WOULD NOT SLIP OUT through the rear of the building or have his car exit from the garage below. Out front, there was still a big crowd in the plaza. In the pictures certain to be taken, he wanted to be seen as the White man standing against the Blacks.

The mayor has his strategy. It is based on dividing the city, the Blacks on one side, the Whites on the other.

In Harlem, it was easy for him to get the kind of pictures he wanted.

He came to the hearing on police brutality, saying and doing before he arrived all that he could to give the impression that the charges being made were without substance.

He had reacted the same way when a minister who was Black charged that he was beaten by the police, first on a Harlem street, again in a paddy wagon, and later, in a precinct station house.

From the mayor, there was no outrage, only expressions of doubt.

In the city, especially in the neighborhoods that are predominantly Black, no issue has been rising faster or is more emotional than the one of police brutality. It has been seething. The efforts to bring the problem to the office of the police commissioner and the mayor were turned away.

The incidents kept stacking up, though. In time an ad hoc committee came together. There were ministers, lawyers, politicians, and even Black cops, in the group. All of them cited incidents of police misconduct. They built their files.

When nobody in the city agreed to listen, they did what Black Americans have usually done in time of trouble: they went to the federal government in search of a remedy there.

They went first to Rep. John Conyers Jr., who heads the House subcommittee on criminal justice. The Michigan Democrat, a former chairman of the Congressional Black Caucus, reviewed the evidence that was brought down from New York. He agreed to bring his subcommittee to Harlem and hold hearings there.

The Ad Hoc Committee did not stop there. It took the documents to the Justice Department in Washington and put the grievances before William Bradford Reynolds, who heads the civil rights division. The promise from Reynolds was that he would look into the charges that were being made.

The congressional hearings were scheduled, and the citizens who could get no hearing in New York had a piece of the federal government come to them. A huge crowd showed up. The hearing room was jammed. It was the same with a larger room upstairs. An even bigger crowd waited outside.

The mayor's attitude was that all this was just some politicians who wanted to run against him stirring up trouble.

The hearing was going forward, and the mayor and the police commissioner who should have come to listen were invited instead to testify. They brought along William Bracey. He was once the chief of patrol in the department, at the time the highest ranking Black man on the force.

He is retired now, but still they called him out because Commissioner Robert McGuire follows the lead of the mayor. He does not promote Blacks in the Police Department. He runs a segregated force, which is what the mayor runs at City Hall.

What happened at the hearing was not surprising. A woman who lost a son to a cop's bullet barged in. She was emotional. It stopped the proceeding before it barely had begun. The politicians used that as an excuse to end the hearing.

It was not a real disruption. The only real reason for not going ahead with the hearing was that city police officials, citing security reasons, had insisted on holding the proceeding in a space that was much too small.

The leadership of the city doesn't know. The leadership has no idea what Blacks in New York feel, or think. The reason is because the city now is a closed shop where Blacks are concerned.

In the morning yesterday, lawyer C. Vernon Mason sat in his office downtown on Broadway. He said that it is not over. "Everyone knows now that police brutality is a real issue in this city," he said. "I don't view what happened as being negative at all."

Vernon Mason was in the forefront of the effort that brought the hearing to Harlem. He would have been a witness, too, had the hearing lasted long enough. His would have been powerful testimony. He had all of his words and documentation on paper. Together, they told a story of what is taking place now in the city.

He had a list of all of the Blacks and the Hispanics who have been victims of police killings since 1957. The list itself tells a story. From 1957 through 1974, there were 18 such killings. After that, it began to change. In 1979 alone, there were 13. Before, there would be one, two -- seldom as many as three -- such killings a year. No more. In 1980, the figure was 10, and in 1981, there were 12 killings. Already this year, there have been six, and, as Vernon Mason said, "This is not all of them, this is just a list of the ones we were able to find out about."

Mason said that 21 was the median age of the ones who died. "As the aunt of (one of the victims) Donald Wright, aged 19, said, 'Black children are becoming an endangered species,'" he said.

Mason quoted Patrick Murphy, a former commissioner of the New York City Police Department: ". . . The most powerful people in policing in the United States are mayors. The mayor who appoints the chief (of police) of course does set policy. He sets the tone. And he certainly can hold his police chief and his police department accountable."

In the testimony he was to give, Mason examined the racial makeup of the city police department. "The unfortunate fact," he said, "is that the department is largely segregated." He said that of about 23,000 officers, just 10 percent are Black. Of sergeants on the force, he said, 6 percent are Black, as are 2 percent of the lieutenants and just 1 percent of those above the rank of captain.

He also was critical of the city's Civilian Complaint Review Board. He pointed out that all seven members are employed by the police department and appointed by the commissioner. He said all investigators are cops and that the board only makes recommendations, which the commissioner can reject if he so chooses. This setup, he said, is the reason that many do not take their complaints to the review board.

"Where does it go from here? Vernon Mason was asked.

"There will be another hearing," he said. "We don't know the date yet, but there will be another hearing scheduled."

After Conyers left, a "people's hearing" was held. Through the afternoon, one after the other, witnesses came, and, in emotional testimony, detailed chilling stories of police abuse.

"The people didn't come here (to the hearing) to riot," Vernon Mason said, "they came to be heard."

1983

HE WORE A DARK BLUE sweatshirt that had the name of the organization, the Guardians Association, printed across the front in golden letters. "They want law enforcement in this town to be anything, but Black," he said. "Just look at the facts."

Johnny Cousar reached across the cluttered table that was in front of him and grabbed a sheet of paper that was filled with long rows of figures. "These are the facts," he said. "The Guardians were struggling with discrimination in the police department 12 years before the court order. So what has happened since the court ruled in 1979?"

His finger moved across a row of figures on the paper that was in his hand. "They say they're doing so much," he said of the city's police department. "But just look at facts."

The figures he had supported his argument: The number of Black males in the police department increased by just 103 men -- from 1,837 in 1978 to 1,940 in 1983. "And that's counting everybody," Johnny Cousar said.

He is out of the police department now. He retired in July 1982. But for 15 years Johnny Cousar was active in the Guardians Association. The Guardians is the organization within the department that belongs to police officers who are Black. From the first of January 1980 until his retirement, Cousar was president of the Guardians Association.

In the police brutality hearings that open this morning in Harlem, Johnny Cousar will lead the testimony that comes from Black police officers. Through the afternoon yesterday, he sat at a table in his apartment in Brooklyn, sifting through documents and affidavits he needed for his testimony.

He begins with the makeup of the department itself.

"If you change the complexion of the department," he said, "you change the level of brutality. You also change the level of service. You even change the quality of life in the city."

In federal court, in 1979, the city's police department lost the discrimination suit brought by the Guardians. The court ruled that to remedy the situation, a third of all the officers hired by the department had to be Black or Hispanic.

"Everybody has done well except Black males," Cousar said, and he went back to his figures. In 1978, Black males were 7.6 percent of the force. In 1983, the figure was 8.9 percent. In 1978, Hispanics were 3.5 percent of the force with 838 officers. In 1983, the figure jumped to 6.6 percent with 1,445 Hispanic officers. White women did even better. It jumped from 109 to 387 in the same period, and Hispanic women increased from 8 to 189.

The department now has 23,288 officers. Of that number, 18,315 or 84.1 percent are White males as compared with 21,350 in 1978.

At the aborted brutality hearing of last July, the police commissioner, in his undelivered testimony, had 17.6 percent of the police department being minority. But he was counting in his figure Blacks, women, Hispanics, Asians and native Americans. "In other words," Johnny Cousar said, "(the police commissioner) was saying that he gave

90 percent of the population 17.6 percent of the jobs, and because he did that, he was doing a good job."

In the room where Cousar worked, a small television sat in a corner. Into the room came the chilling stories that were told on July 18 after the congressional hearing at the Harlem State Office Building was adjourned, and a "people hearing" convened.

"They beat him to death," a father was saying of his son.

"They brought him out in a body bag. His feet were tied and his face was covered with a piece of a sheet."

A man, his voice trembling with emotion, told of a struggle he had in getting a coroner's report. He finally found that his son was "beaten from his head to his feet."

There was a young father who told of being beaten by the cops "for no reason" while in a van with his young son. He told how, in winter weather, his 18-month-old son was stripped of his snowsuit, searched by the cops, and how his son was left alone in the van with the windows open.

Gil Noble's "Like It is," on WABC TV, broadcast the incredible stories of police brutality in New York City. Now, it was an older man who was Black. He was saying the cop told him, "We can do anything we want." The old man was outraged. "When you get involved in this, it blows your mind," he said. "You say, 'This is not Nazi Germany.' I've never been in jail. It's a degrading experience. You are thrown in with any and everything. It is a humbling experience. But you find that everybody there doesn't belong there."

Johnny Cousar had 19 pages of testimony. "We won't have time for everything we want to say," he said. "But we will use all of the time we have, and we'll save the rest for later, for the Brooklyn hearing."

The core of the testimony he shaped yesterday was powerful. In testimony filled with detail, he says that in New York City, the system itself is designed to produce "the brutal White cop." None of it is an accident, Johnny Cousar -- himself once a cop -- said. He builds the case he presents today with compelling evidence.

He shows how the system embraces recruits who are White and rejects others who are Black. He shows how the system itself makes a mockery of sensitivity aspects of police training. "The silly sciences, they call it," he said. He said this cop is then heavily armed and -- with a head full of stereotypes -- is sent into Black areas to patrol.

"He comes out there (into Black areas) like he was going to Vietnam and the department permits that."

Cousar went back to his figures, which showed that in the department, the overwhelming number of control officers, the ones responsible for discipline, are White. His figures showed that with sergeants, 1,985 are White, 124 Black and 54 Hispanic. Among lieutenants, 739 are White, 13 Black and 11 Hispanic.

"That is why there is a double standard of discipline," he said.

Cousar said the department not only produces the brutal policeman but "protects him to the hilt." He had experiences with the civilian review board which he used as proof. It was a powerful case he was building. It said that something very wrong is going on in the New York Police Department.

Editor's Note

A nation-wide survey in the summer of 1994 revealed that the New York City police department had the worst record for hiring African Americans and other minority officers of any urban police force in the nation.

1984

IN TIME THEY WILL CALL it charisma. He wears baggy suits. He has his own special way with the language. Almost always, he looks as though he needs a shave. But he's tough. He has shown that he's not afraid -- not of the cops, the mayor or anybody else. Mario Merola is his own man. The good news is that he's going to investigate the shotgun killing of Eleanor Bumpurs.

The old woman should still be alive. No shotgun should have ever been taken to her apartment, not under any circumstances.

The shotgun is a weapon the cops need. There are so many dangerous weapons in the hands of criminals, it would be stupid to say cops can't use shotguns. But no cop should be allowed to use a shotgun to evict a citizen from his or her apartment. Not under any circumstances.

Even the police commissioner does not understand. He defends the use of the shotgun on Eleanor Bumpurs. He just says that in the future, in such cases, a captain should be called to the scene *before* any killing is done. If the commissioner can't see the wrong in using a shotgun on Eleanor Bumpurs, then his plan to put cops in the schools better be stopped quick. The parents' association of every school in the city ought to meet in emergency session. The commissioner's plan is to put cops in the schools to stop the drug traffic. The cops are going to bring guns. Sooner or later, there is going to be shooting in the hallways. If there is a problem with drugs, give the principals the power they need to deal with it. The cops shotgunned Eleanor Bumpurs. If they don't see anything wrong in that, then they should never be trusted to bring their guns into the schools.

There are people armed and dangerous who beat, rob and rape old women in their apartments. There are people, armed and dangerous, putting cocaine, heroin and angel dust in the hands of kids. To deal with those people the cops, at times, do need shotguns. But Eleanor Bumpurs was not a part of that crowd.

Now it is in the hands of Mario Merola, who is district attorney in the Bronx. It comes to him because it is now being said that Eleanor Bumpurs, an overweight grandmother whom police were there to evict from her apartment, had no knife, as the cops claimed. Two stories are emerging. There is the story the police tell, and another from witnesses. Merola will investigate.

In time, they will call it charisma. It's because he is not fancy. He just takes off his coat, rolls up his sleeves, and tries as best he can to be fair. He tries to stand up for the public trust that is in his hands. In times of trouble, there are not many places people can turn to any more. It's because too many of the people who hold offices are afraid, even afraid to just stand up and be fair.

Mario Merola is different. He doesn't have that paralyzing fear. He wasn't afraid to open up the child abuse cases. In another killing, when the cops wouldn't tell their supervisors what happened, Merola hauled the whole bunch of them into court. And when the medical examiner's office was being taken apart, he stood up for Michael Baden. It didn't scare him that he stood alone. It's courage that Mario Merola has.

1984

THE ISSUE WILL NOT GO AWAY. Now it's the report of the Conyers committee that brings it back to the center of attention.

"The report just confirms what we've been charging all these years," the attorney, C. Vernon Mason, said.

The charge is that in New York City there is a serious problem of racially motivated police violence. It is the worst kind of charge that can be made against the police. But it's more than just a charge now. After a series of tumultuous public hearings, the Conyers committee found that there is substance to the complaints.

Rep. John Conyers (D-Mich) is an old liberal in the House, and chairman of the Subcommittee on Criminal Justice. Last spring, his committee conducted hearings in New York on the issue of race and police violence. The Conyers committee didn't find that it was systemic. It didn't find that it was institutional. But in its report, it said that it was there. It said that "racism appears to be a major factor in alleged police misconduct." It also found that complaints were treated "less than seriously" by city officials.

It's an old issue that keeps coming back. Twenty years ago in the city, a White cop shot and killed a youth who was Black. It was one of those killings that brought back the old anger. It touched off the Harlem riots. The complaints were treated seriously in the city then. In the wake of the riots, officers who were Black were moved to decision-making roles in the police department. Before the riots of 20 years ago, there had never been a Black commanding officer in the city's police department. Not ever. After the riots, Lloyd Sealy was made commanding officer of the 23rd precinct in Harlem. The upward movement of Black officers in the department started there. It went forward. In time, it got lost again.

By the spring of 1983, again, there were no commanders who were Black in the department. "The department is almost 90 percent White, and in the city that is almost half Black and Latino," Vernon Mason said yesterday. Vernon Mason was the lawyer who organized the testimony presented during the Conyers hearings. He said the report only confirms what has been charged. He said the problems still exist. "We should be trying to get a police department that reflects the population of the city," he said. Mason said the issue is so pressing that he urged Archbishop John O'Connor to get involved. "We're talking about the right to life," he said. "The Catholic Church should be involved."

The issue of race and police brutality is not confined to New York. Conyers's committee has held hearings, and made similar findings, in other cities. Two years ago, the national Black United Front had witnesses from around the country testify at hearings in New York on racially motivated police violence.

In New York, the issue had been building for more than five years. There had been marches, rallies, and calls for investigation. But there was none. The protest movement grew. When city officials failed to respond, the complaints were taken to the Justice Department in Washington, then to Rep. Conyers. The hearings and report were the result.

"The people are going to speak on this," Vernon Mason said. "Hopefully, the people will do that in 1985." It's not over. It's an old issue, and it's back again at the center of attention. "It's the department itself," Vernon Mason said. "The department has to be opened up. It has to begin to reflect the population of the city."

1985

NOW, IT'S THE MAYOR saying that the Justice Department from Washington is needed here in the city to investigate the police. But it is too late for that.

The mayor saw all the danger signals that have been rising; but he kept turning his head. Now, it's too late.

Two years ago, he could have headed off all the trouble that has come to the Police Department. Back then, he played politics. Even when a Black minister charged that he was beaten in a Harlem station house, the mayor refused to listen.

"I doubt it," the mayor said, and turned his head the other way.

In the spring of 1983, there were many complaints. There were not just complaints of beatings but charges of killings, too. There were the deaths of Arthur Miller and a kid whose name was Randy Glover in Brooklyn. There were the deaths of Vietnam veteran Peter Funches and Louis Rodriguez in the Bronx. Those were just some of the names in a string of deaths that were laid to police brutality.

The mayor refused to listen. The police commissioner took his cue from the mayor and would not listen either. Back then, complaints that should have been handled in the city were taken to Washington. Even William Bradford Reynolds, the assistant attorney general in Ronald Reagan's Justice Department, said it appeared the complaints had substance. Rep. John Conyers was so moved by the charges that he brought his subcommittee on criminal justice to the city and conducted public hearings.

But the mayor refused to listen. He accused Conyers of playing politics. He called the ones who took the complaints to Washington, Black rednecks. The sore festered. Now, a police department that had been called "The Finest," has been plunged into deep crisis.

"But it's not systemic," the mayor insists. But the evidence says it is. Even the good cops on the force refuse to stand up to the wrong. A cop driving a patrol car ran down and killed a citizen on Park Avenue. But the cops who have information have refused to come forward. The silence grows. Good cops knew of the torture in a Queens stationhouse, but they have refused to come forward. It is the same with beatings. It all says the problem in the department now is systemic.

After the public hearings, the Conyers committee, in its findings, said the problem of police misconduct in the city was being treated less than seriously. It also said that racism appeared to be a major factor in police conduct, and that a serious commitment was needed by local officials to deal with the problem.

Now, the mayor wants Ronald Reagan's Justice Department. It's too late for that.

The good idea came from City Council President Carol Bellamy. She said that the time had come to appoint a special commission and that a full-blown investigation was needed. The mayor accused Bellamy of playing politics. It goes back to what the Conyers committee said: "It's time for a serious commitment."

In the spring of 1983, when a group of local ministers and other citizens took the police brutality complaints to Washington, the Rev. Calvin Butts of Abyssinian Baptist Church in Harlem was asked why such action was necessary. "The attitude of Edward Koch," he said.

Koch was playing politics. He was saying there ought to be a federal investigation of charges of torture. But he scoffed and turned away two years ago, when the charges were that police brutality had actually resulted in death.

In the meeting with Bradford Reynolds two years ago, attorney C. Vernon Mason detailed so many allegations of police misconduct that the assistant attorney general promised an investigation. Yesterday, Mason said the issue had come full circle.

"The one who called us Black rednecks is now calling the Justice Department to investigate. The police department is out of control. The only group that has not been silent about this are the Guardians. The Guardians (the Black police officers' organization) have been consistent about the need to weed out police brutality. Too many good cops have been silent, ethically and morally. That's criminal. It's like the good ones who were silent during the Holocaust."

1986

ADD THE NAME of Edmund Perry to the awful list. His name fits there along with those of Michael Stewart, and Eleanor Bumpers, and Peter Funches, and Arthur Miller, and a long list of others.

In a way, the case of Edmund Perry is the saddest of all. He was just 17. Until last June, when he was killed, his was a life that seemed to have only promise. He had come out of a neighborhood in West Harlem where the cops allow the drug traffic to flourish in a way that makes it almost legal. But he made it through.

He went off to Exeter Academy, which is one of the best prep schools in the nation. He was on the fast track, and he did well. He would have been in his freshman year at Stanford University now. But in June, he was shot and killed by an undercover cop. The way the official story had it, the whole case was cut and dried. Edmund Perry and his 19-year-old brother, Jonah, a sophomore at Cornell, had tried to mug a young White guy on Morningside Drive. But the guy they grabbed, the official story said, was an undercover cop. In the tussle, Edmund was killed. But the pieces in the story the police told never fit. The Perry brothers had grown up on the other side of the park. They came from a family that was solid. They had roots in the community that were deep. It never figured that they would be on the Columbia side of the park doing a mugging.

But when arrests are made, it's always the official story that gets told, and repeated. In time, it gets accepted as the truth.

In this story, the cop who did the shooting was White, the victim was Black. New York has had so many killings of that kind, the credibility the police need to make their stories hold was used up long ago. So when Edmund was killed, in part of New York, the official story took root. It was said that he and his brother, Jonah, could not rise above their environment. But in the other New York, the New York of the minorities, the pieces never fit.

The story from June was in the courtroom in January. Jonah Perry, the brother, was brought to trial on charges of assaulting and attempting to rob cop Lee Van Houten. Alton Maddox was the defense attorney. He came to the trial with the toughest kind of case to win. He argued that there had been no mugging. He argued that the cop was drunk. He argued that young Edmund Perry was murdered. Finally, he argued that there was a coverup, and that Jonah, the older brother, was framed to make the official story stick. He took those arguments into the Supreme Court, to a jury of nine Whites, two Latins, and one Black. He won.

An old truth says that only those who are in the courtroom and see the witnesses and hear all the testimony can truly understand a jury's verdict. When the jury in the Perry trial came back and said not guilty on all charges, Alton Maddox said that he was not the least bit surprised.

"Finally," Maddox said, "there was the character of the two boys." He talked of what both of them had been able to do with their lives. He made the point that both of them had jobs. That took away any motive for them to be out on the street mugging anybody.

Jonah Perry went back to Cornell, to try and put his life back together. His brother, Edmund, is only another name on the awful list of those who were killed by police officers in circumstances that official stories said were justified -- stories one big segment of the city does not believe.

Maddox was one of the lawyers involved in the Michael Stewart case. Two weeks after that, he was tried in court by the Manhattan DA on charges of assaulting a court officer. He was found not guilty. He said the charges against Perry reflected "prosecutorial arrogance." He said it sends, "a dangerous message to Black people as to how they are going to be treated in New York City in the future."

1991

THEY CALL IT "THE BOSTON STORY." Across the country, it has hit Black communities like a bomb. At Abyssinian Baptist Church in Harlem, the Rev. Calvin O. Butts told of the chairman of his board of deacons coming to him and saying, "We have got to do something." Rev. Butts said that on Sunday, he would take the issue to the pulpit.

The so-called "Boston story" is the best reflection yet of what the incredible rise of street crime in urban America has led to. In Boston, a middle class White man apparently wanted to get rid of his pregnant wife to collect insurance money and pursue another love interest. So he drove with his wife into a Black area. He shot his wife (and 17 days later the baby delivered by Caesarean section also died), then shot himself. To cover up the crime, he said that a Black man jumped into their car and did the crime.

Nobody questioned the story that Charles Stuart told. Instead, there was outrage, and quickly, it became another example of vicious Black crime. "A Black man did it," Stuart said. Before long, police in Boston arrested a Black man. That might have been the end of it . But Stuart's brother came forward and offered evidence that the story his brother told was a lie. Charles Stuart committed suicide.

"He (Stuart) was certainly aware of the advantages he would be given by making an accusation against a Black person," said New York attorney C. Vernon Mason. "He created a person. No person existed. It was just a matter of labeling someone who was vulnerable. He knew he could falsely charge a Black person and get an outpouring of sympathy from the White community. He also knew that the system would work in concert with that conspiracy. He knew how to take advantage of whiteness in a racist society."

What happened in Boston is not an isolated case. In New York, there were the recent cases of undercover transit cops charged with falsely accusing Blacks and Latins of crimes that were never committed. They just wanted arrests, and selected, at random, persons who fit a certain profile. The thinking was that Blacks and Latins do subway crimes, so the cops used them. More recently in New Jersey, a prosecutor trying to get reappointed admitted that he invented an attack. He accused two Black drug dealers. It has to do with what Rev. Butts said of the Boston case. "One White man says it, and everybody takes it for granted."

For a long time, especially in the Black community, concern has been growing over the environment being created. Drugs brought an explosion of violent street crime. A lot of that crime involved young Blacks. The concern was that Whites were beginning to look at all Blacks as criminals. Accusations became guilt. The Boston story has stunned Blacks into facing what the crime problem has led to.

"Black people especially, but all people, must be careful not to trade in their liberty for some kind of security," Rev. Butts said. "Everybody is afraid of drug dealers and crime in the streets. They say, 'We need more, bigger jails' and they say, 'it's alright if the cops kick down doors to pick people up.' If this continues, we will have no liberty at all. I know how upset people are because of drugs and crime, but we can't turn over our liberties to a police state. And as bad as it is, all of our children are not criminals; all the Black community is not criminal. We have to stick up for our young people. Because a kid has a cap turned backward on his head and is wearing sneakers does not mean that he's a criminal."

The Boston story scares. It says that worst fears have become real. "Crime has been politicized," Mason said. "Bush knew that when he used Willie Horton; he knew how that would play in White America. We are grouped and judged by persons in our community who do crimes. A White person is presumed to be of good character."

1989

THIS WAS NOT FROM SPIKE LEE'S MOVIE, "Do the Right Thing." This was from the real world of upstate New York in the middle of December 1986.

In Spike Lee's movie of this summer of 1989, White cops trying to restrain a Black kid used the deadly choke hold, and the kid died. In the movie, that prompted all hell to break loose. Rioting erupted, fires got set, and it ended there.

In upstate New York, a White cop also used the choke hold on a Black kid. The kid was 19. He and three buddies were causing a commotion in a movie theater in Wallkill, a little town about 50 miles northwest of New York City.

The cops came and ushered the kids out of the theater. But the trouble that started inside didn't end. Somehow, it resulted in the cops grabbing one of the kids. One of the cops applied the choke hold. The kid whose name was Jimmy Lee Bruce Jr. collapsed on the sidewalk. There was no riot, no fires were set, but Jimmy Lee Bruce was dead.

As it happened, young Bruce's mother was a woman who came to upstate New York from Georgia 22 years ago. She was of that generation of Blacks who grew up with the struggle of the civil rights movement. So when she moved to New York, Maude Bruce continued to be involved. In time, she was elected president of the Ellenville branch of the NAACP.

When Maude Bruce got word of what had happened to her son, she knew that she had to fight.

"They (the cops) didn't know who he was," she said. "All they knew was he was Black. We have so much racism in Orange County. They figured they would get away with this, too. But they messed with the wrong one this time."

The history of the NAACP is to fight through the system. The organization believes in using pressure to make the system work. In the Bruce case, that's what happened.

A defense committee got organized. Word got out. Demonstrations began, and before long, the issue was on the desk of Gov. Cuomo. He ordered an investigation. The report that came back said that something was wrong. The governor turned the case over to the State Commission of Investigation. A grand jury in Orange County had cleared the cops of any wrongdoing. The commission studied the case the district attorney put before the grand jury. The more the commission looked, the more it found that was not right. The report to the governor said a special prosecutor ought to be appointed, and a move ought to be made to reopen the case.

Dennis R. Hawkins became the special prosecutor. He went before State Supreme Court Justice S. Barrett Hickman and made the case for a new presentation to the grand jury. A week ago, the judge handed down his decision. He found that evidence had been omitted in the prior presentation. He accepted the special prosecutor's documentation that some earlier testimony was perjured.

Justice Hickman said the court was "appalled" at what it found in reading the minutes of the grand jury proceedings. He especially decried the way race had been used. Over 200 times, the prosecutor made reference to "the Black kid" or "Black youths" or "Black males" in presenting his case. The DA used race to sway the jury; he made it Black kids against White cops.

In his opinion, the judge wrote: "Although our criminal justice system is admittedly not perfect, great responsibility rests upon those involved to see that all proceedings are conducted in a fair and impartial manner without inappropriate references to age, race, religion, sex or any other irrelevant factor." So he ordered the case back to a grand jury.

After seeing the film, some believe Spike Lee's movie urges Blacks to riot, especially to protest grievances such as those when a White cop uses a choke hold and kills a

Black kid. It happened that way in the movie. But history tells another story. Through the years, Blacks have been involved in an ongoing struggle to make the system work.

The case involving the killing of Jimmy Lee Bruce is not one to hold up as proof that "the system" works. Too many wrongs have already been done for that. But there are times when the system gone wrong can be made to turn around by using the pressure tactics that were the movement's way. The Bruce case has become a very good example of that.

1992

THIS IS NOT JUST ANOTHER UPRISING. The reaction in Los Angeles to the outrageous verdict handed down in the Rodney King case marks the turning of a corner. A door has been opened.

It was not supposed to happen this way. Not in the Rodney King case. This time, there was an ordinary citizen standing in the shadows. That citizen was not just watching the police as they savagely beat Rodney King. He had a video camera. He came up with a piece of videotape that captured the whole crime. It was the kind of evidence that never exists. Always before, it was the police telling one story, the victim telling another. But this time, it was different; this time there was the videotape. That was supposed to make a difference.

The videotape was so compelling that even Richard Thornburg who was then U.S. Attorney General had to respond. He promised to review every complaint of police brutality that had come before the Justice Department in the last six years. When he was questioned, he said that in all, there were *15,000* such complaints in the files.

Before Rodney King, those complaints just sat there, gathering dust. Suddenly, it was different. For a moment, it seemed that a whole new era was about to dawn. As it turned out though, a different history was to be written. A judge in Los Angeles took the trial of the four cops charged with the King beating and moved it away from the jurisdiction where it would have been possible to get a jury that had some mix. The judge moved the trial to one of those suburban sanctuaries -- one of those places where cops who work in the city go home at night to sleep. Once that was done, it did not matter what had been captured on the videotape.

It did not even matter that one of the officers involved broke the so called "blue line" and testified that in the beating of King his fellow officers were out of control. The jury had 11 Whites and one Asian. It was quick to reach verdicts of not guilty.

The next chapter in the story -- and there is a lot yet to come -- was played out in the streets of Los Angeles. The verdict hit with the force of the historic Dred Scott decision delivered in another era by the U.S. Supreme Court. The Dred Scott decision held that a Black had no rights a White man was bound to respect. The decision from the jury in Ventura County said to many that a Black man has no rights a White cop is bound to respect.

It goes back to the 15,000 cases Thornburg mentioned more than a year ago. For a long time, these cases of police brutality have been piling up. The history is that nothing happens. New York is a case in point. In New York City, there is a long list of names that bring back cases where brutality appeared certain, and nothing happened. In the Bronx, there was the killing of Peter Funches, a Vietnam veteran in 1979. Witness told of the way he was kicked and beaten by cops. Still, nothing happened.

Just days after the King beating in Los Angeles, there was the case in Queens involving 21 year-old Frederico Pereira. The fallout from Los Angeles then compelled the DA in Queens to bring murder charges against four city cops. At the time, that was big news. But quietly, in a series of courtroom maneuvers, the case fell apart.

The words of Ron Kuby, one of the attorneys for Pereira, stick in the mind. "The level of judicial concern when police officers are charged is a level unparalled," he said. "You get new constitutional rights with every stroke of the pen."

Los Angeles answers the huge question for now: If not in the courtroom, then where do the victims of police misconduct go for justice? Los Angeles says that a corner has been turned. Issues that ought to have been settled in courtrooms are being played out in the streets. It is what has long been feared. Call it the fire next time.

1992

ACTING POLICE COMMISSIONER RAYMOND KELLY has an answer for dealing with cops who use racial slurs. He said that when officers use such language "absent extreme emotional stress," they will now be fired. In a lot ways, that was the easy part.

The conduct of the cops at their out-of-control demonstration at City Hall has left the commissioner with a much bigger concern. It doesn't involve what the off-duty cops did at City Hall; it was what the on-duty officers there refused to do.

In a preliminary report to Mayor Dinkins, Kelly reviewed what happened at the demonstration. The report raised "serious questions" about the cops' absolute refusal to police other off-duty officers. Kelly said that when the demonstrators surged out-of-control and began knocking over barriers to enter City Hall Plaza, "there was, at best, a lethargic response on the part of officers assigned to the perimeter." In other words, the on-duty cops would not do their job.

He said one on-duty cop, first overheard uttering a racial slur, allowed the cops to storm the barricades, and did nothing. Kelly said, "More commonly, officers appeared to stand by, and observe misconduct without taking action." At the Spruce Street entrance to City Hall Park, where the \demonstrators first began to overrun police barricades, the captain, two sergeants and 10 police officers assigned there have been charged with failure to maintain police policies."

Commissioner Kelly also said that "additional instances of misfeasance or nonfeasance are being investigated."

The preliminary report to Mayor Dinkins says in an unmistakable way that within the police department some important fences have been torn down. So some cops now watch other officers as they break the law. Instead of doing their duty, they turn their heads and do nothing.

It ties into an almost forgotten issue, which is the ongoing investigation of corruption in the department. It cannot be said that the officers who refused to do their job at City Hall only took that position because they believed in the cause of the demonstration. When a cop does not do his job, a fence gets torn down. The problem spreads. Cops who break the law in one area find it easier to break it in another.

So much of the time when something happens that involves an institution as large and important as the Police Department, the resulting investigation amounts to a cover up. Not this time. The report that Kelly handed to Dinkins had the ring of honesty. It was thorough, which is what the situation demanded.

The acting commissioner also made another huge point. That involved Phil Caruso, head of the Policemen's Benevolent Association. He as much as said that Caruso cannot control his men. He said the PBA leadership consistently stressed that the demonstration would be peaceful, and that there would be sufficient marshals on the scene to control it. That is what Caruso said; we know what happened.

The position Kelly took on cops who use racial slurs means, they can use that kind of language if they want, but when they get caught, it means their jobs. That is the kind of clear-cut position the department uses. Never again should a Black woman who sits on the City Council tell of trying to get to her office, and being told no by a cop who calls her a nigger. That's what happened to Una Clarke of Brooklyn.

For a long time, it has been said that a lot of cops use racial slurs. It has also been said that cops refuse to police other cops. Now it is different. Now the head of the department has investigated and found these things to be true.

Yesterday, the talk was reconciliation between City Hall and the cops. There is nothing wrong with that, but it by no means lessens the need to set a lot of crooked places straight in the city's Police Department.

1992

FIRST, IT WAS THE ACCUSED, Larry Davis. Three times, he stood trial on the worst kind of charges. He was acquitted of all except the most minor of the charges. Instead of walking out of court at least on bail, Davis wound up in Attica, the state's maximum security prison.

Now, they've come for the lawyers who defended Davis. When a lawyer wins a trial as big as those involving Davis, that usually changes a lot of things for that attorney.

Michael Warren, of Brooklyn, was chief counsel in the defense that wound up two weeks ago with Davis being cleared of killing a drug dealer in Washington Heights. Instead of acclaim, Warren has gotten hauled onto the carpet. Today, he goes before the trial judge, State Supreme Court Justice Richard B. Lowe III, to face contempt charges.

All of it is part of an old story. In the Davis case, nothing fits, and nothing figures. When he was arrested, Davis was charged with killing drug dealers and trying to kill cops.

The juries that heard the evidence cleared him of all those charges. He wound up being found guilty only of criminal possession of weapons. For that, he got 5 to 15 years, and slapped in Attica. He's got to be the only inmate in a maximum security prison who is there only on a gun charge. But that's the story in this case.

Often, arguments in a courtroom get testy. That's especially so in a trial where points of disagreement are as sharp as they were in the Davis trial. But here is Judge Lowe wasting time in criminal court with a hearing on charges against Warren that should have been dropped two weeks ago.

Warren insists there is more involved than meets the eye -- or has been allowed to come out in the courtroom. In a case presented as being cut and dried, no prosecutor has been able to get a conviction on the serious charges.

The public need to know why? Thus, Warren speaks of a silent issue: cops and drugs. In the trial, he tried to bring that out. He pushed as hard as he could. Maybe he went too far, for that is what got him into trouble with Lowe. Today, he will have attorney C. Vernon Mason defending him.

Mason sees some dirty dealing. He says, "The continued persecution of Davis and his attorney, Warren, is politically and racially motivated. And the federal government and the state government should commence an investigation immediately into the police corruption, and drug dealing by police that underlie all of the Larry Davis cases."

Even Judge Lowe presiding over the trial has been an issue. He's 48 and in his first year on the State Supreme Court. Going into the trial, the speculation in some quarters was that Judge Lowe was under heavy pressure to produce a guilty verdict. He's a former assistant in the Manhattan district attorney's office.

The speculation is, that next time around, he'll run for the job now held by Robert Morgenthau, who is expected to retire. It would make him only the second Black to win election as a DA in the state. The breakthrough win was scored by Robert Johnson in the Bronx.

Lowe comes from a family of police officers. His father was a highly decorated officer. He also has a brother who served with distinction on the New York police force. On Friday, Lowe made another decision involving Davis that drew fire from attorney Warren. Davis has showed up in court in a wheel chair, claiming paralysis suffered from beatings administeed by prison guards.

Lowe ruled that Davis was faking. Warren announced intentions to appeal the decision.

The case involving Larry Davis cries out for investigation. Yet, nothing happens. It makes another reason for losing faith in what is called the criminal justice system.

1993

IN A LOT OF THE NEIGHBORHOODS of New York, these confessions that come now from cops appearing before the Mollen Commission are not even the least bit shocking. In those places, these tales are nothing more than some "we told you so" stories.

Only problem was, when these voices sounded the alarm, those who were supposed to respond chose instead another course of action. They damned the messengers, branded them as rabble-rousers and liars. A good part of the reason it happened that way goes back to what is known as "the blue wall of silence."

You only needed to hear the words of former police officer Bernard Cawley when he testified before the commission looking into police corruption. Cawley, attached to the 46th Precinct in the Bronx, told of the beatings he inflicted on hundreds of citizens. He said he never worried about the consequences.

"Who was gonna catch us?" he asked. "We're the police."

So, there it is, all laid out in a straight line. It is officers themselves saying, 'we are a law unto ourselves.' That being the case, it meant, 'we will do as we please!' That is exactly what a lot of people have been shouting and screaming for a very long time. Those voices told of cops inflicting brutality on citizens as they pleased. They told of cops buying and selling drugs; of cops leaving their beats to engage in all kinds of activity, from sex to drugs. In doing so, they were saying to hell with the citizens.

Once, a congressional subcommittee came to New York to investigate. That body was accused of meddling and playing politics. So many community groups have mobilized through the years to deal with what they call "the problem with the police," the count of those gatherings would be impossible to number.

That day the huge mob of cops converged on City Hall, in an unprecedented show of arrogance, a lot of New Yorkers were scared by the truth they came to witness.

They understood the power of the blue wall of silence.

It is the testimony of the police themselves that tells us that now is the time to act. From these places where the abuses have been worst, all along, those who saw it portrayed the cops as something of an occupying army. Those people told of the cops coming into their neighborhoods, not to protect them, but to exploit and abuse.

They want the cops who work on the force to be citizens of the city.

The truth they know is that it is not so easy to rape and pillage the community where you live, where your kids go to school, and where your wife walks the streets to shop for groceries.

The legislation to require residency is in the hopper at this moment. That has to be made an issue. The city needs it now.

As Police Commissioner, Lee P. Brown was not all bad. His only problem was that he was an intellectual; he dealt in concepts. In his tenure, the concept he brought to the city was called "community policing."

In the end, Lee Brown could not get a grip on the New York City Police Department. Maybe that, too, figured into Brown's decision to leave.

As it happened though, behind Brown stood the ex-Marine, Raymond Kelly. Mayor Dinkins, an ex-Marine himself, knew that Kelly could do what Brown could not; he could take control of the department. Kelly had also bought into the idea and became a disciple of community policing.

That concept now has to be taken to its maximum; cops who are a part of a community come under the scrutiny of that community. In that circumstance it is not so easy to run amuck the way Bernard Cawley and his gang described to members of the Mollen Commission.

Chapter Two, Part One

WHEN THE BOUGH BREAKS

A Lullaby

Rock-a-bye Baby
On The Tree Top
When The Wind Blows
The Cradle Will Rock
When The Bough Breaks
The Cradle Will Fall
And Down Will Come Cradle
Baby And All.

Editor's Note

Earl Caldwell began his column just as the full magnitude of the catastrophe that has been visited on urban children began to unfold. His writings chronicle that disaster, step by step. In many cases. Caldwell's writings are prophetic.

1979

HE IS THE KIND OF KID everybody wants to like. He has a beautiful smile. When he uses it, it lights up his face. Yesterday, when he stood before Justice Howard Bell in Supreme Court in the Bronx, the only thing on his face was fear.

Raul Quinomes was certain that he was going to jail. He is 17, and a jury convicted him of second degree robbery. He was brought before Justice Bell for sentencing.

In the courtroom he stood squarely in front of the bench, next to Stephen Cohen, his lawyer. He said nothing.

Always, it is the same with the kids in the courtroom. They come in, keep their heads down, and their mouths shut.. When questions are directed at them, they mumble answers that can barely be heard.

Stephen Cohen, a young lawyer, was hoping for a break. He pointed out that Quinomes had always made his court appearances, always been on time.

"I'm not worried about that," Justice Bell said, cutting him off.

"Your honor, he's drifting. It's not that he's thumbing his nose at society. He's not a wise guy. It's just that, as a man, he's not strong enough to pull himself out."

And he kept talking about Raul Quinomes. He talked about the neighborhood in the Bronx where Quinomes lives, a neighborhood that sits in the shadow of the courthouse, and about his life there and all of the evils that are a part of it.

"He's like so many young people around here -- out of school and without any work -- and he winds up as so many of the young people do today."

"All right," the judge said again, cutting the lawyer short.

"What I'm saying, your honor, is that he deserves a break. He has been arrested many times, but he has never been involved in anything this serious. Before this, he was never convicted, and his involvement here ... it was very slight."

Now the judge talked to the kid.

"You have a right to be heard before your sentence. Do you wish to say anything."

Raul Quinomes shook his head. The judge told him that he had to speak. He shifted his weight on his feet and ran his hand across his red T-shirt and finally he said, "No," he had nothing to say.

Now the judge, a large and graying Black man, leaned out over the bench and stared down directly at Quinomes. He gave the kid a break. The sentence was five years on probation.

"I hope you have sense enough not to get arrested again," the judge said. "If you violate probation, if you come back, and they will probably bring you here, I can assure you that you're going to jail. I want you to understand that. I'm not sure I'm doing the right thing here. You're always being arrested. If you come back here, you're going to jail.

When he turned to walk away, the youth's face was filled with the light his smile brought. The fear was gone. He had another chance.

"I'm going back to school," he said later, "I haven't been hanging out lately -- just once in a while."

"What was the robbery about?" he was asked.

"A radio," he said. "And there was a medallion and some money. I didn't see the money. I don't know how much it was. And there was some reefer too -- you know, marijuana."

After Quinomes had left, his lawyer was in the hallway outside the courtroom. "That seldom happens," he said. "You know, the judge decided right there to give him a break. You seldom see that."

"Will the kid be back?" he was asked.

He shrugged. "I hope not. He's really a good kid. Even the cops say that he's a good kid but he's out there hanging out and that's how these kids get into trouble. But it's so unfair. There's nothing for the kids. And putting them into jail is not the answer."

Justice Bell is the kids' judge. Nearly all of the cases that involve juveniles come before him, and yesterday was a day for sentencing.

After Quinomes, they brought another kid, Robert Pabon, before Justice Bell. He had pleaded guilty to purse-snatching on the subway, and his sentence was set. The minimum was a year and the maximum three years. When sentence was passed, three officers led him out of the courtroom in handcuffs.

As he neared the door, a friend stood up to reach out to him. But the teenager could not touch him. Pabon disappeared through the doorway with the officers. His friend slouched down in his chair and wiped his hands over his eyes.

Next came Robert Davis. Davis celebrated his 14th birthday four days ago on Rikers Island, a maximum security prison for adults. He has been there almost a year. He was the first 13-year-old charged with murder to be tried as a adult in the state of New York.

Stanley Green, Davis' lawyer, was happy. The case was being sent back to Family Court, where he'd been trying to get it since the child's arrest. The juvenile law has been changed. Now a kid the age of Robert Davis cannot be tried as an adult for felony murder. Only intentional murder. And yesterday intentional murder charges against Davis were dropped and he pleaded guilty to felony murder.

Justice Bell asked him to explain what happened. Robert Davis mumbled. "Speak up," the judge admonished. And finally he did. He said that he had been on a playground with kids he did not know. They had been playing basketball and when they were finished with that, Davis said, one of the kids asked him if he wanted to rob somebody. He said that he did. They went to a subway station and they robbed a kid and he was shot and killed. Davis said he didn't know there was a gun. He said he didn't know the other kids. There were no witnesses, so the state could not prove intentional murder. The kid got a break.

He will not stand trial for intentional murder, thereby escaping the possibility of life imprisonment. His case is in Family Court now, where the maximum punishment is five years in what is called restricted placement.

There are never any good days in Justice Bell's courtroom. It is the story of wasted youth. Yesterday, when court recessed, Stephen Cohen walked outside and said he was tired. "These cases," he said, "they eat you up. I don't like them."

1979

AT THE SCHOOL, THE GUARD stopped the minister and those with him, as soon as they came through the door.

"Who do you want to see?" the husky Black man who sat at a small desk and had a silver badge on his shirt asked.

"The principal," the Rev. Calvin Butts said.

"No, we don't have an appointment," the Rev. Butts said. "But please tell him that we're here."

After the delegation signed in, the guard showed them up the stairs, up to the office the principal at Junior High School 43 occupies, the school that now carries the name of the late Rep. Adam Clayton Powell Jr.

Allen Lewis, the principal, was in his office. He is a lithe, dapper man who has been in the New York City public school system since 1959, when he was a science teacher at JHS 52 in the Bronx.

"We've come to inspect the school," the Rev. Butts said. "We want to talk with you and we'd like to look around. We're interested in visiting some of the classrooms and talking with some of the teachers, too."

Allen Lewis, the principal, wears a thin mustache. It twitched just a bit as a small smile came onto his face.

He had not known that Rev. Butts and the people with him were coming, but, immediately, he understood what was happening.

"We're all community people," the Rev. Butts was saying now. "We're concerned about the general lack of achievement in the schools. We want to see what discipline is in here...We're concerned about reading scores and ..."

Allen Lewis, the principal, interrupted the minister.

"I'm glad you're here," he said. "There's no problem, your touring the school. I don't have a problem, the board has a problem. I have to get permission."

In all of the City of New York there is no school district as troubled as the one that JHS 43 is a part of, District 5. The schools in District 5 are Harlem's schools, and the struggle to bring quality education to these schools never ends.

The appearance of the Rev. Calvin Butts, an assistant pastor at the Abyssinian Baptist Church, signaled the start of another round in the endless effort to do something about the public schools in Harlem.

"I know this is an impromptu visit," the Rev. Butts told the principal. "That's the only way we can get a true picture of what is happening."

The principal invited the group into his office while an effort was made to get Elaine Landrum, the district administrator, on the telephone for the permission the Rev. Butts's group would need to tour the school.

While they waited, the Rev. Butts and his people fired questions at Allen Lewis, the principal.

"How many students do you have?"

"About 1,100," the principal said.

"What is the racial breakdown?"

"I'd say about 70 percent Black, and about 30 percent Dominican and Puerto Rican. I'd say we have about two Whites."

"What about the staff?"

"Of the 63 teachers, about 23 are Black and six, I think it is, are Spanish-speaking."

"What about counselors? How many are Black?"

"One."

"You mean you only have only one counselor who is Black?"

"Oh no, I mean we have only one counselor. That's all we have. I know that's a problem. We should have one for every 350 students, but since the budget cuts..."

While they talked in the principal's office, a secretary came into the room and handed a note to the principal. He read it and looked up. "It's okay," he said. "It's okay for you to look around."

Calvin Butts and the eight people who were with him went from floor to floor, room to room. Each of them carried a notebook. When they were finished, they returned to the principal's office.

Allen Lewis is in his third year as principal at JHS 43. He was brought in by the parents. He came from IS 201. Slowly he has been turning JHS 43 around. The Rev. Butts and his people sensed this. You can tell a lot about a school as soon as you go through the door, and it was that way at JHS 43. No students raced through the halls. Classrooms were quiet. Something was taking place.

"We're trying," the principal said.

The principals at public schools are like captains on ships. No matter what happens, it is their responsibility. "But we need help," Allen Lewis said. "We need all the help we can get."

Later that night, the Rev. Butts and his people were in the Abyssinian Baptist Church. There was a large crowd there to listen to their findings. Next week they'll make another impromptu visit at another school. They'll continue until they've hit every school in the district. Then they will decide on a course of action. "We're prepared to do whatever has to be done," the Rev. Butts said. "We are going to do something about the schools. We're going to do it now. It's our duty. These are our kids, and we owe it to them."

1980

WHEN IT WAS TIME FOR THE KIDS in the classroom to read aloud, an excitement rose in the room. The kids began to squirm in their seats. They smiled and quickly found the right page in their primers.

Claudia Smith, the teacher, was at the front of the classroom. She stood, staring out at her class until all the kids were ready.

"Now let's see what transpires," she said. She began to call out the names of the first-graders who were scattered out in the room in front of her.

"All right, Richard," she said. Over at the side of the room, in the glow of the sunlight that filtered in through the Venetian blinds, a tiny kid dressed in gray slacks, gray jacket, white shirt and red tie began to read. He didn't read long, only for a few minutes, but in that time he went through several paragraphs of one of the fabled old stories of Dick and Jane.

When the boy had read a while, Claudia Smith interrupted.

"All right, Reginald," she said.

Up front in the first row, another of the tiny first-graders began to read. Nobody had to tell him the place. He had been following the story using his finger. When he heard his name he jumped up, read.

"All right, Eric," the teacher interrupted again.

It was the same with the next boy. He picked up the story. Like all the others who had read before him, he didn't stumble over the words. When Claudia Smith's voice interrupted him, there was a wide smile on his face because he knew not only that he could read, but that he did it well.

It went on like that, with the students at the Concord Baptist Church that was Claudia Smith's class, and all of it was beautiful.

So bad is the condition of many public schools, that encountering students who can read well can be astonishing. But it was more than that. It was the whole rhythm of everything in the class. It was like a song, and it was Claudia Smith who established that. She did it with her voice, the way that she would say "all right" as she called out the names. The voice said you did well. The kids understood this. When they were finished, they smiled and squirmed happily in their seats. It was a part of the beauty that was in the classroom, Claudia Smith's first-graders at Concord Baptist Church.

After every child in the classroom had the chance to read, there was a series of drills. Claudia Smith wrote sentences on the blackboard, sentences about the story that was read. As soon as she finished, hands shot up into the air. She called the children by name. They stood in front of what was written and read aloud from the blackboard.

Then it was time to go over the rules.

From the front of the classroom, Claudia Smith's voice was an instrument. It played one part. When the youngsters responded, they sang out the answers.

"What's a sight word?" Claudia Smith asked.

The whole class responded, voices ringing out in unison.

"The short vowels," the teacher said.

The class responded. Claudia Smith kept throwing out the questions.

At noon, when the class was over, the kids dashed off to chapel. Claudia Smith, who has taught at Concord for 16 years, was alone in the classroom. When asked why the first-graders could read, she was ready with the answer.

"I teach phonics," she said. "We still believe in the ABCs." Her smile carried a special pride. "They're reading the newspaper by the time they get out of here."

There are kids in junior high school all over the city who do not read anywhere near as well as the first-graders at Concord Baptist.

"Why?" Claudia Smith was asked.

"They're not teaching them," she said. "You must start in the first grade. They've got to read. It's almost impossible to do anything else if they can't read."

So what makes Concord work, why do the kids here -- even the first-graders -- read so well? "You must teach in a learning situation," she said. "You know, we still use the strap, and we can have discipline here without worrying about the parents' descending on us."

1981

THE HOSPITAL CLOSED MONTHS ago. After that, the day care center went. Nobody has been paid for weeks at the Head Start Center.

"It's the after-school center they're talking about now," Veronica Perry said. "They say they are going to close that down in a few weeks, and when they do, I just don't know what the children up here are going to do. I just don't know."

Closing an after-school center does not sound like much. In other neighborhoods it might not matter. But Veronica Perry lives in Harlem. In her neighborhood, the after-school center is everything.

"You know what the streets are like up here," Veronica Perry says. "The drugs are everywhere. If they close the after-school center, we know what will happen to our kids. It is like putting them out there on the streets and telling the drug dealers to come and get them."

In the City of New York there are areas where the sale of hard drugs is so wide open that the traffic is virtually legalized. In Harlem, it was that way on W. 143rd St. until the block association raised so much noise that finally the police moved it away.

And it is that way yet on W. 114th St. It is so bad that last year, on the Fourth of July, the block association held its meeting in the middle of the street, and the parents used a microphone to scream threats at the drug dealers, but nothing happened.

Even while the meeting was going on, cars with New Jersey, Connecticut and Westchester County license plates kept coming through the block -- the drivers looking for drugs. The cars just inched along, moving so slowly that the block association people became incensed and chased the cars away. Almost a year has passed. Nothing has changed.

It is not the cops on the block or the precinct commanders. It is the higher-ups, the brass, in the police department that have to say, "enough." Despite all the complaints on W. 114th St., nothing has changed.

"Don't put my name in the paper," an older man who lives on the block said. "I don't want any trouble," he said, "but yes, it's really bad up here. Of course the kids need a place to go. These streets are no place for the kids. It's a crime what they let go on up here."

If Veronica Perry is afraid, it is not about what might happen to her for speaking out. She is afraid only of what might happen to her youngest child, a daughter who is 10 years old.

"With girls, you used to worry just about them having babies, but now, it's this drug thing," she said. Veronica Perry is not a transplant to New York. Her family has its roots in the neighborhood where she lives now. "People talk about Kunta Kinte in Africa and all that," she said, "but I got six generations of my family right here. That's why I get so angry about what is happening."

Veronica Perry was born in Metropolitan Hospital. She has 45 years in Memorial Baptist Church. It's the church where she was married. In the morning yesterday, she was among the first to come through the door.

She has a full-time job. She is also a nursing student at Bronx Community College. In the time she has left, she raises her family and also serves as president of the Parents Association at PS 113.

The after-school center is in PS 113, an old elementary school. Once the center was open seven days a week. Then it was cut to five, cut again and again. Now, it operates only on Tuesdays and Thursdays.

From 3 o'clock until 4:45 in the afternoon, it is open for elementary school children. At night, from 6:45 until 10:15, it is open for teenagers. There is supervised recreation, mostly basketball and volleyball, but there are also other games. It is not much, but every day that the center is open, hundreds of young people come. It is a place to go, and there is nothing else. The money to operate comes from the Board of Education. The problem is that now the funds are gone.

"Of course we would like to continue," says Jack Berbarien, the acting superintendent in District 3. "We know how much it's needed, but we have budgetary constraints. And we are one of the few districts still running after-school centers. We know if we close, that they (the kids) are going to get into trouble, but we have no choice."

It is about priorities. The Board of Education says no to after-school centers. At the same time, it keeps dozens of architects on the payroll in the Division of Buildings. It is a way of saying that drawing pictures of buildings is more important than young people.

In addition to her daughter, Veronica Perry has two sons. One is 13; the other, 15. Both went to PS 13. Both were outstanding students and were a part of the enrichment programs in junior high school. Both won scholarships and are about to enter private schools. One is going off to Westminster in Connecticut; the other, to Exeter Academy in New Hampshire.

"People say the public schools can't work," Veronica Perry says. "That is not true. Just look at my sons."

It is said that in the hard times now, the city is balancing its budgets on the backs of the poor. Absolutely not true, officials say.

The hospital is in the same neighborhood as Sydenham Hospital, which was closed months ago. Day care for children is out. Head Start soon will be gone. Now the kids are being put on the streets where the traffic in drugs has been all but legalized. It is a part of what gives strength to the arguments that racism is involved.

1983

THE ISSUE IN THE CITY 15 years ago was community control of the public schools. A part of the fight that came with it centered on Intermediate School 201 in Harlem. The idea was that people in the community where the schools were located, especially the parents, ought to be the ones who had control of those schools.

It was to be the last real fight over education in the city. Since then, there have been arguments and skirmishes. But back in 1967, it was a fight. No morning passed that parents were not there, on the sidewalk, at the schools targeted for community control. The arguments were sharp.

In 1967, Queen Mother Moore, a legendary activist, was in the forefront of the decentralization fight. Reporters and television cameras were at the doorway to the school.

"It's about what this rotten system is doing to our young people," Queen Mother Moore shouted.

On the sidewalk, kids clustered around her. She had a newspaper in her hand. She reached out and grabbed one of the kids.

"I want to see you read this paper," she said.

Queen Mother Moore is a large woman. She had a grip on a teenage boy, and she put the newspaper in his face.

"Now read," she commanded. The boy took the paper and began to stutter and stumble over the words. It was not meant to embarrass the boy. Queen Mother Moore knows how to make a point. That done, she pushed the kids away.

"You see what I'm talking about," she cried out. "These children, they don't even know how to read. How can you teach a kid anything if he doesn't even know how to read?"

The morning and the pictures of another time came back yesterday. They did because of another fight in the city over education. The issue now is the naming of a new school chancellor. It all becomes important because in the city, the crisis in education has not gone away.

In the city's school system, the chancellor is the leader. If any good is to happen in the schools, the impetus and the creativity to make it happen has to come from the top. When he was asked to become a candidate for the job, Gordon Davis, who had been parks commissioner, said no. He said the job was so important it should go to someone who wanted it more than anything else.

I do not know the reason kids are not learning. I only know that too many are not. In the afternoons, when they ought to be in classrooms, they prowl the streets and get into trouble. A part of it is that they know there is nothing for them in the schools. The absentee rate in the city's schools is incredible. The dropout rate is worse. All of it comes back to today and the decision the Board of Education makes on a new chancellor.

The New York Urban League has gone back to 1978 for criteria that was set then for selecting a schools chancellor. At the top of the list of criteria, it stated:

"The chancellor should have a creative vision of the possibilities of education in the City of New York, an informed understanding of the ways in which schools relate to other educative agencies, a sound knowledge of the processes of teaching and learning, and a firm commitment to providing every child with the encouragement and opportunity to master reading, writing, arithmetic and all the other important domains of knowledge, skill and appreciation."

The law puts the selection of a chancellor in the hands of the Board of Education. In the afternoon yesterday, Joseph Barkan who is board president, insisted that it isn't a political decision. "I can only speak for myself," he said, "but the mayor, he'd like me to vote for Wagner or anyone else, and the borough president (Donald Manes of Queens) said he would like me to vote for what is best for New York. I can't speak for the others, though, only myself."

Several other board members echoed Joseph Barkan.

It was different with Miguel O. Martinez. "You would not take me seriously if I said there is no political pressure," he said. He said that while the mayor cannot remove him from office if he does not support his choice, he could make life miserable for him. And if he quits, he said, there is no guarantee that another Hispanic would be appointed in this place.

"As I said before," he said, "the board is not ready for a Hispanic or minority person for chancellor. I'll tell you seriously, if I support Anthony Alvarado, it most likely would be the only vote he would get. I could vote for Dr. (Thomas) Minter, but I would be very surprised if he got more than one or two votes."

1983

HE WORRIED ABOUT THE KIDS. "What really scares me," he said, "is that one day somebody is going to come along and organize them -- and probably for something we don't want them doing. Now they are just out there, striking out on their own. Can you imagine what it would be if they were organized?"

He was in the process of building an office on Madison Ave. It was one of the last times we talked. He got very sick after that, and he never came back. Last year, he died while still a young man.

"I'm worried about the Black family," he said. "The family is key and it's being taken apart."

That afternoon on Madison Ave., Cenie J. Williams, president of the National Association of Black Social Workers, sat in his office and spoke of the dismantling of the family -- the silent issue in Black communities across the country.

"I used to talk about it," Benjamin Hooks, executive director of the NAACP, said. It was late at night, and Hooks was with a group of reporters in a suite at the Fairmont Hotel in New Orleans where the organization he heads was in the midst of its 74th annual convention. "I know that the Black family has problems," he said, "but when I talked about it, I found that would be in the headlines -- the criticism of the Black family -- and everything else I said about the causes would be ignored. So I had to stop talking about it."

"Of course it's something we need to deal with."

On a sidewalk in Harlem, Michael Joseph said, "I'm worried." He turns 17 in November.

"What are you doing? he was asked.

"Staying in school," he said. He is entering his senior year at Julia Richmond High School.

"Doing good in school?" he was asked.

"Doing the best I can," he said.

He sees college next. "The arts," he said, "that's me. That's what I'm all about." He talked of getting into production, but if that doesn't work, he has back up ideas about something in computers. "I'm good with mathematics."

He was asked about the neighborhood. "How is it going?"

"Bad," he said. "But it's been like that every since I was small. It's been bad since I was 3 or 4 years old. Where I grew up, you know the deal. I've seen guys that had money, and they got hooked on drugs. Everybody knows how it is, the environment is bad."

It is going to break soon. Whatever it is that is building with Ronald Reagan in Central America, it is about to explode. If it comes to war, these are the kids who go. Zack Coleman, a tall, muscular 20-year-old. Reggie Payne, dark, wiry and 20 years old. They are the ones the Army takes. Michael Joseph is still a bit young, but Melvin Lake is 19, and has just begun to have hair growing from the smoothness of his face. He is the perfect age.

Yesterday they could not see it. The names are only vaguely familiar. El Salvador, Nicaragua, Honduras. Once, it was that way with names of countries in another section of the world, in southeast Asia. In time, Vietnam and Cambodia and Laos became places that were familiar to every American.

So in the summer heat of yesterday, in a neighborhood where the government comes for soldiers in time of war, the fear was not there. It has not happened yet.

Zack Coleman stretched on the rail across the sidewalk from Melvin Lake. Michael Joseph stood alongside Reggie Payne. In the summer afternoon, what tied them together was work. Each of them had a job in the summer program operated by the W. 131st St. Block Association.

"We've been providing jobs for the kids here for 20 years," said William Byrd, executive director. The program the block association operates is one of the official work sites of the city's Department of Employment.

Close to 40 of the kids are employed in a youth patrol. The patrol is an escort service. It operates within the housing project that stretches for four blocks. In all, St. Nicholas Houses has 14 buildings, each 14 stories high with 108 families.

The escort service has the kids taking adults to meetings, stores, churches and other places in the area. Escorts are needed because older people are afraid to use the streets alone, especially at night. The program operates a nutritional service, sewing services, recreational services and a maintenance program.

The housing projects cover four blocks. In between, the grounds are landscaped. There are benches and trees, and yesterday in the afternoon heat the benches were filled.

The summer jobs program that the four Army-aged kids are part of operates out of the basement of one of the buildings. There is a complex of rooms. One large room is a dining area. Another is a weight room. Another has sewing machines and clothes are made there. Young girls are taught modeling and fashion. In every room the walls have pictures of the kids in sports uniforms, and at meetings and in classes.

"The kids," William Byrd said. "We have to do more for them. I mean we have to do it because these are our kids." That was the way he came to Diana Ross and the concert in Central Park. "She could have done more," he said, "if she wanted to help, by coming up here."

"I feel she doesn't care about us as a race," Zack Coleman said. "She's our color, but she doesn't care about us."

"I heard she doesn't like Blacks," Melvin Lake said. "I'm telling you, money makes you that way. It changes your whole personality."

In the late afternoon they drifted away. "Yo, you breakin?" Reggie Payne called to Melvin Lake. The trouble in countries they do not know does not worry them now.

"I'm here," William Byrd said, "because the kids have nothing to do, but they will find something, and I live here and I don't want them to do it to me."

1987

IT'S THE SAME AT ALL the hospitals. They've taken the little space that could be found, then scrubbed and polished it. That's what they use.

"For our babies," they say.

In the city of New York, where the incredible happens on a daily basis, nothing is more shocking than to see these infants left in hospital cribs. It's that way because their mothers are so addicted to drugs, that either they can't be trusted to take their babies home, or they just walk off without them.

For close to two years, these infants have been collecting in city hospitals. They are known as boarder babies. They are the clearest reflection yet of the kind of damage that drugs are inflicting on people at the bottom.

At the start, the belief was that the boarder baby problem would be short-lived. But it's not happening that way. Instead of getting better, the situation is getting worse.

"It's frightening," said Dr. David Bateman, chief of the neonatal unit at Harlem Hospital. "It's got to be frightening," he explained. "We have almost no tools to deal with the situation, and we know so little."

In New York, the municipal hospitals are huge, monstrous places. But by law, they cannot turn anybody away. They take it as it comes. They are noisy, crowded and often dangerous places. It would seem that these hospitals would be all wrong for the boarder babies. But that hasn't been the case. In caring for the infants, these hospitals, in a way, have achieved their finest hour. Still, it is not ideal.

You see the long rows of white metal cribs that hold these babies. You are struck by two things: almost all the babies are Black; almost all of them are smaller than they ought to be.

The mothers are not only addicted to drugs; many are also heavy cigarette smokers. Dr. Bateman says those two things account for the low birth weight. Some of the infants stay in the hospitals a few weeks. Others stay for months before foster homes are found.

"Nobody knows what happens when a baby is left alone like that," Dr. Bateman says. "What happens when an infant misses the bonding that takes place between a baby and the mother?"

At Kings County, they have paid workers who come into the hospital to rock or just pick up and hold the babies. They also have senior citizens who are volunteers. They come to the nurseries to do the same jobs. It's not just at Kings County. At Harlem Hospital and others, they have the same programs. None of the babies is left alone.

Janet Wise has been involved in social work for 17 years. At Harlem Hospital now, she is social work supervisor. "It's scary," she says. "So much is needed; but we're living in times where human services are not a priority. Poor people need so much. Education is so important. At what age do you begin to reach youngsters?"

"But shouldn't the young women know by now that they risk losing their babies if they continue on drugs while they are pregnant?" she is asked.

"But they don't know. On the streets, we hear people say: 'They're taking people's babies. You'll lose your baby if you go there (to Harlem Hospital).' So instead of coming here early and letting us help them get care and advice, they stay away. By the time they come to deliver, it's too late. By then, the drugs are in the baby's system, too."

"Is it just the young teenagers?"

"Actually, it's not the teenagers. A lot of women are over 25, and some are older. Some of them are homeless, and they have gotten into a situation that is so stressful, they use cocaine. They say it's just recreational. But they come here addicted."

"But what about their families?"

"A lot of these families are just over-loaded. There are already too many babies and there's been a great deal of breakdown. In a lot of cases, grandma would like to help, but she has limited resources. And there's only so much a person can do."

"What does it mean?"

"It means that we all need to work together and put pressure where it's needed. Our future as Black people is definitely at stake here. We're losing a generation of children."

"Is it already too late?"

"I'm an optimist, but to do what has to be done is going to take a lot of work. But we don't have a choice. We're being destroyed from within."

1989

HE GOT ONTO THE STORY quite by accident. He had been working as a foreign correspondent in Africa, mostly covering a war in Angola. Then, as it happened, his young daughter fell sick, and he wanted to be with her. So Leon Dash, a Washington Post reporter, came home.

This was early in 1984. Dash had been in Africa nearly five years. It was a long time. When he came back, he found that he had lost touch, not just with what was going on in the District of Columbia, but in America.

Soon, he found himself doing something reporters often do: He was getting together with friends, "To talk," he would say. But he would really be interviewing them. He would fire questions and challenge statements. He was not trying to be contrary or argumentative. He was merely being what he was, a reporter playing catch up.

What stuck in his mind was a conversation with a friend from one afternoon of that January. Her name was Vernita Fort. Dash was visiting at her apartment in Washington, near American University. They were two Black people talking about "the Black community." He remembers how stunned he was as she told him of the way young girls, just babies really, had begun to have babies. He was told that more than half the Black children born in America are the children of single parents. He was told that more than a third of those mothers were poor and just teenagers.

"I was staggered," he recalled.

Reporters are always looking for their next story. When Leon Dash came back from Africa, he wondered, "What will I do?" It wasn't intended to happen that way but his friend, Vernita Fort, pointed him toward his next assignment.

On the first of February, the start of Black History Month, Leon Dash had his first book published. He calls the book, "When Children Want Children." Leon Dash came away from that afternoon's conversation with his friend, determined to find out "the why" in the story of babies making babies. He did not set out to write a book. That part happened quite by accident. But he was determined to get and to tell the story. He is an excellent reporter. He accomplished what he set out to do.

The book he wrote is really two remarkable stories. Both are remarkable for the same reason. They take readers to places they seldom get to go. First, Dash takes his readers with him into the city-room of the Washington Post. He lets his readers see from the inside the way a newspaper works on a big story. Next, he takes his readers with him to one of the poorest neighborhoods of Washington. He gets himself an apartment there and moves in. He takes his readers along as he goes out and finds the young girls, the babies having babies.

No reporter, no matter how skilled, can walk up to strangers in a neighborhood where he does not belong and say, "Tell me your story. Why are you pregnant? Why are you, a girl just 13, having a baby? Where is the father? How are you going to support this child? What kind of life do you think you can provide for the child?" A reporter can ask the questions. Often, the reporter will get answers. But the truth, that's something else, and not so easy to come by. Leon Dash found all that out. But he did not stop. In time, he wrote an award-winning series for his newspaper. But he had much more to say. So he kept going. His book tells the whole story.

When he started out, the way he had it in his mind, he would stay at home and do interviews for a few weeks and then write his series. As it happened, Bob Woodward, one half of the team that won a Pulitzer Prize for breaking the Watergate scandal that brought down President Nixon, was assigned as Dash's editor. The managing editor told Dash, "take four months," to do the series. Woodward said, "No, take more time. Get an apartment in the right neighborhood. Move in. Take six months or more." As it turned out, Dash lived in the neighborhood a year.

"Don't tell that story," some Blacks told Dash. "Whites don't need to hear that," he was advised. But he wrote of what he found. It's a tough, painful story that has a ring of truth. The girls want babies. They want to prove they are not barren women. They shun birth control. They are out there in a whole different world. Leon Dash has pulled all the pieces together for a story that ought to be required reading this Black History Month.

1989

IT USED TO BE A DIFFERENT STORY for women who were pregnant, and, for a lot of reasons, felt they could not have the baby.

Having an abortion was the way out. To accomplish that, the woman had to go down an awful road.

First, she had to get a handful of cash. Most of the time, she then had to go alone to some secret place. Once there, she had to put her life into the hands of what often turned out to be a butcher.

Not all women who traveled that road made it back. Some paid with their lives. Those who survived were changed forever. What they had been put through left them with an anger that was not soon to subside.

The horrible history that was supposed to be behind us again looms large. It is because the issue is in the hands of the U.S. Supreme Court -- the court that Ronald Reagan and President Bush rebuilt. All the while the two of them were remaking the court, one of issues they had in mind involved a woman's right to abortion.

A woman's right of choice was supposed to have been settled. In 1973, in the landmark case of Roe v. Wade, the Supreme Court seemingly established abortion as a fundamental constitutional right.

In the arguments before the court on Wednesday, Kathryn Kolbert, a lawyer for the American Civil Liberties Union, made a powerful point.

"Never before," she said, "has the Court bestowed and taken back a fundamental right that has been part of the settled rights and expectations of literally millions of Americans for nearly two decades."

It would be good if it were that easy. But it isn't. This now is a different court, one built on right-wing politics. It seems to take the position that nothing is really "settled," and that includes the right of abortion.

As the issue was being put into the hands of the justices, the matter was played out in a familiar way on the streets. There were demonstrations and counter-demonstrations; one side screaming yes; the other, never. Almost forgotten are the children.

It is a fair question. How do we treat the children who are here?

In Washington, the Children's Defense Fund takes no position on abortion. To keep the focus where it ought to be, on the children, the defense fund tries as best it can to operate above politics. But yesterday, Jim Weil talked of what the research gathered by the Defense Fund now shows with regards to the way children in the country are treated.

"The record of the country over the last 20 years has not been very good," he said. The facts show that a child is twice as likely to be living in poverty as an adult.

Among the developed nations, we rank near the bottom in infant mortality, immunizations, child poverty, teenage pregnancy and educational achievement. That is not the whole story.

Even a program as successful as Head Start is funded at levels that are woefully inadequate. "For about a third of the eligible children," Weil said.

Some 10 million kids in the country are not covered by any health insurance. Because we are the only major country with no national health insurance, kids get left out on that level, too.

On Wednesday, the Bush administration had its lawyers appearing before the Supreme Court asking that the most basic right a women has -- that of reproductive choice -- be taken away.

In arguing the case for going back to the awful place of more than 20 years ago, the government insisted that it has a compelling interest in protecting fetal life.

What was not discussed though was the awful record the country has in providing for the children who are here. While that may not fit as part of the legal argument, it ought to at least have some place in the debate.

1990

NOBODY DARES TO USE the word that fits. But in the New Jersey town of Glen Ridge, they were kids from the world of money and privilege. So, nobody says that, for kicks, they too went wilding.

To describe the way a gang of Jersey youths sexually assaulted a teenaged young girl who was mentally retarded, "wilding" is the only word we have that fits.

In Glen Ridge, the girl was assaulted on the 1st of March. The gang took her into the basement in one of those fancy suburban homes. She was forced to commit sexual acts, and who knows what else? Then, because wilding plays on the edge, she was violated with a broomstick and a baseball bat.

In Glen Ridge, this was a crowd of 13 teenagers, all of them described as being "good kids." According to reports, five of the boys were active participants in the attack. But the others who were there did nothing to stop it. When it was over, instead of remorse, the gang of them went out and shared details of what had happened with friends.

So what happens when the rich kids go wilding?

Through all of March, April and most of May, nothing happened. Not until after NBC-TV broke the story did authorities in New Jersey round up the gang and press charges. In the high school in Glen Ridge, students talked of it. Teachers knew about it. There were even markings on a bathroom wall that told of what had been done. It was not only kids and teachers who knew, and did nothing. The police in Glen Ridge also knew. But through part of March, April and most of May, the police, at best, only had the case "under investigation."

Nothing stays under the covers forever. So the rich town's secret kept moving in a wider circle, and reporters got onto it. It finally came out that kids from the world of money and privilege also go wilding.

Until the brutal, late night attack on a young woman jogging in Central Park, wilding was not a word in our vocabulary. Although it was later denied, it was reported that "wilding" was a word the gang involved in the Central Park rape and beating had used. It does not matter whether the kids used the word or not. In the Central Park attack, the word fit. It described a bunch of young people going beyond all bounds. It so happened that in Central Park, they were Black kids from Harlem, pouncing on a White woman from the upper East Side. It was turned into a racial assault. But it was not racial. Those kids who sat in wait in the park would likely have pounced on any woman who came by at that moment. It was a horrible, unacceptable attack. But before a trial, even before formal charges were brought, there rose a cry for those kids lives.

The teenagers involved in the attack in Glen Ridge were White. The girl who was the victim of the attack was White. Even knowing what the kids did, some in Glen Ridge say, so what? They say, they were good kids, and that nothing ought to happen to them.

Nobody has called them animals. Nobody has described the group of them as being a wolf pack. Nobody has called them mutants or any of the other words hung on the kids from Harlem.

After the attack in Central Park, Donald Trump took huge ads in major newspapers, to call for the death penalty, and encourage hate. Trump comes from money and privilege. What ads is he apt to take in newspapers now, or does he, too, play by two sets of rules?

The wilding episode in Central Park involved some kids who were juveniles. The practice has been to afford juveniles certain protections. In news stories, their names and photographs are almost never used. But for those kids, age made no difference. Their names were printed and broadcast. Their addresses were used along with just about everything else that could be learned. Of the kids who went wilding in New Jersey, the juveniles were protected, even though two of them, both 17-year-olds, were arrested and charged in the attack.

The Central Park attack was seen as racial. In a way, that became the whole story. The Trump-led cry for revenge was so loud it blocked out any discussion of reasons why, even though violent sexual attacks on women are increasing in a frightening way. Maybe now it will be different for we know that rich kids from New Jersey go wilding too.

1992

MOTHER HALE WAS A PIECE of the hope, because of what she did with her life. She didn't have a lot of money or a big position. When she saw where she could use what she had to make a difference in her community, she did it.

Hers was a true Christmas story, all about giving.

So many agencies that are supposed to be about helping children wind up as part of the problem. It happens that way when people forget what they are supposed to be about. Instead of helping, they start chasing after position and money. Once on that track, it is not long before they are lost. They wind up a part of the problem.

That never happened to Mother Hale. That was the reason she was able to go so strong for so long. She knew what she was about. She was committed to helping. She never tried to line her own pockets or to make herself important. When President Reagan singled her out as being an American hero, she down-played that. She insisted that she was no hero. She only saw herself as doing the good she knew how to do.

What that involved, mostly, was helping babies whose parents were drug addicts. Mother Hale never built that job up as being one that required a huge amount of expertise. She said that love is what the job really required. That was her strong suit. So she took those babies and nursed them back to health by giving them love. She held them to her bosom, rocked them, sang to them, and, I am sure, she also prayed them through the time it took to rid their tiny bodies of the demons left from drugs.

We may never know just how many young lives Clara Hale saved. That really doesn't matter. We know she saved a lot of them. She did what she did because it was the right thing to do. In this week of Christmas, as she goes to her rest, she leaves a life that stands as a beacon of hope. That's because she showed us that one person can make a difference.

It is different for the principal, Patrick Daly. He was not like Mother Hale; he did not get all of his years. His life was cut short. So in a significant way, what he represents is the challenge.

He believed in children, too. We know from those who knew him well, the students and their parents from PS 15, in the Red Hook section of Brooklyn. They have given a ton of testimonials to all the good work he did. Daly was like Mother Hale. He wasn't after position and money. He wanted to be a part of making things better. Instead of taking a school in a fancier area, and a place that did not have so many social problems, he stayed at Red Hook, ignoring the danger that was eventually to take his life. He ignored it, not only in the school building. He ignored it the day of his death, when he left the campus in search of a troubled student who was missing from class. Near the boy's home, Patrick Daly was caught, and killed, in the crossfire in a gang-war.

So much of the time, people look at the misery and danger around them and ask: "What can we do?" The challenge of Patrick Daly says that ordinary citizens have to stand up and assert: enough is enough. Once a community begins to organize, to move against evil, nothing can stop that movement. In a lot of housing projects -- not just Red Hook, and not just in New York -- that has got to begin to happen. The new beginning in America has to stretch from top to bottom.

Patrick Daly only got 48 years. Then, a bullet from a child's gun snuffed out his life. It is not enough for those who benefited from his work and principles just to say what a good man he was. To make the giving of his life mean something, they have to take up the challenge, which means using the power they have to change the environment that puts guns and drugs in the hands of children.

Chapter Two, Part Two

WHEN THE BOUGH BREAKS

ATLANTA'S MISSING & MURDERED CHILDREN

Editor's Note.

Almost from the beginning of the murder of children in Atlanta, perhaps no journalist in America wrote as frequently and passionately about the case. Earl Caldwell's focus on the murders continued through the trial and guilty verdict of the only person charged in the murders, and for many years thereafter.

Caldwell's writings reveal that the murder of African American children was not unique to Atlanta -- then or now.

1981

THEY FOUND THE BOY'S body exactly where the person who called on the phone said that it was -- in an old, abandoned building on Brooks Ave. in the Bronx.

The boy was 10. He disappeared from his school.

"He was a good kid", Stanley Kaminsky, the principal, said. "He would have grown up to become a really decent human being. That's the shame of it."

"A horrible thing," the medical examiner said. He explained how the boy was killed, how the stab wounds went through the skull, through his neck, then into his spine.

The boy's name was Jack Brewington. He lived in Claremont Village, the city-owned development on Washington Ave. in the Bronx. The Brewingtons have a small fifth-floor apartment. There is LeVan Sr., his wife, Carrie, and there are three remaining children.

LeVan Brewington Sr. is a lean, well-built, muscular man. He supports his family driving a gypsy cab. He cannot prove what he believes happened to his son. But he is certain that his son was killed by a loan shark.

The boy disappeared from school. Brewington and his son LeVan Jr. went to the school that day in the gypsy cab to ride Jack home. He was nowhere to be found. That evening, when the boy had still not been found, the father went back out in his car, and that was when he got the call.

"I got your kid," the voice said.

The voice said that the kid was being held in an abandoned building on Brooks Ave. The father called the police. The police told him not to go alone, to wait for them. Driving any cab is a dangerous job in New York. It is especially dangerous for those who drive the gypsy cabs. One of the ways that the drivers take care of themselves is by sticking together. When there is trouble, they put the word out on their radios, and gypsy cabs from everywhere rush to help. That was what LeVan Brewington did. When he arrived at the building at Brooks Ave., where the voice had told him his son was being held, many other gypsy cabs were already there. Then the police arrived and rushed into the building, searched everywhere, but found nothing.

Wednesday turned to Thursday. Friday morning, the boy's body was found. It was exactly where the caller had said, in the very building on Brooks Ave.

Late in the afternoon last week, Wendell Foster, the city councilman, was at the Brewington's apartment. Councilman Foster's wife teaches in the city schools. On the last Wednesday in January she came home from work and said to her husband, "Two kids disappeared from a school today."

Right away what popped up in Wendell Foster's mind was Atlanta. For a moment, he froze. It is that way with Black people everywhere in America now. As soon as a child is missing, the first thought is of Atlanta.

Foster, who is also a minister, contacted the families. The other kid that was missing showed up. Then he contacted the Brewingtons.

As he sat in the living room, he cross-examined the father. He explained to the father that he had been out in the streets questioning people, and that word was, drugs were involved. The father's face tightened. He called those stories lies. He said that the police had given him two lie detector tests. He had passed both of them. Foster still came at him. There were still more questions. When he finished, Foster apologized.

Carrie Brewington, the mother, sat in a corner of the room. She kept getting up and going out into the kitchen. She did not want anyone to see her cry. "A child has been killed," she said, "and it's being treated like it's some dark secret."

LeVan Brewington Jr., the 11-year old, sat near his mother. He has not been to school since his brother was taken. "And I'm going to keep him here," the mother, a dark, attractive woman, said, "I'll teach him here myself if I have to."

"At first, the police asked me if I killed him," the father said.

"I told them who did it. I told them who the killer was. I recognized the voice on the phone. But they're talking about proof. They know I'm not lying. They kept us at the precinct all night."

"I brought the boy up here," an uncle who was in the room said.

"I had left him back home, in South Carolina," the father explained. "I came up here first, to get started, to get things set up, and then I sent back home for my family. My brother here, he brought the kids up."

"Tell me again what happened," Councilman Foster said.

Then LeVan Brewington told again how he had borrowed $30 from a man he insisted he did not know was a loan shark. He said he tried to pay the man back, but that he would not accept the $30. He wanted $60; then it was $90. From there, it all went up very fast.

He said that he ran across the man on either Friday or Saturday on the weekend before his son was taken, and that the man wanted hundreds of dollars from him . He said that he told him again that he owed him $30 and that he would pay no more. On Wednesday he got the phone call at work, the one that said his kid was in an abandoned building. He said he knew right away who the caller was.

The Brewingtons keep their kids at home now. The worry now is that another child might be taken.

Everywhere the violence grows. Old men and old women are beaten and killed. Some of the victims are rich, others are poor. Some are Black, others are White. It used to be that the kids were safe.

1981

IN ATLANTA, HER SON was the 18th to be found dead.

His name was Jeffrey Mathis. He was 10 years old when he disappeared early in the evening on the 11th of March in 1980. His body was not found until the 19th of this past February, almost a year later.

"It wasn't much left of him," his mother said yesterday. "It was just a skull."

The mother, Willie Mae Mathis, stopped and lowered her head into her right hand. For a while, she kept it there. In time, she took her hand away, raised her head up high. She did not cry.

She said her son was found in some woods, in a very exclusive neighborhood, a place called Cascade Heights. "They found him right at Cascade Road and Subee Road. To identify him, they had to have his dental records."

Willie Mae Mathis remembered all of the details of the day the February before, when she took all of her kids off to the dentist for checkups. That was the reason, when they found the body, that the dental records were readily available.

"They said his teeth were still intact in his skull," she said. "My son saw it. He said they had the skull on a table. There was no feet, no legs, just a little part of the hip and that was all, except for the skull."

Two days after the remains were found, they had the funeral. Yesterday, although all of the hurt is still with her, Willie Mae Mathis was in New York. She spent most of the afternoon rushing from interview to interview, first telling, then retelling the story of what happened to her son.

She is not the only mother who lost a child in Atlanta who is doing the same thing. They have come together and formed a sort of committee. They go everywhere they can.

"We just got to let people know what is happening," Willie Mae Mathis said. "I don't believe Atlanta can take any more of this. I don't know what will happen if another body is found."

Yesterday, she came to New York. She had already been in Toronto. On Monday, she is due to be in Syracuse. Then, she has to fly to Montreal, and then to California and she has promised to keep going as long as she believes that she can help.

"I'm so tired," she said. "I've been on my feet all day and I haven't eaten and, you know, I'm going to march tonight."

She was talking about the candlelight service in Harlem. It was the reason for her visit to New York, and she said it was important. It did not matter that she was tired, she was going to march the entire 25-block length of the demonstration, then tell the Black people of Harlem, of New York, what is happening to the children of the Black people in Atlanta.

"They're saying that it's just street kids that's disappearing," she said, bristling at the thought. "That's not true," she said. "Not one kid has disappeared at night. They are taking our children in the broad daylight."

She talked about her boy, Jeffrey.

He disappeared on the 11th of March. The day before, the body of another Black child who had been killed was found. "That was Angel Lanier," the mother said. "They had it on television, and I got all of my kids and brought them into the room and made them watch. I wanted them to know what had happened, to understand, and they did."

Still, the next day, she lost her son, 10-year-old Jeffrey.

"It was about this time. It wasn't dark yet and I asked him to go up to the filling station to get me some cigarettes. It's just a little over a block away. When he didn't come back by 8:30, I sent two other boys out looking for him. I knew what was going on but Jeffrey was well aware what was happening. He never got to the service station. We did learn that."

In 1974 Willie Mae Mathis lost her husband. He was working as a security guard, and he was shot and killed while trying to stop a burglary. They had six children. Ronald 22, the oldest, and Valerie, 18, are married, and have left home. But three other boys -- 17-year-old Stanley, and Reginald, who is 15, and Frederick, 14 -- live with their mother, and Wanda, a 9-year-old daughter.

For as long as she could, Willie Mae Mathis told her other children that somebody who wanted a child, and did not have any, had taken her son Jeffrey. She said to her other children that Jeffrey would return, as soon as he could get away.

"I couldn't break down," she said. "If I had broke down, they would too. So I just had to be strong."

For nearly a year they waited. It was not until the middle of that June that the Atlanta police officially listed Jeffrey Mathis as being one of the children who had disappeared. It is one of the things that still disturbs the mother.

While she waited, she said, anonymous calls began to come to her home.

"It would be somebody saying that they had Jeffrey. Then they'd hang up. Sometimes when they would call they would say that he was dead. The police came and put a tap on the phone, but they only left it there a week. They come and took it off. I still don't understand why."

She tries not to worry about losing another child.

"I don't think the Lord would let that happen. The Lord tries not to put too much on you, and I know I couldn't bear that."

"My one boy, he has to go to the doctor. He keeps saying that he sees Jeffrey in the house. And the little girl, Wanda, she wouldn't go any further away than the driveway."

Late in the afternoon yesterday, Willie Mae Mathis sat in the studios of radio station WLIB on Second Ave. She sat across from Afeni Shakur, of Harlem Legal Services, an organizer of the candlelight march. The two of them answered questions posed by Pablo Guzman.

WLIB is new in radio. It is the only Black station dealing entirely in news and information. When Pablo Guzman opened his show for callers, the switchboard lit up like a Christmas tree.

"It's the Klan that's doing it," one caller said.

"Boycott," another said. "Nobody should buy anything from anybody White until this thing is solved."

Willie Mae Mathis was asked if she had come to New York to raise money, money for the investigation into the killings that have now claimed the lives of 20 children, all of them Black.

"No," she said right away. "That's not why I'm here. My thought is that the government is the one that should put up the money. I'm not here to raise money. I'm here to let people know what's going on in Atlanta. I'm asking people to keep praying the snake to come out of the grass. If enough people do it, it will happen."

She is a large, dark woman. The pain of all that has happened is etched in her face. But she does not cry. Now Willie Mae Mathis, whose son was 18th to be found dead in Atlanta, prays. Her prayer is that the killing will stop.

"I don't think we can stand another child's body being found," she says. "It's too much. It's too much."

1981

AT THE END, THEY STOOD jammed together in the street and as the candles they carried flickered in the wind, their voices rose in the Harlem night.

"We love you!" they shouted. "We love you!"

They kept repeating the words, over and over again, until finally it became something of a chant.

On the platform in the middle of Harlem, the two women who had come from Atlanta to tell about the murder of their sons stood and waved. In time, tears welled in their eyes.

"It meant so much," Camilla Bell said later. "And I'm still on a high. It was beautiful, just beautiful."

There had not been much time for the word to pass. Only a few days. But notices were sent out. There were blurbs on the radio. But nobody had expected Harlem to do what it did on Friday night for Camilla Bell and Willie Mae Mathis.

"It's because of the children," women said. "Anytime you have somebody messing with the children, people are going to act. It's because of the children," they said. "That's why people are out here."

Camilla Bell lost her son, Yusef, who was 9, and Willie Mae Mathis lost her son, Jefferey, who was 10. Both were victims of the killings of Black children that have been taking place in Atlanta for more than a year and a half now. On Friday, Harlem turned out in a way that had people saying that they could not remember when, or if, they had ever seen anything quite like it before.

Harlem has fallen on hard times. In that, it is no different from most other Black communities. The problems of unemployment, crime, drugs, the schools, housing and medical care are everywhere now. Harlem is not alone.

But in Black communities across the country, there is another issue now, one more important than jobs, medical care, housing, or any of the others.

"We're being killed," people say.

"Did you hear about what's happening in Buffalo?"

"Have you heard about Utah?"

"I heard Blacks are being killed out in Seattle."

On a Saturday early in January, the Black United Front met in an all-day meeting at Hunter College. There were people who came from across the country. One by one, they gave reports of killings that were called mysterious or suspicious. In every case the victims were Black.

The whispered reports have become important stories in the neighborhoods where Blacks lives. Fear grows. Above it all stands Atlanta.

Atlanta is different. Nobody knows who the killer or the killers are. The one thing that is known is that the murders are unsolved. Atlanta is different because it involves children. It is different, too, because the number of victims has reached 20 now, and the killing does not stop.

Harlem was spurred on Friday partly because of the two women, Camilla Bell and Willie Mae Mathis. They are remarkable women. Both still hold the hurt that comes from losing a son. They wanted to be home with their families, but they say it was more important that they travel now, to report what is happening in Atlanta.

Saturday, Vice President and Mrs. Bush were in Atlanta. They met with some of the mothers there who have lost sons. Afterward, the vice president's wife had nothing but praise for the women.

"They are very courageous," she said. "I don't believe I could do the same thing myself."

They are courageous women, and they moved Harlem. Behind it all is the fear that is building, and the core of it is in Atlanta.

"We need to know what is happening," Camilla Bell said. "As parents, as Black people, we need to know."

On Friday night, Harlem rose up and the words were: "We love you." But in its way, the community that prides itself as being the capital of Black America was saying something else.

It was saying that the systematic killing of children has to be dealt with, that the time is now. It was saying that Atlanta has to be put at the front of the nation's agenda, that nothing deserves a higher priority.

Nobody stood around damning Whites. Not much was said even about the Ku Klux Klan. But there was anger. The irony was that most of it seemed to be directed at Atlanta's Black political leadership.

"Where's Coretta been and Andy and Abernathy?"

"Why hasn't Julian been speaking out?"

"Why is it that Atlanta's Black leaders could go all over the country to tell Black people why they should vote for Jimmy Carter, and none of them could come up here to talk to us about the children being killed?"

On Friday night, they were just a few of the tough questions the people in Harlem asked.

1981

THE TOUGHEST DAYS NOW are the ones when they bury the kids who are being murdered. Yesterday, on another warm and sunny afternoon, they put the body of Larry Rogers in a grave.

He was the 23rd victim in the string of unsolved killings. There are two others still missing. Both are boys. One is 10, the other 16. The two of them are the same as all of the others who have died: Black.

The mayor, who is also Black, did not come to Mount Moriah Baptist Church in northwest Atlanta for yesterday's funeral. Nobody explained exactly why. It might have been because he already has been to too many of these funerals. Yesterday, he sent Leon Hall to stand in his place. Hall is a veteran of the civil rights movement. He was a 1960s activist who is now the director of community and consumer affairs for the city of Atlanta. He is good with words in the way that so many of the old movement people are. As he stood on the pulpit yesterday, and looked out at the Black faces on the benches in Mount Moriah Baptist Church, he acknowledged that words now are not enough.

It was an emotional service. They all are. Leon Hall said, mostly, he just wanted people to know that the city cares, that the city loves them. As he went on, he began to call the names of those slain in the last 20 months. But before he could call all 23, he stopped. It became too much.

"It seems like an endless list," he said, "but we assure you, we assure you, we soon will bring this nightmare to an end."

Those were his most important words. A nightmare can last too long. These killings have truly begun to test the city of Atlanta.

1981

THE NUMBER IS 25 NOW. The special police task force investigating a string of mysterious murders of young Blacks yesterday added the name of Michael Cameron McIntosh.

McIntosh's nude body was found Monday afternoon snagged on a sandbar in the Chattahoochee River. He had not been reported missing, and thus, until yesterday, had not been a part of the task force investigation.

As soon as the body was discovered, however, there was speculation that McIntosh was another victim in the string of murders that stretches back to July 1979, and remains unsolved.

Police said that McIntosh's body was badly decomposed, but that the medical examiner was able to draw a clear set of fingerprints. Those prints were then used by police to make an identification. The police gave McIntosh's age as 23.

McIntosh lived alone on the city's southwest side near the homes of two other victims -- Joseph Bell, 15, and Yusef Bell, 9, who were not related. A neighbor said McIntosh had "a host of friends," but the names of Joseph Bell and Yusef Bell were not familiar to her.

The body was discovered just one day after a dirt biker found the body of Joseph (Jo Jo) Bell, 16, in the South River in DeKalb County. Bell had been listed as missing by the task force since shortly after his disappearance on March 2.

Associate Fulton County Medical Examiner John Feegel said yesterday that the "probable cause" in McIntosh's death was suffocation.

Now, five bodies have been found in rivers, two from the South River and three from the Chattahoochee. The place where McIntosh's body was found was just a short distance from where two others were discovered. The body of Timothy Hill, 13, was recovered from the Chattahoochee on March 30. The body of Eddie (Bubba) Duncan, 21, a day later.

At 23, McIntosh is the oldest of those slain. However, the medical examiner pointed out that he was just 5 feet, 5 1/2 inches tall and weighed only about 80 pounds. "He had the build of a boy," the medical examiner said.

While McIntosh's body was completely nude, the others found in the rivers were clad in undershorts. McIntosh is the 14th victim to die from asphyxiation by suffocation.

In addition to the 25 bodies already recovered, one other youngster remains missing. He is 10-year-old Darron Glass, who disappeared last September.

1981

THEY WERE THE BEST of friends. When you saw one, the other was there too. It had been that way for them since they were first-graders.

It was Jimmy Ray and Mike. They were like peas in a pod. Jimmy Ray went out with Mimi, and Mike dated her sister. They were so close. Eventually, when one got into trouble, the other did too. They would end up doing time together.

On Wednesday, Jimmy Ray started out for an old-coin shop over at the Omni. That ended it. Nobody has heard from him since.

"I knew something was wrong on Wednesday," said Mimi Turner, his girlfriend. "When he didn't call me, I just knew it. He always calls me."

"I would have gone with him," said Mike Harrison, his best friend, "but I didn't have train fare."

Jimmy Ray never came back.

Yesterday, on a warm and sunny Sunday afternoon, Jimmy Ray Payne's sister, his girlfriend and Mike, the buddy who was with him everywhere he went, all believed that he had become yet another victim.

A victim to what? They do not know. Nobody knows.

It began in July 1979. At first it was kids. A 14-year-old, then a 13-year-old, and then another, who was 14. After that, it was 9-year-old Yusef Bell. Then, 12-year-old Angel Lanier's body was found, followed by that of Jeffrey Mathis, who was 10. It went on and on. Now, the number is 25.

At first, it was just the police in Atlanta who were on the case. Now, there is a task force of over 100 investigators. The FBI has 40 agents on the case. Still, nothing.

Now, it is the disappearance of Jimmy Ray Payne that Atlanta must deal with. This may turn out to be the most important of all. He is 21 years old. He is the fourth victim to disappear, who was an adult. The other three have already turned up dead.

There was Eddie Duncan, whose body was found in the Chattahoochee River. Then there was Larry Rogers. Although both were 21, the explanation was that the two men could easily be mistaken for kids. It was said that they were both retarded and slightly built. That was supposed to explain it. Then came Michael McIntosh. He was 23, but he didn't weigh much over 100 pounds. It was said that he had problems with alcohol, that he was "slow," and that he, too, might be mistaken for a kid.

It is not that easy to explain away Jimmy Ray Payne. Ask Mike Harrison. He would know. They were best friends.

The police came to ask questions. They had Mike, the best friend, in a room for a whole afternoon. They questioned Mimi, the girlfriend. They took Evelyn, the sister, downtown. One of the questions they kept asking was if Jimmy Ray was homosexual.

"He wasn't into nothing like that," his best friend said.

"That's crazy," the girlfriend said. "He had a strong mind."

"We served time together," Mike said, "me and him in the same dormitory down there at the Middle Georgia Correctional Institute, and he didn't mess around with no sissies. He wasn't like that."

Jimmy Ray lived on Magnolia in northwest Atlanta. It is not far from the Omni, the sports convention and entertainment center in downtown Atlanta.

Up the hill from where Jimmy Ray Payne lived, Magnolia St. changes and becomes Play Lane. There is a housing development there called John J. Eagan Homes. They have the look of old barracks, except some of the buildings have been painted pastel green; others are light tan and yellow.

Mike Harrison lives in the building right next to the renting office. Mimi Turner does too. Yesterday, the two of them stood out front and talked of Jimmy Ray.

Mike had a knife that he kept pulling out of his pocket.

"I'm not going to lie to you," he said, "I'm scared."

"Have you been out looking for Jimmy Ray?" he was asked.

"Been everywhere," he said. "Been everywhere we go. I jumped the train and went to the Omni, to the coin store. The man said he didn't know him. Jimmy Ray had called before he went over there and the man told him he didn't buy foreign coins. That's what he had. One was Mexican, and he had about eight Canadian nickels and some other coins. We used to joke about them. He would carry them with him, and I would tell him that somebody was going to knock him in the head, thinking he had a pocketful of money."

Michael is 21, the same age as his friend Jimmy Ray. He has no job. And Jimmy Ray had no job.

"There's no work here," Mike said. "That's why he went to the Omni to sell those coins. He needed some money."

Joseph Harris is 20. He is two years out of high school, but still has not been able to find a steady job. Yesterday he said that more than anything else he wanted to get out of Atlanta.

"Are you afraid?" he was asked.

"Not really," he said. "I'm mostly around here and I'm usually around a lot of other people. But I want to leave Atlanta because I've never been anywhere else. I've been here all of my life."

He is tall and rangy with a face that is coal black. It is his brother Harmon, 18, he worries about.

"What do you tell him?"

"What can I tell him? It's hard to tell him anything. You know kids now, they got their own theories about things, and besides, he's as big as I am. If I say anything, it would just start a big argument."

He stared out across the street, over to the new houses where Jimmy Ray Payne stayed. "If this was Whites that it was happening to, they'd be snatching up a lot of Blacks until they find something. If it was Whites, I'd bet they'd have the National Guard in here."

"But the mayor and the police commissioner, they're Black men," he was told.

"That's what I hear," he said. "I just know that if the kids were White, they'd find something before 25 was dead.....25 kids killed and nobody knows who. If it was Whites, it would be case closed by now, and the guy would be in jail."

Now it has begun to come into focus. What is tying these cases together is money. All of the kids who were killed had one thing in common: they came from families who were poor. None of the four adults who died had money. Now it's Jimmy Ray and he is like the others: Black and poor. And somewhere in that, he got himself into trouble.

1981

IN ATLANTA, THE FBI had wanted to make the arrest earlier, but Public Safety Commissioner Lee Brown insisted on waiting. He wanted to assure himself he had the strongest case possible. All along he had felt the worst thing that could happen would be for him to make an arrest, and then have his case fall apart. So he refused to rush.

"But when we do make an arrest," he promised, "you can be sure that we will know what we are doing."

When Lee Brown made an arrest, it was the man the FBI wanted. Wayne B. Williams was taken into custody and charged with killing Nathaniel Cater, the last of 28 young Black children and men to die.

The killings of young Blacks has troubled Atlanta for nearly two years. Cater's body was found in the Chattahoochee River on the 24th of May.

That was exactly two and a half days after a stakeout team under a bridge over the river heard a loud splash, and found Williams at the scene.

Since then, he has been under police and FBI surveillance -- and no names have been added to the list of Atlanta victims.

Williams's name first meant nothing to investigators. That night, when Williams retraced his movements for the FBI, he was connected with a place called the Mar Quiett Club . It was later referred to in the newspapers as an Atlanta nightclub. People who know the club have other names for it.

The Mar Quiett Club is on Martin Luther King Jr. Drive in northwest Atlanta. It's just off Ashby St., not far from Paschal's Hotel. Once, this was one of Atlanta's better Black neighborhoods.

That was back in another time, before integration came to Atlanta, and when downtown hotels were reluctant to welcome guests who were not White.

Then, Paschal's was the place to go. The hotel had a top jazz club, a popular restaurant, and people flocked there.

I remembered Paschal's from its glory days. When I returned last month, I found a new neighborhood. That section of King Drive had become a hangout for Black homosexuals. The Mar Quiett had become one of the key places.

The club is known for two things: it's rough, and a hangout for transvestites. Nobody comes into the Mar Quiett without first being searched.

At the door, the men who do the searching have pistols strapped to their waists. The Mar Quiett is not a place where strangers wander in by chance. People who go to the Mar Quiett know what to expect.

Williams supposedly told the FBI that he was at the club to pick up a tape recorder the day he was found at the river.

The purpose of his visit was not important. Once he was linked with the Mar Quiett, he was tied -- not just to transvestites and homosexuals -- but a particularly violent group that frequents the club.

When Williams was first connected with the investigation, the immediate question that arose was motive. Why? Then the connection with the Mar Quiett Club was made. There was no more talk of motive.

1982

FOR THE FIRST TIME SINCE the trial began, jurors have heard testimony that in a subtle way began to portray Wayne Williams as a mass murderer.

The turn in the testimony came after Superior Court Judge Clarence Cooper ruled that it was permissible for the prosecution to introduce evidence linking Williams to 10 more killings.

Until now, the jury had only heard testimony tying Williams to the two murders for which he is on trial, those of 27-year-old Nathaniel Cater and 21-year-old Jimmy Ray Payne.

But before the day was done, the prosecution began the arduous task of bringing the murders of other young Blacks before the jury. Perhaps even more damaging to Williams was testimony that since his arrest, according to the police, the Atlanta murders had stopped.

"We're in an unusual situation now," said Dr. John Feegel, assistant Fulton County medical examiner. "We have not had any children's death from traumatic cause in many months."

The controversial ruling by Judge Cooper allows the prosecution to present evidence that Williams was involved in other killings, "for the limited purpose" of showing pattern, scheme, bent of mind, and identification.

After Judge Cooper's ruling, the defense immediately moved for a mistrial, which the judge denied. Three times during the day, the judge admonished the jurors not to let this evidence form a bias against the defendant.

The prosecution went back to July 1979, almost to the start of the string of Atlanta murders that eventually captured worldwide attention. To start making the link to the 23-year-old Williams, who steadfastly maintains he had nothing to do with the crimes, the prosecution began with the death of Alfred Evans.

The Evans testimony brought back a lot of the old hurt. His body was found in July 1979. The assistant medical examiner, Dr. Feegel, told how the parents refused to admit that it was their son; how the body of the 13-year-old stayed in the morgue more than a year.

1982

THE JUDGE CAME OFF the bench to sit, almost hidden, in a corner at the front of the courtroom. The defense attorneys left their table, and used chairs near the jury box. It was a day for the prosecution, a day when the state's case against Wayne Williams began to come together, exactly as promised, as pieces of a puzzle.

Yesterday, the prosecution played a high card. With painstaking care, it began to put before the jury its fiber evidence. It began with the prosecution's first witness in the morning. When court was recessed for the day, it still was not finished. But the prosecution positioned itself so that when court resumes today, it can play its trump card.

Fiber evidence is one of the big pieces in the state's case against Wayne Williams. It is difficult to make such evidence stick with a jury. Just the same, it is what the state says it has to link Williams to the two bodies recovered from the Chattahoochee River, those of Nathaniel Cater and Jimmy Ray Payne.

The task begun in the courtroom yesterday is to link fibers found on those bodies -- victims in the string of 28 Atlanta murders of young Blacks -- with fibers collected in a search of Williams's station wagon and the bedroom of his residence.

In the morning, the prosecution turned the courtroom into a classroom. The subject was fibers; Herbert Pratt, the expert, is a silver-haired, senior technical specialist from Du Pont, the largest fiber producer in the U.S. All along, the prosecution had said that its toughest job in this trial would be presenting its fiber evidence in a way that the jurors would be able to grasp. Pratt was selected to do the teaching. For this, he used a large movie screen that was placed directly in front of the jury box. That was for his display of slides. Next to the screen, he had a blackboard; alongside that an easel that held large charts and diagrams.

In order to watch Pratt do his work, the judge left the bench, and the lawyers found new seats. Williams, the defendant, was left sitting alone at the defense table.

Pratt started on the witness stand. He was there a full 10 minutes, just to recite his credentials. Then he came down to a lectern that was brought especially for him. He worked awhile at the lectern. Soon, using his pointer, he was at the screen with his slides. Then at the backboard and, in between, he had his charts.

Mostly he talked of man-made fibers. He started from scratch and brought the making of fibers through every stage. At the lectern, he kept one hand jammed into the jacket pocket of the light gray suit he was wearing. He was meticulous in the way he went about his teaching.

"Those short molecules are hooked together," he said "and we end up with a molten soup, so to speak, and that's called polymer. Building blocks, it's called." It was a way of getting to polyester.

On the blackboard he drew pictures of fibers. "If you take a round fiber and put a ray of light on it... You see fibers, and there are ways of measuring these fibers." And soon, he was explaining nylon. "The molecules in that fiber look like a plate of spaghetti. They go every which-a-way..."

He seemed an effective teacher, because he seemed to demonstrate that fibers have characteristics that make one identifiable from another. That brought him to the FBI, and what he called an unusual fiber an agent brought to him last summer.

"I couldn't identify it," he said.

He took it to Du Pont's Applied Research lab, then to other experts. He searched the Du Pont files -- still, nothing.

Then Herbert Pratt told of a luncheon he had one day with a colleague. He drew a picture of the mysterious fiber on a napkin. The colleague, a woman, looked at it and said it was something she had seen before. The fiber the FBI brought was then traced to its producer, the Wellman Co., in Boston. Pratt notified the FBI, and the telling of that story in the courtroom yesterday began the unfolding of a trail that led back to the defendant, Wayne Williams.

In this trial there is no smoking gun for the prosecution to produce, only bits and pieces..."But they fit together like a puzzle," the prosecutor said in his opening statement to the jury.

Pratt was able to link it with the Wellman Co., a manufacturer of synthetic fibers, nylon and polyester.

After Pratt finished, the prosecutor called Henry Poston, director of technical services at Wellman. He testified that his company designed the unusual looking fiber. He said it was a fiber with a crimp and that it had two long lobes at one end and one short lobe.

"I've known no one else in the world that makes a fiber like that," he said. He explained that his company had come up with such a design for a very specific reason. "To circumvent patent laws," he said.

Poston said the particular fiber was designed for making carpet. "These fibers are too big to go into yarn," he said. That was what the prosecution needed. It had identified the fiber, and had testimony that it was used in the making of carpet. From there, the prosecution called Gene Bagget, an employee of the Carpet and Rug Division of West Point-Pepperell, who testified that the carpet it made was sold in the Atlanta area. He examined the sample the prosecutor handed to him and then compared it with one that he had brought and he said, yes the two appeared to be identical.

1982

IN THE PICTURE THE PROSECUTION has painted, Wayne Williams is two people. He is, on one side, bright and ambitious, a hustler determined to succeed as a promoter in the entertainment business. On the other side, the side nobody knew, Williams is pictured as a different person altogether.

That other side, brought alive in the courtroom where he is on trial for murder, was built on the testimony of prosecution witnesses. When that pictures was painted, Williams's father bolted from the courtroom, calling it all "lies, lies."

The picture of the Wayne Williams nobody knew is what the State of Georgia used to tie him not just to the two men he is accused of killing, but to 10 other Atlanta murders. The indication is that in time, the move will be made to accuse him of even more killings.

"He's a Gemini," a woman who knew him as a friend told the jury. "He's two people."

That other Wayne Williams emerged from the testimony. It was a picture of a young man who had an absolute hatred for poor Blacks, especially children who hustled on the streets for money. It was said that he hated them so much that he actually had figures to show what killing a single Black male would do to decrease the population of poor Blacks.

The other Wayne Williams was pictured, too, as being homosexual. It was said he lured young boys into his car with the promise of money. He was pictured as being so strong that even a man who is 6-feet-2 and weighs 292 pounds came into court and said he had wrestled with Williams -- that the suspect was able to give him a go when it came to a test of strength.

There was more. He was also pictured as being a habitual liar. One witness said he had asked Williams how he earned his money. Williams told him, without hesitation, he said, that he was a reserve Air Force pilot who flew F-4's on weekends at Dobbins Air Force Base. "I could tell by those thick glasses he was wearing that he wasn't a pilot," the witness said, "but I didn't say anything to him. I just let on that I didn't know."

But those were prosecution witnesses. As those witnesses were cross-examined, money often was mentioned. "Did anybody offer you money for testifying?" Alvin Binder, the defense attorney, would ask, "Did anybody say that you were going to get some money? Are you expecting to get some money?"

Binder was referring to the reward. Close to $500,000 in reward money for information leading to the arrest and conviction of the killer in the Atlanta murders is still unclaimed. It has become a not-so-silent issue in the trial. The defense maintains that prosecution witnesses have been encouraged to lie in testimony against Williams, having been led to believe they will get a slice of the reward money.

Even Kenneth Lawson, the former Atlanta police recruit who testified for the defense, said reward money was mentioned to recruits on stake-outs around the river where bodies of murdered young Blacks were dumped.

"We were told that since we were recruits, we were still civilians and eligible for reward money," he said.

"Who told you that?" he was asked.

"Our superiors told us that a number of times," he said.

In the Fulton County Courthouse this morning, the trial enters its seventh week. Now defense witnesses are being brought into the courtroom. On Friday, when the defense began presenting its case, it went after Nellie Trammell first. She had been one of the state's star witnesses. An effort was made to depict her as a psychic who had visions every time a body was found.

There was an effort to show that the police stakeout at the river where Williams was first stopped was mishandled, and carried out by beer-drinking officers leery of being alone in the river bank through the night.

By recess Friday, the defense had one of its expert witnesses on the stand, a pathologist from upstate New York. His testimony was that Georgia pathologists who performed autopsies on the victims bungled the case. He said what defense attorney Binder had been saying: that the state could not prove corpus delicti, that there was no evidence that the two men Williams is accused of killing were homicide victims.

It is back and forth. Wayne Williams himself is becoming the key. What will he do? What will he say when it is his turn to sit in the witness box? It is coming down to the defendant himself. Earlier, when the defense did not believe the state had much of a case, there was talk that Williams might not testify. No more. Now the only question is when.

On Friday, Williams came into the courtroom wearing a three-piece tan suit with matching tie, and instead of dropping down at the defense table the way he always has done, he stepped up to the rail and greeted his parents. He used to ignore them. Then he moved to the end of the defense table, to a position facing the jury. He used to sit almost hidden between his lawyers. He seems to be changing. It may have something to do with the picture the prosecution witnesses painted of him, the one that supposedly showed the side nobody knew.

1982

WAYNE B. WILLIAMS, TESTIFYING yesterday in his defense, told his jury: "I haven't killed nobody, I haven't thought about killing nobody, and I don't plan on killing nobody."

After having been portrayed as a mass murderer responsible for many of the murders of 28 young Blacks in the Atlanta area, and standing trial in two of those killings, Williams, 23, seemed confident through most of his 2 1/2 hours of testimony.

It was not a spellbinding story he told the jury. Instead, his testimony yesterday was elicited through a string of well-framed questions put to him by Alvin Binder, chief of his defense team.

Williams's only moment of hesitation came at the outset of his testimony. His mother, who had preceded him on the witness stand, had just undergone a grueling cross-examination. He rose in the crowded courtroom to become the 64th witness for the defense.

His first answers were barely audible. "You speak up," Binder said, "because this is your day in court, and I want the jury to hear you."

"I'm scared," the defendant said.

"You realize you are charged with the murder of Nathaniel Cater and Jimmy Ray Payne?" Binder said . "Have you ever seen or do you know either of them?"

"I don't know 'em, I've never seen 'em before in my life," the defendant said.

Binder then allowed his client time to shed any nervousness, and gain confidence, by concentrating his first line of questioning on the defendant's background. By the time Binder began to ask about the murders and the charges against him, Williams seemed eager and smooth.

Q: "What were you doing on the Jackson Parkway bridge on the morning of May 22?"

A: "To be honest with you, I was trying to get to the other side so I could get home."

Q: "Do you know how fast you were driving?"

A: "At the time, it was dark and foggy. I'd say I was going about 20, maybe 35 miles an hour."

Q: "Were the lights on the car off or on?"

A: "On."

Q: "Did you ever stop on the Jackson Parkway bridge?"

A "No."

Q: "Look at the jury, Wayne. Now tell them, are you a homosexual?"

A: "Ain't no way. No. I don't have any grudge against them as long as they keep their hands to themselves but don't come near me."

Q: "A 15-year-old boy came in here and said you fondled him sexually. Is that true?"

A: "A barefaced lie."

Q: "A witness said he saw you holding hands with Nathaniel Cater. Is that true?"

A: "I ain't holding hands with no man."

Binder asked his client about Lubie Geter, one of the victims of the Atlanta slayings. Two witnesses had testified to seeing Williams with Geter on the last day the youth was seen alive.

Q: "Did you ever take Lubie Geter from a shopping center in your car and do wrong with him?"

A: "I haven't done anything like that to nobody."

Q: "Do you know the deceased Jo-Jo Bell (another murder victim)?"

A: "No."

Q: "Did you harm, maim or kill him?"

A: "No."

Then the lawyer asked Williams the same questions about Larry Rogers and Patrick Baltazar, two more of the victims. Again, the answers were no. Binder said if he called all 10 names of the cases that were introduced plus the names of Cater and Payne, would the answers be the same? Williams replied that they would.

Then Williams looked directly at the jury and said: "I haven't killed nobody, I haven't thought about killing nobody and I don't plan on killing nobody."

Of his parents, the defendant said: "I was scared of both of them when it came to whippings." He added: "Ever since I can remember they told me we don't have any family secrets. They even told me how much money they made, and when there were decisions, we all sat down together. There were no secrets. Even when you went to the bathroom, nobody closed the door."

1982

THE POLISHED COOL that Wayne Williams had displayed through two days of testimony disappeared abruptly yesterday in his third day on the witness stand at his murder trial.

He did not step back from his insistence that he is innocent of killing anyone. He said: "None of those folk (witnesses) saw me stopped on the bridge. Nobody saw me throw anything off the bridge. Nobody saw me kill anybody."

When Assistant District Attorney Jack Mallard, in his relentless cross examination accused Williams of reveling in the publicity of the crimes, the defendant snapped: "You must be a fool."

In the courtroom yesterday morning, the defendant seemed a different person. Immediately he got into a heated argument with Mallard. Then, he had words with Judge Clarence Cooper.

Eight minutes after the session began, Mallard was asking Williams why he was driving home at 3 a.m. May 22 on a road that took him across the Jackson Parkway Bridge over the Chattahoochee River.

"Man, look. What in the world has that got to do with killing anybody?"

Judge Cooper interrupted, ordering Williams to answer the question.

"Sir," he said to the judge, "I can't answer the question. I've explained to this gentleman all day yesterday. We've been over this question time and time again. Now I've been through a lot and I'm tired, and I'm trying to do the best I can to answer this question. He keeps asking me the same thing. The question is, did I kill anybody and I done told this man, I haven't."

Defense attorney Alvin Binder rushed to the bench. Then, he went over to the witness stand and pushed the microphone away. He put an arm around the defendant and the two of them, the Mississippi lawyer and the 23-year-old defendant on trial for two of the 28 Atlanta slayings of young Blacks, whispered a long time to each other.

When Binder moved away, tears welled in the defendant's eyes. But Mallard kept pressing him. His answer came in a broken voice. Tears were on his face.

"Let me ask you, were you concerned about the evidence being found on the bodies?"

"Sir, I didn't kill nobody, so I wouldn't have any reason to be concerned about it. You haven't got no proof I did anything."

It was a day marked by a stunning turn of events in the courtroom. After the display of temper and emotion by the defendant, the prosecution had the breakthrough it wanted. And just after 10 o'clock, Mallard ended his questioning.

"You don't have to be upset now, son," Binder said in a soft voice as he began a brief redirect examination.

"I'm trying not to," the defendant said through his tears, "but it hurts."

As soon as Williams came off the witness stand, Binder rose to say: "The defendant rests his case."

The state immediately began its rebuttal, and the 12th witness it called was a slim 17-year-old, who told the jury a chilling story of how he saw Williams beat and choke his father, Homer Williams, and slap his mother, Faye, in a brawl in the Williams home that ended with the father pulling a shotgun on his son.

Sheldon Kemp was the 17-year-old who told the jury about the fight. He is one of the youths Williams had recruited for a singing group he was organizing.

Kemp said that on the day of the fight, he and his brother were sitting in the living room at the Williams home when Wayne asked his father to write him a check. The youth said the fight began when Homer Williams refused.

"Wayne started cursing. His mom was trying to keep him away from his dad. He (Wayne) slapped her, and then they went in a back room. He (Wayne) jumped on top of his dad. He was choking him. His mom said his dad had some kind of heart condition. His dad was on the bed, and he (Wayne) was sitting on top of him, choking him."

1982

WAYNE BERTRAM WILLIAMS, the pudgy, young Black man who stood trial for two of the mysterious Atlanta slayings of 28 young Blacks, was found guilty on both counts here last night by a jury that had deliberated 11 1/2 hours.

The verdicts for first-degree murder were read in the courtroom at 7:08 p.m. Judge Clarence Cooper sentenced the only son of retired Atlanta schoolteachers to serve consecutive terms of life in prison.

Under Georgia law, however, he becomes eligible for parole review after serving seven years.

Once the verdicts were read and the sentences were passed, the judge asked Williams if he wanted to make any statement. Williams moved to the lectern in the front of the courtroom where his lawyers had argued his case and, in a clear voice, said, "I wish to say one thing.

"I have maintained all along through this trial my innocence," he said, "and I will still do so today. I don't have any malice against the people on the jury, the prosecution or anyone. I, more than anyone, wanted to see this terror end, but I did not do it. I just hope the person or persons who did these crimes can be brought to justice. That is from my heart, I did not do it."

After making the statement, Williams, dressed in a brown suit with his shirt open at the neck, stepped back into the midst of deputy sheriffs who had stood behind him when the verdicts were read.

Cooper asked Homer Williams, the 68-year-old father of the defendant, if he had anything to say, and the retired schoolteacher stepped to the lectern.

"Judge, your honor, jurors, fellow people," the balding father began, "I feel that this is very unjust. I don't see how anybody, anywhere, could find my son guilty of anything. It's unjust, and I will say that anywhere in the world. It is impossible to find a young man like this guilty. We know anybody who sat in the courtroom the last nine weeks can see that. Nobody has brought any evidence to prove my son guilty. Judge, your honor, I think it's very unfair."

The mother, Faye Williams, who is in failing health, was not in the courtroom when the jury delivered its verdict.

Afterward, defense attorney Alvin Binder said he was "sure there would be an appeal." He said it would probably be based, mainly, on Cooper's decision to allow evidence of other killings to be introduced in the trial to show pattern, scheme and the defendant's bent of mind.

Binder also said: "The prosecution, the public or no one else knows how these poor people died. And that's unusual in a murder case."

Clearly, that evidence was a turning point in the trial. Williams was charged with the murders of 27-year-old Nathaniel Cater and 21-year-old Jimmy Ray Payne, but during the trial the judge allowed the prosecution to introduce evidence that tied Williams to 10 or more of the slayings.

The state presented fibers evidence that tied Williams to the 12 slayings.

Assistant District Attorney Gordon Miller, who handed the fibers evidence for the prosecution, said he believed this was "probably the greatest fibers case ever tried."

He added: "It will advance scientific evidence in criminal trials in America more than any other case in this century. I think fibers evidence is good evidence, and has reached a stage now where it is real important."

"In this particular case, we were blessed," Miller said, "because we were dealing with a very unusual fiber, and an association of fibers."

In its case, the prosecution showed that fibers from the rug in the defendant's bedroom were made in an unusual shape, and manufactured only in 1971. There were also other fibers found on the bodies of the victims that matched fibers taken from a bedspread, blanket, and other items in Williams's house and car.

When asked if Williams would now be tried for other slayings, District Attorney Lewis Slaton said that he was not yet in a position to discuss that. He called his case complicated, but said: "I wasn't surprised by the verdict."

Mary Welcome, the Black woman who was the first lawyer to join in Williams's defense, said after the verdict: "He was charged with two murders, but was called on to defend against 12. We were put in a position where we were almost shadowboxing. I don't think that (the state) knew until after the trial started which of the other 26 cases they were going to ask the judge to let in."

But Binder also said "the fibers evidence was the hardest to overcome."

The prosecution had said it would not seek the death penalty. Georgia law allows for no lesser sentence than life imprisonment on a murder conviction. Williams will be eligible for parole review in seven years under a state law that says prisoners must come up for such review.

Deputy Sheriff T. H. Connally said that any defendant sentenced to more than five years in prison is entitled to appeal to a review panel, but must give 30 days notice that he will do so. The defense said it intended to give such notice.

The Atlanta murders go back to the summer of 1979. On July 28 in that summer, the bodies of two young Blacks, Edward Smith and Alfred Evans, were found. In November 1979, two more were found within four days. In 1980, alarm spread in Atlanta as nine more young Blacks were found dead. By that July, a special police task force was created to investigate the killings. Atlanta became a city locked in fear.

The killings went on, police say, until May 24, 1981, when the body of Nathaniel Cater was found in the Chattahoochee River. He was the 28th victim.

By the time Cater was found dead, the police had a suspect -- Wayne Williams.

In the early morning hours of May 21, he was stopped by police who found him on the Jackson Parkway bridge just as a stakeout team reported a loud splash, believed to be a body being dumped into the Chattahoochee.

The story Williams gave to the police that night never checked out. He said he was looking for a woman name Cheryl Johnson. No such person was ever found, but Williams never changed his story.

During the trial, his parents tried to give him an alibi. He said he was sick that night at home in bed until after midnight. Only then did he get up and go out, his parents said. Evidently the jurors did not believe either the defendant or his parents.

1982

POLICE OFFICIALS SWIFTLY CLOSED the books yesterday on 23 of the Atlanta slayings of young Blacks, indicating a belief that Wayne Williams was responsible.

However, Fulton County District Attorney Lewis Slaton said that Williams, convicted and sentenced to two terms of life imprisonment Saturday after standing trial for two of those slayings, would not be indicted again.

"One reason" Slaton said, "is that he (Williams) is already sentenced to two life terms."

Before yesterday, there had been speculation that Williams would not only be tried again, but also that this time the death penalty would be sought.

As it stands now, he is eligible for parole review after seven years of imprisonment under Georgia law.

The announcement alleging that Williams was responsible for 23 slayings in all was made by Police Commissioner Lee Brown at a news conference at the headquarters of the special police task force that was established to investigate the crimes.

Brown also said that 29 slayings actually had been under investigation, not the previously disclosed total of 28. Brown said the additional victim was John Harold Porter, 28, whose name had been withheld for investigative reasons.

Of the total of 29 killings, six were not tied to Williams, he said. Those cases would remain open. A 30th case, that of Darron Glass, 10, also remains open. He disappeared in September 1980 and never has been located.

The press conference came at the end of a meeting attended by law enforcement officials from 11 jurisdictions in the Atlanta area, FBI personnel and the head of the Georgia Bureau of Investigation.

In another development yesterday, Mary Welcome resigned from the defense of the 23-year-old Williams, who is being held at the Fulton County Jail. She reportedly tendered her resignation after Williams refused to meet with her at the jail Sunday night.

1991

THEY WERE KNOWN AS the Atlanta child murders. They go back 10 years and involved the killing of more than two dozen kids, all of them Black, most from poor families. The case was never completely solved; but it was declared closed after the conviction of Wayne Williams.

Although he insisted he had killed no one, Williams, 23, was tried and convicted of two murders, a 27-year-old, and a 24-year-old. To show a pattern involved in the killings, the prosecutor was allowed to offer evidence in killings that Williams was not charged with committing. Ten of these killings were brought into the courtroom; they were kids who were listed among the victims in the child murders.

In the trial, the attornies for Williams argued vehemently against the ruling that linked him with the child murders. They lost that appeal. After that, shrewd arguments by the prosecutor sealed Williams's fate. The prosecutor told the jurors the child murders stopped when Wayne was arrested. "You can put him back on the street," the DA said, "but you have to take responsibility for that." The trial lasted close to three months; the jurors reached their guilty verdict in a matter of hours.

For 10 years, Williams has been in prison; all the while, insisting that he is innocent. He has been granted an important habeas corpus hearing.

From the evidence that has begun to come out, it could be that Williams soon will be cleared of the killings he has always said he did not commit.

In the hearing, in Jackson, Georgia, the most startling revelation has been the introduction of information which showed that a police undercover agent got a tape recording of a known KKK operative. On the tape the man, a Charles T. Sanders, is said to admit killing some of the murdered children.

According to testimony, Sanders said that he killed Lubie Geter, who was 14 years old. It also came out that dog hairs found on many of the bodies were not hairs from Williams"s German Shepherd, as was claimed during the trial.

Rather, the hairs were said to have come either from a Huskie or an Alaskan Malamute. Sanders owned a Huskie.

In the original trial 10 years ago, Williams's defense team was no match for the smooth team of prosecutors it faced in the courtroom.

This time it is different. At his hearing, Williams was represented by a high powered array of lawyers including William Kuntsler and Ron Kuby of New York and well known and respected southern attorney Bobby Lee Cook.

In the hearing, the defense is attempting to show that evidence that would have weighed heavily in the first trial, had it not been suppressed, might have led to a different verdict.

They are especially dwelling on the aspect of evidence involving the Ku Klux Klan. They say that evidence was withheld because authorities feared that if it came out, it might provoke a race war.

So now, in the case of the Atlanta child murders, all of it is again being put on the table for scrutiny. It is what ought to happen. In the trial of 10 years ago, the case was declared closed even though nobody (including Wayne Williams) was ever charged with killing any of the kids and authorities were not even able to determine exactly how the victims died. In many cases the coroner listed asphyxiation as the cause of death. But just how the victims were killed remained a mystery.

Just eight days after Williams was convicted, the task force investigating the murders was disbanded. At the time, there was widespread criticism of what was called a rush to judgment.

The hearing going on now says that, in the matter of the child murders, it is not over. In fact, it may be just the beginning of getting at the truth of what really happened 10 years ago.

1991

IN A WAY THE KILLINGS NOW from a poor, mostly Black neighborhood in Milwaukee bring back pictures from 10 years ago. Then the string of grisly murders that had the attention of the nation was taking place in Atlanta. They became known as "the child murders" and in all, 24 lives were taken.

A common line runs through the two strings of murders involves the victims. In Milwaukee, most of the victims were Black or from other minority groups. With the child murders, all the victims were Black.

As it was to happen, both cases were to provoke charges of racism and shabby police work.

New York attorney William Kuntsler has watched the Milwaukee case from afar. But in the Atlanta case, he remains deeply involved. Yesterday he talked of what he saw when looking at the two cases.

"What they show," he said, "is that Black lives and the lives of other Third World people in the United States aren't worth a dime. So in Atlanta when kids were missing, not a thing was done until parents got together and raised hell. In Milwaukee, when a kid who is not White runs out bleeding and naked, the police say, 'It's just a domestic thing' and they throw him back into the house. Why? Because in this country, Black lives are worth maybe 20 percent of what a White life is worth."

While Kuntsler looked at the killings a 31-year-old White man, Jeffrey Dahmer, has confessed to in Milwaukee, he talked at length of the murders in Atlanta that have had Wayne Williams, a 33-year-old Black man, behind bars in South Georgia for 10 years.

In a recent interview from prison, Williams repeated what he said in the courtroom at the time he was convicted of murder.

"I didn't do it," Williams said.

Kuntsler says Williams is innocent. But he says that is only a part of a massive cover up involved in the case. He said the child murders were carried out by members of the Ku Klux Klan. He says authorities in Atlanta not only know that, he says they also have the proof in their hands.

On the 8th of October, Kuntsler will be at the Valdosta Correctional Institution in Jackson, Georgia where Williams is being held. There, he will argue an appeal on Williams's behalf. The way he tells it, all hell is likely to break loose, for then, he intends to put the state of Georgia up against the wall.

According to Kuntsler, authorities knew the KKK was involved in the child murders but did nothing. "Because they were scared. They believed that if it got out that the Klan was responsible for the killings, there would be a war. They believed Blacks would take to the streets with guns so they had a secret meeting and they just decided that a Black had to be arrested and charged with the killings. That's how they got Wayne. But he didn't do it."

Williams was never actually tried for the child murders. Of the 24 killed, all were kids except for the last two murders. They involved a 24-year-old and a 27-year-old. Williams was convicted of those murders. But in the process, the state was allowed to open a door, "to show a pattern" and in that, they showed associations Williams had with 10 of the murdered children. He was not charged with killing any of those kids but, before the jury, testimony was allowed that linked him to missing and murdered kids.

In the hands of prosecutors, that was powerful ammunition. It got Williams portrayed as being responsible for the child murders. "When we arrested him, the killings stopped," the prosecutor argued. Williams was convicted and although he was not charged with killing any kids, he is regarded as the perpetrator of the child murders.

"But the killings did not stop once he was arrested," Kuntsler said. "They just stopped reporting kids who were missing or murdered."

In Milwaukee, the handling of the Dahmer case has led to the police being charged with incompetence and racism. But Kuntsler believes the bombshell development is the one soon to be dropped in the Atlanta case. "They had a secret meeting in the governor's mansion and decided they couldn't indict a Klansman. So they just suppressed the truth. And we can prove that."

Chapter Three

THE FRUITS OF THEIR LABOR

Editor's Note

Over the last two decades, Earl Caldwell has written of the crises confronting American workers and organized labor. In the lives of ordinary people and hands-on union organizers, he has witnessed the urban flight of businesses, municipal cut-backs, a hostile environment fostered by Ronald Reagan's administration, the move to replace strikers with permanent replacements, the technological displacement of workers, and growing racial conflicts between the largely White leadership of organized labor, and the growing Black and Hispanic work force.

1979

THEY WORE JEANS THAT WERE CUT OFF above the knees and T-shirts of every color.

There were hundreds of them there, lounging on the sun-filled plaza at Columbia University, using the afternoon to play Frisbee, football, and bathe in the sun.

There is trouble again on the campus at Columbia University. For the students who attend school there, only the sun and the games they played seemed to matter.

But the trouble has been building for months. On Thursday, it came out into the open. Before the night was over, buildings were seized. The police came on the campus and 37 arrests were made.

It is not the students who are in the forefront of the trouble that is on the campus now. It is union trouble. The dispute involves the clerical and cafeteria workers at the university, all of them members of local 1199 of the Hospital and Health Care Workers Union.

These are the lowest paid employees at the University. Money is not the root of the issue now. It is a squabble involving the employees' pension program that has been going on since last year.

Basically, the dispute is this: the union wants the university to contribute to its pension plan. The university, on the other hand, is demanding that the employees leave the union plan and join the pension program that Columbia has for its employees.

Yesterday, the 500 union employees found themselves locked out of the buildings in which they worked. Tacked onto the doors of the buildings was a note of explanation. It said:

"Based on your actions of yesterday (Thursday), wherein employees were involved in a sit-in, taking over of offices, trespass, damage to property and other related actions, you are hereby suspended, effective immediately."

There were many versions of what led to Thursday's sit-in and takeover in basement offices at Hogan Hall. But the police were called in and arrests were made. In the offices that were taken over -- including the controller's office -- files were overturned, ledgers destroyed, and other damage was done. It was not just a labor dispute. Something bigger appeared to be building at the university.

"They're trying to force us into a strike," Jesse Olson, who is executive vice president of the union, said. "We don't want to strike. We've appealed to the university not to lock us out. We're prepared to negotiate, but we won't negotiate with a gun at our heads."

The "gun" that Olson referred to was the lockout and the indefinite suspensions.

Ross Rimicci, the director of employee relations and development at Columbia, had little to say.

"There may be more negotiations, and there may not be," he said. "It just depends."

"Depends on what?"

"Read the memo," he said.

There were two paragraphs to the memo posted by the university. The second said that any member of the union who was not involved in the actions at Hogan Hall could send a confidential letter to Rimicci's office.

"It looks as though they're trying to break the union," Olson said. "Hell, the average worker only makes about $250 a week. What do they want? These people have a right to complain. We've been trying to sit down and negotiate with them. But they don't want to negotiate. They want to force a strike and break this union. It's as simple as that."

While the students lounged in the sun and played their games yesterday, the members of the union huddled outside Hogan Hall on Broadway. They wore blue and white paper caps, but the students who passed hustled by without asking questions.

Up on the plaza, in the sun, the students seemed unconcerned about the events of the night before or the trouble that was on the campus now.

"I heard the food service has been disrupted," one student said.

"I don't know what's going on," another student said. "I just hope the library is not closed."

The comparison on the campus of Columbia University was with the '60s, when it was the students who took over the buildings and who were arrested by the cops. Yesterday, the '60s seemed very distant.

In Dodge Hall, the university and union officials were meeting, but not negotiating. Jocelyn Pierre-Louis, 32, one of those arrested Thursday, stood and talked about the students.

"It's very difficult for the students to understand out plight," he said. "They're not poor, and they don't understand the poor. They needed us then, back in the '60s, and we gave them our help, but we don't really expect anything from them now."

The union is made up mostly of Blacks and Hispanics. Many of the Blacks are immigrants from the Caribbean. Pierre-Louis came here 16 years ago from Haiti. He did not worry about what the arrest would do. Instead, he talked about the difference it would make if students were to support the workers.

"But it's a different type of student here now," he said. "The only thing I have to say to them, though, is that the way the economy is going, and with the inflation we have, the old saying about a good education being a guarantee of a good job is no longer true."

1979

HE HAD NOT BEEN TALKING VERY LONG, less than half an hour. You could see that even the men in the audience, hunched forward in their seats, hanging on every word, were biting their lips.

He was talking about his dream, which is building a national union of farm workers. It was what Cesar Chavez always talks about.

He was talking about the struggle in the fields today. He said that four lives had been lost since 1962.

"But the struggle goes on," he said. "We know and we're very fearful that maybe more lives will be lost. But it's our duty. We must continue. We must continue to struggle to do it nonviolently, and hope and pray there won't be any more loss of life. But, nevertheless, we must continue to do it."

Last Saturday, on a rainy afternoon, Chavez talked to a group of the city's Hispanic labor leaders.

He had traced the history of the United Farm Workers Union, of which he is the president. He said that for more than 100 years, farm workers had been trying to organize, and that the odds had been very great against them.

He went back to a time when it was the Chinese who were the immigrants who handled the harvest. In the quiet voice that he always uses, he brought the history forward.

"The boycott is so important," he said. "And it's so easy to do. If you just do that much and spread the word, we should win. We're going to win because our history is one of winning. We've been in worse situations. The victory will give us more hope and encouragement."

He had on a dark bulky sweater. His eyes were bright as they looked out to meet other eyes in the audience. He talked about the union organizers lost in the fields.

"But nothing's going to bring back their lives," he said. "They're gone forever. But that is the way it is with movements for social justice. We're not the only ones who have lost people in this kind of struggle."

It was quiet now as he spoke.

"We need to make sure we don't ever ... don't ever let that life, the giving of the life, be in vain."

When he was finished, everyone stood. For a long time they applauded, and there were tears.

Cesar Chavez is all that is left. He is from another time, from a time when our direction seemed certain, when there was a morality in the speeches that our leaders gave. He is from the time of Robert Kennedy and the Rev. Martin Luther King Jr. But he is different because he got through, and is still out there, still involved in the struggle.

His dream is that, in his time, there will be a national farm workers union. When he talks about it, no matter how great the odds, it seems real and within grasp.

"We have nothing else to do with our lives except to build our union," he says. "We will continue whether it takes one year or 20. We will never give it up."

This was supposed to be the year that Cesar Chavez and his United Farm Workers Union branched out. It was supposed to be the year that they moved into Florida, to organize the citrus workers, then on to Texas to organize. But now, there is trouble again in the fields of the Imperial Valley of California, so the branching out had to be put off.

When he began his speech on Saturday, Chavez was saying how happy he was to be in New York. "I feel like I'm home," he said. "You can see I'm very relaxed. The problem is that we never come to see you when everything is O.K. When you see us coming down the street to New York, you can just know -- you can bet your bottom dollar, we're in trouble."

The trouble this time is a strike. The issue is money. Chavez has imprinted in his mind all of the important figures.

In 1970, when his union signed its first contract with lettuce growers in California, the wage was $2 an hour. In terms of purchasing power, he says, that $2 was worth $1.71. When the contract expired, the hourly wage was $3.70, which he said was worth $1.84.

"In almost nine years, they're earning 13 cents more than in 1970.

The target of the strike is a conglomerate known as United Brands. The offer to Chavez's union was a 7 percent increase. "Not enough," he said. When an impasse developed, he made an offer. "We'll take it," he said, "but if we do, you have to promise that you won't raise prices more than 7 percent." The company refused and the result was the strike.

Chavez said his union could easily have won the strike. Even without a boycott. But the problem, he said, is that strikebreakers are being imported from Mexico. He maintained that the Immigration Service will do nothing about it.

In February, the trouble came. One of his organizers was killed and 12 were wounded when shooting erupted in the fields. The organizer, Rufino Contreras, 27, a lettuce picker, was killed.

Now Chavez has turned to his old weapon, the boycott. The dispute is over lettuce, but he said it's too difficult to boycott. United Brands, the target of the boycott, also owns Chiquita Banana.

After the speeches were finished and the day's work done, Chavez went to the theater. To "Zoot Suit." "I used to be a Zoot-suiter," he said.

"Really."

When the show was over, Chavez was on his feet applauding and smiling.

"Terrific," he said. "I thought it was terrific. You know Danny Valdez, he wrote it. He used to be out in California with us. He used to be in the union."

1979

HE SEES IT FROM THE WORLD of paper from the Bureau of Labor Statistics, where everything is charts, graphs, and endless rows of figures that tell us how bad the unemployment situation is.

The people without jobs are not there in the world of paper where Lewis Siegel works.

Siegel's office is in a skyscraper in Times Square. He had all of the statistics on his desk. They showed that the unemployment rate in the city is dropping.

"It's 8.2 percent for April," he said of the city's unemployment rate.

"That's down a bit from March. It's been that way for 19 consecutive months. That's about 50,000 jobs ahead each month.

"More people are finding work now," he said, "no question about it. There is movement. The only problem ... you know, is when people come out to look. That's why we haven't been able to make a real dent in the unemployment rate."

"What about the summer?" he was asked. "What about the kids who are coming out of school in a month? Are there going to be jobs for them?"

Now the optimism was gone. The figures told a different story.

Nationally, unemployment among teenagers is 15.8 percent. Here in New York, it's worse. The figure is 28.8 percent.

"What about for minorities, for teenaged kids who are not White?"

"That's the highest figure I see," Lewis Siegel said.

For youths between 16 and 19, the unemployment rate is 16.5 percent. Broken down, the rate is 13.9 percent for Whites, and 34.5 percent for Blacks and Puerto Ricans and others.

"And the real figure is probably higher than that, higher than 34.5 percent," Siegel said. "That figure only counts those looking for work. You could say that a good third of the Black teenagers looking for work can't find it."

With only a month left to the school year, that was the prospect for teenagers who will be on the streets looking for work.

Late in the afternoon on Monday, Wesner Thenor, 17 an 11th grader at Brandeis High School, was saying that he had applied for a job with the city's summer youth employment program.

"I need the money," he said. "It's as simple as that. A summer with no money can be very, very boring."

Thenor is an honor student. He says that when he's finished with school he'd like to go on to college. He would like to be a doctor.

"It's hard to get a job," he said. "You know, just to be eligible. Your family can't be earning over $6,000, I think it is.

"What does your father do?"

"He drives a taxi," the kid said. "But my parents can't give me the money I need. This is a good school. I wanted to go to Cardinal Hayes, but my folks couldn't afford it. That costs about $600 a year."

"Will you get a job?" he was asked.

"I'm not worried because I want to work. I could work here, at Brandeis, but the pay is not that great. But if nothing else comes up, I know I can do that."

Beverly Irish, who is 15 and a 10th grader, sat across the classroom. She comes from Harlem, and also has applied for a job in the city youth program.

"Money," she said. It is what all of the kids who are looking for work say when asked why they want a job. "I need the money."

"What will you do if you don't get the job?" she was asked.

Now she squirmed in her seat. Finally, her face lit in a smile. "I don't know," she said. "I don't know what I'll do."

Beverly wants to be a doctor, too. Not all of the kids in the city schools are slow learners whose big interest is cutting classes and smoking dope.

"Why a doctor?"

"My mother is studying to be a doctor," she said, "and my aunt is a doctor, and her husband is a doctor, too, and that's what I want to be. I want to go to college, and, after that, to medical school."

Ronald Gault has not been commissioner for the city's Department of Employment long. Already he is faced with his first major test. Summer jobs for kids.

Yesterday morning, he was in his office saying that there is money now to hire 55,000 teenagers for summer work. The jobs will pay $2.90 an hour, and the kids who get them will work six hours a day, four days a week for seven weeks. They can earn about $500, not a lot, but better than nothing.

"Do you have enough jobs?" the commissioner was asked.

"You could quadruple the number we have," he said. "About 120,000 young people have applied already, and about 95,000 of those have already been determined eligible, and that number is going up."

Mostly, the teenagers hired will work for city agencies, or be assigned jobs with nonprofit groups. Because the number of applicants exceeds the jobs available, a lottery will be held to determine who works, and who does not.

It is Gault's job to make certain that the program works, that the work experience the kids get is real because, as he says, "This is the first work experience for a lot of them. Their lives are being shaped and formed by this experience."

In the morning yesterday, the playground next to Brandeis High School was crowded and filled with noise. In the playground, stripped to the waist, were young men, all of them without jobs. Instead of working, they played games of basketball and handball.

Just before noon, Beraldo Reynoso came out of the school and headed down the block. He saw the guys in the playground. He considered himself lucky. "I've got a job," he said. "In the market, on the corner. I've been there two years. Yeh," he said. "I'm lucky." It is that way now. Only the lucky ones have jobs.

1980

DURING THE STRIKE, when the transit workers were saying it, nobody paid much attention. It was just talk, the men were angry. When they said how much they hate the work they do, nobody listened.

"Productivity," management said. "We've got to have more responsibility It was management's way of telling the workers that what they were doing was not enough, that they had to do better. The men understood. Every time they heard the word, the response was anger.

Before the transit strike began, a group of men who run the Seventh Ave. express were on their break, sitting in the little shack they use uptown in the terminal.

"Bull," one of the men said, when the word productivity was mentioned. "I say bull. Do you have any idea what it's like down there breathing steel all the time? Do you know what all the noise does to a man?"

It went around in a circle, first one of the men, then the next, each saying in his own way how much he hates the work he does.

"I just want to do my eight hours and get out of here," a young mechanic said. "I don't want to work any overtime or anything else. I just want to do my shift and go home."

Nobody listened. It was written off as so much strike talk. Management went ahead talking about productivity. The men who run the trains, they say bull.

The men who run the trains do have their jobs. It is easy to ignore the way they feel about the work that they do. The attitude is that if they don't like their jobs, then let them quit. Let them go someplace else.

But it isn't just the men who work underground in the subway system.

Listen to the voices from New Jersey, from the men who work at the Ford Motor Co. plant at Mahwah, the assembly plant that employs 3,732 people, the one that is going to shut down completely in June.

"I'm glad," Vincent Russell, a welder at the plant, said. "I'm glad it's closing."

It is not the way a man who is losing his job is supposed to talk; especially not for a man who has already put seven years in on the job, with a wife and two kids to support.

But that was Vincent Russell's attitude. The reason is that he hates the job he has on the assembly line at the plant at Mahwah. "This work here, it deprives a man of being a man," he said. "In order to have pride, you gotta be given respect and dignity first. They (Ford) don't understand that."

Vincent Russell was not alone.

Listen to Curtis Mosley. "For me personally," he said, "closing the plant is not all that bad. It gives me the chance to do what I want to do." Curtis Mosley is not without responsibilities either. He is divorced from his wife, but he has custody of their son who is 8. "I should be able to make it," he said. For now, he is going back to school, where he intends to study broadcasting.

"It shows me that if I can get out here and survive, that I can do something other than put a few bolts in a car. Yeh, the money was good but you work for it like anything else."

After Ford announced that it was closing its Mahwah plant, reporters stood outside the gate that employees use and talked to the men as the afternoon shifts changed. Mostly, the men were dazed, unsure of what they would do without jobs. The old men worried. But among those who were young, young enough to believe that they could find something else, they spoke the way that Vincent Russell and Curtis Mosley did.

When Ford announced its intentions to close its Mahwah plant, one of the reasons it gave was the poor quality of the cars it said were produced at the plant. When the men heard it, they boiled.

"Crap," Mosley said. "That's a lie. Ford is only interested in putting out 63 or 64 cars an hour."

"They want quantity," Russell said, "not quality. They're pushing out a car every 52 seconds."

It is not so easy to ignore what the young men at Mahwah say, the men who believe that they are young enough to find something else, even now, as the recession grows, and the threat of a depression begins to loom larger.

What the young men at Mahwah are saying is that Ford is only interested in how much money it can make; that the company doesn't care whether the cars it produces don't hold up, that they waste gasoline. Given the choice, they say, they would just as soon not be a part of it.

It is about these jobs, not just at Ford or in New York with the transit system. It is a growing thing. The people doing the work are beginning to say that to their employers, if you don't care, then we don't either.

In New York, with the transit system, it may be that the men who run the trains understand that management doesn't care that the trains are filthy, that the stations are like sewers, and the noise if deafening. It spills over. In time, the job becomes a place to collect a pay check.

There was a time in this country when management could say to its workers, well, you're finished. That would be it. That was before the American labor movement. The unions have grown strong. It is not so easy for management to turn aside the employees it does not want.

There is talk now about a new form of slavery coming back. About union-busting to create a situation whereby workers will need jobs so badly that they'll do anything. Work under any conditions, accept any salary.

The American worker has changed. Expectations have been raised. The civil rights movement, the anti-war movement, the women's movement, have raised the consciousness of everyone. It spills over. What we are hearing now is the call for improvement in the quality of life at the working place. More than half of a working person's waking hours are spent on the job or getting there. If employers want productivity, they've got to restructure the work to create for the workers pride and dignity in what they do.

1981

HE HAD BEEN ON THE PHONE for hours, making one call after another to just about everyone he knew from around the country. Late in the night, a frown was pressed in his face and anger came through in his voice.

"This just isn't right," Jim Butler said. "Bill Lucy is next; that's the name of the game, and we can't go back now."

Jim Butler, an old union man, began to make his arguments. "History," he said. "Past practices...they always do it the same way. If something happens to the president, they automatically give the blessing to the next in line and Lucy is next."

He mentioned the AFL-CIO. "When George Meany stepped down, Lane Kirkland was next," he said. "There were no other hats in the arena. It was just Kirkland, but what do we have here? We got Gotbaum's hat in the arena, and we got McEntee's hat in the arena. I'm very disturbed. The way I see it, there should only be one hat in the arena: Bill Lucy's hat."

It is about the presidency of one of the nation's largest unions, the million-member American Federation of State, County and Municipal Employees. Five days ago, Jerry Wurf, the union's president, died. The way Jim Butler sees it, what should happen next is cut and dried.

"Bill Lucy is the No. 2 man," he says. "He is the international secretary-treasurer. He has had that position for nine years. There should be no question of his ability to carry out the union's business. We just came back from Singapore. They had a worldwide meeting of public workers there, and he was the one who led the American delegation. I witnessed his ability to carry out the union's business. So what is the problem?"

Jim Butler, the old union man, stopped. For a while he said nothing.

"The one thing I see," he said, finally. "The only shadow over Lucy is the color of his skin. I just feel that if he was White, he would slide in. There wouldn't be any other hats in the arena, just Bill Lucy's hat."

It is another story about race. "There is no other person in the union movement with a position as high as Lucy's," Jim Butler said. "He could be the first now, the first Black man to head a major union. He should be the first, too. It's history, it's the way they've always done it, and Bill Lucy is next. I'm very much disturbed, This is going to set us back in the labor movement. It is going to set us way, way back. And this man (Lucy), he was not just watched here, he was known all over the world."

In the telephone calls that he made through the night on Monday, Jim Butler was doing all that he could to rally support for Bill Lucy. "There is plenty of talk going on around the country. We got a Solidarity movement we're trying to put together right here."

On Monday, Jim Butler went to his office in Harlem early in the evening. At midnight he was still there on the phone. His anger was directed mostly at Victor Gotbaum, executive director of District Council 37. At a board meeting earlier Monday, Gotbaum had announced that he was running for the presidency. He had the support of everyone on the 19-member board except Jim Butler.

"I guess it was loyalty," he said of the other board members. "Either that or fear, but I wouldn't call it loyalty at all. I call it ignorance, people not knowing the history of the labor movement, not knowing that when there is a death, you always go to the second in command."

He singled out Al Diop, an international vice president who is also Black. "He went with him (Gotbaum), too, but that didn't surprise me. He always goes with Gotbaum.

When Gotbaum decided to stay in the closet in the mayoral election, he (Diop) stayed with him."

The city election is a part of it. Nobody had worked harder than Jim Butler to defeat Mayor Koch. It is something that goes back to the closing of Sydenham Hospital. After that, Butler was set against the mayor. It angered him that Gotbaum did not lead the union against Koch.

Victor Gotbaum is not the only candidate for Wurf's job. Gerald W. McEntee, an international vice president and leader of the AFSCME council in Pittsburgh, also is running.

Yesterday, the union leadership was gathering in Washington. After today's memorial service for Jerry Wurf, the union turns to the business of electing a new president. The vote is to take place tomorrow.

Only once on Monday night did the anger go out of Jim Butler's voice. It was when he talked about Jerry Wurf. "There was a man," he said. "He did so much. We remember his struggle, the way he fought for the dignity of public workers. You know, he was the one who stopped the practice of calling us by our first name in the hospitals. We respected him. He did so much."

In the afternoon yesterday, Victor Gotbaum was not in the city. He was already in Washington, building his candidacy. A spokesman in New York said that Jim Butler did not have it right on the succession. "The constitution says that within 15 days (of the death or removal of the president) the executive board is convened, and it votes on a successor," Ed Handman, the spokesman, said.

"No," Jim Butler said. "The practice is that you go to the second in command if something happens to the president. Why are they putting this red light in front of Bill Lucy? Why can't they wait until next convention? If this was convention time, I'd have no comment at all. I'd say 'To each his own,' but now Bill Lucy should be the next and I say that if he isn't, this is going to set us back, way back." The old union man had his say. He then got on one of the buses being used to take his troops to Washington.

1981

THE WORDS KEEP COMING back to him. He has long since split with the mayor and dropped out of the city government. Still the old quotes haunt him. Now he says they are not his words. The burden of the quote has become too much.

In March 1979, when he made the statements, Haskell Ward was deputy mayor. Back then, he did not hesitate. When this reporter asked him about reshaping of the city, how New York could face its future, he said of course it was true that the city would not be able to provide for the poor the way it had in the past.

"Does this mean that some people will have to leave New York?" he was asked.

"Yes," he said.

"Where will they go?"

"I don't know," he said. "Some will go south, and others will have to go west, but it's true, some of them will have to leave New York." In all the time he was involved in the city government, there was nothing that Haskell Ward said that had more truth to it. But he runs from the words. He says he was misquoted, insists that his statements were taken out of context. He refuses to stand up to the words.

It doesn't matter. There are other voices now. What they are saying is no differently from what Haskell Ward said one morning more than two years ago. "I keep telling people who come in that the jobs are in Texas, but the Black people don't want any part of it. I say Texas, and they don't want to hear it. They say, 'What about Alabama or Tennessee or Atlanta?' They just don't want to go for Texas. I don't understand it."

In the office that the New York State Employment Service operates in the Harlem State Office Building, Jack Compton sat in the manager's office, chain-smoking cigarettes. "We used to get the jobs here," he said, "but not anymore. You know why? Because businesses are leaving New York. We just don't have the jobs anymore, and I don't believe New York is ever going to be able to draw business back here. It's too expensive to do business in New York. There are too many regulations, and there's a lot of corruption. So the businesses are leaving, and when people come in here, we can't do much for them."

By "corruption," he said he meant the ways that businesses get around the city's regulations.

"Are you saying that poor people have to leave New York?" Jack Compton was asked.

"The jobs aren't here anymore," he said. "There are jobs in Texas," he said. "In the next five to eight years, there will be more people in Houston than there are in New York City. That is where it's happening, and what I'm saying to people is that if they want to work, they are going to have to start going where the jobs are. But the Black people who come in here, they don't want any part of Texas."

The fight is for jobs. The belief in New York is that the city has more than its share of poor people. So the city embraces the policy called "redistribute the poor."

1982

IT DEPENDS ON THE WAY you look at it. Maybe it was nothing more than the result of good organizing. Maybe. But just the same the signals say: Don't overlook what happened yesterday in the grand ballroom at the Roosevelt Hotel.

There wasn't a seat in the place; it was packed.

It was the kind of gathering that isn't often seen in the city. Mostly, that was because it was a huge gathering. Half the people there were White, the other half, Black.

What happened in the hotel was another good indicator as to where the new hookup taking place between Blacks and certain segments of organized labor is going.

The occasion yesterday was the seventh annual banquet luncheon of the Labor Research Association (LRA) and coupled with it, a salute to the Congressional Black Caucus.

The LRA is an old union organization. It has a history that goes back to 1927. In the labor movement its role has always been educating. In its early days, it did just what its name says: research. Later, when unions were able to provide their own researchers, LRA provided information on the finances of corporations involved in union negotiations, and published books and pamphlets.

The Congressional Black Caucus is new politics. It was organized in 1971 and had 13 members. Richard Nixon was President, and there was an early confrontation. It came when the Caucus asked Nixon for a meeting to discuss concerns of Blacks and poor people, and Nixon refused.

Stung by the refusal, every Black member of the House of Representatives walked out of the chamber during the President's 1971 State of the Union address. The walkout served its purpose. Three months later, Nixon scheduled a meeting with members of the Caucus.

The Black Caucus has 18 members now. After January, the number will be 21. John Conyers of Detroit, who is a senior member of the caucus, came to the Roosevelt Hotel to accept honors from the LRA. Conyers, in a stunning speech, said that the time has come for members of the Congressional Black Caucus to begin taking some risks.

He said that members of the Caucus, all of them Democrats, get elected by landslides. "But we don't take any risks," he added. He said it doesn't make sense because "the fact is, the more challenges we make, the more support we get back in our districts."

Conyers used the alternative budget for fiscal 1983 proposed by the Black Caucus as an example. He said the attitude among the House leadership is that "they're tolerating us." He said the attitude is, "Give 'em all the time they want, let 'em make their speeches." But the vote is the same, Conyers said.

"They (House leaders and other Democrats) even come to us afterward and say how brilliant our speeches were. But some of us are beginning to realize we're in a trick bag. We're giving Congress a good name, advertising progressive proposals that don't stand a chance. It's part of this cute, unspoken arrangement."

Conyers said, "It's time for action." He said, "The time has come to stop quoting Frederick Douglass on the price of struggle. The time has come to stop quoting (Martin Luther) King and Malcolm (X) and (W.E.B.) Du Bois, all of whom were risk takers, and become risk takers ourselves."

He said the caucus should say, "We want change, or we're going to get new leadership."

He said he noticed that the "boll weevils" (the 39 southern Democrat conservatives who support Reaganomics) won reelection, and still have their chairmanships and party positions.

Conyers admitted that the Black Caucus doesn't have the votes to overturn the party leadership. "But the impact of voting against the leadership would be profound," he said. "That would send tremendous shock waves. You have all these Democrats getting elected on the votes of Blacks."

That brought it back into the ballroom at the Roosevelt Hotel. The word was coalition. It meant Blacks, Latinos, women, and labor joining, in coalition, to elect progressive candidates.

Conyers turned to the figures. He said the Democrats won 26 new House seats. Then, he mentioned the governorships. He said that the majorities were provided by the coalition, but the Democrats were representing moderate/conservative politics.

"Jobs, equality and peace," he said, "that's what it's about. You can't have one without the other. Martin (King) taught us that."

Conyers said the country is "on the eve of an incredibly important movement." He compared it to the '30s when Franklin Roosevelt and the New Deal came to power. He said the way minorities voted in the last election was proof "there is a hope among the people that there can be change." He said the objective should be full employment, but added, "It's not even being debated."

He said, "We are in a depression as we meet; so the question then becomes, 'What are we to do?' If a risk is attached, we ought to begin taking it now because 11 million people are out of work. It's time for action."

Before Conyers spoke, Major Owens, who was elected to Congress in part because of the coalition represented in the ballroom, came to the lectern. He looked to Conyers, and said, "He's my kind of congressman. If I have a model, he is it. He is the kind of congressman I want to be."

When it was his turn, Conyers looked to Major Owens and said his election was particularly important. "When you choose a Black member of Congress, it's a lifetime appointment."

It depends on the way you look at it. Maybe it wasn't much, but yesterday, in the ballroom at the Roosevelt Hotel, there was evidence that coalitions are building and it may be, as John Conyers said, the eve of an incredibly important movement.

1982

BY YESTERDAY, WHAT WAS LEFT on the corner was a boarded up shell, another remnant; not much different from the one a block away that was once Sydenham Hospital.

"I hear it's gonna be another restaurant," an old woman who waited at the bus stop said.

"I believe they was doing some work there a while ago," she said.

What is coming down is Thomforde's. To say that Thomforde's was just another restaurant is like calling the Empire State Building just another skyscraper. Thomforde's was one of those special places that bridged time. It never changed. In a way, it was every bit as much an anchor in that part of Harlem as Sydenham, the hospital that went before it.

It was the politics of now that Sydenham fell victim to. Taking the hospital out was the easy part.

What is left of Sydenham is a neighborhood clinic, and some promises the politicians made.

In the days when Sydenham was still an issue, the argument for keeping the hospital open was that it was needed. "This is one of the most medically deprived communities in the country," the experts said; but the politics of now said, "So what? Money is tight."

That meant the second part of the keep-Sydenham-open argument didn't stand a chance. That was the part about jobs. Sydenham was a big employer in Harlem. There were jobs for janitors, orderlies, nurses' aides, and secretaries -- in all, hundreds of jobs.

In Harlem, it touched a woman whose name is Marion Anderson. For close to 20 years, she worked around the corner from Sydenham. She liked her work and believed that she had a blue-chip job. It would always be there. She was a waitress and short-order cook at Thomforde's.

There were just a dozen employees in the restaurant, not many, but that is what ties it together -- a few jobs here, a few over there, and a whole bunch down the street. Only now, it keeps coming apart. Marion Anderson sat in her apartment in the Lenox Terrace apartments, smoked cigarettes, and said: "I'm hoping I'll get something. I'm in a good union, Local 6, and they are trying to get us jobs. But you know, it's really tough out there now. It's really bad."

It was a strike that put her on unemployment. Last July, the waitresses at Thomforde's walked out when the employer tried to take the union away. "We came out on strike a little after 11 that morning," Marion Anderson said yesterday. "Then around 1 o'clock, they closed the store. We had one meeting with them. They wanted us to go back without the union. We wouldn't do it. That was what the strike was about."

Thomforde's never opened again. On the old sign over the front on the restaurant it said, "Thomforde's, established in 1903." It was one of those places that stayed busy. It had good food, good prices, and stayed clean. At Thomforde's, they made their own ice cream, their own candy and cakes. They had an old-time way of displaying everything. But it was the people who worked there who made it special. They weren't coming and going; they stayed. Marion Anderson put in 20 years. A woman whose name is Frances Atkins was a waitress there for 35 years.

They didn't earn much money, either. Atkins started at $40 a week. She was earning $135 when the strike came. Marion Anderson's salary was $68.75. But there were tips, and they were a part of a place that had good vibes. The only time they balked was the time the owner said no union. They walked out. It ended there. They stayed on the sidewalk with their picket signs through the middle of the next winter. Thomforde's began to come apart. Now, it is just a shell.

Marion Anderson used to start to work at 8 o'clock in the morning, but she always came in early. "I opened up the place," she said. "I'd be in there by 7, and I would get the oatmeal and the grits and the sausages ready and put the potatoes on."

Frances Atkins has found another job.

"She was lucky," Marion Anderson was told.

She bristled. "Not lucky," she said, "She's a good waitress."

Yesterday, the hope that Marion Anderson had was that the union would call, saying there was a job for her.

"I like waitress work," she said. "It's a hard job, it's sure not easy because you stay on your feet. The big thing is, you have to be nice. You have to be courteous to people. But I don't want no summer job. I want something permanent because when I get on a job, I stay there."

"Where do you look for a job?" Marion Anderson was asked.

"I've been to the employment office, but they didn't have anything," she said. "But the union, they're doing everything they can to get me work."

James Williams, with Local 6 of the Hotel, Restaurant, Club Employees and Bartenders Union, spoke about the women from Thomforde's.

"I know about Mrs. Anderson," he said, "and we're working on it. But the problem is that with most of the jobs we have now, they are dealing only in young boys and girls. It seems that everything is geared for youth. It poses a problem, a terrible problem and it hurts, it really hurts that we can't help these people."

"What happened at Thomforde's?" he was asked.

"The man just put a padlock on the door," James Williams said. "Nothing came of the hearing. There was supposed to be a hearing, but as far as I know, the man never even showed up."

It is about the politics of now. Yesterday, Marion Anderson, a woman who believed her job was secure, was another of the victims.

1983

BY THEN, HE HAD BEGUN to center his attention on economic issues. That night in New York in the speech he delivered, he talked of what he called the other America, and it was a part of the building of his dream, a Poor People's Campaign.

This was 1968, the 10th of March. In less than a month, he would be dead.

He would be shot and killed in Memphis. He would never be able to go ahead with his idea to gather up the poor from all parts of the country, bring them to Washington, to engage in a massive campaign of civil disobedience. The goal of that campaign would be to bring about the enactment of legislation that would provide for jobs or a guaranteed annual income for the poor.

It would have been the most ambitious campaign Dr. Martin Luther King Jr. ever attempted. It was to be, as he said then, his final effort to bring about real change through nonviolent protest.

He came to New York that March to speak at a Freedom Salute dinner sponsored by Local 1199 of municipal workers.

The union took the words that came from Dr. King that night, and had them pressed into records. Yesterday, at the end of the weekend that celebrated his birth, the words were brought back.

"Probably the most critical problem in the other America," he said, "is the economic problem. By the millions, people in the other America find themselves perishing on a lonely island of poverty in the midst of a vast ocean of material prosperity."

He said: "The fact is that the Black man in the United States is now facing a literal depression."

He brought the people to their feet with applause. "When there is massive unemployment in the Black community, it is called a social problem," he said. "When there is massive unemployment in the White community, it's called a depression."

He said unemployment was not the only problem. "It's under or subemployment. People work full-time jobs for part-time wages. Most of the poor people in our country are working every day, but they're making wages so inadequate that they cannot begin to function in the mainstream of the economic life of the nation. We look around and we see thousands and millions of people making inadequate wages every day. Not only do they work in our hospitals, they work in domestic service. They find themselves underemployed. You see, no labor is really menial unless you're not getting adequate wages. People are always talking about menial labor. That isn't menial labor. What makes it menial is the income, the wages.

"Now what we got to do is attack the problem of poverty, and really mobilize the forces of our country to have an all-out war against poverty, because what we have now is not even a good skirmish against poverty. Every year about this time, our newspapers and television people generally begin to talk about the long hot summer ahead, and what really bothers me about this is that long hot summer has always been preceded by a long cold winter. And the tragedy is that the nation has failed to use its winters creatively, compassionately, and with enough concern, and our nation's summers of riots are still caused by our nation's winters of delay.

say it in no uncertain terms. And I simply say to you that I'm afraid that our government is more concerned about winning an unjust war abroad, than in the war against poverty right here at home, and I say if we will stand and work together, we will bring into being that day when justice will roll down like waters and righteousness like a mighty stream. We will bring into being that day when America will not longer be two nations but one."

He left New York that night in 1968, and went ahead with his plans for a Poor People's Campaign. He was opposed by the newspapers that feared violence. He was even opposed by other civil rights leaders. But he believed that a confrontation on economic issues was vital, and he would not step away from his idea.

Then came Memphis. He was sidetracked by the garbage collectors in Memphis who were losing a strike they had against the city, and they asked his help and he went to Memphis.

On the day before he was to die, he stood on the balcony of his hotel, on the identical spot where he was to fall victim to an assassin's bullet, and he said he would not step back from his Poor People's Campaign.

"I'm aware of the opposition," he told me, "but we cannot call off our efforts because some few people might be violent."

That night, Dr. King was to make another speech. This one would be the last that he would ever deliver.

"And some began to talk about the threats, that are out, or what would happen to me from some of our sick White brothers. Well, I don't know what will happen now. We've got some difficult days ahead. But it really doesn't matter with me now because I've been to the mountaintop. I don't mind. Like anybody, I would like to live a long life. Longevity has its place, but I'm not concerned about that now. I just want to do God's will and He's allowed me to go up to the mountain and I've looked over and I've seen the promised land. I may not get there with you but I want you to know tonight that we as a people will get to the promised land. So I'm happy tonight. I'm not worried about anything. I'm not fearing any man. Mine eyes have seen the glory of the coming of the Lord..."

Then, his voice was stilled by the assassin's bullet. He was not there to make his Poor People's Campaign work. He saw that it was an economic problem in the country, but once he did, it was what got him killed, and it comes back now, on the celebration of his birth.

1983

THE TWO STORIES THAT LINK UP tell an important part of what is happening now in the labor movement in New York. One story is of a union strike. The other is of a union election. They both say that something very important has taken root, and is building in the labor movement.

The strike involves the Greyhound Bus Lines.

The election was held late last month, and involved a hotel that sits in the shadow of LaGuardia Airport. It had been billed as an important election. The stakes were high, and the outcome figured to be very close. On one side there was the Marriott Hotel Corp. On the other was Local 6 of Hotel, Restaurant, Club Employees and Bartenders Union.

On the night of the election, David Nadel went to the hotel to await the results. "I was completely shocked," he said. The vote wasn't even close. Nearly every eligible employee at the hotel voted. In all, 212 ballots were cast. Of that total, 170 went against the union. Just 28 voted in favor of the union, and 14 ballots were challenged. It wasn't just the margin of defeat that stunned Nadel.

He said he had been in the labor movement 28 years. Never before, he said, had he seen anything like what took place at the LaGuardia Marriott on the night of the union election.

"I just signed up for a job," said one of the hotel's new workers, in his 20s. He said he dropped out of college because he needed a job.

"It's been so long since I've seen money that I've forgotten what it looks like," he said. "Yes, I know these guys are on strike, but they're striking for more money. I need a job. I don't have any money. It may be wrong, but they (Greyhound) said they are hiring, and I need the job. It's not just that I want a job. I need one; I have to have a job."

It was the other side of the story, and David Nadel, the union man, said yes, he understood the way it all links up. He remembered the old days, how different it is now. "In 1938, he said. "I had just come to New York. We were organizing drugstores. We had a picket line at one store, and nobody went in. The attitude of the public kept people out, but the climate has changed. This is a time the labor movement has to go to work."

At the Marriott LaGuardia, Michael Hollander, manager of the hotel, was not surprised that his employees voted against the union. "We're not running a sweatshop," he said. "Our wages and benefits are competitive with the union. Personally, I think some unions are out of date."

David Nadel recalled the vote. "When it came down that we had lost, the workers were all jumping up and down, hugging and kissing their bosses, shouting that 'we won, we won'. I never saw anything like it. The only thought that went through my mind was that this is the wave of the future. The whole thing was like Japan. They (the employees) were saying 'our hotel' and 'we won.' I was just completely shattered."

There was a lot about what happened at the Marriott LaGuardia that was disturbing to David Nadel, an old union man. "About half of the new employees were minorities, too," he said. "Usually, minorities don't relate to establishment institutions, but they did this time."

"The way Marriott handled the campaign," he said. "They didn't have an anti-union attitude. Instead, they projected a positive image of what they were doing. They built up the hotel, talked about profit-sharing, and made the employees a part of what they were doing. We learned a tremendous lesson."

It is a lesson that says the labor movement in 1983 is not what it was at another time. Another piece of the evidence was visible on the lower level of the Port Authority terminal where Greyhound has a piece of the operation. On the lower level, Greyhound is located right alongside Trailways, one of its prime competitors. In front of Greyhound, though, there was a picket line, and the young men and women, Blacks and Whites and Hispanics, shouted their anger. "Respect the strike," they yelled. "If you want to get home for Thanksgiving, don't go Greyhound because it's not safe. Trailways will get you there safe; respect the strike."

They also shouted something else. "Those are scabs working back there. Don't support the scabs."

Greyhound had all of its ticket booths open, and there were workers. Yesterday, the Greyhound buses began to make routes in face of the strike. At the terminal, each time a customer crossed the picket line, the strikers closed in. "They're trying to cut our salaries $4,000. This strike is supported by 99 percent of the employees." But in the face of the argument, some still bought tickets and rode Greyhound.

Cops stood behind the picket line. At the gate where the buses were loaded, security guards allowed only those with tickets to pass.

1983

ON THE SIDEWALK, outside the union's headquarters, her voice rose above the noontime noise. "How could this happen?" Margarita Lopez asked. "How could this happen in a union that is supposed to be so liberal?"

In one hand, she held a microphone. In the other she clutched a thick sheath of documents. "The Blacks, the Hispanics, the Chinese," she said, "those are the workers. The dues come from those people, but the housing, the housing is all White and middle class."

She was surrounded by a thin knot of supporters who applauded her words. When she was finished she passed the microphone on. The others took turns at saying how the International Ladies Garment Workers Union discriminates against minorities in four union-sponsored cooperatives on the lower East Side.

The issue already is in federal court. Still, the workers were determined to raise the issue on the union's doorstep.

"Because we want this brought up at the convention," Fred Seiden said, "This is not just simply segregation on Grand St., it's union-financed segregation. It's being done with union dues money."

"This is some of the best housing in the city we're talking about," Fran Goldin said. "These are large, very inexpensive apartments, and they're on the East River."

The lawsuit goes back to 1977. It was brought by the Lower East Side Joint Planning Council and garment-district workers. The suit, which now is before District Judge Robert Carter, was directed at the boards of directors of four cooperatives on the lower East Side -- the Amalgamated Houses, Hillman Houses, East River Houses and Seward Park Houses.

Lopez heads the lower East Side Joint Planning Council. The documents she waved in her hand at a press conference outside ILGWU headquarters were ones she said showed the union's ongoing involvement in the housing.

One document had a listing of directors of East River Houses. The vice president is Sol C. Chaikin, president of the ILGWU. Another document was a commendation from directors of the Seward Park Houses. It praised Chaikin for his role in securing the union's help in refinancing the Seward Park mortgage.

"Those were union pension funds," Lopez said. "They give union funds, but union workers who are Black and Hispanic and Chinese cannot live in those houses?"

The cooperatives were built by the United Housing Federation with funds from major unions, and Lopez said that the most prominent union involved was the ILGWU. The lawsuit that charges discrimination used as its basis figures which showed that of 4,439 apartments, only 2.5 percent of the rentals were to Blacks and Hispanics.

Fran Goldin said that a proposed settlement of the suit would have resulted in less than 9 percent minority occupancy of the buildings after 10 years. "We found that insulting and unacceptable," she said. The plaintiffs in the suit want a settlement that would give qualified minorities first call on two of every three available apartments in an arrangement they say would make the complex 20 percent minority in 10 years.

On the day last week that Lopez and the others made their charges to reporters outside the union's headquarters, a spokesman for the ILGWU appeared with a statement from the union.

The statement said the union did invest money in the housing, but it said the ILGWU "never managed, operated or controlled the project." The statement said the ILGWU encouraged its members to apply for East River housing apartments, and even offered to lend money to members who wanted to buy into the cooperatives. "These members," the statement read, "included people of all races and national origins."

At the press conference on the sidewalk, there was an older woman with Lopez who was Hispanic. She told a story of applying for an apartment in the complex. She said she was told that the waiting list was so long that it would take 20 years for her to get an apartment.

Lopez had others with her. The stories they told were similar to one the older woman told. All except the story of Fred Seiden.

Seiden is White. He said when he applied, he was offered an apartment in just a few months. He said he was told not to take the first apartment he was shown but to "wait a while, and look at five or six apartments." Seiden's story was carried into court. His story became prime testimony in the discrimination case.

It connects with a story that was in the newspaper yesterday. The story said that union membership in the country is on the decline. According to the Bureau of Labor Statistics, membership in labor organizations was 22.4 million in 1980, about 20.9 percent of the labor force. In 1970, 24.7 percent of the labor force was unionized.

One of the unions that has a declining membership is the ILGWU. The union has 283,000 members now. In 1979, the ILGWU membership was 341,000. There are many reasons for the decline in membership. Jobs are disappearing. Layoffs are everywhere. And that knocks down union membership. But the other side of what is happening in the union movement goes back to the sidewalk outside ILGWU headquarters and the words that Lopez hollered over the noontime noise.

"The union leaders are saying the hell with the workers," she said, "and the workers are earning a lot less than they (the leaders) are but they don't care. That's why we're out here."

1983

IN THE MORNING, HIS SEARCH for a job took him to Koff Graphics, in the Village. He went through the plant. What he saw scared him.

"It's passing me by," he said afterward. "There are so many new techniques they are using. I was totally aghast. The way they use computers, I couldn't believe it. I could see it's passing me by. There is a very big difference in the way things are done since I graduated."

Peter Ramirez came out of C.W. Post College just a year and a half ago. It all looked so good for him then. It was partly because he was the first in his family to stand in a college graduation ceremony, and have a degree placed in his hands.

Back then, in his family, everyone kept telling him how lucky he was. He had an education; he had his degree. To them, it meant his life would be different. He would not just be chasing dreams. In his life, the promise would be real. At the graduation ceremony, as he stood in cap and gown with his parents watching, it was the best moment in his life.

He came out of college and decided he would stay on Long Island to work. On Long Island, there were many companies. He believed that, with the talent and the training he had, he would get off to a fine start on a good job. Only it didn't work out that way. None of it worked out. The dream faded. The promise disappeared, and the words about how lucky he was became a cruel echo that stuck in his mind.

"I'm just trying to hang on to my sanity," he said yesterday. "I keep watching the news, and I hear them say the economy is getting better, that another 1,000,000 jobs have been created, and I wonder why I'm not one of those people. Why can't I get a job? It has been so long. I begin to wonder if it's me. I'm not even shooting for getting anything in the art field now. I'm just looking for something to bring in some money. I can do anything somebody throws at me."

His field is graphic design. He wanted to be a cartoonist. When he came out of college, and just began to move around looking for work, he carried a big, oversized notebook with samples of his work, including a comic strip that he originated.

In graphic design, though, nothing materialized.

"I don't even remember how many companies I interviewed with," he said. "It could have been 25 or 35, maybe more. And there were four agencies, but . . ."

When there was nothing in his field, he began to look other places.

"I tried everything," he said, "everything from pumping gas to McDonald's fast-food restaurants. I don't know how many job interviews you're supposed to go on before something happens, but I just don't know where to go anymore."

He is 23 now. "It sounds like a young age, I know, but I feel I'm really getting old. Each day I feel so much older. This really does something to you. I even feel that I'm losing my vocabulary. It's been particularly bad for me because I don't have anyone to talk to about this."

He says that the search for the job that he cannot find has begun to have an effect on every facet of his life. "I really don't want to take it out on anybody, but at home, you know, I try to stay away from everyone else. All I do is look at my mom and shrug my shoulders."

His dark hair is cut short. In college he played football. He still has an athlete's body. "People tell me to be patient, that I'll get lucky," he said. "I wish it wouldn't have to come down to luck. Those years (at college) I worked hard. It shouldn't come down to luck to get any little job."

He lives at home, on the Grand Concourse in the Bronx. He was the son who had the advantage of education, the son who earned the degree. His life was filled with promise. Now, he baby-sits while his mother works at a new part-time job she found.

"When I'm home, I try to work at my drawing. I read the want ads, and try to find something, but it always comes down to the same thing: I go out and interview and they say we'll let you know, and nothing happens."

The doubts have begun to build. "I'm not second guessing myself anymore," he said. "It's third and fourth guessing."

"What do you need that would help?" he was asked.

"A portfolio," he said. "But to get a portfolio, you need a job. It is a Catch-22 situation."

"What will you do?"

"I will keep on looking," Peter Ramirez said. "I can't give up. That's the one thing I can't do. But it's been a year and a half. You would think that by now I would have found something. I just need a job."

1984

IT BEGINS TO COME INTO FOCUS. Now it is possible to see the way the two events are related, the convention just finished in Dallas and the strike that drags on in the City of New York.

In Dallas, the Republicans were setting the atmosphere. "America's Party," they called themselves. The important business was nominating President Reagan for a second term. It ties in with New York and the hospital and nursing home strike that moves to a crucial point.

On the night of his nomination, even at age 73, all the signals say Ronald Reagan figures to be a formidable candidate. His reelection seems assured. His margin of victory, the pollsters say, should reach landslide proportions. It comes back to the strike.

The strike is in its 42nd day. On one side is the union, District 1199 of the Retail, Wholesale and Department Store Union, AFL-CIO. On the other side is the bargaining agent for the struck hospitals and nursing homes, the League of Voluntary Hospitals and Homes. The moment of settlement came, but slipped past. It was said that agreement had been hammered out, and word of that was being announced. Doris Turner, the union's president, says the league backed out. James S. Vlasto, a spokesman for the league, puts the blame on the union. The result is that the strike moves on. Now, the hospital's threat is to fire the strikers, and hire permanent replacements. It ties in with Dallas.

In the early days of his time as President, Ronald Reagan was confronted with a strike of air traffic controllers. It was to be the beginning of a new atmosphere. The air traffic controllers had made a no-strike pledge. Reagan ordered them back to their jobs. The controllers refused. Reagan fired the bunch of them. It was a stunning move. He did what had always been said couldn't be done. Labor hollered and made threats. At the end of all that, Reagan's popularity rose. That was how the issue of permanent replacements for strikers came to confront the labor movement.

It has to do with the climate in the country which continues to go against organized labor. When Reagan acted against the traffic controllers, it was a move unprecedented. But the idea took root. When Greyhound had trouble settling a strike, it hired replacements. "Because the way the labor market is now, there are always dozens of people wanting your job," a Greyhound driver said back then.

"The people without jobs just want a chance to earn some money. They don't worry about what is right by us (strikers), and all of the union issues. They want to work. Management knows that, and they take advantage of the situation."

Now it's the hospitals issuing the ultimatums. "I cannot give assurances what some workers will do when someone tries to take their jobs away," Doris Turner said. The strike involves 52,000 workers. They include clerks and housekeepers and orderlies. They are the ones that figure to be fired if the hospital carries out its threat. There are also social workers, technicians and physical therapists on strike. These are employees not easily replaced because licensing is involved. So they do not figure to be fired. Only the employees at the bottom, mostly minorities, and they are already at the bottom of the salary scale.

It begins to come into focus, Reagan's firing of the traffic controllers was the test. It created a climate. Back then, it was the doing of anti-union Republicans. Not now. It calls itself "America's Party," and it's in New York, a union town, where the strikers are threatened with wholesale firings. It tells a part of the story of where organized labor stands in the summer of 1984, on the verge of what is called "Labor Day."

1984

GENIUS. NO OTHER WORD describes it. The best part is that it comes right at the perfect time, on Labor Day.

The newspapers, the television and the radio have the story covered from all angles. The big news was the numbers. A lot of the newspapers had them posted right on the front page. They had nice little boxes and inside, the numbers were set in a row: 26-43-30-3-10-2.

Genius. The great national gambling game is taking hold. For now, the focus of attention is in Illinois. In one swoop, $40 million. Just pick the right numbers, six of 'em. Just do that and get the money.

The word out of Chicago was that close to 22 million tickets had been sold. It was said that they were selling close to 14,000 tickets a minute. Some folks were coming to buy tickets from places so distant it was taking a whole day to make the trip. There were so many stories of folks buying $500 and $1000 worth of tickets at one swoop, they weren't even news anymore.

Genius. It's the new national pastime that's building. It's still just a baby. All this is just getting started. Just wait until the Feds grab a piece of the action. It may be set up then so you just pick up the phone and call in your numbers.

Jackpots of $100 million, that'll be nothing. It's absolutely genius. The timing for all of it is perfect. It is because nobody wants to deal with the real story of where labor is headed in 1984.

There is still a labor movement. Only thing is, it's headed backward. Just look at New York City. In the heart of Manhattan there is rising now what promises to be an incredible hotel. It's in Times Square. Nowhere in New York is there anything to match it.

But the great hotel that is soon to be opened is not likely to have a single union job, and that's a Labor Day story too. It's not just one hotel in Manhattan. It's the direction labor is headed in the whole country. It's supposed to be a big story now, on Labor Day, but it isn't happening that way. The attention is on Illinois and the six numbers and the $40 million jackpot.

It ought to be pointed out, though, that while it's genius the way they're doing it, it did take some big stealing. The so-called "illegal" numbers games have homes. They have deep roots in communities. Many of the numbers operators made loans to folks who couldn't go to banks. They did a lot of other good things to boost economic development in urban areas.

Now, it's called the lottery. In the old days, it all had another name. "The numbers racket," the cops called it. In the community, they just called it "the numbers." But it got stolen, and, on Labor Day of 1984, it's all dressed up. The figures are something else. For now, the big one is $40 million, but this is a baby we're talking about. Some really big stuff is just around the corner. It's really something. Genius, that's the word that describes it.

1986

THEY HAVE A LOT THAT WORKS against them. The old image hurts. "All that coffee, tea or me stuff," Yvonne Norman explained. "A lot of people really believe the most important thing a flight attendant does is serve drinks," she said. "We do a lot more than that."

Her best example had to do with safety. "If there's an emergency, passengers depend on us," she said. "In the air, we're the first line of safety. And we're trained in what to do. That's what the public should be aware of." Since 1975, Yvonne Norman has been a flight attendant on Eastern Airlines. "This wasn't a job," she said. "I looked on this as a career." She had many reasons. The pay was good. The hours were good, and the benefits offered were special.

It had been different in the old days. Flight attendants were known as stewardesses then. Mostly, they were young, single, pretty women. The jobs had glamor, but the rules were restrictive. Just getting married, or having a baby, also meant the end of the line.

All that kept stewardesses from making flying a career. In time, those barriers were knocked down. Instead of stewardess, the name became flight attendant. It wasn't just a word. In a way, it signaled the putting into place what was virtually a whole new job -- a career for many women. It was the kind of job Yvonne Norman saw in 1975.

Suddenly, the unthinkable is happening. Airlines are looking at the salaries flight attendants are being paid, and they're saying, we won't pay that, and making it stick.

"You grow up, and the whole thing is get a good job," Yvonne Norman said. She told a kind of story that flight attendants with most airlines are beginning to tell. Hers was a story of the way a meat ax was taken to her salary. She had a $5,000 cut in the last two years. Then, in January, yet another. While taking a 40 percent cut, she said the company demanded 40 percent more in output. The airlines now are another industry that is shaking out. Companies are creative in finding ways to get out of the costly contracts. They've put unions in check. They tell them: Strike, and the company will go bankrupt.

As Eastern was teetering between bankruptcy and takeover, Yvonne Norman said what many flight attendants say. "Ever since Continental got away with what they did, other airlines are looking to do the same." She mentioned Frank Lorenzo. "I just hope he doesn't get control of Eastern," she said.

Lorenzo, who owns Texas Air, had all but completed a buyout of Eastern. In the airline industry, Lorenzo is the boogeyman. It goes back to 1983. He was operating Continental Airlines. A pilots' strike shut him down. Lorenzo filed for bankruptcy, and used that fact to rip up existing labor contracts, impose new work rules, and new, lower wage scales on employees. Workers all over the airline industry screamed. But Continental went from a money losing operation to one of the most profitable in the industry.

"That's how they got us," Yvonne Norman said. "And it's so easy now. Everything is about union busting -- all over America." Fences that protected workers and wages are being torn down. The flight attendants are learning that it means you do more for less.

1990

HIS IS A UNION THAT REPRESENTS a lot of people who do not have much money. So, it is easy to understand what Stanley Hill is getting at when he says, "I cannot stand by and allow my members to be the mayor's political and sacrificial lambs to Wall Street."

The history that Stanley Hill knows is that every time government gets into financial trouble, it's the little guy who takes the hit. The bankers and the big investors who are the money people always get paid. Their money comes off the top.

At the bottom, it is another story. When times are tough, those who can least afford it always take it on the chin. If jobs have to be cut, that cutting starts at the bottom where losing a job can put a person on the street. It is the same way with programs, no matter how crucial. When the money gets tight, programs get slashed. If the emergency room has to close, that is just too bad. If the drug treatment center has to get padlocked, so be it.

Stanley Hill's union, District Council 37 of the American Federation of State, County and Municipal Employees, has 140,000 members. What they are looking at in New York is what municipal unions are looking at in cities, large and small, all around the country. They are looking at governments that are short on money.

In New York, the spectacle has been one of those unions piling their people behind barricades screaming insults at a mayor they did maybe more than anyone else to get elected. It is easy to understand the anger. But just to scream and make threats on Mayor Dinkins is not being entirely honest. The union leaders who damn the mayor through the budget crisis, also have a responsibility to wake their people up to the forgotten issue.

Deputy Mayor Bill Lynch took a few minutes to talk about what could be in this summer of 1991. "If we were funded at the same rate as we were in 1980 from the federal government, we would have $2 billion more to work with. The $2 billion is about the size of the budget gap."

For the Republicans of the conservative right, these have got to be times better than even they could have imagined. For nobody seems to remember what they did and how that has brought urban centers to a crisis worse than is even discussed. President Bush knows it well. When he heard Ronald Reagan (then a presidential candidate) discuss the plan, Bush called it "voodoo economics." But Reagan made it to the White House, and the plan went forward. Reagan gave the rich a huge tax cut, and told the cities of America to go fend for themselves, which of course they could not do. Those chickens have come home to roost.

Nobody is at the door of President Bush raising hell; instead the crowds are at doors of a lot of mayors, and they had no part in making the dirty deal.

In the meantime, the Republicans celebrate. While union leaders are damning mayors they helped elect, right wing Republicans gloat, and dance at the prospect of another conservative on the U.S. Supreme Court. They also are taken up in the delight of sanctioning the kicking of little people in the rump.

The union leaders who damn the mayors ought to be in the streets explaining to people how the going, for them, is going to get worse before it gets better. In cities, infrastructures are falling apart. Problems of AIDS, homelessness, crime and drugs are all mounting and federal policies now say to cities, "it's your problem." The leaders in urban American have to wake up; instead of fighting each other, they need to get their eyes back on the prize. Even doing that may just be too late.

1993

IN THE MORNING YESTERDAY, when he was bid a last goodbye, the picture of Jim Bell that came to mind was from a wintry day of last December. It was not much after 7 a.m. and he was at the UN Plaza Hotel, in the suite of Nelson Mandela.

That morning Mandela was in the midst of what was to be a hectic trip across the United States. His schedule was filled with days that were to start early and run late into the night.

As long as he was in New York, one of the people Mandela had to lean on was Jim Bell. Early that morning the two of them stood before the picture window that framed the room. As Mandela would ask about various buildings on the piece of the Manhattan skyline that was his view, Jim Bell would explain.

As the two of them stood there, it became another of those times that Bell showed himself to be a classic model of the kind of greatness Dr. Martin Luther King Jr. championed.

"Everybody can be great," King said, "because anybody can serve." And that was Jim Bell. He was great, because he was always there, always serving.

He was, by title, a vice president of District 65 of the United Auto Workers, AFL-CIO. He was also president of the New York City chapter of the Coalition of Black Trade Unionists. He used those positions to work toward accomplishing a lot of what he believed in as a trade unionist.

He was at the center of creating and building educational programs. He was in the forefront of organizing political coalitions. He was an activist in politics, both from the ground floor of voter registration, to being in the leadership ranks of the New York piece in the two Jesse Jackson runs for President.

Jim Bell was also a staunch fighter in the movement against South African apartheid. In 1986, there was a huge rally against apartheid held in Central Park. At the time, it was perhaps the single largest mobilization in New York against the evil and oppressive system in South Africa. Maybe nobody worked harder, or did more to make the rally work, than Jim Bell.

Jim Bell was unique. At one level, he held important titles and mixed with many of the most powerful leaders in the city.

At another level, he was highly respected for his willingness to do the work so many shun -- he was always there and ready to serve. He was there, with his sleeves rolled up, for the kind of work that does not draw a lot of credit, or get attention in the media. It was like the morning at the UN Plaza with Mandela. By 7 a.m. he had been up for hours. He made his way to the hotel, making certain that he was there and ready to serve in whatever role he was needed to aide Mandela.

So much of the time, sports stars and entertainers get looked on as being the real role models and heroes.

A lot of those who are Jim Bell types get overlooked. Because it is that way, it gets said that there are no role models for the young. Jim Bell was one. Yesterday, when a big crowd gathered at Riverside Church for his funeral, Mayor Dinkins was among those to accord him his due. Dinkins knew what Jim Bell was all about.

Bell worked in the mayor's campaign. More than that, the two worked side by side in a lot of other projects, from fighting apartheid to voter registration. Dinkins called Bell "a warrior in the struggle." In his life, Jim Bell did not get a lot of time. He had but 48 years and then, he fell victim to lung cancer. "He was like a brother," Deputy Mayor Bill Lynch said. "He knew how to bring people together," he said. "He had that kind of respect."

At his funeral, Jesse Jackson delivered the eulogy. Jackson declared that Jim Bell's life was a performance deserving of an Oscar and an Emmy."

Chapter Four

DO NO HARM

Editor's Note

The total onslaught on the health of urban dwellers, especially African Americans, has left them with life expectancies that, unlike the rest of the nation, are in decline. The Infants have a lower life expectancy than those in Bangladesh.

The health statistics, along with the relative absence of health facilities and insurance in African American communities, has had a devastating impact on the health in urban areas.

Whether death comes from guns, drugs, or AIDS and other terminal disease, like cancer, Earl Caldwell's writings reveal that poverty, American citizenship, and dark skin form a lethal combination..

1987

THE STORY HE TELLS ABOUT HIS LIFE goes back to the 1840s. He says that was when his great-great-grandfather bought his freedom from slavery. "And that's where my name comes from," he explains. "My great-great-grandfather took the words 'free man' and made that his name."

His son, Robert Freeman, became the first Black dentist in America, finishing Harvard Dental School in 1869.

"My grandfather, Henry Freeman, was a practicing physician in Washington, D.C., where I grew up. My father, who was a lawyer there, died prematurely. I finished Howard Medical School in 1958 and then I went to Freedmen's Hospital. That was the hospital established in Washington for former slaves."

In the world of medicine, Dr. Freeman has made his mark with studies that make the link between disease and poverty. More than anything else, he has focused on cancer and that's because the disease strikes at poor people more than any other Americans.

Dr. Freeman was a student of the late Dr. Jack E. White. More than two decades ago, Dr. White, then a cancer specialist at Howard University, found that cancer struck at Blacks more than any other Americans. Dr. White found that especially in urban areas Black cancer rates were especially high. He kept digging into the why of his findings.

At Howard, Dr. White had a hand in training a huge number of Black physicians. Among them was Dr. Harold P. Freeman. As it turned out, Dr. Freeman was to take up the work started by his mentor. For 24 years, he has studied cancer and Black Americans. For the last 10 years he has been so consumed with that work that he has not seen much of anything else. Finally, he has some answers. What he has found prompts him to look at those places once known as ghettos, and know that was not the right name.

"Third World Zones," is what Dr. Freeman says ghettos should be called, citing a wide range of health statistics in inner-city African American neighborhoods.

Dr. Freeman found that cancer rates, for example, among Blacks were higher than for any other group. Dr. Freeman found the link between Blacks and cancer was not a story of race but, rather, a story of poverty.

Among Blacks, cancer strikes between 6 and 10 percent more often than it does among Whites. With certain cancers, the rate is even higher. In urban areas, prostate and lung cancer run 60 to 70 percent higher among Blacks and cervical cancer is twice as high. But those figures have a flip side, and that's the link to poverty. A third of Blacks live below the poverty line; for White America, only 12 percent are in that category. Dr. Freeman took three areas in America to conduct his study. The powerful conclusion was that Blacks would have a lower cancer rate than Whites if the situations were reversed -- that if Whites (instead of Blacks) had less income and less education and lived in the substandard conditions of poverty.

Among Blacks, the jobless rate has not been above depression levels for most of the last 20 years. Which means there is a large population with no incomes and no medical insurance. Which prompts Dr. Freeman to concluded that economic status is crucial in determining who does and does not get medical care.

For a long time, the gap in life expectancy between Whites and Black had been closing. In 1910, it was 50.3 years for Whites; 35.6 for non-Whites. By 1940, that had closed to 64.2 for Whites and 53.1 for non-Whites. That reflected the changing America, mostly the enactment of social programs that impacted on life for those at the bottom. The gap continued to close until this year, when, according to national health statistics, Black life expectancy, for the first time this century, began to fall. Black men recorded the steepest decline -- from 65.2 years to 64.9. For Black women, the decline was from 73.6 to 73.4. Life expectancy for White women remained stable -- at 78.9 years; while it actually increased for White men -- from 72.2 years to 73.3.

The homicides that often come from drug wars have begun to have a huge impact, especially among Blacks. The statistics show the rate of homicides to be six times greater among Blacks than Whites, and is the leading cause of death of young Black men.

"If poverty is the main problem, then you have to aim your guns correctly, rather than aiming at race," Dr. Freeman said. In other words, to fight cancer, Dr. Freeman says "you have to correct root causes."

For the last 20 years, Dr. Harold Freeman has been at Harlem Hospital. He's director of surgery there, and an associate professor of clinical surgery at Columbia University.

Dr. Freeman's search for the causes of the higher Black cancer rates, inevitably, led to cigarettes.

"What we know," Dr. Freeman says, "is that 1,000 Americans die prematurely every day because they smoke -- 365,000 deaths a year, an outrageous number. This would be six times the number of (American) deaths that occurred in the Vietnamese war. So with cigarette smoking, six Vietnams are repeated every year."

Early in his career, Dr. Freeman became a cancer specialist. When he left Washington he came to New York to study at the Sloan-Kettering Institute. In 1967, he left there to come to Harlem.

"I wanted to work with my people," he said. So he came to Harlem, and what he found was unreal.

"I was struck by what I saw, the very advanced cancers. In four years in midtown, I had not seen this. I became very interested in what was causing this difference. And the mortality rates were much higher in Harlem. I looked at 165 consecutive cases in the 1970s. I found that half were incurable when they walked through the door. In five years only 35 percent were alive."

He pointed out that the overall incidence of cancer went up 27 percent among Blacks while the increase for Whites was only 12 percent. The figures reflected a part of what Dr. Freeman called "the tragedy at the bottom" in America.

What is the link between Blacks and cigarettes? "What we know," Freeman said, "is that Black males smoke more than any other group in the country. About 38 percent of Black males smoke cigarettes, compared with 32 percent of White males. And 32 percent of Black females versus 28 percent of White females.

Why do Blacks smoke more? "I'm not sure I have the answer to that," Freeman says. "The tobacco industry does a good job of selling to Blacks and minorities," Freeman says. He also says that Black leaders, especially elected officials, have been reluctant to take on the issue of cigarette smoking.

Dr. Freeman cites a study that shows that if you take middle-class and affluent Blacks and separate them from poor Blacks, then Blacks smoke at about the same rate as Whites.

"The single most important reason we have a high cancer rate is not racial or genetic. If it is not that, then we have to look at what people are doing and not doing. And what we are doing is smoking cigarettes. I believe it's as simple as that."

Next November, Dr. Freeman will head the American Cancer Society. He is going to take on the issue of smoking in the Black community. But Dr. Freeman also wants to do something about the truth he's found; that just being poor can cause you to have a higher death rate from cancer.

1985

IT WAS ONE OF THOSE BRAGGING kind of photographs that said: "Hey, look at what I'm doing!" It had Attorney General Edwin Meese in an old airplane hangar. Alongside Meese stood a drug agent. The two of them were scrutinizing a huge pile of marijuana plants. They were carrying out one of the biggest crackdowns ever on marijuana growers, a 50-state sweep that involved more than 2,200 federal, state and local agents. Meese said the idea was to send a strong message. The picture from a raid in Arkansas was part of all that. But there was another side.

Yesterday, a young doctor sat in a small office outside the psychiatric emergency room at Harlem Hospital. He talked about phencyclidine (PCP), the drug that is epidemic on urban streets. Like most drugs, PCP, has many names. It's called "crystal," "peace" and "angel dust." It's also known as "hog," "rocket fuel" and "super weed." It can be smoked, snorted, taken orally or mainlined. And as Dr. Douglas Cooper said yesterday, it's a drug that "literally destroys the brain."

In just a month, he said, about 350 patients come through the psychiatric emergency room. "A third are PCP cases. And it's going to get worse. We're breeding a whole generation of urban savages out there."

It's not language he uses loosely. He said PCP is a drug of the young, and it tends to make users violent. "They hear voices telling them to kill -- to kill other people or to kill themselves."

At the hospital yesterday, there were four pages from the manual "Management of Drug Abuse Emergencies" being passed around. The four pages had to do with PCP, and included was a warning to medical personnel. The warning said that because PCP abusers often have acute paranoid reactions and enormous strength and feel no pain, "they must be approached with great caution. With one dose a person can become violent, destructive and confused. Many persons taking PCP have been known to go berserk and kill their friends and loved ones. The incredible strength of the PCP-intoxicated person requires that enough personnel (at least five people) be available to apply restraints."

Dr. Cooper said a dose of PCP can last up to four days. But that's not the end of it. He said flashbacks that trigger hallucinations are common.

What is the attraction? "People are always looking for something to escape reality," Dr. Cooper said. "And some people like the feeling of losing control completely. It becomes their escape. It's their thing. They just do whatever they want and they know that all that will happen is that the police will bring them here. They are doing crimes they wouldn't do, if it wasn't for PCP. But it's cheap and it's freely available."

PCP was originally introduced as a surgical anesthetic. But because of the side effects, it was discontinued. It is partly a psychedelic drug, partly a sedative. The combination makes it popular on the illicit market. As the pages from the manual point out, anybody with a high school chemistry set and a few pennies can produce it in large quantities.

Marijuana does not have the kind of record that PCP is making. Yet, the PCP trade flourishes. Dr. Cooper says he has learned that of the 20,000 PCP arrests, there have been only some 200 convictions. And PCP is a drug that makes everybody pay. Its poison lodges in the brain. "And it's a big drain on us," said Dr. Cooper, meaning, the number of PCP cases has made it impossible for the hospital staff to practice the kind of psychiatric medicine that was the unit's purpose.

Why is this dangerous drug allowed to move so freely on the streets? Why is it being allowed to destroy so many lives? Questions to ponder as Ed Meese stands in a field of marijuana.

1990

FOUR YEARS AGO, the National Medical Association met in New York. Dr. David Musto of the Yale School of Medicine delivered a stunning lesson in Black History.

Dr. Musto went back 100 years to detail the forgotten but chilling experience that Black America had once before with the drug cocaine. His argument was that those who cannot remember the past are condemned to repeat it.

At the height of the cocaine craze in late 1800s, there were no drug laws. For cocaine, America was the land of opportunity. Americans virtually fell in love with the drug. Athletes used it to boost their skills. Hay fever sufferers used it to shrink their nasal and sinus tissues. Some employers were said to discover that cocaine got more work out of employees. But cocaine then was a new drug. It took time to learn the harmful effects. But that happened, and in the 1890s, cocaine's image began to tarnish.

"By World War I," Dr. Musto said, "the image of cocaine had changed from being the ideal tonic to the most hated and feared drug in America." He pointed out that the drug had been used by Whites and Blacks. But when the image changed, "it became associated by White legislators, drug experts and writers, with the Black community."

President Teddy Roosevelt determined cocaine to be "out of control," and launched an effort to restrict drugs at the international level. Cocaine was determined to be a "creator of criminals" and "unusual forms of violence." The federal government wanted to strike nationwide at the drug traffic. But, as Dr. Musto, who is a professor of psychiatry and the history of medicine told the story, the old south, strong advocates of states' rights, stood in the way -- at first. But once Blacks, most of whom then lived in the south, were linked to cocaine and violence, southern Whites agreed to abandon states rights objections, paving the way for the crack-down the federal government wanted.

Dr. Musto said he did not believe there was any greater use of cocaine by Blacks than Whites in the south. But for southern Whites, cocaine justified the oppression that was already underway, and it grew. Laws were passed. The fear and hatred of cocaine became so great that it disappeared. But Blacks were scapegoats. In 1914, the New York Times quoted a leading drug expert regarding the "Negro cocaine fiends" who terrorized the south. At the same time, the Whites used the crackdown to increase the oppression that was already there.

The lesson in Black history that Dr. Musto delivered more than three years ago comes back now, in February, which is Black History Month.

In the summer of 1986, Dr. Musto warned Blacks to take all actions they could to rid their communities of drugs. Otherwise, he said that Blacks again would be scapegoats once the country turned against cocaine. In just three years, what Dr. Musto warned of has begun to happen. Yesterday, he sat in his office in New Haven. He worries about what is happening. The country has begun to turn against cocaine. "More than at any time since 1979," he said. He sees the inner cities, particularly Blacks and Latins, being blamed for the problem.

"The tendency is to try and find a simple explanation," he said. "We tend to symbolize the drug problem, and link it to other fears we have in society." It was a way of pointing to Black crime.

Musto said the real danger now is that people are likely to see all inner-city residents as drug users, ignoring that those are the people who die defending parks, their homes and playgrounds. He said that the more the drug problem is seen as an inner-city problem, the less the middle class wants to spend money for anything except law enforcement and to build prisons. "They ignore the plight of people trying to reclaim their neighborhoods."

In the eyes of Dr. Musto, the worst has begun to happen. "At a time when we should be paying attention as to how the cities can be helped, we are to reject them because all of the people are seen as drug users and, thus, not deserving of help and resources." In Black History Month, 1990, Dr. Musto's lesson in history comes back in a scary way.

1990

SHE CALLS IT "THE STREET." She stood on the sidewalk in front of the building where she lives, and said, "The street has become a model for the whole city."

It is even more than that. The street has become a model for the whole country.

"It makes everybody look good," she said. The warm September sun was on her face. "What are we doing?" she asked. "Aren't we making the system work? Isn't this the American dream?"

Her face, chocolate brown, was smooth,and curls of her jet black hair fell across her forehead. "It shows what can be done," she said.

She is Rita Smith. She was the leader, along with Gertrude Russell, who is 70 years old now, and a handful of others. Almost all of them were women. They took a street in Harlem that was one of the worst drug blocks in New York, and turned the street into a model. The W. 143rd St., Block Association was their organization. Rita Smith was president. What the women did was make a miracle. No other word describes what they did.

Their Block is W. 143rd St., between Seventh and Lenox Aves. In the late '70s, most of the buildings were abandoned. Drug dealers were thick as bees on this block, Gertrude Russell says. "It was us or them," Rita Smith said. "Either we were going to run them out or they were going to run us out, and we didn't have anywhere else to go." Once, W. 143rd St was famous because it was the most densely populated block in all of New York. At the height of the fight the woman had against the drug crowd, there were not 50 families left.

After the women declared war they never took a step back. "We had no place to go," Rita Smith said. "This was home. I was born in the building where I live now, and I was determined that I wasn't going to let the drug crowd run me off." She never backed off, not even when her son was grabbed at the doorway to her building and shot in the mouth. It only made her more determined.

Rita Smith had twin girls, three sons and two other daughters. She was divorced. To make ends meet, she needed public assistance. It was not the kind of life she wanted. She went back to school. She decided to go into law. At Fordham, she earned a bachelor's degree. Law, she found, was not the field for her, so she changed to social work. She earned a master's degree and the expertise she got, she applied to her block.

"What can you do?" Gertrude Russell was asked when the fight was on. "I am going to make a pot of lye," she said, "and I'm going to put honey in it, and when I see them (the drug crowd) come into my building, I'm going to dump that lye right on 'em."

"Why the honey in the lye?" she was asked.

"It makes it stick on 'em," she said. Gertrude Russell was close to 70 when she got into the fight. She laughed at the threats and sat in her window with a bucket of lye that had honey in it. "If they come in this building," she said of the drug crowd. "'I'm going to jam 'em. I mean I'm going to jam 'em good."

The women were watchers, and when drugs moved, they were on the phone to the precinct. "They're not doing it right," they complained at first. "The cops come in one way with sirens screaming, and the drug crowd runs out the other way." They went to the precinct captain. Soon it was different. "Oh, Capt. Vincent got them today," Gertrude Russell began to say. "He brought the police cars in both ends of the block at the same time, and he jammed the drug crowd up in there. He really jammed them."

Gertrude Russell has a five room apartment on one side of 143rd St. and Rita Smith had seven kids and a ten room apartment on the other.

"What came first, the drugs or the abandoned buildings?" Rita Smith was asked.

"It was the bombed out buildings," she said. After the drugs were gone the two women went to work on the abandoned buildings. "We didn't save this block for nothing," Rita Smith said.

The block association came up with a proposal for the federal Housing and Urban Development Department to renovate the abandoned buildings. The drug-fighting proposal was a good one. Eleven million dollars of federal money went to the group from W. 143rd St. On the afternoon of the celebration, the buildings the drug crowd once used had construction equipment around them. W. 143rd St. was on the way back.

Rita Smith has opened an all-purpose center she calls a survival clinic. In the afternoon, she sat in her office. On the wall, there were plaques, certificates of achievement, and a host of other awards. "Everybody is proud of what we've done. We wanted to make a more humane situation," she said. The result was the Harriet Tubman Family Living Center.

At one end of the block, the city saw a cluster of houses it wanted to use for the homeless. Rita Smith didn't like the way it was being done. "They (the homeless) shouldn't be coming in here as victims," she said. "not in a block that's getting itself together. Now these people (homeless) will be our guests on the block," she said. And more important, she said services would be coordinated and instead of a hostile situation, the people who come in would be a part of the block.

In the block, construction is under way on three projects. Each has a special name. There is Malcolm X Project One, Malcolm X Project Two, and the Harriet Tubman Family Living Center.

The fight against drugs was only a part of what the women of the W. 143rd St. Block Association had in mind. In the last week of August they had in the block a celebration they called Human Possibilities Day.

Human Possibilities Day was a celebration of the turnaround, and the families who left were invited back. "Everybody is proud of what we've done," she said. "The street has become a model for the whole city."

"The mayor's office, the borough president, the police, HPD -- it was all of them, along with the people of the community, that's what made it happen. But what happened here shows it can work. This is a story that comes out right."

"A miracle?" she was asked.

"You could call it that, but we worked."

1991

IN THE KILLING OF MARIA HERNANDEZ of Brooklyn, it did not take the police long to get a handle on what had happened. She was a woman determined to stand up to drug dealers in her neighborhood of Bushwick. For that, she paid with her life.

Mrs. Hernandez and her husband, Carlos, were two more of the ordinary citizens who have drawn the line. "Not here," they said to drug dealers. "Not in our building, not on our block." But they did more than talk. They learned that to ask drug dealers to back off means nothing. So the Hernandezes decided to fight. They did not go outside the law. They went to the police and had the courage to provide names and information about trafficking in their area. Maybe they were afraid but they did not back off.

The police say that early on Tuesday, in the ground-floor apartment where the Hernandez family lived, five shots were fired through a bedroom window. Six hours later, Maria Hernandez died at Wyckoff Heights Hospital.

When drug dealers settle into neighborhoods where business is good, nothing seems to scare them away. They take over. They are armed and use the guns to threaten and intimidate. They also kill. Maria Hernandez is not the first to die. Hers is another name on a growing list. We saw all this coming. Bit by bit the last 20 years the fences that stood against dealing of illegal drugs have been torn down. By 1979, drug dealing was no longer something kept underground. Carl McCall was then a young state legislator. He actually took reporters around in his Harlem district and said, "Here it is, out in the open. We have open-air drug markets." Talk of a war on drugs started then.

In neighborhoods, people began to fight. In Harlem, a man named Wilson operated a fine restaurant. A lot of people flocked to Wilson's to eat soul food. The restaurant was a neighborhood center. It was always busy, always crowded. It was a perfect place for drug dealers to set up shop. They did exactly that. "Not here," the restaurant owner said. "Not around my place." He was shot dead. It was more tearing down of fences that stood against lawlessness.

The promise was it would not happen this way. The government vowed to draw a line. A "war on drugs" was promised. Now, there is a war. But instead of the government mobilizing, it is the other way around. The drug dealers are the ones who have declared war. Stand against them and you die, they say. Unlike government, they are not just mouthing words. How many ordinary citizens who have stood up have been killed for their courage? The list of victims keeps getting longer.

In Brooklyn, police believe the shots fired into the Hernandez home were intended to intimidate. Carlos Hernandez was to testify before a grand jury. He lost his wife, but, nonetheless, had the courage to go ahead and testify. "I am going to keep fighting," he pledged.

At times, it takes ordinary citizens to stand up to make government do its job. It is happening that way in the drug wars. But there are casualties. Now add the name of Maria Hernandez. She was 34.

1991

HIS NAME WAS CEFERINO VIERA. He is another of those New Yorkers to wind up in a morgue because he, too, dared to say to drug dealers, "not here, not on our block."

His life was taken in the most callous kind of way. He was run down by a van and killed almost in front of his home as his son and wife watched in horror.

He is not the first to have his life taken that way. So he becomes another victim. He was a man strong enough to do what Mayor Dinkins has asked: to stand and fight against the pushers. In his neighborhood, the Sunset Park section of Brooklyn, those who knew say that is what Ceferino Viera did. They say that when the drugs came, he stood and fought. But like a lot of the others who are the victims, he found himself virtually standing alone. So his life is gone.

He understood what he was fighting against. He was a veteran who had served in World War II and the Korean War. Those veterans came home to good benefits. A way was provided for them to buy a home, and to get started in raising a family. That's what Viera did for 28 years. He found a house, and he and his wife raised eight children. He made himself an asset in his neighborhood. And when he saw the wrong that was coming, he refused to run. Some tried to encourage him to get out, to run to another safer place. But he understood that to run was not a solution. He chose to stand and fight in the neighborhood where he had been a builder. He did not go outside the law. He did not try to shoot anybody, or attack anyone, but he had the courage to challenge those who came onto his block to sell drugs.

The pushing of drugs has become an enormous business. And those who are in are bold. When they encounter opposition, they try to smash it. They have no regard for the law. They do what they want, and use fear to scare off those who stand against them. When that does not work, they kill.

In Harlem, Rita Smith talked of the death of Ceferino Viera. In her block of W. 143rd St., she, too, stood against drug dealers. She led a block association that was mostly women. It took them a long time, but eventually, they won in clearing the pushers from their doorsteps.

"But we were never alone," Rita Smith said. "We had a lot of men -- nationalists and Muslims. They knew what we were trying to do. They put the word out to the drug dealers. They told them, 'If you harm any of these women, we are coming after you.' That was the difference; we were not alone."

Still, a price was paid. Rita Smith had a son shot down on her doorstep. But the women in the block did not stop. They had lookouts and kept badgering the police to stay in the block and as they identified pushers, they turned them in to the police. "But we always had people covering our backs," Rita Smith said. "To fight against the drug crowd, you have to coordinate what you're doing with all the various groups. You have to network. You cannot be out there alone. If you are, you can't survive. They will kill you."

The fight is for neighborhoods. Ceferino Viera, a veteran of two foreign wars, enlisted in this one at home, for home. He died on the battlefield. A part of it was that he did not have the whole neighborhood moving with him. When officials encourage citizens to fight against drugs, they also have an obligation to give them support. Ceferino Viera did not have the back-up he was entitled to have for the stand he knew he had to take.

In the case an arrest has been made. That is not enough. The drug trafficking Viera challenged goes on. When a life is given, it has to be made to stand for something. It should not end only with those who knew the victim saying, "It's too bad; he was a good person." Anytime a life is given, it has to mean something. Ceferino Viera is dead; nothing is going to bring him back. For what he did, something is owed. That account can be squared only when others take up the fight which he had the courage to start. Ceferino Viera was 68.

1992

IN THE NEIGHBORHOOD, the father was not subjected to criticism. "This was his daughter," one resident said. "If it was his son, it might be different; but this was a young girl, and she was staying out for three days straight. He had no choice. He had to do something."

In the eyes of the system, what Eliezer Marrero did to save his daughter was seen as being so extreme that he landed in jail. The judgement in the Bronx neighborhood where it happened said the system was wrong. To save his daughter from the peddlers of the crack, when he believed he had no other choice, Marrero chained the young girl to a radiator to keep her away from the drug.

The system ruled that Marrero was wrong. The action he felt compelled to take, though, says what parents in the city are up against once their kids get hooked on crack. It means they lose their kids. No matter how strong the family ties have been; no matter how strong the parents, once a kid gets hooked on crack, the drug rules. It becomes the master. To save his 15-year-old daughter, to deal with a desperate situation, Marrero knew he had to take desperate action.

Marrero and his wife wound up in jail. They were seen by the system as being guilty of child abuse. They did not run away from the decision they made. They told authorities they had chained their daughter, Linda, to the living room radiator at night for two months because, "she started hanging out with bad people," which was their way of identifying the drug crowd.

The issue has wound up in criminal court in Bronx County. A spokesman for District Attorney Robert Johnson says that a part of any solution should involve counseling for all parties. But that does not get to the hard part -- the hold crack gets on a teenager once the youth is hooked.

There are many stories, all of them real, of how teenage girls (and boys) are turned to prostitution to feed their drug habit. Once they are on crack, they will do anything.

So were the Marreros wrong? "You have to understand, her parents are Latin and they believe in having control," a resident of the area said. "Maybe it was wrong to chain her up, but he didn't know what else he could do."

A lot of stories get told of the way crack drives young people to commit crimes, to leave school, and wind up on the streets and in crack dens. There is another side. That has to do with the damage kids hooked on drugs do to themselves. Young girls are the most vulnerable. The history on the streets is that once hooked, there is nothing they will not do.

In the poor neighborhoods of the city, despite all the efforts of law enforcement, crack is still an easy drug for kids to get into their hands.

"If they have $10, they can get high," residents say. The proof is in the numbers of damaged lives.

Instead of putting them in jail, the system ought to be able to see their side of the hell that drugs bring into the lives.

1992

SO LITTLE OF THE WAR on drugs has been aimed at the top, where the big money gets raked in. Instead of a war on drugs, some have begun to see what is taking place as being not much more than a war on poor Blacks and others at the bottom.

Two days ago, Manhattan District Attorney Robert Morgenthau went after top executives of the huge Bank of Credit and Commerce International. The action Morgenthau took was not entirely unheard of. But seldom has there been such a bold strike at those in high places, who have their hands in the big pot of drug money. Morgenthau was showing the road that has to be traveled. In fighting drugs, no real victory was possible, he said, "unless we can interfere with the money supply."

The BCCI link to drug lords had to do with the lucrative, but illegal, business of money laundering. The trafficking in drugs produces what is known as "dirty money." Just to be caught with too much of that kind of money can lead to a prison sentence. That is what creates the demand for money laundering, the service Morgenthau said BCCI was providing. He said the bank was so deeply involved that it established more than 30 branches in Columbia alone. In his eyes, BCCI did not expand that massively in Columbia to keep track of Juan Valdez's coffee accounts. The bank, according to prosecutors, went to the South American country with the specific intention of giving the bank access to drug money.

So much of the time, the way the trafficking of drugs is portrayed, it gets looked on as being an enterprise that mostly involves heavily armed young Blacks. The kind of legislation the Bush administration is asking for in its proposed Violent Crime Control Act adds to that false impression. The administration virtually declares war on kids involved in selling crack. It wants those juveniles caught with five grams of crack tried as adults, and if convicted, given mandatory five year sentences in adult prisons.

As Morgenthau points out, neither the state nor the federal government has any mandatory sentencing for crimes bankers commit, such as money laundering. Yet, Morgenthau says, "The (drug) money is so big, it almost has to go through the banking system. It is so much, you cannot hide it under a mattress or in cookie jars."

BCCI had no slick scheme for laundering money. It just simply did not report huge cash deposits as required by U.S. regulations. BCCI had a way for getting around that. "It was very clever," a spokesman for the DA said. "BCCI was established in Luxembourg where they have tough secrecy laws, and you cannot look into what banks there do."

The BCCI operation, though, was far flung. It had a world headquarters in London, and although it could not legally own American banks, it did have "some big pieces" of banking operations in the U.S. So Morgenthau says federal laws have to be strengthened. "When we tried to get records, we couldn't; bank secrecy. I'm not an isolationist, but I don't think that kind of bank should be allowed in here. What kept this bank (BCCI) alive was the drug money, and the bribes they were paying bank officers to get central bank deposits."

In moving against BCCI, Morgenthau says he hopes he sent a message that says, "When you launder drug money, if we have to chase you around the world, we'll catch up with you." His explanation of "why" was in drug arrest statistics.

"Last year in Manhattan, between Sterling Johnson (the special prosecutor) and myself, we prosecuted 11,500 (felony drug) cases, and the DA's office had another 1,500 misdemeanor cases. Unless we can cut off the dollars, the economic chain, we'll be doing this until the end of time. We have to cut off the people who are making the big bucks. We just can't be going after the small guys. If you do that, you'll lose your credibility. We have to get those who are making and transmitting the big dollars."

1991

FINALLY, WE HAVE SEEN "THE TAPE." Even though the images were gray and grainy, the pictures were still clear enough for all to see Marion Barry, the mayor of Washington, D.C., standing before a lamp in a hotel room taking two heavy drags from a pipe of crack cocaine.

At first impression, it would appear that for Mayor Barry, it's all over. The videotape delivered as promised -- clear evidence that he was indeed a user of crack. Barry had sworn under oath that he never used the drug. In the courtroom though where he is standing trial on charges of perjury and possessing cocaine, the tape appeared to make a liar of the mayor.

So for Marion Barry, is it all over? The tape runs for 83 minutes. What it offers amounts to a devastating blow to a mayor who once was considered one of the bright lights among Black elected officials.

No matter what the outcome of the trial, as a political leader Barry is finished. For him, the worst has happened. One thing an elected official can't overcome is using crack, especially a mayor of a city that has the kind of drug problem that exists in the nation's capital. The perjury counts against Barry are felony charges and if convicted, a jail term seems almost certain. But yet, as stunning as the pictures on the tape were, alone they do not seal Barry's fate. Far from it.

The tape raises a lot of questions. How far should federal officials go in trying to expose elected officials. And in the Barry case, did officials cross the line and go too far? Was Barry caught redhanded doing what he does, or was his a case pure and simple of entrapment?

When they finally got him, it was the result of perhaps the most questionable "sting" operation ever mounted by the federal government. In the sting, to rope in the mayor, the feds used a woman the mayor had been involved with for some 10 years. In sting operations, the Justice Department has guidelines that are supposed to be adhered to. In the Barry case, lines were crossed. A number of former prosecutors have acknowledged that.

In the Barry case, the "sting" used a woman to lure him to a downtown hotel in the District. The woman was told by the FBI not to have any sexual contact with him. The plan was to get him to use drugs. It succeeded. But sources say that it took so much doing, that it may have given Barry a way out of his legal problems.

The mayor has to represent him one of Washington's best criminal lawyers, R. Kenneth Mundy. In D.C., Mundy has been credited with inventing the so-called "Kunta Kinte defense," which seems perfect for Mayor Barry. Kunta Kinte was a character from "Roots," which was Alex Haley's story of his ancestors' sojourn from Africa to American slavery. Kunta Kinte was the young slave whipped by his White slave master for refusing to renounce his African past and accept his slave name. So the Kunta Kinte defense centers around race.

Not too long ago, Washington used to be called "Chocolate City" because the Black population was so large. It was close to 80 percent; it's fallen some, but the city is still mostly Black. This means the jury that will sit in the Barry case, is apt to be mostly Black. The Kunta Kinte defense invites jurors to nullify the law. It tells them that they are the law, and they can do what they want to do.

Mundy describes the charges against Barry as being "penny ante" and says, "I wish all my cases were that weak." The mayor is charged with five misdemeanor counts of cocaine possession and three felony counts of perjury. All of the charges stem from the government's hot pursuit and from the questionable sting.

"I've seen Mundy walk a lot of Blacks out of the courtroom because he was using the Kunta Kinte defense," says former Washington Star reporter Kenneth Walker who covered criminal court in the District. Barry has given Mundy exactly the kind of ammunition he needs. He called his indictment "a political lynching." Which is a way of his saying that it is these (White) prosecutors out to get me (Black mayor), and they don't care how they do it.

Which brings up the other thing Barry has on his side. Many Blacks in Washington fear what is sometimes called "the plan." Many believe that Whites (who have begun to move back into the city) want control of the government. So not many Blacks have urged Barry to resign. That's because David Clarke (chairman of the city council) would become mayor, and Clarke is White

Barry was lured to a room at the Vista Hotel in downtown Washington in the middle of last January. He was walking into a trap. The woman who lured him to the room, Hazel Diane "Rasheeda" Moore, was a former girlfriend of Barry, and now the state's prime witness against him. In testimony before the tape was shown, she told of having used cocaine with the mayor more than 100 times. All that, though, was just talk. The tape was something to grab ahold of. When it was shown in the courtroom last Thursday, the whole nation saw a part of what the jurors saw. Those gray, grainy pictures showed the mayor in shirtsleeves with the crack pipe to his mouth, taking two long drags of the drug. But there was more.

Before he drew on the pipe, the mayor said he didn't know how to use it. Why? Since he did not know that he was being secretly spied on by a videotape, why would the mayor say to a person he had used drugs with 100 times that he didn't know what he was doing? It gives Barry's defense something to work with. But there is more. He didn't telephone his old girlfriend and say, "Hey, let's get together and do some crack." He was, as he said later in the tape, the victim of a sting. He was, in his own words, "set up." But did the government go too far? Once Barry had possession of the drug, he had set himself up for arrest. But the FBI officials went further. They allowed him to use the drug, knowing even then that crack can be deadly. The question comes back: Why would authorities deliberately allow the mayor to endanger himself?

Some scenes on the tape are frightening. Once the mayor has used the drug, from next door, agents storm the room and converge on Barry. It is as though they are on a bust in a strange and dangerous place, not in a hotel where they had a hand in luring the D.C. mayor.

Obviously, Mayor Barry is sick. It appears that he is an addict. Federal authorities spent millions (some estimates range as high as $40 million) to take him down. It has been offered by some that Barry is an example of double standards from the Justice Department. Even that he was not allowed to plead to a misdemeanor count of possession -- which is the routine for first offenders -- has been questioned. And it's not over.

The showing of "the tape" was the highlight of a stunning day in the courtroom. But outside, there was another piece of drama. Nation of Islam leader Louis Farrakhan showed up for the trial accompanied by more than a dozen of his followers. Farrakhan was barred. The judge ruled that his presence "would be potentially disruptive" and "likely intimidating" and he was declared persona non grata for the rest of the trial.

Barry's is a story that can bring tears to your eyes. Go back a quarter of a century, back to the other America where on almost every front Blacks were locked out. A lot has been written of what King did, what the NAACP and Roy Wilkins did, and what CORE and James Farmer were able to do. Together, the contributions of those men and their organizations in the civil rights movement was immeasurable. They did a lot, but they didn't do it all.

The other side of the movement was what the young people did. They were kids, so many of them barely teenagers. Many left school and home -- forgot about everything else, to work in the movement. In so many places, they were the front line. They were the first to sit at the segregated lunch counters; filled the Freedom buses; fearlessly filled in the march lines of the most dangerous protest demonstrations. A lot of the time, they didn't even get credit for being there. Often they saw the credit go to others, who came later. They knew the contribution they were making. They leaned on each other. When the movement as we know it ended in the mid 60s, a lot of those who were young together in the movement continued to hang together. Marion Barry came through with that class.

Barry, like many others, gravitated to the nation's capital. He was a guy who came out of Mississippi, the son of a sharecropper. He was never much of a speaker, but that was a part of the glory in the movement. Every leader didn't have to be fancy with the language. Barry had a presence, and the movement people around him more than anything else, were organizers. It got him propelled from activist to insider. In D.C., he got elected to the school board, then the city council. In 1978, he scored one of those political upsets that made him a person to watch. He beat Walter Washington, the incumbent, in a mayoral primary. Twice he got reelected, but somewhere in that second term, something began to go wrong. Barry changed. The rumors that began to circulate said he was into drugs. He was fierce in his denials. But once those kind of rumors start, they are not easily put to rest. The media scrutinized his every move. The U.S. Attorney in the District had him under investigation. Then came the night of Jan. 18 that was to change his life. In the FBI sting, he was caught on video tape smoking crack cocaine. After his arrest, he went public, saying he was not a cocaine addict, but rather, addicted to alcohol and "mood altering chemicals."

Barry earlier had testified under oath that he had never used cocaine. After his arrest, he was slapped with felony perjury charges. Jury selection for his trial has begun and two days ago, in the midst of that, he announced that he would not seek reelection to a fourth term.

"I'm proud to say to you tonight with the grace of God, and a good treatment program, today is my 145th day clean of any chemicals," he said. "For some, that's a short time. For those of us in the recovering community, it's a long time. I continue to try to keep this achievement -- one day at a time."

Once, a lot of hopes were in Barry's hands. He came up from the bottom, chosen to lead because of what he did. That he won three terms says that as mayor, he contributed. That he wound up in the place where he was arrested last January, says that he is sick and in need of care. "I hope that you clearly understand the decision which I have announced is my personal decision. No one forced me into it," he said shortly thereafter.

Barry chose his closing words from the Bible. "For everything there is a season and time to purpose under the heavens: a time to get and a time to lose, a time to keep and a time to cast away. Tonight, it's time to cast away."

1992

FROM TIME TO TIME, in the old debate of "what to do about the drug problem," there comes the suggestion that perhaps the best way out is to knuckle under and legalize everything.

Always, before the idea gets any semblance of a fair hearing, it gets snowed under by the arguments of the nay sayers.

They say that to legalize drugs would only wind up creating more addicts. They say that to legalize drugs would be no more than making the government the pusher. They have their bottom line argument which centers on morality. Pure and simple, they say that to legalize drugs would be immoral.

But there is another side in this season of hope that, too, ought to be seen. A new administration is about to take charge of the government. More than anything else, what the Clinton administration promises is change. President-elect Clinton made that one word -- change -- a hallmark in his campaign. He pleaded with voters not to be afraid of change.

It will not take long for Clinton to learn what mayors, especially those in big cities, already know. The drug problem is so far out of control and has reached such proportions that it is no longer even manageable. That means that the American way of dealing with the drug problem just does not work. That ought to mean that it is time to bite the bullet and go another way.

Last Sunday, on the CBS broadcast "60 Minutes," Ed Bradley had a story which he brought back from Britain. It was about dealing with the drug problem -- and decidedly not the America way. As Bradley said at the top of the broadcast, they (the English) tried our (American) hard line methods in the 70s and 80s. All they got was more drugs, crime and addicts. So they went back to a system that allows doctors to prescribe whatever drugs an addict is hooked on. And the state pays.

To a lot of Americans, that is an approach that could never make sense. But before they holler, those nay sayers need to see the piece Bradley had on CBS. It shows just how far behind we in the U.S. are in our thinking on the "what do we do" side of the discussion about drugs. The British approach now being tried in Liverpool is not costly. As Bradley points out, a gram of pure heroin, which would be cut here 10 or 15 times, would cost some $2,000 on the street. It costs the government $10.

All of New York was outraged when a gun battle among teenagers took the life of a well respected and effective school principal in Brooklyn. Only one thing puts 9 mm guns into the hands of kids -- drugs. So much of the crazy violence goes back to the drugs. And the way we in the U.S. have chosen to fight makes no sense. It is a no win proposition. We cannot stop the flow of drugs into the country. It costs a ton of money to arm and bankroll the cops, and all the other agencies involved in what is known as the war on drugs. But the bottom line remains the same: the business of drugs flourishes. That will not change, and the reason is that too much money is involved.

So what do we do? It would seem that at the very least, we would begin to look around and try to see if there is another approach -- an approach that works. And that gets back to CBS, 60 Minutes and Ed Bradley's story.

In England, they do not just let addicts walk in and get drugs, and be on their way. They test them to make certain they use the drugs they say they use. That keeps addicts healthier -- again saving society money. Street drugs are cut with all kinds of dangerous additives -- the government makes sure the drugs are pure. As for encouraging addiction, it may be just the opposite.

In Britain, they make no pretense about trying to cure addicts. "Nobody can," said Dr. John Marks on the CBS broadcast. "Regardless of whether you stick them (addicts) in prison, put them in mental hospitals and give them electric shocks --- we've done all these things," he said.

He also said that it doesn't matter if you put them (addicts) in fancy rehab centers in the country or whatever. He said the fact is, only five percent -- one in 20 -- get off drugs this way. But what Dr. Marks has found is that after 10 years, addicts tend to "mature out of addiction." They just stop. The British system keeps them healthy and alive until then.

Americans like to believe that they know best, but in the dealing with the drug problem, they would be wise to do what Ed Bradley did --- look at an approach that makes some sense.

1987

THE WOMAN THREW UP HER HANDS. "Guns, guns, guns," she said. "You keep talking about guns. Sure people got guns. There's guns here in my building, but don't say that guns is the only problem we got."

"Who has guns in your building?"

"Who? I don't know who, but we got teenagers here, I mean boys, and yes, they have guns. You know they have guns. And they aren't the only ones here with guns. But, like I said, guns is just one problem."

"What is worse than the problems with guns?" she was asked.

"We got problems with empty buildings and problems with drugs and problems with unemployment and not having any money and the schools and our kids out there in the streets in the middle of all that, and I can't say what problem is worse. But what I'm saying is that we got more problems than just with guns."

The woman shut the door and went back inside her apartment in the project that sits in the Bronx.

Around the corner on Willis Ave., a kid who said his name was Face stood with two other teenagers in the afternoon sun and watched the traffic.

"How did you find me?" the kid whose name was Face said. He did not wait for an answer. "Oh, you saw my name," he said.

He was referring to a wall a few blocks away that was filled with graffiti. Right in the middle, in red letters with a blue line underneath, was the name Face. It was just one of many names scrawled on the wall, but yesterday in the sunny afternoon, when the kid looked at it, he smiled.

"Naw," he said. "I don't have no gun. I know some who do, but not me."

"You can buy one," one of the other kids said, but he left it there. "No," he said, "I don't know where."

When school was mentioned, the kid whose name was Face looked into the street and said, "School? School for what?"

Then he said, "Listen, me and my boys, we got to walk."

In the afternoon, all along Willis Ave. the corners were crowded. There were older men and some women. Mostly, there were teenage kids who were out of school and out of work. They were a part of what the Black woman in the project meant when she said, "We got more problems here than just with guns."

Still, guns today remain the most immediate and deadliest problem in many African American communities.

There is a small poster put out by an organization called Handgun Control Inc. The poster has a picture of a handgun, and the gun is done up in red, white and blue. In bold letters above the gun, it reads:

In 1980, handguns killed.
77 people in Japan.
8 in Great Britain.
24 in Switzerland.
18 in Sweden.
4 in Australia.
11,522 in the United States.

At the Bronx County Courthouse, the chief of the Juvenile Offense Bureau sat in an office and went over the figures. "In the last six months," he said, "we've had 26 juveniles involved in crimes where guns were used. One was a murder."

He picked through the papers, then brought out another set of figures. "Since September of 1978," he said, "we've had 25 juveniles indicted for 27 murders, and there is one other case still pending."

He went back to September of 1978 because that was when the State of New York put into law its get-tough-on-violent-juvenile-crime program.

"What do the figures say?" Eric Warner was asked.

"I guess they say that the law hasn't cut down on juvenile crime, on violent crime."

The district attorney's office is on the sixth floor of the Bronx courthouse. It is a large suite, and from the conference table that sits in front of the DA's desk, the view looks down to right inside Yankee Stadium.

Mario Merola, the Bronx DA, did not sit at the conference table yesterday. There was nothing in Yankee Stadium to watch, and he stayed at his desk. Yesterday he was also one of those who wrestled with the problems of crime and the young and guns.

But Merola was not one of those who mixed all of the problems together. He said juvenile crime was one thing, and the problems with guns was another. "The juveniles," he said, "are just taking advantage of the proliferation of guns."

But what worried the DA is that more than half the crime is being committed by kids under the age of 20. But he said he was certain that it was an area where something could be done.

"The older ones," he said of the criminals, "those who are 35 and 40, it may be too late to do anything with them. But with the young, there is where we can do something. We are talking about kids who are crying for leadership, who want us to know that they are here." And then the DA talked about the tremendous energy the young possess. He said they turn to crime and carry guns because it gives them a sense of identity and importance.

"Right now," the DA said, "they feel that they are not a part of us."

Merola said he would fire Family Court judges. "I'd hire (New York Knicks basketball star) Earl Monroe in their place," he said. "Don't laugh," he said. "I mean it. He would reach the kids and the programs that we have. They (the judges) never do that, they never reach the ones who need to be reached."

The example the DA used when he argued that the young want to be involved, that they want leadership, and that they need to be noticed, was the Guardian Angels. It was a perfect example.

It is like the woman in the project said: "We have a lot of problems. It is not just guns." And as the afternoon turned warm and the streets filled with kids out of school and out of work, there were more scary reminders of just how many problems there are in the city.

1990

AT FIRST, THE IMPULSE is to get pretty doggone angry. You read these stories that link the origin of the deadly disease AIDS to Africa, and right away you think: It's another plot, another effort to stick it to Africa and the Africans.

And you go off. You do what Black students at Columbia University did when the student newspaper, The Spectator, came up with a special issue on the disease. One piece concluded that the fact it comes from Africa is about the only thing known about AIDS.

The Black students went off. They said in a letter to the editor that they seldom get solidly behind any issue or cause. But in damming The Spectator and the articles linking AIDS to Africa, they were together. They called it suspect journalism and a subtle, although dangerous, form of racism.

To make the Africa-AIDS link, one article reported seeing Africans eating monkey meat and said that, as a form of birth control, Africans had turned to anal sexual practices. That got the students especially angry.

It's not just the student paper at Columbia. Yesterday, The New York Times published a story that started on Page 1 and continued on an entire page inside. The single purpose was to explore the question: Did AIDS come from Africa?

The article came up with tons of bits and scraps. A lot of them had evidence linking AIDS to Africa. But Lawrence K. Altman, who wrote the story, concluded: "...Finding the origin now is a bit like trying to do a jigsaw puzzle with only a few pieces in the box -- no knowledge of its dimensions, and no picture on the cover."

And if it did, how did the disease become epidemic in the western world, especially here in New York?

The awful truth, as we know, is that there are diseases that exist only in Africa. Some are horrible, killing diseases. There is something called Lassa Fever (always deadly) and something called Marbug Virus (also presumed to be carried by the African green monkey), and those are not all. There are also diseases such as malaria and cholera, not seen in many places, but a problem in Africa.

One of the things visitors to Africa don't like is all the vaccinations they need. But Africa is at the equator. The tropical climate is an incubator of viruses. The continent has the problem of most of the so-called Third World: a lack of preventive medical care.

Look again at the question: Is it possible AIDS had its origins in Africa? The evidence that suggests it may be true is not necessarily a racial plot. It could be an African disease that has been killing Africans for a thousand years. It may be that until now nobody cared because only Africans were dying.

Then another question: If AIDS did start in Africa, how did it move from remote villages a world away to become epidemic in the largest, most influential cities in the West?

Well, if the disease is transmitted sexually, as we're being told, the answer is easy. It means somebody had sex with somebody who had sex with somebody....and so on. It also means that people who say no to affirmative action in the daytime have another standard at night. That has to be true because the awful disease didn't just leap across color lines or from one nation to another.

After the anger, it's some of what you think of when you read of the AIDS-African connection they are trying so hard to make.

1990

WITH THE AIDS EPIDEMIC, the shocks keep coming. Now the federal government, in an almost routine kind of way, drops another bombshell.

A study prepared for the Government Accounting Office (GAO) says the bad news about the spread of the virus is a lot worse than had been expected.

Until now, official estimates predicted that by 1991, AIDS cases in the country would number between 195,000 and 320,000. Those were stunning figures. But now comes the study -- two years in the making -- prepared for the GAO.

It finds that previous estimates of the AIDS epidemic were nowhere close to being accurate. The new report estimates that by 1991, some 300,000 to 485,000 Americans will have been diagnosed as having AIDS.

So just like that, almost from out of the blue, another group of those considered experts tell us the AIDS epidemic has been underestimated to the point that as many as a third more people than believed may come down with the disease.

The full GAO study gets released today. All this is bound to raise a lot of questions and further arouse fears and suspicion.

Recently, a whole new round of attention has focused on AIDS. Partly, that's because of the just concluded meeting in Montreal, where 11,000 officials and experts from 87 countries gathered to share information and ideas on the epidemic. At the same time, though, more and more of the most startling kind of information has been made public.

Before the Montreal meeting convened came the disclosure that the test widely depended on to detect the AIDS virus had been found not to be anywhere near reliable. The conclusion was that maybe through as many as three years, there was no reliable way of testing for the virus. So the report that cast doubt on testing had a bombshell impact.

Just after that, in New York, it was disclosed that some testing had been done in an effort to determine the degree AIDS was striking among the homeless. A study was conducted at the municipal shelter on Wards Island. Again, the findings were shocking. Of 169 men tested, 105 were found to be infected.

In each of these instances, the information released has been stunning. When all the pieces are pulled together, it gets very clear that somebody is trying to tell us something.

Obviously, we are being told that the AIDS epidemic is more widely spread through the population than (1) anyone knew or (2) we were led to believe. What is not being discussed, though, is the agenda.

What do public health officials have in mind? What drastic actions are being considered to cope with the new realities?

The GAO is expected to recommend that national studies be carried out by the Centers for Disease Control to get a better handle on the AIDS crisis. Mostly, it wants a study of sexual habits in America. Not in 40 years, not since the heralded Kinsey Report, has there been such a study.

The GAO also has questions about the reporting of AIDS cases. New York was cited as one of the cities where a lot more people have died of AIDS than first reported. So from its perspective, government has begun to say, "We want more information, and we want it now."

But there are other sides. Cliff Goodman sits on the board of one of those organization that challenges a lot of the official information about AIDS.

His organization, HEAL (Health, Education, Aids Liaison), questions whether AIDS is 100 percent fatal as reported; or whether the HIV virus has been proven to cause AIDS, and also whether the AZT drug prolongs life.

Once when organizations raised questions about AIDS the way HEAL and others do now, not a lot of people listened. But that's changing. Government has been saying, "We know, we know." But more and more information keeps coming out that says, "They don't know" or, "they're not telling us." The GAO report which gets released today seems more of the unmistakable proof that with AIDS, we still are not getting the whole story.

1991

CLIFF KALI GOODMAN died last October. As the cause of death, the medical examiner listed the disease AIDS. That sent Michael Ellner into a rage.

"Nobody dies from AIDS," he said. "AIDS is just a word. You die from a specific infection."

Ellner insisted on an autopsy. "They told me that would take nine months," he said. So Ellner still does not know the cause of his friend's death. "He hadn't been sick. He was about to move into a new apartment, so he took a few days off. When he didn't show up, I got worried. I didn't want to meddle, but I knew something was wrong. So we checked, and they found him in his old apartment, in a pool of blood."

The death of Cliff Goodman, who was 33, gnaws at Ellner. In part it is because they were friends. But a lot more is involved. The two of them were out in the deep water in the business of what they call "telling the truth about HIV and AIDS." The two of them were leaders in the organization known as HEAL (Health, Education, AIDS Liaison). Its most important work involves spreading the word about alternative treatment for HIV and AIDS. Ellner is the organization's president; Goodman was a co-vice president.

It used to be that the two of them were almost everywhere. In a way, it did matter that Ellner is White and Goodman was Black. The mix gave them a lot of entree. But there was more; they were from different worlds, had different styles, but together, they were a powerful team.

Then, the threats began. "There would be phone calls," Ellner said. "Things like, 'You are a dead man.' But we didn't pay any attention. We just kept on getting information out to people.

"The scary part was that just after Cliff was found dead, I got a phone call. The caller said, 'We got Cliff; you are next.'" That worried Ellner, especially after a break in at the HEAL offices. "Somebody just trashed the office. It used to be that when somebody called for information, we had the answers right there. But now, everything is a mess. I called the police. They said it was nothing to worry about."

Ellner worries because he is one of those who are out there challenging the medical establishment, and in doing that, making himself a part of the growing effort that has begun to more than just annoy.

He mentions an AIDS conference he attended along with some 300 activists. Ellner said that at one point a prominent scientist got riled by charges that HIV does not cause AIDS, and that AZT and DDL, two drugs widely prescribed as treatment, are so toxic that they actually break the body down and eventually lead to death.

Ellner said the scientist went off. "He told us, 'You guys are scrutinizing the scientists too much. If you continue to watch us and breathe down our neck, we're going to go back to studying cancer, and the hell with you.' I jumped up and yelled, 'Then, we'll all live with this disease; we'll start surviving.'"

Ellner, trained as a hypnotist, is not a believer in conspiracy theories about AIDS. "I don't understand the conspiracy," he said. "But I do understand the hypnosis part of it. Many doctors prescribe AZT because they're hypnotized, not because they are evil. They just don't know what is going on. They've been told to do something (use AZT), and everything they know says do it. Many are culturally hypnotized. They just don't know what is going on."

As to what is going on, HEAL has some very definite ideas.

They see the current hypothesis that says HIV causes AIDS as being bogus. They have other, many esteemed scientists who offer a competing hypothesis. They say there is more statistical evidence on their side. And what they say is that lifestyle -- especially drugs -- is behind the disease. They say that all kinds of drugs figure into the picture.

It is not just a few voices from HEAL. A new book delving deep into questions of AIDS is about to be published by Maxwell Macmillan books. It is called, "Rethinking AIDS -- The Tragic Cost of Premature Consensus," and it was written by Dr. Robert S. Root-Bernstein, who held a MacArthur Prize Fellowship from 1981-1986 and is an associate professor of physiology at Michigan State University.

The new book is yet another part of what is becoming a whirlwind against the orthodox way of going at AIDS.

A lot of what Ellner says and what Dr. Root-Bernstein discusses ties into what New York nutritionist Dr. Gary Null says. For 10 months before he died, Arthur Ashe was in consultation with Null. Ashe had spent months studying alternative treatment and Null says he was close to breaking with his doctors and AZT. In the end, though, Ashe ran out of time; pneumonia took his life.

Null compares AIDS treatment now with cancer treatment. He said that some 525,000 Americans had died of cancer. He asks, "What percentage died because treatment was immune suppressive? Because of 40 sessions of radiation the patient lost all appetite and withered away. Clearly, the treatment killed them. You can kill every patient in the world as long as it is done in the name of orthodoxy."

1992

DURING THE LAST 10 MONTHS of his life, Arthur Ashe wrestled with the possibility of breaking away from the medical establishment to seek alternative treatment for AIDS.

"He was real close," says Doug Henderson. "He just ran out of time."

When Henderson, a long-time ally of Jimmy Connors, met Ashe in 1974, a friendship blossomed. "I knew he had AIDS," Henderson says. "I knew it before he made the announcement. I never said anything to him, but I began to give him information. I just wanted to make sure that he knew as much as possible. When I told him some of what was being accomplished in alternative medicine, he was surprised. He said, 'if that's true, it ought to be on the front page of the New York Times.'

In April, Ashe told the world what Doug Henderson already knew. Less than two weeks later, Ashe began the chase for information at the Walter Reed Theater in Lincoln Center. That day, Henderson had arranged for a special showing of a documentary film made by the nutritionist, Dr. Gary Null. Just as the house lights dimmed for the showing of the film, Ashe slipped into the theater and took a seat in the last row. The film was called, "The Pain, Profit and Politics of AIDS." After seeing the film, Ashe met with Dr. Null. "We must have spoken at least twenty times by phone," the physician said. "And we had about five personal meetings. He promised to give blood so that it could be examined. He wanted to do it, but he would say, 'what will I tell my doctors?'"

The film got into what the mainstream treatment, AZT and DDL, does to the body," Henderson said. "Everyone who takes that treatment dies; that's what Arthur found out, and that's the reason he was talking with Dr. Gary Null. That's why he was so close to breaking away from his doctors." Both Dr. Null and Henderson knew how loyal Ashe was. For him to walk away from his doctors would not have been an easy thing. But both of them are sure he was -- however slowly -- moving in that direction.

Dr. Null spoke of the volumes of material he sent to Ashe. "I even set him case reports on a number of persons who had advanced AIDS, and were treated successfully. He read everything. He studied what we gave him, and he asked a lot of questions. He just never made it to the point where he was ready to try this treatment.

"I believe it would have saved his life. A hundred times, he said he was going to come into the office and start a program. Every time, his fear caused him to delay."

For 27 years, Null has been involved in alternative medicine. He has a doctorate in human nutrition and public health science. He has written and lectured widely on an alternative treatment for AIDS. He also has been one of the leading critics of the treatment offered by the medical establishment -- a treatment which centers mostly around AZT (which he calls a failed cancer drug) and DDL. He said that both drugs are so toxic that they tear the immune system down, instead of building it up. Dr. Null's alternative approach, by contrast, seeks to bolster the immune system with massive doses of Vitamin C, and various nutritional approaches. He cites cases where persons with advanced AIDS adopted his approach and were brought back to full health.

With AIDS," Dr. Null said, "I am saying that we could be saving 90 percent of those who are HIV, and 50 percent of those who have AIDS. What we have now is death by prescription. It is the biggest scandal of the '90s. But by the end of the '90s, we are going to wake up and see this is prescription AIDS -- where every symptom can be produced by the drugs we are giving the AIDS patients.

Dr. Null sees Ashe as a victim. Instead of healing him, he says, conventional treatment let Arthur Ashe down, and eventually, cost him his life.

1991

THIS GOES BACK ALMOST TWO YEARS, to a press conference held in the East African country of Kenya. By then, through a lot of Africa, whole countries were being devastated by the AIDS epidemic. That day it was announced that, finally, there had been a breakthrough in dealing with the killer disease.

The news from the Kenya Medical Research Institute (KEMRI) hailed the development of Kemron, a technique for treatment of AIDS in humans that had produced impressive results. It was not put forward as being a cure; that would have been expecting too much. But initial findings disclosed at the Nairobi press conference were stunning nonetheless.

It was said that more than 1,200 persons, all HIV positive, had received Kemron, which involved the use of interferons in low dosages. It was said that of those who used the treatment, a high percentage showed no AIDS-related symptoms (fatigue, lack of appetite, rashes, pneumonia, etc.) after just six weeks. Also, 5 to 10 percent showed no evidence of HIV at all.

Any promise of a breakthrough in the treatment of AIDS would be expected to draw great enthusiasm. So the Kenyans had to be stunned at what happened. Outside Africa, the news was virtually ignored. At the time, AIDS had begun reaching scary levels in Black communities in urban areas. So a delegation of Black New Yorkers journeyed to Kenya. After meeting with officials of KEMRI, they came home to report that it was true, that breakthrough treatment had been developed in Kenya.

The hope raised was just as quick to vanish. The why of that is still not known. But it does tie into a growing argument that says the whole truth is not being put forward -- not about the AIDS disease, and not about what treatment is most effective.

Again this week the New York based newspaper, The Native, published an article by reporter Charles Ortieb charging that fraud exists around the whole issue of AIDS and treatment. Some say the research done in Kenya was dismissed, not because it was faulty, but because the medical establishment is so solid behind the use of the drug AZT in treatment. Ortieb quoted scientists who argue that AZT, because of its toxic nature, actually shortens the lives of AIDS patients. Ortieb cited the research of Peter Duesberg, described as "one of the scientists who doesn't believe that HIV is the cause of AIDS." According to Ortieb, Duesberg says that government's big mistake about what causes AIDS has been the development of toxic drugs which are supposed to help the patient, but that ultimately make the patient worse -- or, in fact, help cause the disease itself. Duesberg has called AZT "poison" and those who prescribe it, "guilty of genocide."

So with AIDS, what is not known may be a significant part of the problem. Consider this: While the research from Africa involving he use of interferons was dismissed, similar studies now are underway here, including one at Mt. Sinai Medical Center in New York. Mt. Sinai hospital recently took a full page advertisement to reach readers of the paper which circulates primarily in the gay community.

The ad explained: "Mt. Sinai Medical Center, New York City is currently conducting clinical trial of a low dose oral liquid preparation of alpha interferon (human leukocyte derived). The study is being conducted in HIV-positive patients."

With AIDS, the time has come to ferret out truth from fiction and fraud. Now, there are too many pieces of information that make for jagged edges that tell us with AIDS, we are still not getting the real story.

1991

BEFORE IT WAS THE CITY'S HEALTH commissioner touting the experiment. Dr. Stephen Joseph was so convinced the future of the AIDS epidemic was tied to drug abuse, that no matter how fierce the criticism, he wouldn't back away from a controversial idea which involved giving addicts clean needles to shoot illegal drugs.

It wasn't Dr. Joseph's contention that clean hypodermic needles were the answer. He just kept describing the problem, a way of showing that something had to be done, and he saw the experiment as a starting place.

Dr. Joseph had his time as health commissioner during the Koch years. The New York of that era saw AIDS rise to epidemic levels. Since then, not a lot has changed; AIDS is still epidemic and a formidable problem. For the most part, the deadly virus gets transmitted through sexual intercourse and by intravenous drug users sharing dirty needles.

In curbing the way the virus moves through sexual intercourse, a lot of progress has been made. A massive educational campaign had an impact; word of what the deadly virus can do led to significant changes in lifestyle and so called "safe sex" practices. Among IV drug users, though, a different history is being written. It's believed the city has 200,000 such drug users. Estimates are that over half that population carries the AIDS virus. That was the ammunition Dr. Joseph used to push for the experiment he wanted.

The opposition was fierce. The most vocal of those critics were from the Black and Hispanic community. The story of AIDS has also become a story of race. Over half of all AIDS cases now are in the Black and Hispanic communities. Of all the women with AIDS, 80 percent are Black and Hispanic. Ninety percent of the children with AIDS are Black and Hispanic.

Black and Hispanic leaders see drugs as the problem that produced AIDS in their communities. AIDS isn't the only problem they've seen come from drugs. Whole communities have been devastated. So those leaders say no to any idea that encourages drug use, which they say giving out clean needles does.

The Joseph experiment has been characterized by some as being racist. Others have called it genocidal. But the health commissioner prevailed. U.S. Rep. Charles Rangel (D-NY) was so angered that he got legislation to prohibit federal funds in such an experiment. Instead of giving clean needles to shoot illegal drugs, Rangel argued for money to open treatment centers and to educate against the danger involved in drug use.

"If we tripled the amount of money available for treatment, it wouldn't be enough. We would have room for 100,000 addicts but we'd still have another 100,000 on the streets," Dr. Joseph replied. "Each day an IV drug user can go without an HIV-infected needle is another contribution to containing the spread of AIDS," he argued. When Koch went down in his bid for reelection, Joseph went out as health commissioner. Mayor Dinkins refused to have any part of the experiment. "I do not wish to see people assisted in becoming addicted," he said, and the experiment ended. But not the issue.

The Rev. James Allen, head of the Addicts Rehabilitation Center (ARC) on upper Park Ave. has more than 30 years in drug treatment work. "Why make needles legal," he asks, "when drugs aren't legal? If you make both legal, it would make sense, and I'm against that. All this (clean needles) is just part of the undercurrent of support for legalization." It's Rev. Allen who has a finger on something.

1990

THE ESTIMATE IS THAT SO MANY KIDS in America now smoke cigarettes that in a year's time, they spend well over $1 billion.

Health and Human Services Secretary Louis Sullivan believes that a lot of it has to do with what kids don't know. He understands that kids are head strong and so, when they are told that one day they'll regret ever having started with cigarettes, they don't believe it. They are not old enough to know the truth that longtime smokers know, which is that quitting is not an easy thing to do.

Some smokers spend years trying to kick the habit. Some spend a lot of money getting treatment and hypnotized. Even then, they are not able to kick the addiction. Kids say, "I can quit anytime I want." Dr. Sullivan knows better; he understand that smokers become addicted to nicotine and any addiction becomes a hard thing to beat.

With kids, though, there's another side to the story and that's what has the secretary boiling. In all but six states, it's illegal for kids to buy cigarettes. But when they spend $1.23 billion a year doing just that, Dr. Sullivan says some cracking down needs to be done.

"We have found it convenient to look the other way as cigarettes are openly sold to our nation's youth," he said. And he's gone to the Congress, asking that something be done about it. As a start, Dr. Sullivan wants cigarette vending machines outlawed. He said that 16 percent of cigarette sales to minors come from machines. He gets disputed on that. "Most cigarette vending machines are not in places where teenagers can get at them," argues Mark Dlugoss, editor of Automatic Merchandiser, a monthly trade publication. In Dr. Sullivan's eyes, that's beside the point. He says the machine is a source of illegal sales and that's reason enough to get rid of them.

Dr. Sullivan also has a couple of other ideas. He'd like to see tobacco retailers licensed. That would enable government to have a hold on the people who sell cigarettes so that when they sell to minors, they put themselves at risk of being fined or possibly losing their license to operate. Dr. Sullivan is getting at the fact that there's very little activity aimed at keeping kids from buying smokes. He points out that 44 states have laws against tobacco sales to minors. But when the checking was done, only five states had records of violations and in those five states, in all there were just 32 violations.

Dr. Sullivan calls it "a national disgrace. "We know that almost one billion packs of cigarettes are illegally sold to our youngsters every year."

In the Reagan years then Surgeon General Dr. C. Everett Koop used his office to crusade against cigarette smoking. He did a lot to lead in waking up America as to dangers involved in smoking. And he went further. He got tougher warning labels on packages and encouraged the move toward banning the use of cigarettes in work places and in a lot of government buildings. He set the goal of trying to make ours a smoke free society by the year 2000. Dr. Koop left Washington with Reagan. Now, it's Health and Human Services Secretary Sullivan taking up where Dr. Koop left off.

The companies that make cigarettes are creative and they find a ton of ways to advertise their product. The Rev. Calvin Butts, senior minister at Abyssinian Baptist Church in Harlem, grew tired of all the billboards in his community that advertise booze and cigarettes. He decided to do something about it. So on Saturday mornings, he gets a bucket of whitewash and a roller on a long stick and he sets out from the church with a group of supporters. Each time they see a billboard pushing booze or smokes, they paint it over. Kids notice, and it sends a message. Secretary Sullivan ought to call Rev. Butts.

1991

BY MY COUNT, I HAD SIX GOOD DAYS off cigarettes. Or was it five? I know that first day it got really hot, I mean nasty hot, that's the day I threw my pack away and I haven't been back.

Yeh, that was six days ago and right then, I swore that no matter what, I was not going back to smoking.

This was going to be my little "free at last" story. Finally, me and cigarettes were on a permanent split.

Or, at least that's the way I had it figured. Then I pick up the morning paper and there, jumping at me off the page like who would have thought it, is this big headline.

"Black Smokers Got a Habit Of Quitting," I read.

Underneath that, in smaller type, was the clincher.

"But Black Smokers Always Go Back."

Now my experience with quitting cigarettes is well documented. I've been telling that story in the newspaper for a very long time. And everybody knows the beat to that tune -- this time Caldwell quit, the next time Caldwell's back.

Until I'm reading this story in the paper, I always believed it was just me. I thought it was just Caldwell who was always quitting and starting right back. According to the paper, it isn't just me. It's the whole group of us, whatever name you want to use: Blacks, African-Americans, coloreds or, as Ross Perot says, "You people." According to the story, we got a cigarette thing and what we know is that's not good.

Who is saying this? The predominately Black National Medical Association, that's who. And where are the Black doctors getting their information? From the federal Centers for Disease Control and Prevention (CDC), that's where.

But on this, there's no need to argue. It rings true.

After reading the story, I telephoned a friend who goes by the name I.B. Complex. I reported what I had read in the paper.

Complex said, "They got it right, didn't they?"

Once, Complex (a writer, too) put on paper a part of his own struggle to get off cigarettes. He wrote:

"I've tried a multitude of techniques to wrestle the nicotine monkey from my back: cold turkey (five or six times), hypnosis (once) and tapering down (more times than you could count). Switching to brands with less tar and nicotine than the usual lung busters. Putting mayonnaise jars stuffed with butts on the desk, night stand and bathroom shelf as nauseating reminders of what smoking was doing to my lungs. Chomping on golf ball-size wads of foul-tasting nicotine chewing gum."

None of that worked; Complex kept puffing. And yes, he's Black.

All of it is a very serious thing. It's deadly serious. The spokesman for the National Medical Association says that 45,000 African Americans die each year because of smoking related disease. Overall, cigarette smoking is the most compelling public health issue for Blacks.

So why can't Blacks quit, and not go back? The CDC says that maybe it is because Blacks are more likely to use high-tar and high-nicotine brands of cigarettes. I know we have a lock on menthols, especially Kools and Newports, but those aren't the strongest cigarettes. It is also said that Blacks have less access to preventive health services. I'll buy that. But Blacks also know the truth that Whites know and Hispanics know and Asians know and that truth is that cigarettes kill.

The CDC and the National Medical Association have decided to try and do something to about this problem. They have an ad campaign coming up and they're going to use Martin Luther King Jr. and Malcolm X as examples of Blacks who died for their beliefs.

And they plan to link that to the cigarette thing: "Today Black men and women are still dying because of their beliefs -- beliefs like they can't quit smoking."

At the end, it gets hard to see much humor in the story. And that gets back to what the ads have to say.

"Are these beliefs worth dying for? To die from smoking is to die for nothing."

Chapter Five, Part One

FRIENDS

AND

ENEMIES

Editor's Note

Given a definition of power as the ability and willingness to reward one's friends and punish one's enemies, the absence of it lies at the heart of the African American dilemma. Over the years, Earl Caldwell has chronicled the Black pursuit of political power. This chapter focuses on the political campaigns of two individuals -- David Dinkins in New York, and Jesse Jackson's pursuit of the Democratic nomination for president of the United States. The political campaigns of these individuals are classic case-studies of the dynamics of African American political struggles and aspirations.

1979

ED KOCH HAD SENT THE PAPERS on Tuesday. Until yesterday, David Dinkins had ignored them.

It was now all official. So David Dinkins took the papers off his desk. As he began to study them, he shook his head a bit and for a moment, but a hint of a smile came into his face.

"You know," he said, "it's almost amusing . . . if it wasn't so tragic."

On top of the stack of papers was a letter from the mayor.

"Pursuant to Paragraph E of Section 81 of Chapter 4 of the New York City Charter, I have called a session of the Council members representing the Borough of the Bronx, to be held at the Office of the Mayor, City Hall, Borough of Manhattan, on Friday, Jan. 5, 1979, at 3 p.m. for the purpose of electing a borough president for the Bronx to fill the vacancy caused by the election of Robert Abrams to the office of the attorney general of the State of New York."

Everything was official, so David Dinkins, who is city clerk, went about his job, which meant preparing for the election of Stanley Simon to the borough presidency of the Bronx.

It was painful duty for Dinkins, who had run unsuccessfully for the borough presidency of Manhattan in 1976.

"We couldn't get people to acknowledge then that there was a need for minority representation on the Board of Estimates," he said.

"When we would make that argument, people would always say, 'You mean you should be elected just because you are Black.'"

He came out from behind his desk, pulled off his blue blazer, and began to stalk about in the gloom of his office.

"That wasn't the question," he said. "They knew that wasn't the question. Of course, I didn't feel that I should be elected just because I'm Black. I'm qualified. I felt I was superior to the other three candidates. But the point is, minorities must have a voice."

In the City of New York, it is the Board of Estimates that decides how all of the money is spent. You do not have a say in how the city is run if you do not have a voice in determining how the money is spent. The opportunity was there to make sure that New York is not ruled by an all-White board. It did not happen.

Until the election in 1976, for nearly 25 years, there had been Black representation on the board. It was lost when Percy Sutton resigned as Manhattan borough president to run for mayor. Dinkins had tried to win the office that Sutton left. He did not come even close. He would not even guess when a non-White would again sit on the Board of Estimates.

"But it's wrong," he said, "and it can't continue to go on this way."

"So what do you do?" he was asked.

"You keep trying," he said. "You can't say, well, let's drop out of the system. You can't say the hell with it. I'm an American. I'm not going back to Africa or anywhere else. I'm staying right here, and I'm going to continue to fight. You know, we're all to blame."

David Dinkins is 42 years old now. He grew up across the river in New Jersey, in Trenton, but New York City has been his home since 1951.

He is a lawyer. When he talks, it comes through. He measures his words always.

Now he held up three fingers.

"There are three reasons why non-Whites have got to be included," he said.

He mentioned politics first. He talked about loyalty that those voters who are not White have shown to the Democratic Party.

"Who," he asked, "has been more loyal to the party than us?"

Yet the party has not made certain that minorities have a voice.

Next he mentioned morality.

"It's just plain fair and just that we have some representation," he said. "It's a moral thing. It's something that ought to be done for that reason if no other."

His last reason was, perhaps, the most important.

"The ability to govern," he said. "How can you govern if you continue to push people down, down, down? It won't work. You can't do that. And that's what we're talking about now, the ability to govern."

David Dinkins is always careful with his language. Inflammatory statements do not fall from his lips. He understands that we make it together, or we fall together. So yesterday he was extra careful with the words he used.

"What are you predicting?" he was asked.

"I'm not predicting anything. I'm only saying that somebody had better recognize the need for people of all backgrounds to participate in government."

He ran his hand through the gray in his hair, then he put his jacket back on. It was almost time for him to go across the street, over to the mayor's office to participate in an election he wanted nothing to do with.

1979

AT THE TABLE JUST IN FRONT of the voting machine, Bessie Monroe sat across from Lucille Freeman. Up at the end, with her back against a pillar, was Helen Simmons.

"Talk to her," Bessie Monroe said, pointing a finger toward Helen Simmons.

"It's her birthday. She's 80-something today. You ought to talk to her."

Helen Simmons laughed. "No," she said, "I'm not 80 yet. I'm 72."

The three of them there at the table in a big room on the ground floor of PS 90 in the Bronx laughed. Soon they went back to their conversation.

The women had those small stickers on their jackets that identify them as inspectors of the election. As the morning wore on, there was virtually nothing for them to do.

Occasionally a voter came into the room, causing them to interrupt their conversation. Mostly, the women were free to sit and talk among themselves.

In certain neighborhoods in the city, it is always that way, especially in places such as the one in the Bronx where PS 90 is situated. It is a neighborhood that is occupied mostly by Blacks and Puerto Ricans.

In this neighborhood, it is not a matter of turnout. If every registered voter went to the polls yesterday, the majority still would not have voted. Turnout is only a small part of the problem. The real problem is registration.

On the table where the three women sat, there was a stack of books bound with heavy black covers. Those are the registration books. You could see that there were not enough pages, that the books were much too thin. As long as it stays that way, the women who work on Election Day as inspectors will never be busy on election day.

"It used to be better," said Helen Simmons. "I've been here since 1973 and I remember when we had two voting machines and over 800 people were registered. Now we don't have 400. That's right, we don't have 400 registered."

"Why?" she was asked.

"There's not half as many people left in the district, that's why," she said. "The Jews left. The only ones who haven't left are the old ones who live in rent-controlled apartments."

"What about the Blacks and Puerto Ricans? What about them, why aren't they registered? Why don't they vote?"

Mrs. Simmons was just like everyone else. She didn't have the answers.

"I've talked, and I've talked, and I've begged, and I've begged, and nothing happens. The building I live in, there's 16 families in there; I'd say that 12 of them are not registered. I don't know why."

Lucille Freeman interrupted. "People came out to vote for Carter," she said. "They came out and what did they get? Nothing. They are still in unemployment lines. My son is unemployed. Many peoples is out of work."

Across the table, Bessie Monroe nodded her head in agreement. "The candidates are not interested," she said. "They don't want people to vote."

"I'll tell you another thing," Helen Simmons said. She leaned across the table and spoke in a near-whisper. "Puerto Ricans register more than Negroes," she said. "Yep, that's right. They register more than we do. They vote better too," the Black women said.

"What should be done?" the women were asked.

"I don't see why they can't make these people on social services register," Lucille Freeman said, referring to welfare recipients. "You know, we got a lot of people on social service."

"You'd think they'd learn something from what's happening down South," Simmons added.

"Why do Blacks in the South vote better than up here in New York?"

"I guess it's like I told a friend of mine," she said. "He was talking about joining a church, the Jehovah Witnesses. I told 'em, 'Thank God you found out that the same God that was in Griffin, Georgia, is here in New York, even if you do call him by a different name up here.' Can you imagine, coming to New York, and didn't know where the church was? Now, I'm talking about someone who went to church every Sunday down South, but gets up here and forgets where the church is."

It is not everywhere that Blacks do not vote. In Mississippi yesterday, Blacks were talking about electing 17 mayors and perhaps as many as 25 state legislators. But here, in New York, not a single Black or Puerto Rican occupies high office. Up in the Bronx where there was an opportunity to elect a non-White to an office that would bring some non-White representation to the Board of Estimates, nothing happened. It didn't because the large majority was not registered.

David Dinkins, who is the city clerk, was downtown in his office in the Municipal Building talking about the election.

"Why?" he was asked. "Why don't Blacks vote?"

"I wish I had the answer," he said. "But I don't. But the only thing we can do is keep on trying, trying to get people registered and trying to let them know how important it is."

Dinkins did not say it, but in the City of New York, the old practice of not registering, and not voting, is one that Blacks and Puerto Ricans can no longer afford. It is expected that the 1980 census will show that a majority of the population in the city is non-White. If minorities are going to live in the city, if they are going to have a piece of the action, they will have to take it.

If Blacks and Puerto Ricans continue to ignore the voting process, soon they are going to be pushed out of the city. There are forces here now aiming to build a smaller city. And those without a voice are going to be left out.

When he was deputy mayor, Haskell Ward warned about that. "Where will they go?" he was asked. "I don't know," he said. The truth is that it's easy to push around people who don't vote. Eventually, they can be pushed out. In the Bronx yesterday, the women at PS 90 understood this.

1981

DAVID DINKINS, THE CANDIDATE, sits facing the door that opens onto Adam Clayton Powell Jr. Blvd. in Harlem.

Dinkins says nothing, but hangs on every word. On the table in front of him is pad and pencil. As he listens, he makes notes.

Dave Dinkins is presently city clerk and is running for borough president in Manhattan. The storefront on Powell Blvd. is Harlem headquarters. Dinkins's people identify it as being across from the Red Rooster, next to the Renaissance, down from Lickety Split, and ("for the religious folks") around the corner from Abyssinian Baptist Church.

It's the kind of talk that comes from the volunteers in the campaign when they are sitting out front. They have tables there, one with a huge yellow and white umbrella over it. Most often, late in the day, they sit there on the sidewalk. Somebody orders a bucket of fried chicken. They talk politics and Harlem, the election that is coming up, and all of it becomes a happening.

All of this used to be regular down on W.125th St. But no more. On 125th, the movie theater's closed. So has the Apollo and Frank's restaurant . When night comes, heavy metal gates drop over the storefronts. The people disappear. Some say it is because Asians and Arabs run most of the businesses on 125th St. now, and that they close early and go home to other communities.

Up where Dinkins has his headquarters, it's different. At night, there are jam sessions in the club that is called Lickety Split, and the Red Rooster is still legend. This is the section of Harlem not far from Lionel Hampton Houses and Riverton. On up, there is Esplanade Gardens and Riverbend. Together, the area houses what might be the largest concentration of middle income Blacks anywhere in the world.

It's where there are always people on the streets. Cars park two deep at the curb. It makes no difference because the street is a real boulevard. It is another of those special touches that makes the land in Harlem so desirable. It's why the real estate moguls are never caught asking, "Who would want to live in Harlem?" They know about the gems that are there, which is why they keep pumping money into the mayor's campaign and urging that the city-owned property in Harlem be put on the auction block.

New York is changing. The battle now is for space to survive in. That is what makes the Dinkins campaign so important. When he went out of the storefront and into the streets, there was urgency in his voice.

In the afternoon, in the 300 block of W. 139th St., the block association held its annual party. The men and the women wore gold-colored T-shirts, cooked hot dogs and hamburgers, and sold fried chicken sandwiches.

When he arrived, he shook hands all through the block. Then, they handed Dave Dinkins the microphone . "Our kids," he said. "We have to think about our children now. We owe them a chance." And he began to talk about the schools, health care and jobs -- how important it is in the city of New York that all voices be heard. He took the pieces of the speech, and brought it all back to the race for the borough president's office.

"It's very important," he said. "We have no voice, no representation on the Board of Estimates that will decide how all of the money in the city is spent -- more than $14 billion. I need your help." When he finished, the people applauded. It was the same later with the Hamilton Park block association, which was also holding its festival.

It is a David vs. Goliath battle. Stein has unlimited money. He is the one who holds the office and has the support of the Democratic organization.

"But we are going to win," Jean Booker said. "No question that we are going to win." Jean Booker was one of the 10 who sat at the table in the Harlem storefront headquarters. The 10 are co-chairmen in what is called the "governing council" in the

Dinkins campaign.

Eddie O'Jay, the radio personality, sat across from the Rev. James Manning at the table. The Rev. James Bullock was next to the Rev. Oberia Dempsey. There was Raleigh Bell, William Byrd, Claudette Jefferson and Carrie Goodwyn. They are Harlem names and a cross-section of the community.

"We are not going to make the mistakes we made in Percy Sutton's campaign," William Byrd said.

1981

DAVID DINKINS STARTED OUT in Harlem. He went first to Mount Zion AME Church, then to Mother AME Zion Church.

Mother Zion is known as the Freedom Church. It's called that because of a history that goes back to the time of slavery and the underground railroad. In church literature, they say that Mother Zion was "the beginning of the Black church in the City of New York." It goes back that far.

It was a Sunday set apart. The why of it was told partly with a huge banner that hung from the top of the pulpit. It said that Mother Zion was celebrating its 185th anniversary.

As he stood in the pulpit, the minister, the Rev. George W. McMurray, went back and picked up the history of Mother Zion. He called names that range in Black history from Sojourner Truth to Frederick Douglass. When he was done, he looked out at the congregation and said, "It is the church, this is our strength, the church."

Rev. McMurray stopped and for a moment, put his sermon aside, and looked out into the second pew where David Dinkins sat. Then the minister brought the politics of the City of New York into the pulpit.

"Let me tell you one thing," David Dinkins said later: "What you saw this morning, that is not done very often, especially not on a day like today. But that was their way of saying that it's important and that they also believe now that we can win."

After he left Mother Zion yesterday, Dinkins went on to another church, this time to St. Philip's Church.

By the time he arrived at St. Philip's, the morning services were over, but a good part of the congregation had stayed behind. Those who did waited for Dinkins in a basement meeting room.

"This is the first such meeting we've held here in 25 years," the minister, the Rev. M. Moran Weston, said.

David Dinkins had everyone in the room with him . He took two fingers and held them just inches apart. "We came that close," he said. "We came that close, and they said we didn't have a chance. They said Blacks don't vote, but what we know now is that on Sept. 22, we sent a message, and what we know now is that we can win, that we will win." And in the room in the basement at St. Philip's, the people began to respond. At the end, some stood, and all of them clapped as they hung on Dinkins's last words.

"Our cause is just," he said. "Where people didn't think we could succeed, we came that close. Now, I know we can win."

Weston stood, "These people carry considerable influence," he said to Dinkins, "They will go out and work for you."

It is not over yet. The Democratic primary was supposed to be it, the one last chance that minorities had to get back into the city government. In the primary, David Dinkins, in his race against incumbent Andrew Stein, was considered the best bet. The race was close, but Dinkins lost. It was supposed to be over. The Democrat was supposed to be in. But the evidence began to grow that the real race is in November -- when Dinkins, who has the Liberal Party Line, will go against Stein again.

"But this is greater than any individual," Weston continued. "A city that does not have balanced leadership is a city in trouble, and we are going to do what we can to see that this city gets back in balance."

In the middle of last week, Stein turned tough in his race against Dinkins. He did it with the kind of words that usually cause trouble.

"What has David Dinkins done to deserve being borough president besides being Black?" Stein asked. "That's a racist viewpoint. He has no record of achievement in any area."

The words that Stein had used had made the rounds and there was no trouble. Dinkins laughed. "He's desperate," Dinkins said. "That's all that shows."

At the Dinkins campaign headquarters in Harlem, the words that Stein used were seen as a good omen. "He (Stein) knows that Blacks don't vote in primaries, and he almost lost," one campaign worker said. "I guess he is worried. He knows that in November we will come in really big numbers and so I guess he's trying to persuade liberal Whites not to vote for Dinkins."

After he had made the rounds in Harlem, Dinkins headed downtown to Gramercy Park and the Brotherhood Synagogue, where both he and Stein spoke and took questions.

"It's wrong," Stein said, "to throw me out just because somebody else says they need any representation. Why should Andrew Stein be kicked out?" he said. Then, he repeated his charges that Dinkins had no record of achievement.

In the synagogue, they applauded for Stein when he made his arguments. Then it was Dinkins's turn. He started with the issue of minority representation in the city government. "It's distressing," he said, "to hear that so many of you don't feel that is important. He talked about the price that is being paid by keeping the government in New York City buttoned down. His voice was filled with emotion. Clearly, his was the speech that moved the crowd. When he was finished, applause rose for him.

There is a mantra that is heard around the Dinkins headquarters in Harlem. "We are not going to repeat the mistake that Percy Sutton made," they keep saying.

"What mistake?" they are asked.

"The mistake of not first securing our base," they say. "Our base is here, with Black people and in Harlem. We start here and build on that. Before we can go to anyone else, we have to show that our base is secure."

That is what worries Andrew Stein now. The Dinkins campaign has shown that its base is secure. It has begun to reach out. It can do that because the real issue is representation, and that is on Dinkins's side.

1981

"WE'VE GOT THE MOMENTUM," David Dinkins said. "I can feel it and it's just what we need."

He was standing in the middle of the block named for the poet Edgar Allen Poe. There was a street festival there. What excited David Dinkins was the way people kept coming up to him, grabbing for his hand.

"We can use you," and older, graying woman said. "We've got a real, honest shot at it," David Dinkins said. Right behind the woman came an older man, who also reached out for Dinkins. "We hope you make it," the man said.

"It's important," Dinkins said. "If we're able to do this, we'll give encouragement to others. It will show that you don't have to have all of the money to win," he said.

"How much money has your campaign been able to raise?" he was asked.

"More than twice what we raised the last time," he said. "I'd say we've raised close to $400,000."

"What was the difference this time?" someone asked.

"That I have the 100 percent solid support of the Black community. That's the difference this time," he said. "The last time I ran there was confusion. You know, Percy Sutton was running for mayor and I was running for the board, and there was some confusion. But we don't have that now."

At the festival, the sky turned gray. The wind blew cold, but it did not bother David Dinkins. "My kind of weather," he said. Although he wore only a dark blue blazer, he meant it, and laughed. It was about the kind of reception he was getting in the middle of the last weekend of the campaign.

In the election of 1981, David Dinkins has emerged as the good story. He does have the momentum. There was something real in the way people embraced him on Saturday.

"We want you to make it; we really do." "We can use you."

There are other sides to this election. A part of that was there late in the morning yesterday when Assemblyman Frank Barbaro stood in the pulpit and spoke to the congregation at Canaan Baptist Church in Harlem.

All of the words that Barbaro used were the right ones. The reception for him in the church was warm. But there was something missing. You noticed it afterward, when he went outside, stood on the sidewalk and talked with a reporter.

The Black elected officials were not with him. Diane Lacey, a co-chairman of the Citywide Coalition of Blacks for Barbaro, was there -- nobody else. The elected officials, except for a very few, have not just stayed clear of Frank Barbaro and his campaign, they have refused to get involved in the mayoral election at any level.

It has been the missing link in the campaign. This is the election where Blacks were supposed to get even with Mayor Koch. It is the election where the closing of Sydenham Hospital was supposed to be an issue. It is when that "Nigger in the woodpile" remark Koch made would be remembered. This was supposed to be the election Black voters had been waiting for.

Not too long ago, Congressman Charles Rangel was comparing the mayor of New York City to Bull Connor, the racist Alabama sheriff from the days of the civil rights movement. When Sydenham Hospital was being closed, City Councilman Fred Samuels was saying that Blacks needed to remember, and "punish our enemies."

This was to be the get-even election. The promise was that the leadership would be out in front. But except in those few cases, it hasn't happened. The leadership has been quiet, so quiet that last week the Amsterdam News, the Black weekly newspaper, came up with a major story by just publishing a poll of where Black elected officials stood on the mayoral race.

It is another side of the primary of 1981.

Then, there is the thing with the City Council. The effort is to blame the mayor for the bad redistricting plan. He did sign it; he is the one who let it go through. But the blame really sits with the minorities on the Council. They are the ones who were supposed to stand up and say no. They are the ones who failed. They sat quietly and went along. So the real blame lies with them.

In Harlem yesterday, after Frank Barbaro had spoken his piece at Canaan Baptist Church and left, the minister, the Rev. Wyatt Tee Walker, stood in the pulpit.

"Above all else, he said, "go to the polls on Tuesday. If you don't vote, you can't stand on the corner and bellyache. Anybody would be a better mayor than Koch. You know that, but if you don't turn out, if you don't vote, don't come around later bellyaching,"

Walker is one of the real leaders. They are the ones who are out front now, the ones who are not afraid.

1983

THEY HELD A POLITICAL rally in Chicago. It did not make the kind of news that moves across the country. So nobody noticed. But it was one of the signals that said something unusual was building in the mayoral election in the city of Chicago.

The rally was in support of the candidacy of U.S. Rep. Harold Washington. More than 12,000 showed up at the Circle Campus of the University of Illinois.

The size of the crowd was impressive. In Chicago, it snowed that day. Still, 12,000 came through the storm. The ones who came out on that Sunday afternoon, the 6th of February, were mostly Black, and they jammed the hall. It was a powerful signal that Chicago's Democratic mayoral primary was more than a race between Mayor Jane Byrne and Richard M. Daley, as advertised. "Traditionally, winning the Democratic nomination in Chicago has been tantamount to winning the election.

Early in the primary campaign, when Harold Washington came into the race, his candidacy raised no eyebrows. He didn't have the money. He didn't have the machine or a name as familiar as Byrne and Daley.

Besides all that, he was a Black man. In Chicago, no candidate who was Black had ever been able to mount even a serious challenge for the office of mayor. So Washington was overlooked and counted out.

In cities across the country, though, there are stirrings that in time could change the face of politics. It is something that is happening on the bottom. It keeps popping up as it did last November here in New York. In the cities, Blacks, Latins and Whites who are poor are registering in record numbers. In New York, it was those voters who made the difference in the gubernatorial race that swept Mario Cuomo into office.

It is something that has to do with Reaganomics, and it is taking place in Chicago, too.

Since last summer in Chicago, Blacks have registered in record numbers. More than 100,000 were registered before the Illinois gubernatorial race in November. It was that drive, in part, that accounted for the upset that Democrat Adlai Stevenson III almost pulled off. Since that race, another 100,000 Blacks have been registered. Now, in that city, Black voters account for 40 percent of the 1.6 million registered to vote in the primary.

As the election in Chicago neared, the polls kept showing that Washington was running strong. By the end of last week, those polls showed that he had overtaken Daley and was running a strong second to Mayor Byrne.

On Monday night, election eve, Vernon Jarrett, a veteran Chicago newspaper columnist, was on national television and he was saying that he had never seen in the Black community the fervor and depth of involvement that Washington's campaign has aroused.

The column that Jarrett writes is published in the Chicago Sun Times. On election eve he was saying that he believes it will take about 460,000 votes for Washington to win. "He's in if we can get between 80 and 90 percent of the Black vote," Jarrett said, "because he should get at least 10 percent of the white vote."

In California last year, right up until Election Day, the polls showed that Tom Bradley, mayor of Los Angeles, was leading in the race and the odds-on favorite to win election as governor. But Bradley, who is Black, lost by about 50,000 votes, and polls showed that 5 percent of the white voters would not vote for a Black man regardless of his qualifications.

In Chicago last week, U.S. Rep. Mervyn D. Dymally (D-Calif.), who also is Black, was campaigning for Washington. One of the things that he pointed out about Bradley's defeat was that too many Blacks, 72,000, who were registered, did not bother to vote.

The question was why. Jarrett wrote that Bradley took the Black vote in California for granted. He said Bradley never really campaigned among Blacks. He said Bradley's strategist assumed that he automatically would win all Blacks to his side. As it turned out, 2 percent to 4 percent fewer Blacks voted for Bradley, than voted for Gov. Jerry Brown in 1978.

In New York, it is still widely believed that Percy Sutton lost his mayoral campaign chiefly because he took the Black vote for granted. Last year, when he ran for lieutenant governor, Carl McCall made a strong showing. His base was in the Black community. He secured that first, then built out from there.

Which comes back to Chicago and Rep. Washington and his rally on the snowy Sunday just over two weeks ago. The big crowd showed that he has secured his base.

"The bottom line in Chicago politics is race," Milton Rakove, a professor of political science at the University of Illinois, said in a discussion of yesterday's election. Jarrett wrote that he had no doubt that some White communities would be bombarded with propaganda designed to show that Blacks are going to "take over Chicago if something isn't done in a hurry."

On television, on election eve, Jarrett was saying that it was not only because Washington had secured his base, but also because the 60-year-old congressman was the best qualified of the three candidates to be mayor of Chicago.

1985

ONCE, IT ALL SEEMED TO BE breaking in a perfect way. That was back when it seemed certain that Basil Paterson would be the candidate. There was nobody better.

Basil was known. He had the kind of across-the-board support that it would take to beat Koch. The money was also there for the race that everyone was sure Basil would make. At a dinner that was looked on then as his coming out, more than $200,000 was raised. Back then, it was all coming together in a perfect way.

The other piece is history. At the moment he was expected to announce, Basil Paterson said no, he would not make the race for mayor of New York. It was a stunning blow. It had seemed that it was all cut and dried.

But direct no criticism at Basil Paterson. He had a crisis situation within his family. He says his family needs him, and family calls must always be answered. Family is a cornerstone. "I'll help," Basil said, "but I can't run." Fair enough.

Basil stepped back and Herman Badillo stepped to the front. Badillo and Paterson come for the same class. They are senior and seasoned, and they know the city and have all the tools to lead. But Badillo, like Paterson, understands that only a unity candidate can win. "I'll wait for the decision of the Black leadership." Badillo said. Fair enough.

The Black leadership group has, perhaps by accident, begun to send an awful message. It seems to be saying that it can't find anyone qualified. It's a message that doesn't square with the facts.

Could Franklin Thomas, who is president of the Ford Foundation, be persuaded to run? Would Carl McCall, who ran a strong race for lieutenant governor, make the mayoral race if the money was there? Former U.S. Rep. Shirley Chisholm could be a very good candidate who could address the crisis the city has with educating the young. And there are others. Ossie Davis's voice has grown strong in city affairs. Would he run? Attorney C. Vernon Mason is a rising talent. Would he run?

Look to the women. Federal Judge Constance Baker Motley stands tall. The same is true of Amalya Kearse, who also sits on the federal bench. And there is also Jewell Jackson McCabe, who has been in the forefront of building voter registration.

The list of qualified people is long, but that is only a part of the story. It used to be said that Blacks and Puerto Ricans don't vote. It was attributed to apathy and laziness, but all that is yesterday's story. As many as 400,000 Blacks may vote in the mayoral primary on the Democratic side. The Hispanic vote will approach 300,000. That vote unified doesn't have to link up with much else to make for winning figures.

In New York, Blacks and Hispanics still have no say in government. The voter registration figures say that is likely to change.

At the mayoral level, it had all seemed cut and dried. Basil Paterson would be the unity candidate. The call of family pulled Basil back. Now, the Black leadership group is sending an awful signal. It is saying by default that it can't find anyone qualified. But it's a signal that doesn't square with the facts.

There is, though, no time for argument. Now it's the moment of truth. The Black leadership group comes forward with it candidate, or it embraces Herman Badillo. There is no time left to waste.

1988

WITH ENVY AND ANGER, they have watched as it happened in so many other sections of the country. In Newark, Los Angeles and Detroit. In Chicago, Philadelphia and Gary, Ind. Even in Birmingham, Atlanta and New Orleans. In all those places, candidates who were Black broke through and won election as mayor.

Not in New York. For close to two decades, Blacks have looked at the city's highest elective office, and nurtured the belief that "our time has come." For many reasons, though, it has not happened. It remains another dream deferred.

Looking back over those 20 years of disappointment, Percy Sutton represents the opportunity that was missed.

When he left his post as Manhattan borough president to seek the mayoralty, he figured to be a formidable candidate. It seemed that, in every respect, he was a candidate whose time had come. He had a clear vision of where he wanted to take the city. He had the tools and the savvy to do the job. It even seemed that he had the strong base that it would take to make the run. For Percy Sutton, it was not to be. Instead of winning election as mayor, his campaign became a bitter last hurrah.

After Sutton's defeat came the promise of a race from Basil Paterson. He seemed to have even more pluses. It was widely proclaimed that "Basil can win."

As it turned out, his was a race never to be run. For personal reasons, Paterson decided to stand aside.

So again, the promise of breaking through turned sour. The history written was to be no more than another dismal chapter in the book of dreams deferred.

In the world of politics, though, dreams die hard. Many moments of triumph have roots that are tied to bitter disappointments.

In politics, the old truth says that you keep working and building. In time, good things will happen.

Now the 1989 mayoral race has come into sight. Koch, the incumbent, has staked out his ground. He is off and running.

A large piece of the opposition to Koch will come from the Black community. Which raises questions: Will the Black community again offer a candidate? If so, who will it be?

Former U.S. Rep. Shirley Chisholm has already positioned herself for a race. However, she says she will stand back if Manhattan borough President David Dinkins decides to run.

Dinkins has begun to make moves in that direction. He has polls that say the time for him is right. He has formed an exploratory committee. But his decision remains on hold.

In politics, moments that seem insignificant often grow to become telling events. In New York's mayoral election of 1989, such a moment may have occurred last Saturday. On that morning, a wide cross-section of leaders and activists of the Black community gathered at the Harlem State Office Building. The subject was politics. The mayoral race was the issue. The pressing matter had to do with the role Blacks are to play.

From that meeting came a big idea. For the mayoral race, the decision was to embrace what was called "the Philadelphia Plan." It was a way of trying to make certain that whatever Blacks do, they agree to do together.

So instead of a small group picking a candidate, or having aspirants move on their own, the decision was to hold a convention and select a candidate through that process.

That has never been done in New York. But years of bitter history have made an impact. So in the meeting at the State Office Building, plans were drawn and a convention date was set (Feb.26). From the ashes of past defeats, hopes were raised.

Even in tough times, New York has maintained its standing as the capital city of the United States. To win New York is indeed to win the Big Apple. The mayoral election is 11 months away. For now, the meeting in Harlem is no more than a footnote. In time, though, it could be looked back on as the moment the tide turned for the dream deferred.

1989

WITH THE APPROPRIATE HOOPLA, mayoral candidate David Dinkins opened his campaign headquarters in midtown, on the sixth floor of an old building.

In the course of the campaign, a lot of strategy and some big decisions are likely to get made in the cluttered rooms Dinkins has. But the outcome in his bid for the city's highest office is more apt to turn on what happens in another suite of offices, those on the 8th floor of the Puck Building at 295 Lafayette St. That's where Hulbert James is holed up. From there, he's masterminding what is perhaps the most ambitious effort of voter registration ever to take place in New York for a non presidential election.

In elective politics, almost nothing happens without money. Money has come to be key. On almost every front, money decides. So much so, it has been dubbed the mother's milk of politics. In the city's mayoral race, it will be no different; money will be important. But there is another piece: voter registration. That is where Hulbert James comes into the picture.

In the world of politics, where so much has stayed the same for so long, the significant trend has to do with the emergence of minorities, especially Blacks. The most visible symbol of this has been Jesse Jackson with his presidential campaigns. Behind Jesse has come Ron Brown. His considerable achievement was winning the election that made him the head of the Democratic Party. But these were not "gimmies" or minority set asides. They were reflective of political skills, which have been developed in recent years by the outsiders. In big league politics, Whites used to control everything. They picked the candidates. They developed the strategies; they ran the campaigns. In the major parties, they held onto all the decision-making.

The passage of the Voting Rights Act in 1965 was the signal that change was bound to come. The Voting Rights Act changed the equation. It meant a whole lot of Americans who had been counted out would soon be counted in, where politics and elections were concerned. That's what Jesse saw and a reason he began to see himself as being presidential timber. Because he was the candidate and such a charismatic one, Jesse stayed in the spotlight. So a lot of the significant development didn't get notice. But all across the country, in big towns and small, people who never had the chance were learning how to do. They got experience in running campaigns and voter registration drives. They got experience in pulling out votes, putting together coalitions and raising and spending money. That gets back to Hulbert James.

He's an imposing figure. He's dark, husky, a studious thinker and doer. His is not a new face on the scene. When the Run, Jesse, Run campaigns were registering all those voters, Hulbert James was the genius in the back room quietly making it happen. The effort involved more than just looking at what had been done before and saying, "We can do that." James was a part of building new systems. Of devising solid yet creative ways to register those once considered lost causes.

The mayoral race of 1989 is the test. In a way, the whole Dinkins campaign rides on the voter registration effort headed by James. Dinkins, more than any other candidate, needs a successful voter registration drive. The reason is simple: he's the candidate whose base is among minorities, which is where the unregistered are. How many are there? Some say as many as a million Blacks and half that number of Latins. That gets back to Hulbert James and his work from the suite of offices on the 8th floor of the Puck Building on Lafayette St.

In 1988, it took most of eight months, but over 500,000 new voters were registered. Hulbert James was behind that effort. Now, he has three months to be successful. He has to register 250,000 voters. "The pieces are in place," he says. "We can do it."

In the world of politics, 1989 is not altogether another round of business as usual. A lot of new faces, in the colors of the rainbow coalition, are emerging at the top. In New York, they have a shot at writing a big chapter in the city's politics.

1989

FROM THE START, DAVID DINKINS understood. He knew how much a racial tinderbox the city of New York had become. So, not even for a moment, would he allow himself to be portrayed as "the Black candidate" in the race.

Most of the largest cities in the country have elected mayors who were Black. In most of those races, the Blacks who broke through to win made race a large part of the campaign. Before anything else, they organized formidable bases in the Black community, then moved from there to win election. It happened that way in Detroit, Philadelphia, Chicago, Atlanta, and a lot of other cities. For a long time, the belief was that it would happen that way in New York, too. Long before David Dinkins announced, before it was even considered that he would run, through many circles in the city, the political talk was of "a Black candidate" in the field against Koch in 1989.

But it didn't happen that way. David Dinkins was his own man. On the chilly day of last February, when he announced his candidacy, he put a quick stop to talk of his being the Black candidate. "It's not a question of the city being ready for a Black mayor," he said. "That's not it at all. As things have evolved, I'm the best choice," he said. "I can get elected."

In the race, Gov. Cuomo has refused to make any endorsement. But, for Dinkins, he did the next best thing. He framed the issues that he says ought to decide.

Cuomo said, "The person who is going to win is the leader who will say to the people of the city of New York, the state of New York: I will bring you together."

It was almost as though the governor was reading from Dinkins campaign literature. From day one in his campaign, that's been the Dinkins message. "The leadership has not been sufficient," he said in announcing. "I am prepared to lead the city in the direction we so sorely need." He said the city "needs a new direction, the spirit of hope and optimism."

In the campaign, that was the message he sharpened. On the hot days of July, he said: "We have to renew our sense of values -- as citizens, as a city, as a society. It won't be easy, but we have to begin; and this is a battle we have to win. We have to put an end to this political era of cynical manipulation and divisiveness."

Koch cannot pass the test that Cuomo set. You reap what you sow. Through his three terms as mayor, more than anything else, the mayor at times almost seemed set on turning one group against another. He played the most dangerous of racial games. In time, a price had to be paid. So the names Howard Beach and Bensonhurst have come to be equated with the worst of Mississippi and Alabama of the 1950s. And the mayor with his mouth, and the signals he sent, had a lot to do with taking neighborhoods of New York City to that place.

Dinkins understood, a long time ago, the damage Koch was doing to the city. Back when he was running for Manhattan Borough President, he warned of the kind of polarization that was taking place in New York. He said that using race would win elections, but he worried about something else: "Are you going to be able to govern?"

It surprised a lot of people when Dinkins gave up his sure job as borough president to run for mayor. But he saw back then what has become clear. "I"m the best choice," he explained. "I can get elected."

Of Koch ask, are we better off now in New York than four years? Of Dinkins, match him to the challenge laid down by Cuomo. "Who will say to the people of New York....'I will bring you together.'"

1989

EVEN WHEN THE POLLS had him sitting on a fat 20-point lead, David Dinkins knew that in the mayoral election it wasn't over. It has to do with race. He's Black and in New York, like most places in the country, Whites seldom vote for Blacks. Dinkins understood that for him to get to the mayor's office it was going to be a struggle every step of the way.

It didn't matter that he had said early on that he wasn't running as "the Black candidate." He wasn't just mouthing words. From the start, the whole impetus in his campaign has been toward building a coalition. It wasn't an idea he came onto only when he decided to run for mayor. Over the last decade, maybe more than any political leader in the city, Dinkins has been in the forefront of trying to build a coalition movement, which is not an easy thing to do in the city that Edward Koch has made.

For a long time in New York, a lot of Blacks believed the "Harold Washington model" was the one to follow. The late mayor of Chicago ran, and got elected, as "the Black candidate." Before he agreed to run, he laid down a "show me" challenge to the Black community. He told Blacks, you get organized and registered and then come to me and say you want me to run. In Chicago, it happened that way. In the Democratic primary, Washington got a three-way race. It was perfect. He prevailed. In the general election, it was another story. It was all he could do to defeat an obscure Republican in a city where the holder of the Democratic nomination always wins.

So the victory Harold Washington won represented an "our time has come" triumph for Blacks. That was to produce a lot of confrontations. It was a long time before Washington was really able to govern. New York is not Chicago. The Black community of New York has nothing near the kind of cohesiveness that existed in Chicago. New York is a "do your own thing" kind of town. Four years ago, Denny Farrell ran for mayor trying to use the Black community as a base. It didn't work. Blacks would not rally behind a candidate just because the candidate was Black. So Farrell was not even a good threat to Koch in the primary.

In the polls, Dinkins doesn't have a fat lead anymore. Partly because of mistakes he made, and partly because of tardiness in responding to his opponent's negative campaigning, he lost a lot of ground. In the week that was, Dinkins found himself under a lot of pressure. Mostly, he was under pressure to explain himself. He had a questionable stock transaction. He had Sonny Carson to explain. And because polls showed him losing considerable support among Jewish voters, he also had to explain again his friendship with the Rev. Jesse Jackson.

It is always good to see a leader under pressure. When times are good and the sailing smooth, a lot of people make good captains. It's when the water gets choppy, though, that you learn something about the captain in charge. Say that Dinkins passed his test but it's not over. It takes a lot to hold a coalition together. Between now and election day that's what he's got to do. Can he hold Jewish support without alienating other segments? Are Blacks poised to vote in the general election as they turned out in the primary? For the coalition to prevail, each piece needs to see what it stands to gain, and each piece needs to deliver.

In the media, here and across the country, Dinkins gets portrayed as being "the Black candidate." That's not it. A lot of circumstances have come together in New York to create a climate that's made it right for a coalition -- maybe even one headed by a Black man -- to win election as mayor. New York is in dire need of a government that can create a new attitude. If successful, that's what the Dinkins coalition is committed to. It says that if it can get people to turn to each other, and not on each other, then it becomes possible to change the condition in a city sorely in need of change.

1991

NEW YORK HAS NEVER BEEN in this place. Even though it has elected a mayor who is Black, more new ground is about to be broken. For the first time, the city has a big election that, maybe more than anything else, is about removing some significant power from the hands of the White community.

That means New York has never had an election like the one coming up next week.

So it is no surprise that a lot of candidates for the City Council who are not White say what Larry Warden of the Bronx said about the election.

"It's crucial," he said.

The "why" in Warden's assessment is an issue that has reverberated through a lot of councilmanic districts.

"It is critical," explains Warden, "because this (election) is about empowerment. It is about allowing African Americans to have a say in our representation. It is about our saying, 'Hey, we can do the job.'"

The city has been stubborn in arriving at this place. In fact, had the federal courts not intervened, the power sharing likely to be the by-product of the elections surely would not be occurring. The city was pushed. A lot of history says the Voting Rights Act, which goes back to 1965, had its greatest impact in giving Blacks the vote especially in the Deep South. That may be true. But that isn't all the legislation did; minorities in New York, too, used the Voting Rights Act to get Justice Department scrutiny of the way political power was distributed. Almost everywhere federal officials looked, New York was found to be in violation of the concept of one person, one vote. Changes were ordered. The elections are one more piece of the fallout.

A lot of the power at stake in the election had been in the hands of the body known as the Board of Estimates. That body, though, was found to be so much in violation of the one person, one vote concept, that it had to be disbanded. In its place, the City Charter Revision Commission urged a larger and more powerful City Council. The idea won approval, and in the larger council, districts were carved in a way to ensure greater representation for minorities.

The law does not say a Black must represent Blacks or that a Puerto Rican must represent Puerto Ricans. The districts are carved in a way, though, to give minority groups the largest number of potential votes in areas where they are the predominate population. It is what Larry Warden alludes to. He runs in the north Bronx, in the 12th District. When he says, "Hey, we can do the job," it is his way of saying the time has come for minorities to be their own advocates in places of power. Which is the reason he says, "crucial" when asked to describe the importance of the election.

Larry Warden may not make it to the council. He has opposition, both Black and White. But he does run in a district where 62 percent of the voters are Black. The district is a part of the community he grew up in and with the help of good endorsements and public financing, he figures to be a force in the race. He is a district leader, and chairman of the Northeast Bronx Redevelopment Corp.

District 12 has Co-Op City on one side of the highway and a heavily Black community on the other. The 22 percent White vote in the district is most in Co-Op City. The Co-Op City vote that went against Mayor Dinkins is also what Warden figures he has to overcome. That's the way the district has been balanced. The tilt, while not necessarily in Warden's favor, does give the intended edge to a minority candidate.

In all this, there is an odd twist. The new City Council will have much of the power once in the hands of the Board of Estimates. Candidates who run have public money. But in a lot of the districts carved out for minority "empowerment," campaigns seem to have more "ho-hum" than fires of enthusiasm.

1992

IN THE COALITION DAVID DINKINS used to win election as mayor, no piece seemed stronger or more solid behind him than that of organized labor. The relationship appeared to be one that nothing could interfere with.

Now, in just a few months, it has become a story of the way things fall apart.

Among the unions Dinkins had with him, none was more enthusiastic in its support than Jim Butler's Local 420, the 15,000 city hospital workers.

But late in the afternoon yesterday Butler took a lot of the troops he has to Harlem, on the ground of another piece of the Dinkins base. There the union demonstrated against the administration it did so much to put in place.

Butler was a part of a demonstration outside Harlem Hospital. "They (the administration) are treating us like third-class citizens," he said. "Teachers go into the classroom and teach our kids; they deserve an increase in pay. I have nothing against the percentage they receive. But in the meantime, we have 15,000 health care workers. A lot of our people have been on their jobs 20 and 25 years, and for the mayor to divide us the way he did is not fair.

"My members get up early in the morning and go to all the city hospitals, and they mop the floors and handle those reds, (medical waste), and get stuck by needles, and give baths to patients, and care for those who have AIDS, and they do it, and don't fear those patients... To offer us an increase of one and 11/2 or 3 percent is not fair. Our people go to the same supermarkets on Saturday, push around the same baskets the teachers do. Mr. Dinkins doesn't give us any discount cards to use. We have to pay the same as anyone else. We shouldn't be treated this way."

It is not just Jim Butler and Local 420. While Butler was mobilizing his workers to demonstrate in Harlem, two other powerful unions were coming together to form a joint negotiating team to get more muscle to use against the administration they, too, did so much to put in place.

"City Hall will not balance the books on the backs of workers," said Barry Feinstein, who heads Teamsters Local 237.

So he took his union and joined with Stanley Hill who heads the biggest municipal labor union, District Council 37. Hill represents some 140,000 city workers and Feinstein, 23,000 (about 11,000 involved in current negotiations). "The two unions will go to the negotiating table together," Hill said.

In the Koch years, these unions went to the streets many times. But it was different then; they were not part of any coalition with Koch. In the Koch years, they often found themselves on the other side of the barricades.

With Dinkins, it was supposed to be different. It was supposed to be the unions moving together with an administration they were a part of. So what has gone wrong? Is all this just posturing by union leaders to get for their members the best contract possible?

"It's deeper than that," Stanley Hill said. "It involves the basic integrity of communications of allies who have been friends... political friends for years."

Jim Butler also says that a lack of communications is a part of the problem. But he goes further. "Many of our folks are disappointed. They don't believe we got a Black mayor. We supported him; we believe he's brilliant. But he's got some people around him who are giving bad advice."

All this doesn't mean the relationship between the Dinkins administration and labor is over.

Hill and Feinstein met with the mayor at Gracie Mansion two nights ago. "A good meeting," Hill said. "We talked for four hours." And Butler says, "I would still vote for him again."

The unions, as Butler says, are fighting for "our piece of the pie."

1993

WHAT YOU HAVE TO KNOW about the Rev. Benjamin Chavis is that he is a child of the civil rights movement. He grew up in the fight. It is what he knows, and what shapes his decisions. So for the battle of New York, he borrowed some old strategy from the days of the movement.

In the 1960s, they were called the "freedom rides." Then, buses rolled across the south, carrying mostly young people -- many of them just teenagers. In time, they helped change the course of history.

The way Chavis sees it, the battle grounds have changed, but some of the old strategy still has value. So Chavis has brought the concept of freedom rides back. Only this time, the buses moved in a new direction.

The buses that were a 1993 version on the freedom rides rolled into New York. As it was 30 years ago, these riders were young and full of the belief that they could make a difference.

But the missions are not the same. In the early 1960s, the freedom riders set out across the segregated south to knock down barriers. Many suffered beatings and some were left crippled. Others found new homes in the cemetary. It was a dangerous time but in the end, they prevailed.

The task the riders who came to New York face is not so dangerous. They are not going up against mobs armed with clubs. They do not have to worry about threats and beatings.

But the mission they have in many ways is even more difficult. It is their job, in the time they have in New York, to arouse the Black electorate and impact on the turnout for Tuesday's mayoral election.

"Around the nation, people look at Mayor Dinkins as a hero," Rev. Chavis said.

Benjamin Chavis is in his first year as national director of the National Association for the Advancement of Colored People (NAACP). Among African-Americans, he stands as part of a new generation of leadership.

Chavis represents what former U.S. Rep. Shirley Chisholm called "the continuity." Which is a way of saying that each generation is called on to advance the cause. The last generation won the vote for Blacks.

That was the time of civil rights giants Martin Luther King Jr. and Roy Wilkins. For this generation, the job is to build on the gains that have been made.

So yesterday, they began to move from neighborhood to neighborhood. They are young freedom riders of now and decked out in bright yellow jackets, they yelled and shouted the message they brought to New York.

"Get out the vote," they said. "Go to the polls."

In a way, all this is new ground for New York. Always, it has been the other way around.

It was New Yorkers going to Mississippi, Alabama and Georgia.

"I'm sure it will help," said a woman who stood on 125th as the freedom riders moved through the block. "There is so much apathy up here; maybe this will help wake people up."

It is exactly what Benjamin Chavis had in mind. It dovetails with his history.

"Use what you've got," was the credo of the movement. A part of that is history. The history of the struggle Blacks made for the vote in this country.

"A lot of lives were lost in the struggle to get the vote," Chavis said yesterday. "We cannot let that be forgotten."

So, true to the movement that says "you do something," Chavis has brought an excitement to corners in the city where there had been none around this election.

1992

AT THE FINISH LINE in the mayoral campaign, Bill Lynch only reiterated what he's been saying since the start. "Turnout, turnout, turnout," he said. "That's the key."

Mayor Dinkins has a special way of making reference to Lynch, his former Deputy Mayor who took leave from that job to manage his reelection campaign. With fondness in his voice, Dinkins calls Lynch, "Our rumpled genius."

The two of them have a lot of history together. Never though have they been in a campaign to match the one that draws to a close today. Still, Lynch sounds an optimistic note. "It's coming together," he said. "I think we're ready to do it."

To bolster turnout, Lynch said the Dinkins campaign is ready with what he calls a "humongous" field operation. But that's not the whole of it. No matter how effective the get out of the vote effort, what he knows is that for the mayor to be successful, a lot of people have to be ready to move on their own. And that's especially true of those who make up the mayor's base, the Black community.

"All the polls have the Black vote at 21 percent (of the total vote)," Lynch said. "We have to get that (the Black vote) to 28 percent." How reasonable is it to expect that? "That's what we did in 1989," Lynch said. "That's what the exit polls (in '89) showed."

In looking back at the campaign, Lynch cringed at the rough spots. "I wish August had not happened," he said. That was when the Crown Heights controversy peaked, and also, when the PVB scandal broke. "We weren't counting on that," he said, "but everything else was on target."

"I always said that we wanted to be neck and neck in the stretch -- other than having an insurmountable lead. So we're where we want to be. Our media and our message has been right on target." That was Lynch's way of saying that in this campaign, the issues are on the mayor's side. Republican challenger Rudolph Giuliani is a throwback to Reaganomics.

Giuliani says the city has lost 400,000 jobs under Dinkins. He says Clinton hasn't pumped any money into New York. The only thing he leaves out of those arguments is the role Republicans have played. How much did the city lose because of the Reagan/Bush policies that ignored urban America? And when Clinton tried with his stimulus package to make funds available to cities, U.S. Senate Republican leader Robert Dole of Kansas led the fight to kill that relief. That, too, is a part of the story Giuliani does not tell.

In the campaign, Giuliani blamed Dinkins for what he calls the poor relations in the city among the races. But it was Giuliani who went before a mob of drunken cops at City Hall to deliver what was widely viewed as an inflammatory speech.

New York is the same as all of urban America. It has suffered mightily from the nightmare years of Reagan and Bush. Reagan was the architect of the policy. He treated the cities as though they didn't exist. And the result was that jobs were lost, drug traffic became rampant, even the smallest training programs were eliminated and there was no financial help. Mayor Dinkins was a voice against Reaganomics; Giuliani was on the other side.

Now, the national politics in the country have turned around. President Clinton has made it clear that he stands with the cities. For the first time in a long while, there is an urban policy. Twice Clinton came to New York in the campaign to support Dinkins. He knows the role the mayor played in his election. His promise to Dinkins is fairness for his administration.

Maybe no group has more at stake than African-Americans. As it happens, maybe no group stands to have more impact at the polls. But that gets back to what Bill Lynch said: "Turnout, turnout, turnout." In this election, that's the key.

It used to be that people were not registered. Then, they couldn't vote even if they wanted. Now, it's different. The registration is on the books. The numbers are there. And what will decide on this Election Day is whether or not those who are registered use what they've got. Which gets back to the key word: turnout.

Chapter Five, Part Two

FRIENDS

AND

ENEMIES

1980

THE FIRST TIME HE SAID IT, silence hung over the auditorium. It took time for what he said to sink in, but now, the voice of the Rev. Jesse Jackson came booming back into the microphone.

"Ten million," he shouted.

"We have got 10 million registered Black voters now." He paused there, stopping just long enough to make certain that everyone realized exactly what he was saying. And then Jesse went on to shout his conclusion: "We have got power," he said. "Power," he shouted again and then noise rose in the auditorium.

Never before had so many Blacks been registered to vote. Ten million. Silence came back into the auditorium and now, Jesse's voice was rising again.

"In 1960," he was saying, "Kennedy beat Nixon by 112,000 votes. We got 10 million." Then he went to 1968. "Nixon beat Humphrey by a half-million votes," he said, and he waited there. Then he shouted, "We got 10 million." He came to 1976, pointing out how Carter beat Ford by 1.7 million votes. And again, he picked up the chorus. "We got 10 million."

Outside, the Saturday afternoon was filled with wind and rain. October was moving closer to November, and the presidential campaign was moving to another level.

It is about registered voters now. They are the only ones who count. The field has been narrowed. It is a different set of numbers that interests the politicians. "How many people do you have registered?" has become the important question.

"Ten million," the Rev. Jesse Jackson says. He is giving the Black report.

Jesse Jackson was delivering the keynote address at an all-day meeting at Columbia University that was sponsored by the political action committee of The Coalition of 100 Black Women.

"A day of political action to mobilize the Black vote," it was called. But it was, in reality, something else. It was the beginning of the hard sell of Jimmy Carter. It is coming to the wire now. The gloves are coming off. The 10 million votes are crucial.

In 1976, there were 7 million Blacks who were registered, and nearly 50 percent of them voted. The numbers have been swelled for the election of 1980, and now the push is to take the 10 million to President Carter.

Last week, Black Enterprise magazine endorsed President Carter. The magazine never had endorsed a presidential candidate. And just after that, Ebony and Jet, two of the most popular, widely circulated magazines in the Black community followed with endorsements of President Carter. Again, it was the first time.

On Saturday, the program listed Jesse Jackson as the keynote speaker. It turned out to be a rousing endorsement for President Carter.

Jesse disposed of the John Anderson candidacy with ease. "He had the chance to put a Black man or a Black woman on his ticket," the former aide to Martin Luther King Jr. said. "Had he done it, he could have created a whole new dynamic in American politics. With a strong Black on his ticket, the Republicans and the Democrats would have caught hell trying to stop them." Anderson chose Pat Lucey. "Let him sink and go back to where he came from," the Rev. Jesse Jackson said.

Then he moved to Ronald Reagan. "It's strange," he said. "At General Motors and other big corporations they make people retire at age 65, and then they (the Republicans) reach back and get somebody who is 70 to run the whole country. That's a little off right there," he said. And everybody laughed. Then came a stream of criticism directed at Reagan, and it went from his position on the Panama Canal to China and then Africa.

"He does not want to recognize Zimbabwe and Mugabe. He wants to recognize Ian Smith and says unashamedly that we should recognize South Africa. Those are Tarzan politics for Africa," Jesse shouted and again there was laughter.

"As I see it, there is no room in Reagan's world for us," he said, and then he turned to Carter.

"His human rights policy to us means that he did not lift the sanctions against Rhodesia," he said.

"In the last four years not one boy from the choir loft, street corner or a college chair has been sent abroad to die for some macho politics -- that's important to us," he said.

Next he mentioned that Carter had appointed more Blacks, women and Browns as federal judges than any other President. He said some Blacks say that judges are not important, that jobs are what is needed.

"In slavery, everybody had a job," Jesse said. "It ain't enough to have a job. In slavery we were fully employed, but we had no justice, no health care, no housing. Man does not live by bread nor jobs alone," He blamed the loss of jobs, the high unemployment, on what he called the "unprecedented collapse in the private economy." And he had an explanation for that.

"We were locked out," he said. "That is not the President's fault." And then there was only one thing shouted. "There is nothing more powerful in the whole world than a made-up mind. Make up your minds now." It was about the 10 million.

Dr. Gloria E.A. Toote followed Jesse to the platform, and she made a strong, emotional argument for Ronald Reagan. "Let's not deal in rhetoric any more," she said. "Let's evaluate the candidates, but both candidates," she said. But the weight was against her. It was clear that the candidacy of Ronald Reagan scares Blacks who are registered to vote.

No applause came for Dr. Toote. It did not matter how eloquent she was in her arguments.

Ernest Green, Carter's man, was up now and he was saying that the forms were in the back and that what was really needed was for the people, the ones in the room, to sign up and commit themselves to work at bringing out the vote.

On one side of Ernest Green was Mary Pinkett, who serves on the City Council from Brooklyn, and David Dinkins, the city clerk, was on the other, and the two of them were shaking their heads in agreement. When Jewell Jackson McCabe, president of The Coalition of 100 Black Women, rose to adjourn the meeting, the crowd flocked around the desk in the hallway, and the names were taken of those who were willing to work for the reelection of President Carter.

"Ten million," a woman who had a handful of fliers said. "We got 10 million registered now. All we have to do is vote."

1983

THERE WAS A GROUP of them, and together they made up the inner circle that Dr. Martin Luther King Jr. leaned on. There were Ralph Abernathy, Hosea Williams, Jim Bevel, Andrew Young and Jesse Jackson. They were all ministers, the closest aides to King. Where he led, they followed. It was that way in the spring of 1968 when the group of them arrived in Memphis. The second day they were there, as twilight gathered over the Lorraine Motel, they lost their leader to an assassin's bullet.

As it happened, they were all together in the parking lot and King stood above them on the balcony just outside his motel room. They watched as the bullet that took his life exploded in his neck.

Memphis had been a detour that they had argued against. There was the Poor People's Campaign in Washington. That was the important project they had, but the garbage collectors in Memphis were on strike. They called Dr. King, and he responded. There was no question of King going to Memphis alone. His men -- Abernathy, Hosea, Bevel, Andy and Jesse -- would be there too, because in a way, they were one. It took an assassin's bullet to break that relationship.

After the assassination, the group of them tried to go ahead with the Poor People's Campaign, but they had no chance. King was the center, and he was gone. That took away whatever chance the Poor People's Campaign had. The group of them began to go their separate ways.

For awhile, Abernathy stood in King's place as head of the Southern Christian Leadership Conference. Jim Bevel disappeared. Hosea Williams and Andrew Young went into politics. It was different with the Rev. Jesse Jackson. He had his own ideas and, in Chicago, he created his own organization, Operation PUSH. He was the one who was to become a leader in the style of Martin Luther King Jr.

In the afternoon yesterday, Jesse Jackson was in New York. He was pushing the boycott he has called against Anheuser-Busch Co. It has become his toughest fight. In a way, it puts him in the kind of position that King was in when he called for his Poor People's Campaign. King had many critics, including other leaders in the civil rights movement, but he would not back down from his challenge to Washington. His vow was to use demonstrators in civil disobedience to stop the business of government if necessary, until the issues of jobs and income were dealt with by the national government.

All of that was 15 years ago, but yesterday, at Leviticus International, it came back, and it was Jesse Jackson who made it that way. It had to do with the way he is standing up to fight with the giant corporation that is Anheuser-Busch.

The boycott that Jesse called focuses on Budweiser, which is Anheuser-Busch's best selling beer.

"Why Budweiser?" Jesse was asked.

"It's not just Budweiser," he said, "it's the whole beverage industry, but right now, we're focusing on Budweiser."

He went over his figures again -- the figures that say how much support Blacks give to Budweiser. The figures say how little Black Americans get in turn from Anheuser-Busch. He kept honing in on his arguments and, in the language he uses, he said: "We don't want aid, we want trade." That was the crux of it. He was saying that the time has come for Black Americans to quit begging. He was saying that the time has come for Americans who are Black to quit asking the government to do everything. He said what the President says, that the private sector has to stand up to its responsibility; that it's the private sector, not the government, that has the jobs. In so many different ways, that was what the Rev. Jesse Jackson said.

He said Black Americans spend $660 million a year on beer. He argued that some of the money has to come back into Black communities. He called that a trade agreement.

"How should Anheuser-Busch do that?" he was asked.

It was a question he wanted, and he spoke for a long time and he waved an arm around the room that was filled with young executives, all of them Black and involved in the National Association of Black Promoters. He used them as an example. He took the "BudFest" entertainment fairs that Anheuser-Busch sponsors. He pointed out that they use Black entertainers and rely upon Black audiences. The fairs, Jackson pointed out, are promotions for Budweiser beer. But, he said, the fact is that Blacks have no piece of the action.

The promoters who were at Leviticus yesterday told how they had approached Anheuser-Busch, trying to get a share of the BudFest action. They told how their efforts were rebuffed. They said they were offered "a sharecropping arrangement" where-by they would not make any major decisions. The primary contracts would continue to go to White agencies. In a statement the Black promoters released, it was said that "Anheuser-Busch's economic exploitation takes consumer dollars out of the Black community, but does not return our fair share in jobs or trade with Black business persons. If Blacks had their fair share of business with Anheuser-Busch, it would tend to keep a maximum amount of money circulating in the Black community by hiring Black workers and trading with other Black businesses."

The National Association of Black Promoters endorsed the boycott. Their decision was to use the muscle they have to make it work. They promised to leaflet against Budweiser at concerts they sponsor, and call on Black artists and Blacks who buy tickets to withdraw from BudFests. Jesse Jackson said he was going on campuses around the country to try and bring students, too, over to his side in the boycott.

"It's been five months; how effective have you been?" he was asked.

His answer went back to Alabama and the famed Montgomery bus boycott that propelled Martin Luther King Jr. into the forefront of Black leadership.

"That boycott wasn't won overnight," Jesse said. "It took nine months and, at first, there was opposition. A lot of people have no sense of history, and they believe that Rosa Parks just sat down and Martin made a speech and that was all it took, but that was a nine-month struggle."

He used that to point out that the Montgomery boycott was conducted just for the right of Blacks to sit on the bus. "Not to drive the buses or paint the buses or buy them or repair them. It was just for the most basic expression: the right to sit on the buses. But what we're talking about now is boycotting to change the economic order, and as we move toward opening the doors of corporate America, we cannot put a timetable on it."

He entered the club yesterday dressed in a tailored three-piece suit that was light gray. As he stood on the platform that entertainers use, he was impressive in the arguments he made. It brought back another time. He has hit on something. There is soundness in the arguments he makes. He says it is time to quit begging. He says there is no need to beg, not if you get your fair share from these huge corporations that turn such huge profits. He mentions all of the money the corporations spend. He says it cannot all be spent in the same place, which brings him to what he calls trade agreements.

It has become his toughest fight. After he met with reporters, he went upstairs to a luncheon with the promoters. Before they ate, he led a prayer. "Thank you for life, for living, and a chance to grow," he said. "Give us the tenacity to hold on until daylight comes. And as we go to battle, protect our soldiers because there may be some casualties."

1983

IT'S TOO GOOD TO TURN away from. The fallout from the upset Rep. Harold Washington scored in the Democratic mayoral primary in Chicago is everywhere and it's not settled yet.

To see it best, though, you go to Washington, D.C., which is what I did last week.

It was downright funny the way the Chicago election came barging in to the office of Rep. Charles B. Rangel, the Manhattan Democrat, one sunny afternoon.

Rangel has grown up to become a wily old politician. In the middle of this particular afternoon, he had a delegation of folks in his office who came to give him some of their ideas about the restructuring of Social Security. He was on his feet behind his desk when the phone interrupted the Social Security talk.

"You have to excuse me; I have to take this call," the congressman said as he picked up the phone.

"Mr. Vice President," he said to Walter F. Mondale on the other end of the line. "You caught me at a bad time. I'm right in the middle of the meeting and ..."

The telephone conversation didn't end, though, and soon the words the congressman began to use indicated that Mondale was calling to talk about Chicago and the mess he was in because of his role in the mayoral primary. It was a part of the fallout.

In the primary, Mondale jumped out and endorsed Richard J. Daley's son. It had something to do with Mayor Jane Byrne endorsing Sen. Edward Kennedy in the presidential primary over Jimmy Carter and Mondale. Mondale's explanation is that he was paying off a debt to young Daley. But he's catching hell because Washington beat both Daley and Byrne in the primary. That left Mondale calling Rangel for help and advice.

"It's always nice to talk to you," Rangel said as he put the phone down, a sheepish grin on his face.

"I don't like to do that," he said. "I wasn't trying to embarrass the vice president, but that was the third time he called today. I had to take the call."

Later that afternoon Rangel was questioned about Mondale's call.

"It was insanity for him to get involved in that primary," he said. "I told him that he should be calling Washington."

"What did Mondale say?" Rangel was asked.

"He said he's been calling him but he said Washington won't return his calls." And Rangel had to laugh. "It's bigger than Chicago now," he said, and what he meant was that Mondale's role in the primary could wind up dealing a devastating blow to his front-running position for the Democratic nomination in 1984.

Chicago has put the Black vote front and center now. It is not that voters who are Black are about to sweep elections across the country. As Rangel says, "The geographic layout in Chicago isn't something we enjoy in a lot of other cities." But the fallout from what happened in Chicago is everywhere in the nation's capital, especially among Democrats, and it hasn't settled yet.

On the afternoon Mondale was burning up the telephone line to Rangel's office, Tip O'Neill, the speaker of the House, was trying to do his part to head off another potentially explosive problem for the Democrats. That has to do with the general election in Chicago. In elections past, winning the Democratic nomination was tantamount to winning the election, but that is something that is not at all certain this time around.

House Speaker Tip O'Neill knows this to be true, and he sent a letter to Washington. "The national Democratic Party has a great stake in helping you win the general election. As the Democratic leader in the House of Representatives, I am offering you my full support in your efforts. Please let me know how I can be helpful."

What O'Neill was reacting to were reports going around in Chicago that Rep. Washington, who is Black, will not have the support of some Democratic leaders in the general election against Republican Bernard Epton.

"It has a lot to do with how Washington postures himself in the next six weeks," Rep. Dan Rostenkowski (D-Ill) said.

"What does Harold Washington have to do to win in the general election?" Rostenkowski was asked.

"He is going to have to temper the Black community and convince the White community, and that is not going to be an easy task," he said. "I just hope that Harold understands that he's a candidate and he should be asking people to help him."

"Do you think it's possible that Washington could be beaten?"

"I know it's possible," he said.

In the days before the primary an old newspaperman I know said that something heavy was building. "I haven't seen this much excitement in the Black community since Joe Louis fought Jimmy Braddock for the heavyweight crown at Comiskey Park." Now, in Chicago, they call the election "a political riot" and the fallout is everywhere.

Editor's Note.

While Jesse Jackson had been considering a race for the Democratic nomination for president for some time, what he termed the "insult" of leading White Democrats' failure to endorse Harold Washington's bid to become the first Black mayor of Chicago was the catalyst that launched Jackson into the race.

1983

IT IS STILL JUST AN IDEA in the talking stage, but suddenly, the talk is coming fast and furious. Indications were that a Black presidential candidacy in the 1984 Democratic primaries is an idea whose time has come.

The idea itself is an old one, one that goes back to 1972 and the national Black political convention held in Gary, Ind. In Gary, the idea didn't take hold. Blacks did not unite on a presidential candidate.

As it turned out, though, in the 1972 Democratic primaries, Rep. Shirley Chisholm, a Black woman from Brooklyn, did make a run for the presidency. In her race, Chisholm won more than 100 convention votes but hers was not looked on as a Black candidacy in the sense that is being discussed now.

Chisholm, now retired from politics, ran on her own. Her campaign was to be identified more with women's issues than with Black issues. Partly because of that, she never received across-the-board support from Black leadership.

What is being discussed now is something that has never happened. Now, the idea is to offer a Black candidate in the primaries, a candidate who would run as a populist, with hopes of winning a block of votes large enough to wield real influence in the selection of the Democratic candidate and the shaping of the platform that candidate would run on.

For several months now, at various locations around the country, a small group of Black political and civil rights leaders has been meeting and discussing the idea. It is still not a go. It is still just talk. But the idea is taking hold and growing.

The recent mayoral primary in Chicago figures into it. The stunning upset that Rep. Harold Washington scored in the Democratic primary is evidence of the increasing participation by Blacks in elective politics. And it is not just Chicago.

Black voter registration and voter turnout are on the rise. In the elections last fall, the Black vote was crucial in electing Democrats in governorships in New York and Texas. In Illinois, the Black turnout almost led to the heavily favored Republican governor being upset.

As a result of last fall's vote, the Congressional Black Caucus grew from 18 members to 21. In state legislatures, Blacks gained 17 more seats. Across the country there are now Black mayors in close to 100 cities. In Black communities, voter registration continues to grow.

The idea of a presidential candidate is a flexing of newfound muscle and a reflection of the frustration Blacks in the Democratic Party feel.

The frustration is in the figures, which show that Blacks, in the last three presidential elections, have given over 85 percent of their votes to the Democratic nominee. In all, according to Black elected officials, this accounts for 20 percent of the Democratic vote. The complaint that comes from Black leadership is that Blacks support the Democrats but that the Democrats do not, in turn, support the issues that concern Blacks, or Black Democratic candidates, as was shown in Harold Washington's mayoral election. It is the kind of argument that allows the idea of a Black presidential candidacy in the primaries to take hold.

In a speech here last December, Rep. John Conyers (D-Mich.) said it was time for Blacks in Congress to begin to take risks. He said that each year the Congressional Black Caucus offers an alternative budget but said that it is routinely dismissed. He spoke of the ongoing effort to get a meaningful jobs bill through Congress but, he said, those efforts always end in rejection.

In his New York speech, Conyers did not mention a Black presidential candidate but the idea was building.

"What good does it do us to be here in a Democratic-controlled Congress," Rep. Louis Stokes (D-Ohio) asked, "and we cannot get these pressing problems that confront Black people addressed through legislation sponsored by the Democratic Party?"

Stokes asked another question: "How do you say to Black people that their legitimate aspirations should be manifest through a Black candidate for President of the United States?"

The move by Black elected officials takes on added significance because at the same time, across the country voter registration among Latinos is also on the rise. Gov. Tony Anaya, of New Mexico, said the effort now is to double the Latino registration in the country to seven million.

"It's time for us to renegotiate the agreement with the Democratic Party," the Rev. Jesse Jackson said, and his suggestion was that fielding a Black presidential candidate was the proper route. He compared presidential politics to football, "The primaries are the regular season," he said. "The (nominating) convention is the Super Bowl. When we get to the Super Bowl, the best we can hope for is a ticket to get in if there are any left."

The discussions concerning a Black presidential candidate involve a who's who in Black leadership. Included are Jackson, former Manhattan Borough President Percy E. Sutton, Atlanta Mayor Andrew Young, District of Columbia delegate Walter E. Fauntroy, Stokes, Los Angeles Mayor Tom Bradley, Mayor Richard G. Hatcher of Gary. Ind., M. Carl Holman of the National Urban Coalition, the Rev. Joseph E. Lowery of the Southern Christian Leadership Conference, and Coretta Scott King.

"It's not an empty, symbolic gesture," Jesse Jackson said. "We'll win our self-respect if we don't win anything else."

1983

ONCE THE MOMENT CAME, he turned away from his words. He had intended to come ever so close to saying that he, too, was a presidential candidate. He had intended to do it here, in the sweltering heat, before the huge March on Washington crowd at the Lincoln Memorial.

In the early afternoon it became his turn to address the crowd. He stood where Martin Luther King Jr. had stood 20 years before. He needed only to say the words, and this would become his moment. He moved through his speech. An air of expectation hung over the crowd.

"Run Jesse, run", came the chant.

He moved closer. He brought his words to politics. "David has unused rocks," he said. "The Rainbow Coalition has promise and power," he continued. "What do I mean?" he shouted.

In the brilliant sunlight, Jesse Jackson stood on the edge. But on this humid afternoon, in a setting like no other, he turned away. He left the words unsaid.

He called the nation-wide response among Blacks to the idea of his running for president "most gratifying." "In just four months we've gone from the ridiculous to the rational." He said he has found that running for office is in itself a strategy. "The fact is," he said, "the more traditional the approach, the lower the turnout." He used Chicago and the mayoral race as his example. "Many disgruntled Democrats have an option now -- the Rainbow Coalition," he said.

He is filled with the fever of making a run for the Democratic presidential nomination. "We have 10 percent (in the polls), and we're moving up," he said.

"Why did you abandon the words in your speech?" he was asked.

"It wasn't appropriate," he explained.

He had left the speakers platform. Now, he stood in the shadows behind the Lincoln Memorial. A crowd had moved with him. They pressed in close to hear his words. "There will be many other forums available to project the political agenda for 1984," the Rev. Jesse Jackson said.

But earlier, once he finished with his speech, a familiar shout rose from the crowd. "Run Jesse, run," were the words. They were repeated over and over again.

1983

ON THE AFTERNOON, HE WAS in Harlem for the congressional hearing on police brutality, Jesse Jackson walked through a few blocks of Lenox Ave.

No sound truck announced his presence. No advance man lined up crowds. It was just Jesse on the sidewalk and, in the afternoon that day, it became clear just how much the idea of Jesse running for the presidency has caught on among the Black masses.

On Lenox Ave., he was awarded the kind of celebrity attention usually reserved for Richard Pryor or Stevie Wonder. It was one more bit of evidence that said something special is coming together around Jesse Jackson's candidacy.

Jesse is back in New York today. He will be in the city most of the week and when he leaves, he wants one thing said: He's just registered 250,000. "Registration," Jesse says, "is my first mission."

In New York this week, Jesse is leading the kind of voter registration effort that has never before been seen in this city. In the south, the hope is that registration will produce at least one Black congressman elected from each Southern state. What would be the impact of 10 Blacks, coupled with the loss of 10 boll weevils (conservative southern Democrats)?

North Carolina was an example he used. He said the state also has 505,000 unregistered Blacks. "If those Blacks were registered, at the minimum we're talking about two Black congressmen from North Carolina."

Jesse asks: "What does 4 million new players on the field mean?"

He has carved out a piece of space for himself. "It's not important that I'm the first one across the finish line. It's (his presidential race) about public negotiation for parity, not a private deal for a job. The absence of Reagan does not mean parity, but if we empower Blacks and Hispanics at the bottom, they will change things at that top."

For now, the important round is New York. It begins in Brooklyn this morning. Tomorrow it is the Bronx, and then Queens. And the idea, as Jesse said, is to come away from the week and say: We just registered 250,000. It is the important part of Run, Jesse, Run.

Voter registration, it is the big piece of Run, Jesse, Run.

"The race is not about one person running for the White House," Jackson says. "The race is about one wagon pulling a lot of other people to other houses. It's about how many new voters are pulled, how many Congress people win, how many state legislators win."

Registration is key. Jesse says critics look at the lack of Black registration as something wrong with us. He says nothing is said of what he calls "the disincentive factors." He speaks of "ego castration" and talks of how that leads to "many levels of frustration." In turn, he says that what happens is "Blacks end up spreading misery instead of spreading miracles."

Jesse sees his job as turning all of that around. "The hope of our people is very important," he said.

One morning last week, Jesse was in New York. He told a room crowded with reporters, almost all of them Black, of the race he is certain to make. "We're in the last phase of exploration now. This is a major, major decision."

Now, Jesse believes the time is right. "There is an upswing factor in Black America," he said. He mentioned the political victories Blacks won in Chicago and Philadelphia. He mentioned the Black astronaut and the Black woman who won the Miss America title. He said each of these has, to some degree, overcome the media image of Blacks. "They project us as being more violent than we are, as being less hard-working than we are, as being less intelligent than we are."

It is all a part of his building a climate for his race in the Democratic presidential primaries. "We have to know what is at stake so we can be inspired to fight," he says.

Then, he comes to his figures:

"In Mississippi, Reagan won by 11,000. We (the voter registration crusade) put 40,000 new voters on the board. Ronald Reagan won Massachusetts by 2,500. The state has 50,000 unregistered Blacks. Pennsylvania was won by 300,000. Pennsylvania has 600,000 unregistered Blacks. Reagan won New York by 137,000. New York has 900,000 unregistered Blacks."

1983

HE MENTIONS A MOMENT from Saturday because it does not go away. He was in Trenton. As he moves closer to the announcement that he is a candidate for president of the United States, his family moves with him. It was that way in the afternoon on Saturday in the moment he heard the chilling words and everything froze.

"Get down," was the shout. "Hit the floor," was the order.

He was grabbed and pushed. Once his attention came into focus, he was on the floor. His eyes were looking into the eyes of his oldest son, Jesse Jackson Jr., who was on the floor alongside him.

It had been a false alarm. There had been no real threat, but afterward, as the Rev. Jesse Jackson said, "It was a heavy moment."

He understands what he is getting into, but he keeps moving forward. Tomorrow, in Washington, he will make it official. He will announce that he is in the race for the presidential nomination of the Democratic Party.

He is not the first Black American to run for the presidency. He is not even the only Black in the race now. But never before in the history of the republic has a Black man with the kind of support that Jesse Jackson has mounted a presidential campaign.

"It's a dangerous mission," he said.

It is late to be starting a presidential campaign. The primaries are just around the corner, and Jackson finds himself putting pieces of an organization in place, and raising money. "But this campaign is different," he said. He said his hope is to develop a crusade because, as he added, "crusades have a history of beating campaigns." He is testing themes, sifting for pieces. "We intend to struggle for as many delegates as we can, everywhere that we can," he said.

"What is it that sets you apart from the others in the race?" he was asked.

"They want to provide social service," he said. "We need social change. They want the state Democratic Parties to endorse them; we want the state Democratic Parties to open up."

He seems sure of his ground. It was that way, even when the question was money. He told a story from Chicago. In the mayoral race there, he said, incumbent Mayor Jane Byrne had $12 million for her campaign, Richard J. Daley had 4 million, and "Harold Washington didn't even have $1 million." He said he made his point.

"No, I can't compete with them (the other candidates) in raising money," he said. "But they can't compete with me in raising issues."

He is about to take the words, *Run, Jesse, Run*, and make them real, and yesterday, in the afternoon, he was starting out in New York. He said, "It's about empowerment which leads to improvement." The picture that stuck in his mind, though, was the one from Saturday and the way he found himself looking into the eyes of his son.

Never before has a Black man with the kind of support that Jesse Jackson has mounted a presidential campaign.

"It's a dangerous mission," he said.

As president of Operation Push, his Chicago-based organization, Jesse had developed a relationship with just about every segment of the Black community. Nowhere was that relationship more special than with businessmen. A part of it stems from the agreements (he calls them trade agreements) Jesse has been signing with major corporations. In those pacts, corporations agree to do more business with the Black community. Those relationships are a part of what is being tapped into now in Jesse's budding campaign.

All this is the new Black talent, wealth and influence that is coming into the campaign. It is a flowering of successes from another time, the old civil rights movement. All of it is a part of what makes Jesse Jackson's run now so different.

And it is taking hold. A recent ABC-TV poll showed that Jesse's approval rating among Blacks rose from 30 percemt in June to 36 percent in September and was at 46 percent by mid October. And it is not a campaign for the Black vote only that Jesse Jackson is running. He keeps coming back to the words, Rainbow Coalition, and he says his campaign, if nothing else, will move to give life to the words.

"At every level," he said, "the campaign has got to represent the rainbow, male and female. We are going to make functional the Rainbow Coalition."

It's an old idea that comes back now with the words, Rainbow Coalition. The idea says that change can be brought to society, but only if there is a coming together that gets beyond race, sex, and sexual orientation, and the other things in society that pit one group against another.

1983

THE NIGHT BEFORE, **IN HARLEM**, he stood in the pulpit of the Abyssinian Baptist Church. He had one more speech. It would be there, at Abyssinian. Then he would move on to Washington and, as he said, launch our movement. He could find no place more appropriate than Abyssinian. It is a church 175 years old, older than any Baptist church in all of New York, and on this night, it was perfect for the Rev. Jesse Jackson because he was standing in the doorway of history.

On this night of history there were no seats left in the church, and many stood in long rows along the walls. Nearly all of the faces were Black, and there was in Abyssinian an air of electricity.

The young minister, the Rev. Calvin O. Butts, associate pastor at Abyssinian, recalled that at another time, from this same pulpit, the political career of Adam Clayton Powell Jr. was launched.

Now it was the Rev. Jesse Jackson. The movement he spoke of was a drive to win the presidential nomination of the Democratic party. He piled on names: Dr. Randall Forsberg, director of the Institute for Defense and Disarmament Strategy, Vern Bellecourt, of the American Indian Movement, former Attorney General Ramsey Clark and Lars Isaacson, president of the Student Association of the State University of New York. Those were only some of the ones who stood with Jesse yesterday and made the idea of a Rainbow Coalition more than just words.

By the first hour of the afternoon, it was Shirley Chisholm of Brooklyn who was at the microphone. She went back 11 years, to the presidential campaign of 1972 and her candidacy. She had been the first Black woman since Reconstruction to sit in the House of Representatives. Eleven years ago she tried for the Democratic Party's nomination. Now, she looked to Jesse's candidacy. She said, "This is a part of the continuity."

It was all history. "We are about to reach a plateau, a turning point, a crossroads," she said. "The Rainbow Coalition is moving to finalize its awesome potential at the highest level," she said.

At 12:20 in the afternoon, Shirley Chisholm handed the moment to Jesse Jackson. "A new day in national politics unfolds at this moment," she said. There was an explosion of noise that became *Run, Jesse, Run*. He stood at the center of the platform in a dark suit. His words from Abyssinian in Harlem from the night before came into focus. "We must get bigger than ourselves."

It was possible in the convention center yesterday to hear many echoes in his voice.

"So again, the gauntlet of destiny has been tossed to a new generation."

"Let peace be written in the sky."

It is different now. The campaign of 1984 is, from this point on, set apart. It is what Jesse and the promise of the Rainbow Coalition together have done. It could be seen here yesterday, in Washington.

The day before, at historical Abyssinian, as keynote speaker at the 41st convention of the National Council of Negro Women, Jesse reached back for one more piece of support that would be the strength to lean on. He came to the front of the pulpit with Dorothy Height, the organization's president, at one side of him and at the other, Betty Shabazz, the widow of Malcolm X.

"It's an opportunity, it's our challenge," he said. "You can do anything with a made-up mind. We cannot wallow in yesterday's achievements. Give us this day to go a step higher."

He looked out from the pulpit. With his voice rising, he said, "At this moment in history, we are called on to be great, to get bigger than ourselves. All of us cannot be famous, but we can all be great because we are called to serve."

Applause exploded for him in the church. But what stuck in the mind was the call he made for Black people to get bigger than themselves because, as he said, history demands it.

"This is our challenge at this hour," he said. "We must use our numbers and make up our minds. Our time has come."

Then he went out into the night. That was the way he left Abyssinian and Harlem, and moved to the moment of launching what he called "our movement."

By mid-morning, the huge convention center here in Washington began to fill. The entrance that Jesse Jackson would make into the presidential race would be like no other. It would be part theater, part church, part crusade.

He had said that his would not be a Black campaign. Instead, it would be an effort of what he called the Rainbow Coalition. As he moved to his announcement, it was the Rainbow that he showed. He had an audience of thousands there in the convention center awaiting his announcement. He had, too, an enormous press corps. But the way Jesse staged it, before anything else was to move, he would show that there was, indeed, a Rainbow Coalition in the making.

He showed it with the endorsements that came from White farmers, Hispanic, Native American and Asian political leaders, as well as a former U.S. Cabinet member, Ramsey Clark , Lyndon Johnson's Attorney General. It was all history, and it could be seen here yesterday, in Washington.

1983

THE CAMPAIGN THAT IS *Run, Jesse, Run* is back in New York, but it's a little different now. Jesse has some bruises he wasn't showing the last time he was in the city.

It has to do with what happened down in Alabama. The Deep South is supposed to be fertile ground for *Run, Jesse, Run*. But in Alabama, Jackson hooked up with Walter Mondale, and the fact is, Jesse took a licking.

The fight was for the endorsement of the Alabama Democratic Conference. The reason Jesse called the fight is that this is a group of Black Democrats. It turned out to be a big mistake. Democrats are Democrats, and Mondale won it. As a consolation prize, the group gave Jesse its endorsement for vice president. The real damage, though, was that by losing 4-to-1 in Alabama, it gives the impression that Jackson does not have big support in the Black community, which is crucial in his building the "Rainbow Coalition" that is the cornerstone of his campaign.

Late in the afternoon yesterday, the Rev. Jesse Jackson brought the campaign for the presidential nomination of the Democratic Party back to New York. He started out late in the day in Buffalo. This morning, he is supposed to be in Rochester early and then in Syracuse. Tonight, he'll be in Queens, and after moving around on Long Island in the morning, he'll come into the city.

It will be different this time around. On his last visit to New York, he was at the Waldorf, and big-shot New York had his attention. Tomorrow, he will be in Harlem and in Brooklyn. It says he learned something from the licking he took down in Alabama.

A reporter who was with Jesse in Alabama when he went before the Black Democrats there to try to win their endorsement, said that the speech he gave was his best of the campaign. It was a speech so good that glimpses of it were snatched and shown later on television. Jesse can make a speech, but that was already known. The lesson of Alabama is that words alone, no matter how eloquent, do not change anything.

What sticks in the mind now is something that Jesse said in New York about a month before he announced that he was going after the presidential nomination. He had a group of reporters in a room. He was explaining that his race was important, not because he might win, but because of what his candidacy could do to arouse the energy it takes to put on the books the big numbers of Blacks in the country who are still unregistered voters.

"If I get over the finish line first, and my wagon is empty, we still lose," he said.

He said that if the registration rises, then everything else changes too. "Because then, we can elect sheriffs and tax collectors and congressmen and councilmen." And he went on, and it came into focus that this was the basis for the real excitement in *Run, Jesse, Run*.

But in Alabama, Jesse went the other way. He got into a contest with Mondale that made no sense. In Alabama too, Jesse's wagon getting across the finish line first was not enough. In Alabama too, it is about putting the unregistered on the books. It has nothing to do with trying to beat out Walter Mondale for an endorsement.

In Buffalo last night, Jesse started out on Fillmore St., which is a big name in the Black community. His schedule has him working his base down the state right into the heart of Bedford Stuyvesant in Brooklyn, which is the largest Black community in the United States.

Nobody puts it in the newspapers or on television, but in Brooklyn, there are so many Black people that once a year, when they throw that big parade, the one that highlights the West Indian festival, they have, by conservative count, two million Black people on the streets.

New York also has something else: It has a million unregistered Blacks. It also has a half million unregistered Hispanics. On Sunday, Jesse starts out early, meeting first with Puerto Rican leaders and then coordinators of his campaign in the Latin community. This time around in New York he is working his base.

But no, it is not the same as it was the last time he was in town. Jesse has got some bruises on him now.

What does it mean? It means the Rev. Jesse Jackson learned a powerful lesson about politics down there in Alabama. The lesson was that, in civil rights, a big speech can sometimes move people, but in politics, it takes organizing. The way you can tell he learned this is by the attention he is paying now to organizing his base.

1984

JUST A FEW DAYS BEFORE the New Hampshire primary, there was some criticism of Jesse's decision.

"You should stay here and campaign," he was advised.

Jesse saw it another way. "There's going to be a crowd of 2,000 in Chicago," he argued. "It's going to be very big."

The crucial decision was made. Jesse Jackson flew to Chicago and joined Louis Farrakhan at the Muslim's Saviours' Day celebration.

Farrakhan was not supposed to speak. It was to be Jesse's night. He would address the big crowd.

The idea was that it would be a big move toward bringing the Black Muslims into the kind of traditional politics the organization always had shunned.

Farrakhan then was still an all-but-anonymous figure in the Jackson campaign. Before that night was over, that was to change in a very dramatic way.

Louis Farrakhan rose to make the introduction. It was to turn into a speech that would have a stunning impact on Jesse's campaign.

Farrakhan spoke of threats that had been made against the candidate.

"And I am not going to let our brother go down into the valley of the shadow by himself," Farrakhan said.

Then, his voice rising with anger, he called out his warning: "My Jewish friends," he said. "If you harm this brother (Jesse), it will be the last one you harm."

"We can afford to lose an election," he said, "but we cannot afford to lose this brother."

He said that if anything happened to Jackson, the Jewish community would be held responsible.

When Farrakhan sat down, it was Jesse's turn, but nothing Jesse said that night sticks in the mind. Farrakhan took the moment.

He rose from here to become a focal point in the campaign. After that night, every word he uttered was scrutinized.

Last week, Jesse Jackson broke with Louis Farrakhan.

There was only one moment that Jesse seemed weary. He had just finished with his meeting in Nicaragua. He had won the promise of a region-wide summit meeting.

The Sandanista government had set a firm date for elections. Jackson's "moral offensive" for peace had made some progress.

It figured to be a good time for him.

It did not work out that way. Even in Central America he was dogged by the words of Louis Farrakhan.

From Nicaragua, he was returning to Cuba and he knew that Castro was planning another warm welcome.

But it was Farrakhan that occupied his thoughts.

He had been on the phone to his office in Washington. A statement had been drafted. He had taken that and reworked the words again and again, until he had the language he wanted. It all had to do with making the break with Farrakhan.

Over the phone, it had been laid out for him. Farrakhan's speech was detailed, but more than that, he was told of the rising backlash.

It was all coming back. Walter Mondale was being pressured to break with him. There was an effort building to keep him from addressing the convention.

He felt that he had no choice.

He had promised his supporters that at the convention, that "this time around," it would be different. He built whole speeches around that remark.

"This time around, we'll be on the inside," he would say. "This time around, we'll have our say." Now it was all threatened. Farrakhan's words were standing in the way.

In Washington, it was not the moral offensives that was discussed. Instead, it was the break Jesse was making with Louis Farrakhan's words.

It all goes back to last winter. It began back then on a cold night in Chicago when Louis Farrakhan made a promise to the group he called "my Jewish friends."

1984

GENIUS. IT'S GENIUS THE WAY they have taken the outrageous thing the reporter did, covered it over, and made it a badge of honor.

The reporter is Milton Coleman of the Washington Post. Milton is a veteran in the business -- by many standards, a good reporter. He is dogged. There is nothing that comes past him that he will not put in the newspaper. He has all that on the record he has made for himself. Digging up information and getting it published. That's a reporter's job. On that score, Milton comes out all right. In his work on the presidential campaign, Milton messed up. He did the kind of thing that can get a reporter in very serious trouble. But now, the history of Milton and the campaign of 1984 is being tampered with. At the Sheraton Centre on Wednesday night, Sen. Edward Kennedy, who ought to know better, got involved in tampering with the facts.

This was at the dinner for Basil Patterson. Mostly, it was a good speech that Kennedy made. But with Milton, he was all wrong. He said the Washington Post reporter's life was threatened just for doing his job, and that was not the truth. First, Milton Coleman was not threatened. More importantly, he got into trouble because he broke some basic rules of newspaper reporting. The genius now is the way it's being turned around.

Milton agreed to sit down in an off-the-record discussion with Jesse Jackson. It's a reporter's way of saying to a source: okay, this conversation is not taking place. It's the rule. Good reporters usually want no part of the off-the-record talk. They do not want secrets to carry around in their pockets. They want information on the record, which is valuable, because it's information that can be used.

Milton took Jesse's private talk and put it in his pocket. He carried it around for nearly a month. He then took that information and handed it to another Washington Post reporter. That reporter took the information and dropped it down in one of the more controversial stories The Post published involving Jackson. It was just a word. Hymie. Milton told another reporter that in an off-the-record conversation, presidential candidate Jesse Jackson used the word Hymie when referring to Jews.

"... Just doing his job," Senator Kennedy said. No, he wasn't just doing his job. Milton could have come away from this conversation with Jesse and gone straight to his typewriter. He could have leveled with his readers. He could have said, I know I shouldn't be writing this. I know our conversation was off-the-record, but this is too important, I can't keep this silent. This, readers, you ought to know.

Milton could have done it that way. He could also have taken that off-the-record conversation, and could have done what a good reporter would have done. He could have dogged Jesse, stayed right on because, if that was the language that Jesse used in private, before long it would have come out another way and the reporter would have it clean, on the record. Then, there would be truth in Kennedy's words, "...He was just doing his job."

Anytime a reporter sucks up to a source, takes information off-the record and then uses that information, the reporter is asking for trouble. That is rule No. 1. It has nothing to do with race. Being Black doesn't figure into it; no way at all.

Genius. Just change the rules. Make the reporter a hero. Don't even bother to ask what other off-the-record information did Washington Post reporters pick up during the campaign.

As for the threat that Kennedy mentions, that, too, is turned around. It's said the threat came from Louis Farrakhan of the Nation of Islam. Authorities investigated, but no threat was found. The reporters who heard Farrakhan denounce Milton in a public speech didn't believe any threat was made. But in the rewriting of history that is taking place now, it keeps coming back as a threat to the Black reporter.

Milton Coleman made a mistake. He caught a lot of heat for the mistake he made, which is exactly what he should expect considering what it was that he did. It's genius, though, the way it's all being turned around. It's genius or a damn big coverup.

1984

IN ALL, THERE WERE THREE PIECES of his day and, together, they tell a story of the way Jesse Jackson's strategy and direction have begun to shift. It's still early, but it might be the first hint that the climate is right for Blacks to begin an exodus from the Democratic Party in wholesale numbers.

Jesse never mentioned an exodus, and he made no threats. But in the three pieces of his day on Monday, it was easy to see that his strategy and direction are shifting.

Late in the afternoon, he was on a train, moving from New York to Philadelphia. "I'm not going to argue about it anymore," he said. "If the Democrats want 22 percent of the vote to be 7 percent of the delegates, then...it means two thirds of our people are unrepresented. But let the convention decide. Let the nation see, and let the chips fall where they may."

It was a part of the shift in strategy. Jesse has 300 delegates. He believes he ought to have many more, at least 600, but he has decided now to push his fight no more. Instead, he is ready to lose on the floor of the convention, and that ties in with another piece of his day on Monday.

At night, he was in a hotel room in Philadelphia. In the Pennsylvania primary, he carried Philadelphia. He did it even though Wilson Goode, the newly elected Black mayor of the city, supported Walter Mondale. In the hotel room, Jesse stood before the delegates, his suit jacket off, his tie loose and his voice soft.

"This thing we represent, it cannot be pulled back any more," he said. "We're early in the morning in where we have to go, so one of my appeals to you is to carry this toughness. We may leave there (the convention) naked as jaybirds, but we'll have our self respect. They (the Democrats) may get our vote (in November) but not our enthusiasm. It depends on how they treat us. We're going to get some seats, but we made an impact when we had no seats. The ball is in their court. What shall they do? But our self-respect, we'll have that."

In the hotel room, he began to recite the words of the old movement song: "Before I'll be a slave, I'll be buried in my grave, and go home to my Lord and be free."

It was the piece that had a message to the party. "We intend to concentrate on local races," he said. "It may be that we are paying too much attention to the presidential race." It ties in with the other words he used: "They (Democrats) will have our vote but not our enthusiasm."

1984

IT'S ANOTHER TROPHY FOR JESSE. Don't expect Mondale or any of the other bigwigs in the party to admit it, but it was the Rev. Jesse Jackson who got a woman on the Democratic ticket.

Jesse never backed off. From the time he came into the race, he carried arguments that said the party's vice presidential candidate ought to be a woman. He was so strong, so effective in pushing the ideas, that the women's movement picked up on it. And the idea took hold.

But it's Jesse's trophy, and right behind him comes Geraldine Ferraro. Once the idea of a woman on the ticket began to take root, it put her into a position to be noticed. It wasn't that she stood up to the scrutiny. She flourished.

When the spotlight was on her, she put meaning to the words that Jesse Jackson used in the pulpit of the Abyssinian Baptist Church in Harlem on the night before he went to Washington and announced his candidacy.

"We must get bigger than ourselves," he said. It was that way with Geraldine Ferraro.

"She's from Queens; what has she ever done?" a critic asked yesterday.

It is not the record of her time in Congress that has her on the ticket. Her record counts, but the crucial performance was the one that she gave when the attention of the country was focused on her. She came away from that looking and sounding better than any of the men or the other women who were mentioned as possible running mates for Walter Mondale. She earned her selection. She won it, and so now, our best election in 25 years has the possibility of getting even better. Just having Geraldine Ferraro on the ticket does that.

She is like Jesse now. Her name is in the history books. Like Jesse, she gets there by being first. But it's also a big shot that she has.

It is not possible to put a finger on any one quality and say, this is what makes a leader. But there are some who have it, and others don't. Jesse Jackson has it. Ronald Reagan has it. And if the glimpse of what we're seeing now is real, Geraldine Ferraro has it, too.

That leaves Walter Mondale. It seems certain now that the Democratic Party's presidential ticket will be Mondale and Ferraro. It's not bad. The only problem is, it's upside down. Mondale is not a No. 1 man. He is not a leader. He was very good as vice president. On a Ferraro-Mondale ticket, he would serve the party well.

But all that is conjecture. The ticket for the Democrats is set. But for the first time in the history of the republic, a major party has a woman on its ticket. It's because of the Rev. Jesse Jackson. It's another of the trophies he brings back from the best election we've had in 25 years.

1993

FOR THE CONGRESSIONAL BLACK CAUCUS, the year of the promise has finally arrived.

This goes back to 1984. That was when the Rev. Jesse Jackson made his first run for President. In that campaign, in his first try at elective politics, Jackson did what many saw as the impossible. He actually won in some 60 congressional districts.

At the time, the Black Caucus in Congress barely had 20 members. So in way, the Jackson race showed what was possible. Eight years later, the moment of promise has arrived.

At present, the caucus has 26 members. That is about to change -- and in the minds of many, change significantly. In the elections of 1992, the ambitious prediction is that the number of Blacks in the Congress could as much as double. That may not happen. What is certain, though, is that the numbers in the Congressional Black Caucus are sure to swell.

Already, discussion has begun as to what the new numbers in the Black Caucus will mean in the Congress. All the new Blacks will be Democrats and allied with the progressive wing of the party. Once that block of votes becomes more than 40, it becomes enough to have a deciding impact on a lot of close votes. It becomes enough to set an agenda.

So on Labor Day in Brooklyn, when the West Indian Day parade was the feature, politics played more than a passing role. At the center of it was Jesse Jackson and mostly, his concern centered on the congressional race in the 10th district. What Jackson stressed was the importance of the race involving Edolphus (Ed) Towns.

It used to be that once a Black was elected to the Congress, that seat belonged to the person for as long as he (or she) wanted the office. In 1982, Towns won election in Brooklyn. Since then, he was reelected every two years. It seemed that he was on the verge of establishing the kind of seniority that makes a congressman especially important to a district. This year, he came to reelection not just as a favorite but, also, holding the important credential as being chairman of the Congressional Black Caucus.

What was supposed to be a shoo-in for him, though, has turned into a fight. He is opposed by Susan Alter, a member of the City Council. Had Towns been in his old district, it would be different. But redistricting recarved the lines and has made a race where there was not supposed to be any real fight. So on Labor Day, Jackson huddled with virtually all important political figures in Brooklyn, and the reminder from Jesse had to do with just what is at stake in the congressional race involving Towns.

At a time when the Black Caucus appears on the verge of gaining real muscle, to lose a veteran such as Towns would be more than just a blow. In the words of Jackson, it would amount to a serious step in the wrong direction.

The new 10th district has a makeup that is 57 percent Black. It also has some 24 percent White voters, 20 percent Hispanic and about 2 percent Asian. In recent days, Towns forces have accused Alter of attempting to win by using questionable racial tactics. They have latched onto one particular piece of campaign literature that shows two brains, one of normal size and the other, peanut size. "We know what that means," a Towns campaign spokesman said yesterday. "It is trying to send a racial code that says something is wrong with the brains of Blacks." In the literature, beneath the small brain is the notation that says: "Size of brain Edolphus Towns gives you credit for having."

What has hurt Towns, though, in the minds of some observers, is not the Alter campaign but, rather, the lack of the entire Black community being enthusiastic about his reelection. And that was where Jesse Jackson came in; he served to rally the Blacks around Towns with the reminder that this is not just another race.

The complaint against Towns is that he has not been strong enough. The other side is that he is on the verge of gaining serious seniority. The Alter race is a sort of wake up call; it has sent the message that just being Black is not enough. In the new, larger Congressional Black Caucus, constituents have greater expectations.

Chapter Six, Part One

CAIN AND ABEL

BLACKS AND JEWS

Editor's Note

Although racial conflict in America is as old as the Spaniards' landfall in the hemisphere, many observers believe that the tenures of Ronald Reagan as President and Ed Koch as mayor of New York ushered an especially violent phase of racial and ethnic conflict throughout the nation, as well as in that great city.

Often bloody racial conflicts began to occur throughout America. Nowhere was this trend more pronounced than in New York City: Christians, Jews, Muslims, Blacks, Italians, Koreans, Irish and others -- Americans all -- seemed to be at one another's throats.

Part one of Cain and Abel concerns the explosive relationship between African Americans and Jews.

1979

HE WENT TO WASHINGTON amid all of the talk of his being reprimanded, perhaps even fired. Andrew Young had already taken charge. No longer was he reacting. This was to be his moment. He seized the time.

He had made a decision the night before. At the ambassador's apartment in the tower of the Waldorf-Astoria, Young talked it over with his wife. He understood that it was time for him to resign.

It was late in the evening when he finished speaking with his wife. Young then called his closest aides to ask that they meet him at his office. He dictated his resignation. They put it all down on paper. It was not a decision the secretary of state or even the President would make. This would be Andrew Young's decision.

Now, he was alone in his office. "It was an easy decision," he said. "It really was. I've loved this job, but I've loved every job I've ever had. But I've always known when it was time to move on. I'm free," he said.

He never liked the ambassador's desk, and did not use it now. He sat up front in the office, up near the windows that overlook the United Nations Plaza. He recalled those times in the past when he had been urged to use his resignation as a threat. "But I never played those games," he said. He said that he did not even offer his resignation during that famous cabinet meeting several weeks ago. In response to President Carter's determination to shift his cabinet after declaring a national "malaise," one by one the members of the President's cabinet had raised their hands, signaling that they would resign. But Andrew Young did not play the game. His was the only hand that was not raised.

Though he had been up through most of Tuesday night, he was up early Wednesday for the first shuttle flight to Washington. He had called Jesse Hill, his friend from Atlanta and a presidential confidant. Hill met him when he arrived in Washington. He handed Hill a letter. It was his resignation. He instructed his friend to deliver it to the President.

Andrew Young then made his way to the office of the secretary of state. When he arrived, the first thing that he was to do was put his resignation on the desk. Then, he and Cyrus Vance, the secretary of state, began to talk. While they talked, the President called and asked the ambassador to come to the White House. But it was already done.

"It might have been my pride," he said now. "But I knew I was not going to apologize for anything I'd done. I was not going to put myself in an embarrassing position of recanting or apologizing. That's why I insisted that it could not be the President's decision. I had to decide what was best, and it was best for me to serve this administration as a private citizen."

Thursday was filled with the fallout. The clamor for his resignation had come primarily from the Jewish community. That is fact. The backlash that Andrew Young had warned the Israeli ambassador about what was rising. Downstairs, on the steps of the U.S. mission to the UN, the Rev. Jesse Jackson was saying that Andrew Young was "the fall guy." Jackson took the issue that had been silent, head on -- the issue of the pressure from the Israeli lobby that had led to Young's resignation. Jackson talked about the growing tension between old allies, the Blacks and the Jews. Jesse Jackson had the rhythm of the pulpit working as he stood there on the steps in the sun. He was saying that it was not the Klan that deals with Southern Africa, and that it was not the Klan that brought the pressure to fire Andrew Young. "It was our former allies," and the backlash was building more.

Upstairs Young talked of his relationship with Ambassador Yehuda Blum. He called him a good friend and spoke of the ambassador's young son and how the boy had twice read "Roots," Alex Haley's book, and the conversations they had about it. Young said that he had read "The Holocaust" and he remembered the two of them, him and the boy, discussing the experiences of the Blacks and the Jews. And he was saying now how much the two people share in background and why it is that Blacks expect so much of Jews. "It's not the leaders," he said. "Black and Jewish leaders have always been close. The problem is ... there are others."

He talked about his much-discussed meeting with Ambassador Blum, the meeting where he explained his encounter with Zehdi Terzi, the Palestinian representative at the UN. "He understood it," the American ambassador said. "But they didn't understand it in Israel. They didn't make a decision on the basis of U.S. domestic politics. I tried to warn them. I tried to explain."

So now in the fallout, there are many questions to be answered. Questions about Israeli spying on U.S. officials. Questions about Israeli pressures that are so great they can force an American official from office. And behind that, the rising tensions between old allies.

"I had been running from this one for two and a half years," Andrew Young said. "I didn't want anything to do with the Middle East." Had the Israeli government made a quiet, diplomatic protest of Young's meeting with Terzi instead of going public, there would have been no resignation. "But when it becomes a public issue," Young said, "when the Israelis made it public, it was an issue I couldn't win on. I had become, you know, the problem. I sensed this would become another long flap. The country doesn't need it. The President doesn't need it, and I don't need it."

The irony is that here is a man who in the early days of his tenure as UN ambassador was often criticized for his open, say-what-you-believe style. He was told to be diplomatic. On this issue he was. He played the diplomatic game. He acted the way diplomats do. It got him run out of office.

When he came into office, he was criticized for taking the job. But he made something of it. He made friends for the U.S. where there were none. "My position became powerful," he said, "because I made it powerful." He stood up. He spoke out. But in the end, it cost him his job. "Finally the bureaucracy got me," he said. "Had I played the games, it would have worked out. But the bureaucracy didn't have any vested interest in protecting me."

1979

NOT SINCE THE DEATH OF THE REV. MARTIN LUTHER KING JR. has it been this way. Not in more than a decade has the press paid the kind of attention to Black Americans that it is doing now.

At the center of it is the Southern Christian Leadership Conference. This was King's organization. It was the organization that he founded, and the vehicle he used to become an international figure. After the assassination of King, SCLC fell on hard times. Its support and influence dwindled. When it opened its annual convention in Virginia, it was a gathering that was largely ignored. Then came the sudden resignation of Andrew Young, and everything changed.

Yesterday, the preacher who leads SCLC now, the Rev. Joseph Lowery, stepped into a conference room on the eighth floor of the building in United Nations Plaza occupied by the United Methodist Church.

Rev. Lowery came to the press conference after a long meeting with Israeli representatives to the United Nations.

"We're on the side of human rights for all of God's children," he said. "We're messengers of peace. Violence should come to an end."

Back in the room, the men who were behind the television cameras shoved their competitors. Reporters were on their feet, shouting questions.

"We make no apologies for our support for human rights for the Palestinians," the minister said. "We're asking both sides -- as preachers of the Gospel -- we're saying let's stop the killing, and work out problems. That's our plea. That's our hope."

Rev. Walter E. Fauntroy, the congressman from Washington, D.C., and a longtime leader in the Southern Christian Leadership Conference, spoke next.

"We want peace in the Mideast," he said. "We do not believe we can move toward peace as long as there is violence on either side. We say that we support the nationhood of Israel. And we say that we support the rights of Palestinians."

The press conference did not last long, less than 30 minutes. It ended with only the slightest mention of Andrew Young. But the event was part of the legacy the ambassador leaves behind.

In choosing his moment to quit, Young has picked up Black America. His action has taken Black America off the back burner. His resignation has brought Black Americans together in a way that they have not been in more than a decade.

There is concern now that there is something anti-Jewish rising in Black America. It is partly because Blacks, with the resignation of Young, have begun to reexamine their relationships with Jews. They are looking again at Israel and Israeli policies, particularly those regarding South Africa. But more than anything else, Blacks are speaking out on the Middle East. They are saying, as the Rev. Lowery said, that they have nothing against the Palestinians.

All of it is part of the legacy of Andrew Young. It's not about being anti-Jewish. It's about growing up, and a community whose time has come.

1984

HE WAS THE SAME AS MOST of the others. Before his question, there was a statement. "Nobody talks of the contributions Blacks made to Jews," he said. "Black soldiers in World War II rescued Jews. We were not fighting for Black liberation."

"You've seen the response, evaluated the facts," he began. "Can we now divorce in peace with Jews taking any position they want, and do what we think is best, holding no malice to each other?"

In the front of the room the Rev. Wyatt Tee Walker sat at one end of the table and Nathan Perlmutter was at the other. It was Walker's turn to answer first.

"That so-called division between Blacks and Jews is not reconcilable until the Jewish community goes along with us as we seek our goals and aspirations. But if you won't go, we're going on without you."

Perlmutter's eyes were on the faces of the audience. "We don't have to hold hands," he said. "I'm not even inclined to hold hands with all of you. However, I do know that the basic thrust of Black aspiration is good, and I know the basic voting patterns and attitudes of Jews is good. So we can walk parallel, and I suspect we'll get to the same promised land."

It had gone back and forth for close to two hours. First it was Perlmutter and then Walker. They had as their subject, "Blacks, Jews, Jesse Jackson and other issues," and the exchanges were so sharp they kept the World Room in the journalism building at Columbia University filled with emotion.

"The Klan is being absolved as public enemy No. 1 in the Black community -- and being substituted (is) me," Perlmutter said.

"You who have once been our allies are now over there blocking the door," Walker said. "There are no affirmative-action programs without goals -- or, to use your word, quotas. You have to have something to measure it by. Jews see it as quotas; we see it as opportunity. We insist on what *our* perception is in our best interest."

"I'll continue on Jesse Jackson, and why I'm concerned as a Jew," Perlmutter said. "He says...Zionism is a poisonous weed choking Black aspirations. Anybody sitting in this room that likes that is self-hating."

"It is a fact," Walker said, "there isn't anything Jesse Jackson could have said, or could have done, or can do, or can say to ever get the blessing of the bureaucracy of Jewish organizations. Jesse Jackson, like some of us in the Black community, will no longer bow to the paternalistic treatment that White folks and Jews have historically thrust upon us."

Nathan Perlmutter is national director of the Anti-Defamation League of B'nai B'rith and a leading critic of Jesse Jackson. Wyatt Walker is minister at Canaan Baptist Church in Harlem and prominent in the Jackson for President campaign. The New York Association of Black Journalists brought the two together in a forum last Thursday night. At the end, it all intended to show how much distance and strong feeling there is now between Blacks and Jews. Much of it has to do with Jackson, but another emotional issue has to do with Israel and South Africa.

This was Perlmutter: "I feel that trade with South Africa on the part of Israel and any other nation is undesirable. I would welcome similar criticism of the 46 Black African countries which do 20 times the trade Israel does with South Africa."

Walker: "You misrepresent the case, Nathan. When you talk about 46 nations who trade with South Africa, most of those nations have to do it to survive. Israel does not have to trade with South Africa."

Perlmutter brought up Jackson's reference to Jews as "Hymies."

Walker replied: "Israeli fighter planes are named Kaffir and you're getting upset about Hymie. Kaffir in South Africa means Nigger."

Perlmutter accused Jackson of saying he was tired of hearing about the Holocaust. "Can people who object to the phrase 'benign neglect' understand the concern others have when someone says, 'I'm sick and tired of hearing about the Holocaust'?"

"Jews give the impression nobody had a Holocaust but you," Walker replied. "We have 60 to 90 million dead, a genocide unmatched in the history of mankind."

"Nothing I've said about Jesse Jackson is other than what Jesse Jackson said," Perlmutter added.

"Who decreed that criticism of Jews is off-limits?" Walker said. "My experience has been when you criticize a Jew or Jews, then you get labeled racist or anti-Semitic."

Through most of two hours it went that way. It all served to put into good perspective the relevant question at the end: "Can we now divorce in peace...holding no malice to each other?"

1981

JIM LAWSON WAS READY with his explanation. "I was just telling the truth," he said yesterday. "The only thing I said was that we have five borough presidents and four of them are Jewish. Now is that the truth or isn't it?"

It was a part of the residue from Tuesday's vote. The election itself is history. But in one of many post-election analyses, one of the things being said was that the anti-Semitic charge that Andrew Stein hung on David Dinkins seemed to have made a difference. That was how Jim Lawson got into it.

Jim Lawson is a big, husky-looking guy who is getting up there in years because, as he says himself, he has been working the streets for better than 45 years. He identifies himself as a Black nationalist. You find him on what is still the most famous corner in Harlem -- 125th St. and Seventh Ave. Lawson's spot is next to the old Theresa Hotel. Whatever it is he is peddling at the moment, you find him there.

In the election campaign, once Andrew Stein began to worry that the office of borough president was slipping away from him, he decided he could best help himself by picturing Dinkins, his opponent, as being ant-Semitic. To do it, one of the people he used was Jim Lawson.

In the afternoon yesterday, Lawson was not on his street corner. He said it didn't have anything to do with anti-Semitic charges. He did not back away from the words that he had put in his writing. "I was just saying that we should have some ethnic balance, that's all. If something goes wrong, they (the Jews) are going to get blamed because they don't let anybody else help them rule."

The anti-Semitic charge was also put on Fred Weaver, a newspaper columnist. He writes for the Amsterdam News, the city's oldest Black-owned newspaper. Weaver calls his column "The Lash and Cross" and right under the title, in italics, he says: "You shall know the truth and the truth shall set you free."

In his column published yesterday, one of the things Weaver wrote about was Tuesday's election. In part, he said, "...cries of anti-Semitism are raised if a candidate is described as Jewish but if an opponent is described as Black, that's not racism."

He went back to the ugliness of the campaign to point out how Stein in the closing days kept saying that Dinkins's only excuse for running was that he was Black. "What could be more racist than that?" Weaver wrote. Then he explained what happened to him. "Because we termed him (Stein) a wealthy Jewish politician, we are supposed to be anti-Semitic. Horse manure -- if you know what I mean," he wrote.

It goes back to the 60s, and Albert Shanker, the head of the teachers union, was one of the ones who started it. The issue then was community control of public schools. In the fight, one of the demands was that more principals who were Black should be hired. "Because most of the students were Black," was the logic. When it was pointed out that most of the principals were Jewish, those who said it were tagged by Shanker as being anti-Semitic.

The ant-Semitic charge did not cost David Dinkins the election. He got beat. It was a race almost impossible to win but in the campaign, he did manage to put so much pressure on his opponent that he made him panic and when that happened, the anti-Semitic charge was made. And that was how Jim Lawson and Fred Weaver were brought into it.

"We have five borough presidents and four are Jewish," Jim Lawson said again yesterday. "Is that true or isn't it true? That is the only thing that counts."

In his column Fred Weaver reached back for some of Shakespeare's words and he directed them at Stein and "to anyone else who wants to fight me as anti-Semitic." He wrote: "Lay on, MacDuff, and damn be he who first cries hold enough!"

1983

IN THE LATE AFTERNOON HE SAT in his office, fingering the gray in the hair that framed his face, and shaking his head.

"If someone had said we were going to have a problem when it came to the 20-year anniversary," Albert Chernin said, "I would have said, you're crazy."

It is approaching 20 years since the historic March on Washington. The 1963 march was like no other, not just because of the huge crowd, or because it was to be the scene of Martin Luther King Jr.'s famed "I Have a Dream" speech.

"It's a regrettable issue," Albert Chernin said. "It's a symbol of the fragmentation, of the division in the civil rights movement today."

Albert Chernin is executive vice president of the National Jewish Community Relations Advisory Council. The letter that urged Jewish organizations across the country to shun the anniversary march went out from his office. Today, the council meets in New York and is expected to make official the action which Chernin and his staff suggest.

"My feeling and the feeling of many is one of deep disappointment that we find ourselves placed in a position where we cannot participate in what should be a meaningful observance in Washington," Chernin said. "I think the feeling is pretty widespread. Sadness is the best way of describing it. But we also have to be true to our own principles. History as far as we're concerned did not end in 1963."

Over 100 national organizations have agreed to participate in the march and a "call to the nation" has been written and endorsed by the conveners of the march.

It is that call and some of the participating groups that have led the advisory council to urge Jewish groups not to participate.

"The call is too far-reaching in all kinds of areas," Chernin said. "We use the Middle East as illustrative," he said. In the call, it says: "We oppose the militarization of internal conflicts, often abetted and even encouraged by massive U.S. arms exports, in areas of the world such as the Middle East and Central America, while their basic human problems are neglected."

Chernin singled out former Sen. James Abourezk among the conveners. Abourezk now heads the Arab American Anti-Discrimination Committee. "They're not going to talk about civil rights," he said. "I've never heard them talk about civil rights, not 20 years ago or not last year on the Voting Rights Act. But I know where we were," he said.

In his office late in the afternoon on Friday, Albert Chernin went back to 1963 and the March on Washington. "For 20 years prior to that (the march)," he said, "the civil rights movement came down to the Black community, the Jewish community and the trade union movement. We were pretty much alone." He said that back then, in the late 1930s and the mid-40s, the Blacks and the Jews shared the same values and had the same self-interests and that they worked together because they felt the same pressures. He mentioned quotas that kept Jews and Blacks out of professional schools. He mentioned Nazi rallies and marches that threatened Jews and Blacks. And he mentioned the Ku Klux Klan. "Congress wouldn't even pass an anti-lynching bill," he said. "You had segregation in America then in the most blatant way."

By 1963, the coalition suddenly began to expand and other groups began to play significant roles in the civil rights movement. But while the March on Washington was one of the first events to have full participation of the White churches, Dr. Joachim Prinz was one of the chairmen, and virtually every major Jewish organization, religious and secular, endorsed the march and was heavily represented.

In the '60s, the relationships between Blacks and Jews began to change.

Chernin mentioned that merchants who were Jewish and did business in Black areas began to be attacked. He said the position of Jews regarding affirmative action was misunderstood. "What we opposed were quotas," he said.

Israel's relationship with African nations also became a factor, he said. "But up to 1967, the relationships between African nations and Israel were good," he said. "It was oil, not politics that changed that," he said. "I still believe the Saudis bludgeoned the Africans to break relations with Israel. The Jewish community didn't walk away from the civil rights movement," he emphasized.

The Advisory Council was organized in 1944 and includes 11 national Jewish agencies and 111 others that operate at the community level. The national groups include the American Jewish Committee, the American Jewish Congress and B'nai B'rith Anti-Defamation League.

Today's meeting in New York is the organization's scheduled quarterly meeting, and the prime business is the adoption of a joint program plan for Jewish community relations. It would have been routine except for the issue of the march that is scheduled for Washington next month. It is a part of the story of shifting relationships.

"We are not walking away from civil rights," Albert Chernin says. The question is, he says, "What is the way of enabling the Jewish community to continue being an active partner? We wouldn't say to them that you have to buy our position on the Middle East, although we would like them to because it's the right position. But I would presume we all have many items on our agendas not all our partners can buy. We will not impose ours on others, and by the same token, we do not want them to impose their agendas on us. We will work together where we have common cause. On civil rights, we do have common cause."

The chairmen of the march next month are Martin Luther King Jr.'s widow, Coretta Scott King, and the Rev. James Lowery, the president of the Southern Christian Leadership Conference, the organization that King led. Their names are the first that appear under the call to the nation.

The advisory council acknowledges that the absence of Jewish groups in Washington at the march next month will not be overlooked. It had suggested a campaign, including newspaper ads, to explain its position. But at the bottom, it's a story of old allies who find themselves in the summer of 1983 moving in different directions.

1985

AT HARLEM'S CANAAN BAPTIST CHURCH of Christ, it was Communion Sunday. There were barely enough seats in the church to handle the crowd. But before Communion, before they sang the special hymns, even before the sermon, the issue of Louis Farrakhan's appearance at the Garden tonight came into the pulpit.

The Rev. Wyatt Tee Walker, in a bright red and white cassock, rose to speak to what he called, "the furor surrounding the appearance of Louis Farrakhan in New York City." He had received many calls from reporters, asking for his reaction. On Communion Sunday, he brought his response to the pulpit.

He pointed out that the media had heralded as Black leaders those who denounced Farrakhan. The subsequent furor, he said, had produced "some curious revelations about leaders in the Black community and to whom they are accountable."

He said, "I would be glad to join in denouncing hatred and bigotry any time, but where is the evidence or judgement of Farrakhan's hatred and bigotry?"

Applause erupted as he said: "The whole scenario smacks of hypocrisy."

From the pulpit his voice rose. "Where were these forces when the Rev. Jerry Falwell assailed Desmond Tutu as a phony and announced to the world his program to prop up apartheid?" His words were barely audible over the applause. "Jerry Falwell," he added, "is far more dangerous to the American ideal of democracy than Louis Farrakhan could ever be.

"Some of these Black spokesmen -- not leaders, spokesmen -- hold credentials that are suspect." He mentioned Bayard Rustin. "Bayard Rustin abandoned Dr. King. He attacked Rev. Joseph Lowery (head of the Southern Christian Leadership Conference) and others who had the temerity to talk with Yaser Arafat. He opposed the candidacy of Jesse Jackson. Rustin's penchant for Zionism is well-documented." Walker's conclusion: "Rustin cannot be trusted on any Black issue." The applause swelled through the church.

"As to the substance of the present furor, and the concomitant charges, my perception is that Farrakhan makes Whites with submerged racist tendencies uneasy, and much of the Zionist element in Jewry is antagonized by his truth-speaking." Walker mentioned the New York Post and said the newspaper attributed the phrase "gutter religion," to Farrakhan. "Mr. Farrakhan admits to the phrase "dirty religion," which was the reference to the use of violence, war and death to achieve a nation's (Israel's) goals." Walker said, "Whatever rhetoric one chooses, soft or hard -- a nation, a religion, a people leave themselves morally and spiritually suspect when they declare over and over again, 'We will never forgive...and never forget.'"

He said, "The nub of the matter is that few of Farrakhan's critics have even listened to him other than by means of the snippets reported in the media. I have listened to his broadcasts. I have listened to his tapes. Indeed, he has spoken at the church I serve in Harlem. To say he is an apostle of hatred and bigotry is grossly unfair. His pronouncements are indeed harsh, but accurate.

"Whatever Louis Farrakhan is, for good or ill, he was made in the U.S.A."

1988

ON THE FIRST DAY OF THE CAMPAIGN in the most important presidential primary of 1988, Mayor Ed Koch resorted to political terrorism. He began with the most outrageous statement even he could imagine. He said that Jews would be crazy to vote for Jesse Jackson. What the mayor said had nothing to do with presidential politics. His was a terrorist strike.

Koch saw the kind of powerful coalitions the Jackson campaign was building. He saw the way Jesse was bringing even the most divergent of groups together. He saw Jesse reaching out to Jews, and even with all that has happened, the way Jews were responding.

Koch needs the climate he has built in the city. He has encouraged groups to turn on each other. He has made sure everything revolves around attacks. In his time, he has been careful to nurture that. It didn't just happen.

In 1988, the state of New York was handed the most important primary of all. In the race for the Democratic Party's presidential nomination, New York was called on to decide. For a moment, New York seemed the perfect place. Then, by himself, the mayor poisoned the air.

He created a situation so tense that through the last days of the campaign, Jackson could not move around the city without lugging the weight of a dark blue raincoat his Secret Service bodyguards insisted he wear. The coat has bullet-proof shields that weigh a ton. The environment the mayor created forced the Secret Service to make certain that Jesse carried that weight every time he stepped into the streets of the city.

In New York City now, Koch desperately needs to divert attention. He cannot answer for the neglect so pronounced that even important bridges now face closing, before they fall down. Already, the Williamsburg Bridge has been shut down; soon many more will follow. The mayor cannot explain the reason drugs have been permitted to flourish to the point that trafficking on the streets has become all but legal. He cannot explain the way public schools have deteriorated, or corruption that has resulted in systematic looting of the city treasury. He cannot answer for housing policies that keep whole blocks of city-owned buildings empty while the number of homeless swells, and welfare families are stuffed into costly, but run-down and dangerous hotels.

So the presidential primary came to New York at the best of times for Ed Koch. He used the primary to divide. He cannot run on his record, so instead, he has chosen to run on race. His act of terror was to foment trouble between Blacks and Jews in the city. He is a politician running so scared he cannot risk any campaign that involves a discussion of the issues. He needs the climate he has set in concrete and to preserve that, he has resorted to calculated political terrorism.

1991

ON THE NIGHT OF 1984 that the New York Association of Black Journalists had the Muslim minister Louis Farrakhan as its guest speaker, the organization was in need of two things: members and money. Farrakhan, with his appearance, helped solved both problems. Once word got out that Farrakhan was speaking, so many showed up a decision was made to hold most seats for members. That night, memberships sold like hot cakes. Farrakhan was a hot ticket.

In 1984, White America discovered Louis Farrakhan. Jesse Jackson was just starting out as a presidential candidate. To build a base, he was trying to pull together every segment of the Black community. He was especially taken with the idea of getting the Muslims, who never get involved in politics, to cross over, and register to support and vote for his candidacy. Jesse always had an eye for the sensational. He sold the idea to Farrakhan, leader in the Nation of Islam, and the bargain was struck.

The Jackson campaign was to be Farrakhan's coming out for White America. In the Black community, Farrakhan was widely known. He had been since the late 1960s. In the feud between Malcolm X and the Nation of Islam, Farrakhan was on the side of Elijah Muhammad. After Malcolm, Farrakhan mended a lot of fences. In time, Farrakhan became the Muslim voice in the Black community, and, perhaps, one of the nation's most effective speakers. Even Jesse is hard put to beat Farrakhan in addressing a crowd. Some lines Jackson won't cross; Farrakhan knows no bounds.

For awhile, in '84, Jackson's campaign was skyrocketing. After he went to Syria and brought back captured Navy Lt. Goodman, his campaign took off. In New Hampshire, he had begun to make a big move in the polls. Then, the "Hymietown" issue exploded. From the start, Jesse had opposition from Jews. After it came out that he used the word "Hymie" in private, a lot of Jews tried to hound him out of the race. Then Farrakhan stepped up.

It was in Chicago, a huge Nation of Islam rally, and Jesse and Farrakhan were both to speak. Farrakhan went first. Jackson had been getting a lot of threats, according to the Secret Service -- some of them from people identifying themselves as Jews. That night, Farrakhan delivered his explosive "come to your senses, Jewish leaders" speech. His language was tough and blunt. He said that if anything happened to Jesse, he personally would lead the charge in holding Jews responsible. Maybe never had a Black man stood in public and talked to Jewish leaders the way Farrakhan did that night.

Jackson never recovered. Farrakhan became the center of attention. At the Black Journalists meeting, when he rose to speak, he threw back his head and laughed. "They (White media) have given me the kind of publicity that money can't buy," he said. Since 1984, a fear and fascination with Farrakhan has only grown.

The Washington Post has standing as one of the most important newspapers in America. Recently, the Post invited Farrakhan to a private meeting with editors and reporters. Just that was a bit surprising. But the stunning part had to do with what happened next. A day later, the Post took two full pages and published a word for word transcript of almost everything that Farrakhan had to say.

It's seldom that a newspaper takes two whole pages to deal with anything. But that's what one of the most important papers gave for Farrakhan. The "why" in what the Post has done is not so easy to put a finger on. He did spell out his views on a lot of issues concerning Jews. But he didn't settle anything. Some who were there came away saying he was anti-Semitic. Farrakhan did say that he believed a government plot to bring about his assassination was afoot. He said the crack epidemic in Black areas began in 1985, just after he began moving from one of those communities to another, addressing huge crowds. He also said that AIDS, as some have charged, may be a manufactured virus.

Farrakhan spoke the day after it came out that one in four Black men within a certain age group were in prison or under supervision of the courts. Farrakhan talked of the "brilliance that's hiding in prisons all over America" and talked of plans his organization has to recruit among that group. "All they (inmates) need is a chance."

1991

I DON'T KNOW THIS MICHAEL LEVIN of City College. The record is that he's a tenured professor of philosophy. Recently, he's been doing all he can to make a name for himself by mouthing a lot of stupid ideas that he knows are sure to create a ton of controversy.

What Levin is doing, though, makes you ask: "What in the world is going on at City College?"

It used to be that for those at the bottom, education was the way out. It was a badge of pride for a student to say that he or she was "the first in our family" to make it to college. College meant one thing: learning. You got into school, and you had professors who knew that they were there to teach. At one time, all that made City College of New York one of the finest institutions of higher learning in the country. Now, from City College, we're getting something else.

Here is Levin who is supposed to teach. Instead, he's using his position at the school to make himself a celebrity by pushing half-truths based on bigotry. To do this, he uses the taxpayers' money. Levin ought to be fired. City College President Bernard Harleston ought to call him, and give him two hours to clear out his desk.

But that doesn't happen. On the campus now a professor can go off in any crack pot direction he or she wants, and get away with it. They lay claim to some kind of intellectual freedom which they say allows the spouting of any kind of nonsense a professor cares to utter. The worst part is that faculties stand behind this; they say this freedom is crucial to airing of views of all stripe. Which is hogwash.

Take Levin. He hasn't distinguished himself in any way as an academic. But he's found out that he could rise from obscurity if he persisted in stirring the racial pot. He made a splash in the news by claiming that Blacks are intellectually inferior to Whites. He has nothing to base that on. But he knows that just the words, and his standing as a City College professor, are enough. He says that 25 percent of Black men are likely to commit crimes. He says that, but doesn't offer an iota of data to back up his claim.

Then, Levin goes a step further. He advocates public policy based on his ideas. He says Black males are so violent that on subway cars, they ought to be required to ride on separate police patrolled cars; that curfews ought to be imposed on Black youth. Levin is a Jew. At another time, in another place, Hitler had a lot of baseless ideas about Jews. He used those ideas to make policy that took a lot of lives.

The point is, aside from the students who rightfully tried to run him off a stage at Long Island University, there has been no outcry against Levin. He's a man who obviously has a lot of access to the media so that he can peddle his poison. Jews have been quick to force Black leaders and public officials to repudiate remarks made by Blacks they feel are bigoted. Levin has clearly used bigotry as the basis for his positions. Instead of being repudiated, he's been given a larger arena to sound his ideas.

Levin says he doesn't believe there is much racial discrimination today. It is a statement based on ignorance. Yet, except for Black students, he has not gotten challenged. He actually said that it would "be a great deal" to be a Black male. He says, "I don't think the Black male has anything to complain about." How much racism and bigotry is allowed to come through the door saved for academics under the name of intellectual freedom?

That gets a long way from what a student was supposed to get in a college classroom. The worst part is that it's the taxpayer who is the patsy paying for the scam that is going down.

1991

WHEN THE NEWSPAPER GOT FINISHED with him, the demand was that Dr. Leonard Jeffries Jr. do some explaining. If he had any interest in keeping his job at City College, it was made clear that he had to do that explaining fast.

A good thing happened though. Dr. Jeffries was out of the country. He was in Africa. So, he could not defend himself. What made that a good thing was that it sent a lot of people back checking on the kind of reporting the newspaper had done in selling the story to New York.

When the checking was done, it was not Dr. Jeffries who came up short. It was the newspaper, the New York Post, that was out there making charges it could not defend.

The Post accused Jeffries of so many sins, it had a bevy of political heavyweights demanding his resignation. Sen. Al D'Amato even went so far as to indicate that federal funds would be jeopardized if Jeffries remained as chairman of the African-American studies department at City College. But D'Amato, like a lot of others, spoke before they did their homework. They did not bother to get hold of all that Jeffries said in a speech before a cultural gathering in Albany. Instead, they just took the few quotes and the charges from the newspaper, and formed opinions.

The newspaper they put their trust in was playing a vicious game. Even though New York is a racial tinderbox, The Post was race baiting. By its actions, it was encouraging trouble.

But before they responded, a lot of New Yorkers did what the Rev. Herbert Daughtry of Brooklyn did. "My wife and I stayed up all night watching the tape (of the speech Dr. Jeffries delivered). We kept running it back and running it back. I just wanted to be sure as to what was on that tape when I stand with him. He (Jeffries) is a friend. He has lectured at the church every year. I've always admired him as a human being, and always thought that he was a consummate scholar."

After his scrutiny of the tape, Daughtry found Jeffries had basically raised six issues.

(1)--"The questions of Africa's role in world history and how that is to be put into the educational system of America."

(2)--"Who enslaved us? His contention is that rich Jews (in the tape he says, 'I'm not talking about all Jews.') He points out that the mass of Jews were beaten and persecuted up and down Europe. But he says there were rich Jews who participated in the slave trade. And not just Jews. He says that after the fall of the Roman Empire, rich Jews in an alliance with the Catholic church, began to enslave White people in Europe."

(3)--"This had to do with the stereotype of us on film. He says that Russian Jews in an alliance with the Mafia took control of Hollywood and hatched these stereotypes."

(4)--"This was about what he says is an alliance of some Jews with the conservative element to deny Africa's role in history as presented in the educational system."

(5) --"He questions the sincerity of Whites. He's raising a question we've been raising ever since we've been here: to what extent can we trust Whites when it comes to an accurate portrayal of our history."

(6) --"Is there a different value system between Europe and Africa?"

Rev. Daughtry noted that when Jeffries rose to speak, that he had in front of him a table stacked with books. He quoted Jeffries as saying, "I've got my ammunition." So as Daughtry said, the speech was not just some mouthing off.

But why was the newspaper selling racial hatred? It used to be that vehicles such as the Journalism Review published at Columbia University would monitor the press and then have such answers. But Columbia abandoned that responsibility some time ago. Those who have watched The Post lately have found that it has been following an anti-Black slant. So much so that CEMOTAP, an organization headed by Betty Dopson, has ordered a boycott of the newspaper.

But why did the newspaper go after Dr. Jeffries? A lot of Blacks say it has to do with the newspaper's opposition to a curriculum of inclusion.

1991

IN BROOKLYN, THEY HOLD FUNERAL SERVICES today for 7 year-old Gavin Cato. For now, his is the name that frames the trouble in Crown Heights. Crown Heights is a community that has so much trouble that, on Friday, for the first time in 25 years, officials came to a weekend worried that a community in New York was about to explode.

It gets said the trouble in Crown Heights is between Blacks (mostly Caribbeans) and Jews (mostly of the Lubavitch Hasidim). To say the trouble is between people who have power, and others who do not, may be a better way to put it.

Not too long ago, a lot of New Yorkers believed the election of David Dinkins as mayor would end exactly the kind of trouble that has been so persistent in Crown Heights. The events of last week put an end to that notion. When Dinkins went to Crown Heights he made the mistake of asking for peace. "We want justice," the mayor was told, and the message was sent with a barrage of rocks and bottles.

This latest round of trouble in Crown Heights was touched off by the killing of young Gavin Cato. Blacks, mostly Caribbeans, were so outraged at all that happened around the death of young Cato, they took to the streets. On the day he died, the Cato youth happened to be on the sidewalk when a car ran a red light, collided with another vehicle, and, then, according to witnesses, jumped the curb to hit two youngsters. One of the kids was seriously injured; the other, Gavin Cato lost his life. The Cato youth was Caribbean; the driver of the car was Hasidim.

What those who were there say happened next produced so much anger that soon, riots were in the streets. The driver of the vehicle was whisked away without being charged. It is said that the dead boy's father was beaten by the police even as he tried to free his son from the weight of the car. That was seen as evidence of the difference in treatment for powerless Caribbeans and the influence the Hasidics have in Crown Heights.

Colin Moore is both a candidate for election to the City Council and a highly respected lawyer, who operates largely in the Caribbean community of Brooklyn. He represents the Cato family. When he talks of the case, he does not try to hide his anger. He says the driver of the car should have been arrested. "Nobody is saying he ought to be hung," Moore said. "We are just saying that he should have been charged. There were four laws he violated." Moore said the driver of the car had run a red light, was speeding, driving in a reckless manner, then left the scene of an accident, which he said was a felony.

"For the Police Commissioner to come out and say that no laws were broken is ridiculous," Moore said. He also accused the police of acting improperly. He said that after the accident, even though a kid was dead, the police conspired in spiriting the Hasidics away from the area. "They did that," Moore said, "but they didn't do their job. They did not even question people who were there and witnessed what happened. All they were interested in was protecting those (Hasidic) individuals. It was a combination of callousness, arrogance, racism and bad police work. And all we are saying to the mayor is, Do your job. Enforce the law.'"

Colin Moore says the case brings to mind the incident that led to the boycott of the Korean market in Brooklyn. "A woman was abused; all that people were saying was arrest somebody. They wanted to see authorities do their job, but nothing happened. They (authorities) are always telling us to wait for justice. In the St. John's case, we waited, and look at what we got. When Blacks violate the law, they act right away. Now they're telling us to wait for justice. They got to be joking.

1992

THIS IS A PIECE OF THE REST of the story in another of the controversies involving Dr. Leonard Jeffries of City College. This goes back to the statement Jeffries made about Jews and the slave trade. In a speech, he said, "Everyone knows rich Jews helped finance the slave trade."

For that statement, Jeffries caught so much flak that in a lot of circles it was just assumed that he didn't know what he was talking about. His critics, for the most part, said Jews were not involved in the slave trade. Others conceded there may have been some involvement, but they said that was only in the most peripheral way.

In time, the controversy died, and the issue went away. Now, it comes back. That's because of a reporter who went digging for the facts. David Mills of the Washington Post took on the assignment. His findings were published in the Sunday edition of the newspaper in a lengthy article. Were Jews involved in the slave trade? Mills found that they were, and that it wasn't just in a peripheral way.

So Jeffries was right? Mills says not exactly. He says Jeffries misuses historical facts. But while he says that, his article tends to support the Jeffries assertion.

Jewish involvement in slave trading, according to the Mills article, began in Brazil. The sources in the article say that it also took place in the British and French West Indies, the Dutch Colonies and Colonial North America. In Brazil, the finding was that Sephardic Jews were the predominant retailers of slaves in the colony. In looking at Brazil in the 1600s, a telling quote is taken from Arnold Wiznitzer's "Jews In Colonial Brazil." He writes, "The buyers who appeared at the auctions were almost always Jews."

In the British and French West Indies, where there were more than a million slaves, the finding was that Jewish involvement was limited. Of that region, Mills found that those Jews who were involved mostly dealt with sickly slaves who were bought cheaply and resold at considerable profit.

In the Dutch Colonies, the finding was that Sephardic Jews had "a direct hand in wholesale slaving." In Colonial North America, the Sephardic Jews were also involved. However, the finding was that gentiles overwhelmingly controlled the slaving business.

In his article, Mills builds his case on information mostly from historians and scholars. Many he cites are Jewish. Reporter Mills asks, "Why are so many people ignorant of such a well documented point of history?

He answers: "One reason is that popular histories of New World slavery tend to omit any mention of Sephardic Jews while cataloging the activities of many other ethnic communities. He points out that James A. Rawley's "The Transatlantic Slave Trade" does not make a single mention of the involvement of Sephardic Jews. Mills said that because the Jewish involvement in slaving is not mentioned in many texts, that is taken to mean the role was negligible.

So while the reporter Mills does not come down on the side of Jeffries, his article is a significant victory for the head of the Black Studies department at City College. And Jeffries has been getting his share of victories lately. The largest of those victories he won in a courtroom. City College had intended to dump him as a department head. There was even a move afoot to get him off the campus. All that failed, though. Jeffries had made controversial statements in a speech. That provoked a storm of protest but when college officials tried to oust Jeffries, he went to court. And he won.

What he wasn't free of, though, was the charge that he doesn't know what he's talking about when he delves into history. His statement about Jews and slave trading had been a kind of exhibit A. Now that some digging has been done, it seems that Jeffries wasn't so far off base on this either.

1992

MAYOR DINKINS POINTS to the hostility directed at Rev. Jesse L. Jackson by the Jewish community, and asks: "I wonder, when does it subside?"

That the mayor raises the issue now is no surprise. He is headed toward a tough reelection campaign. Jesse and the mayor are long-time allies; they will be together in the campaign.

Will Jackson's presence be used by Jews as a reason for opposing Dinkins?

The matter of Jesse and the Jews has resurfaced largely because of what happened in Tuesday's presidential primary.

Jackson all but endorsed Jerry Brown. On occasion, the two campaigned together. Brown, in his most daring assertion, announced that Jackson would be his choice as running mate.

Brown earlier had hinted as much. But it was not until the New York campaign that he went all out in embracing Jesse.

He appears to have paid a heavy price for doing so. Polls show that before embracing Jackson, Brown was winning some 20 percent of the Jewish vote. By primary day, Jackson was strongly identified with the Brown campaign, and Jewish support for Brown had plummeted to the point that exit polls showed him winding up with just 8 percent of that vote

Jackson's standing with Jews exploded during the 1984 presidential campaign when it came out that in private conversation he had referred to Jews as "Hymies," and to New York as "Hymietown."

At first, Jackson insisted that he had not intended to slur Jews with his remarks. Then, in the midst of the primary campaign in New Hampshire visited a synagogue where he delivered a memorable apology.

It was not enough.

Jackson supporters argued that nothing Jackson could do would ever be enough. They pointed out that long before the "Hymietown" remark, Jews had opposed the Jackson campaign.

In fact, a group of Jews tried to disrupt his rally in Washington on the day he announced his presidential bid.

Jackson's friendship with Muslim minister Louis Farrakhan also became an issue. In time, Jesse disassociated himself and his campaign from Farrakhan, but that did not solve the differences. Which leads back to Dinkins's question -- when does it subside?

A part of the answer may be reflected in the case of Jitu Weusi, a former Brooklyn school teacher and long-time political activist.

In the late 1960s, Weusi (then Les Campbell) was a teacher in the Ocean Hill-Brownsville district, which was then embroiled in a heated controversy about decentralization.

That fight brought to the forefront a lot of tensions between Blacks and Jews. In that atmosphere, Weusi became a target when he read a poem entitled, "Jew Boy," which was written by a student. The poem contained language conceded to be anti-Semitic. Weusi denounced the poem, but still read it in his classroom. He said it was done for reasons of discussion.

He later apologized, saying that he had made a mistake. But after more than 20 years, Weusi is still ostracized and accused of being anti-Semitic.

"How long do I have to keep paying?" Weusi asked. It is a question that links up with what the mayor asked about Jesse.

When trouble broke out in Crown Heights, some city officials wanted to use Weusi to help keep the peace. But they couldn't. He was still paying for something he apologized for 20 years ago. Something of value was lost. Jesse Jackson also has something of value to offer. But he, too, is being made to keep paying for an old mistake.

Chapter Six, Part Two

CAIN AND ABEL

NEIGHBORHOODS

Dutchess County
1988

THEY WERE THE WORST KIND of racial attacks, but they always happened someplace else -- in Mississippi, Alabama or Arkansas. Almost never would it be here, in New York. "We don't have that kind of problem," New Yorkers would said. In a way, it was true.

Not any more.

It seems as though the change has come all of a sudden; that it just blew up yesterday.

But that has not been the case either. Bit by bit over the last 10 years, it has been building.

What has come into focus now is that more horrible racial attacks have begun to take place in New York than maybe any place else in the country.

New York has a long string of recent cases that center on race. There was the killing of Michael Stewart. There was the killing of Eleanor Bumpers, an elderly grandmother shot-gunned to death because she resisted -- with a kitchen knife, police say -- eviction from her home.

Then came the case of Bernard Goetz, the subway rider who shot Black kids in the back. After that came Howard Beach, where a mob of Whites attacked Blacks.

There was so little confidence on the part of Blacks that authorities would investigate and prosecute, that the victims refused to cooperate with any investigation. A special prosecutor had to be appointed; only then did the victims of the attack come forward.

Now the case being held up for the whole nation to see is that of Tawana Brawley of Wappinger Falls.

In a way, the Brawley case has become the perfect reflection of race relations in New York. Once again, the breakdown is so great that the 16-year-old girl who says she was the victim of a sex attack by a White mob refuses even to talk to authorities about what happened to her two days before Thanksgiving.

Gov. Cuomo appointed Atty. Gen. Robert Abrams as special prosecutor in the case. But lawyers for Tawana Brawley have advised her not to cooperate.

Abrams was promising the most vigorous kind of investigation. He said he would be hands on; and that he had the governor's promise that any and all resources needed to do the job would be available.

Still, he could not get the confidence needed to persuade the young girl to come forward.

In the Brawley case, before Abrams took charge, several prosecutors began investigations, then quit.

They saw something so wrong they wanted no part of it. Brawley lawyer Vernon Mason said the governor knows what those prosecutors saw. "He ought to tell the people what's going on."

What is going on is the story Tawana Brawley first gave investigators before she stopped cooperating. She said she was kidnapped, raped and sodomized by a gang of White men, including one with a badge. After being held four days, she was found with feces smeared on her body, and the initials, "KKK," and the word, "Nigger" scrawled on her.

The earlier prosecutors quit because initial suspects included a state trooper, an assistant Dutchess County District Attorney, and a former part-time police officer, who, since, has committed suicide.

Last November, just after he came into the case, Alton Maddox called on the investigating Dutchess County DA to resign because of a conflict of interest; last week, the district attorney did just that.

Always it used to be someplace else where the horrible racial attacks happened. But now, it's New York.

1988

ON THE DAY LAST WEEK he was putting up reward money, Bill Cosby said the horror of the Tawana Brawley case took him back to a time 25 years ago. "People are doing things they used to do in 1963," he said.

Maybe Cosby had in front of his mind the horror those in the civil rights movement called, "the Mississippi Summer."

In the summer of 1964, that kind of attention focused on Neshoba County in rural Mississippi. Three young men, active in the movement to get Blacks the right to vote, were arrested for no legitimate reason and held in a country jail. The horror was in the way they were taken from the jail in the middle of the night and delivered into the hands of racist terrorists. The belief was that not even the bodies would be found because the killers had the protection of a code of silence. Many knew who they were, but nobody would say. So through 43 days, there were only the names of the victims -- James Chaney, Andrew Goodman and Michael Schwerner.

This would have been just three more lives for the racial terrorists of Mississippi, but the outrage was too great. To find the informant who was needed, the FBI put up money. The amount got larger, until finally, it was enough. Once there was an informant, the FBI got a bulldozer and a drag-line. They went to a precise location at a dam just outside the Mississippi town of Philadelphia. They dug down an exact number of feet, then got shovels, and uncovered the 44-day-old remains of Chaney, Goodman and Schwerner.

In the Brawley case, Bill Cosby and Ed Lewis of Essence Magazine put up $25,000. The Brawley case also involves racial terrorism in Dutchess County, N.Y. Cosby and Lewis are acting to break a code of silence.

In the summer of 1964, the racial climate in Mississippi embraced, and, in a way, encouraged the attacks on Chaney, Goodman and Schwerner. Chaney was a young Mississippian, but he was Black and the system approved any attack on him because he stepped out of "his place" by getting involved in the movement. Goodman and Schwerner were Jewish students from New York who gave up their summer to go to Mississippi and work in the movement.

But the movement prevailed: the system of 25 years ago that encouraged racial terrorism in Mississippi was broken. So what takes us back?

Maybe a part of it is this: When he was just starting out, the place Ronald Reagan went to announce his candidacy for President was Philadelphia, Miss. In 1964, when he was running for President, George Wallace wouldn't go to Philadelphia. It was different with Reagan. Intended or not, that sent a signal. The KKK picked up on it and endorsed the Reagan candidacy. Reagan said he didn't want the Klan's support, but just going to Philadelphia was seen as a wink and a nod.

Maybe that signal stretched all the way to Dutchess County, N.Y.

East Brooklyn
1979

THE TWO PRIESTS CAME from Flatlands Ave. It was late in the morning, and when they reached the corner, when they turned onto E. 45th St., in Brooklyn, every eye in the block was on them.

Across the street was a group of women who stood in the shade of a leafy tree. Farther up the block, there were two others who sat on the steps of a clapboard house, and, across from there, there was another group.

In the morning, there were only women on the street. All of them were White. They had their eyes glued on the two men in black, the priests who came onto their street.

Nobody said anything. The priests, jaws set, moved at a brisk stride, heading directly for the second house from the corner. It was the house where the Black family moved in 10 days ago, the house that Monday night was the target of a cross-burning.

Father Pote was up the steps first. Father McNeils followed. Ivy Morgan was there at the front door when they arrived. The door was only partly opened, and she looked out from behind it.

"We're from St. Thomas," the older man, Father Pote, said. He had his pipe in his left hand, and he kept it behind him as he talked.

"We came to apologize," he said. "We don't have cross-burnings. We have statue breaking." A small smile came onto his face. Mrs. Morgan smiled back at him.

"It's the kids," Father Pote said. "They see this stuff on television. That's where they get it, and then they think they have to go out and do it."

Ivy Morgan did not want to come out to greet the priests. She was not dressed. She still had on her blue slippers and her long, flowered housecoat. It had been a busy morning. First came the police, then the reporters. Now, there were the priests, and, through it all, there had been no time for her to get dressed.

She stood in the doorway and briefly, the three of them talked. Father Pote spoke about what had happened at his church, at St. Thomas Aquinas.

"They broke out the stained glass windows," he said. Then, he mentioned the statues and, as he talked, anger rose in him. "You know who did it?" the priest said. "Graduates from Aquinas. Yeah, they were graduated in '74. Three drunken louts."

Now Father McNeils chimed in. "Tell her what you called them last Sunday," he said.

Father Pote smiled. "I called 'em drunken louts whose brains and bellies were loaded with beer," he said. The two priests apologized again, said goodby, and left Ivy Morgan standing behind her front door that was still only partly open.

"Are you afraid?' she was asked.

Now, it was her turn to bristle. "We don't scare easily," she said. "We're West Indians, and we don't back off that easy. No way. We're strong, hard-working people, and we've worked hard to come by everything we have. We earned it. This is what America has to offer everybody, and I'm staying in America because I like it. This won't sway me at all. Not one bit."

From her doorway, Mrs. Morgan could see her neighbors who stood in clusters along the streets. "This is so unfair to these people," she said. "They have been so nice. They're really warm, friendly people. I don't believe that it was anyone from around here that did it. It's totally unfair to the homeowners."

The Morgans moved into the house just 10 days ago. It's a big, red brick house, but sits in a modest neighborhood.

"What is the big deal in living in an area like this?" Mrs. Morgan said. "We only moved here because we needed more space."

While Ivy Morgan stood in her doorway and answered questions, her husband, Jocelyn, was away at work. They own a 35-unit apartment house, and he manages the property. The two children still at home, a daughter who is 15 and son who is 12, were away at school. A third daughter is in California, where she is in school, studying medicine.

"What did you do last night, when it happened?" Mrs. Morgan was asked.

"I didn't even know it," she said. "I didn't know anything until the firemen came. That was about 11:30 at night."

"What happened?"

"I asked them why they were here," Mrs. Morgan said, "and this fireman tells me that there's a cross burning on my lawn. I told him, I don't have any lawn. I didn't even see the darn thing."

Yesterday the cross was gone. It had been placed just inside the gate, in a small patch of greenery off the front porch. After it was lit, somebody called the Fire Department. And now, in the morning, the block was filled with neighbors who were trying to understand what it meant.

"There was no reason for it," a woman who stood across the street said. "I know nobody from this block did it."

"How do you know?" she was asked.

"Most of us came out here to better ourselves, and they're no different," the woman said. "They're (the Morgans) just like us. I don't know them, though. They keep to themselves, but they seem like nice people. They contributed to the block party we had, I know that."

None of the neighbors wanted to give their names. "We don't want any trouble," a woman from across the street said. "The last thing my husband told me this morning was don't say anything to anybody. On this block, everybody minds their own business."

Now, across the street, there were two cops at the Morgan house. One of the officers, a Black man, who said that his name was Jackson. He was from the community relations department of Brooklyn South, and he talked with Mrs. Morgan.

"I don't think it's organized," he said. "I'm sure it's the kids."

"Exactly," Ivy Morgan said. And finally she shut the door at her new house.

Fort Wayne, Indiana
1980

OUT IN FORT WAYNE, the federal agents involved in the investigation have quit taking questions. All the inquiries that were handled by the field office just after the shooting are now directed to Washington.

"We're not issuing any more statements," an agent in Fort Wayne said.

Everything about the investigation into the ambush shooting of Vernon Jordan has been shifted to the national headquarters of the Federal Bureau of Investigation.

But even at FBI headquarters, little is being said. "The investigation is continuing," a Washington spokesman for the FBI said yesterday.

"Is there any progress?" the spokesman was asked.

"We're still running down leads," he said. "It's an ongoing investigation, and we're checking out leads from all over the country." It's FBI talk. It is the way that the Federal Bureau of Investigation deals with reporters when it has nothing to say. The spokesmen are polite, proper and brief. But they say little, and that is the way it is now with the investigation around the shooting of Vernon Jordan.

Two months have passed since Jordan was shot in the back by a sniper using a high-powered rifle. By all accounts, he was lucky to escape with his life. Although he has been moved from Indiana to New York, he is still hospitalized.

When he was first brought back to New York, the few who were able to see him in the hospital remarked about how well he was doing.

Then suddenly that changed. There was talk of a fever and infections. It was whispered that he was not doing as well as many thought. Then, a week ago, that changed. The fever left, the infections cleared, and it was said again that, considering that he had a hole in his back as big as a fist, he was doing very well.

It was so different from May, in the days just after the ambush attack. President Carter spoke out, calling it an assassination attempt. Right behind the President was William Webster, director of the FBI, who said immediately that there was evidence that the shooting of Jordan involved a conspiracy.

Conspiracy is the word officials always hesitate to use, but in the Jordan case, Webster spoke out right away. His quick assessment came as a surprise, and even drew some objections from local officials in Fort Wayne.

Yesterday, while the FBI was saying little about the status of the investigation, it was sticking to the notion that a conspiracy was involved in the shooting.

"There is more than one individual being sought," an FBI spokesman said. "That has not changed. We still have reason to believe that there were co-conspirators in this."

For a variety of reasons, more than the usual amount of attention centers on this year's Urban League convention.

Partly it is because of the shooting of the organization's national director and the circumstances surrounding the incident. It is partly because this is a year of presidential politics.

And beyond that, there are other factors. Basically, those involve the recent violent outbursts that have taken place in Black communities.

It started in Miami, with the deadliest riots in decades. Since Miami, there have been other outbreaks. It has not been a replay of the '60s, when riots swept from one Black community to another across the country.

But it was the pictures of the '60s that came back with the violence in Miami. Because of that, the conventions of the major Black organizations have taken on added significance this year. There is this year an urgency in the national meetings.

"Nobody is going to riot because the FBI hasn't caught the people who shot Vernon Jordan," an Urban League staffer was saying yesterday. "But it's one more thing in a troubled time.

Gravesend, Brooklyn
1983

IT WAS A PIECE OF THE CITY'S business that was so important, the politicians were not allowed anywhere close to it. Instead, it was put into the hands of 12 ordinary citizens.

It involved the killing of Willie Turks, 34, who lived in Far Rockaway, Queens. It was a racial killing. Turks was a Black man, a transit worker. He was killed on a warm night last June outside a bagel shop in the Gravesend section of Brooklyn.

Just after the killing the report was that Turks was beaten to death by a mob of young Whites. There were witnesses, the police made arrests, the system moved forward and by February, the issue was in State Supreme Court in Brooklyn.

Gino Bova, a kid of 18, was the first of the ones accused of the beating that ended in death to be brought to trail.

The killing of Willie Turks came into the courtroom an explosive issue. Presiding over the trial was Justice Sybil Hart Cooper. Before any of the evidence was heard, before even a single witness was called, the court, as the law requires, took 12 ordinary citizens and put the important business of deciding the case in their hands.

It is still true. When it comes to matters which are really important, those matters cannot be left to the politicians. It takes ordinary citizens who are willing to be fair and honest to do the important work.

In the trial of Gino Bova the jurors were the ones who sat in the courtroom and heard every word of testimony. Once that was done, the lawyers had their say and the judge lectured on the law. Then, the important business of deciding was left to ordinary citizens.

The jury convicted Gino Bova of second-degree manslaughter, of assault, rioting and two civil rights violations. The ordinary citizens, the jurors, do not pass sentence. The sentencing is left to judges.

Later, Justice Sybil Hart Cooper came onto the bench to impose the sentence. Before the judge could come to sentencing, Paul Callan, who is Bova's lawyer, rose to make one last effort to pull his client away from imprisonment. He took excerpts from a letter he had, and argued that it was a witness recanting her testimony. He asked that the conviction be set aside. The judge listened, then Andy Plump, the prosecutor, argued the other way.

The judge then took the letter, and she read all of it in the courtroom. She put the letter aside. She said it was rather sad but no more than an apology from a witness who had testified against Bova in the trial. Then, she turned the proceeding back to the business of sentencing.

The prosecutor rose to ask that the maximum sentence be imposed. He talked of Turks, who was 34 years old, and he said that he was an Army veteran and a father, and then Andy Plump looked back in the courtroom and he called the dead man's mother, Willie Ann Lee, to the front. She was seated on the aisle, four rows back, and she came forward with her face filled with pain. "I just want to say I'm glad this did not go without punishment," she said. "What I'm going through is not easy. Death is death, and we all have to do it, but not this way." She said no more. She turned and went back to her seat.

Andy Plump finished his words and then it was Paul Callan's turn. " I shudder at the thought of what the New York State prison system may do to this young man," he said. "I urge the court not to act in the spirit of revenge."

Then, it was Gino Bova's turn. "I'm truthfully sorry a man died, he said." "I truthfully am." His words became lost in his tears and he looked back into the courtroom at his parents. "There is so much more," he said. "All I can say is I hope I haven't failed my parents."

Now it was Justice Cooper's turn. "It's not my practice to make speeches with sentencing," Justice Cooper said, "but this much is owed to Willie Turks."

In the steamy courtroom the judge picked up a white tablet and the words she read were strong. "I would like to dismiss the indictment against the Gravesend community," she said. "It is unfair that the whole neighborhood should become infamous because of the actions of the defendant."

From the bench, she looked down at Gino Bova. "I listened to you very carefully," she said. "You said you are sorry a man's dead. You didn't say you're sorry you killed him. I was waiting for you to do it."

It was sealed right there. It was a passing of sentence, but there were still more words to come from the bench. Justice Cooper described the way that Willie Turks died, and she said, "It takes a lot of hate to beat someone like that." She said it was "reminiscent of the worst day of the Deep South."

She reached back and pulled out the language that came from the night that Willie Turks was killed and, she brought it back into the courtroom.

"Niggers, get out of here."

"This is a free country, we have a right to be here."

"Gino Bova hit him over the head with a stick. He was dead at 3 a.m. He was 34. He was 5-11. He weighed 170 pounds. He died of multiple blows to the head. It is interesting to note that nobody wielded a stick but the defendant. He feels no remorse. The jury has spoken. It was a lynch mob on Avenue X that night. The only thing missing was a rope and a tree. Willie Turks was forced out of the car by the mob. His arm was in a cast. He tried to run as his friends had done but he didn't make it. Gino Bova stopped him. Gino Bova was looking for trouble. He found it. He killed a man. Only Gino Bova sees his actions as being justified. Perhaps in prison he will see his actions were wrong."

Now, the words from the judge came quickly. "Wasn't Willie Turks summarily executed?" she asked rhetorically. It was 3:35 in the afternoon. There were no more words, only figures now, and the judge was reading them off. "Five to 15 years," she said of the manslaughter conviction. "Five to 15 years," she said of the conviction of assault. "One and a third to four" for the riot conviction. "One year, one year," she said of each of the civil rights convictions, and then it was over.

Gino Bova stood. He looked back into the courtroom. The officers pulled his arms behind his back and handcuffs were put in place. Four of the officers hurried him out of the courtroom.

Paul Callan, the lawyer, leaned over and spoke to a reporter. "I expect to file an appeal, first thing tomorrow," he said.

It was the way the trial of Gino Bova ended yesterday. None of it went very fast the way it usually does. It was that kind of case.

Brooklyn
1991

THE WAY IT COMES OUT, the judicial system stands on one side saying to the Rev. Al Sharpton, "We are going to teach you a lesson." On the other side, the activist minister stands his ground while sending the message back that says, "Do you really know what you are doing?"

The lesson to Sharpton seems designed to teach him that he'll have a big price to pay if he ever dares to lead another demonstration of the kind that took place in Brooklyn on the 12th of December in 1968. That day (which had the name a Day of Rage) a good piece of business in the city couldn't happen. In Brooklyn, subways were stopped, traffic was a mess. By the time Sharpton was eventually arrested, he was in the subway, down on the tracks, and no trains could move.

From that day until this, a lot of the time the courts say they do not have has been given over to this matter. There have been at least 24 separate actions. And the way the courts work, that means paperwork which involves everything from judges to clerks and all the others in between who function as part of "the system."

Why? To what end? It has to be about teaching Sharpton a lesson; there is nothing else to explain why so much supposedly valuable time (to say nothing of resources) has been spent on the case. Sharpton had a trial. The verdict in that came on Feb. 13 of 1990. He was found guilty of obstruction of government administration, of criminal trespass in the 4th degree, and of disorderly conduct. All that got him a jail term of 45 days. Sharpton fought that right up to last week, when the last word came down from State Court of Appeals Judge Joseph Bellacosa. He denied Sharpton's appeal, which means that as early as today -- and surely no later than a month from now -- Sharpton is likely to wind up in a jail cell on Rikers Island.

"I come out of the King movement," Sharpton said. "I'm going where I belong."

More than a "Do they know what they are doing?" question, Sharpton is really asking, "Do they know what that means?"

Rikers is like almost all lockups in the state of New York. About 95 percent of the inmates are Black and Latins, and most of them are poor. In a way, that means they are a lot of the Sharpton constituency. In his eyes, Sharpton sees the trip to jail as a chance to organize on grounds where a lot of organizing is needed.

That does not mean that Sharpton agrees that he ought to go to jail. "A double standard," he calls his 45-day term. And he goes back to December of 1968 and brings back what the atmosphere was then in New York. It was the time of Howard Beach and the attack on Michael Griffin that took his life. It was the anger around that which prompted the Day of Outrage. So Sharpton sees the demonstration in a different way. "It channeled that anger," he said. "We didn't have people in the streets going crazy; we didn't have riots around that." To explain what that means, he points to Los Angeles, and what took place after the verdict in the Rodney King trial. He said that later, U.S. Rep. Maxine Waters of Los Angeles told him that had there been an Al Sharpton in Los Angeles to properly focus the anger after the verdict, that there probably would have been no riot.

The case against Sharpton was prosecuted by former Brooklyn DA Liz Holtzman. In all, some 73 persons were arrested. All the cases were disposed of -- mostly through pleas -- except that of Sharpton, activist Charles Barron and the Rev. Timothy Mitchell of Queens. Mitchell's sentence was dropped because of his health. Barron and Sharpton could go behind bars today.

To put Sharpton behind bars may stir up trouble where trouble is not needed -- in an overcrowded jail where there is already a lot of tension.

Bensonhurst
1991

ONLY IN THE HOWARD BEACH CASE did it happen. Early on, a special prosecutor was appointed. Once that happened, the way was cleared to build a formidable case against the defendants. At the end of the trial, the special prosecutor won convictions.

Since then, in almost every case involving serious racial attack, the demand has been for the appointment of a special prosecutor. But that almost never happens. So instead of special attention, the cases are just thrown into the hopper with a ton of others. That means they get routine treatment from prosecutors who already have more cases than can be properly handled. As a result often there are no convictions; prosecutions that ought to be strong wind up falling apart.

Last August in the Bensonhurst section of Brooklyn, 16-year-old Yusef Hawkins fell victim to racial attack. According to official reports, he and three other Blacks were set upon by a mob of some 30 Whites, many of them wielding bats and clubs. One of the Whites shot and killed Hawkins. At the time, the city was in the midst of a hotly contested mayoral election. The killing hit like a bomb. Politicians issued statements to condemn what had happened; they urged a full investigation and prosecution. Later, many of the state's leading elected officials attended the boy's funeral. But what got ignored was the cry for a special prosecutor.

The case was put into the hands of the district attorney's office in Brooklyn. At the time, it seemed to be cut and dried. Authorities had eye witness accounts of what had happened. Convictions seemed certain. The case was supposed to have gone to trial last week. But it didn't happen. Instead, the DA's office was in court begging for a delay. The worst had happened; the prosecution's case had fallen apart.

The DA's office had to go into court and concede that it had lost track of its key witness. How could such a thing happen? That wasn't all. Further, the DA's office then went to the family of the dead boy, the victims, and asked them to go public in an appeal to the Bensonhurst community for witnesses in the case to come forward and offer testimony. Hawkins was killed over six months ago. The police said he was attacked by a mob. Yet, by the March trial date, only six persons had been charged in the crime. Where were the others who were a part of the mob? Why weren't the police and the DA's office leaning on the community (as they routinely do when they want information) to get what was needed? All this in a case that set the city on edge and attracted national attention.

By last week, the dead boy's parents were so disgusted with the prosecution that they vowed to wash their hands of the case. Moses Stewart, Yusef's father, told the City Sun, a weekly newspaper published in Brooklyn, that he was particularly angered with the conduct of newly elected Brooklyn DA Charles Hynes.

"I put my trust in him, and he has totally ignored my wishes. My posture with Hynes is that I don't even particularly care to talk with him anymore. I placed my trust in him and in the process. All we got was lies, deceit and trickery. No one is cooperating with us. He (Hynes) has totally disrespected us."

What angered Moses was the disappearance of a key witnesses, John Vento, who later surfaced in Dayton, Ohio but then, told the DA through a lawyer that he would not act as a prosecution witness. Vento had earlier told a grand jury that Joseph Fama, 19, had fired the shots that killed Hawkins. Vento, after changing his position and refusing to testify, was charged by Hynes with second-degree murder.

If nothing else, the botching of the Bensonhurst case clearly points up the pressing need for Gov. Cuomo to establish a permanent special prosecutor to deal with serious racial violence. Special prosecutors get appointed to deal with corruption and with drugs and other pressing matters. Why not racial violence? In Howard Beach, the victims refused all cooperation until they got a special prosecutor. Cuomo assigned the case to Hynes and he was given all he needed to build an effective prosecution and he got convictions. Hynes came away from the case with so much acclaim that he rode it to election as Brooklyn DA. But Hynes didn't join in the call for a permanent special prosecutor and so now, in the Yusef Hawkins case, he's paying the price.

A Community of 12
1991

IN THE HOWARD BEACH CASE the idea was to keep Blacks off the jury. In the case involving Larry Davis, the effort was to get a jury that didn't have any Whites.

For years, in the courtroom, jury selection has involved a piece of messy business. A lawyer can virtually say, "I don't want any Blacks or this jury" or, "I don't want any Whites" and in the courtroom, the lawyer can get away with that. The lawyers used the peremptory challenge as the tool for striking down a prospective juror even when the only objection to that person was skin color.

Until last month, all this was a part of the history played out in courtrooms across New York. Then the Court of Appeals, the state's highest tribunal, said no more. Justice Fritz Alexander authored the opinion handed down. In part, he wrote: "We hold today that such racial discrimination has no place in our courtrooms and that such conduct by defense counsel is prohibited by both the civil rights clause and the equal protection clause of our state constitution."

The court was unanimous in a decision certain to have immediate and telling impact. Maybe no trials carry more emotion than those which involve the issue of race. So when a prosecutor or a defense attorney in those courtrooms attempts to shape a jury on the basis of race, it prompts an uproar. That happened in the Howard Beach trial; the Davis cop shooting trial too. But now the court has spoken and so, in the Bensonhurst trial around the killing of Yusef Hawkins, there can be none of the messy business of eliminating prospective jurors solely on the basis of race.

The fight to end racial shaping of juries began nearly 10 years ago. That was about the time Elizabeth Holtzman, the first woman elected a big city district attorney, was taking office in Brooklyn. The DA there had just lost a case that involved picking a jury on the basis of race. The DA was positioned to appeal, but Holtzman got elected and when she came into office and examined the issue, right away she said there would be no appeal. More than that, she joined the other side. She became an advocate; she said it was wrong for prosecutors to be involved in such practices. And she went further; when the issue was tested at the Supreme Court level, she became the only DA in the country to stand against discrimination. Four years ago, in a landmark case (Batson v. Kentucky), the U.S. Supreme Court ruled against prosecutors using challenges to seat all White juries in cases involving nonWhite defendants.

Holtzman reasoned that, if it was wrong for prosecutors to shape juries on the basis of race, then it was wrong for defense attorneys too. She was moved by a handwritten note from one of the ordinary citizens who make up so many juries. It told of how embarrassing it was for a prospective juror to have a lawyer say no, we don't want you because you're White or, we don't want you because you're Black. Holtzman agreed and she became an advocate. The court decision was based on an appeal from the Howard Beach case where a judge ruled that peremptory challenges were being used to exclude Blacks from the jury.

"Of course, we've very proud," Holtzman said. As a DA, she broke new ground just getting elected. The role she played in getting rid of racial discrimination in shaping juries has become her legacy.

Not all lawyers agreed. William Kunstler who defended Larry Davis called it a "terrible" decision. Attorneys for the Howard Beach defendants hinted at an appeal.

But for now, at least in the courtrooms of New York, a stop has been put to the old and messy practice.

Church Ave., Brooklyn
1991

THE WAY THE ISSUE COMES BACK, it is as though there had been no earlier version of the trouble. But all that is taking place has a history. Now the targets are two stores in Brooklyn. Before, the store was in Harlem and then, as now, the Black community was on one side and Korean merchants were on the other.

Lloyd Williams, who heads the Uptown Chamber of Commerce, was at the center of the dispute when the focus was a fruit and vegetable market in Harlem. And he says, "What is happening in Brooklyn is not an anti-Korean effort any more than what happened in Harlem.

If what happened in Harlem was anti-Korean, then all Korean businesses would have been picketed. That wasn't the case. The demonstrations were only conducted where specific incidents took place and that is exactly what is happening in Brooklyn. They are not picketing all Korean stores; it's only where incidents have taken place."

Williams argues that issues have gotten blurred because "Koreans work well with the White media." He accuses them of using that arrangement now to "portray themselves as victims of reverse racism," and he calls that "a blatant lie."

"Should the Black community not be able to demonstrate before any business where abusive incidents take place?

The real issue is that nowhere are Korean businessmen welcomed more than in the Black community. Nowhere has he been more appreciated. But when Korean, Jewish, Italian, Arab or African-Americans operate businesses where abusive incidents take place, they should be the target of demonstrations.

On Park Ave.. when Whites demonstrated against a Korean business, that was no front page issue.

In Italian and Jewish communities, a lot of the time they prevent Koreans from coming in; they run them out and nothing is said. But when it's the African-American community, they (the media) pit one group against the other."

In Brooklyn, it's happening that way now. No groups are attempting to force all Korean businesses out of the Black community. The Red Apple grocery at 1823 Church Ave. and another store nearby are targets but for specific reasons. The contention is that at the Red Apple, a Haitian woman was roughed up by employees and a boycott and demonstrations are almost entirely in response to that. And that's the way it was in Harlem.

The demonstrations there were aimed at a store on 125th St. Three times in six years, there were boycotts. But while those actions were being carried out, some 70 other Korean businesses continued doing business in Harlem without harassment.

"If this was an issue of racism against Yellow people," Lloyd Williams asked, "then why were there no problems with businesses operated by Chinese people?

"They have a lot of restaurants, laundries and grocery stores and they have been in the community for 60 to 70 years and with no problem. To portray this as Black against Yellow is an absolute lie. We have all put ourselves on the line to build an integrated business community in Harlem and Bedford-Stuyvesant. The problem is that a lot of Koreans see us (Blacks) as being shiftless and lazy drug addicts. They don't respect us and that's what is behind this trouble. There is going to be a race riot, though,if something doesn't change because one of these days, some old woman or a kid is going to get attacked, or get killed, and all hell is going to jump off.

"We (in the Black community) are not coming up with rules for Koreans, but rules for the community. The Koreans don't respect us, our communities or our culture, and if that doesn't change, there are going to be a lot of problems."

Williams acknowledged that, on the picket lines at demonstrations, a lot of anti-Korean statements do get shouted. He does not read racism into that. "There has been some inflammatory rhetoric," he said. "But sometimes you have to have that to secure your base of support.

"But remember, the demonstrations are not against Koreans. They are against specific stores. The December 12th Movement should be applauded for keeping these issues in the forefront; somebody ought to do it. This is an issue of community control and an issue of community respect."

So the dispute that's going on now in Brooklyn has a history. It goes back through most of a decade, and Lloyd Williams is another of those who has a finger on the cause of the trouble that gets played out in the media as being Black racism aimed at Korean merchants.

The history goes back even further. From the start, Martin Luther King, Jr. used the boycott. In 1955, when he was just 25 years old, he was the leader in the effort to desegregate public transportation in Montgomery, Alabama. King needed an effective tool to change the minds of the city's White leaders who were saying never to the demand for desegregation.

King would not resort to violence. He argued that there was another way to deal with the situation and to do that, he told his supporters they didn't need guns, clubs or knives.

It was King's idea that Blacks had to "use what you've got." So his decision was to implement economic sanctions. To do that, a boycott of the public transportation system was organized.

It takes some doing to make a boycott effective. The issue has to be so clear that it's easy to see. The issue also has to be so important that once implemented, the boycott has the support of masses of people. Then, it takes commitment.

At first in Montgomery, as Blacks walked and used car pools rather than support the segregated system, Whites snickered and hurled insults. The belief was that Blacks were only hurting themselves.

Early on, it sometimes seems that way with boycotts. But that changes; in time economic sanctions take their toll. "Just don't ride the bus," King counseled Blacks in Montgomery. "Just do that and we'll win."

What King understood was that the system that treated Black as less than citizens could not operate without the support of Blacks. That was a truth that eventually all of Montgomery came to understand.

When Blacks quit riding, service got cut and jobs got lost, and Whites who had been laughing and shouting insults took to violence in trying to force Blacks to break the boycott.

But a commitment had been made and the boycott stood. King and the movement that began in Montgomery was to win a huge victory. And the history made then was never forgotten. In subsequent battles, the boycott was a tool used successfully again and again.

Chapter Seven, Part One

THE AFRICANS

AND

THE AMERICANS

LEGACY OF RESPECT

Editor's Note

Over the years, no journalist working for a major U.S. news organization has reported more frequently or comprehensively on African leaders and events -- without being based there -- than Earl Caldwell. He has repeatedly identified the many links between African and American policies and populations. While much of this coverage concerned the liberation struggles in Southern Africa, Caldwell also explored much of the rest of the continent -- in countries large and small.

1980

IN THE EVENING, AFTER THE SUN has dropped in the west, twilight stills the water in the lagoon and, in the quiet, music rises.

You cannot see the church. It is farther over, hidden somewhere among the mud huts in the village. But it doesn't matter. The music says it's there. It is the kind of music that rises on Sunday mornings from churches in Harlem and Bedford Stuyvesant in Brooklyn. Now, in the twilight, it is here in this village that sits isolated on the banks of a lagoon just off the South Atlantic in Nigeria on the continent of Africa.

The Africans have languages only they understand. Still you strain for the words. The music is that familiar. It is music Black Americans are brought up with; old Negro spirituals they are called. When you stand here at twilight along a sliver of blacktop that is the road, you do not notice the women who pass with babies strapped to their backs. You do not notice the brown goats, the chickens, or even the kids. You are frozen by the music.

The Rev. Wyatt Tee Walker said that it was that way. He said that what is Black and has survived in the West is mostly that which is connected with the church. Rev. Walker is a pastor at Canaan Baptist Church, in Harlem. He made the trip here to Africa, studied the music, and made the connection which he wrote about in his book, "Somebody's Calling My Name." He wrote that the Black church is the American fruit of an African root. At twilight, here in Badagry, you hear the echo of his words.

Sooner or later, if you are Black, American and traveling in this section of Africa, somebody picks you up and brings you here to the coast, to Badagry.

"You haven't been to Badagry," Kayode Otufale said. "Oh God," he said. Kayode Otufale is 28, of the Yoruba tribe, and grew up in Lagos, the capital city of Nigeria, which is 20 miles to the west of Badagry.

"This is something," he says, "Rosalynn Carter comes here, and right away they take her to Badagry. If I was in government, she wouldn't see that. No way she would see that. She doesn't need to see that. For what?"

Badagry is roots. The connection that links many Americans who are Black to Africa begins here at the end of a dusty road that comes down to the water, to the lagoon, where, in another time, slave ships docked.

Just off the road, away from the village, there is one building that stands larger than any of the others. It is a barn-like building, fenced in. The lock at the door is new.

A row of smaller houses sits just up from the barn. An old heavyset woman in African dress sits alone on one of the porches. She spoke first to Kayode, then to a small boy who came onto the porch. Then the three of them headed for the barn, the old woman, the small boy, and the tall African who studied in the United States, first at Southern University, then at Prairie View A&M.

The old woman unlocked the door and propped it open. Just inside was a grave where the headstone read, "In memory of our dearly beloved Father."

Underneath it said. "Chief Simbu Mober of Beokah, Badagry, who died Oct. 16, 1893."

The woman who was a grandchild of Chief Mober carried a stick. She leaned on it as she made her way to the center of the barn. As she moved, the small boy moved with her. There was a table at the center of the room, a long table. On top were boxes, a small cannon and other pieces of metal. The woman leaned on the side at the end of the table. She did not say a word. Only the small boy spoke.

Without any prompting, he began, and words spilled out. There was a heavy hoarse sound to his voice. The words came in a rush, at first so rapidly that the woman had to stop him because she knew that no one could understand.

"Twenty-four people on the left, 24 people on the right, 24 in the front, 24 in the back." As the small boy went on, he would point to show how the collected Africans, those who would be sold into slavery, were positioned around in the barn in rows of 24 each.

He opened a musty wooden box that was filled with piles of rusting chains and then began to speak again. "This one for the left leg," he said, holding up one chain. "This one for the stubborn slaves," he said, holding up heavy irons. "This one for two people...this one for small children..." He kept racing through the litany. All the while, the old woman watched and listened.

Now, the kid pointed to the cannon, saying that it was sounded three times every day. "Once in the morning, once in the afternoon, once at night." He raced on. "After the last one, if they see someone on down the road, they take them off as slaves."

"Why did it happen?" Kayode asked the woman.

She spoke no English. She used her tribal tongue. Kayode listened, then translated. "She says it happened in the old days, and they didn't know too much. As of today, she said she really feels bad about it, but it happened and it's a sad story.

"She said the chief didn't go around capturing slaves. She said he had money. The Whites started him out as a financier. He was buying slaves for them. He was the broker."

"How did they decide who would be sold into slavery?"

Again the woman spoke in the language of the tribe, and the small boy listened and then Kayode repeated in English.

"Anyone who was disrespectful to the chief. Anyone they caught out late at night, after the cannon was fired. But she says it was a long time ago. She said she's sorry."

The old woman began to make her way towards the door. When she was questioned about her age, and how the story had been passed along to her, she would not answer.

"What does the name Badagry mean?" Kayode Otufale was asked.

He said that was not really the name of the town at all. He spelled the name: Abgadarigi. "The Whites changed it," he said. "They couldn't pronounce the real name so they just changed it."

Outside, the sun was gone and the twilight was changing to darkness. Now, there was no music. Only the quiet.

1992

ON A NIGHT ALMOST six years ago in Lusaka, the capital of Zambia in southern Africa, Kenneth Kaunda, the country's president, was hosting a reception for a delegation of Americans led by the Rev. Jesse Jackson.

As he spoke that night, Kaunda talked of the way life was across so much of the African continent. He mentioned the disease, the poverty, the illiteracy and a long list of other problems. When he finished describing the conditions that wrack the continent, Kaunda talked of how important it was that Africa be changed.

"Because," he said, "the Black man will never be respected anywhere in the world as long as Africa remains the way that it is."

That night Kaunda talked of many things. More than anything else, he stressed the importance of ending the apartheid regime in South Africa. His is a land-locked country that sits to the north of South Africa. He talked of how the powerful military machine in South Africa had virtually ruined his country's economy. Then, South Africa was punishing Zambia because Kaunda had allowed Nelson Mandela's African National Congress to establish its base and headquarters there. So the rail lines that Zambia needed to reach ports in Mozambique were constantly bombed. And because the Zambian military was little more than a token force, South Africa also made routine bombing raids on Lusaka.

Kaunda insisted that eventually apartheid would fall. He worried, though, that it would take a blood bath. But in the post-apartheid era, he saw the chance for prosperity all across southern Africa.

Two days ago, when the White minority approved a referendum that clears the way for the South African government to continue negotiations with Black groups over a new, non-racial constitution, what Kaunda saw as only a glimmer of hope suddenly rises boldly on the horizon

As South African President F. W. de Klerk declared, "Today we have closed the book on apartheid."

South Africa does not yet have its new, non-racial democracy. But that's the prospect that now looms large. That brings to the front something that Pik Botha, South Africa's foreign minister, said to Mayor David Dinkins on his visit to South Africa last fall. At the time, Botha was trying to persuade Dinkins to change his position on sanctions. Dinkins would not be moved. "Don't try and convince me to change," Dinkins said to Botha. "You convince Mandela; I support Mandela's position."

The argument Botha pressed on Dinkins, though, was an important one; he sketched out for the mayor a vision of what southern Africa could be once it got past its problems of race. Botha told Dinkins almost exactly what Kaunda told Jesse Jackson and his party a half dozen years earlier.

The truth about southern Africa is that the region is one of the treasure troves of the world. It's not just South Africa that has a wealth of raw materials. The whole region has one precious reserve after another. What it has not had is the environment to take advantage of it. The region of southern Africa has been at war over race almost continually since Whites arrived. But the vote in South Africa two days ago signaled what may be the beginning of the end.

And as Botha said to Dinkins, that means something. With apartheid an issue of the past, Botha envisions governments in the region acting in concert. He sees the development of a common market. He believes that once it becomes the reality, the economies of all the nations in the area have the potential to boom.

"Change South Africa," Kaunda said, "and you begin to change all of Africa."

That now appears to be the reality that is on the horizon.

1980

SALISBURY, RHODESIA -- THE PATTERN has not yet been broken. Each day still begins much the same as the one before. At dawn in downtown Salisbury, the streets begin to fill with Blacks, and in the early morning virtually none of what is unfolding here is visible.

At first light, the movement of Blacks into the city is only a trickle. There are the women, some in uniforms that are white, starched and pressed, and with them others who wear plain, print dresses. Then come the old men in work clothes and after them younger, stronger men in heavy shoes. And it does not stop. Others come, young boys on bicycles and on foot and girls in summer dresses. All of them are Black.

Before 7 o'clock the trickle has turned to a stream. Nobody stands around. All of them hurry along, some almost running to the garages, hotels, office buildings and the stores, shops and government buildings where they work serving White people.

In the morning, when the city comes alive, there is nothing that says that the life and the rule of the White minority, which has existed here since the 1800s, is coming apart. Thee Africans still are obedient to their work. In the hotels when they serve their customers, almost all of whom are White, they still bow. Some call their employers Boss. When they take their instructions, their heads nod in agreement and obediently they keep saying: "Yessir, yessir, yessir."

Here in Salisbury, the facade is that everything is still in place. Whites come leisurely into the city after the sun is up. They come in their cars, wearing suits and ties. When they go into their buildings, the Blacks bow. The appearance is that everything is in place. But it is only a facade.

Now the liberation movement that has swept through most of Black Africa in the last 20 years is here. Rhodesia is on the verge of yielding to Black majority rule, but the end does not come easy.

Through the last seven years, the country has been torn by a bloody war of liberation waged by Blacks with such intensity that even the so-called internal settlement it provoked last year, one that brought a Black man, Bishop Abel Muzorewa, to power as Prime Minister, did not end the fighting.

There are no accurate figures as to how many deaths the war brought. Estimates begin at 20,000. Even when figures twice that high are used, many say that even more died. But the breakthrough that produced the ceasefire, ending the war, finally came late last year in London.

This country has had many names: Rhodesia and Southern Rhodesia, and last year at London it was Zimbabwe-Rhodesia. The agreement for majority rule first produced a new constitution, one providing for a Parliament of 100 seats. The White minority, now estimated at 200,000, would have 20 seats. The Black majority, estimated at seven million, would have the remaining 80 seats. It was agreed in London that there would be a transition period, during which the country would be recolonized by the British, and in this interim, a governor sent from England would rule. On December 21, the ceasefire agreement was signed.

Now the transition period is drawing to a close. The time is approaching for the Whites in Rhodesia to turn the power loose. This is a country whose leadership once responded to the call for Black majority rule by saying: "Never in a thousand years."

There is no question as to why the White minority continues to grasp for control. Rhodesia is not what is called an underdeveloped Africa nation. Rhodesia is modern and rich. Even with the burden of war, and the limitations of sanctions placed on it, it thrives.

It is a beautiful country. There is not even the slightest hint of pollution in the air. Everyday the sky is the brightest blue. Now, in the summertime, it is green and lush.

The huge farms and ranches that stretch out in the countryside just beyond the cities are, without doubt, among the best and most productive in the world.

They call this a country that has everything. Even the weather is perfect. Everyday the temperatures are in the 80s, the sun always seems to shine, and there is little humidity. The people here say that it is nice even when it rains.

It has gold mines. Chrome is plentiful. The farms produce not only enough to feed Rhodesians but manage surpluses to export.

Salisbury is the centerpiece. It is not simply a clean city: it sparkles. There is not a speck of litter anywhere. The lawns around the city's building are not just neat. They are painstakingly and perfectly manicured. Outside the core of the city, in the neighborhoods where the Whites live, it is the same. Every home has lawns and gardens filled with flowers of every kind. Every tree, hedge and bush is finely pruned.

But the real part of what makes Rhodesia so attractive to the White minority, what makes it so difficult for them to release their hold on any piece of the country, is that it is not expensive for them. Everything except gasoline is inexpensive.

"We've got the best farms in the world out here," a husky businessman, a White who has lived in Rhodesia for 15 years, said. "Better than you've got in America. We got better beef, too."

"Why is it so inexpensive?" he was asked.

"You know why," he snapped.

Everyone knows why. The Whites do not discuss it, particularly not with Blacks. But the answer is cheap labor. There are millions and millions of Black Africans to clip the lawns, prune the gardens, work the ranches, and tend the crops on the farms. There is no such thing as a minimum wage. Whites who earn $15,000 a year can afford to hire two, sometimes three Blacks to do the work. Now, it's coming apart.

It was evident here yesterday, which was the start of the election that is supposed to turn control of the country over to Blacks. The election is being held in two parts. Yesterday, the Whites voted. For three days, beginning February 27, the Blacks will vote.

What was evident here on White election day was that the White vote is irrelevant. This is a Black election. It is the Black vote that will decide. That is what has brought tension, fear, killing and worry as to what is to come to this country in southern Africa where Whites have ruled for hundreds of years.

What will the Blacks do? Will they take the farms? Will they take the jobs? It is a country filled with questions. Already some Whites have begun to leave. The papers are filled with excellent opportunities to buy good property at low prices.

There are nine Black parties contesting for leadership of the country. But only three are given any real chance of organizing the new government. There is the party led by Muzorewa, another led by Joshua Nkomo, and a third led by Robert Mugabe.

The Whites know Muzorewa. He is the candidate they would like to see lead the new government. Nkomo and Mugabe are symbols of the war and neither is acceptable to the Whites. Nkomo led the guerrilla forces that were largely based and given sanctuary in Zambia on the north. Mugabe's army, the largest, operated out of Mozambique. The two fought together in London. But now, each is in the election with his own party, vying for leadership.

It is Mugabe who is especially feared by the Whites. He is an avowed Marxist, and Whites are certain that his election would mean that they would lose the big farms; that the system that now works for them will be twisted to drive them out. But it is not the Whites who will decide. It is the millions of Blacks.

THE SOLDIER'S NAME IS TAKAWIRA Topfumanei. His face is smooth, clear and dark -- a young man's face. Even with the bulky, camouflage-colored fatigues, the ammunition strapped at his waist and the gear tied on his back, you notice that the body is lean and strong.

He keeps an AK-47 slung over his shoulder. The weapon is Russian-made. He does not explain how it got into his hands. He never puts it down.

"Best assault weapon in the world," he says.

"How old are you?"

"Old enough to be a commander," he says.

There are other soldiers with him, many of them even younger. Young girls and young boys who have not yet acquired the look of teenagers. But when you ask their ages, they keep saying 18 and 19. Topfumanei, the commander is right: With soldiers, age does not matter. It is said that the young fight best, and it is true. Those who have not lived do not fear death.

It is early in the afternoon, and Topfumanei stands in a clearing in the bush in a remote section of Northern Rhodesia, less than 10 kilometers from where the country borders Mozambique. There is the cluster of soldiers around him and others farther back. When you look hard, hundreds more come into focus in the bush.

All of them are a part of the Zimbabwe African National Liberation Army (ZANLA), the guerrilla army of Robert Mugabe, the man many feel will be elected Prime Minister of the new independent Republic of Zimbabwe next week.

These are the soldiers that White Rhodesians always refer to as terrorists. Outsiders call them guerrillas. But to Black Africans, they are the boys, the boys in the bush.

Without the ZANLA, fighting together with the army of Joshua Nkomo as the Patriotic Front, there would have been no elections in Rhodesia this week. There would not be the anticipation here that there is now, the anticipation of real power passing from the White minority to the Black majority. The ZANLA of Robert Mugabe and the Zimbabwe Independent People Revolutionary Army (ZIPRA) of Joshua Nkomo forced the issue.

The armies are still now. The ceasefire is still intact and the soldiers they call the boys are collected in remote sections of the country in places known as assembly points. The camps carry names such as Alpha and Bravo and Charlie. They are not real camps. Just clearings in the bush. In some there are hundreds of "the boys" and in others, there are thousands.

"We're people's soldiers."

Takawira Topfumanei is an officer in the assembly point called Delta, wedged between a dirt road, a picturesque lake, a stream where the boys sometimes fish and the foothills of the mountains that stretch out to Mozambique.

"We're people's soldiers," Topfumanei says. "We don't fight for money. We're not like the Rhodesian soldiers. We're not mercenaries. We need no praise or money for fighting for the people. I've been in it for nearly a decade and I've never got a cent."

As Topfumanei moves through the camp, the young soldiers who stand in the clearing watch. When he comes close, they snap to attention. Some salute.

"Yes, comrade," he says.

In Delta, the ZANLA camp, all of the soldiers address each other as comrade.

"Why do you fight?" Topfumanei is asked.

"For political objectives," he says. "To free our people, to free our people from foreign rule, and from exploitation."

The site where Delta is located rises off the dirt road where a large blue and white sign stating, "ceasefire assembly point" sticks out from the trees. Just beyond the sign, a small camp houses what is called the monitoring force. There are 37 monitors; all except three are Australians. The others are British. The boys, the ZANLA boys, are deeper in the bush. At Delta, there are 2,777 of them.

Yesterday, on the last day of the elections here, portable polling booths were brought into the camp. The boys cast their ballots. Bit by bit now they are taking the camps apart. The boys are being integrated into the Rhodesian army. The outward signs are that the war is over.

But listen to Topfumanei, the young officer.

"We can fight for years if necessary. We are not tired. We promise not to be tired until our people are free -- or until death."

His English is perfect. He also speaks good Swahili and another language, his tribal tongue, but he will not say what that is. "Tribe is not important," he says. "If we were divided as tribes, we could not have fought the war for such a long time."

"Where were you educated?" he is asked.

"Here," the young officer says. "I was educated in the bush."

When the young officer says that ZANLA is political, outsiders do not understand. But the Africans who live here in the bush, in the tribal Trustlands - called TTLs and in the protected villages, they know. They've lived with the boys for years. In that time, they've been organized and politicized by them. Next Tuesday morning, when the election results are disclosed, all of Rhodesia will understand.

George Marimo, who calls himself a Zimbabwean -- he never uses the word Rhodesia -- says it is those who live in the TTL's who have fared the worst during the war.

"Why?"

"Because their villages were burned.," he said. It is a tactic the Rhodesian army borrowed from the American pacification program in Vietnam. After a village is burned, the government tries to move the people to so-called "protected villages." "Many of them run to the city hoping they can get some help," Marimo added. "They've been through it all. Nobody has it worse than the people in the TTL's."

A woman who lives in a TTL south of here talked about the boys. When she did, right away she mentioned the meetings they held every night during the war. They call the meetings "Pungwe." And everybody goes. Nobody says not this week, or I'm too busy. When the boys call a meeting, everybody shows up.

"Meetings about what?" she is asked.

"Politics and everything," she said. "But mostly, it's politics. Everything you do, you have to consult with the boys. Even if my father wants to visit me, he has to tell the boys.

"People believe in the boys," she said. "They believe in the boys so much. They believe anything they do is good. You know, these people in the TTL don't have enough to eat, but they always manage to cook something good for the boys. You know, like chicken and eggs and stuff."

The Africans worry now about the boys. As part of the ceasefire agreement, they came into the assembly points around the county. People worry that the Rhodesian army might try a sneak attack, surround the boys and slaughter them. When you say that you have been to a camp, excitement comes into their faces.

"You've seen the boys? You mean it? Are they all right? You sure?"

The boys in Mugabe's army are Marxist-oriented, and that is the politics they teach in the meetings they call Pungwe. They have been in the bush for seven years fighting the war, but even longer than that, every night, they teach. All of the boys are teachers. The election will tell just how effective they've been.

These are the young sons and the young daughters of the Africans isolated on the reservations called TTLs. They are the sons and daughters of the Africans who are crammed into the townships. For years they have been fighting and teaching. Whites in Rhodesia shake their heads with incomprehension. They do not understand why Blacks would vote for a communist like Mugabe.

A part of the answer is up here in the bush. These young kids, men and women, dress in anything they can find. But all of them are armed. With AK-47s and with machine guns and rocket launchers, with long strips of ammunition criss-crossing their shoulders and chests. "We control this area. Sure, we are subjected to bombardment but we control the people."

The young officer, the comrade, looked at the boys. He would smile. "You can see the whole process," he said.

"We're prepared to do whatever is necessary. And we will win. Whether it comes through the ballot or through the barrel of a gun."

ALL THROUGH THE CAMPAIGN, the Africans had been quiet. They just went on serving, lifting and bowing, assuring their White bosses that everything was all right by always answering. "Yessir, yessir, yessir."

They played the role to the hilt. It was difficult to know that one of the most important elections in African history was about to take place, if you watched the Africans when they were close to their White employers.

They stood obediently when they were lectured on the evils of communism. They nodded agreement when urged to vote for Bishop Abel Muzorewa. When strangers asked, they were quick to disavow any interest in politics.

Then, last Wednesday, it was time to vote. It was time for the Black Africans to select the government they wanted. In Rhodesia, Blacks have never had a voice. Always, Whites decided.

On Wednesday, the Africans came streaming out of every hut and shanty, in the bush and in the townships, from everywhere they came in a stream to the polls. They stood in enormous lines. They waited for hours. They were long, quiet lines, filled with people who, for the first time, were making a real decision about their country. But still, they never tipped their hand. They did their voting quietly through three days, and Rhodesia waited to learn what the Blacks had decided.

In the early morning yesterday, when the word came, it was so overwhelming, so decisive, that it left the White minority stunned.

In the morning sun, Blacks were on the street as they always are, walking, sometimes running, to their jobs -- but yesterday was different.

There was a light in their faces. When they greeted each other, many raised a fist. Sometimes, it was only a smile. Whatever the gesture, when they greeted each other, they knew they had struck a decisive blow. They had delivered up the one thing the Whites could not take. They elected the Marxist party of Robert Mugabe, and they did it in the grandest of styles.

The forecast was for a close election. No party was given a real chance of winning an absolute majority. But Mugabe, the Marxist, swept in, his party winning 57 seats and nearly 63 percent of the vote.

If Muzorewa was the candidate of the Whites, Blacks treated him as such. It has been estimated that he spent $30 million in his lavish campaign. Much of the money came from South Africa. Whenever he was questioned about his finances during the campaign, Muzorewa's answer was the same. "None of your business," he always snapped.

Muzorewa won only 8 percent of the vote. The party he led captured just three seats. It was a humiliating defeat.

Except for a handful, what votes Mugabe did not get went to Joshua Nkomo. His party polled 24 percent of the vote and finished with 20 seats in Parliament, the governing body of the soon-to-be-independent Republic of Zimbabwe.

There was no great celebration in Rhodesia yesterday. No boisterous crowds filled the streets. There were no parades. There were no rallies. The army and all the various kinds of police that are called security forces made certain of that. The celebrating that was done was slipped past the soldiers.

It didn't matter. It was a historic day, and that was enough. In Rhodesia, the Black Africans took another step in the steady move towards taking control from the White minority. Independence is not being granted. It is being taken.

In the early afternoon, Mugabe came out of the modest house in the Mount Pleasant neighborhood where he lives, and crossed the lawn to meet reporters. As he moved, his supporters kept calling to him "Prime Minister," they shouted. "Prime Minister."

His politics of liberation had caused him to spend 10 years in prison. His only child died while he was jailed. There was so much, it welled up in him and it was, as he said, "a great moment."

The British governor who is in charge here as part of the agreement that led to elections had already asked Mugabe to form a new government. Now, as he sat facing reporters, his victory certain, there must have been the urge somewhere inside Robert Mugabe to gloat, to say, "We showed them." But he didn't.

"We cannot talk of losers," he said. "We all belong to the same country." And soon he was saying that his government would nationalize no property, that it would take nothing from anyone. He talked of being just and fair, and was saying that people of all races would be considered for his cabinet.

As he talked, it was clear that he understood that the struggle was not yet over. He measured every word. He was filled with caution.

Beyond the fence that surrounds his yard, army trucks moved past and the machine guns that were mounted on top were easily visible. The word coup came to mind. It explained the caution Mugabe displayed. It is not over yet.

Whites in Rhodesia have been telling Blacks over and over again of the evils of communism. They have been saying in almost hysterical tones how bad Marxism will be for the country. Blacks made their own choice and the Marxists won the election. What is clear is that it is Whites who worry. Whites fear Mugabe. The question now is whether they will accept his government.

Earlier in the morning, in the backyard of another modest house, in another neighborhood, Joshua Nkomo came out to meet reporters. There were some who applauded him when he came to the microphone. More than anything else, Joshua Nkomo had wanted to win this election. More than anything, he wanted to be the first prime minister of Zimbabwe. But as he came out before the press, he knew it was not to be.

Nkomo is a huge bear of a man. His hair is mostly gray, and he uses his booming voce like an instrument. He likes to laugh, and when he does, his whole body shakes.

They call him Josh. He's considered the father of the nationalist movement here. He has been in it for 30 years, and like Mugabe, he was imprisoned for 10 years because he was determined to end the system that allowed 200,000 Whites to rule seven million Blacks.

"We fought for Zimbabwe," Nkomo said. "We fought for the independence of our country. Finally we've got it. This is what is vital. Results don't always please everybody. But the people of the country made a decision. It has to be accepted."

Now, he forgot his dreams and talked of unity. He fought with Mugabe against the White Rhodesian regime. He had thought the two would wage a joint campaign in the election. It was not to be. Mugabe ran alone, and he won.

Nkomo is of the Ndebele tribe. In those sections of the country where the Ndebele rule, he won easily. But the Mashona have the numbers, and they delivered their votes to Mugabe. Nkomo forgot all of that. He spoke instead of the importance of being united. He also understood that it was not over yet.

It is said that there are three tribes in Rhodesia, the Mashona, the Ndebele and the Whites. The question now is whether the three can get together to build a new nation, Zimbabwe.

THEY CALL THEM AFRICAN BARS. They are really beer gardens, but in Rhodesia, they are known as African bars because all of the customers are Black.

The African bar is another slice of the segregated society in Rhodesia that has not yet disappeared. The African bar is still here.

In downtown Salisbury the bar Africans use sits on a busy street next to the Ambassador Hotel. It is a big place with a high ceiling, bright lights and a long, L-shaped bar. An hour before noon yesterday, it already was crowded and noisy and everybody seemed to have a grip on a bottle that was either Castle or Lion.

"You from America?"

"You mean it?"

This has not been just a segregated society for Blacks. It also has been a closed one. Rhodesian Blacks have not been permitted, and most could not afford, to travel. It is seldom that outsiders, especially Black Americans, have been allowed to visit here.

"You from America, you mean it?"

They say it with amazement in their voices, and they stare, and keep looking, and then they smile.

"America," they ask, "what is it like?"

When outsiders come into the company of White Rhodesians it is different. They like to say how great the country is, and after that, it is not long before they mention sanctions.

"We beat sanctions," they say. An elderly man with steel gray hair who was once the mayor of Hartley, a small town southwest of Salisbury, said that sanctions saved the country.

"We had to pull together," he said. "All of us." Before he was mayor he owned two gasoline stations. When sanctions came, he closed one. He went into another business. "Metal business," he said. "We could fix anything. A part breaks, you bring it to us. We could make anything. Some people came to us just to use our equipment. We had a damn good business."

Beating sanctions is what Whites are quick to talk about. They tell of all the things they had to do, all the laws they had to break. But it didn't matter, only beating the sanctions that were imposed on Rhodesia by the international community was important. That enabled Whites to keep the segregated society from falling apart.

Everyone was involved; even Chris Anderson, the minister of justice, who boasts even now about how he was able to slip into the United States illegally. He laughs when he talks about it.

The Africans had no stake in beating sanctions. In the bars where they gather, they talk of other things. Black Africans are beer drinkers. When strangers come into their bars, they brag about the beer.

"The Castle," they say, "It's really good." It is the same way with the Lion. "The best beer in Africa," they say. As they drink they begin to argue the point. But it is all in fun. You know this because sometimes the men who are close hold hands as they talk. When Africans are friendly with one another, they show affection.

But on this morning in the African bar next to the Ambassador Hotel there was no talk of beer, of the Castle or the Lion.

"Smith," said a young fellow who wore jeans and a dark shirt. "He was talking to Smith. Yeah, yesterday he was talking to Smith. Can you believe that? I can't believe it."

"He's gonna put Whites in the government," another older man said. "That was in the newspaper."

Yesterday morning all of the talk was about Robert Mugabe, the man Black Africans elected so overwhelmingly to lead the government when Rhodesia becomes Zimbabwe.

Control in the new, independent state passed from the White minority to the Black majority.

Before the elections Blacks in their bars never argued politics. Especially when strangers were around. But on this morning there was no other topic of conversation.

And at the center of it was a meeting Robert Mugabe held with former Prime Minister Ian Smith, who said later that he would accept a cabinet post in the new government if asked. To Black Africans, Ian Smith is the symbol of racist oppression. Until now they had been careful about using his name. Since the election it has been different.

"To hell with Smith," another African in the bar said. His back stiffened. "There's no need to talk with Smith. That's why we voted ZANU-PF. That's why we voted for the cock."

ZANU-PF is the acronym for the Zimbabwe African National Union-Patriotic Front, the political party of Robert Mugabe. The rooster, the cock, is the party symbol. It is the symbol Mugabe's people used so effectively to let those who cannot read know where to mark their ballots. In the bar, the arguments were punctuated with Africans imitating the crow of the cock. Every time it happened, a great noise rose in the bar.

In a corner, a man whose name was Elton Mutasa listened. "You got to understand," he said, "that's why people voted for Mugabe. They thought he would be the hardest on Whites. They thought he was going to change everything right away."

"But Mugabe has to go slow, doesn't he?"

"I know that. You know that, But a lot of these people, they don't understand. They don't care about Whites leaving. They want them to leave. They believe that if the Whites leave, they'll get their cars and the houses Whites live in. They believe they'll get the jobs that Whites have, and make the money Whites make. They want the Whites to leave. They expected them to leave."

One of the reasons Mugabe is moving slowly is because he does not yet have control of the army, and a coup here is still considered a real possibility.

In the evening yesterday Eddison Zvobgo, a spokesman for Mugabe, went before the press to announce that the prime minister-elect was determined to end martial law and the curfew imposed on Blacks as soon as possible. When asked to be specific, he hedged. He also hedged when asked when the roadblocks would end. It was the same when he was asked, when the army would discontinue the show of force that it continues to carry on in the streets and towns throughout the country. Zvobgo had no real answers because Mugabe is moving slow. Mugabe has even asked the British to stay on in Rhodesia a while longer, delaying independence, and thus delaying his takeover as prime minister.

"The problem," Zvobgo said "is that we don't have a system for the orderly transfer of power. I understand now why the Americans have a definite system to handle the transition of governments. It's a good system they have. Very innovative. Here, you are either in or you are out."

Yesterday, Mugabe and the government that Blacks elected overwhelmingly last week was still out. In the African bars, a lot of people had trouble understanding.

ONCE THE CRY WAS NEVER, never in a thousand years. But tomorrow, it happens. Tomorrow Rhodesia dies.

In ceremonies in the capital city of Salisbury, Rhodesia becomes the independent nation of Zimbabwe. Once it does, control of the strategic, wealthy state in southern Africa passes from a White minority to a Black majority.

It was Ian Smith who said never. He was prime minister then, and to Rhodesians the symbol of White supremacy. "Never in my lifetime," was his response to the call for majority rule. "Never in a thousand years."

It was a promise that Ian Smith could not keep.

The Africans fought. Through more than seven years, they waged guerrilla war against Smith's government. It was a bloody, costly war, and many died. In time, it became too much. Finally there was compromise, which produced elections. One person, one vote.

Still, Ian Smith tried.

He argued that the concept of one man, one vote was wrong for Rhodesia. "It means that we're giving the vote to our laziest, most incompetent citizens," he said. It was an argument made in desperation. Ian Smith understood arithmetic. Rhodesia had seven million Blacks and fewer than 200,000 Whites. Elections meant Black rule. The only question was what Blacks would take control.

That was decided late in February. In three days of voting, nearly 95 percent of the Africans, who were eligible went to the polls. At times, they stood in lines that were more than a mile long. They were patient. They waited. They voted, and when the ballots were counted, the Africans gave a stunning victory to the Marxist party of Robert Mugabe.

Mugabe was the candidate that Whites had feared most. "The Communist," they called him. "Anybody but Mugabe," they said. But it was one man, one vote and it did not matter what Whites thought. That was what Smith understood.

Rhodesia is one of the jewels of southern Africa. It had been a paradise for Whites. It is a country of spectacular beauty. Unlike much of Africa, it is modern and highly developed.

Before the election, it was widely believed that if Mugabe won, there would be a mass exodus of Whites. The fear of Mugabe was that great. But once he was elected, Mugabe immediately made overtures to Whites. "We don't want anyone to leave," he said.

"Everyone will be treated the same," he said. "We are going to build a true multiracial society."

Mugabe also made another promise. He said that his government would not confiscate land or any other property owned by Whites. He especially encouraged the White farmers to stay. Agriculture in Rhodesia, at least for now, defuses somewhat the explosive racial conflict in southern Africa. But South Africa is still here. The Africans say that there can be no real peace in the region until the question of South Africa is settled. In South Africa 22 million Blacks live under the domination of four million Whites.

As long as the war in Rhodesia went on, the threat was that South Africa would come in. The fear was that if that happened, the resulting conflict would be such that it would touch off a war of frightening dimensions.

It was largely because of that threat that the United States took an active role in bringing about the settlement in Rhodesia. Tomorrow, when Rhodesia falls and Zimbabwe is born, it will represent an important foreign policy victory for the Carter administration.

"Had the United States dropped sanctions," Rhodesia's White justice minister said, "and supported the Muzorewa government, the internal settlement, we would have won the war. There's no doubt about it, we would have won the war."

The internal settlement was an arrangement engineered by Ian Smith. It brought into office as prime minister a Black man, Muzorewa, but it excluded the leaders of the guerrilla armies, Mugabe and Joshua Nkomo, who waged the war together as the Patriotic Front.

As part of the internal settlement, Smith resigned as prime minister. He had hoped that by resigning, clearing the way for Muzorewa, the new government would win international recognition and an end to the sanctions.

"Had that happened," Anderson said, "we would have defeated the terrorists." He always calls the soldiers who fought with Mugabe and Nkomo, "terrorists."

In the morning yesterday, the official American delegation to the Zimbabwe independence celebration was flying toward Africa. At the head of the group was W. Averell Harriman, the former governor of New York, and Andrew Young. The selection of Harriman was a surprise. Young was a logical choice.

While he was chief U.S. representative to the United Nations, one of the places where Andrew Young had a real impact was in shaping American policy toward Africa, particularly southern Africa. It was Young who counseled the Carter administration against recognizing the Muzorewa government. The U.S., he said, should recognize no settlement in Rhodesia that did not include the Patriotic Front.

Last summer, in the middle of July, Muzorewa made a crucial visit to the U.S. He came at the urging of Sen. Jesse Helms, the conservative Republican from North Carolina, and his most prominent supporter in the U.S. Muzorewa came to ask Carter to recognize his government and drop the sanctions. Carter, at the urging of Young, refused.

It was Young's contention that the Muzorewa government did not represent the majority, that it was a puppet regime. The elections that were held in February proved him right. Muzorewa's party ran, but managed to win only three of the 80 seats reserved for Blacks in the new parliament. Mugabe's party won 57 and the party of Nkomo won the other 20 seats.

The Carter administration has been criticized for much of its foreign policy. Tomorrow, when the torch is passed and Rhodesia becomes Zimbabwe, the Americans who are there will sit on the right side.

1980

NOBODY WANTED TO SAY VERY MUCH, especially not the Africans who were seated around the long conference table. "It would be premature to say anything now," Souradjou Ibrahim said.

Frank Ofei was seated next to Ibrahim and he was quick to voice agreement. "Yes, yes," he said. "It would be premature."

Still, the room that was on the 17th floor of the State Office Building in Harlem was filled with optimism. The Africans had long yellow pads in front of them at the table. Through the morning, they listened, then asked questions. They kept making notes on the sheets of paper. They were painstaking in their examination of the charts and graphs and intricate plans that were passed around.

"It's a first step," Jacob Henderson of Washington said. "But I'd say it's important, very important."

"It's significant," Elowame Williams of Nigeria said. "Quite significant."

Below on the streets, Harlem went through the morning that was much the same as any other Sunday. The sidewalks belonged to churchgoers. Metal gates covered the front of shops. Kids romped in the playgrounds and the idle gathered on stoops and street corners.

But on the 17th floor of the office building, in the suite of rooms occupied by the Harlem Urban Development Corporation (HUDC), the meeting was a benchmark on the road to establishing important economic ties between the nations of Black Africa and Black communities of the United States.

The Africans scattered about at the conference table were representatives of the Economic Community of West African States (ECOWAS), the official economic organization of 16 West African nations. It is sometimes referred to as the West African counterpart of the European Economic Community -- the Common Market.

The idea of building economic links between Black Africa and Blacks in the United States is not new. But yesterday's coming together was important because, for the first time, the machinery to make such links real is close to being in place on both sides.

ECOWAS was formed in 1975. It is the apparatus the Africans needed. And yesterday, around the conference table in Harlem, the Africans were briefed on the plans for development of the vehicle that Black Americans put into place, an international Third World Trade Center that is to rise in Harlem.

Some of the funds have already been earmarked for the trade center. Vice President Mondale, in as visit to Harlem, pledged the administration's support towards construction. Rep. Charles Rangel, one of the foremost advocates of the center, says without reservation that it will be built.

Construction of the trade center is scheduled to begin this fall and the talk now is of a completion date in 1983. The trade center is to be located on the Lenox Ave. end of the block where the State Office Building sits. Yesterday the effort began to bring Africans into the center of the plan.

The ECOWAS delegation did not come to the United States just to learn about the trade center. They are in the United States to build business ties. This week in Washington a two-day conference has been organized to that end. While in America, they will meet with many businessmen, including some whose companies rank in the Fortune 500. But, the first stop the Africans made was in Harlem, in a Black community.

"It is about re-establishing the links broken by slavery," John J. Edwards Jr., general manager of HUDC, said. "Essentially what we're talking about is Africans rejoining after many years. We're trying to put some substance behind the symbolism."

Just off from the room in the State Office Building where the Africans sat with HUDC officials, there is a large picture window. The view is a sweeping one that looks south. From there, all of Harlem north from the park is visible and what is seen is a community that needs. Mostly, what Harlem needs is money. Money to build, repair, and grow.

There is the threat now of an ugly fight in Harlem for control of the illegal numbers gambling industry. It is about money. The numbers, though illegal, represent Harlem's major industry. Money from numbers operations was used to start many Harlem businesses. It was used to purchase buildings. In Harlem, for many years there was no other money available to Black entrepreneurs.

Two weeks ago, the organization that is called the 100 Black Men held an urgent meeting at the State Office Building. The only issue that was on the agenda for discussion was the prospects for Black business in the '80s. The conclusion was that the prospects were not good. The reason was that the money that it takes for business to expand and grow was not available to businessmen who were Black.

It was money that made yesterday's meeting in the rooms on the 17th floor of the State Office Building so important. The dream is that, through the trade center, Black and Hispanic businessmen can gain access to international markets. In time, by linking up with African markets, they can attain the size, and eventually control the kind of wealth, that will make it possible for them to begin to repair and rebuild communities such as Harlem.

It is not a one-way street. The countries of West Africa also need. Blacks in America suffer from the legacy of slavery. In West Africa, the still newly independent nations suffer from other legacies of years of colonial domination.

Souradjou Ibrahim of Lome, Togo, deputy director of ECOWAS, understands the need for West African states to build international trade. It is the same with Frank Ofei, an economist from Ghana. They need links with major American companies. But they also know that the ties between Blacks in America and the nations of West Africa are real. When most Blacks trace their roots, they find that they go back to West Africa.

The Africans also realize that the stronger the Black communities in the United States grow, the more they are in a position to influence American policies that deal with Africa. It is a two-way street . Yesterday, nobody was ready to say very much, but the feeling was that important progress was being made.

It is as John Edwards said. "We need these linkages. We cannot do it alone." It is a part of what makes the talking on the 17th floor of the State Office Building in Harlem yesterday, "quite significant," as the Nigerian said.

1980

THE SON WAS IN NEW YORK a month ago. He was going around, trying to stir things up. "Idi Amin," he says to anyone who will listen. "He is the new Idi Amin of Africa." He uses Amin's name again and again. The son understands. He knows that when he uses Amin's name, people will listen.

The son is Gilchrist Olympio. His father is Sylvanus Olympio. The names are not familiar. But from 1958 until 1963, the father was chief of state of the tiny west African nation Togo.

On the 13th of January in 1963, there was a coup d'etat in Togo. The government was overthrown and in the process, Sylvanus Olympio was killed.

The son is a tall, handsome man in his mid 40s. "I'm not a politician," he says. "I'm a businessman. I'm doing this because it's something that must be done. The world needs to know." Gilchrist Olympio is persuasive and confident.

"Does revenge figure into it?" he is asked. "Oh no," he says. "Revenge has nothing to do with it. I tell you, the man is worse than Idi Amin. That is the reason I'm doing this."

The target of Gilchrist Olympio's comments is Etienne Gnassingbe Eyadema, the president of Togo.

"Our president is very popular with the people," Anai Akakpo Ahianyo says. Ahianyo is foreign minister of the Togolese government. "If the things that he (Olympio) says were true, how could President Eyadema remain in power, and have the trust of the people?"

It is late in the morning on Saturday, and Foreign Minister Ahianyo is seated on a plush couch in the living room of the house that the Togolese government provides for its diplomats. The house is in New Rochelle, in Westchester County. It sits back from the road, amid a clump of tall trees, in a quiet residential district.

Seated across from Foreign Minister Ahianyo is Akanyi Awunyo Kodjovi, the minister of justice in the ruling government in Togo. He keeps looking at his watch. In three hours he must board an airplane for Paris, the first leg of the trip that will carry him back to Lome, the capital of Togo.

"We are a free country," the minister of justice says. "We have nothing to hide."

Across from him, the foreign minister nods in agreement. "We are a developing nation," he says. "We know our weaknesses, but we have a good situation. We know that, no matter what Mr. Gilchrist Olympio says."

It keeps going back and forth between the two officials who represent the government of Togo. The foreign minister speaks in perfect English, the minister of justice struggles with his English and sometimes lapses back into French, but the two of them, they keep making their points.

This Saturday morning was similar to the day a month ago when Gilchrist Olympio was in New York. He sat in an expensive French restaurant in Midtown Manhattan and kept calling on all that he could to say, first one way and then in another, that the President of Togo was an evil force and that he had to be removed from office. "He is another Amin," Gilchrist said. "Put the two names together: Idi Amin and President Eyadema."

Gilchrist had a briefcase that bulged with papers. He kept pulling them out and shoving them on the table to make his points. In the living room of the diplomat's residence in Westchester, the two ministers -- Kodjovi and Ahianyo -- did the same. They kept shoving papers they hoped would help make their points.

"But don't take our word for it," the foreign minister said. "Come to Togo, come, and see for yourself. Come and see that there is no truth to these charges that he (Olympio) keeps going around and making. There is no truth to what he says. Absolutely none." And Kodjovi, the minister of justice, nodded his approval.

In every story, there is what editors call the so-what paragraph. It is the paragraph that explains why a story is important, why a reader needs to know about Gilchrist Olympio, and ministers whose names are Kodjovi and Ahianyo, and a tiny West African state by the name of Togo. The answer is that because, even though Togo is thousands of miles away, has no great resources that the United States depends on, and no particular strategic importance, its officials bring this argument here because they take seriously the concern that the United States voices about human rights.

Togo is wedged between Benin and Ghana on the west coast of Africa. It has a population of close to 2.5 million. The leaders of Togo talk of the country becoming the "Switzerland of Africa." It is, for now, a dream. But Togo has the capability of making the dream real. Its economy is fairly stable. Industry is growing. New hotels are being built, and roads are being extended and expanded. Togo has the promise, and that is one of the reasons it is so important to solve the controversy that is flying now around President Eyadema. So they come to the United States, to New York. "It will be decided here," Olympio says. "The United States is very important," Minister Kodjovi says. Foreign Minister Ahianyo agrees.

1982

THE LIGHTS THAT HAD BEEN DIMMED were brought back, and now Franklin Williams was at the front of the small room. He stood with his hands gripping the edges of the lectern.

"These beautiful photographs," he said, and then he caught himself.

"I cannot say 'beautiful'," he continued. His voice was soft and everyone who was there in the room understood.

The photographs had been stunning, and there was beauty in them. They were pictures that were filled with the colors of Christmas -- the brightest reds and deep shades of green, brilliant blues and yellows. The whole spectrum of color was in the photographs. These were classic pictures, ones that gave meaning to the old truth that says one picture is worth a thousand words.

The photographs were the work of Peter Magubane, who is a Black South African. In the afternoon yesterday, in a darkened room on the second floor of the Phelps Stokes Fund Building, slides of the pictures that were from refugee camps in Somalia, in the eastern Horn of Africa, were in a slide projector. One after another they were flashed onto a silvery screen.

Magubane, husky with gray in his hair, stood at the projector. He knew each slide. The pictures were an incredible story of the horror and the beauty found in the refugee camps.

The horror came through in photographs of children who had patches of flies nesting around their mouths; children so weak from hunger, they did not even have the strength to flick the flies from their faces. The horror was in the photographs of children who walked naked, with bellies swollen from hunger. There was the horror that came through in the face of an old woman, whom Magubane said he watched and photographed for three days. The old African woman's face was carved with deep lines and filled with pain. "After three days, she died," Magubane said.

There was an incredible photograph of a young girl who carried her younger brother, who was naked and starving, in her arms. The young girl's face was African -- Black and smooth -- but the pain was there. When the picture came onto the screen, Magubane said, "I watched them for 10 days." He came to another picture. It was filled with beauty because it was a photograph of the same boy and his sister. The girl, who had been wrapped in rags, now had on a bright-colored African dress. The boy, who was very dark, was clothed in a pure white robe, and health had come into his face.

Peter Magubane went to Somalia to take pictures because he believed his photographs would help the people survive. He brought the pictures back to New York and delivered them to a photographic agency. They were stunning pictures, of the camp and the people there. There was the beauty in the faces of those who were not starving, the smooth skin, the white teeth and the hopeful smiles. He had a photograph of a herd of 200 camels, a brilliant picture of the animals as they stood in long, straight lines. "The Somalian government gave them to the refugees to slaughter so they could have some meat to eat," he said of the camels.

Magubane brought the pictures back. What he found was that they were photographs that nobody wanted. "We were only able to move three pictures," he said yesterday. "Just three."

The story of the refugees in Somalia, in the Horn of Africa, has been one that nobody wants to hear. Yesterday, Magubane had the pictures at the Phelps Stokes Fund. Franklin Williams, the former American ambassador to Ghana in West Africa, arranged for Magubane to show the pictures at a luncheon. Afterwards, he asked for help to raise $6,000 to have the photographs mounted for a exhibit.

"We'd like to show them here in New York," he said, "and then move the exhibit around the country because we believe that if people see the work of this gifted artist, they will respond and help with the refugee crisis in Somalia."

In the spring of 1978, when he was 46 years old, Peter Magubane was profiled in a New York Times article that was written by C. Gerald Fraser. In that piece, Fraser wrote:

"He (Magubane) has been a newspaper photographer in Johannesburg, where he has worked for the Rand Daily Mail, for more than 20 years. For five of those years, he was restricted by government banning orders. He could not go into a building that had a printing press. He could not talk to more than two persons at one time. He was confined to home in a Black township. He had to report regularly to the police. For a total of two years, he was imprisoned. He spent six months in ordinary confinement and 586 days in solitary confinement. He has never been convicted of any crime."

In the article, it said: "While working (in South Africa), Mr. Magubane has felt the muzzle of a policeman's machine gun against his temple. He has been struck across the face with the butt of a gun, and his film and Nikon camera have been taken from him." It also said that in 1976, Magubane became the first Black journalist to win South Africa's main journalism award, the Stellenbosch-Farmers Winery Award, also called the Enterprising Journalism Award. He was in jail then, and colleagues had submitted his photographs. The award was presented to him in 1977 by Walter Cronkite in Johannesburg.

Iris Haynes of the Health Commission on Refugees at the United Nations said that "a tremendous emergency" still exists in Somalia, where refugees have gone since 1978, victims of drought and the Ogaden war. She said 80 percent of the refugees are women and children and she estimated the number to be around 700,000. She said there had been as many as 1.5 million of these refugees and that "there has been a relative stabilization of the influx."

"This has been the kind of work I wanted to do," Peter Magubane said of the photographs he brought back from Somalia. "Let me give some assistance to help them survive. I once depended on the help of other people, not as a refugee, but as a banned peasant."

That was in South Africa. He was asked why he had been banned?

"They never give you any reasons," he said.

In the Daily News, almost two years ago, Dr. Kevin Cahill wrote of Somalia and the crisis involving refugees. His words do not go away. "The call of death is common today along the Ogaden-Somalia border, and it is the children who are summoned most often," he wrote. "As one sees the starved skeletal frames of the innocent young and appreciates the overwhelming burden of poverty, illness and the violence of war on the largest refugee population in the world today, even the physician can appreciate death as a gentle release from suffering."

Now comes Peter Magubane and his photographs that have the colors of Christmas. They are pictures that give new meaning to the words Dr. Cahill wrote.

1983

HE WENT BACK TO THE FIRST TIME he came to New York. It was in 1955, and he came to visit the United Nations. "I was a petitioner," he said. "I was petitioning for the independence of my country."

He did not see Harlem during that trip. "I was restricted," he explained. "I could not leave a certain area of New York." In 1956 he was in New York again. "That time," he said, "I came to Harlem, and I spoke. I spoke more freely then than I am likely to speak now. At that time, I was an agitator. I am not supposed to be an agitator anymore, so I'll choose my words very carefully."

On Wednesday, President Julius K. Nyerere of Tanzania stood at the front of the conference room on the second floor of the State Office Building in Harlem. With the October sun pressing at the windows before him, he stayed true to his promise. He was careful with his words. "When I came to New York the first time, my country was not free," he said, "but your country was not very free either."

In that first trip Nyerere made to New York there was a chance meeting he had with a man at the UN. It was, for him, one of those things that sticks in the mind. In Harlem, he recalled what it was that made the meeting important. "He was one of your professionals, a lawyer," Nyerere said. "I spoke very confidently to him that my country would become independent -- that the whole of Africa would become independent." President Nyerere said the man was so taken by his confidence that he broke down and began to cry. It became a moment he never forgot.

He did not say much after that. It was not necessary. It was the perfect message. It ties in with the agenda of now, which is the matter of the million unregistered Blacks that New York has. "You can help in the decision making," Nyerere said. In all of Africa, he is one of the most experienced and respected leaders. He was careful with his words. He was saying that you Black Americans can help Africa, but only if you are registered and vote, because then you have influence in the making of policy that the government of the United States carries out.

In the city on Sunday night, a voter-registration campaign like no other in the history of New York starts in Brooklyn. "A crusade" it is being called, and the immediate goal is the registering of 250,000 of the million who are off the books.

It ties into yesterday when the outrage in New York was the death of Michael Stewart, who was 25. The newspaper story of his death called him a fledgling artist. The police arrested him in the subway 14 days ago. He was delivered to Bellvue Hospital in a coma. The charge is that he was yet another victim of police brutality.

In Harlem, Julius Nyerere, the president of Tanzania, spoke in the same conference room that was, in July, jammed beyond its capacity when the issue was police brutality. The city still ignores the issue. It is because of the million unregistered. "You can help in the decision making," Nyerere said on the afternoon he came back to Harlem.

In Harlem, in the afternoon, the room where Nyerere spoke was filled with Harlem people, the African leader said, "You are now more free (than in 1951)." But the shouts from the audience interrupted.

"No! No Way!" were the shouts that rose.

Julius Nyerere smiled at the faces framed in the sunlight.

"I told you I was going to be very careful," he said. "But the United States is a lot more free now than the United States of 1955-56. We aren't free yet; freedom is a process. It's a struggle. We are more free. You are more free. The world is more free.

The shouts came again, but fewer now. The Tanzanian said, "You are one country. You are not one people yet."

He said he had not intended to speak. He had a theme, and he spoke of the need for the international community, especially the richer countries, to come to oneness with the world," . . . (to) begin to tackle the global problem of poverty," he said. "Wealth is not being used properly in the world. Where there is wealth, there should not be poverty. But in the world where we live, poverty can live side by side with great wealth. People say charity begins at home, but any government that tolerates poverty in its own country is not likely to be particularly interested in abolishing poverty elsewhere. Governments that cannot begin to deal with the poverty of the people who voted them into power are not likely to deal with the poverty of a Bangladesh or . . . this country of yours...." Words from the audience stopped him again.

"We are Africans," was the shout.

"It's no sin to remember where your ancestors came from," Nyerere said, "but you can help us better here."

1984

HE HAS A FACE FILLED WITH YOUTH. It's an African face, smooth and dark and, at the UN, it's his turn tomorrow to stand before the General Assembly and have his say.

He is Thomas Sankara. He arrived in New York two days ago. He came through the airport wearing combat fatigues and beret, clothes that identified him as being a revolutionary leader.

He is Captain Thomas Sankara and, by title, chairman of the National Revolutionary Council of the tiny West African state of Burkina Faso.

Sankara also carries another title. He's prime minister. The country, Burkina Faso, is also known by another name. Until recently, until the Aug. 4, 1983, revolution that brought Thomas Sankara to power, the country had the name Upper Volta.

So it's a country starting over. "To give people the right to decent housing, the right to decent education, the right to decent health," Sankara explained.

Burkina Faso is poor. Sankara estimates that 90 percent of the population of 7 million is illiterate. But he sings a happy song of what the revolution, in time, will do.

On his first visit to the United States, he said, "For us, the American people are friendly people." He made distinctions between the American people and the American government.

He said the government sees Africa as "an open field where they can do what they want." He said the government has an attitude of "Africa for the Americans."

He sat at a long table surrounded by reporters. He did not wear fatigues; he wore a white African robe with black stripes, laced with fancy embroidery. The language he used was French.

Still, what came through was his distaste for imperialism, which he called "a living evil." He said his revolution was a coming together of patriotic forces, the students and military. He spoke, too, of a new society that is being built.

He also said it is his country's desire to remain unaligned, something he said is not so easy to do. He used examples of the American government trying to pressure him to vote (in the UN) the American way. He used other examples of the Russians telling him he was voting "the American way."

In his meeting with reporters, what he dwelled on was the promise he saw for his country, the nation that now has the name of Burkina Faso.

He spoke of the way women were being received into all aspects of life in the country. "Traditionally, (women) were used to get the milk out, the babies out and the work out of them," he said. "African youth," he said, "look with an envy to our country, to what we are doing."

He said that there has been so much change in the country that even the army is no longer aloof. "We brought the army down to live with people," he said. "We have demystified the army."

Burkina Faso is about the size of the state of Colorado. A part of its promise is in untapped mineral wealth. It has gold, silver, large deposits of manganese and zinc.

But it is still promise. It's because Burkina Faso, once a colony of France, is a country still throwing off the shackles of colonialism. The old name, Upper Volta, was the first to go.

The Moss are the country's largest group. Burkina is a Moss word. Faso belongs to the Diola, the third largest group.

In the afternoon today, Thomas Sankara brought greetings from his country to Harlem to the state office building. Tonight, at 7 o'clock, he'll make a public speech at Harriet Tubman School in Harlem..

"Harlem is my White House," he said and he laughed. But when the smile was gone from his face, he said, "We have an open international policy. We have a message of friendship. Dialogue will be welcome, but you (United States) have to expect a new type of language, a frank language."

1986

IN HIS INTRODUCTION, SAMORI MARKSMAN searched for the word to describe the moment. He said it was "unusual," and then, to make that stronger, he called it "unprecedented."

Neither word was strong enough. What happened at the Harriet Tubman School in Harlem on Saturday was mind-boggling.

Since the Black liberation movements were spawned more than 25 years ago, there have been suspicions of illegal activity by the CIA across the continent of Africa.

On many occasions, leaders of those movements came to Harlem, stood in the auditorium in the Harriet Tubman School, and made serious charges against the CIA.

Until Saturday, they were only charges, with almost nothing to back them up.

John Stockwell changed all that in two hours on Saturday that were, for those who were there, mind-boggling.

Stockwell is a former high-ranking agent in the CIA. He was a GS-14 ("That's like a Colonel.") and a station chief.

Once he sat in on meetings of the National Security Council. On Saturday, Stockwell came to Harlem. Before a packed house in the school auditorium, he told incredible stories of CIA dirty work.

He focused on Africa. He said all the suspicions and charges, as serious as they have been, do not even begin to tell half of what the CIA has done in Africa. The bottom line of the story he told was that he was there. He was on the inside. In Angola, he headed the CIA operation that conducted what he called "an invisible war" against the government the United States wanted overthrown.

Stockwell's telling of CIA secrets is not entirely new. He gave testimony to a Congressional committee that he says should have put Henry Kissinger and former CIA Director William Colby in jail.

He also put all of his CIA record on paper, and that was published in his book, "In Search of Enemies." But his appearance in Harlem, as Samori Marksman (of the African-Caribbean Resource Center) said, was unusual and unprecedented.

He told how the CIA worked to overthrow governments in the Congo (now Zaire) in Angola and in Ghana.

Stockwell, who grew up in Africa, went to Angola after serving in Vietnam. He had been a Marine, and said he looked on joining the CIA as "going to graduate school."

In Angola, where he headed the operation, he said the CIA worked hand-in-hand with the government of South Africa. "We brought in the South African army," he said. He said Cuban leader Fidel Castro sent 42,000 troops to Angola and "eventually sent the South African army packing."

Of the involvement in Angola, he said Russia, Cuba and the Chinese all admitted to involvement in Angola. "The United States lied," he said. He said the American government refused to acknowledge any role. "The truth had nothing to do with it; we were vying for people's minds," he said.

Stockwell said the United States had 50 covert actions going, including 13 that are very large. He mentioned Nicaragua as one of the large efforts, and said the United States is on the brink of war in Central America.

1986

OUSANE SEMBENE BROUGHT his film, "Emitai," to tell his story of Africa.

"I did not make the film in the spirit of revenge," he said. "The film itself is a story. I took my inspiration from a true story. It's our history."

In his native Senegal, they call him the "grandfather of African cinema." He is a filmmaker and writer. On Wednesday he was another of the Africans to speak at the UN.

Sembene did not show his fil, and he did not speak before the assembly. That was for diplomats only. While foreign ministers and ministers of finance were speaking of Africa's economic woes, another story was being told in the Dag Hammarskjold auditorium. That was where Ousane Sembene was found.

He is short, muscular for a film-maker, and African Black. He is also shy. After his film was shown, he came to the front of the auditorium to answer questions.

"I don't have all the solutions," he said. "I don't know all the answers."

Sembene came to the UN with his film to show another side of Africa. In the General Assembly, the African states were given a lot of advice about the need to improve economic conditions on the continent. They were told to encourage free markets. They were told that government must step back and let private enterprise move to the front. They were told many things. But in the assembly, all of it was diplomats talking to diplomats. Sembene and a host of others -- writers, painters, dancers and musicians -- came to the UN to speak of African culture.

"Ours is a consciousness-raising effort," Sembene said. "You can take a rich White man from the United States, a rich White man in France, and a rich Black man in Africa, and they will join hands to exploit the little man. We are seeing what is happening around the world. Not Russia, France, or the U.S. is going to free Africa. It's the African men and the African women who are going to free Africa."

Sembene's film "Emitai" was set in Casamance, the southern Senegal village of Efok, near the end of World War II. Senegal was still a colonial possession of France. The film ends with a stunning massacre of all the men in the village. The film brought the issue of colonialism to the UN in a way that none of the speeches did. Sembene also showed how little the French knew of the Africa they controlled. The men who were killed did not control the rice, that was the point of contention between the French and the villagers. The women did.

"For better or worse, I was born not far from this village," Sembene said. "I went to primary school in the area. When I was 10, I spoke three African languages and maybe two more badly. I had six years of Western education. Then, I punched the headmaster, and had to go out and work. So I never lost my identity. I speak only French. I care nothing about Russian or English. I have no problem with any God, and with or without any God, I sleep very well."

In his film, when the French took over the town and demanded the rice, Sembene showed the way the men in then village turned to religion and witchcraft for a solution. Sembene told of the way he later saw the people of his town turn to religion and superstition when faced with drought. "But it didn't rain," he said. "But had they worked, and built dams and fertilized the land..."

At the end of his film, Sembene chose not to show the massacre. He showed the way the men were lined up to be killed and the movie ended with the sound of gunfire.

"We could have shown the blood," he said. "We could have filled up the screen with blood, and showed the village being burned. But for what? We did not make the film in the spirit of revenge. We paid with our lives for the freedom of a lot of other people. But if my father and grandfather were colonized, their children and my children will never be colonized again."

1989

IN ANGOLA, IN SOUTHERN AFRICA, something big is brewing. Foreign Minister Pedro de Castro Van Dunem can see it coming; the only problem is, he doesn't know what it is that his troubled country is looking at.

Last week, the Angolan minister was in New York. He came here from Washington. For now, it seems that officials in the American capital may know more of what is brewing in Angola than the foreign minister of that country.

Over breakfast at the UN Plaza Hotel, as he talked of what is to come for Angola, Minister Van Dunem, at times, seemed a sort of Jekyll and Hyde. One moment he saw good, another, evil.

At one point, he spoke of peace, at another, of more war.

Across southern Africa almost no leaders like to talk of what is. Instead they prefer to talk of what could be. That's because almost every nation is either engaged in some sort of war, or has just come out of war.

Angola has 15 years of a civil strife that has been so bloody that it has produced more victims than any other place in the region. So what Minister Van Dunem hopes, more than anything else, is that the something big that's brewing has to do with fostering a peace between his government and the rebel troops of Jonas Savimbi.

He stressed the positive. "Over the next few days," he said, "direct contacts with UNITA will begin." UNITA (the National Union for the Total Independence of Angola) is Savimbi's movement.

It has backing from the United States and South Africa. "I don't know where the conversations will take place, but the Angolan government has decided to enter into direct talks." Just that represents a big step.

For the Angolan government, Savimbi is the equivalent of the devil himself. His forces control significant areas in the country, and they have the ability to inflict damage at a level that keeps Angola in turmoil.

So, it means something when the foreign minister says, "The Angolan government intends to create all the conditions, so that we can enter into dialogue. There is no cease fire yet, but we hope to agree on principles to construct conversations to reach a cease fire."

A cease fire in the long war is the something big that Van Dunem would like to see realized. But there is another prospect.

"South Africa has resumed its support to UNITA," Van Dunem said. He said Pretoria was providing logistical supplies and military advisers. Minister Van Dunem also said that Savimbi's support from the United States has been increased.

"That support is extremely harmful to the negotiating stance we're trying to establish," he said. "We believe it will encourage UNITA not to sit down with us. For us, it is very difficult to understand how the United States feels it can promote talks while supplying the weapons for war. The talks are to begin in days. Yet we hear that additional support (for Savimbi) is coming from the United States."

Minister Van Dunem sees a worst case scenario. He says that with increased support from the U.S. and South African governments, UNITA may be on the verge of carrying out an attack on Luanda, the Angolan capital.

A moment after expressing fear of an escalation in the war, the minister turned to say, "I am convinced the United States may be changing its attitude over the next few weeks. I want to believe, and it is the wish of my government that there will be an end of (U.S.) aid to Savimbi within a month."

Why the optimism? Minister Van Dunem says Angola, too, is moving away from its Marxist past, and is in the process of establishing a free market economy. On the political level also, he said change was coming. Soon, multi-party elections would be a reality in a country where one party rule now exists under President Jose Eduardo dos Santos.

Angola is changing. Cuban troops are leaving, and the Marxist influence is in decline. Heavy negotiations are taking place -- a turning point moment could be in the making. But it's not at all clear exactly what Angola is looking at.

1989

THEIRS IS ANOTHER OF THOSE COUNTRIES that has just found its freedom. But for Namibia, in Southern Africa, freedom didn't come easy. The Namibians had to fight. For 23 years they had to stand against the strongest army on the continent, but that didn't stop them. Once a people have their mind set on freedom, they don't worry about the price they have to pay; they just do what they have to do to be free.

To get their freedom, Namibians had to go deep into the bush. With almost no weapons at all, they began to prepare to make war on South Africa. That wasn't the way they wanted it; they had no choice. South Africa took over the former German colony in 1915, and the Afrikaners wouldn't let go. It didn't matter what any government in the world said, South Africa would not let go of its illegal occupation of Namibia. The United Nations ordered South Africa out; the government in Pretoria thumbed its nose at the UN.

In 1966, when Namibia began its armed struggle against South Africa, Sam Nujoma was a young man. He was a member of SWAPO, the South-West Africa People's Organization. SWAPO was the organization of Black Africans in Namibia and for a long time, SWAPO had tried to find a peaceful route to freedom. But there was none. South Africa was saying never to majority rule, never in a thousand years. So SWAPO's decision was forced. To raise money and support for the guerrilla war, Nujoma made regular trips to the United States. He would come to Harlem and Brooklyn, and to a lot of other Black communities across the country. He would tell of the fight and ask for support. It got to the point that he could walk into a room in New York and call dozens by their first name. Two years ago, he came with a special excitement in his voice. "We're winning," he exclaimed. "We are winning the war."

When they started out, he recalled days when they had less than a dozen rifles for their whole army. But the Namibians had time on their side. It was their country they were fighting for. They were not going anywhere. The only plan they had was to keep getting stronger, and to keep on fighting.

SWAPO did not defeat South Africa. But what they did was a part of an effort that, in time, forced Pretoria to the conference table. A negotiated settlement was reached last year. Elections were held and SWAPO, the people's organization, was victorious. A new constitution was written, one establishing a non-racial democracy.

On Wednesday of this week, independence for Namibia becomes official, and Sam Nujoma gets installed as the country's first president under majority rule.

A country, and a people, who have been through all that the Namibians have experienced, need a lot of help to make their democracy work. So they look to the wealthy nations of the world. In a way, their future is in the hands of those nations. Namibia looked to the United States; what Namibia got amounts to a slap in the face.

To Poland and Hungry, the U.S. aid packages approach $1 billion. It is the same with Panama and Nicaragua. To Namibia, the U.S. offered a mere $500,000. That's not as much as the average big league baseball player gets in a year's salary.

In Angola, where the Bush administration supports guerrilla leader Jonas Savimbi, it's a different story. Aid to Savimbi is estimated at $50 million a year. But the money to Savimbi is stuffed in another envelope. It is not to build; the aid to him is to destroy, and do damage.

In 1991, aid to Namibia is expected to rise to nearly $8 million. Even that is not enough. In the scheme of things, it amounts to spare change. The Namibians fought long and hard for their freedom. They have adopted a constitution that's perhaps the most democratic in all of Africa. But at the moment they most need help, what the government of the U.S. holds out, amounts to an insult. For a people who have struggled the way Namibians have, on the eve of their independence, they deserve better.

1989

HE SEIZED POWER in the small West African country of Liberia 10 years ago. He was Master Sergeant Samuel K. Doe. Although he was just 28 years old, he raised a lot of hopes. He promised elections; vowed to build a democracy. His pledge was that more than anything else, in Liberia, the rule of law would prevail.

But from the start, the hopes were tinged with apprehension; for good reason. The coup that brought Doe to power was not just bloody, it had a side that all but glorified brutality.

Doe did not jail his opponents or attempt to drive them out of the country. Instead, he rounded them up, and in public view, he staged executions. The president he overthrew, William Tolbert, was strapped to a telephone pole. His body was riddled with bullets. The same happened to Tolbert's son, and to foreign minister C. Cecil Dennis. On one bloody day, 13 high officials of the government were executed on a downtown street. What aroused fear was the way soldiers of the revolution then posed standing over the bodies as though they were no more than animals shot down in the jungle.

Hopes were raised though, because the Tolbert government had been repressive. Tolbert had lived in grand style in a country that was desperately poor. Doe was to be a new beginning. Liberia is a country with strong ties to the United States, and Doe, too, shared those ties. He was trained by the American military. Indeed, on the day he presented himself as the country's new president, he showed up dressed in American military fatigues. He was an army sergeant, and an 11th grade dropout from a Liberian high school. That prompted him to be asked if he was qualified to run the country. He insisted he was, and he got the boost he needed when the government he established was recognized by the United States.

All that was 10 years ago. The hopes that Doe raised were never realized and by yesterday, the stories coming back from Liberia told of a country in turmoil. Government troops were reported to have raided a compound of the United Nations Development Program, killing one civilian security guard. Some 40 refugees at the center were said to have been kidnapped, and reportedly later killed. Doe denied that his troops were responsible, but even as he was making that claim, it was being disputed.

In the meantime, his government was at war with rebel troops led by one of his former cabinet members, Charles Taylor. The rebels are said to be in control of large sections of the country. So little stability now exists in Liberia that the UN Secretary General has ordered all UN personnel out of the country.

The developments in Liberia come at a bad time for Africa. Opponents of one person, one vote in South Africa are sure to point to Liberia, and see it as proof that Blacks cannot government themselves. They are sure to hold up Samuel Doe as a prime example in making the argument.

Even though the Doe government came into power with a lot of blood on its hands, it was by no means doomed from the start. What Doe really represents is an opportunity lost. A part of the blame has to fall on the American government. The United States had tremendous influence over Doe. He had been trained by Americans, and he courted the relationship. But no pressure was put on him to live up to the promises he made when he came into office. Bit by bit, Doe kept stepping backward. In time, he proclaimed himself a general, and, like his predecessor, he began to govern as a dictator, and took the high style of living. He started out driving a Chevrolet. He dropped that for a limousine. He cracked down on dissent. Newspapers were closed or taken over. Opponents were killed. Doe had presented himself to the United States as one who would stand against the advances Libya was making in the area. The government of the United States saw that and little else.

The special relationship the United States has with Liberia goes back to when the country was founded as a haven for freed American slaves. Even now, Liberia uses American money as its currency. Its police officials dress in American styled uniform. The largest hospital is the John F. Kennedy Memorial Medical Center. Even the Liberian flag is patterned after the American flag except Liberia has but one star.

In a way, what is surprising is that Doe has lasted 10 years. While he may be losing his grip, questions are being asked about rebel leader Charles Taylor. Where does he get his support? How has he been able to muster a force large enough to take over significant portions of the country? Are Kadafy and Libya behind his movement?

As for Samuel Doe, he is seen now, not as hero but a pathetic figure typical of those dictators who have led many African countries to ruin. Liberia becomes another country on the continent of Africa without hope and waiting now for a new generation of leadership.

1993

HERS IS THE OTHER SIDE of the African story. She is Pascaline Bongo and she is foreign minister of the nation of Gabon.

Gabon?

When a lot of people hear the name, they ask, "Where is that?"

Or they say, "I've never heard of It."

Foreign Minister Bongo understands. She knows that so much of the time, the nations on the continent of Africa get portrayed only in terms of the problems they have at the moment. Which means that one country gets known because of starvation, conflict and war.

Which gets back to Gabon. It is a small country that sits on the west coast of Central Africa. "We're an OPEC country," minister Bongo says. That always rings a bell. OPEC means oil and oil means money. In Sub-Saharan Africa, no country has a higher per capita income than Gabon.

That's not all. Gabon, with its 1.1 million people, has political stability. It has a budding democracy. It also has its first presidential election coming up in two months.

For the elections, the foreign minister says, "Everything is set up. We have a new electoral code. The government is doing everything to insure free and fair elections."

Minister Bongo has a favorite among the candidates -- the incumbent, her father, President El Hadj Omar Bongo. For 26 years, he has led the country. In the eyes of his daughter, he is a big part of the reason Gabon is not troubled by so many of the kinds of problems that wrack so much of Africa.

"He did not wait for the streets to dictate," she says. "He took the initiative. He was the initiator of change. He did not wait for change to be thrust upon him."

That was her way of telling how her father responded to the winds of change blowing across Africa. The change being demanded is democracy. Gabon has already held legislative elections. It has a newly adopted democratic constitution. Many democratic institutions have been put in place. Only the presidential election is awaited. While she says that all is in place for the vote, Minister Bongo worries for her father.

"Because a lot of people believe that to have democracy, you have to throw out whoever is in," she said. "They believe that to have democracy, President Bongo needs to be removed." But she also knows that is what the campaign is about; making the people understand what democracy really means.

Of all the diplomats from around the world who are in New York this fall for the annual session of the General Assembly at the United Nations, Minister Bongo had, in many ways, some of the most important stories to tell.

One had to do with Somalia. "It is the one country of Africa that should not have a problem," she said. "They basically speak the same language, practice the same religion and have no tribal differences. That's what plagues the rest of Africa."

She also says she and others on the continent saw the trouble in Somalia coming. "At the OAU (Organization of African Unity) summit, Ethiopia tried to attract attention to the problems of Somalia. As their President said, they (Ethiopia) had a similar problem -- the problem of no state. That there was no state; it didn't exist. Even at the summit (OAU, there was a question of who would represent the country (of Somalia). In Mogadishu now you hear about chiefs. They say they are coming to speak on behalf of the Somali people. They do not represent the Somali people; they are neighborhood chiefs...just like gang leaders."

Minister Bongo said she, along with most others, applauded UN intervention. That was when the specter of starvation was great and, as she said, "you can't just go in and drop food. No type of aid can be brought in and just dropped." So, at the UN, her question asks, "are we still on track with our good intentions?"

Of the trouble in Angola, she lays blame on Jonas Savimbi, who lost in the presidential election. She said his action is typical in Africa. "The loser doesn't want to accept that he lost."

On the wars that wrack the continent, she asks a good question: "Why can't we as Africans stop killing each other?"

At the UN this fall, Pascaline Bongo stands out from the crowd. And that is because she does not speak in diplomatic double talk; she says what is on her mind. Of course, she is different; in her country, her father is President.

Chapter Seven, Part Two

THE AFRICANS

AND

THE AMERICANS

SOUTH AFRICA

Editor's Note

Long before it became popular, or even note-worthy, Earl Caldwell wrote about the struggle for freedom in South Africa. His writings began in the bleakest days of that effort, and continued to the nativity of a new day in South Africa.

1979

FOR A MOMENT, IT APPEARED that the cover-up was over. Finally, it seemed that the lie had been exposed, and the truth was out in the open.

For many years, there had been rumors and suspicions that the government of South Africa was close to developing a nuclear capability.

But always, the South Africans said no. They called the rumors lies. The government of the United States led us to accept the notion that there was nothing to the speculation.

Until last Friday, it was that way. There were the headlines that screamed off the front pages of the newspapers. Finally, it appeared that we had the truth.

We were told that there was unmistakable evidence, that the most racist regime in all the world had exploded a nuclear warhead.

Even before, we felt we knew. Still, when it appeared that there was verification, it struck like a thunderbolt. It was not good news for anyone.

Even without introduction of nuclear weaponry, the situation in South Africa is extremely dangerous. The war in Zimbabwe-Rhodesia always seemed to be growing. Even while the peace talks in London went on, the war in Rhodesia did not stop. But the hope was always that a settlement could be reached, that the White minority would somehow be persuaded to relinquish real power. There were days when the news came from London, and it seemed that there was progress.

Then came the news last Friday. The news that the government of South Africa apparently had The Bomb. The government of South Africa is desperate. There is determination to hang onto the racist policies at all costs. Desperate people do desperate things. Last Friday, we learned that in the region where there had been no nuclear weapons, there may well be a new reality.

When the word came that there might have been a nuclear explosion in the Indian Ocean, the government of South Africa was quick to issue a denial. More lies, the South Africa spokesman said.

Still, they tried to mask the truth. But we felt that we knew, and here in New York, as the word flashed across the city, there was another word that was heard -- holocaust.

There are many in the City of New York who know what the word means. It's a word we've tried to put deep in our past, but it does not go away. It sticks with us like a dread disease

Rep. Stephen Solarz, the Brooklyn Democrat who is chairman of the African subcommittee of the House Foreign Affairs Committee, spoke with anger in his voice.

He called it a deeply disturbing and destabilizing development. He had already ordered hearings. "First thing Monday morning," he said. Congressman Solarz understands how much the world has changed. He understands that Africa can no longer be looked on a as distant place far removed from the center of our lives.

"Next to the Middle East," he said, "I can't think of another region in the world where the introduction of nuclear weapons can have more catastrophic consequences than in South Africa."

But that was in the morning on Friday. By midday, spokesmen for the Pentagon and then the State Department began to hedge. "We're not sure," they said. Bit by bit, they began to backtrack.

By late afternoon, Congressman Solarz was on the phone again. He was holding up the hearings that he had scheduled. It kept going that way. On Saturday, spokesmen from the State Department had done a complete about-face. Slowly, everything that had been said was taken away.

The story had fallen out of the news completely. It was not even discussed. It was as though there had never been any evidence of a nuclear explosion.

The American government is saying is that it doesn't know. It seems to be saying that maybe the South Africans exploded a nuclear device; maybe they didn't. It is a position that is not easy to understand.

If you ask Randall Robinson, executive director of the TransAfrica Lobby, the Black American lobby for Africa and the Caribbean, he scoffs at the idea that the government of the United States does not know.

"What is curious to me," he says, "is that, on one hand, we're saying we can't verify a nuclear explosion in the Indian Ocean off South Africa. But, on the other, we're saying that we can monitor the many-faceted arms program of the Soviet Union."

Is the American public being misled on the government's ability to verify compliance with the SALT pact? Or do we know full well from our surveillance that South Africa did, indeed, detonate a nuclear warhead?

Or, is it as Robinson suggests: that the American government is prepared to watch the Soviet Union closely, but that we've never been prepared or committed to turning our monitoring technology to watch the South Africans.

We are entitled to have the truth. We should know if the nuclear weapon has spread so that now it is in the hands of the most racist country in the world. The South Africans may not be able to use nuclear weapons against their own Black majority, but there is little question that the weapons can be used to threaten neighboring states that would give aid to a guerrilla army. And the word comes back: holocaust.

1981

IT'S BEEN MORE THAN A WEEK now, but at the South Africa embassy here yesterday nobody was willing to say a word.

"If that's what you want to talk about, a woman in the press office said, "then don't come over here."

"Can you just tell me if they are still here?" she was asked.

"We are not saying anything," she said, "nothing at all."

It remains a mystery. For almost a full week, five high-ranking South African military officers were in the United States. Officials of the U.S. State Department said yesterday that the South Africans have left. They were in a plane out last Saturday night. But the reasons for their visit was still mostly a mystery.

"Wasn't it an illegal visit?" a State Department official was asked.

"Not illegal," the officer said, "just against policy."

"How did it happen? How did they get visas?"

"Didn't you see the statement that was issued today?" the State Department official said. "That is all we have to say about it now."

The statement that was issued was vague. It offered no real explanation why the South African military men were in the United States; or how it happened, that, while they were in Washington, they had meetings at the National Security Council and at the Defense Intelligence Agency.

By late in the afternoon yesterday, it was not really necessary for the South Africans to make any statements. They did not have to explain. They could play it coy. The reality is that the relationship between the government of the United States and South Africa has changed.

Jimmy Carter said it would happen. In the last days of the campaign, when the polls began to show that his presidency was slipping away, he warned Black Americans that if he was ousted, the American policy toward Africa would change. On that matter, Jimmy Carter was right.

The prime evidence came on the night Ronald Reagan gave an exclusive interview to Walter Cronkite on CBS-TV. Reagan repeatedly referred to South Africa as being a friendly nation. He said that the South Africans had supported the U.S. in every war, something he used as a test of friendship. He conveniently omitted any reference to the known sympathies of most White South Africans for Nazi Germany's position during World War II. Reagan dismissed the apartheid policies of South Africa as being little more than routine racial problems. What the President was doing was sending a signal.

The South Africans were quick to pick up on it, and the day after the Cronkite interview, Reagan was hailed as a hero in Johannesburg, South Africa. The morning newspaper, The Star, carried a banner headline on page one that said, "Reagan Pledges to Stand by South Africa."

The shift in American policy comes at a time when, at the United Nations, the move is toward isolating South Africa. The immediate issue is Namibia, the South African-ruled territory that lies between South Africa and Zimbabwe.

Since 1941, more than 50 African nations have achieved independence. Today, only two countries in Africa remain under White rule -- South Africa and Namibia. Guerrilla war is growing in Namibia. After the elections last year that turned White-ruled Rhodesia into majority-ruled Zimbabwe, the hope had been that free elections could be held in Namibia. The Carter administration was a key supporter of a U.N. plan for a ceasefire and then elections in Namibia. But now that has changed. The signals that are being sent by the Reagan administration are not being ignored.

A part of the evidence was that Dirk F. Mudge, head of the Namibian political party that South Africa supports, is in the nation's capital, busy trying to influence American policy. What Mudge said was that the vibrations he was getting were encouraging.

There is the party led by Dirk Mudge and supported by South Africa on one side. On the other side is the South-West Africa People's Organization (SWAPO), which has led the guerrilla war in Namibia and is backed by most Black African states, and the United Nations. Among the people that Mudge saw was Sen. Jesse Helms (R-N.C.) and it was one of the places where he got his good vibrations.

But in Washington, there was also another side. Late in the afternoon, Randall Robinson, executive director of TransAfrica, the Black American lobby on Africa, sat in his downtown office and talked of how quickly and totally American policy on Africa has changed under Reagan.

"It's mind-boggling," he said. "We're talking about the most heinous nation in the world (South Africa), and we want to have a relationship with them."

In a larger room outside his office, students were busy making signs and preparing for a demonstration that was to take place at a building in Dupont Circle where Dirk Mudge was to speak.

"Furious," Randall Robinson said. "That's how I feel about the Reagan policy -- furious."

On the wall behind him was a huge poster, and across the room on another wall was a map of the United States that had push pins stuck in clusters at various points. Robinson explained that replicas of the poster were being made into metal signs and that in every city on the map where the pins were, ministers had agreed to install the signs in front of their churches.

"We've got 44 cities already."

At the top of the poster, in bold letters, it said: "Let's end U.S. support for South Africa." Below was the message. It said, in part, that South Africa is a nation where four million Whites dominate 20 million Blacks. It said that the Whites control 87 percent of the land, 70 percent of the national income, and that it is the only country in the world where the right to elect or be elected to the country's decision-making bodies is exclusively reserved for a single race.

It said that Blacks have no freedom of speech, assembly, right to fair trial, bear arms, own land, travel, or due process of law.

That was only part of the message. It was only a part of the story of apartheid. And what is new is that now, the President of the United States calls the nation where apartheid is a practice a friend of America. It is cause for worry.

1981

AT THE UNITED STATES MISSION at the UN Plaza yesterday all of the questions were turned away.

"She's out of town," a spokesman for Ambassador Jeane J. Kirkpatrick said.

"She is in Washington today," the spokesman said," and no statements are going to be made."

Jeane J. Kirkpatrick is the chief American delegate to the United Nations. It has been two weeks now since she met secretly with a group of high-ranking South African military officials who slipped into the country.

Among the South Africans in the meeting with Kirkpatrick was Lt. Gen. P.W. Van der Westhuizen, the head of South Africa's military intelligence. The American ambassador's explanation is that she did not know, that she thought the South Africans were private officials, and that she met with them because she listens to opinions of a lot of different kinds of people.

That was an explanation that came in bits and pieces. Just on the face of it, it doesn't answer questions, it raises them. By late in the afternoon on Thursday the Congressional Black Caucus stepped out in front of the surprisingly modest controversy that the Kirkpatrick meeting with the South Africans has sparked.

Rep. William H. Gray III (D-PA), vice chairman of the caucus, said at a press conference in Washington that Kirkpatrick ought to be fired. He said that her explanation, that she did not know who the South Africans were, was "extremely hard to believe."

It is an understatement. What came to mind yesterday was the controversy that flashed around Andrew Young when he was the U.S. ambassador to the UN and he was caught in a meeting that was not supposed to have taken place.

That was back in the middle of August of 1979. As soon as it was discovered that Ambassador Young had carried out an unauthorized meeting with a representative of the Palestine Liberation Organization, a furious protest arose.

"Fire him," a newspaper headline demanded.

There was never any doubt that his resignation would be forced. It was. And yesterday the Black Caucus was saying that it should not be any different now with Ambassador Kirkpatrick.

But there was no outcry. The newspapers were silent. The voices that were raised against Andrew Young were silent.

The change in American policy toward South Africa is swift now. It does not go unnoticed. In the middle of the week, a group of Black African leaders went to the secretary general at the UN to voice their concern at the sudden tilt in American policy. The concerns were such that Secretary General Kurt Waldheim got on the phone to Ambassador Kirkpatrick.

The newspapers are filled with stories of the crisis in Poland and the crisis in El Salvador. But in the two months that it has been in place, the Reagan administration has given enough signals to the South Africans to encourage them to step up their aggressive stance toward their neighbors and bring real tensions to Africa.

It is a serious matter. It is time now to know the whole story as to how and why five of the top-ranking officers of the South African army came into the United States in a clear violation of policy. It is time now also to find out exactly what Ambassador Kirkpatrick knew, and when she knew it.

In Washington, when the Black Caucus members called for Kirkpatrick's resignation, theirs were the only voices raised. When there should have been some visible sign of support for the Caucus' position, there was nothing.

It goes back to Andrew Young and August 1979. Andy fell. He was taken off as the American ambassador at the United Nations. But while he was there, he brought Blacks into the area of foreign policy. That was his legacy and the promise was that while Young himself was gone, Blacks would never again be kept out of foreign affairs.

There was a challenge; Blacks promised to try and do for Africa what Jews in this country do for Israel.

1982

IT IS NOT A COMPLICATED ISSUE. It is all very easy to understand. It is cut and dried. It comes down to another moment of truth for the government of the United States.

It is about South Africa, the most racist, repressive government in the world.

The issue is this: The South African government is in the midst of a severe economic crisis, and needs help. It needs big help. Without it, the government could collapse under its own weight. To secure the help it needs, it must have the support of the government of the United States.

It would seem that there would be no real decision to be made here; that the American government would say no, we will not prop up your racist apparatus. Do not look to us.

It would seem that there would be no real decision, because the American government would say clearly to the South Africans that we are true believers in the idea of human rights, and not for any reason would we position ourselves on the side of evil.

It all seems cut and dried, but it is not working out that way.

At the end of last week, the word came from Washington that the American government is supporting a South African request for $1.1 billion in loans to solve its economic problems.

The Reagan administration is not using American tax dollars to bail out the South Africans. It is doing it another way, but the result is the same. The money would prop up South Africa's policy of apartheid. And the most criminal government in the world would grow strong.

South Africa wants the money in the form of loans from the International Monetary Fund, a specialized agency of the United Nations. South Africa is a country whose policies are so objectionable to the world, that in 1974 it was ousted from the General Assembly and suspended from memberships in other UN agencies.

The General Assembly repeatedly has asked the IMF not to approve loans to South Africa, but the fund is not bound to adhere to those resolutions. The biggest block of votes in the IMF is held by the United States. The U.S. holds 20 percent of the stock and has 19 percent of the votes. Now the Americans are expected to go along with the South African request.

The question that arises is, why? Why would the Unites States go along with a country that embraces so much of what Americans stand against?

The U.S. Treasury Department, which supervises American activities in the fund, supports the loans, it is said, because there are no technical or economic grounds for opposing it. In other words, it is saying that South Africa has good credit and that is all that should count. It says the fund should not be politicized.

"It's absolutely shameful," said Randall Robinson, executive director of TransAfrica, a Black American African lobby in Washington.

"It's a way for the United States to bail out a sagging economy...instead of direct assistance, it is hiding behind the insulation of the IMF." It is another way of saying that, since Reagan cannot hope to get South African aid through the Congress, it seeks to do so indirectly.

On his desk Robinson had a copy of a confidential memorandum the Treasury Department had prepared two months ago for delivery to Herman Nichols, American ambassador in South Africa.

The memorandum was intercepted. It asked the ambassador to inquire about the South African plan to ask for the loans. He was instructed to inform the South Africans that the American government would not oppose the loans on the basis of that government's racial policies. The memo said the loans would be dealt with, as far as the Americans were concerned, strictly on merit.

But the memo warned South Africa that its loan requests might spark a movement to have it expelled from the IMF. "Handle with great caution and care," were the instructions to Ambassador Nichols. It had been thought the South Africans would seek the loans at an IMF meeting last month in Toronto.

South Africa said it had no such plans. That was a lie. Now it is out in the open. The request has been made and will go before the IMF Nov.3 at its executive board meeting in Washington.

"The United States could suffer an enormous embarrassment here," Randall Robinson said. What he meant is that there is going to be a fight. And in the fight the United States is going to be on the wrong side.

Robinson said the Scandinavian countries already were lining up against the loans and Third World countries were doing the same. "The countries of Western Europe are the key," he said, "especially the French."

So battle lines are being drawn in a fight that should never be taking place. The Congressional Black Caucus is mobilizing. A group of Democrats, including Thomas J. Downey of Long Island, plans to call special preelection hearings.

South Africa's economic problems have been caused in great part by a decline in the price of gold, which accounts for about half of its earnings. But its heavy military spending -- in the fight against Namibians and Angolans -- has contributed to its economic woes. Fighting to keep its racist policies intact has been expensive. Now, South Africa needs help. It needs big help and it needs it now. The IMF loan and the support of the government of the United States are the key. And the American government is leaning its way.

"Shameful," Randall Robinson said, "it is absolutely shameful."

The words are not strong enough. We stand against oppression in Poland and it is right. It is what America should do, but the same should be true in South Africa. It is cut-and-dried, and it comes down now to a moment of truth for the government of the United States.

1982

IN THE CENTER OF THE ROOM there was a long table and it was piled high with the flyers and on top were the ones that had the picture of Ray Charles.

On the top of the flyer, just above the picture of Ray Charles, the bold letters carried the message.

"Protest Against 'Bro' Ray Charles (for) artistic collaboration with racist South Africa."

Tomorrow night, Ray Charles, who has always been just this side of sainthood among Blacks, has a concert scheduled at the Beacon Theater on Broadway at 75th St. It was supposed to be a big night: Ray Charles, number one, soul singer supreme.

Now, it shapes up as an evening of pain, and that is what South Africa is doing.

In the room, on the third floor of an old building in Harlem, the African whose name was David Ndaba sat at the end of the table. His face was dark and smooth and filled with youth.

"This is a very important issue to us," he was saying. "Inside South Africa itself, it is very important."

The sin for Ray Charles is that he performed in South Africa.

"By sending your artists there (South Africa), you're helping them," David Ndaba was saying. "Black artists should not be depending on South Africa to help their development. When you hit them (South Africa) there, culturally, you're hitting them in their weakest spot."

David Ndaba is a part of the African National Congress (ANC), the main liberation organization operating inside South Africa, and Wednesday night he was in Harlem to give impetus to the drive to halt Black American entertainers appearing in South Africa.

He had one word that he kept using.

"Isolation," he said. "They (South Africa) have to be isolated. Especially it has to be culturally, and we feel the time is right and the time is right now. There is no myth about it. We are not struggling to listen to that music or to eat at restaurants. The people are starving for freedom."

Another stack of leaflets announced a meeting that is scheduled for 5 o'clock in the evening on Sunday at the State Office Building in Harlem and Elombe Brath, who sat at another side of the table, said that the meeting on Sunday is to decide what should be done next to punish the Black American entertainers who appear in South America.

"We can't let that happen," said Brath, head of Harlem's Patrice Lumumba Coalition.. "If they insist on going to South Africa, we have to let them know that they will pay a price, and the price is going to be that they are not going to appear in Harlem or anywhere in New York without a demonstration. I love Ray Charles too, but he went to South Africa, and he has to pay for it."

South Africa. It comes back and it will continue to be that way as long as the government there is one of Whites that dominates the Black majority in the most criminal way possible. It spills over.

In the afternoon yesterday, the issue was at the United Nations before the General Assembly. Yesterday, the General Assembly had before it a resolution that urged the International Monetary Fund to turn down a South Africa request for a $1.1 billion loan. South Africa, too, is in the midst of a severe economics crisis and it has come to the UN agency, the IMF, for help.

The vote wasn't even close. The countries of the world had their say yesterday, and South Africa took a licking.

By count, there were 121 nations that said yes, supporting the resolution that urged the IMF to deny South Africa the loan.

There were 23 other nations that abstained.

South Africa managed to win while losing. It turned out that way because there were three other votes cast: the American vote and the British vote and the West German vote. Those went in favor of South Africa and there are indications, because of the influence of these wealthy countries, that South Africa may get the $1.1 billion loan it needs to prop up its ailing economy.

Just before the vote was taken, the American delegate, Gordon Luce, rose before the General Assembly to say no, that the IMF should not be used to punish South Africa.

"The United States believes the demise of apartheid can best come from peaceful reform within South Africa itself," he said, "rather than from further assaults on South Africa, actions in the international arena."

He said, "We (the United States) believe that constructive change is taking place, and we are determined to continue to encourage South Africa to hold to a firm course in that direction."

They were good words, but they were not enough.

Shettima Ali Monguno, the Nigerian delegate, followed the American speaker. He said that giving the loan to South Africa was wrong. He said the money would help build South Africa's war machine, that it would aid the government in policing its apartheid state.

He said that the loan would also send a signal to corporations and banks, a signal that would say that it is all right to deal with South Africa and that, he said, "is quite intolerable."

The Nigerian in his words was saying what David Ndaba was saying in Harlem and the message was that South Africa has to be isolated.

"You treat them as a pariah," Elombe Brath said. "That is the way you deal with South Africa."

All of it becomes important now because South Africa is hurting. South Africa feels the pinch of the worldwide recession. But South Africa is different because it has in place the most racist, oppressive government in the world.

"People are dying," David Ndaba said. "My people are dying, they are dying every day in the struggle against this regime and they ask us (ANC), 'What is happening in America?' They ask us, 'Don't we have the support of the people in the United States?' We say yes, but then they see these things, they see Black artists come to South Africa, and it hurts because it helps the racist regime that we are fighting against."

1983

IN THE TOWNSHIP OF SHARPEVILLE, it was a day the Black Africans said no.

The system of racial discrimination that is known as apartheid has many laws, hundreds in all. On this day in 1960, in numbers that were measured in the tens of thousands, Africans who were Black said no to the law that required them to carry passes anytime they ventured out of their neighborhoods.

In 1960, the American civil rights movement had become a mighty force, and its impact stretched across the world, including South Africa. Nothing just happens, though. It takes organizing and leadership. Behind that comes courage. On that day in Sharpeville, more than 20,000 Black Africans converged on the police station.

It was the plan of the organization known as the Pan Africanist Congress. That day, through underground channels, the Blacks were urged to walk out with no passes. They were to walk to the police station and say no, no more, and give themselves up for arrest, rather than continue the indignity of not being able even to walk the streets without a pass for the government of Whites.

The news that came out of South Africa that day came as it always does from places where governments restrict the flow of information. It came in bits and pieces, and it was many months before the whole story was known. Then the events at the police station became known as the Sharpeville Massacre.

The police had barbed wire around the police station, and armored cars around that. That morning, the Black Africans threw stones, and the police, armed with submachine guns, began to fire into the crowd. The first report said 25 were killed, and then that was raised to 50. By June, The New York Times was reporting that 72 Africans had been killed.

Sharpeville was a township, and it had no hospital. The wounded were taken to nearby Vereenging. Soon, the hospital was filled, and many were treated outside on the lawn. A senior police official was quoted as saying, "I don't know how many we've shot. If they (Blacks) do these things they must learn the hard way."

In Sharpeville that day, the demonstration began in the morning. The first time the police opened fire, one demonstrator was killed, two others were injured. The Africans who came to protest would not be turned around. It is that way in movements. They go on, and they build steam. There comes a moment when, as a group, they say no, nothing is going to turn us around. It was that way in 1960 in the township of Sharpeville, which sits 30 miles south of Johannesburg in South Africa.

Police fired warning shots. Still, the crowd would not be moved. The police opened fire with machine guns. "People fell like ninepins," a news dispatch quoted an observer as saying. In May of that year, there was an inquiry and two physicians said they found that more than 250 of the Blacks had been shot in the back.

The pass laws go back to 1807. There were demonstrations against them as early as 1903. Never was there anything to match what happened at Sharpeville. It became a name burned into memory, and because it did, it also became something that had to be destroyed.

Ten years later, the South African government moved to take Sharpeville off the map. The entire population of 40,000 Blacks was to be moved to a new township. Sharpeville was
to become a residential area for Whites and an industrial site.

All that happened in Sharpeville comes back now, on the first day of this spring, because there are moments in history that never disappear. The United Nations took the

Sharpeville Massacre and used it to proclaim the first day of every spring as International Day Against Racial Discrimination.

At the UN, appropriate ceremonies are scheduled when the whole problem of apartheid and South Africa again comes before the world organization.

An hour before that ceremony, also at the UN, Dr. Bernard W. Harleston, the president of City College, and the ambassador from Nigeria to the UN will meet to announce an unprecedented honorary doctorate to Nelson Mandela, an attorney and founder of the African National Congress.

The ANC is the prime mover in the freedom movement in South Africa. Leadership involves risks. Nelson Mandela sits now imprisoned in Capetown, South Africa. Disobedience to the same kind of laws that led to the Sharpeville Massacre led to Mandela's imprisonment.

Tonight, at Music and Art High School in Harlem, the day-student government of City College joins with Unity in Action Network in a program, "Artists Against Apartheid." It is one more coming together of forces that move now to isolate South Africa culturally. The program is to benefit victims of South African raids on refugee camps in Angola and Mozambique and Lesotho.

South Africa. It stays on the back burner. Across the country now, students have begun to rise in protest against American involvement in El Salvador. It is said that the movement on the campuses is growing because American involvement in El Salvador is wrong, and that may be a part of it. But what the students fear is another Vietnam.

But South Africa, it stays on the back burner. Only on days such as this, the first of spring, which brings back the Sharpeville Massacre, does attention focus on apartheid and the system that is compared with Nazism and the Germany of 50 years ago.

1983

THE RITUAL OF GRADUATION DAY was unfolding. On the platform, it came to the awarding of honorary degrees. It was the moment yesterday that made the 137th Commencement Exercises at City College special.

The honorary degrees were given. One was put into the hands of Bernard Taub Feld, a nuclear physicist. Another was given to Walter F. Mondale, former senator, former vice president, and now the front-runner in the race for the 1984 Democratic presidential nomination.

But it was the other honorary degree that was given, the one conferred on Nelson Mandela, that was to make this an afternoon set apart.

Mandela was not on the platform at South Campus Field, but at first mention of his name, small applause began to grow, and it built. The students in cap and gown, who were sitting on folding chairs, began to stand. By the time the citation for Nelson Mandela was read, the huge crowd that filled the grounds was on its feet, and the applause was loud.

Nelson Mandela. Since 1962, he has been imprisoned in South Africa. His sentence is life, and it is said that he will never get out. But his name has become a powerful symbol of the struggle in South Africa that grows against the system of apartheid.

Never before in its history had City College awarded an honorary degree to a recipient who was not there on the platform on graduation day to receive the honor.

In South Africa, Nelson Mandela has long been a part of the leadership of the African National Congress. The ANC is the preeminent anti-government organization in South Africa. It has been in existence since 1912. In that time, it has been in the forefront of the struggle against apartheid in every significant way. For more than 40 years, Mandela has been a central figure in the ANC.

Mandela was one of the leaders with the ANC in the forming of an armed unit; Unkhonto We Sizwe, it is called, meaning the spear of the nation. On May 20, the ANC's armed wing struck at the South African government, exploding a powerful bomb that killed 16 people and injured nearly 200. The ANC called it an escalation of the struggle. Yesterday, at CCNY, the whole struggle of South Africa came to the center of attention.

The magic in the afternoon belonged to Nelson Mandela and to the Rev. Maxime Rafransoa, general secretary of the All-Africa Council of Churches, who accepted the award in Mandela's place.

Mandela, who is a lawyer, had been at Robbin Island prison in South Africa. Last year, he was removed to Pollsmoor, a maximum security prison. He is a symbol of defiance.

On the day he was sentenced to a term of life in prison, he spoke to the court and his words have become legend.

"I do not believe," he said, "that this court, in inflicting penalties on me for the crimes for which I am convicted, should be moved by the belief that penalties deter men from the course that they believe is right. History shows that penalties do not deter men when their conscience is aroused, nor will they deter my people or the colleagues with whom I have worked before."

In his trial, Mandela was charged and convicted under the South Africa sabotage and suppression of communism acts.

"I am prepared to pay the penalty even though I know how bitter and desperate is the situation of an African in prisons of this country," he said at sentencing. "I know how gross is the discrimination, even behind the walls, against Africans, how much worse is the treatment meted out to African prisoners than that accorded to Whites."

"Nevertheless, these considerations do not sway me from the path that I have taken, nor will they sway others like me. For to me, freedom in their own land is the pinnacle of their ambitions, from which nothing can turn men of conviction aside. More powerful than my fear of the dreaded conditions to which I might be subjected is my hatred for the dreadful conditions to which my people are subjected outside prison throughout this country."

"You teach us," Rev. Rafransoa said of Mandela. He was going back to words that Mandela spoke to the South African court at his sentencing.

"Whatever sentence Your Worship sees fit to impose on me for the crime for which I have been convicted before this court, may it rest assured that when my sentence has been completed, I will still be moved, as men are always moved, by their consciences; I will still be moved by my dislike of race discrimination against my people when I come out from serving my sentence, to take up again, as best I can, the struggle for the removal of those injustices until they are finally abolished once and for all."

In the afternoon yesterday, in the sun on South Campus Field, the special moment in the CCNY graduation was the moment that was given to Nelson Mandela. It was because of the struggle he makes in South Africa against the system of race discrimination that is apartheid.

1984

IN THE MORNING, THE REV. JESSE JACKSON started with the news that Bishop Desmond Tutu had been awarded the Nobel Peace Prize. "A tremendous thing has happened," he said.

He understood what the placing of the prize in Bishop Tutu's hands would mean. Two decades ago, the prize was conferred on Martin Luther King Jr. who was then the young leader of the American civil rights movement. Jesse was just linking up with King then, and he saw up close the impact the Nobel Peace Prize had. He saw the way it lifted King and the civil rights movement onto the world stage. In the morning yesterday, all that came back, and Jesse knew the attention that would now focus on Bishop Tutu and the struggle he has led against the apartheid laws of South Africa.

Jesse said how timely it was that it happens now. It has to do with Sunday, and the second Reagan-Mondale debate. "South Africa will be on the agenda now," he said. The site of Sunday's debate is Kansas City. Jesse said he would be there. "And I'll be leading a prayer vigil," he said. It comes back to South Africa. "We have to make certain that (South Africa) is on the agenda," he said.

His campaign for the presidency is over, but yesterday Jesse had some old business to occupy his time. The old business had to do with a promise he made months ago when he was a candidate for the Democratic Party's nomination. He promised then to send a signal to his supporters, a signal that would make it clear what he thought they ought to do in the election. "The stakes are high in Nov. 6," he said. "You have a thousand reasons to vote," he said and made a long list of arguments as to why Mondale ought to be supported.

He started the Cathedral Church of St. John the Divine and went from there to John Jay College. At both stops, Jesse worked for Mondale the way he had worked for himself in the primaries. Tutu had appeared with him at rallies. On those occasions, Jesse introduced Tutu as "the Martin Luther King Jr. of his country." When Jesse said that "a tremendous thing has happened," it was because he saw the issue of apartheid and South Africa coming to the front the way the civil rights movement did when the prize was awarded to Dr. King 20 years ago.

Africa was the center for Jesse yesterday, and his vow was to make certain that it becomes an issue in next Sunday's debate. He went back to the time when he was a candidate, and the Democrats who were in the race for the nomination debated at Harvard. "We went through three quarters of that debate," he said, "and left out two thirds of the people in the world." He played that off against what he called the facts -- "that most of the people of the world are Yellow, Black or Brown and poor, and don't speak English." But he kept coming back to South Africa.

He said that under Reagan the United States had become "the number one trading partner of South Africa." He made a long and detailed argument of the ways the administration had aided and "reinforced the arrogance of apartheid." He brought it all back to Sunday and the debate in Kansas City. "It (the American relationship with South Africa) should be discussed, and on Nov. 6th, you can do something about it."

"It's a beautiful day," Jesse said. He mentioned that in El Salvador the peace proposal he helped set in motion was taking root. He mentioned a lawsuit that was initiated in New York against second primaries. But he came back to Bishop Tutu and the Nobel Peace Prize. "A tremendous thing," he called it.

1984

THE NEWS COMES IN BITS and pieces. It does not even say for sure how the killing was done. The details are always sketchy, but they come to the figures that are a count for the dead.

In the news from yesterday, the report was that 10 more Blacks had been killed inside South Africa. It figured to happen that way.

More than anything else, the American election had been holding the South Africans back. Now the campaign is over, and the South Africans have begun to cut loose. Yesterday's count of the dead was 10. It was nothing. The figures that measure the killing are going to be much bigger.

The hope was that somehow the whole issue of South Africa and the apartheid laws that enslave 22 million Blacks would have come to the front in the American political campaign. The hope was that it would have all been brought out and put before the American people, but it didn't happen. In the primaries, when he was a candidate, Jesse Jackson tried to put South Africa on the agenda. Alone, he couldn't do it. He would raise the issue, but it would be quickly passed over and then dropped.

In the second Reagan-Mondale debate, which had an audience of 100 million, the reporters who asked the questions never raised the issue of South Africa. Not once. They toyed with questions involving human rights, but ignored the oppression inflicted by the most brutal government of all. Now nothing holds the government of South Africa back. The campaign is over.

In sketchy details from Johannesburg, it was reported that in the Black townships of South Africa, resistance to government's apartheid laws grows despite the killing. It was reported that both workers and students struck out at the government. The reports that came back supported what David Ndaba said in New York. Ndaba is a member of the observer group that the African National Congress (ANC) has at the United Nations. He said that "a true people's war" is now under way in South Africa. He said the people were striking out at the government in almost every way possible. And the sketchy details that came back said that David Ndaba was right. The reports were of strikes and boycotts and of gasoline bombings, stonings and disruptions of business and services. But the reports were also of the government's response, which was the killing, and yesterday the number of deaths was 10. And now the number of killings will grow. It's because there is nothing to hold the government of South Africa back. The American election is over.

The Reagan administration calls South Africa "an ally." They argue that the South Africans stand against communism. But on the day he accepted the Nobel Peace Prize, Bishop Desmond Tutu said the American policy of "constructive engagement" with South Africa has discouraged the government from making changes in its policies toward Blacks. Bishop Tutu counseled Blacks to work for non-violent change. The ANC, banned inside the country, counsels armed resistance. David Ndaba hailed the "people's war" and said, they are just being ungovernable.

Once the hope was that South Africa would be a country so isolated in the world that it would be forced to change its racist policies. That has not happened. It is going the other way. Yesterday the prominent picture in the news was of Roelof Botha, South Africa's foreign minister, sitting and smiling and greeting Yitzhak Shamir, Israel's foreign minister, in a meeting in Jerusalem. The hope was that there would be shame in dealing with South Africa. It hasn't worked out that way. It was revealed that the ties between the nation of Israel and South Africa are so strong that trade between the two countries amounted to $250 million in 1983 alone. But the true people's war is rising.

1984

IT DIDN'T TAKE THE SOUTH AFRICANS long to see the kind of trouble that was building. One after another, important figures in Black America were stepping forward at their embassy in Washington and subjecting themselves to arrest.

The South Africans could see it taking root. Each day they would peer out from the windows at the embassy. The demonstrators would be there, and the fervor in the words they shouted was rising.

The South Africans did not wait. They knew the demonstrations had in them the potential to become movement. Even in South Africa, it is legend what the American civil rights movement did in its time. The South Africans did not wait. They went to the State Department and made strong arguments that the demonstrations be stopped. They even went so far as to compare the protest to the Iranian takeover of the American embassy in Teheran.

"This must stop," the South Africans demanded.

That was where the Constitution of the United States came into the picture. The South Africans were told that nothing could be done, that it was not the same as the embassy takeover in Iran. It was the Constitution working. The Constitution guarantees the right of assembly, and the right of free speech. At the South African embassy in Washington, it was rights guaranteed in the Constitution that were being exercised.

The law says that no demonstration can be carried out within 500 feet of the embassy. But each day, to build the movement, an important figure in Black America stepped within that boundary and accepted arrest. Black members of Congress stepped forward and were handcuffed. Martin Luther King's daughter was arrested. Labor leaders came to the front. Then Whites joined in. It was an old tactic. It was from the civil rights movement that, in its day, was so successful it achieved every goal. It knocked down every law in the United States that sanctioned discrimination of any kind. It was a movement so powerful that it became a blueprint for protest in the world. But it was most effective here, in the United States. That was because of the Constitution.

On the Fourth of July in 1979, the Supreme Court upheld the NAACP's right to use economic boycotts as a means of forcing social change. On the day the decision came down, Benjamin Hooks, executive director of the civil rights organization, hailed the strength of the Constitution.

He told the story of a group of Blacks from South Africa who came to the United States to study first-hand the reasons the American civil rights movement had been so successful.

"One of the first things they did when they got here," Benjamin Hooks said, "was read the American Constitution." As soon as they had done that, the Blacks from South Africa said, "We can stop right here. We can see why you (the civil rights movement) were so successful. It's your Constitution. Your Constitution here works for you. South African law works against us."

The South Africans were right. The demonstrations that started in the middle of last month do have in them the potential to become a movement so powerful that it can arouse and force change. It can force the American government to change its friendly policy toward South Africa. It can even force South Africa to change, and knock down the apartheid laws that enslave 22 million Blacks. It is not a movement yet, but the roots are growing. In November, it was just Washington. By yesterday, it had spread to Los Angeles and to Park Ave. in Manhattan, outside the South African consulate there. It keeps growing. The fear that the government of South Africa has is that it may become a movement. It's because they know what a movement can do.

1985

HE STARTED OUT WITH a story from his old newspaper, The Washington Star. It was a story from 1976. Kenneth Walker said he remembers it as if it were yesterday. He was at his desk in the cityroom. For the first time in the newspaper's 128 years, South Africa was on the front page. It was at the height of the Soweto uprising and the headline told that 200 were dead.

He said an editor noticed him reading the paper. "And in his insensitive way, he tried to make a joke." The editor hollered, "I see we're finally getting rid of some of you people...heh, heh, heh." The editor was White. Kenneth Walker is Black.

On Wednesday night at a forum at Columbia University, Walker had many stories to tell. None was more compelling than the one from the cityroom of the newspaper that died four summers ago. Walker said the joke did not strike him as funny. But "rather than react with my initial instincts," Walker said, he decided that day to visit South Africa as a reporter, and to do all he could to "help expose the incomprehensible oppression of apartheid and White racism."

It took five years, and he had to pay his own way, but he made it. He saw apartheid up close. He came back to write an award-winning series. The last piece of that series was published the day before The Washington Star went out of business.

Kenneth Walker recently returned from another trip to South Africa. This time, he went as a correspondent for ABC. His reports were part of the unprecedented Nightline shows broadcast live from South Africa. On Wednesday night, Walker was the featured speaker at a forum sponsored by the New York Association of Black Journalists.

Walker built his speech around the question: What is the difference between now and then -- why the Washington Star dragged its feet on South Africa then, and why did ABC go after the story so aggressively now? His conclusion was that it had to do with the Constitution we have in the United States, and the way the American media are changing; of opening up to reflect the diverse population. He pointed out that South Africa was put on the front of this country's agenda by Americans using their Constitutional right to protest at South African embassies and chanceries around the country.

At the forum, Walker had many stories to tell. He finished with the story of a woman named Ellen Kuzwayo, who helped found the YWCA in South Africa. She told Walker of her first trip to the U.S., which was in 1969. She said she had heard much of Harlem, and was determined to visit this capital of the Black Americans. She said she was stunned by what she found. "Buildings falling down, people without jobs, young men on drugs, women selling their bodies."

She said she sat on a curb and wept. "Is this the curse of Black people all over the world?" she asked. Harlem was supposed to be different." Kenneth Walker said there was another side to Ellen Kuzwayo's experience.

The next day, she was taken to another building in Harlem, the Schomburg Center, which is the premier repository of Black history in the U.S. He said, that as she was being shown the history of Black America, the history that starts with slavery, the African woman stopped her hosts. "Does your government know what you are doing here?" she asked. "Do the police know?"

She was astonished. She was seeing up close the difference between South Africa and the U.S. "In my country, they do not allow such things to be discussed," she said.

"The America I've come to love is Ellen Kuzwayo's America, where we have the right to discuss openly the problems in our society," Kenneth Walker said. And he tied that to the way the students on the campuses use that freedom now to protest apartheid. At Columbia, at the finish, he said his finding was: "Yes, the end of apartheid is near."

1986

SUDDENLY, FROM INSIDE South Africa, almost nothing can be reported. The government has virtually locked up the news media, and given the keys to the police.

The restrictions are so great that a White opposition legislator stood in the Parliament, and declared that a blood-bath could have taken place in South Africa without people knowing.

Moderate voices from inside South Africa have warned that the situation has grown so critical that a million, or millions, of people could die. Words such as "holocaust," and "Armageddon," were used to sound the alarm. But always, behind the scary language, was the feeling that forces in the world would permit the racist regime to go only so far.

The other side was that the media were always counted on to tell the world exactly what was taking place inside South Africa.

That's the reason concerns were voiced early on when the South Africans first began to clamp down on the media. Back then, the government in Pretoria argued that the media, especially television, were fanning the unrest in the Black townships. The cameras were kept out. But the violence didn't end. It didn't even subside the way the government had predicted. A big piece of the story inside South Africa was taken off television. That was what the government wanted. Now, another big step has been taken. The media have been removed almost entirely. From inside South Africa, there is virtually nothing that can be reported.

Suddenly, they have in South Africa the darkness that's needed for the government to do anything.

The situation the legislator spoke of in the South African Parliament has become real: A blood-bath can take place without people knowing.

Imagine one whole section of New York City being under siege and nobody outside that area knowing anything. It's almost impossible just to imagine such a thing happening here. We know the media will tell the story. They may botch the story. They may not get it right. There may be too much or too little. But we know there will be something, and we depend on it.

In time, word will slip out as to what is happening now in South Africa. In tirne, people will know. But by then, it will be too late. Whatever happened will have been done.

Through everything, President Reagan has stood by his policy of constructive engagement with South Africa. When Reagan called Botha, he was told, the reports say, to "bug off," which means, "get lost."

The policies of the South African government don't shock anyone. Not anymore. The whole world knows the kind of regime that rules in Pretoria. But with the world watching, there are lines that even the South Africans care not to cross. With the world watching, and that means the media, even the Botha government can go too far.

But take away the media. Create a situation where nobody can see and nobody can tell what goes on. Do that, and anything can happen.

Do that, and you have the environment to carry out a bloodbath, a holocaust, a pogrom.

But it always takes darkness. No reporters were on the slave ships to tell of the millions of Africans killed during the Middle Passage. The media didn't tell of the slaughter of the Jews until it was done. The Turks used the darkness to butcher the Armenians. Only now has word begun to come out. It's always that way. Start with the bloodbath, killing of the American Indians.

In South Africa, the restrictions on the media are so great that just reporting movements of security forces breaks the law. So the news from South Africa is that we don't know. We don't know because the media cannot look and say what is taking place.

So anything can happen. In South Africa, they have now the kind of darkness that permits the slaughter of millions. In time, it will come out. In time, we'll know. But by then, it will be too late. The killing will have been done.

1989

FIRST THEY BROUGHT SOUTH AFRICAN Archbishop Desmond Tutu to the front of the pulpit. There they put into his hands one of the highest honors the synagogue has to give, the George Brussel Jr. award for human rights.

At the Stephen Wise Free Synagogue, where only a few seats were left empty, all who were there stood, and the applause for Tutu rose until it became special.

"Courage and commitment is what the Brussel award is all about," Tutu was told. He was the 26th recipient. The applause was the congregation's way of saying it was an honor Tutu had earned.

For the role he has played in the fight against apartheid in his native South Africa, Tutu has made himself one of the most admired religious leaders in the world. Nothing has ever stopped him from using his voice and position to stand up to the regime. Whenever needed, Tutu has been there with the commitment and the courage to say (and do) what the situation demanded.

On Monday night, Tutu did not come to the synagogue on the upper West Side only to be honored. Again, he was called on to exhibit the courage that has earned him esteem, the Nobel Peace Prize and a good place in history. Before an audience made up mostly of Jews, Tutu was asked to speak about the unspoken -- the relationship between the nation of Israel and the racist regime in South Africa.

In New York, where relations between Blacks and Jews have been strained, the Israel-South Africa connection has been an explosive issue. So what would Tutu say? How far would he dare to go?

By himself, no matter how eloquent, Tutu cannot square matters between the Black and Jewish communities. But it was in his hands to put a thorny issue on the table, and Tutu did exactly that.

"What a wonderful gift God gave us through the Jews," he said. "You have been a tremendous light to the world.

"We give thanks to God for the Jewish people. Your history is our history. At home (South Africa), many of those in the forefront of our struggle have been Jews -- and we salute them."

But on this night, Tutu had two stories to tell. "We Blacks in South Africa cannot understand how you (Jews) allow the government of Israel to have the relationship with South Africa that it has." He told of how the two nations collaborated even in matters that involve defense and nuclear know-how. "We cannot understand how Jews cooperate with a government that collaborated with Hitler."

Tutu also spoke of the price to be paid. "Black-Jewish relations in South Africa and the United States will suffer grievously as long as the Israeli-South Africa link exists," he said.

Before his speech at the Stephen Wise synagogue, Tutu had not spoken on the matter. But once the time had come, he also questioned other Israeli initiatives. "I find it very, very difficult to understand Israel's policy regarding the Palestinians," he said. Tutu said descriptions of what is happening on the West Bank and Gaza Strip sounded to him like descriptions of South Africa.

He used more than an hour to make his case. Then he laid down a challenge.

"Press Israel hard for justice for the Palestinians," he said. "Press Israel hard to change its policy on South Africa."

After he had his say, Tutu looked into the audience. "All this comes from the heart," he said. Again, everybody in the synagogue stood, and applause began to build. The senior rabbi, Balfour Brickner, went to Tutu, put his arms around the Black South African and for a long moment, the two embraced.

"A powerful message," Brickner said. "Words that come from the heart go to the heart."

One speech will not change Israeli policy toward South Africa. Neither will it heal the deep divisions between Blacks and Jews in the U.S. In time, though, the speech Tutu made at Stephen Wise Free Synagogue may be looked back upon as a turning point. For old allies, it brought into the open a very big problem.

1989

OF "THE MEETING," ONLY THE BAREST of details were released. But that figured. For a long time now, there has been no free flow of information from South Africa. The only news the Afrikaner government allows to get out is news the government wants the world to know.

So it was the government in Pretoria -- and only the government -- heralding a meeting between ailing State President P. W. Botha and the imprisoned black leader, Nelson Mandela.

The official release said "the meeting" took place last Wednesday at the presidential office in Cape Town. Along with Botha and Mandela, Justice Minister Kobie Coetsee also attended. He said the session lasted 45 minutes.

Of the Botha-Mandela meeting, Coetsee was the designated government spokesman. He said, "Their conversation took place in a pleasant spirit." He also said, "President Botha and Mr. Mandela availed themselves of the opportunity to confirm their support for peaceful development in South Africa."

Mandela said nothing. But that also figured. For 27 years, the ruling regime in Pretoria has seen to it that Mandela has had no freedom whatsoever. So whatever happened last week in Cape Town, it was entirely the government's doing. Mandela is a prisoner. He was one of the African National Congress leaders locked up in 1962 and never released.

Mandela did not summon Botha to his prison quarters for a sit down chat. The meeting was Botha's doing. He said to prison authorities, "Bring Mandela here." The question is, what is Botha up to?

The winds of change suddenly are blowing big time through southern Africa. From out of nowhere, a cease fire has been arranged and implemented in Angola. In Namibia -- the last colony of Africa -- elections to establish independent rule are scheduled for November. But in the politics of southern Africa, decisions made in Pretoria are key. So what is happening now?

In South Africa, the media have been virtually held under lock and key for some time. South Africa used to brag of having the freest press in Africa. The government boasted of how few restrictions media had and argued also that the free press reflected democratic values. But the government wasn't telling the whole story. The media were all White and saw almost everything only through the White man's eyes.

With freedom, the test is always decided by what happens in tough times. Freedom may not exist during periods of crisis. In South Africa when the Black majority began to rebel in a violent way against apartheid, media got banned from covering the story. At first, the ban was supposed to last just through the crisis. Then it was stretched through a year and then two. Now, it has become the reality in South Africa.

For years, Botha was South Africa's strong man. He was the defiant figure the Afrikaners held up to the world. But Botha's time is past. He is expected to leave office after the September elections. Education minister F. W. de Klerk is expected to be Botha's successor as head of the ruling National Party. Where Botha was loud and rough, de Klerk is soft and smooth.

Suddenly, South Africa needs what Botha could not deliver -- allies in the international community. Ronald Reagan is gone. Sanctions have begun to hurt. Pressure on Pretoria keeps increasing. Maybe "the meeting" was no publicity stunt; maybe it was proof that the government in Pretoria is in a bind and that it needs a deal.

When the country to the north of South Africa was Rhodesia, and the ruler was Ian Smith, he too said no Black majority rule. He was like Botha; he said never in a thousand years. But war and sanctions took a toll and in time, the White government fell. At the end, Ian Smith tried to make a deal but he waited too long.

The winds of change blowing through southern Africa suggest the Afrikaners are looking to make a deal. If that's the case, then for starters, they ought to free Mandela, clear the jails of political prisoners, end the state of emergency and scrap the constitution that embraces apartheid. Maybe that's what Mandela told Botha.

1990

WINNIE MANDELA DOES NOT CHANGE. No matter how the government in South Africa comes at her, she never takes a step back. She is always strong and always defiant.

Through most of 30 years, hers has been a voice the regime in Pretoria has tried to silence. Even when she was banned, which was supposed to stop her from even speaking in public, she ignored the law, and did what she believed she had to do.

First, the government imprisoned Nelson Mandela, her husband. Soon after that, she was taken into custody. For nearly two years, she was kept in solitary confinement. The effort was to break her; the government insisted she tell of crimes that never were, in order to put a noose around her husband's neck. But Winnie Mandela showed herself to be a woman too strong. It was in her blood to fight, and that was what she did. When they could not break her, they banned her. They tried to make her a non-person. That did not work either. Winnie Mandela always kept finding a way to do what she had to do.

The government in South Africa never forgets those leaders in the anti-apartheid movement who are strong. By what she did, Winnie Mandela made herself one of those targets. She again finds herself in serious trouble. She has been charged with four counts of kidnapping and four of assault with intent to commit grievous bodily harm and soon, she is expected to face trial.

She remains defiant. Of the government's decision to bring charges, she said, "Suffice to say I welcome the decision in the sense that at last, I will be able to stand a proper trial and clear my name properly."

The charges go back to late 1988. It was said that she organized a club of young men, mostly teenagers, and that she used the group as bodyguards. It was also said that the group, organized as a soccer club, took to violence to beat and intimidate others with political differences in the Black township of Soweto. South African authorities charged that on Dec. 31, 1988, the group kidnapped a 14-year-old who was said to be a police informant, and that at Mandela's home, the youth was beaten, then taken away and stabbed to death.

The murder of the youth, Stompie Seipei, was out at Winnie Mandela's doorstep. She took a lot of heat. There was even an effort to force her out of the anti-apartheid movement. In a raid on her home, authorities said they found a blood stained knife.

Government officials had pictures taken of the raid on the Mandela home. That footage was made available to American television networks and was shown on prime time newscasts. All of it, Mandela supporters insisted, was part of a plot to finally put Winnie Mandela in check and quiet her voice in the movement. It didn't work. She refused to walk away from her role as a political activist and she continued to speak in blunt language.

Just after the killing of Stompie Seipei, when the criticism of Winnie Mandela was strong, her oldest daughter came to New York. She is Zenani Mandela who is married to Prince Thumbumuzi Dlamini, the son of the King of Swaziland.

"This (the charges against her mother) is just another hurdle," Zenani Mandela said. "But I know this: they (the South African government) will never break the spirit of my mother or my father. I am deeply hurt. They have hurt my mom. They have hurt my father. But the truth will come out one day. We know that."

1990

IT TOOK 42 YEARS, BUT, FIINALLY, in South Africa the struggle against apartheid has reached a point where there can be no turning back. The door that state President Frederik W. de Klerk has opened can never be closed.

In his turning point speech to parliament, what de Klerk said in a way said to South Africa's Blacks, "Here is a bit of freedom. Take this now, but be mindful that more is to come. So be patient."

With freedom, history teaches us that it doesn't work that way. A bit of freedom merely whets the appetite. It's a turn-on that only sparks the reaching for more and more and it doesn't stop. Which means that it's a big door that's been opened in South Africa.

When de Klerk lifted restrictions on the African National Congress, and freed virtually all other groups to resume full political activity in South Africa, he was clearing the way for Blacks and their allies to embark on the kind of mass political mobilization that can sweep a government away.

What Blacks in South Africa have on their side is numbers. That's the reason the ANC was outlawed; the organization of Nelson Mandela was involved in organizing the numbers that were on their side.

So long as they are unorganized, the numbers don't mean so much. But once those masses begin to move together, they create what is called "people power" and what that kind of mobilization means has been demonstrated in the clearest way all across Eastern Europe. So is it to happen that way now in South Africa?

Soon, the de Klerk government has to free Mandela from his long imprisonment. Mandela is a formidable figure.

What happens when he walks out onto the streets free to lead as he sees fit? It would seem that Mandela returning to Soweto would be an event so large that it would have the potential to spark in the townships of South Africa the kind of fervor that Iran was faced with when the Ayatollah Khomeini returned from exile.

Even before de Klerk announced his reforms, the process of change was underway in South Africa. Black labor unions organized before they were legalized. The pass laws were repealed, but that happened only after Blacks just began to ignore them and go where they wanted.

By the time the government desegregated beaches, Blacks were already using them. Those were signs that "people power" was beginning to rise. But all that was unorganized; now it's different.

What is to happen in South Africa, once the ANC and COSATU, the big labor federation and the United Democratic Front, together all begin to mobilize mass political activity? With the numbers they have to work with, and the freedom to organize, the potential is there to put millions into the streets. That's the big hammer the opponents of the government in Pretoria have on their side.

The plan of the de Klerk government is to enter into negotiations with Black groups, a process the government says may take five to 10 years before an acceptable power-sharing arrangement is reached.

In the past, when the South Africa government has talked of "negotiations" and "reforms" not much has happened, except that the status quo, apartheid, has remained intact.

Now, Black leaders believe the situation is different. Free to organize and mobilize Black support, they see their movement getting stronger. At the same time, they believe the government is no longer in a position to call out the police dogs and use oppressive law to turn back the clock.

When he stood in parliament and announced his sweeping changes, President de Klerk was without doubt hoping to buy some much needed good will from the international community. The White government sorely needs to be freed of the economic and cultural sanctions that have been imposed on the country. In giving Blacks a bit of freedom, de Klerk has opened a door that can never be closed. And that's because a bit of freedom only whets the appetite.

1991

FOR NELSON MANDELA, IT DIDN'T BEGIN that April in 1964. The South African government was already holding him prisoner. He had been convicted of leaving the country without a permit and of inciting Blacks to go on strike and for that, he was serving a sentence of five years.

But Mandela was a leader the White government desperately wanted to get rid of and in 1964, to accomplish that, they brought him to trial on charges of sabotage. Mandela knew that he would be convicted. He also knew that once that was done, that he would be given either the death penalty or sentenced to life in prison.

He was strong and vigorous, in his mid 40s. He was married and had a family. Surely he did not want to give up his life, or to spend the rest of his time in the worst kind of imprisonment. But facing even that, Mandela did not waver. He chose to stand for what he believed. He would not fight for his life as the rulers of the White government wanted. He would not grant them that satisfaction. So at the trial, he did not allow any evidence to be submitted on his behalf. And he refused to be cross examined. But he did speak.

Mandela rose in the courtroom in Pretoria and used the trial where his life was at risk, to deliver a most damning indictment of apartheid. His words were never forgotten. He spoke for a long time, telling at the start of life in his homeland before the White man came, to an eloquent summation of what the struggle led by his organization, the African National Congress, was all about.

"Above all," he said, "We want equal political rights, because without them our disabilities will be permanent. I know this sounds revolutionary to the Whites in this country because the majority of voters will be Africans. This makes the White man fear democracy.

"But this fear cannot be allowed to stand in the way of the only solution which will guarantee racial harmony and freedom for all. It is not true that the enfranchisement of all will result in racial domination. Political division, based on color, is entirely artificial and, when it disappears, so will the domination of one color group by another. The ANC has spent half a century fighting against racialism. When it triumphs it will not change that policy.

"This then is what the ANC is fighting. Their struggle is a truly national one. It is a struggle of the African people, inspired by their own suffering and their own experience. It is a struggle for the right to live.

"During my lifetime, I have dedicated myself to this struggle of the African people. I have fought against White domination, and I have fought against Black domination. I have cherished the ideal of a democratic and free society in which all persons live together in harmony and with equal opportunities. It is an ideal which I hope to live for and to achieve. But if needs be, it is an ideal for which I am prepared to die."

On the 11th of June, 1964, at the conclusion of the trial, Mandela and seven others were convicted. Mandela was found guilty on four charges of sabotage and like the others, was sentenced to life imprisonment.

Mandela served 27 years. He did hard time. Most of his years were spent in South Africa's notorious maximum security prison on Robbin Island. But even that couldn't break him. Through the 27 years he exhibited so much strength that more than anyone else, he became the symbol of resistance to South African apartheid.

Mandela showed what it is possible for one man to do and yesterday after he walked out of prison, arm and arm with his wife Winnie, he stood before a huge crowd in Cape Town and his voice had nothing in it but strength. He is 71; the black hair he had in 1964 had turned white but still, his voice inspired.

"Our struggle has reached a decisive moment," he said. We have waited too long for our freedom; we can no longer wait. Now is the time to intensify the struggle on all fronts."

South Africa did all that it could to break Nelson Mandela; it couldn't do it. Which means that the anti-apartheid movement has the leader to conclude what Mandela called, "the final chapter of our struggle."

Chapter Eight, Part Two

HIDDEN HAND

Editor's Note

During his reign at the Federal Bureau of Investigation, the late director J. Edgar Hoover launched a counter-intelligence program aimed at progressive organizations and individuals in the United States. African Americans were especially targeted for illegal surveillance, burglaries, infiltration, provocation, and, many believe, even assassination.

The purpose of this program, according to top FBI officials, was "to prevent the emergence of a Black nationalist messiah who could unite Blacks" against racist U.S. policies.

The African American targets, in addition to Dr. Martin Luther King Jr., included leaders and members of the Black Panther Party, and many, many others.

Earl Caldwell was at the center of much of this controversy. While a reporter for The New York Times, FBI agents first requested, then demanded that Earl Caldwell serve as a bureau spy on Panther activities. When he refused, the bureau subpoenaed him to appear before a federal grand jury to testify about his confidential sources in the Black Panther Party. His refusal led to a landmark First Amendment case before the U.S. Supreme Court.

Although the court ruled against him in a narrow decision, Caldwell's case led to the enactment in 27 states of so-called "shield laws" that give varying protection to reporters trying to protect confidential sources.

1979

WHEN SOMETHING OF GREAT IMPORTANCE happens in our lives, we never forget. We think of it frequently. On the anniversaries of that occasion, the memories come back with special force.

It was 11 years ago tonight down in Memphis, at a sprawling old motel there that sits in the shadow of Beale St., that the Rev. Martin Luther King Jr. was shot and killed.

It has been 11 years, but the mind has its own way. It can blot things out. It can allow them to grow fuzzy and dim, and in time they disappear.

But some images never seem to fade. They always remain sharp. They stick there in the mind as though waiting to be understood, aware that the present, as Robert Frost wrote, is too crowded, too confused to contemplate.

We look back on that night in Memphis when the Rev. King was killed, recalling where we were, what we did. Still, we do not know what we should know about the assassination.

It is that way, even though books have been written about the killing; even though many newspapers have made exhaustive investigations, and a full blown congressional inquiry has been held.

Last night, Andrew Young, who is now the American ambassador to the United Nations, was asked about the assassination. On that night 11 years ago, Young was in Memphis. He was one of the Rev. King's closest aides. He was there in that cluster of people underneath the balcony at the motel, and he witnessed the killing.

Young is asked if he believed that James Earl Ray was the lone assassin.

"No, I don't," he said. He paused ever so slightly. "I'll never believe he was," Young said.

Being there when something really important happens is an obsession with many reporters. They tell themselves that they do not want to see anything terrible happen, that they wish no one ill. Their reasoning is only that if something is to happen, they want to be there.

The dream of being there comes from the frustration of near-misses, of always arriving on an assignment after whatever it is already has happened. And of being told, "Geez, you should have been here an hour ago." Or last night or yesterday. Then the reporter must try to piece the story together. Seldom, though, does it come out right.

"Stick to the facts," an editor admonishes. But the reporter knows the facts can mislead. "We don't want opinions," the editor says. "Let the columnist express the opinions."

But what are the facts? Are they the accounts that officials provide? Or are they a consensus of opinions?

Being there, it is believed, would solve the problem. If just once you were there, then you would know, and then you could say. As a reporter, it always was that way for me until that spring evening 11 years ago as twilight gathered over Memphis, bringing with it the feel of an oncoming chill. Then it was my turn to come as close as a reporter ever does to being there.

It was a Thursday. It was near 6 p.m. and the evening light was still good. I was in my room at the Lorraine Motel. I was in Room 215, on the ground floor of the motel, only a few doors from the room that the Rev. King occupied. It was deadline time, and I had been trying to get a long distance line to telephone to New York the story that I had been working on.

The shot sounded like an explosion. I took it to be a bomb. It was my fear working. Bombing was something I identified at that time with the Deep South. Homes, schools and churches had been bombed, and on this night I was certain the motel was the target.

Bombing was one of the terrorists tactics used against Blacks, and -- as all this welled up inside me. My response was automatic. There was no hesitation. I was already on my feet. The door, which opened to the balcony, was open. There was the split second needed to identify the sound and then, in one, two, three strides, I was in the doorway.

There was no smoke, no fire, no mass of debris. There was, off to my right, a knot of people. They were jumping about, and it occurred to me that perhaps someone had set off a firecracker.

"What a lousy joke," I thought.

From the doorway, my view was of the thicket across the street and my attention was drawn to a man who was stooping low in the bushes. He did nothing strange or suspicious. My attention focused on him only because he was there. There was no one else, and my eyes stayed glued on him. He was off to my right. He appeared to be coming out of a crouched position. He was alone, partly hidden in the thicket. He did not look in my direction. His attention was trained on something else -- something that I could not see.

He was White, and he seemed rather chunky. It could have been his clothing. He was wearing something white, and I took it to be a pair of overalls. As he straightened up, he seemed to twist his body, yet his eyes stayed riveted on something else.

What? What was it he was watching?

He began to move, slowly, in that twisting manner, off toward his right, as though he were about to run to the firehouse on the corner.

Now, from the yard, came the moans and then the cries. I learned that attention was behind me, up on the balcony. It was Rev. King. It had not been a bombing. It had been a rifle fire, and the Rev. King was the target.

It was 11 years ago. Still I, wonder about the man who climbed up from the bushes that night. The police, in their reports, say the man did not exist. But I know better. I was there. And today, I'm like Andy Young. I do not believe that James Earl Ray alone was responsible for the assassination.

1980

THERE WAS DEATH IN HIS FACE when they took him off the balcony. The huge wound the bullet had left in his neck said that Martin Luther King Jr. would not live.

The assassination was carried out. But that evening at the old Lorraine Motel in Memphis, the police came from everywhere. They were shouting that nobody would be allowed in or out of the motel grounds. Then they went through all the motions of setting up a cordon.

And for a while it looked as though the investigation was real. It looked that way until it became clear that there was no cordon. Anyone who wanted could wander in or out of the motel. And that was only the beginning.

Through the night, people who were registered at the Lorraine waited for the cops to come and ask questions. Where were you standing? What did you see? What did you notice earlier? They are the kinds of questions that police ask when there is an investigation. There are no magic solutions for solving crimes. It is what the police do, when they go door to door and ask questions. It is a procedure that has never been improved upon.

But that night in Memphis, the police never got around to asking questions. And by morning, officials were saying that they were certain that there was no conspiracy. They said they had found on the street a bundle of evidence that had everything they needed. And that the evidence pointed to James Earl Ray, and the police looked no further.

And now it all comes back. In the morning on Thursday, when word came from Indiana that Vernon Jordan had been shot, the thoughts that raced through the mind were of Memphis and King. It will always be that way because there was an emotional attachment to King, the kind of attachment that Blacks no longer have with their leaders.

The killing of Martin Luther King Jr. still is considered an unsolved crime. A year ago when there was a congressional inquiry into his death, and Andrew Young, who had been one of his chief lieutenants, was asked about the killing, he never hesitated. Right away, he said that he believed that there was a conspiracy. He said that he would never believe that Ray had acted alone in killing Martin Luther King Jr. And he is not alone.

Now comes Vernon Jordan. Yesterday, the doctors in Fort Wayne were saying that there should be a complete recovery. They said that he is not yet out of the woods but, barring complications, he should be able to resume his work as head of the Urban League.

And that leaves the police work. It was the FBI of J. Edgar Hoover that investigated the assassination of King. It was a long and costly job and, when it was over, the bureau said that there had never been an investigation in its history to match it. Never had so many agents been used in solving a single case; never had so much money been spent. But the doubts about Ray's being a lone gunman never disappeared.

It was the FBI itself that was questioned. How can they investigate King's death, people asked. The feeling was that the FBI wanted to see King dead. Later, there was evidence that the FBI had tried, using secret tapes, to embarrass King into committing suicide.

That was 12 years ago. Now J. Edgar Hoover is gone. It is a revamped FBI headed by William Webster, a former judge, that is investigating the shooting of Vernon Jordan. When word of the shooting of Jordan came, there wasn't the same kind of reaction. People have set up a shield. People are numb. They just took the news and they waited. They waited for the official story.

On Thursday night from Washington, FBI director William Webster was the first to use the word. "Conspiracy," he said. He said that the shooting of the head of the Urban

League was "in furtherance of an apparent conspiracy to deprive Jordan of his civil rights."

Before the director of the FBI issues his statement, the reports from Fort Wayne were scoffed at. There was vagueness about a "domestic" situation and then local officials were saying they were certain that the shooting was not racially motivated. Then, Webster, the head of the FBI spoke out.

Always, there has been a reluctance to use the word conspiracy. Always, the tendency has been to say no, it wasn't planned, it was just one kook out there, nothing more. But the head of the FBI is saying now that the evidence from Fort Wayne tells another story. Conspiracy. Now, the question is: Where does this lead?

Out in Indiana, Jesse Jackson wondered if the shooting of Vernon Jordan was part of an effort to assassinate Black leaders. He was thinking conspiracy.

The attempt on the life of Vernon Jordan came out of nowhere. But on the streets on Thursday and yesterday, Blacks who talked about it kept coming back to one thing: Indiana. It is one of the things that Black people know. Certain information is passed down. One of the things that Blacks say about Indiana is that it's Klan country. It was the reason Blacks scoffed at early reports that said no racism was involved. Blacks know the territory.

Early in the evening on Tuesday, two days before Jordan was shot, the 100 Black Men met uptown in Harlem. It was a dinner meeting, and a bar was set up in a corner but almost nobody drank.

One Hundred Black Men is considered one of the most prestigious and powerful of all Black organizations in the city. It is a distinguished group that includes bankers, businessmen, educators and professionals from many other fields. It is a group of the Black elite, and on Tuesday night when they gathered at the Harlem State Office Building, the room was filled with urgency. It was part of the impact of Miami.

The speaker was Earl Graves, editor and publisher of Black Enterprise magazine. Graves is a member of the 100 Black Men. On this night, he was supposed to talk about Black business, and its prospects for the 80s. But it didn't turn out that way.

The room was crowded, and when Graves stood he spoke in a voice that was filled with emotion. He began talking about business and its importance in the Black community. But soon he went beyond that, and he talked about what many in the Black community talk about now, the great need for leadership. Graves looked out at his colleagues, and he said that the difficult times that are now demand that everyone do more.

Nobody in the room disagreed. And that was before Fort Wayne. Before the shooting of Vernon Jordan. Nobody doubted the need for effective leadership. The question is, can any leadership survive now in the time of politics by assassination? It is a question that makes the FBI investigation in Fort Wayne so important.

1983

OUT IN THAT PART OF THE YARD that doubled as a parking lot, Solomon Jones, who chauffeured Martin Luther King Jr. about in Memphis, slid behind the wheel of a sleek blue Cadillac. He started the motor and eased the car over close to the balcony. He wanted everything to be convenient for Dr. King. While he waited he thought about the rally that had been held the night before and the speech Dr. King had delivered. He could still hear the echo of the words.

". . . Mine eyes have seen the glory of the coming of the Lord."

The pictures were sharp in his mind. He could see Ralph Abernathy, Jesse Jackson, Bernard Lee and Andrew Young, all of them ministers, as they came leaping forward. Their arms were out and ready to embrace Martin as he delivered that last line, stiff with emotion, spinning away from the microphone as he spoke. They had never heard him speak that way, and neither had Solomon Jones, and he too had been on his feet. It had been a moving experience -- one he would never forget.

He wondered what Dr. King had meant. He wanted to know more. He thought of that as he sat there, and while he waited, he could hear the voices of Jesse, Jim Bevel, Andy and the others who milled about in the yard near the car. They too waited for Dr. King.

They would not go off to eat, nor to the hall where another rally was to be held, nor any place else until after Dr. King had left. It was not an order. Nobody told them to wait. Yet, it was always done that way. It was just another of the ways they had of showing their respect and devotion to his leadership. It was the same with Solomon Jones. Nobody had asked him to pull the car up close to the balcony. He just did it.

Solomon Jones, who was in the car, could not see Dr. King as he was struck by the bullet, as his spine stiffened, and he pitched backward, then down onto the balcony. But at the instant of the explosion, because he could not see Dr. King, Jones's head whipped away. It jerked backward, back toward the explosion. In that moment, he saw a figure across the street rise in the bushes. He did not look at the man long. Only a few seconds. Immediately his attention went back to the balcony where Dr. King had been standing. He knew now that it was a shot, that somebody was shooting. He saw the man across the street in the bushes, and now he knew that Dr. King was hit.

He did not intend to abandon Dr. King. He did not intend to run. It was a reflex action. His foot came down heavy on the gas pedal and unleashed the tremendous horse power of the Cadillac. The car sprang forward. The sudden movement jolted him. Instantly he hit the brakes. He yanked the gear shift into reverse. His foot came heavy on the gas pedal again. The car jumped backward, and without realizing what was happening, what he was doing, and with his thoughts swirling through his brain, he shifted gears again, and again, he sent the car leaping forward. This time the car went further ahead. When he finally hit the brakes, he could not hear the shouts. He could not hear anything. His foot was jammed down hard on the brakes, and he sat there, spent, his head slumped over the steering wheel.

1983

THE PICTURES NEVER FADE. Even after 25 years , they stick in the mind. But after a quarter of a century, when the pictures from Dallas and the slaying of President John F. Kennedy come back, mostly they are a reminder of what we still do not know.

The official history tells us that Lee Harvey Oswald, acting by himself, killed the President. That, though, has never been the end of the story. The questions keep coming.

In the current issue of Time magazine, the cover story looks back 25 years and asks of JFK's assassination: Who was the real target? The article, an excerpt from a forthcoming book by James Reston, Jr., offers yet another scenario. Reston accepts that documentation that Oswald was the assassin. His compelling argument, though, theorizes that Texas Gov. John Connally, not Kennedy, was the target Oswald intended to take out. Connally, who was riding with Kennedy in the presidential limousine, did suffer a gunshot wound. Could it be that we lost Kennedy, and so much of the tide of history was turned, all because of an errant shot?

Oddly, in the same issue of Time, another assassination story poses another, deeper question: "Did the mob kill JFK?" The "mob" angle gets dismissed as "the trendy theory," and yet the article carries some telling quotes from underworld figures.

From a Florida mobster to an FBI informant in 1962: "Kennedy's not going to make it to the (1964) election. He's going to be hit." From another voice of the underworld in April 1963: "There is a price on the President's head. Somebody will kill Kennedy when he comes down South."

We still do not know. With assassinations, it tends to be that way.

Who killed Martin Luther King Jr.?

Good police work always begins at the scene of the crime. With the King assassination, it did not happen that way. The official story admits to following but one trail, the one that led to the arrest (and subsequent guilty plea) of James Earl Ray. So with King, too, we still do not know.

What is very clear and easy to see is the damage assassins' bullets have done. The pictures from Kennedy's time stick in the mind for a reason. It has to do with the promise of the best America yet. A lot of the historians tell of the Kennedy myth. They argue that in the thousand days he had as President, not much was accomplished. They say he holds a high place, not because of substance, but mostly because of his style, wit, and good looks and attractive family.

All those attributes, Kennedy had. But there was much more. You still find JFK's picture tacked onto a lot of walls in unlikely places. He had a voice that made people believe that, in his time, we could have the best America yet. He had a way of saying that we could be better than we are, and people who listened believed the words.

Assassinations do more than take out bright lights. They alter the course of history. So where would we be had the presidency of JFK been allowed to reach full bloom? What did we lose because King was cut down? And what difference would Robert Kennedy have made had he finished his quest?

1985

A GOOD PART OF THE STORY of what the FBI did to Martin Luther King Jr. was published in 1976 by the U.S. Government Printing Office.

It's an incredible, scary story, all of it based on fact.

The green-covered book that has 989 pages is the final report of a Select Committee of the United States Senate whose work was the study of governmental operations with respect to intelligence activities. It is Book III, Report No. 94-755.

The chilling story in the book is a case study of the FBI and Martin Luther King Jr. It goes back more than 20 years, back to January of 1962. It did not end until after King's assassination in 1968.

In the language of the report, a "war" was conducted by the FBI against Dr. King. The person the bureau had in charge of the war was to say: "No holds were barred. We have used (similar) techniques against Soviet agents."

It is obscene what Jesse Helms is doing. So obscene that even President Reagan wants no part of it, and yesterday he had Justice Department lawyers in court to block Jesse Helms.

In Washington, Jesse Helms is trying, as other have, to stand in the way of history. The United States Senate is scheduled to vote today on making the first Monday of each January a national holiday in the name of Dr. King. It is legislation that has already passed the House, and the President is expected to sign the measure into law. Jesse Helms is certainly aware that the movement of now involves registering and voting. Jesse Helms sees all of this, and, in the Senate, it has made him a desperate man.

In another time, when there were other movements, sheriffs stood in courthouse doors and blocked voter registration. And politicians stood in schoolhouse doors and blocked integration. But the movements always prevailed. Those who tried to stand in the way of history were swept away, which is the destiny that awaits Jesse Helms.

The Select Committee found the purpose of the FBI's program was clear. The introduction to its report begins, "From Dec. 1963 until his death in 1968, Martin Luther King Jr. was the target of an intensive campaign by the FBI to 'neutralize' him as an effective civil rights leader."

The move against King was a part of COINTELPRO, a counter-intelligence program carried out by the FBI. The Senate committee used testimony from FBI agents and documents from FBI files to build its report. The report tells how the intelligence gathering against Dr. King began with telephone taps. It went from there to the placement of microphones in hotel and motel rooms where King stayed. From an intelligence gathering operation, the move against King was widened and an effort to discredit him began. There were moves to discredit him with members of Congress; and then with universities, churches, and even the Pope. There was an attempt to discredit him during his receipt of the Nobel Peace Prize. Attempts were made to block publication of articles he wrote. Tapes of conversations were mailed to his wife. There was even an effort made to try and force him to commit suicide.

There were attempts made to discredit him with heads of government agencies, with major political and financial leaders, and in the news media.

As the FBI said, no holds were barred.

There is on one page of the document a long list of names of hotels and behind each name is a date. The FBI explained that it was a record of hotels where microphones were hidden inside Dr. King's room.

Why was all this done? The FBI says it was because it had reason to believe that King was involved with the Communist Party. When did it stop? It never stopped. Even after his death by assassination, the effort to discredit Dr. King continued, and it is all there, in the 989 pages of the green-covered book published by the government's own printing office.

What the FBI did to Martin Luther King Jr. was a national disgrace. What brings it back now are the demands being made by Jesse Helms, a right-winged Republican and a member of the United States Senate.

In Washington yesterday, Jesse Helms was trying to use the law to force public closure of FBI files. He is about to be swept over by the rising tide of Back voter participation.

In his North Carolina, in 1980 there were 915,000 votes for Reagan and 874,000 votes for Carter. There were also more than 500,000 unregistered Blacks. Jesse Helms goes before the United States Senate and says not a word of the way the FBI broke the law with microphones it hid in hotel rooms. It's a desperate man bringing back an ugly chapter from the past.

1985

IT HAS BEEN DONE, MARTIN. It's official now and this time around we celebrate your birthday as a national holiday.

Just the same, you should know that it's not a very good time, especially here in the City of New York.

More and more, the poor people are suffering. Many are living in the streets. They have no place else to go, and it's very bad now. Just last week we were hit with a cold wave. So many people from the streets crowded into shelters to keep from freezing that not even during the Great Depression was there anything like it.

Yes, Martin, it's that bad. There are an awful lot of people now who have no work at all. You said once the real emergency we face is economic and that it is a desperate and worsening situation.

I remember your words. You said, "In our society it is murder, psychologically, to deprive a man of a job or an income." You said, "In substance, (you are) saying to that man that he has no right to exist."

Those words of yours come back to us on the cold days of this winter, Martin, because more and more the victims themselves are being blamed for the situation that exists. In your time, you saw this attitude taking shape.

Your words still stick in the mind. You said, "All too many of those who live in affluent America ignore those who exist in poor America."

You said, "In doing so (ignoring the poor), the affluent Americans will eventually have to face themselves with the question that Eichmann chose to ignore: How responsible am I for the well-being of my fellows? To ignore evil is to become an accomplice to it."

In New York, Martin, we also have a terrible problem with crime. It's especially bad on the subways. There is so much fear on the subways now that people cheered when a rider took a gun and shot, in the back, four teenagers he thought were about to rob him.

It doesn't square with your words. You said, "Hatred and bitterness can never cure the disease of fear; only love can do that." You said, "Hatred paralyzes life; love releases it." You said, " Hatred confuses life; love harmonizes it." Those are words not heard much any more, Martin.

You said, "Love is the only force capable of transforming an enemy into a friend." You said, " We must develop and maintain the capacity to forgive." You said, "He who is devoid of the power to forgive is devoid of the power to love."

It is a troubling time, Martin, but there is a sunny side, too. You'd be proud the way nonviolent techniques you taught were brought back and used with great skill to make South Africa's racist, apartheid system a world issue.

Bishop Desmond Tutu raised his voice in a way that reminded us so much of you. He was so eloquent and so courageous that he became the first Black person to receive the Nobel Peace Prize, since the honor was bestowed on you 20 years ago.

And, Martin, there was all the work you did to get the vote for everyone. Well, the fruits from those efforts have begun to ripen.

Jesse Jackson ran an incredible race in the Democratic Party's presidential primaries. He leaned on an idea you were building. In the Poor People's Campaign you spoke of bringing people of all colors and backgrounds together in a rainbow revolution.

Jesse picked up on that. He called it the Rainbow Coalition. His idea was to get people of all colors and background to turn "to each other and not on each other."

In all, Martin, I suppose the good news is that the struggle continues. Some say not enough is being done. Some others question the direction we're moving in, but even in your time, doubts were raised.

The national holiday we have in your name is very important. For one thing, it brings your words back. You said, "There is little hope for us until we become tough-minded enough to break loose from the shackles of prejudice, half truths and downright ignorance."

1988

AFTER 20 YEARS, IT IS STILL THE SAME. We know the way Martin Luther King Jr. was gunned down as he stood on the balcony at the Lorraine Motel in Memphis. We know that he died almost instantly. We also know that is not the whole story.

So after 20 years, almost nothing has changed. We look back to the evening of April 1968, and the assassination of Martin Luther King Jr. Still, we do not know.

We have the official story. That's the FBI's version, but that never really held up.

We have the so-called "true story," which is the claim for the book that Gerald Frank wrote, "An American Death."

But Frank was not there. He did a remarkable reporting job. He brought together a wealth of information, but he paid a price for not being there. He was not able to evaluate properly the material he dug up. So Gerald Frank did not get the story right either.

But what difference does it make? Twenty years have passed. The assassination and the incredible outbreak of violence the killing sparked are distant memories. So what is the good in looking back and asking yet again: What really happened in Memphis? Who killed Martin Luther King Jr? And why?

They are not just idle questions. The haunting truth tells us that a people who do not know their history are bound to repeat it. What does that say to us now?

The official story tells us that James Earl Ray killed Martin Luther King Jr. Supposedly, he leaned from the bathroom window of a flophouse across from the motel, and, using a rifle that had a telescopic lens, pulled off the shot that exploded in King's neck.

The official story says that Ray then dashed back to his room, wrapped the rifle in a blanket with a lot of other personal items, and dashed down the stairs. The incredible story says, that once down stairs, Ray then dropped the whole bundle of damning evidence on the sidewalk, jumped into a white Mustang, and fled.

Later, after a search that stretched across a good part of the world, Ray was arrested. He was brought back to Tennessee to stand trial.

He engaged Percy Foreman, a formidable criminal lawyer, to handle his defense. Ray said he didn't kill King.

A widely held belief was that the state would have trouble winning a conviction of first-degree murder. But there was no trial. Nothing ever came out. James Earl Ray entered a guilty plea to the killing and was sentenced to 99 years in prison.

The official story, though, still didn't hold up. The FBI overplayed its hand. The bureau boasted of using more agents and putting more hours into the investigation of the King assassination than any other in FBI history.

But it came out that the investigation was so shabby that no police or FBI agents even went door-to-door at the Lorraine to ask those guests whose rooms faced the flophouse, what, if anything, they had seen.

The failure to do such basic police work was no oversight. Instead of conducting an investigation, police and FBI officials were following the bundle of evidence left on the street that pointed toward James Earl Ray.

Nothing else mattered. So there was no need to start out at the motel, the scene of the killing, which is what police investigators always do when trying to solve a crime.

The author Gerald Frank found three witnesses who saw a man rise from the bushes in front of the flophouse at the moment of the shooting.

But Frank did not see the man himself. He had nothing to convince him the man was there. So, in his "true story," Frank followed the FBI; the man in the bushes got left out.

In the assassination of Dr, King, we still look back. But after 20 years, just that is not enough: We need the real story of the killing at the Lorraine Motel in April, 1968.

1991

THE OFFICIAL STORY SAYS that James Earl Ray was the trigger man in the killing and authorities insist that he acted alone. The guilt of Ray was not proven during a trial; he was pleaded guilty by his lawyer. So, in the courtroom, not much evidence was ever disclosed.

Not long after he began serving his term of life in prison, Ray reversed himself. He told of having been deceived by his lawyer. He swears that in the assassination, instead of being a participant, he was really the fall guy.

Ray has since demanded a trial but on that, he has gotten nowhere. The court says, case closed.

The official story of what happened in Memphis at twilight on the first Thursday in April of 1968 has in significant ways become more a preposterous tale with jagged edges.

The investigation into the killing of King was led by the FBI. After it was done, it was said the probe conducted was the most exhaustive in the bureau's history. But the investigation the FBI once bragged of now gets pointed at as a prime piece of the proof that in the killing of King, no first rate murder investigation ever took place.

Every good murder investigation begins at the scene of the crime. Investigators are especially thorough in looking for witnesses. When they find them, they ask a ton of questions. Exactly where were you? What did you see? When did you notice it? Are you sure? Did anyone see what you saw?

At the scene of the crime, the investigator goes from room to room. Nothing gets overlooked. In time, all those who were there get questioned as to what they saw. The bits and pieces of information picked up get organized. That's how the investigation begins to come together. In Memphis, with the King assassination, it didn't happen that way. No FBI agents or any other cops ever went door to door at the motel where King was killed and asked questions. I know; I was reporter in Memphis that evening and my room at the Lorraine Motel was just beneath, and to the right of King's room. The doorway to my room looked directly across the parking lot and the weeded embankment to the flop house where James Earl Ray, according to the official story, leaned from a bathroom window and ambushed King.

No witnesses saw Ray pull the trigger. No witnesses saw him lean from the bathroom window. What the official story involved, nobody saw. It says that after Ray shot King, he went back to his room and wrapped the gun he used and a lot of other damning evidence into a sheet. He then took all that and ran down the stairs, stopping only to drop the sheet containing the evidence onto the sidewalk. Ray supposedly jumped into a white Mustang car and sped away.

All that was a part of what officials say happened, but nobody saw. Those who were there were to tell another story. It involves a man who witnesses saw standing in the high weeds on the embankment at the rear of the flop house.

When the fatal shot was fired, I could not see King from the doorway of my room. He was down on the balcony, out of my sight. So at the moment of the blast, not knowing King had been shot, my sight was trained on the direction of the explosion. I saw a figure huddled in the weeds. Solomon Jones, who was King's driver, was in the car when the shot was fired. He couldn't see the balcony either, but his head whipped toward the embankment. He, too, saw the man in the bushes. Across the street, an old man who had been sitting in the weeds "watching the big doings" at the Lorraine while drinking wine with a friend, also told of seeing the man in the bushes. The old man who drank wine said he saw what Solomon Jones had seen, which was that the shot that killed King came from where the man in the bushes was perched.

The official story makes no mention of any man in the bushes. In the official story, he did not exist. The official story points only to James Earl Ray. Which means that in the assassination of Martin Luther King Jr., after 23 years, nothing has changed --- we still don't know.

1993

THERE ARE NOT MANY OF US. We are the ones who were there in Memphis with Martin Luther King Jr. 25 years ago, on the night a bullet fired from an assassin's rifle snuffed out his life.

Most of us share one thing; we never had a chance to tell of what we saw, not in a courtroom, anyhow. But that is about to change. James Earl Ray is going to stand trial.

Only problem is, this is not the real deal. This is sort of like the movie, JFK. It is people who want answers coming up with some creative ideas. With JFK, Oliver Stone got a lot of information out with his movie. It had some impact; some files concerning the death of President Kennedy are being unsealed.

With the assassination of King, Ray actually had his moment. He went into court but instead of pleading innocent then, he made a deal that got him 99 years.

He insists, though, that he is innocent. Maybe he is. A lot of people do not believe that Ray, acting alone, carried out the assassination of Dr. King. But that is what the official story says.

Ray has since recanted. He says he was duped into offering a guilty plea. Maybe he was.

Ray ought to be heard. He wrote a book, "Who Killed Martin Luther King?" but a book is just one side of the story. In a courtroom, the story you build up, a prosecutor tears down. Ray needs to be subjected to that. Everybody ought to have a chance to hear and see what happens. That is about to come to pass.

In January, Ray will stand trial. It will be recorded on videotape, and in April, on the 25th anniversary of King's death, the trial will be shown on television. The series of shows that will comprise the trial will be shown over Thames Television of Great Britain and on HBO in the United States. It will be a trial as close as possible to the real thing that never was. A jury will be empaneled; witnesses will be called. Ray will have his defense attorney and a skilled prosecutor will be on the other side. There will be no actors, no script.

What does it matter? A lot. That's because it may wind up throwing some needed light on the truth of these political assassinations that have changed the course of history. We have a right, not just to the truth, but also to believe we have been told the truth. With the killing of King, that's not true as it now stands.

That's the reason I agreed to "testify" for Ray, who from all I'm told, has more than a bit of the bigot in him.

Did Ray do it? I don't believe so. Why? Because the FBI never conducted a thorough investigation at the scene of the crime. When that is not done at the murder scene, the investigation is flawed. J. Edgar Hoover, then the director of the FBI, said the King investigation used more man hours and more resources than any in the bureau's history. Sounds good until you realize that nobody went door to door at the motel, asking basic questions. Where were you standing? What did you see? Did you notice anything the night before, or earlier that day? Did you hear anything strange? You have to ask questions. A lot of the time, people don't know that they might have witnessed something important. That's because they do not have the big picture; but asking questions, that's what investigators draw -- the big picture.

A big and important movie on Malcolm X is in the theaters now. On that project, filmmaker Spike Lee did a tremendous job. But with Malcolm, more than anything else, we need to know about his death. Who killed Malcolm? Again, too many people do not believe the official story.

With the killing of King, authorities were quick to say that no conspiracy was involved. But how can they say that without a proper investigation? And that, they didn't do.

It is almost 25 years since twilight gathered over the old motel just off Beale Street in Memphis, and Martin Luther King Jr. was shot to death. One old, poor, bigoted, criminal was arrested. The official story says that's it. That cannot be it; so bless Thames TV and HBO, because in putting on a trial for James Earl Ray, maybe we will finally be getting at some truth we need to know in the assassination of a leader so great he had his name attached to a national holiday.

Editor's Note

The jury in the HBO "trial" of James Earl Ray returned a verdict of "not guilty."

1994

IT IS STILL THE SAME. Every time another bit of new information that deals with the assassination of the Rev. Martin Luther King Jr. comes to light, you grab for it, and you wonder.

Is this it? Is this the link to the real story? Are we finally going to know what happened that April night in 1968 at the Lorraine Motel in Memphis?

We have the official story. It says that James Earl Ray did it, acting alone. Ray is in prison. The case is closed. But the questions persist.

With the King assassination, there will always be questions. That's mostly because the FBI bungled the investigation. Even the bureau admits that once it got onto Ray's trail, it didn't look in any other direction.

So it is not surprising that this year, as the Jan. 17 King national holiday approaches, new charges are being made as to who killed King. This time, the report says Ray was a patsy, that he had nothing to do with the killing. Those reports, aired on national television, say a retired Memphis businessman claims he hired the assassin, and that he was acting on behalf of a New Orleans crime family. Maybe there's something here; maybe it is just another story. The FBI has been asked to investigate.

This all has to do with the story John McFerren told the day that King was killed.

McFerren is a Black man who lives in Somerville, Tenn. He's an older man, and for a good part of his life, he was involved in the civil rights movement. In fact, he never stopped being active. McFerren operates a gas station and a kind of community store. The way he tells it, a lot of people in his little town started leaning on him because of his civil rights work. They shut off nearly all his supplies. The idea was that if he couldn't get supplies, he'd be out of business, and without that, he'd be out of town.

Only thing was, McFerren was not that easy to get rid of. He says he took to driving to Memphis to pick up his own supplies. He was in Memphis picking up supplies at a produce house early in the afternoon that Thursday in April 1968. He says there were two White men in an office talking loud and ignoring him. He says they were treating him as though he didn't exist. But he was there, and, the way he tells it, eavesdropping.

He believes he heard one of the men give the order to kill King. He says he heard one of the men say: "Shoot the SOB right on the balcony." What ties in with the new charges is that Lloyd Jowers, the businessman, who is the sources, is a produce operator.

In 1968, the FBI talked to McFerren. His story was dismissed as fantasy or paranoia.

McFerren also had another piece of information from that day. He said that while at the produce house, he also listened in on a telephone call. He said he heard one of the men say into the phone, "no, you can pick up the five thousand bucks from my brother in New Orleans." So, like Jowers, he put it on the record that there was a New Orleans connection.

McFerren told all this the day that King was killed. He said that he left the produce market after hearing the conversation that afternoon. Later, when King was killed while standing on the balcony at the Lorraine Motel, McFerren was sure that he was onto something, and went to the authorities.

Only problem was, the FBI was not following leads like the one that came from McFerren. The bureau was onto James Earl Ray, and that's the way the investigation was pointed -- the entire investigation.

The Rev. Joseph Lowery, president of the Southern Christian Leadership Conference, King's old organization, has asked the Justice Department to look into the new assertions.

Chapter Eight, Part Two

HIDDEN HAND

Editor's Note.

During his reign at the Federal Bureau of Investigation, the late director J. Edgar Hoover launched a counter-intelligence program aimed at progressive organizations and individuals in the United States. African Americans were especially targeted for illegal surveillance, burglaries, infiltration, provocation, and even assassination.

The purpose of this program, according to top FBI officials, was "to prevent the emergence of a Black nationalist messiah who could unite Blacks" against racist U.S. policies.

The African American targets, in addition to Dr. Martin Luther King Jr., included leaders and members of the Black Panther Party, and many, many others.

Earl Caldwell was at the center of much of this controversy. While a reporter for The New York Times, a federal grand jury subpoenaed him to appear and testify about his confidential sources in the Black Panther Party. His refusal led to a landmark First Amendment case before the U.S. Supreme Court.

Although the court ruled against him in a narrow decision, Caldwell's case led to the enactment in 27 states of so-called "shield laws" that give varying protection to reporters trying to protect confidential sources.

1980

EVERY PAGE OF THE DOCUMENTS carries the stamp. In bold letters it reads: "All information contained herein is unclassified." Then there is the date of declassification and, underneath that, the initials of the appropriate official.

The documents provide one more look into the way the FBI operated through the late '60s and early '70s.

The pages are full of revelations. They confirm many old fears. Still, they do not tell all that happened. I know. I was one of the reporters caught up in the counterintelligence program the FBI conducted in its effort to destroy the Black Panther Party.

One of the declassified documents is dated Jan. 12, 1970. It is a memorandum that carries the code name "Airtel," and was sent by the special agent in charge of the FBI's San Francisco office to Washington, to the national director.

Regarding subject, the memo says: Black Panther Party. Racial matter. Smith Act of 1940, seditious conspiracy, rebellion and insurrection.

It was a two paragraph memo, directed to J. Edgar Hoover, the longtime head of the FBI. It begins: "Re: Bureau Airtel Dated: 12/18/69 Concerning interview of Earl Caldwell of the San Francisco office of The New York Times. Special agents of the San Francisco office have made six calls at The New York Times office, leaving messages that an appointment was desired."

The memo goes on to say that Caldwell, the reporter, was never available, but that his secretary had been advised of interest in an interview Caldwell had with a Panther leader, David Hilliard. The memo says the secretary volunteered that she believed the Hilliard interview had been tape-recorded.

Then, the declassified FBI memorandum concludes: "In view of the lack of response from Caldwell, no further attempt is being made to conduct the interview."

It did not happen that way, and it did not end there.

The memo says nothing about the FBI first asking, then demanding, that I become an informant. It does mention the threats that were made. It says nothing of the court fight that followed, one that wound up before the Supreme Court of the United States with its historic ruling in 1972 that dealt with reporters' rights.

It goes back to 1969. I was a national correspondent with The New York Times then, based in the newspaper's San Francisco bureau. A part of my responsibility was covering groups that were considered radical. At the forefront was the Black Panther Party.

In the middle of December 1969, there were almost constant battles between the Panthers and the police. Not a week went by that there was not some kind of confrontation. Some ended in killings; most involved shooting. The Panthers argued that nobody would say what was really happening to them, that they were being set up, and that the FBI was behind what was taking place.

At the time, I spent every night that I could at the Party's national headquarters, which was in an old two-story wood frame building on Shadduck Ave. in Oakland. The nightly fear was that a police raid would take place.

"Why don't you write this?" Hilliard, who was the Panther's national chief of staff, screamed one night. "Why don't you tell people what the FBI is doing to us?"

There was nothing to say. I understood what Hilliard meant, and I believed the raids that were taking place were not chance happenings. There were obvious planning and coordination. The raids were being executed with military precision. But reporters cannot always say what they would like to say in their newspaper stories. Editors demand facts.

They want proof. They say to their reporters, "Prove it, then we'll print it." The proof needed to say what Hilliard wanted to say was proof I did not have,

It was then that the FBI came for me. It was the middle of December 1969. The FBI approached me to ask if I would be willing to become an informant, to spy on the Black Panther Party.

"You are around the Panthers all of the time. You are there everyday," an agent said to me over the telephone. "What we would like you to do is call us, and let us know what you see, and what you hear. You could call us every few days."

At the time, it surprised me what the FBI was asking, and my answer was no. It was something that no reporter could do. A reporter could not be a cop. Over the phone that afternoon I tried to explain this as best I could to the agent who called. But when I was finished, he did not want to leave it there. He pressed it. Finally, the conversation ended with my saying that I did not even want to talk to him or any other agents again.

But the next day, the FBI called back, again the next day, and the day after that. But I would not take the phone calls. Still the FBI continued to call saying now that they wanted information about Hilliard. I continued to refuse to speak to them on the telephone. Then came the threat.

Over the phone the agent said to the secretary in The Times bureau that the FBI was tired of playing games.

"You tell Caldwell that we've had it with him," the agent said. "You tell him that if he does not want to meet with us, that if he won't tell us anything, that he can tell it in court."

That was on a Friday. On the Monday morning that followed, a federal marshall showed up at The Times bureau and he had a subpoena in hand.

The subpoena that was served ordered me to appear before a federal grand jury that was investigating the Panthers. The subpoena further said that when I come I should bring all of my notebooks, tape-recordings, and anything else I had that dealt with the Black Panther Party.

That day, right then, my reporting on the activities of the Black Panther Party was finished. It was over. Checkmate.

It meant that I could not stay out there and watch as my editors had wanted. The Panthers had been making charges, saying that there were no provocateurs, that they were being set up, that FBI agents were using phony documents, and a lot of other devises to create dissention, then trouble with the Party. But the Panthers had no proof.

Getting the proof is the reporter's job. We want the facts, editors say. It is the reporter who must go back and dig. The reporter hopes that, in time, the facts that show the truth will emerge. The reporter goes back and stands watch. The reporter does this because what the reporter understands is that if he stays out there long enough, if everything is right, that, sooner or later, there is the chance of getting the evidence that is needed.

With the issuing of the subpoena, the FBI took away any chance that I had of getting the facts. From that Monday morning on, my time was spent with lawyers, fighting first one subpoena, then another. Before it was over, the issue was in the hands of the Supreme Court.

It never occurred to me then. I did not realize that the FBI did not want reporters out there looking, asking questions, standing watch, because there was fear that, in time, the reporter might just be lucky enough to stumble onto what they, the agents of the Federal Bureau of Investigation, were doing.

This is part of what the document, the one numbered 105-165706 and directed to the attention of J. Edgar Hoover, does not say.

1980

WE GOT THERE THE BEST way we could. If our newspapers would pay, we used their credit cards. Those who had the money took the days off and paid their own way. Whatever was necessary was done. Quietly, in a small central Missouri town of Jefferson County, Black journalists from across the country came together. It was to be part conference, part survival meeting, part reunion. It was also to be a highly charged and emotional meeting. Certainly there never before had been a gathering quite like it.

Many of us did not know one another, but we did not come together entirely as strangers. Everyone seemed to know somebody from an NAACP convention, from a riot or from some assignment in a ghetto somewhere when there had been trouble. There were reporters who came out of New York and Philadelphia and Boston. Others came from Chicago. There were a few from the Deep South. There were others from St. Louis and from California.

We had organized the conference out of the San Francisco Bay area, using the Ball and Chain Review, our newspaper. It was the subpoena issue, and the Caldwell Case that mobilized us, and suggested the conference for those of us who were reporters and Black. We had to know more about what was happening. We needed to sit down in an atmosphere where we could compare notes.

We agreed to meet in Jefferson City. It was a central location for a national meeting and also because Lincoln University was there, which for many years was the only predominately Black college with a journalism department in the country.

We met there through three days. Out of those meetings came a strategy to publicize the issues of the Caldwell Case.

We set up an apparatus to carry the issue to every convention and meeting of the major predominately Black groups. We drew up model resolutions that we would persuade these groups to pass. The resolutions condemned the Justice Department's action and urged support for reporters who refused to honor subpoenas. We also made preparations to raise funds, if that became necessary. Each of the journalists agreed to write stories about the Caldwell Case to raise the issue in his or her home area. Some of the most effective pieces that would be written came from journalists who attended those meetings.

Many of the newspapers where we worked were hiring Black reporters for the first time. Many of the papers had only one or two Blacks on the staff. We were symbols of a change that was taking place in journalism. Our presence on the papers had broadened coverage because, as Blacks, we found new sources, and took our newspapers places where they had not been able to go before.

Now the police were attempting to turn us into spies. They were demanding our notebooks, demanding tapes of interviews we made, and, in the process, destroying our relationships with sources. We felt that they were, in short, attempting to drive us out of the newspaper business.

In Jefferson City that weekend, we vowed that we would not go quietly. We believed that it was in our blood to fight. We made the decision that we would fight as journalists.

It was the gun that set the Panthers apart. The embracing of the gun made H. Rap Brown different. The police used the gun as an open symbol, too.

But the gun was not our weapon. We would not enlist in that army. We understood those who did, but we were different. We were journalists, and our fight was for our rights and freedom to function as reporters. We would not become informants and we would not be run off. We would fight.

1981

AT THE END OF THE PRESS CONFERENCE, reporters jumped from their chairs and rushed toward Fulani Sunni Ali. The Black woman whom authorities called Cynthia Boston was seated in the front of the courtroom. The rush was for one more question, and nobody had any objections.

"Great press conference," said William Kuntsler, one of the attorneys who stood watching. "I'd say this was the best conference we've had in a long, long, time."

Fulani Sunni Ali had told her story well. Kuntsler and the other lawyers who were there on Friday at the State Office Building in Harlem knew it. Much of the story had been chilling, especially the part about the children.

"The children," Fulani Sunni Ali had said. "I salute the children. They were as calm as could be. All the children down to age 6 were handcuffed. They simply had none (handcuffs) small enough for the babes. All of the children were brought to the middle of the road, handcuffed behind their backs and grabbed and told to run, to run away from the driveway leading to the house and to the (police) cars. They frightened the children. After being told to run, they dragged them immediately afterwards so they would run. It was quite frightening for the chidden."

The chilling story that Fulani Sunni Ali had to tell was about her arrest. It took place near dawn on Tuesday, the 27th of October, at the old farmhouse in rural Mississippi where she had been living. As she told it on Friday, there were 15 people in the house.

"At 6 o'clock I peeped out the window and saw a camouflaged-colored tank," she said. "Then suddenly I saw four of these tanks. Once I was out in the road they looked at each other and said, 'Is this her? Is that her?' The female agents nodded. I had a hat on my head which they snatched off and they were tickled that my hair was in braids. They said, "that ought to make a good shot."

It could not have been better for the lawyers. It was a story that fit in perfectly with exactly what they had been saying ever since the raid on the Brink's truck in Rockland County in which two cops and a guard were killed. The raid took place on the 20th of October. It all goes back to that.

According to law enforcement officials, the bungled Rockland County raid was the work of 60s era radicals gone underground, but now linked up and active again. As proof, two of those arrested in Rockland County were tied to the Weather Underground. Later, another was linked to the Black Liberation Army, then another to the Black Panther Party.

It was all part of a wide conspiracy, the authorities said. Then came the early-morning raid on the Mississippi farmhouse. Among those who had been listed as being wanted was a William Johnson, also known as Bilal Sunni Ali and husband of Fulani Sunni Ali. Thus, the making of the Mississippi connection. But authorities also said they had a witness who had seen Fulani Ali at an apartment in Mount Vernon, N.Y., that was described as being a "safe house" for those involved in the Brink's attack. The way authorities told it, there were no loose ends. It was all cut and dried. The press conference on Friday was the other side.

"A war plan" were the words Fulani Ali used on Friday when describing the Mississippi raid. Then, she talked of helicopters, tanks (armored vehicles), and hundreds of agents.

They released the woman they called Cynthia Boston from jail on Thursday. As it turned out, it was just as attorney William Kuntsler had said in court. At the time she was supposedly seen in Mount Vernon, she was actually in New Orleans, and they were able to prove it.

At the press conference Kuntsler sat on one side of Fulani Ali. On the other was Vernon Mason, general counsel of the National Conference of Black Lawyers. Just after the Rockland County raid, as police began to tie one radical group after another to the attack, Vernon Mason began to speak out. "I'm worried," he said then. "This gives them (police) an excuse to go kicking down doors in the middle of the night."

He went back to an old case that he has been handling. "You remember 92 Morningside Ave.," he said. That was last year and the tenants who live in the building still tell incredible stories of the night FBI agents raided the apartment house and terrorized tenants, saying they had information that Joanne Chesimard was holing up there.

All through the press conference on Friday another lawyer stood directly behind Fulani Ali. This was Chokwe Lumumba. He had come from Detroit. Chokwe Lumumba and Fulani Sunni Ali are part of the same organization, the Republic of New Afrika. She is minister of information, and he is a vice president. It is another old name being brought back now. The Republic of New Afrika is a separatist organization that wants land and independence for Black Americans. Chokwe Lumumba said his organization is not involved with the Black Liberation Army.

"When we sponsored the camp for the kids," Fulani Sunni Ali said, "that was when the surveillance began. We were supposed to be training the young children in terrorism. We have a right to educate our children. We have the right to teach our children self-defense."

"It seems we ought to have a clarification when we talk about terrorism," Chokwe Lumumba said.

Chokwe Lumumba is a member of the latest group that authorities are attempting to tie to what they say is a new threat from radicals they describe as terrorists.

1982

"DON'T BE SO ANXIOUS to go to court," the newspaper's lawyer said.

"You go to court, and if you lose, I'll tell you what will happen: You may end up getting some bad law written, and reporters will suffer. You will see many reporters going to jail."

They are words from another time, words from the late '60s. For reporters those were the worst of times.

Richard Nixon was in the White House. John Mitchell was Attorney General. One of Mitchell's chief assistants in the Justice Department was William Rehnquist, a lawyer from Arizona, who is now an associate justice of the Supreme Court.

It was another time, but it comes back now. It does so because of the reunion Nixon and his inner circle celebrated in Washington at the end of last week. It has come full circle and it is as the newspaper's lawyer said. Reporters suffer. Reporters go to jail.

The 10-year reunion for Nixon and the President's men celebrates the election won in 1972. It brings back the decision that the press lost before the Supreme Court that same year.

In the winter of 1968, I was a reporter on assignment in California covering the activities of the Black Panther Party. That winter the FBI came to me.

At first the demand was for me to become an informant. "You are around the Panthers all the time. You talk to them, you see a lot. We want you to give us regular reports."

That was where it began. I refused to act as a spy, but it did not end there. Next came the subpoena. From the Justice Department. A federal grand jury was investigating the Panthers. The investigation was not going well. The government needed an insider. It had nothing of its own and so the decision was made: use the newspaper reporter.

The subpoena that was written did not just demand my appearance before the grand jury. The subpoena was also for every notebook, every tape recording, every unpublished interview, everything that had been collected in 14 months of reporting on the Black Panther Party.

It was the beginning of the taking away of everything the reporter needs.

"There is no established law in this area," the lawyer said then. "Both sides (the government and the press) assume certain rights. If you go to court, you are going to get some bad law written."

But there was no choice, and the issue was litigated. I refused to appear before the grand jury. The notebooks and tape recordings and the interviews, those were all destroyed. But the issue began to move through the courts. In June 1972, the Supreme Court of the United States ruled. Its 5-4 decision went against the press.

The late Justice William O. Douglas was one of those on the court who said no, that the decision against the press was wrong.

It was to be one of his major cases. He wrote his own dissenting opinion. At the end he said:

"The intrusion of government into this domain is symptomatic of the disease of this society. As the years pass the power of government becomes more and more pervasive. It is power to suffocate both people and causes. Those in power, whatever their politics, want only to perpetuate it. Now that the fences of the law and the tradition that has protected the press are broken down, the people are the victims. The First Amendment, as I read it, was designed precisely to prevent that tragedy."

In the mail from Washington yesterday came the latest issue of the magazine published by The Reporters Committee for Freedom of the Press. The magazine details cases from around the country that infringe on reporters' rights. The committee was organized 12 years ago, when the issue of reporters' rights was moving through the courts, and the government was just beginning to make outrageous demands on journalists. There were only a few cases then, written about on a few sheets of paper. It takes a magazine to handle the number of cases now.

"And we're only able to deal with about a 10th of what we know," Jack Landau, editor of the magazine and head of the committee, said yesterday.

"It's (demands on reporters) become institutionalized now," he said. "We thought the reporters committee would go away when Nixon went away, but that has not happened."

Landau, a journalist with Newhouse Newspapers, then began to detail what he called "a process that feeds on itself." That was his way of explaining the way it has passed down. A decade ago, it was the federal government that made demands on the press, the U.S. Justice Department.

Now it is local governments and police departments. It began with criminal cases. Civil cases are involved now. It keeps spreading. It has spilled over into the area of libel and nobody even keeps track anymore of the number of reporters who wind up in jail because they refuse to disclose sources or information.

The words of the newspaper's lawyer come back: Reporters will suffer. Reporters will go to jail.

And it is as Justice Douglas said. The fences of the law, and the tradition that has protected the press, are broken down.

None of it fades. It sticks in the mind. Last week it came back when the pictures in Washington were of Nixon and the President's men.

1983

IT HAS BEEN ALMOST 25 YEARS since J. Edgar Hoover declared the Black Panther Party to be the greatest single threat to the internal security of the U.S. What happened to the Black Panthers after that is well documented. The party was virtually destroyed. Many members were jailed. Others, fearing arrest, fled the country. Others, not so fortunate, wound up in cemeteries.

Now, after nearly a quarter of a century, many of those who were in the party when it held the attention of the nation, have begun to resurface. Some have begun to tell what they know in revealing books. Almost every month now, groups of Panthers are released from prison. They, too, have stories to tell.

Much of what happened to the Panthers has in it a thread that goes back to the FBI, J. Edgar Hoover, and the massive counter-intelligence program he launched in the mid-'60's. Hoover was not aiming at the Panthers alone with the program code-named COINTELPRO. He targeted Dr. Martin Luther King Jr. He targeted many of the White radicals who were then active on campuses. He targeted Black activists he deemed to be militant. But the Panthers were a prime target.

Much of what the FBI did to the Panthers turns out to have been illegal. Some already has been documented; more is coming out now, through discovery motions that compel the FBI to release documents that often shed significant light on what was done a quarter-century ago. One such case is unfolding now in New York. It involves two cops who were shot dead while on patrol at a housing project, and three inmates serving 25-years-to-life terms in state prisons. The two cops, Waverly Jones and his partner, Joseph Pagentini, were killed in 1971. After one trial ended in a hung jury, three former Panthers, then members of the Black Liberation Army (BLA) were convicted of the killings. The BLA was part of the Black Panther Party: It served as the organization's military wing. BLA members were a special target of the FBI.

Through more than 20 years, the three Panthers convicted in the case -- Anthony Bottom, Herman Bell and Albert Washington -- have insisted they were innocent. They believe they were victims, caught up in the COINTELPRO net that Hoover swung far and wide.

The cops were shot with a .45. When Bell and Washington were later arrested in California, they had a .45, and they also had the weapon belonging to the dead officer, Pagentini. The other officer's gun was found on a farm in Mississippi -- on land owned by the Bottom family. That alone gave the appearance of an airtight case. It was far from it. So much so that the case is now before U.S. District Court Judge Morris Lasker on a Habeas Corpus proceeding. Lawyers for the defendants use the word conspiracy to describe what they believe the prosecutors did to obtain a guilty verdict.

At issue is evidence not given and testimony said to be perjurious.

The evidence not given involves an FBI report. Agents tested bullets fired from the .45; those bullets did not match the weapon introduced at trial. Why was the evidence withheld? The prosecutor said he did not know of the FBI test. Hard to believe? That's what defense attorneys say.

Testimony said to be tainted came from the state's ballistics expert. He said he made a match with bullets he tested and the .45 said to be the murder weapon. But when he made the test, he said, he did not tell anyone. Not his boss, not others in ballistics, not the FBI, not anyone. As for the FBI report, the state's ballistics expert said the bullets he sent to the bureau were too deformed to be of any value. What makes all this questionable is that the ballistics expert testified only in the second trial making the match; in prior testimony, he said the match was made in San Francisco, where the arrests were made and the weapon confiscated.

A part of what makes each of these cases so important is that they offer windows through which can be seen what really happened in the '60s. In this, the case before Lasker is Exhibit A.

1980

THEY HAD WANTED TO SPEAK when they were in the courtroom. They tried to, but Federal Judge Joel Tyler stopped them.

"I don't want any statement," the judge said as he peered down from the bench. "I'm a little worried about any statement from them."

Judge Tyler understood. He had before him the two men who climbed the Statue of Liberty. The tiny courtroom on the third floor of the Federal Courthouse where they now were being arraigned was jammed. There was no room left anywhere, not even space to stand.

Judge Tyler knew that it was the news media that crowded the courtroom. He wasn't surprised that the two men before him, Edwin Drummond and Stephen Rutherford, wanted to speak. They had climbed the Statue of Liberty to get the attention of the media. It was a publicity stunt, and they had pulled it off. Now the judge was making certain that his courtroom would not be used as a forum.

"Any statement from them may deal with something other than what we're here for," the judge said.

Then the lawyer, William Kuntsler, stepped out of the crowd to guarantee bail, Drummond was released. Rutherford was sent back to jail. "I want his father to come up here," Judge Tyler said.

In the middle of the afternoon, when Edwin Drummond walked out of Federal Courthouse in Foley Square, reporters were on the steps waiting. And quickly they surrounded him and a barrage of questions began. They were not the kind of questions that Drummond wanted. The reporters kept asking about the Statue of Liberty, about the damage that had been done, and Drummond kept shaking his head and saying that the national monument had not been harmed.

He had not been able to change his clothes since Saturday, when he climbed the statue, and now, in the afternoon as he stood on the courthouse steps, he looked strange in blue tights and a green turtleneck sweater, and another sweater that was wine colored but sleeveless pulled over the one that was green.

The people who were in Foley Square saw the reporters and the strangely dressed man on the steps. They pushed in and began to ask what was going on? When they heard that it was one of the guys who had climbed the Statue of Liberty, right away they began to speak in harsh tones. They stood and heard Drummond, a tall, blond man of 35 years, say over and over again that he and his partner had not used any pitons (nails) in their climb, that it was not they who hammered against the statue, that it was the police who did that, and that no damage had been done.

They were not the questions, though, that Drummond wanted. He and his friend Rutherford had not climbed the statue just to see if they could do it. The climb had a purpose. It was political, and now, in the afternoon, it was Geronimo Pratt, the Black Panthers, the FBI and the 60s that Edwin Drummond wanted to talk about.

"Liberty is a real thing," he said. "Liberty is something that affects people's lives. It's not a statue."

There was something in the way that Drummond talked. He was quiet, patient and, even though he did not like the questions, he was painstaking with his answers. The people who had wandered by listened. Many of them when they walked away said that they understood what Drummond and his friend Rutherford had been trying to do.

There were three of them involved in the climb at the Statue of Liberty. Along with Rutherford and Drummond, there was a man named David Flatley, 35, who went along as publicity man, and was arrested on three misdemeanor charges, including littering. All three live in San Francisco. They plotted the climb out there, then came to New York and pulled it off. "For G," they said. Pratt's real name is Elmer, but he is known as Geronimo, and those close to him say "G," and that is enough.

Pratt is a 32-year-old Black man who is serving time now in California in San Quentin Prison. He is charged with killing a woman in a $30 robbery that took place in Southern California in 1968. That was back when Pratt was active in the leadership of the Black Panther Party. Pratt was an important figure in the Black Panthers. He headed the chapter in Los Angeles and was a member of its policy-making central committee. He insists that he did not kill the woman. His supporters say he was framed. They point the finger at the FBI.

At the time Pratt was active in the Panthers, the party was labeled by J. Edgar Hoover, then director of the FBI, as the "single greatest threat" to the internal security of the United States. At Hoover's urging, the FBI undertook a program of counterintelligence that was designed, in the FBI's words, to "neutralize" the Panthers. By its own admission, the FBI are responsible for his imprisonment. To prove his case, he wants documents from the FBI that detail its illegal surveillance.

The FBI's counterintelligence program was known as COINTELPRO. There is now a quiet effort under way in the Congress to have a full-scale investigation of COINTELPRO. It is said that the program led to the imprisonment of some and the deaths of others. It is even charged that COINTELPRO activities were involved in the assassination of Martin Luther King, Jr. There are too many charges. COINTELPRO cannot be passed off as the bad judgement of another era. It must be examined.

In the morning yesterday, David L. Moffitt, superintendent of the national monument that is the Statue of Liberty, was saying that scaffolding would be raised to see what damage, if any, resulted from the climb for Geronimo Pratt.

"It wasn't as bad as the original estimates," he said. "That $80,000 figure was very high. But it was in excess of $100; I know that."

Edwin Drummond is a poet from England who climbs mountains and buildings for causes. Stephen Rutherford is the 27-year-old son of F. James Rutherford, a former professor at New York University. Today the elder Rutherford was in New York getting his son out of jail. Tomorrow he is scheduled to be in Washington, where confirmation hearings will be held on his nomination as assistant secretary of education. David Flatley is the son of a former vice admiral in the Navy, and brother of the commander of the carrier Saratoga, now patrolling in the waters of the Persian Gulf off Iran. Together the three of them were an unlikely trio to bring the case of Geronimo Pratt to New York.

1986

IN HIS PRESIDENTIAL CAMPAIGN, in 1984, Jesse Jackson was very good at getting free time on television. But that wasn't his real ace in the hole. To reach his primary constituency, Black Americans, Jesse used radio; but not just any radio. He made big use of Black radio.

Radio is the communications link the Black community leans on. Maybe nowhere in the country is that more true than in New York.

The station in New York that Blacks listen to more than any other for news and "talk" is WLIB-AM. It's the only "talk radio" station in the country aimed primarily at a Black audience. On any given day, on any issue, the Black discussion in New York builds on WLIB.

On the station, the "talk" begins early and continues right through the day. When it happens that a trial is the primary issue, the station has reporters in the courtroom. Reports are fed to the station, then put on the airwaves. When the trial is one that has particular interest, listeners are invited to phone in, and the conversation develops. It's not just trials. WLIB deals with the whole spectrum of issues. Often, the discussion is buttressed by on-the-air interviews of leaders in the Black community. On some occasions, lawyers are in the studio. Other times, elected officials, ministers or community activists are there. Some of the talk centers on local issues. At other times, national and international matters are discussed. Together, it has made listening to the station a must for growing numbers, especially in the Black community.

Now comes word that intelligence units of the city Police Department have also begun to listen to WLIB. The police have also begun to use the station to build dossiers on Black leaders.

"Now we are going back to the FBI era of J. Edgar Hoover," attorney C. Vernon Mason said.

Mason was particularly outraged that the Rev. Calvin Butts of Abyssinian Baptist Church in Harlem was among those the police admit to building a file on.

"Rev. Butts is not underground," Mason said. "But our status does not matter to the White establishment. You can be at Abyssinian 15 years, and that doesn't matter. Abyssinian is a church going into its 179th year. This is an international outrage. But it is not going to intimidate us. This will only serve to further mobilize our people."

In the afternoon yesterday, in a speech to a gathering of Ethiopian Hebrews at a synagogue in Harlem, Mason blamed Police Commissioner Benjamin Ward.

"He ought to hang his head in shame and resign immediately. But this is not Ward's idea: This is Koch. He can see the organizing that is taking place, and the way that people in the Black community are coming together. Not in 15 years have I seen the level of organizing that we have now. And that is what this is all about."

In the late 1960s, when the FBI was headed by Hoover, the bureau initiated a campaign of widespread surveillance in the Black community. That was known as COINTELPRO (counter-intelligence program). That program not only infiltrated organizations and carried out surveillance, but it also made use of agents to disrupt, and attempt to institute illegal activity. Now, in New York, a program comes back that smacks of Hoover and 20 years ago.

In the report of the activity directed at WLIB, memorandums from the police department involved, among others, statements made by Butts, associate minister s at Abyssinian; Brooklyn activist Sonny Carson and Michael Warren, who has represented the family of Michael Steward, who died in police custody.

The dossier involving Rev. Butts had a very distinct resemblance to the COINTELPRO operation. In part, the intelligence file had statements quoting Rev. Butts as saying:

"Turn the other cheek is not a successful strategy," when "violence is directed against Blacks."

It was grabbing at little pieces and fitting them together to destroy. Recently, Rev. Butts has indicated that he may move into elective politics. Many believe that because of his church ties, and appeal at the grass-roots level, he would be a formidable candidate. So alarm bells have begun to sound, and for good reason. Maybe COINTELPRO did not end with J. Edgar Hoover.

1987

WE WERE REPORTERS. Paul Branzburg was with a newspaper in Kentucky. Ike Pappas was with a television station in Connecticut. I was a reporter on the staff of the New York Times.

This was early in the 1970s, and each of us got into trouble for the same reason: for refusing to share with police investigators information and sources we had gathered as reporters.

Branzburg had written about the manufacturing of illegal drugs in Louisville. The police demanded his sources.

Pappas was on an interview inside an office of the Black Panther Party during a confrontation with the police. Later, authorities wanted to use him as though he had been there as an undercover cop.

I covered the Panthers on the West Coast. After more than a year on that assignment, the FBI insisted that I act as a spy.

The old truth is that reporters are no better than their sources. A reporter has to find people willing to given information. At times, the reporter has to assure those persons, the sources, that the information gathered will go no further. That's one of the reasons people will open up. In the early 1970s, all that seemed clear. Reporters were on one side; police investigators were on the other. Then came the cases of Branzburg Pappas and Caldwell.

The demands made on the three of us so outraged legislators that many states rose up and said no. They passed "shield laws," designed to help reporters trying to protect their sources.

One of the places that happened was in new York. In Albany, the state Legislature passed a shield law -- legislation intended to protect reporters.

As it happened in the early 1970s, the cases involving Branzburg, Pappas and Caldwell went all the way to the Supreme Court of the United States. In the high court, in a 5-4 decision, the reporters lost.

In Albany County, recently, a district attorney who needed information leaned on a reporter, who refused. The issue wound up in court with the reporter counting on the shield law for protection, not the Constitution.

The reporter lost. The state Court of Appeals last week decided that the shield law applied solely to confidential sources or to information supplied by confidential sources.

So it happens exactly the way critics of the shield law predicted. The Constitution is there: It's solid. It's a rock. Legislative bodies change. At one time they may be receptive to the needs of reporters; at other times, they may not be.

The suggestion now is that New York's shield law needs to be strengthened. But that may not happen. In 1981, the New York Legislature refused to pass an amendment to the shield law explicitly to include nonconfidential materials.

Increasingly, the news media find themselves in disfavor with general public. Minorities challenge news organizations for discriminatory practices in employment and their portrayals of ethnic groups. The general public is increasingly estranged by a news media that seems, at times, fixated on crime, invasions of privacy, scandal and horse-race political coverage -- all the while screaming a First Amendment right to do it all.

Journalists used to be among the most respected members of society. Recent polls place them near used-car salesmen.

In some ways, the news media have not been responsible custodians of the rights bestowed them in the Constitution. Increasingly, the public, and legislators, are unwilling to grant legislative relief to a group often viewed as privileged and arrogant.

Despite the news media abuses, this loss of freedom to protect confidential sources impairs the essential function of an independent press in a free society.

In my case, the late Justice William O. Douglas was perhaps the strongest defender of First Amendment rights. In a dissenting opinion, he wrote: "If what the court sanctions today becomes settled law, then the reporter's main function in American society will be to pass on to the public the press releases which the various departments of government issue."

Chapter Nine

THE SHOULDERS OF GIANTS

Editor's note

Earl Caldwell repeatedly has written of the giants of his time. Some were widely known; others, only to a few. He conducted interviews with most of them. Many, he knew personally.

Oliver and Leola Brown

THE HIGH COURT HANDED down its decision on the 17th of May in 1954.

Yesterday, it was 30 years. In the grand ballroom at the Hilton Hotel, all of the tables were filled. It was, by title, the annual Civil Rights Institute, sponsored by the NAACP Legal Defense Fund. It was the marking of three decades since the U.S. Supreme Court ruling, in one of its most important cases ever, Brown vs the Board of Education.

This was the case in which the highest court in the land said no to segregation. It is the case that outlawed the Jim Crow concept of separate but equal. It was a decision so significant that yesterday Andrew Young, who is now mayor of Atlanta, said there would have been no civil rights movement "without that decision." He pointed out that he is now mayor of Atlanta. "The only reason I'm there is because of the Supreme Court decision of 1954."

Each year, the anniversary of Brown vs. the Board of Education has been special. It is a day those with roots in the civil rights movement never let pass unnoticed. But yesterday was made special. A good part of it had to do with the presidential election. Always on the anniversary of Brown, the questions asked involved the degree of progress Blacks have made since the legal outlawing of segregation. The stunning run Jesse Jackson is making for the presidency has, more than anything else, mirrored the Black progress in the country since 1954. But, as Andrew Young said: "We've seen the nation turn around in a way we couldn't imagine. Don't let anyone tell you there hasn't been progress," he said.

"We still have problems," he said. That brought him to President Reagan, and the election of 1984. He said the president that wins would have three, four and maybe even five appointments to the Supreme Court. "If the present President makes those appointments, we will lose the one branch of government that has consistently been with us," he said. And then he balanced the gains that have been made since Brown, and the losses he said were suffered under Reagan. "To continue four more years would be a disaster for the nation and the world, so we can't possibly relax. We've come too far to give up now," he said.

Another piece of what set the day apart was that Linda Brown was in the ballroom. She is Linda Brown Smith now. She is 41, and has a daughter in college and a son in Topeka, Kan., where she still lives. In the lawsuit that led to the landmark court decision, she was the Brown whose name is set in history. It was her father, Oliver Brown, and her mother, Leola, who made the decision to try and have her enrolled in the school two blocks from her home, even though that school was reserved for Whites only.

"Black children don't have to live with the stigma of second-class citizenship that we had to," she said in the afternoon yesterday. "I see strides being made in all facets of American life." She remembered the decision and "the spark it set off," and it set her to calling names. She mentioned Rosa Parks and Martin Luther King Jr. She came down the line to now, and the name that came to her lips was Jesse Jackson. "I've always been an optimist," she said. "I'm not surprised it's come this far. But there's still more," she said. "The struggle continues."

Nothing just happens, and it was that way with the case, Brown vs Board of Education. The Legal Defense Fund is sometimes called the country's greatest law firm. It built its reputation trying cases in the civil rights movement. For the LDF, Exhibit A is the work it did in Brown vs Board of Education. The history of the case has been gathered, and forms the core of the best selling book, "Simple Justice," which was written by Richard Kluger and published in 1975. Yesterday, on the 30th anniversary, the LDF had soft-cover copies of the 823 page book, and the organization put a copy of that history into the hands of all who crowded the ballroom.

Yesterday was special, too, because at the LDF, it was in a sense a changing of the guard. In his opening remarks, William T. Coleman (transportation secretary in the Ford administration) announced that Jack Greenberg, the longtime director-counsel of the LDF, was leaving the organization to become a law professor at the Columbia Law School.

At the Legal Defense Fund, Jack Greenberg goes back to the old days. He is finishing his 35th year. He goes back to the days when the work on Brown vs. Board of Education was taking shape. The LDF was led then by Thurgood Marshall, now an associate justice of the Supreme Court. Yesterday, Greenberg had in his eyes reflections of LDF's work from his time. It's a big mark that LDF has made. It took the best and brightest lawyers. They went into courtrooms everywhere. They made the arguments, and won the cases that turned a nation around.

It was all there yesterday, a day made special in the history of the country because of what good people did at another time.

Justice Thurgood Marshall

FIRST, IT WAS ASSOCIATE JUSTICE John Paul Stevens who spoke out. That was last August, and his criticism was so strong it became front-page news.

Justice Stevens said that his conservative colleagues on the Supreme Court were in such a rush to move the law in this country to the right, that they were casting aside judicial restraint. It was tough talk, the kind that almost never comes from the justices of the Supreme Court. It didn't end with Justice Stevens.

A week ago, in a speech to the judges of the Second U.S. Circuit, Associate Justice Thurgood Marshall leveled blunt criticism at the conservatives on the high court. Justice Marshall spoke of "grave concern" at certain decisions of the Supreme Court which, he said, "illustrate a very disturbing pattern -- a pattern that has become more and more common." He said that, with such decisions, "those who need protection (of the law) will have reason to turn away from the legal system. They will be convinced that their rights are being trivialized more than they are being protected."

Justice Marshall spoke out last Friday. Two days ago in Washington, Associate Justice Harry F. Blackmun added his voice to the criticism from within of the conservatives. He said the court is "moving to the right" and doing it "by hook or by crook." He went so far as to say that "extremism" was showing up in opinions. He said his work as a justice on the court had become a "rotten way to make a living."

It's all heavy stuff, and it comes up now because of the November elections. One of the things that the president elected in November is certain to have is the opportunity to make a number of appointments to the Supreme Court.

Almost always now, when a member of the Supreme Court is mentioned, a number follows the name. The number is the age of the justice. It's important now because five of the nine members of the court are past 75. Chief Justice Warren Burger is 77. Associate Justice Lewis F. Powell is also 77. Marshall is 76; Blackmun turns 76 in November, and Associate Justice William J. Brennan of New Jersey is 78. The youngest members of the court are the conservatives. Even now, they form the majority. With the reelection of President Reagan, that majority likely would grow, and become so solid that it would easily stretch into the next century.

All this brings the criticism into focus. Justice Stevens says that, in important cases, the conservatives are coming up with ill-considered opinions just to move the law to the right. Justice Marshall cited five cases from the last term.

"The court seems to concede in each case that important federal rights are at issue, and that they may have been violated," he said, but added that "(the court) then denies the victims the only effective remedies to those violations." He continued: "When rights are violated, courts should normally craft memories that attempt to make the victims 'whole' and deter future violations." Blackmun also cited specific rulings from the last term. He concluded that as a result of one decision "affirmative action was pretty well interred."

It's not often that justices of the Supreme Court go public with criticism of their colleagues. But it's happening now, in the midst of the campaign. Everything says that it's a signal the justices are sending.

It's a signal becoming strong enough to be important in the making of the president in the election of 1984.

IN THE AFTERNOON, HE SAT in a conference room next to his office. He had the sleeves of his white shirt rolled to his elbow. On the table in front of him were stacks of manilla folders.

He came away from the table, pulling off his glasses, rising to greet a visitor.

It's stunning the way he's come back. For a long time, the picture of Thurgood Marshall that stuck in the mind is one from a few years back. That was when he had been in and out of the hospital. He appeared frail and unsure on his feet. Then, it seemed certain that his days as an associate justice of the Supreme Court were numbered.

He was very sensitive then to every comment that had to do with his health. He saw it all as part of an effort to force him into retirement that he was not ready to face. At the time, he wasn't much past 70. He understood that, for an associate justice of the Supreme Court, that wasn't even old age. So he hung on, and rode it out. Now he's all the way back.

Thurgood Marshall is two months into his 76th year. He leaned back in his chair, and took both hands and ran them through his hair, which is long and silvery and very thick. He knew he looked good. His words and movements said that he felt good, too. Thurgood Marshall is looking ahead.

Two things at once are happening. One has to do with what is called the "graying of America." As incredible as it sounds, the fastest growing age group in the country is the one 85 and over. And as quiet as it's kept, not everybody over 65 is content to sit and waste their days on park benches.

"Sit down and take it easy," the young say to the old.

"Sit down and do what?" the old ask. "Sit down and die."

There is a wheel that is turning in America. Yesterday, a writer who lives in New York but has his roots in Georgia, was speaking of his father.

"He's been retired for five years, and now he says he's going back to work. My father is 70 years old."

But the way it came out, his father was like Thurgood Marshall. He feels good. He's healthy. He wants to stay active.

With Justice Marshall, though, there is another side. He is the first African-American to sit as an associate justice on the high court. He was appointed by a Southerner, Lyndon Johnson. And the irony was that, as a lawyer with the NAACP Defense Fund, Marshall had played perhaps the greatest role in the school desegregation case, Brown vs. the Board of Education. President Johnson appointed him first solicitor general and, when an opening came, nominated him for the Supreme Court. At the time of his appointment, the court's majority was made up of liberals. Now, it has swung the other way. Now, it's the conservatives on the court writing the law.

In recent weeks, though, there have been increasing signals of unrest among the justices. First, it was John Paul Stevens. Then Thurgood Marshall and, after him, Harry Blackmun. And each of them, in tough language, accused the conservatives of pushing aside judicial restraint in a rush to move the law in the country to the right.

It comes back to age. It may be that some justices who had thoughts of retirement have changed their minds. Age does not determine when justices of the Supreme Court retire. So the issue of now, the moving of the law to the right, may be changing some minds.

Justice Marshall has an old rule. He says no to all requests for interviews. But he has his health back. It's stunning the way he looks. And his movements now say that he also has four more years in mind.

HE IS 78-YEARS-OLD, and, for 20 years, he has sat as an associate justice of the United States Supreme Court. But in that time, never has Justice Thurgood Marshall made himself a center of controversy the way he has now.

Justice Marshall has always been quiet and cautious. Only rarely does he make a public speech. And mostly, those are low-key affairs. So the role that Justice Marshall has taken for himself in the bicentennial celebration of the American Constitution comes as a major surprise. He has changed the whole debate. He has come up against former Chief Justice Warren Burger. Indeed, he has gone up against the President.

As far back as last January, in his State of the Union address, Ronald Reagan was pointing to the bicentennial. The President began then to say how important the Constitution was in the country's history. He praised the framers as "giants." He called them "men whose words and deeds put wind in the sails of freedom."

President Reagan appointed former chief Justice Burger head of his commission on the bicentennial celebration. Burger, like Reagan, was very narrow in his view of the history of the Constitution. He looked back at the document drafted 200 years ago, and called it "the best thing of its kind that was ever put together."

But Justice Marshall saw all of it another way. He saw the work of the framers as part of the "perpetuation of slavery," and he said the celebration now "invites a complacent belief" in the perfection of their work. Three weeks ago, in advance of the celebration that began on Memorial day, Justice Marshall spoke out.

"I do not believe that the meaning of the Constitution was forever 'fixed' at the Philadelphia Convention," he said. "Nor do I find the wisdom, foresight and sense of justice exhibited by the framers to be particularly profound. To the contrary, the government they devised was defective from the start, requiring several amendments, a civil war and momentous social transformation to attain the system of constitutional government, and its respect for the individual freedoms and human rights we hold as fundamental today."

His language was very direct. But Justice Marshall, perhaps more than anyone, knows that the "We the people," the framers spoke of in 1787 did not include all Americans. "'We the people' no longer enslave, but the credit does not belong to the framers," he said. "It belongs to those who refused to acquiesce in outdated notions of 'liberty,' 'justice,' and 'equality,' and who strived to better them."

Justice Marshall noted that the record of the framers on the slave question is especially clear. The Constitution explicitly extended the slave trade until 1808. He said, "It took a bloody civil war before the 13th Amendment could be adopted to abolish slavery, though not the consequences slavery would have for future Americans."

He said that even after the 14th Amendment (which guaranteed equal protection of the laws to Blacks) was passed; "almost another century would pass before any significant recognition was obtained of the right of Black Americans to share equally even in such basic opportunities as education, housing and employment, and to have their votes counted, and counted equally."

ONLY ON THE RAREST OF OCCASIONS does he make public speeches, and his rule against granting interviews doesn't bend. So now, it's not what Justice Thurgood Marshall has said that's so startling. The surprise is that after 20 years, he let a reporter sit him down and, in front of a camera, answered questions.

He had some good stories to tell and some very astute observations. But more than anything else, what got attention in his interview was the way he rated President Reagan on the matter of civil rights.

"The bottom," he said. "Honestly, I think he's down with Hoover and that group. Wilson. When we (Blacks) really didn't have a chance."

Justice Marshall has spent his whole life on the front lines of what in his time became "the movement." The misconception, though, is that it centered almost entirely on people demonstrating at barricades. That was not the case. The big battles, the ones that rewrote the law of the United States, were played out in courtrooms. Marshall was in the forefront of that. He earned his law degree and almost immediately put it to work in the fight to earn African Americans equality under the law.

For him, the Reagan years have been the worst of times. The administration has kept up a steady drive to knock down the legislation Marshall spent a lifetime building up. And where there was no effort to knock down laws, the administration did something that in Marshall's eyes had to be even worse. It just refused to enforce certain civil rights laws.

Of course Marshall would rate President Reagan at the bottom. But the Supreme Court is bound by tradition. Almost never does a sitting justice criticize a president. This may be Marshall's way of saying to Reagan: I know what you're doing, and I am going to put it on the record so the whole world will also know.

On an afternoon late in September 1984, when there were only six weeks left in the presidential campaign and Reagan's reelection seemed certain, I met with Marshall in Washington. I found him seated at a conference table outside his private quarters. The ground rule was that it had to be an off-the-record talk, so there was no news to report. But I came away from our meeting that day certain that more than anything else, he wanted me to see and pass the word along that he was in good health. And that being in good health, he was prepared to stick it out through the Reagan years.

So he rolled up his sleeves and ran a finger through his long, mostly white hair in a vigorous way. And at the end, he said: "Come walk with me." And we strolled through the hallway where he met Justice Brennan, and the two of them went to lunch.

The Reagan years are winding down. In his two terms, he has already had two Supreme Court appointments and elevated William Rehnquist to Chief Justice. In Marshall's interview with columnist Carl Rowan, mostly to talk of the 200 years of the Constitution, he mentioned that once, when hospitalized during Richard Nixon's time, the President called to get a condition report. "Not yet," he affixed to the report. Now he is close to outlasting Reagan.

Marshall said the best Presidents for civil rights were Harry Truman and Lyndon Johnson. He said Robert Kennedy held back his brother, the President. Marshall said he didn't believe Roosevelt did much.

"But Johnson," he said, "his plans were unbelievable -- the things he was going to do. But he was too far out for Negroes and civil rights. He wasn't thrown out because of Vietnam. They just used that as an excuse to get rid of him." That was the surprising comment from Justice Marshall.

Everybody knew that Reagan would be at the bottom in civil rights.

ON THE U.S. SUPREME COURT, he had become a defiant figure. He did not intend to give a conservative Republican in the White House the opportunity to appoint his successor. For as long as he could, Associate Justice Thurgood Marshall kept holding on.

He took delight in saying, "I have a lifetime appointment and I intend to serve it."

Marshall advanced to become the court's oldest member, but at 83, with his health failing, he came to the point where he could no longer meet the demands of his office. Late in the morning yesterday, he sent his letter of resignation to the White House. It was not a signal of surrender; even on his last day, in his last opinion, he was having his say. He accused those in the court's conservative majority of being more interested in power than in reasoning. He offered that assessment in a dissent of a decision that allows victim impact testimony to be introduced in capital cases. To reach that decision the court again ignored precedent which Marshall said threatens a host of constitutional liberties.

Justice Marshall had nearly a quarter of a century on the High Court. In 1967, when Earl Warren was Chief Justice, President Lyndon Johnson nominated Marshall, his Solicitor General, to become the first African American to serve in such a position. Marshall won confirmation and through most of the following two decades he was a part of a court that had a liberal majority. For Marshall, those were to be his "good years" on the Supreme Court. He admired and liked Justice Warren whom he called "the boss," but more than that, he was a part of making the law that put the weight of the Constitution on the side of the issues he had been associated with since his days as the NAACP's most prominent lawyer.

But just as Marshall saw the liberals on the court rule, he also had what was for him the painful experience of seeing the court change. A year ago, the retirement of Justice William J. Brennan left Marshall as the last of the court's unwavering liberal voices. Brennan, a native of Newark, had 34 years as an associate justice. Among the justices, he had been Marshall's closest friend. The two of them often lunched together and Marshall acknowledged that Brennan was the only justice whose chambers he visited.

In 1967, when Marshall was confirmed as an associate justice, it marked a huge breakthrough. It came soon after passage of the Voting Rights Act, at a time when important civil rights legislation began to move through Congress, and to many stood as the proof that Blacks could move into every area of American government. The anthem of the movement said, "We shall overcome" and Marshall was the symbol of that. He was to proclaimed as "the most important Black man in America," and the voice he developed with his decisions on the court gave substance to that.

Marshall had said that as far back as when Richard Nixon was President, that conservative Republicans wanted him to resign his seat. Not because they didn't want a Black in the position; the motive wasn't race. It was ideology. As he moved along in advancing age, Marshall took a kind of pleasure in holding onto his seat. "I'm not going anywhere," he would assure visitors. And it was that way until yesterday.

In submitting his resignation now, Marshall in a way puts President Bush on the spot. Bush has already indicated that he will veto a civil rights bill for the second year in a row. In modern history only two presidents, Reagan and Bush, have vetoed civil rights bills. Bush will nominate Marshall's successor.

To nominate a Black is something Bush may very well be inclined to do. But what is not likely is that he will select a Black with the kind of liberal credentials that Thurgood Marshall carried. Marshall was the court's last true liberal, and it's not likely that there will be another one like him anytime soon.

THE ONLY SAD PART IS THAT when he is buried today at Arlington National Cemetery, he takes too much with him to his grave. It did not have to end that way.

A part of his legacy should have included the book he wanted to write. But there is no memoir, because a publisher made the mistake of thinking that Justice Marshall could be persuaded to turn away from what he believed in if the money was big enough.

On an afternoon when he was into his 80s, and not yet retired as an Associate Justice of the U.S. Supreme Court, Marshall sat in his chambers and displayed the check in the amount of $250,000 that had arrived from the publisher.

"I'm sending it back," he said. ""Sure we could use the money,"" he went on. "But what they (publisher) want, I am not going to do."" The demand on Justice Marshall was that he include in his book a lot of the stories Associate Justices never tell. The publisher wanted details from some of the conferences justices convene in their private (and secret) deliberations of important issues before the court.

That was something Justice Marshall would not do. He had too much regard for The Court. His life was not about making money. He lived to change the wrong he saw in his country. In all of American history, few individuals have had the kind of impact that Thurgood Marshall did in his life. The whole American society is different because of his work. He was perhaps the most important lawyer not just of his time, but maybe for a whole century. He was truly a giant in his time.

So you cry no tears for Justice Marshall. He did it all, and so much of the time, he did it his way and in his style. And what a style that was. He even had his own peppery language. And one of the joys in his life was story telling. He was so good, you can only imagine what a joy a Thurgood Marshall book would have been.

He not only argued the landmark cases in the civil rights movement, he also lent his considerable legal skills to African countries coming out of colonialism. He wrote the Constitution for Kenya. In recalling that experience, he told of a state dinner he would never forget with the legendary Jomo Kenyatta. It was in Kenya. President Kenyatta, who had asked Marshall to write the Constitution, hosted him at a special dinner.

""He was wearing a white suit that night,"" Marshall said of Kenyatta.

"'They (waiters) began serving the dinner. One waiter tripped. Everything went right on the President.'" Marshall demonstrated a karate chop. '"Just like that,"' he said. '"He (Kenyatta) hit him and he went down. He didn't move. The next day, I inquired," he said. "I was told the man was dead."

That was Thurgood Marshall; a man with an endless number of stories to tell. But there will be no more; not now. He even said that after his death, he would have all his papers destroyed.

But what a life Thurgood Marshall had, all 84 years. And what a joy he took in living.

He said once that as far back as the Nixon era, there was some pressure to try and persuade him to retire from the Supreme Court. He especially liked telling stories about that, too. And always, he had the same ending.

"I am not going anywhere," he would say. "I have a lifetime appointment and I intend to serve it."

SO THE ARGUMENT RAGES. It is not just Chief Justice William Rehnquist saying the Library of Congress has done the late Justice Thurgood Marshall wrong.

Justice Rehnquist is fierce in his protest. The chief justice has many allies who agree with him when he says that, in opening all of the papers of Justice Marshall to public scrutiny, the Library of Congress has exhibited "bad judgement." The late justice's wife and the lawyer for his estate make the same argument.

There are also the voices of former clerks to the former justice, and they are very specific in pointing to the ways the library wronged Marshall. But in the end, they lean on the argument that says: "We know Justice Marshall. We worked with him. He told us what he wanted, and he was against anything like this happening."

All that is powerful stuff. It makes it appear as though the case against what the library did is so overwhelming that there is no other side. And maybe that is what part of the effort is all about -- to make it appear as though there is no other side.

But there is. And the reason I know is because, for 10 years, Thurgood Marshall made it a point of inviting me to his chambers and he would take a lot of time -- on some occasions, a whole afternoon -- and tell me important truths about the Supreme Court of the United States. Sometimes, as I would listen, the question that crossed my mind was: "Why is he telling me this?" I believe that now I know.

Marshall had a lot of wisdom. He also knew there were a lot of ways to get to where he wanted to go. And one of the things he wanted to do was shed some light on the way the justices sitting on the court now talk and the way they think, and the kind of people they are. I know he wanted that because he told me. And he knew that if he told a reporter, he was telling somebody who would tell somebody else.

He told me of the animosity that existed in the hallways and chambers of the court. He told me it had gotten bad, "real bad. I don't step foot in their chambers and they don't come in here," he said of his colleagues. The one exception was Justice William Brennan.

But it was different with the others. And that "difference" Marshall spoke of began to come out in decisions handed down by the court. The Reagan-Bush appointees were not the same kind of people Marshall said he had encountered when he came to the court. And, of course, the biggest difference was with the chief justice of that era, Earl Warren.

He told of Warren coming to his office to chat. "I told him, 'you don't have to come here. When you want to see me, just call. I'll come to you.'" Marshall said Justice Warren replied: "I don't operate that way."

He used that memory to tell the way the court had changed. And it wasn't long after that, that veteran observers of the court began to notice that so much animosity had developed that it was noticeable in opinions handed down. Marshall was not on the sidelines. His opinions, too, began to have very pointed lines directed at certain colleagues.

In light of the controversy now, I look back on those sessions in his chambers and what I see is Marshall telling a journalist that all is not as it ought to be in this building. But how could the larger public ever know? My mind tells me that is what Thurgood was doing in passing all his papers to the Library of Congress and leaving the way open for those papers to be scrutinized so soon after his death.

The consequences of Marshall's act are enormous. Whether it's what he intended or not, the result is that something valuable has been put into a library. The challenge is for people to go and see what is there.

Chaney, Goodman and Schwerner

IT IS A FOUR-BLOCK STRETCH of Riverside Drive, Freedom Place. In the evening sunlight that was where they gathered.

Ruth Messenger was the first to speak, and she called them "three extraordinary young men."

She wore a suit that was bright red, and the sun that came from over the West Side Highway was in her face. "They were together," she said, "Black and White, Christian and Jew, and they chose to live what they believed, and ...(they) were brutally murdered because they did. (But) they inspired a revolution."

It goes back to the summer of 1964, the Mississippi Freedom Summer. In the history of the civil rights movement, it stands as one of the high points and in it, the names which are Chaney, Goodman and Schwerner are special.

"They chose to live what they believed," Ruth Messenger said.

There was an army of them. Kids, they were called. They were young and they had ideals that were high. In the summer of 1964 in America, they went South, to Mississippi, which was a bastion of racism, and they went to work in the movement. The Mississippi Summer became famous in the world. A part of it was because hundreds and hundreds of young people, mostly students, answered the call and went south and took part in a project. A part of it was because there were three who gave their lives. This was James Chaney, Andrew Goodman and Michael Schwerner..

It goes back to the night of June 21, of 1964. That was the night the three of them disappeared from a Mississippi town that had the name Philadelphia. The nation stopped, and attention focused not just on them but on the issue of civil rights. And through 44 days there was a search, and then the bodies were found, buried beneath a newly constructed dam.

Schwerner and Goodman were New Yorkers. Mississippi was home for James Chaney. Two young men who were Jews and another who was Black, together in the struggle to overcome racism, and the price they paid was their lives. But their names are special. They came to be powerful symbols in a movement that, in time, did wipe out the segregationist laws and brought the right to vote where it had been denied.

In New York, a plaque was put in the sidewalk and the four blocks of Riverside Drive at 70th. were given the name Freedom Place, and it was done in the names of Schwerner, Goodman and Chaney. And in the evening on Wednesday in the sunlight a crowd gathered on the sidewalk, on Freedom Place, and looking back was a part of it. But it was more than that. The movement was a glorious moment, but time has its way of changing issues and the trouble of now was evident in the words that were spoken at Freedom Place.

"Those of us who fought together for civil rights and voting rights are talking against each other now," Roscoe Brown, the president of Bronx Community College, said. "It's time to stop arguing," he said. "We must rededicate ourselves. We must fight racism here in New York City."

Carolyn Goodman Eisner, who was Andrew Goodman's mother, spoke. And after her, Julia Chaney Moss, who was James Chaney's sister, spoke. And then it was Basil Paterson. "We've come a long way since those days," he said. "But we should not just talk of the past. We should rededicate ourselves to the fight for human dignity."

Bill Kuntsler, who was the movement's lawyer, read poetry. Bill Tatum, publisher of the Amsterdam News, called for unity.

"It reminds us that together, we did win a lot of victories," Councilwoman Messenger said. "It's been an important 20 years, but we still have a lot more to do."

The sunlight was still there when they put the roses down and went away.

It goes back to the summer of 1964, the Mississippi Freedom Summer. In the civil rights movement, it was a high point, and the names Chaney, Goodman and Schwerner stick in the mind. "They inspired a revolution," Ruth Messenger said.

Roy Wilkins

THEY STILL MISS THE OLD MAN. He built the organization. He took it when there were just a few hundred branches, and he built on that. Once he was finished, the NAACP was everywhere. And now, it suffers because of what the old man did.

This is no slap at Benjamin Hooks, who stands now in the old man's place. He didn't create the problems the organization has. The problems are ones Hooks inherited. But the organization misses the old man who was Roy Wilkins because Wilkins was the general who knew every button to push and the precise moment it needed to be done. That was the way he made the organization work.

The time of Roy Wilkins, though, was the 1940s, the '50s and the '60s. The issues were sharper then. The targets were clear. And Wilkins, the general, had loyal people. He gave orders; the orders were carried out and the organization put a lot of important achievements in the books.

Roy Wilkins and Benjamin Hooks. They are as different as possible in style and approach. Wilkins, an old newspaperman, didn't believe in charisma. To him, a speech was a means of getting information out and no more. He was quiet, knew how to fight and always made sure of his ground. Benjamin Hooks is the other side. He is charisma. He uses a speech to move a crowd and his background is rooted in the Baptist Church and the law.

They are as different as two men can be, one who built on what he learned as a reporter, the other using the experience he acquired as a judge. Wilkins and Hooks, executive directors of the NAACP.

For the NAACP, it is the best of times and the worst of times. In the week just past in New Orleans, the organization moved through its 74th convention. The moment of truth was Tuesday night. Kelly Alexander, vice chairman of the board, puts his finger on the problem in the keynote address.

"It's a shame and a disgrace," he said, "the way Black people support their organizations."

He was talking about the NAACP and the membership that now hovers around 350,000. He was saying what the NAACP needs: It needs to be retooled. Like many American corporations, it is outdated. It needs to be streamlined. What Roy Wilkins built at another time was fine. Today, it's obsolete.

In the lobbies of hotels and around the pressroom at the convention, the problems of the NAACP were argued.

"They're all too old," some said. "Just look at the board; it's nothing but a bunch of old people."

There is some truth in the argument. Julian Bond, the Georgia legislator, is an exception. He is not much past 40. Ernie Green, an undersecretary of labor in the Carter administration, is on the board, and he is about the same age as Bond. But by and large, the board is made up of older men and women. It does need new blood.

"The organization is irrelevant," some argued. It was an argument that was made but there was no supporting evidence. During its convention, the organization showed it has some very impressive programs. On the afternoon of the first day of the convention, in the huge hall at the Rivergate center, awards in a program called ACT-SO were made.

ACT-SO means Afro-Academic Cultural Technological and Scientific Olympics.

This is a program the NAACP has devised to promote classroom excellence and it is a creative program, and on the afternoon it was in the spotlight the huge hall was crowded. The roars for scholastic excellence were the kind usually reserved for basketball games. In ACT-SO, the NAACP is into something heavy. But at the convention the program didn't get much attention, and that was because the reporters were in another room and the talk was of internal problems. But ACT-SO grows, and at the convention, the winners in physics and higher mathematics and science competition were being awarded computers and scholarships.

"They aren't doing anything," some said of the NAACP. "That's why they are not getting the support they want from Black people."

On the day after the ACT-SO awards, the same hall was crowded with delegates from every section of the country and that morning the issue was voter registration. The NAACP, because it is everywhere, brought into the hall that morning voter registration figures that said something important is going on at the bottom in Black America. And it links up, because on the last day of the convention Vice President George Bush stood before the delegates and, in emotional language, accused the organization of giving the Reagan administration a bum rap.

Vice President Bush didn't come to the NAACP convention looking for Black votes. He came because he understands what an organization can do and he had the information on the kind of voter registration drive the NAACP has going everywhere in the country.

It comes back to what Kelly Alexander said in his keynote. "Blacks do not support their organizations," he said. "A shame and a disgrace," he called it.

Money. The NAACP needs money. It needs money to retool its plant the way American automobile and steel companies do. It needs today's technology. It needs computers that can take the 1,800 pieces of the organization, the pieces that are everywhere, and bring them together in the way that the operation can be made effective. The organization is in need. It needs the resources to reach out and go into the pool of Black talent, the greatest pool of Black talent that has ever existed in the history of the country, and get its share of brains and know-how and use that expertise in the building of programs for now.

"Hooks is an old-time preacher," was one of the charges made. "We don't need that old-time stuff anymore."

It is another charge that doesn't hold up. It is not style, it's substance that makes the difference. Wilkins was dry in his approach but it worked. Hooks raised a crowd in a way Baptist ministers do and it works.

It is there; the organization is in place. The old man in his time as executive director saw to that. It is time, though, to take the organization to another level and to do that, it takes money. It takes Black people to go into their pockets to support their own.

"It's a shame and a disgrace," Kelly Alexander said.

It is the best of times and the worst of times for the organization that the old man built. It is good because it is there. It is everywhere. It is the worst of times because of the shame and disgrace: The ones the organization works for keep refusing to do their share, to take part in supporting the organization the old man built.

IN HIS BOOK, "STANDING FAST," Roy Wilkins tells a lot of very good stories. Some of the best come back now because they have to do with the times of John F. Kennedy.

"He first caught our eye at the NAACP in the very early 1950's," Wilkins wrote, and that was the introduction he used to a story.

"One day Clarence Mitchell was on the Hill making rounds and bumped into Adam Clayton Powell, who was talking to a thin young man with a broad Boston accent. Powell waved Clarence over and introduced him to the young congressman from the 11th District of Massachusetts.

After Powell's lean colleague left, Powell nodded toward the receding politician and said to Clarence, "You know, you ought to keep an eye on Jack Kennedy. He's going to be somebody very important one of these days."

The history books deal with Roy Wilkins as a leader in the civil rights movement. He was executive director of the NAACP, and in his time he built the NAACP into the largest civil rights organization there has ever been in the country.

All that is confirmed in the history books. But Wilkins was also a newspaperman, and a piece of the reporter always stayed alive in him. And that's what makes his book, his autobiography, so special.

He never lost the habit of writing everything down. "If you don't have it in your notebook, you don't have it," editors tell reporters. Roy Wilkins was from the old school. He wrote everything down.

Since 1960, no President of the United States has ever been inaugurated without bringing John Kennedy to mind. A part of it has to do with the assassination. Kennedy never had time for even one full term. But the image looms large.

The tendency is to look back and say that it was the best of times. In a way, that was true. Kennedy was young; had a style and a voice that gave hope. But there was another side.

"When John F. Kennedy became President, everyone expected him to come in and tear up the pea patch for civil rights," Wilkins writes. "But it didn't happen that way. Through all the years I knew and watched Kennedy, I did not for a moment doubt his moral fervor, and his sympathy for Black Americans was real enough as well.

"But getting him to turn those emotions into tangible political action was a matter of an entirely different order. Until the last six months of his life, he moved very, very cautiously on civil rights."

The issues that involve race have confronted every President. Even on the eve of his inauguration for a second term, President Reagan was being challenged on his handling of issues involving Black Americans. But it's different with Reagan. He won his second term with almost no support from Blacks. In his book, Wilkins points out that Kennedy's margin of victory was thin and that it was Black support that gave him the edge. And it followed that there were expectations that Kennedy would "tear up the pea patch for civil rights."

Roy Wilkins wrote of the reality. "One of the hardest problems the NAACP faced in those years was to complete his (Kennedy's) education on race and to keep his feet to the fire on Capitol Hill."

The kind of civil rights legislation the NAACP wanted never came in Kennedy's time. The bill that was to become the Civil Rights Act of 1964 was reported out of committee on Nov. 20, 1963. As Wilkins wrote, "And that's where things stood when John Kennedy left for Dallas."

Of that day, the NAACP leader wrote: "When the first news bulletin came over the radio I scoffed at it. Hell, he's down in Texas now, I thought. Nothing can happen to him there. A few minutes later I picked up my hat and coat and headed out for lunch. When the elevator doors opened in the lobby, I saw people pressed against their radios; on Fifth Ave., grown men were weeping. It was a miserable moment. Kennedy had contributed significantly to changing, the first step before civil rights legislation could be passed."

It's all from another time, and the Inauguration brings it back now. But the hope from then is missing now, and nobody looks to Reagan to "tear up the pea patch for civil rights."

Martin Luther King, Sr.

THANKSGIVING HAS ITS OWN WAY of being special. If nothing else, it makes us stop and take stock. For just that, thanks.

But at Thanksgiving, 1984, that's not all of it.

Thanks for Daddy King, too. The moment that sticks in the mind is from the Sunday after Martin was assassinated. Ebenezer Baptist Church, Daddy King's church in Atlanta, has seen many moments, but that Sunday was set apart. Dizzy Gillespie came with his horn; Mahalia Jackson with her magnificent voice and nowhere in the church was there room to just stand. The moment that does not fade was when Daddy King stood at the pulpit.

"I know you didn't think I'd be here this morning," he said. He tried to tell how deep the hurt for him was. Tears came to his face. That was the moment he reached out and he said, "But we must never let it get so dark that we can't see the stars."

Thanks for a will as strong as Daddy King's. He was in the pulpit at Ebenezer the morning a crazy man rose from the congregation and shot his wife dead. He lost a second son to a mysterious death. He was found in a pool, and it was said that death was accidental from drowning. Daddy King could have said some things about hate. He went out preaching love.

Thanks. Thanks for the idea of the Rainbow Coalition. It's the idea that says regardless of race, or background and religion, that people can come together. It's the idea that says that there is a way out. It says that we must turn to each other and not on each other. It says we must go another way, and at Thanksgiving, 1984, it's an idea that sounds right.

Thanks for Evelina Antonetty, another of the good who died young. She was like Daddy King. She did not make it to Thanksgiving '84 but the spirit she had is legend in the Bronx. She was not one of those people who asked, "What can I do?" She never waited to be asked. She stayed on the front lines and gave energy and wisdom to every movement.

"She fought for what she believed in," Richard Perez said. "She was considered the 'mother' of the movement. She was keenly aware of the need to develop young leaders. She always reached out for the young." She founded the organization, United Bronx Parents. "Her belief," Perez said, "was that the only way education could succeed was in having a closeness between the schools and the parents."

It is said that Thanksgiving '84 is the worst of times. It is put that way mostly because of Reagan's overwhelming victory in the election. But it's not true. These are not the worst times. It's a different and trying time. It's a time of testing. But these are not the worst of times, and thanks for that.

And thanks to the Blacks in Soweto and all the other townships in South Africa. Against great odds, they are standing up, daring to struggle, daring to win. Thanks for that.

Thanks for Bernice Bolar. She was so much like Evelina Antonetty. She believed in community and last month when she went out, she was still trying to do all she could to make it better. "She was a person out there fighting for the survival of the Harlem community," Alice Kornegay said. "She always felt that our children could be educated and that people should have a decent place to live and raise their children. No matter what it was, Bernice would always be there, in the front, fighting for Harlem."

Thanks for the fighters. Thanks for the way they stood up for Eleanor Bumpurs who lost her life because she was poor and couldn't pay the rent, and, at the end didn't get the same chance to live that killer dogs get. But thanks to the people who weren't afraid and stood up and made her dying mean something.

Coretta Scott King

IT HAS BEEN 18 YEARS since the April night an assassin's bullet took her husband's life. But a lot of the horror of what happened at the Lorraine Motel in Memphis is still there, etched in her face.

At times, it seems she is still in mourning. Her critics accuse her of being a professional widow.

Coretta Scott King is a tough and determined woman. In the 18 years since the death of Martin Luther King Jr., she has become one of the best known women in the world. The irony is that, until the assassination, she had always been in the background.

It was never Martin and Coretta. In the limelight, he stood alone. He was the leader, the brilliant speaker and scholar, winner of the Nobel Peace Prize. She was housewife and mother. Her only moments on center stage were those Sunday mornings she stood in the pulpit of her husband's church and sang.

Her training was in music. She studied voice and piano, and once her ambition was to perform professionally. But that never happened. She gave up her career for marriage.

Coretta, like Martin, was a Southerner. But he came from a family of ministers. His father had a big church in Atlanta. It was different for her. She was born April 27, 1927, one of three children. As a child in Heiberger, Ala., she hoed and chopped cotton during the Depression.

Like Martin, she moved to get the best education she could. He skipped two grades, and, at 15, entered Morehouse College in Atlanta. In 1945, she entered Antioch College in Yellow Springs, Ohio, on a scholarship to study education and music.

Coretta dropped plans to teach and pursued music. Martin had entered college with an eye on medicine, then the law. But he turned to the ministry, and in 1948, was in Crozer Theological Seminary in Pennsylvania. Coretta entered the New England Conservatory of Music in Boston. Martin was graduated first in his class and won a fellowship to study for a doctorate degree.

They met in Boston. She was studying music. He was doing graduate work at Boston University. the way the story is told, theirs was a whirlwind romance. In 1953, they were married in Mario, Ala. But there was not a lot of time for the two of them. They both had to go back to school. A year later, Coretta completed her studies, and her bright husband was appointed pastor of the Dexter Avenue Baptist Church in Montgomery, Ala.

After that, there was almost no time. Martin earned his doctorate in 1955. Yolanda, their first child, was born. And Rosa Parks, a woman neither of them knew, refused to give up her seat to a White passenger on a segregated bus in Montgomery, which touched off the famous bus boycott. The Montgomery Improvement Association was formed to coordinate boycott activities. They elected Coretta's husband their president. She did not know it then, but she was giving her husband to a movement.

By 1964, Coretta was the mother of four children: After Yolanda, came Martin III (1957), Dexter Scott (1961), and Bernice Albertine (1963). King had met with President Eisenhower, and, later, President Kennedy. He delivered one of the most memorable speeches ever before a crowd of 250,000 at the Lincoln Memorial in Washington.

But the dangers were already apparent. Their home had been bombed. He had been stabbed by a deranged woman in Harlem, and had come close to dying.

In 1964, he won the Nobel Peace Prize. He and Coretta went to Oslo, Norway to receive the award. On the way home, they met with Pope Paul VI. The movement had changed their lives, and she began to sense she would not get her husband back.

The telephone call came just after 7 o'clock in the evening on Thursday, the 4th of April, 1968. Martin had been shot. Coretta dropped the phone and raced to the airport to fly to Memphis. At the airport, another telephone call awaited her. Coretta's husband was dead. She went back home to be with her family.

Coretta never really had Martin. When they met, there was the pressure of their studies. And after that, the pressure of a new job, a new town, her husband's first church. They had only moments together. Then came the movement, which took him altogether.

The second life for Coretta Scott King began when Martin died. She left no details of the funeral -- or anything else -- to others. It was done her way. She had always been the woman behind the man. But now, she began to assert herself. She put on a black dress and a black veil and vowed to be strong. And she was.

Four days later, she went to Memphis and stood in his place to lead a march on behalf of striking garbage collectors. After that, it was expected that she would step back. She did not. Instead, she reclaimed her husband's work, and, to some degree, his place in the movement.

One of her goals was the build a Martin Luther King Jr., Center for Nonviolent Social Change in Atlanta -- "a mecca for people from all over the world who seek a better understanding of the life and work of Martin Luther King Jr.," she said. The cost was figured at close to $10 million. Nobody spoke against the idea, but once she began to raise funds, the criticism started. "She's just building a monument to her husband," others charged. But Coretta ignored the critics and went on.

It took 14 years, but the Freedom Hall Complex and center were built exactly as she envisioned. She raised $8 million, and in January of 1982, she stood in the pulpit of the church where her husband had been pastor, the Ebenezer Baptist Church in Atlanta, and said, "This is truly a day The Lord hath made." Her husband would have been 53.

In her fund-raising mission, Coretta went everywhere. The woman who always stood in the back became comfortable at the front. She spoke out on women's issues, took a leadership role in civil rights matters, used her influence in the political arena.

In a way, all that came to a head at the Democratic National Convention in San Francisco in 1984. She had not supported Jesse Jackson. She and Atlanta Mayor Andrew Young were Mondale supporters. In a tumultuous night at the convention, Andy was booed loudly by Black delegates when he spoke against a platform change supported by Jesse.

The next morning, she addressed a caucus of Black delegates. "Those of you who wronged Andy last night should say I'm sorry," she said. The delegates began to boo Coretta as they had booed Andy the night before. Tears came to her eyes. "My heart is heavy," she said. The words brought a mixture of cheers and more boos, and Coretta came off the speaker's platform and sat down.

Then Jesse stepped to the microphone. "When I think of the road that me and Andy walked together," he said, "and when I think of Mrs. King -- her house bombed, her husband assassinated, raising her children all alone....She's earned the right to be heard."

Jesse's words broke the tension. But it was a stunning moment for Coretta. She had never been challenged that way. She was always held in a special place. She was Martin's wife. She had given her husband to the movement; and the pain of what happened was in her face for everyone to see. She has her memories and Martin's name. And, as Jesse said, she had raised her children alone. Her husband left a modest house. He did not have any money, but there was a legacy. And Coretta took charge of that.

On that cool morning in November 1983, when President Reagan signed the bill making the third Monday of January a national holiday in King's name, Coretta was there in the Rose Garden. After the President spoke, he handed the microphone to her. Coretta Scott King, Keeper of The Dream.

Rosa Parks

SHE GETS CALLED THE "mother of the civil rights movement." But those are just words. The movement was not a family; the movement was about many people, both Blacks and Whites, coming from many places, and together they changed a lot of America.

Rosa Parks was not "the mother" in that movement; she was, though, that remarkable, courageous person who was grabbed by history and measured up to the moment.

On Friday, Rosa Parks was in New York. She is 75. Her hair, still long and full, is white.

But when she walks, her body has almost none of the stiffness of age. And her face is smooth and clear. She speaks in a soft voice, but even yet, she is a woman who can fill up a room.

You sit with her for a while and you know the reason she gets called the mother of the movement. She has that certain quality.

She is everybody's mom. And yet, she is a formidable person and in a room with her, you feel that too.

She does not use caffeine. She does not drink alcohol. She does not use cigarettes. She uses only natural foods. She mentions those things when she is asked how she manages to look so good at 75.

"What about that moment in 1955?" she is asked. "Does all that happened to you back then stay in the front of your mind?"

She smiles and shakes her head. The answer is no.

"You have to live in the present," she says. "And you have to think of the future."

It was 34 years ago. The American South then had a system of segregation as rigid as that now in South Africa. Rosa Parks grew up in that system.

As it turned out, she never completely bowed to it. On the night of December 1, 1955, she was on her way home. She worked as a seamstress; she was tired and it was late when she climbed on the bus and found a seat in the White section.

In those days, in that place, when Blacks wanted to sit in the White section, it was against the law. If you sat there, it was challenging segregation, a serious offense.

To build a movement, it takes many things, both large and small, to come together at once. Months earlier, at an NAACP meeting, Rosa Parks had seen a young minister. "I was so surprised at how young he seemed." The new minister, 25-year-old Martin Luther King Jr., had come to Montgomery to serve at the Dexter Ave. Baptist Church.

The first time they met was by chance, but the lives of King and Rosa Parks were destined to become linked in history.

As it turned out, that night in December 1955, when the laws of segregation demanded that Rosa Parks move to the back of the bus, she refused. And she would not back down, not even when they took her to jail.

Blacks were outraged; a bus boycott followed. King was to emerge as the leader of the boycott, and, eventually, the voice of the movement that ensued.

An assassin's bullet took King's life at 39. Rosa Parks is still on the case. She heads the Rosa and Raymond Parks Institute for Self-Development in Detroit. King would be proud.

Her institute identifies, reaches out and does what it can to pull up and along young people who have leadership skills. "You think of the future," Rosa Parks explains.

On Martin Luther King Day 1989, it gets asked, how is it going? What shape is the holiday taking? All is not what it ought to be. But there are some very good points of light.

It took 20 years to get the King Holiday. It's not possible to make it all it needs to be in just a few years. But the momentum is in that direction. That's why Rosa Parks, at 75, keeps going strong. We need the King Holiday to work. To those who ask why, the late Bayard Rustin had the perfect answer:

"By honoring (King), America would be doing justice to itself, for it would be creating a symbol -- a day of national observance -- of how we must behave...if we are...to realize the principles upon which this nation was established."

Marian Anderson

EASTER SUNDAY OF 1939 will always be a day set apart, because of Marian Anderson.

The story has been told and retold many times. Now, at the end of this Easter season, it is being told again -- because, at age 96, the great Marian Anderson has died.

As an artist, she had a talent so large that some called her perhaps the greatest singer ever. Or, as Arturo Tuscanini told her, "A voice like yours is heard once in a hundred years."

The woman who was this enormous talent was an African American born in Philadelphia, the oldest of three children. She began singing in church as a child. Even as early as that, it was easy to see that hers was a special talent. By the time she was 15, she was taking formal voice lessons.

But it was a different America that the young Marian Anderson encountered. Her gifts began to blossom in the late '20s, long before the civil rights movement. So when the time came for her to rise and be recognized, she ran into the wall of segregation that said to Blacks: This is as far as you can go.

In 1930, Marian Anderson did what many talented Black artists of her generation had to do: She left the country of her birth. She toured Europe and was a tremendous hit.

But all that lasts only so long. Sooner or later, you yearn to go home again. In 1935, Marian Anderson came back to New York and made a triumphant return to Town Hall. From there, she toured the country, billed as "one of the great singers of our time."

Then, in 1939, as the rumblings of World War II were heard, she was about to be booked to appear in Washington at Constitution Hall, the national headquarters of the Daughters of the American Revolution. Instead of being given a date to appear, Marian Anderson, in a blatant display of discrimination, was told that all dates were taken. It was an excuse that fooled no one. It caused an uproar.

In 1939, the White House was occupied by Franklin D. Roosevelt. It was not the President, but his wife, Eleanor, who was known as the great champion of minorities.

When word of the DAR's snub got to the White House, Eleanor Roosevelt came to the support of Marian Anderson. What followed would become a piece of American history.

First, Eleanor resigned from the DAR. Then, Secretary of the Interior Harold Ickes, at Roosevelt's urging, offered Marian Anderson another platform on which to deliver the concert she was not allowed to give at Constitution Hall. His suggestion was that she appear at the Lincoln Memorial. Sometimes, the worst has to happen in order to bring out the best. That was how it went on Easter Sunday 1939. Marian Anderson accepted the Ickes offer and appeared at the Lincoln Memorial. An enormous crowd, some say as many as 75,000, came to the national monument. The concert, and the enthusiastic reception the singer received, are now part of American lore.

Marian Anderson went on from there. She encountered segregation and discrimination on other fronts. But, as with the DAR, she did not let those slights deter her. She had a lot of talent, and over the years, kept using the gift she had. In 1940, the DAR even had to back up and invite her to appear at Constitution Hall, which she did.

In her career, she had a lot of range with her voice. She sang the classics and performed the work of the masters. But she was also a woman who started out in church. She used her voice to elevate the songs known as spirituals. In her time, Marian Anderson made her mark. In the late '50s, then-President Eisenhower sent her to the United Nations as an alternate representative to the Human Rights Committee. Later, in 1963, she sang at the great March on Washington, where Martin Luther King Jr., delivered his "I Have a Dream" speech.

Marian Anderson's life ended in the Easter season. She was an Easter person.

Rev. Ralph D. Abernathy

IN THE HISTORY THAT'S BEING written of the civil rights movement, mostly the status accorded the Rev. Ralph David Abernathy is little more than that of a footnote. He had but a few years as a leader at the top. When he was elevated to that position, it was not so much that he was the man for the moment but rather, because Martin Luther King Jr. was assassinated. And even through those years, whatever he did was not enough and so, Abernathy took a ton of the kind of criticism he didn't deserve.

That he came up short when he was called on to stand in King's place was no surprise. Abernathy was not King. But it was written down that if anything happened to King who was the leader, that Abernathy would take over. At twilight on the 4th of April, 1968, King was felled by as assassin's bullet. King had been virtually all that could be asked of a leader. He was a scholar, a brilliant speaker and he had the kind of charisma that compels the crowd the follow. Abernathy was the other side. He had no advanced degree; he was not much of a speaker and most of all, he was simply an ordinary southern Baptist minister.

On the day after King was killed, though, he walked out of the Lorraine Motel in Memphis and he spoke of the "awesome burden" that was on his shoulders, and through nine years of tough times, he did try with all that he had to carry on "for Martin." He led the Poor People's Campaign that King had envisioned. Without King, though, it ended in disappointment and failure, and much of the blame for that got heaped on Abernathy.

Yesterday word of Abernathy's death came from Atlanta. He had wanted to die a long time ago. He and King had talked of the dangers involved in their work and they always understood that assassination was a possibility. What they shared was the hope that if the worst was to happen, that the two of them could go together. They were closer than brothers; the bond they shared was a story unmatched in the movement. Abernathy was the one who was always there for King. The leader is the one who stands in the bright light, but the other side has moments of doubt and periods of loneliness. A leader needs someone to lean on, and for King, Abernathy was that person.

It gets forgotten that in 1955 when he started out on his journey of leadership, King was only in his mid 20s. Abernathy was but five years older. But yet, they had an enormous impact in changing America. And even today freedom movements all across the world borrow from what King and Abernathy did three decades ago.

More than anything else, Abernathy was a preacher. He had as his base the West Hunter Street Baptist Church in Atlanta. When King headed the Southern Christian Leadership Conference, Abernathy was his chief aide. And King had it written down that should anything happen to him, Abernathy would be the leader. In 1968, King was killed, and the mantel of leadership of the non violent movement was in Abernathy's hands. After nine years, he stood aside. He was unsuccessful in a bid to win a seat in Congress, and as the movement changed, he got pushed deep into the background and retired back to his church.

For Abernathy, the last years of his life must have been the most painful. That was because of "the book." A lot of books have been written on the civil rights movement but in many ways, none was more insightful than Abernathy's autobiography, "And the Walls Came Tumbling Down." But from the time it was published by Harper and Row, it brought him nothing but grief. That was because he dared to write of King's relationships with women. Although that was only a few paragraphs of the book, it raised such a storm that nothing else got noticed. Abernathy wrote a good book. He had many important stories to tell. Still, a lot of ridicule was heaped on Abernathy; he was cast from disfavor to disgrace and in time, his health which was already poor began to get worse. Yesterday he died, at 64.

Malcolm X

HE WAS BORN IN 1925 IN OMAHA, NEB. His father was a Baptist minister. Malcolm was a seventh son.

Ossie Davis delivered his eulogy in 1965: Ossie Davis, who knew Malcolm, said it best.

"Many will ask what Harlem finds to honor in this stormy, controversial and bold young captain -- and we will smile. They will say that he is of hate -- a fanatic, a racist -- who can only bring evil to the cause for which you struggle...

"Malcolm was our manhood, our living, Black manhood!"

Malcolm X. He was, perhaps, more than anything else, a teacher. On his birthday, look back. Listen to his words:

"Our people have to become registered voters," he said. "But they should not become involved actively in politics until we have gotten a much better understanding than we now have of the gains to be made from politics in this country. We go into politics in a sort of gullible way, an emotional way; whereas politics, especially in this country, is cold-blooded and heartless. We have to be given a better understanding of the science of politics as well as becoming registered voters. And then, we shouldn't take sides either way with any of these parties. In my opinion, we should reserve our political action for the situation at hand, in no way identifying with either party or selling ourselves to either party; but taking political action that's for the good of human beings; and that will eliminate these injustices."

Malcolm spoke of many things.

"The only person who can organize the man in the street is the one who is unacceptable to the White community."

He was asked if hate was a tool to use to organize?

"I won't permit you to call it hate," he said. "Let's say I'm going to create an awareness of what has been done to them. This awareness will produce an abundance of energy, both negative and positive, that can be channeled constructively. The greatest mistake of the movement has been trying to organize a sleeping people around specific goals. You have to wake the people first, then you'll get action."

"Awaken the people to what?" he was asked.

"To their humanity, to their own worth, and to their heritage. The biggest difference between the parallel oppression of the Jew and the Negro is that the Jew never lost his pride in being a Jew. He never ceased to be a man. He knew he had made a significant contribution to the world; and his sense of his own value gave him the courage to fight back."

In 1964, he spoke at Harvard. He was asked the difference between White and Black racism.

"Usually, the Black racist has been produced by the White racist," he said. "In most cases, where you see it, it is the reaction to White racism: And if you analyze it closely, it's not really Black racism. I think Black people have shown less racist tendencies than any people since the beginning of history."

In January of 1965, Malcolm spoke of the causes of race prejudice in the United States. Listen to his words.

"Ignorance and greed," he said, "and a skillfully designed program of miseducation that goes right along with the American system of exploitation and oppression. If the entire American population were properly educated -- by properly educated, I mean, given a true picture of the history and contributions of the Black man -- I think many whites would be less racist in their feelings. They would have more respect for the Black man as a human being."

Malcolm. In that eulogy from a day in February 20 years ago, Ossie Davis said of Malcolm:

"We will know him for what he was and is -- a prince -- our own Black shining prince; who didn't hesitate to die, because he loved us so."

Malcolm. On his birthday, the words, a part of the legacy he left, come back.

"Remember this," he said. "nobody puts words in my mouth."

IT USED TO BE THAT with Malcolm X, his name came back mostly around the anniversary of his death. That wasn't so surprising. It had to do with the way he died.

Malcolm X was another of those Black leaders to fall victim to assassination. On the 21st of February, in 1965, as he was rising to address a rally at the Audubon Ballroom in Harlem, he was met with a hail of gunfire and he never made it off the speakers' platform alive. For a long time, Malcolm was frozen in the events of that Sunday. The question of "who killed Malcolm?" became so important that he got discussed almost only in that context. Some said his death was a "hit" ordered by the Nation of Islam. That was hotly disputed by others who blamed the government and said the killing was carried out by local police.

It was true that in 1965 the Federal Bureau of Investigation was in the hands of J. Edgar Hoover and Hoover's FBI then had a counterintelligence operation that, among other things, had the stated goal of preventing "the rise of a Black messiah." Documents later made public said Hoover feared a Black leader "who could unify and electrify the militant Black nationalist movement."

In the weeks before his assassination, Malcolm had been barred from entering France. Some raised the question, "Did the French government expect an assassination attempt there?" Five days later, his home in New York was fire bombed. Less than a week later, during a talk at the Audubon, his speech was interrupted by a scuffle. Some were later to ask, was that a rehearsal for the assassination. Six days later, Malcolm died. Just as before, a scuffle developed as he rose to speak and this time, out of that confusion came men with guns and his life was snuffed out there.

Assassinations leave a lot of questions. And all that gets doubled when the victim is a figure as large and plays as pivotal a role as Malcolm was moving into in Black America. So after his death, for a long time, the debate that raged centered on his death. It is that way yet with Dr. Martin Luther King Jr. King's name gets brought back because of the national holiday but still, the most intense discussions about King have to do with his death. With King there is still no serious, concentrated delving into his work and ideas and philosophy. It gets said that he was a dreamer, but the nuts and bolts of what he stood for have yet to get examined in a serious, meaningful way. Until now, it had been that way with Malcolm but no more.

A year ago on the occasion of Malcolm's birthday, a rally was held at the Abyssinian Baptist Church in Harlem. It turned out to be a stunning event; so many people showed up that finally, the iron gates in front of the church had to be closed. But still, close to a thousand people waited in the night, hoping to somehow get into the church. A part of what got noticed then was how many of the people were young; many so young they had not even been born when Malcolm was killed. But they cheered those who cited his words and ideas and they embraced what they knew of his philosophy.

What came into view a year ago, has been built on and is flowering this weekend, the anniversary of Malcolm's birth, which was the 19th of May, 1925, in Omaha, Nebraska. Starting at Medgar Evers College in Brooklyn and ending in Harlem, attention focuses on Malcolm. But now it's different; instead of his death, the focus in 1991 is on the fire that illuminated his words and ideas.

Malcolm was always clear. He was a teacher who gave direction. For example, when asked about Blacks building alliances with other groups, he was clear. "Whites can help us, but they can't join us. There can be no Black-White unity until there is first some Black unity. There can be no workers solidarity until there is first some racial solidarity. We cannot think of uniting with others, until we have first united among ourselves."

Congress of Racial Equality

IN THE CIVIL RIGHTS MOVEMENT, the Congress of Racial Equality was one of the key organizations. At its national convention that summer among the important business CORE had on its agenda was the electing of a new national chairman. That election was to be a turning point first for CORE and in time, for the movement.

The leadership of CORE was then in the hands of James Farmer, its scholarly national director and founder of the organization. Two decades later Farmer was later to write an autobiography of the movement, which he called, "Lay Bare the Heart." The chapter that dealt with the important business from the summer of 1963 was called, "The Cannibalizing of the Movement."

Among some in CORE the election was seen as no more than some routine shuffling at the top. Charlie Oldham was stepping down as national chairman. As Farmer recalled, when he arrived in New York for a meeting of the National Action Council, he was told by Oldham that it had been discussed and decided that Alan Gartner would be the new national chairman.

"What!" Farmer shouted.

"I'll be damned if it's all set."

Oldham tried to explain. "Marv (Rich) and I just decided that Alan is the best qualified person to chair the organization through these troubled times, and we thought you would agree with that."

Farmer bristled. "Marv and you thought," he said. "Neither of you found it necessary to ask what I thought. Maybe you thought my opinion was irrelevant. Now, let me make it clear. Alan is a friend of mine and I have the highest regard for his intelligence and his abilities. He has served the organization well as chairman of the Boston chapter and as a key member of the National Action Council. But there is no way that a white man can be titular head of what Louie Lomax has called the 'Negro revolt' at this point in history."

Farmer said, "What I was doing-- what I felt I had to do -- tore me up inside." He had been so instrumental in building and guiding the development of CORE as a "color blind" organization. He said that was why it was "of Racial Equality" rather than "on Racial Equality." But in the summer of 1963, CORE was being attacked by its enemies and criticized by its friends as being basically a white-led organization with a Black front. "This was its Achilles' heel," Farmer wrote, "and mine, even within the community of activist civil rights organizations. That picture had to be changed if CORE was to consolidate its image as the cutting edge of the movement. It could not be a Black organization, but it had to be Black-led. Now that the attacks upon us for being White-led were mounting in the Black community, I felt that the stand I was taking, tactical rather than principled, was the correct one for the organization."

But to win the election, Farmer needed the right person. That became the moment Floyd McKissick, the Durham, North Carolina lawyer, rose to national leadership in CORE. Farmer asked McKissick to run. He agreed, and at the convention there was no vote. Lincoln Lynch, who was then chairman of Long Island CORE, rose on the convention floor and moved that McKissick be elected national chairman by acclamation, and that was the way it happened.

In another three years, McKissick was to replace Farmer as head of CORE. He called himself "a country lawyer," but McKissick's time as head of CORE was to be momentous.

McKissick came to national leadership because the time had come for Blacks to lead Black organizations. Before the end of the 1960s, the issue became Black power. It was a concept shunned by the NAACP, the Urban League and Martin Luther King Jr.'s Southern Christian Leadership Conference. But not by McKissick. He sided with Stokely

Carmichael and the young militants of the Student Nonviolent Coordinating Committee who believed the time had come for Blacks to use their organizations to build Black power. The Black power debate was to split the movement but McKissick never wavered. He then began to champion Black economic development. His speeches were emotional and often tears would well in his eyes. He was so committed to the ideas of Black power and Black economic development that he left CORE to try and build an all Black town in rural North Carolina. In that, he was not successful but, he never let go of the idea of Blacks building for Blacks.

The events from the summer of 1963 come back now with the news of McKissick's death from his native North Carolina. He spent most of his life in the movement and at a pivotal time, he emerged an important leader at the top. He was 69.

Jackie Robinson

THE WAY THAT JACKIE REMEMBERED IT, on the 9th of April in 1947, just before the Dodgers were to play an exhibition game, reporters in the press box received a single sheet of paper with a one-line announcement.

It read: "Brooklyn announces the purchase of the contract of Jack Roosevelt Robinson from Montreal."

"Less than a week after I became No. 42 on the Brooklyn club, I played my first game with the team," Jackie Robinson wrote. "I did a miserable job. There was an overflow crowd at Ebbet's Field. If they expected any miracles out of Robinson, they were sadly disappointed. I grounded out to the third baseman, flied out to left field, bounced into a double play, was safe on an error, and, later, was removed. The next four games reflected my deep slump. I went to the plate 20 times without one base hit."

The book, "I Never Had It Made," is Jackie's side of the story. It was published in 1972. April and baseball bring the story back.

"Early in the season, the Philadelphia Phillies came to Ebbet's field for a three-game series. I was still in a slump. Starting to the plate in the first inning, I could scarcely believe my ears. Almost as if it had been synchronized by some master conductor, hate poured from the Phillies dugout.

"'Hey, nigger, why don't you go back to the cotton field where you belong?'

"'They're waiting for you in the jungles, Black boy.'

"'Hey, snowflake, which one of those White boys' wives are you dating tonight?'

"'We don't want you here, nigger.'

"I have to admit," Jackie wrote, "that this day, of all the unpleasant days in my life, brought me nearer to cracking up than I ever had been. For one wild and rage-crazed minute, I thought, "to hell with Mr. Rickey's (Dodger club owner Branch Rickey) noble experiment. The haters almost won that round."

But, Jackie wrote, the game was still scoreless and the insults were still coming when he batted in the bottom of the eighth. On the second pitch, he singled to center. "Gene Hermanski came up to hit, and I took my lead." The Phillies had a knuckleball pitcher on the mound. "I cut out for second. The throw was wide." And Jackie went to third and Hermanski singled him home. "And that was the game," Jackie wrote.

But the next day, and the day after, the name-calling kept up. Finally his teammate, Ed Stanky exploded. "He started yelling at the Phillies, 'listen, you yellow-bellied cowards, why don't you yell at somebody who can answer back?' It was then that I began to feel better. I remembered Mr. Rickey's prediction: If I won the respect of the team and got them solidly behind me, there would be no question about the success of the experiment."

In May, it was St. Louis. "The Cards were planning to pull a last-minute protest strike against my playing in the game. If successful, the plan could have had a chain reaction throughout the baseball world with other players agreeing to unite in a strong bid to keep baseball White." The plot was exposed by a newspaper reporter, and Jackie said that Baseball Commissioner Ford Frick reacted immediately.

"If you do this you will be suspended from the league," Frick warned the St. Louis team. "I do not care if half the league strikes....they will be suspended. And I don't care if it wrecks the National League for five years. This is the United States of America, and one citizen has as much right to play as another. The National League will go down the line with Robinson whatever the consequences."

In 1947, The Year of Jackie, the Dodgers won the pennant. "We were joyfully received by our fans," Jackie wrote. "Their enthusiasm for me was great. I had started the season as a lonely man, often feeling like a Black Don Quixote, tilting at a lot of White windmills. I ended it feeling like a member of a solid team. The Dodgers were a championship team because all of us had learned something. I had learned how to exercise self-control; to answer insults, violence and injustice -- with silence. I had learned how to earn the respect of my teammates. They had learned that it's not skin-color, but talent and ability that count. Maybe even the bigots had learned that too."

Fannie Lee Chaney

IN THE AFTERNOON ON MOTHER'S DAY, she sits in the living room of her small apartment on Columbus Ave., her back to the picture window that is framed with plants, her quilting on the sofa across the room.

The bright print dress she wears is one that she has made. She has quit cigarettes. Her hands are folded across her lap. Now, in the afternoon, she sits near the phone and waits for the Mother's Day call she is expecting from her son.

You do not forget this woman, whose name is Fannie Lee Chaney. Once, the central story in her life was so important that it was reported at the top of every newscast, and written of in newspapers in towns and villages everywhere in the country. Now, in the living room of her apartment, the only reminder of that time gone by is a picture that hangs on the wall behind the sofa.

The picture has the faces of three very young men and all of the faces are strong. On one side of the picture the face is of Andrew Goodman. In the middle, it is Michael Schwerner and the other is of James Chaney, who was her son.

"That was a very long time ago," she says. "Yes, it will be 19 years this June."

She can never forget. That was the summer of 1964, the Mississippi Freedom Summer. There was an army of college students that flocked to Mississippi that June to work in a voter registration project that was part of the civil rights movement. Andrew Goodman and Michael Schwerner had come down from New York and on the 21st of June, they were with James Chaney, who was Fannie Lee's older boy. The three of them were arrested. It was the Old South, and as soon as they were arrested, they knew their lives were in danger.

The story of what happened to them is the history that was delivered on television and in the newspapers. They were in jail until late at night and then, when they were released, they were virtually put into the hands of a racist mob, and the three of them were murdered.

After that, nothing went right for Fannie Lee Chaney. She lost her job, her house was firebombed, and so many threats were made on her life that she had to leave her native Mississippi. The civil rights movement in the South was linked up with good people in the North and Fannie Lee Chaney moved to New York, to the apartment on Columbia Ave. where she lives now.

But hers was to remain a troubled life. Seven years after she moved to New York, her younger son, Ben, went back South. He made the trip with two friends. One of them, a 24-year-old veteran who came back from Vietnam with mental problems, went on a shooting spree. He killed four people before he was shot and killed himself and young Ben Chaney was there and because he was, in the eyes of the law, it made him guilty of felony murder.

"When Ben left here he was 17," his mother said yesterday. "He's been locked up ever since."

He is imprisoned in Florida, in a place called Clermont. Fannie Lee Chaney scrimps and saves all she can and she uses the money to ride the bus to Florida, to the prison, to see her son.

"It costs so much," she says. "Yes, the bus ride is hard on you. The last time I went down, I left here at 10 o'clock in the morning on Friday and it was 4 o'clock on Saturday when I got off the bus in Clermont. They just drop you off on the side of the highway and you have to find your way around."

Her dream now is that one day soon her son will win parole.

"He's suppose to go back for a parole hearing soon," she said. "We're waiting for the parole date now."

To get the money that it takes to make the trip to Florida, she makes quilts. "I been doing it since I was 8 years old," she said.

Yesterday, Her quilting was put aside. "Because I can't get any cotton," she said. "That's my trouble now. I usually get some from Meridian (Mississippi), my hometown, but I can't even get any from down there now."

The kind of quilts that she learned to make as a child are popular now. A few months ago several of the quilts she made were shown in a gallery in Brooklyn, and one night not long ago, she was in a gallery in midtown to look at an exhibit. "I got a new pattern that I'm trying out now, too," she said. "If I can just get the cotton."

She was talking about the quilts, and how much the work means to her -- "it keep me occupied so my mind doesn't go running off" -- when the call that she had been waiting for came through from her son in Florida.

She was not on the telephone long but when she came back into the room there was a light in her face. "I knew he was going to call," she said. "He says he's doing all right. They got him in a dormitory, he's not off in a cell by himself. He sure has been away a long time. He's really grown up a lot. He says he wants to get out so he can get his life back together and do something for himself."

Fannie Lee Chaney also has three daughters. She counted a while, then said she now has 15 grandchildren and three great grandchildren.

But it is Ben, her younger son, whom she worries about. "How long does he have to pay for that?" she asked. Then she told how her son had tried to stop the killings, how he broke off and ran away from the gunman.

She mentioned Ramsey Clark, the former attorney general. "He's helping us with the case now," she said. But what she needs more than anything else is influential people to come forward and appeal to the authorities in Florida to grant her son parole. "We need people to write, too," she said.

"What are your plans?" she was asked.

"I want to leave New York now," she said. "It isn't like it used to be." She mentioned drugs, and the way that young people have changed. "Even their parents don't have control over them," she said. "It looks like they turn them loose too quick."

"Where will you go once you leave New York City?" she was asked.

"I don't know," she said. "I know I can't go back to Mississippi. But when Ben gets out from down there, we'll go someplace and live."

Melville T. Miller

HE KEEPS THE DOG OUTSIDE. It's a big, shaggy-haired animal, completely black, and every day it lies out there, always staying close to the front door and when kids come along, it's the dog that they know about.

And last week, in the rain that fell late on this afternoon, the kids who played their way through the block stopped and shook their heads in puzzlement when asked about Melville Thornhill Miller.

Time has played a trick on Melville Miller. Now he's a part of the past. His is a forgotten history. But the man is a hero. He's history.

He lives now out in Brooklyn, out in that section of Crown Heights that is all Black. His is a quiet street, Sterling Place, and the houses on his block are all attached and every one has a yard out front and they are wrapped with metal gates.

Melville Miller is in the history books because he was a part of the 369th Infantry Regiment, the all Black volunteer unit in World War I. When it was formed, nobody wanted the 369th. These were soldiers who all through the war were never allowed to fight. The American Army then was White. Blacks could cook and clean and serve. But then, they could not fight for their country.

But the 369th overcame that. It became legend. They were nicknamed the Harlem Hellfighters, and so distinguished was their record that when they came home, here in New York, the city did what it does best. They threw a parade up Fifth Ave. for them and the city acclaimed them as heroes.

The 369th got into the war, into the fighting, through the back door. Because U.S. Army regulations then kept soldiers who were Black from combat, the 369th was sent to France for other duties, unloading piers and building railroad tracks and loading ships. But the Allied armies were pressed and the French needed help and the 369th was there.

On April 13, 1918, the 369th was attached to the French 4th Army. They fought at Bois d'Hauza and at Minacaurt. They fought in the great battle of Maison en Champagne that carried them to the Rhine River and, after that, many other battles. They served 191 days in action -- longer than any other American regiment. They were the first of the Allies to reach the Rhine, and in all of the battles, they never lost a foot of ground and not one of their men was captured. They were honored by the French. Eleven times the entire unit was cited for bravery, and the entire unit was awarded the French Croix de Guerre for gallantry.

In addition to all that, 171 men of the 369th were decorated individually with the Croix de Guerre or the Legion of Honor. One of those was Pvt. Melville Miller of Brooklyn, who had lied about his age and enlisted when he was 16 years old.

The 369th paid a price. The regiment had nearly 3,000 men, and almost half were wounded or killed in action. When they came home, the first combat regiment to return, they marched up Fifth Ave.

"It was the best day of my life," Melville Miller reminisced yesterday. "It was the one day when the Black man was in power. It was a great day."

He's 79 years old now. Time has added a thickness to his body and the beard he wears is pure white. And his wife, whom he met at a reception after the big parade, died in 1972.

On the walls of the living room in his house on Sterling Place are the mementos. The plaques, the citations and the medals. The kids don't know him but Melville Miller is not unknown in Brooklyn. He has been honored by the community and, as he says, "I've got quite a fan club."

When he came home from the war, back to his old neighborhood, which was Underhill Ave., a neighborhood that was mostly Irish and Italian, Miller fell in with his old buddies.

"But it was the same old thing," he said.

He went with two friends who had told him about jobs that were available at the post office. One of his friends was Irish and the other Italian. The three of them went together. The others got the jobs; Miller didn't. But he kept trying. "Nobody ever accused me of being stupid," he said. He went through civil service and finally got the job. He stayed at the post office until he retired.

"How is it here in Brooklyn?" he was asked.

"It's different. It's a Black town now. How could it be better? It's worse. The houses are deteriorating and you're afraid to go out at night and there's no jobs for people..."

He is like many New Yorkers now. He finds it hard to see anything that is happening that is good and right, and within his grasp. "The prices," he said. "Everything costs so much and ...the kids. They're just jailhouse fodder, that's all."

"Tell me a good story?"

"I can't," he said. "and it's no use for me to lie."

He did not mention Sunday. But tomorrow, up Fifth Ave. the 369th Veterans Association will hold its 12th annual Martin Luther King Jr. parade. Whatever the differences, regardless of the problems, New Yorkers put them aside for a parade. It makes no difference if it's the Irish or the Poles or the Italians or Greeks. It may not be much but in New York now, where some people find it difficult to tell any story that is good, the tradition of the parade is till intact.

"Will you be there on Sunday?"

"Oh yes," Melville Thornhill Miller said. "I'll be there somewhere."

Howard University Students

THEY WERE THE FIRST WORDS out of his mouth. As soon as the students forced him to beat his hasty retreat and resign from the board of trustees at Howard University, Lee Atwater was quick to let the students know that for their action, they would pay a price. He had nine ways of saying it, but each time the message was the same: Over and over, Atwater kept saying, I could have got you money.

He told of how he could have helped the school with fund raising. He told of the impact he could have had in building the scholarship endowment, which also means money. He told of how helpful he could have been in identifying job opportunities for graduates and in opening scholastic opportunities such as student internships at the White House and Republican National Committee. The message gets slick. For in saying what he could have done had he been allowed to remain as a member of the board of trustees, Atwater was also sending a message. He was saying, you messed up. He was telling the students that yes, your protest cost me my position, but you lose the money, and I know and you know, that not getting the money my presence on the board represented, in the end will hurt you most.

Maybe not in 20 years has an issue on any predominantly Black campus erupted the way the Atwater episode did at Howard. The students were so aroused and the anger so great, that during their protest the students would not even allow Bill Cosby to carry out a scheduled appearance at the school.

Atwater was appointed a trustee at Howard in January. It took a month for the anger at what was done to explode. More than any other person, Lee Atwater was the symbol of the way race is exploited, especially in politics. Atwater was the genius who took the convicted murderer Willie Horton and made the Black man a centerpiece for fear in the Bush campaign. Bush won the White House and Atwater got elected head of the Republican Party. It never seemed to occur to either Bush or Atwater that they might have to pay a price for the way they exploited the racism in the country to win an election. Indeed, Atwater talked of the big plans he had of wooing Blacks to the Republican Party.

But then came David Duke. By title, before running for the state legislature in Louisiana, he was a grand wizard in the Ku Klux Klan. Duke saw himself as a Republican. "I feel comfortable in the Republican Party," he said. In other words, he was tuned in to the signals Atwater had been sending. It embarrassed Republicans at the top that David Duke surfaced as their man, and they tried to read him out of the party. But he ran and won. Right in the midst of that, Atwater got his coming out as a trustee at Howard University.

Atwater called it right. Howard and many of the students are ones who need. So the students who decided to stand up, knew they would have to pay a price. One of those students, in an interview with a Washington Post reporter, explained the decision to fight. "It's the principle," he said. "They say Atwater's going to bring a lot of money in. I say, we don't need to stoop that low. But the main thing is the Willie Horton issue. I believe Mr. Atwater -- and I don't really feel hate for him in spite of saying this -- knew subconsciously he could instill fear in the country with those ads. I've seen it in myself. People see me, a Black male, and think I can fight, or whatever. They think I'm street wise. I'm not street wise at all. But I'm a young Black male, and there you are."

What happened at Howard was no small thing. Obviously it rocked the Howard administration that dared to play the Atwater game. Just as clearly, it was a stunning blow to Atwater and the Republicans. Atwater tells of all the ways that Howard loses because of what the students did. But he's not telling the whole story. He does not talk of what he and the Republicans lose. He does not say that his strategy to woo Blacks gets knocked into a cocked hat. It is not all one way. The students at Howard called some high cards and came away having won something very big -- self respect, for themselves and their school. To the crowd that has money, they made it clear that some things are not for sale.

Ancestors of Earl Caldwell

THE MOTEL SITS HIGH in the mountains overlooking the highway, Interstate route 80, and now, in the evening, with twilight closing in, the blacktop parking lot outside began to fill.

Inside the lobby, there was a truck driver, a young man dressed in faded Levis and stained T-shirt, and he stood by the front desk frowning at the assistant manager.

"I can't believe you don't have any room," the trucker said. "You've always got rooms here."

"Not tonight," the manager said. As he talked, he kept scanning a sheaf of papers on the counter in front of him and occasionally he used a pencil to jot notations on the papers.

"It's this Caldwell reunion," this manager said. "It has taken every room we've got."

"Every room?" the trucker asked.

"Everything," the manager said.

Now, as he turned toward the door, the trucker stopped and looked back at the man behind the desk. "That must be some kind of family," he said.

This was a Friday and up here in the mountains in the center of Pennsylvania our family, the Caldwell family, came together for the great ritual that is the family reunion.

This wasn't our first reunion. There were others. I still remember the one 31 years ago. That was when we met in New York, out in Mount Vernon in Westchester County. But that was nothing like the gathering that was taking place here. Everything about this reunion was different.

Just meeting here made it different. This is a remote section of Pennsylvania high in the Allegheny Mountains, where all of the population, except for a tiny fraction, is White and ours is a Black family.

We came here to Clearfield County because this is where my father settled 61 years ago. Where he raised his family and where he sill lives with his wife of 70 years. And now he is in this 98th year and the senior member of the family, and so this reunion was brought to him.

The oldest sister, Janie Smith, journeyed a thousand miles, coming from Asheville, N.C. She is 90 years old but still a strong, stately woman. And there was another sister, Mattie Hughes, who came from Mount Vernon, and the youngest sister, Eula Fletcher El, in her 70s, who came from Detroit.

It spread out from there. By Saturday, there were 241 members of the Caldwell family in the motel. The local people were saying that they had never seen so large a gathering of Blacks. Members of the family came from every section of the country. From the West Coast, the Midwest, the South, and from across the Eastern seaboard.

Hovering over this reunion like a giant shadow was the legacy of Alex Haley, the author, and his book called "Roots." It was in the book that Haley made the connection, tracing his ancestors from slave plantations in the old South back to Black Africa.

What Haley accomplished inspired Blacks everywhere. And now, any time a Black family meets in a reunion, the impact of Haley is there. And it was no different for us.

We traced the family back to 1820, back to Clinton, S.C. Back to slavery and a plantation where a slave girl, whose name we still do not know, bore the child of her slavemaster.

There was an excitement in the search. But always, for the Black American, there is pain in learning. It was no different for us.

Johnny Woods, who lives in Mount Vernon, eldest child of Janie Woods, led our search for roots. He came to the reunion brimming because of his findings and lugging stacks of notes and papers and documents. When he laid it all out, it took the family back to the plantation of a man whose name was Copeland.

His research found that Copeland, the slavemaster, fathered a child to a slave girl. The child would have the name Janie Copeland. She was to marry a man whose name was Simpson. They were to have a daughter, Etta Simpson, who was to marry Gus Caldwell, my father's father.

Gus and Etta, in Clinton, S.C., were to have 21 children. Five are still living and four of them were at the reunion, bloodline of the family.

But Johnny Woods, in his search, also found a word: Kwashie. An African word. From West Africa. We have learned that it is Ghanaian. That it is associated with perhaps the Ga or Ewe tribes there. So the search goes on, but now with even more pieces of the puzzle.

From Clinton, in the northwestern region of South Carolina, the family moved to Asheville, 110 miles northwest in North Carolina, in the Smoky Mountains. And from there, it scattered.

My mother, Pearl, was asked how it happened that my father and his elder brother, Lonnie, were to move from the Carolinas to the mountains of Pennsylvania.

"To work," she explained. And she remembered clearly the recruiter who came South searching for men to work in the brickyards of central Pennsylvania. And now, during the reunion, they talked about this and about the South they grew up in and the family that is ours.

So what difference does it make?

It was Ivan Warner, the Supreme Court justice in the Criminal Court in the Bronx, who answered. Warner married into the family, his wife being a sister of Johnny Woods and daughter of Janie Smith.

He was saying how important the search for roots is for the children. "If they don't know where they come from," he said, "they don't know where they're going." And it's true. So we continue to search. When we meet now in family reunions, they are strong, emotional and powerful affairs.

THIS IS ONE OF THOSE STORIES that comes out right. It is about two people who started out together when they were young and strong and filled with dreams. About two people who took chances to build their lives together. They are up there in years now, but both of them are still going strong. Dad's birthday was the day after Christmas, and this year he was 100 years old. Mom turned 90 last September.

They are still here, in the mountains of Pennsylvania, in a place called Clearfield. Ask anyone where they live; it doesn't make any difference. Just say, "George and Pearl Caldwell," and they'll know. They still live in the little white house on Wrigley St., the house they built themselves.

They were married on the day before Christmas in 1909. In the family Bible, where the records are kept, it says that the minister who married them was a Rev. Jordan, and that the ceremony was at the home of Mr. and Mrs. Singleton.

"We have been truly blessed," Mom says.

"We've been as happy as any two people could ask," Dad adds.

They look back and they laugh. Time has not dimmed any of the memories. They are still there, sharp in the mind. When they settled in Pennsylvania, Dad wanted to buy a farm. He picked one out called Fruit Hill. "It was nice," he says. "It even had a place where you could dig your own coal."

"I said I wasn't going on no farm," Mom says. "Clearfield is farm enough."

Dad built the house on Wrigley St. He dug the foundation with a shovel. "By himself," Mom says. "He would come home from work, put his lunch bucket on the porch and then go over there and start digging. Even the preacher came by and said, 'If there is ever a house built here, I want to see it.'" Dad laughs.

When they bought the land on Wrigley St., it had a shanty on it. Dad says it was a nice shanty. He tried to get Mom to live in it, but she wouldn't. "I said 'I'm not going to live in no shanty. I'd be stuck in it.'" Mom says.

"I said, 'Oh, God, I got a problem,'" Dad says, and they laugh.

Work is what brought Mom and Dad to Pennsylvania. "Everything was going then," my father says. "All the work you wanted. You could work until your tongue dropped." Mom always says it was Dad's brother, my Uncle Lonnie, who talked them into leaving Asheville, N.C., and moving so far up into the mountains of Pennsylvania. "Lonnie came up here, and as soon as he got settled, he sent word back that he wanted George to come up, too," Mom said.

Dad came north first. He worked about a year, and then he went back for his family. He and Mom had been married for nine years. They had three kids, but two died before they were a year old. The other boy, Raymond, was 6 when they came north in 1919.

The family grew. But of the next three kids who were born, two more died as infants. Of six children born to Mom and Dad, four now had died. Then Joetta, the oldest girl, fell sick. The doctor said she would not last the night. On the morning she was supposed to die, she began to get well. She survived, and after that, there was not another death in the immediate family. Not one. After Joetta, another girl, Mildred, was born. Then two more boys, first William Franklin and then Nathaniel.

I am the youngest. It is no secret that parents do not tell any of their children very much. But the youngest, they tell the youngest next to nothing at all. That's part of the reason it took so long for me to understand how it happened that my parents ended up in such a remote section of Pennsylvania, in a region where nearly all of the people are White.

I knew my parents had come from the South. Home for Mom, Pearl Tinsley, was Mountville, S.C. Dad was born in South Carolina, too, but they did not meet until both were living and working in Asheville, N.C. Since nobody said anything, and because we lived in such an out-of-the-way place, as I began to learn how life was for Blacks in the

South just after the turn of the century, I assumed that racism had something to do with my parents' leaving. I guessed there might have been some sort of trouble, that something had happened.

My oldest brother, Raymond, straightened me out. "What do you mean, how did we get up here?" he said. "We came on the train, what did you think? You had an uncle who worked on the train."

"What is it that makes a marriage last through 72 years?" Mom was asked. She said that one of the important things was to know when to talk and when to shut up.

Dad was big and strong. Mom was little. Dad says he never made much money, but he worked until he was into his 80's. "But it's not what you make," he says. "I found that out long ago. It's not what you make, it's what you do with it. You can get anything you want, if you're willing to sacrifice."

Family. The family was at the center of everything for Mom and Dad. "If she wasn't here (at home), then I was coming," Dad says. "We didn't put our children out. We said we'd never leave our kids alone."

The life they had was not easy. But they keep going. Dad fires the coal furnace in the wintertime. He mows the lawn and trims the hedges and makes a garden every spring. "You stop and you die," he says. Mom has some trouble with her eyesight, but she doesn't let it slow her down. She is up early too, and makes Dad his breakfast. It has always been that way. "He eats three meals a day," she says, "and no matter what else, I make sure he has his meals on time." Any time it is mentioned that she ought to slow down, she bristles. "I'm not ready to die," she says. "Work is what keeps you going."

Yesterday the celebration at the little white house on Wrigley St. was for a marriage that has lasted through 72 years and for Dad who made it to 100 years. There was a box full of cards that came, including one from President Reagan. "Nancy and I congratulate you," the President wrote.

All of the family was gathered. Down from Raymond, the oldest son, there were five generations. And it was the same with Mildred. Five generations down to a 3-month-old whose name is Jamyl.

"Family," Dad says, "family is the important thing. That's what we've worked for. The family."

They have been together nearly three quarters of a century. "I got everything out of life a man could get," Dad says. "We've had a good life," Mom says. "We worked hard, but it didn't hurt us." It is one of those stories that comes out right.

THE WAY IT HAPPENED for my father was beautiful. All the way to his 100th birthday, he was climbing the smooth side of the mountain. Nothing seemed to go wrong. He hardly had a day when he didn't feel good and no matter what the weather, he was outdoors with sunshine in his life.

He made 100 the way you want to see those who live that long do it. He even had perfect recall, and so, on many days, he would sit with kids who were writing projects for school, and tell them of experiences far back in his life.

My Dad was a model for growing old. He was up early every day. And he kept busy clipping hedges, mowing the lawn, tending his garden, chopping wood. And when he took a break from his work, he used that time to visit with friends and neighbors.

His birthday was the day after Christmas. On the snowy night that he turned 100, the family was there and we had a memorable celebration in the house that he built in the mountains of Pennsylvania.

It doesn't always happen the way it did for my father. A lot of people die early; they don't even get to know old age. And often, for those who do get a lot of years, life can become a kind of hell.

My mother turns 100 today. "You're so lucky," people say. "Both of your parents lived to be a hundred."

But the outer reaches of old age don't always bring joy; often, it comes with a ton of problems. That's the way it's been for my mother. She has made it to be 100 years old, but for the last 10 years, she has had to climb the rough side of the mountain.

Mom had about 85 years that were very good. For what she did in that time, you could spell her middle name, "love." She loved her children and her husband. She loved her flowers, her neighbors and her church. She loved to cook and sew and read. She loved to see about others, especially those who were sick, and couldn't see after themselves. And every Sunday in her life was special. She loved it from the prayer she always said at breakfast before she was off to church; to dinner in the afternoon; to the quiet time she used to go through the newspapers at night.

Then her eyesight began to fail. To take sight from a person who is a doer is the worst thing to happen. Mom fought it with all she had. When she was almost totally blind, she pretended that she could see, and she kept going. She and Dad had celebrated 75 years of marriage when he found her one morning on the floor outside their bedroom. Sometime during the night, she had tried to get up; a massive stroke knocked her down. The doctor gave her two weeks to live. That was nearly eight years ago.

The worst nightmare for old people is that, in their old age, they'll fall into bad health. So they worry about winding up in a nursing home: And even worse, they worry about becoming a burden to their children. My Dad and Mom worried about that.

They had their own home, and the modest way they lived. As long as their health held out, they knew they would be all right.

When Mom had the stroke, it changed everything. She couldn't get out of bed. Because everyone believed she would soon be dead, she got no therapy. The paralysis froze the right side of her body. It broke Dad's heart. He just made himself sick; at 100, he died.

Sunday is still Mom's good day. Her minister and his wife bring church to her bedroom. She may have rambled all week long, and not been able to hear anything. But, miraculously, somehow, the words to the prayers and the songs come to the front of her mind, and she joins in. But except for those moments, she has to have total care.

A lot of people remember her good years, and they help in a lot of ways. But to keep an old person who needs total care at home puts an awesome burden on someone. How do you cope with that? Some say, let the old person die. Others have no choice but to put that person in a nursing home.

My oldest sister, Joetta, has given her life to taking care of my mother. She cooks all the meals Mom loves, and spends the time it takes to feed her. She washes her, massages her body, and even when there is no answer, she spends hours telling her of family and friends.

To get to 100, Dad made it up the smooth side of the mountain: Mom had to come the other way. But she made it. So Mom, Happy Birthday! May it be a Sunday in your life.

I HAD HOPED THAT SHE could hold on until spring: That was because she had such a love for flowers. Except for when the snow is fresh, it gets so bleak in the winter here in the mountains. But nobody gets to choose when death comes; and so, on the day after Martin Luther King, Jr.'s birthday, my mother died.

Mom lived to be the oldest in the neighborhood. She made it to her 100th birthday last September. That takes some doing in our little community, though, since we've had a nice group to live past 100. My mother made it; so did my father. Mrs. Nipson, who lives a block over, made it too.

To get to 100, Mom had to climb the rough side of the mountain. A stroke left her paralyzed. Through the last seven years of her life, she was not able to get out of bed, and she needed total care. The death certificate listed her passing as being of natural causes. I suppose that was true. At her wake, many spoke of the way old people die. My mother stopped eating.

"That's the way it happened with my mother, too," I heard others say. Old people seem to hang on as long as they can, and then a time comes when they stop. Maybe t he death certificate is right; maybe that is the natural course.

A wake can be an awful time. You have friends who come and take your hand, and they struggle to find words they hope can ease your pain. You hang onto those people; and later, you realize that, just by being there, they made you feel better. Mom's wake turned out to be wonderful. So many came. At the funeral home, they crowded three rooms; and it was more a celebration of life than grieving our a death.

The wake for my mother was a gathering of young and old, and of Black and White. Race was not a part of it. But you notice the mix because of the way so many people in so many places are at one another's throats; not because of what anybody said or did, but just because of the difference in skin color. At times, in our neighborhood, there were disagreements. But, for the most part, the people, Black and White, had respect and love and a way of sharing. And through good times and bad, they hung together.

Death takes you into a sort of time capsule. You forget now and tomorrow; and instead, you go back in that person's life to good old days, and you talk of that. What sticks in the mind is often humorous. I remember the lunch Mom packed that I would carry to elementary school. We ate at our desk. I always dreaded opening my lunch. Mom would pack sandwiches made with bread she had baked. The other kids had sandwiches made of store-bought "light" bread.

My parents never bought much from the store. Dad grew most of what we ate. Mom baked bread: And so, my lunch had sandwiches with thick slices of bread cut from a loaf with a kitchen knife. It took a lot of years to pass before I was to realize how lucky I was to have a mother who baked bread.

So in the old neighborhood, another page turns. The oldest now is Domonic Rodi. He's in his 94th year, and going strong. "He's already talking about planting his garden," said Eugene, his oldest son. Rodi's wife died a month ago at 86. Had she lived another month, the two of them would have celebrated 70 years of marriage.

He still lives up the street in the house where he raised seven children. He has a daughter, Frances, who is there, and she cares for him the way my oldest sister, Joetta, did for my mother. But Mom was bed-ridden: Rodi, always a strong and hard-working man, has not had to give in to the years. His son laughed and told of a day last summer when his father wanted to climb an old tree to trim some limbs. "He believes he can still do what he did 30 years ago."

Mom was tough, but she couldn't hold on until the flowers of spring. They published her obituary on the front page of The Progress, the local newspaper, and so many who knew and heard of her came to make the wake a memorable celebration of a remarkable life.

She was Pearl Tinsley Caldwell. And she lived to be 100.

EVEN AT 100, HE WAS STILL going strong. He cut the hedges that framed his property, mowed his lawns and tended a very productive vegetable garden. In a neighborhood of gardeners, he was one the others studied. He was especially good at growing tomatoes.

He fathered 10 kids; all of them were born at home. Of the first four, not one lived to be a year. But after that, through more than 70 years, he never saw another of his kids get so much as a serious illness.

He believed that eating habits had a lot to do with health. "Most of what my family ate, I raised," he said. He always ate three meals a day. "And you have to drink eight glasses of water," he said. He made everybody in his family do it, and he did it himself.

He was a tough disciplinarian. To spare the rod was not a part of his philosophy. If a whipping was in order, he would cut a nice little switch from a tree in the yard, and use that to do the job.

He taught that nobody got by without working. "I can't make you stay in school," he would say. "But, if you quit school, you get a job or you go to the Army. You cannot just sit around here. Everybody has to work."

He believed that you got ahead by saving. "If you earn a dollar, you ought to be able to save at least a dime out of that." He did not believe in wasting anything. "You learn to use what you've got because if you have to go to the store every time you need something, you'll find that gets very expensive," he would say.

His family was the most important thing in his life. He helped build his church; he had strong ties with his neighbors.

But his wife and kids were the center of his life. "Me and my wife never believed in leaving our kids alone. Even when both of us were working, we had it arranged so that one of us was always there with the kids."

He was a baseball fan. He followed the Dodgers and the Pittsburgh Pirates. The only big-league events he ever saw were baseball games he took his sons to watch at the old Forbes Field in Pittsburgh.

He believed in hard work. "My wife and I both worked hard all our lives," he would say. "Hard work does not hurt anybody."

As a young man, he smoked Camel cigarettes. Later, he gave up cigarettes, but he never stopped smoking. In the last 50 years of his life, he smoked a pipe, and on most evenings, and Sunday afternoons, he had at least one inexpensive cigar. He always stayed clear of liquor.

He was a carpenter, a brick mason, and a barber. He was an artist at firing a coal furnace -- not an easy thing to do in the severe winters of central Pennsylvania. He loved the country. He especially loved the mountains. "No matter how hot it gets up here in the daytime, it cools off, and you can get a good rest at night," he would say.

He was an excellent hunter. He did not care much for big game, but in his younger years, he spent many evenings and Saturdays in the woods hunting for rabbits, pheasant and grouse. "Most of what I didn't raise for my family," he would say, "I got in the woods."

He loved his wife. They had 73 very good years together. Then she was felled by a stroke that left her paralyzed and bedridden. That was the moment the bright light went out in his life. It did what ravages of time had not done; the stroke his wife suffered made him an old man.

"You don't know what it's like to be with somebody as long as me and my wife have been together. You get to be like one person," he often said.

He knew death was coming.

"This old age isn't fun anymore," he said, not long after his wife had the stroke. Before that, his health always had been excellent. He died three years ago. He was my father, who lived to be 103. I got lucky. You remember that, on Father's Day.

Chapter Ten

SECOND RENAISSANCE

Editor's Note

Recent years have seen an explosion of cultural activity among African Americans -- in art, music, film, dance and literature. Considering the racial barriers confronting Blacks earlier in the century, this recent flowering almost certainly surpasses, in its scope, the Harlem Renaissance. Over the years, Earl Caldwell has chronicled much of this new proliferation.

Expatriates

THEIR NAMES FORM A KIND of Who's Who for Black America. Josephine Baker, James Baldwin, Richard Wright and Henry O. Tanner. There is Miles Davis, Lois Mailou Jones, Claude McKay and Dexter Gordon. Those are but a few of the names in the list that runs long.

They are all a part of a history that Blacks know well but a history that even yet remains largely untold for most of America.

It was just over a hundred years ago that Henry O. Tanner, a young and talented painter, decided to call it quits in America. Tanner was a Black man. He left the United States for the sanctuary he was to find in Paris. He left, he said, because he "could not fight prejudice and paint at the same time."

He was to be among the first of the expatriates. In time, the numbers would grow and in a way, they became the best reflection of the toll racism was to take on the most creative of Black Americans -- the writers, the artists and entertainers.

Lois Mailoui Jones, another painter, left the country of her birth in the 1930s. Once in Paris, she said, "I forgot I was Black. It was like being free for the first time -- my paintings were exhibited at the Salon des Artistes, and the Galerie de Paris, and the Galerie Charpentier, purely on merit." In Paris, she found all that she had been denied in the United States because of her race.

This huge piece of history comes to New York with a show and the introduction of a book that has the history. The show and a book signing "celebration" opens at the Cinque Gallery, the perfect place for the show that has the name Paris Connections. The Cinque Gallery was founded in 1969 by three prominent Black artists: Romare Bearden, Ernest Crichlow and Norman Lewis. In founding the Cinque Gallery, the artists were creating a place "to ensure Black artists were afforded the opportunity to exhibit their work and gain necessary exposure."

The show comes to New York from San Francisco where it opened at Bomani Gallery, owned and operated by Asake Bomani, and her husband and business partner, actor Danny Glover. The show features the work of 17 African-American artists. Many are like the artists who founded the Cinque Galley -- brilliant artists who have made huge contributions, but artists who have not been given their full due, largely because they are artists who are not White.

So in a significant way, the show and the book connect with the biggest story in the country -- the story from Los Angeles. The uprising of last week has set many to looking at Black America and asking, "Why?" Why are Blacks rioting? Why are Blacks not content the way others are with life in America? Why do Blacks still feel they are relegated to second class status?

The book has a lot of the answers. It tells many of the stories about why so many of the most talented and brilliant Blacks of successive generations fled the so called "land of the free" in search of freedom to express themselves and their art.

The book is the work of Asake Bomani and Belvie Rooks. The work the two of them have put together makes for yet another good argument for the demand from Blacks of now -- a curriculum of inclusion in the schools. Which means a history that includes the experiences of all Americans, regardless of race.

Who knows the work of Ernest Crichlow? Yet, he lives in New York City, in Brooklyn. There is also Herbert Gentry. His work is included in the show. He, too, is a New Yorker. "I was brought up in Harlem," he said. "When I grew up there, Harlem prepared you for a city like Paris. In Harlem, we liked people from the whole world, and the first place artists from the whole world wanted to visit was Harlem. Foreign languages were not strange to us, nor were different types of people." But in 1946, Gentry found the need to leave the New York he knew for Paris. The show, the book, "Paris Connections," and the opening tonight at the Cinque Gallery not only answer a lot of the why. They also shed needed light on another of the important stories not told.

Dexter Gordon

ON THE RADIO, WBGO from Newark is the jazz station that serves most of New York City. Like so many of the stations that feature jazz, WBGO struggles for the money it takes to stay in business. So as it turned out, on the day that Dexter Gordon's death was reported, WBGO (Jazz 88) was in the midst of a fund raising effort. But once Gordon's death was announced, WBGO asked for no more money. Instead, all that was left in the day was given to Dexter Gordon, the man and his music.

Dexter Gordon was a figure who stood larger than life. His talent as a tenor saxophonist was enormous. As a jazz musician, he wrote a huge chapter. His name stands right in the front line with Bird, Mingus, Parker, Monk, Coletrain, and so many others.

On a lot of summer nights he performed with the Jazzmobile when it was at Grant's Tomb. On those occasions, he was truly a prince of the city. The crowds would be enormous. No matter how many were there, when Dexter played, those who listened accorded him the kind of respect that was a way of acknowledging that he was one of the giants.

The nights with Dexter Gordon at Grant's Tomb are not the only ones that stick in the mind. Jazz is the American music. Almost all of its roots are here. Yet, in a city as large and as much a cultural center as New York, no major radio station in the city features jazz. But what New York does have are more clubs with jazz music than any city in America. Among those clubs, the Village Vanguard is among those that are special.

The Vanguard was one of the places Dexter Gordon played. The Vanguard is the classic jazz club. You go down a flight of steep steps into a dark, crowded, smoky place. For Dexter Gordon, it was the perfect place. When Dexter Gordon played there, he always appeared to be especially at ease.

Maybe it had to do with where he had come from, and where he had been. He was born in Los Angeles in 1923. By age 13, he was into music. He started with the clarinet, then moved on to the saxophone. He was among those who created the bebop style. He found what the long line of jazz greats were to discover -- which was that America had no great music halls reserved for them and their music. Jazz got relegated to clubs on a lot of ghetto streets. But it survived and grew. In time, it gained standing in the world. Dexter Gordon was a part of that. On a lot of streets, nobody knew his name. But in the jazz clubs, in places like the Village Vanguard in New York, he got his due. On the nights he was there, a kind of magic was in the room and all that too sticks in the mind

Another piece in the life of Dexter Gordon has to do with "the movie." He got the starring role in a film called "Round Midnight" that was released in 1986. He was so great that his performance won for him a nomination for the Academy Award as best actor. Later, it came out that he almost didn't get the job. His voice was deep and raspy and the fear was that on film, he would not be understood. As it turned out he was perfect in the role. But the film's appearance marked the start of questions from those who knew him: "Is Dexter alright?"

Some said that Dexter was playing himself in the movie. The role was built around the life of an aging jazz musician, a Black American, who was living the life of an expatriate in Paris. For nearly 15 years, he played the jazz clubs of Europe, and lived the life of the expatriate. That was the role he made in "Round Midnight." He played it to the hilt. Nobody questioned his nomination for the Academy Award. The questions about his health started then. And even then, the cancer was eating at his throat. He was hospitalized last month and two days ago, he died in Philadelphia. He was in his 68th year.

Miles Davis

WHEN NEWS CAME FROM CALIFORNIA reporting the death of Miles Davis, it was shocking, even though rumors of his serious illness had circulated for weeks.

As a man, his style, flair and famed wild side gave him a larger-than-life aura. He had 40 years at the center in music.

Miles Davis's talent was special, and then some. Maybe the best way it was ever put into words was the way it was done by the author, playwright and poet Amiri Baraka.

In the summer of 1985, a profile of Davis that Baraka wrote was published in the Sunday magazine of The New York Times.

"For many years of my life, Miles Davis was my ultimate cultural hero; artist, cool man, bad dude, hipster, clear as daylight and funky as revelation."

What Baraka captured in words was a feeling a whole generation had about Miles Davis. Not all of them were Black. Of course, he was special to Black people. But millions of all colors gravitated to Miles Davis's music.

He was born Miles Dewey Davis III, on the 25th of May, 1926, in a place called Calton, Ill. He grew up in East St. Louis. To say that a person is Black, and grew up in that town usually means that person's story has its roots in poverty.

Not Miles Davis.

He was the son of a well-to-do dentist. His father's father was affluent, too.

"When I graduated from high school, I was an A student, because I wasn't going to be caught dead in St. Louis," Davis told Lena Sherrod of New York in an interview for Essence magazine in 1984. "My mother said, 'now you'll go down to Fisk University with Dorothy (his only sister).' I said, 'no, no; not me. Is Dizzy down there?'"

Davis told Sherrod, "I made up my mind when I was 10 that I was going to be a musician." He said his father got the word from his high school instructor. "He told my father, 'don't expect Miles to be a doctor; he's got too much of that trumpet in him.'"

On his 13th birthday, Davis said his father bought him a trumpet.

He said his mother told his father, "Do you know your son is crazy?"

He said his father replied, "Well, just remember he's crazy, and don't mess with him."

Davis played his first job as a musician at age 16. "I used to watch people I liked. When guys would come to town, I watched the way they moved, the way they dressed and the way they talked. If they talked funny, and dressed funny, I knew they weren't going to be playing anything."

After high school, Miles Davis came to New York. He enrolled in the Julliard School of Music in September of 1944. At the school, he studied classical music, but at night, he took his trumpet to the clubs, and the music was jazz.

"Everything I've done, White people name it, not me," he said. "They name it so they can catalogue it. First it was cool. I was supposed to be so cool. I didn't say I was cool; they did."

"I develop music," he said. "I'm a stylist. I have that gift, and I know it. So whatever other musicians say about me doesn't matter, because I love music.

"If I can't add to it, I wouldn't be in it. I would just stop. I love music too much to spoil it."

In his time, Miles Davis launched many major musical changes. He developed "cool jazz" and "hard bob" and "electric fusion."

Miles Davis died last Saturday at a hospital in Santa Monica, Calif. He had suffered a stroke. Doctors said that death was caused by pneumonia. He was 65.

Dizzy Gillespie

THE SUNDAY AFTER THE ASSASSINATION of Dr. Martin Luther King Jr., Dizzy Gillespie took his horn, went to Atlanta, and sat in a pew in the front of Ebenezer Baptist Church.

It was "Daddy King" who called him to the pulpit. Dizzy took his horn with him. "This is what I know," he said. He lifted the trumpet with its trademark upsweep on the bell. As he began to play for the slain leader he so admired, as his cheeks ballooned, tears welled in his eyes. That was a side of Dizzy Gillespie too.

In the world of music, nobody questioned that Dizzy earned a place at the top. Giant, legend, genius, and master are the words people use to describe him But he was much more than that. He was truly a man of many sides. A lot of artists who make it to the top wind up as being very one-dimensional people. In that place where they use their talent, they shine. But to get to that place, they have to use a kind of tunnel vision that shuts out all else. Often, other facets of their lives become a horror and a shambles. It didn't happen that way with Dizzy, and that too was a part of his greatness.

His humor was legendary. In 1978, he played at the White House jazz festival organized by George Wein. Late that night on the White House lawn, then President Jimmy Carter came to the bandstand. Dizzy had written a song called "Salt Peanuts." Before his presidency, Carter was a peanut farmer. Along with the drummer Max Roach, Dizzy and the President sang his song.

Over the noise of applause, Dizzy said to the President: "I just want to know one thing: Can you go on the road with us?" Carter replied: "I might have to after tonight."

That was Dizzy. He was comfortable with anyone, even a President of the United States.

He was born John Birks Gillespie. One of his best-known compositions has the name, "Birks' Works." It has been said that Dizzy never studied music, that his was all natural talent. Of course, that was not true. Early on, he studied under Phillmore "Shorty" Hall at the Laurinberg Institute in North Carolina. His work reflected that. He was very technical. He was also an innovator and, along with the late Charlie "Yardbird" Parker, Dizzy was in the front line of those jazz musicians presiding over the progression of the music from the swing to the modern jazz era.

Dizzy Gillespie's music spanned six decades.

So many who wanted to be the best looked up to Dizzy Gillespie. He influenced not only trumpeters, but those the players of other instruments, and composers studied him as well.

On radio, all through yesterday on WBGO, the jazz station of New York out of Newark and on WKCR, the jazz station from Columbia University, they played no other music except that of the great Dizzy Gillespie. It is a kind of tradition. When one of the truly greats from the jazz world passes, they celebrate the life and the talent with sort of non stop concerts of their works.

The giants in the generations that shaped so much of the evolution of jazz music keep passing on. In that group, nobody was more special than Dizzy. The pictures of him stick in the mind. Dizzy Gillespie in those plaid pants with that odd shaped horn and those huge jowls doing his thing, which was making people happy and music great.

Dizzy Gillespie had one marriage. On the last anniversary, he and his wife celebrated being together for 52 years. It is said that he was never into dope, that he sought out and ate good foods, and he practiced his religion. He worked hard, often performing hundreds of concerts in a year. He lived to be 75 years old.

Billy Eckstine

HIS WAS ONE OF THE VOICES that identified the era. He was Billy Eckstine. As a singer, he reached such a high place, that he became known simply as Mr. B.

A year ago, at 77, he suffered a stroke. After that he went back to his roots, to Pennsylvania. On Monday, he died in Pittsburgh, which is where he was born.

For a lot of reasons, you have to stop and acknowledge Billy Eckstine. In the world, Americans are known for the music they create. Mr. B was a part of that. He was there with Dizzy Gillespie, Charlie Parker, Miles Davis, Earl "Fatha" Hines, Sarah Vaughan and the list goes on and on. They were all giants and they lasted. Mr. B's time at the top is measured in decades. Through the 40's, 50's, 60's and 70's, he was right there.

He put together a remarkable band that had a big ride. He was a trombonist in the era the piece of jazz known as be-bop was created. But there is no mistaking what made Billy Eckstine special. He knew how to sing a song.

There are many middle-aged persons who can mark the eras of their lives with Mr. B's songs.

He had, "I Apologize," "Skylark," and, "Jelly, Jelly."

There was "Stormy Monday Blue,." "Fools Rush In," and "My Foolish Heart."

Music plays a huge part in our lives. It gets us through so many of the rough places.

Billy Eckstine was involved with music almost all his life. My oldest brother, Raymond, went to school with Mr. B. That was before he had that name but even then he was singing. "And he was extraordinary even then," my brother recalled." They were students together at St. Paul Normal and Industrial School in Lawrenceville. My brother said that, in those days, Mr. B was the star singer with the school band.

He also had an eye for talent. He hired Sarah Vaughan as his vocalist, when he had his band. He had Dizzy in his group; Miles, Bird, Dexter Gordon and Art Blakey among others.

What you notice in that group now, is that they are all gone. Sarah, Dizzy, Miles, Bird, Dexter, and Blakey. What it means is that the book is closing on an era that represents a huge chapter in American music. They were more than just creative; their generation gets defined in terms of genius. The music they created mostly in Black clubs which is where they started out, now has standing in the world as something important and special.

Maybe no other male singer in that era had the kind of popularity he enjoyed. His was a voice so sweet, he had standing as a kind of king of the Black world. But his music stretched beyond race. He won popularity on all sides of town. When segregation barriers fell, he played the country's major nightclubs.

As the giants of that time pass away, one after another, it often gets asked, "What was it that created the spark that brought so much talent together and uncovered so much genius."

Maybe a part of it is that music and clubs were a big part of the era. That meant the opportunity was there. But also, maybe even segregation played a part; it kept so much talent together, and artists fed off each other. When Billy Eckstine put together his great band, he was asked how did he do it; how did he collect so much talent. His answer was that it was easy, because "we were all hanging out together." Segregation played a role in that.

Now, the book on that time made special is closing. So we stop to say farewell to Billy Eckstine. At the end, he went home to die. He was 78.

Eubie Blake

ALL THROUGH THE WEEK, everybody kept saying how incredible it was. Nobody wanted to believe that Eubie Blake was really 96 years old.

At 96, it's supposed to be over -- and for most people it is.

But, last week, there came Eubie Blake, showing everybody in the City of New York the proper way to grow old..

It was not what he did. He didn't have to perform. It wasn't what he said. Speeches were unnecessary. It was quite simply the style of the man.

There he was, smoking the cigarettes that he loves, one after the other, and as clean as he could be in a black suit that was tailor-made, and fit him like a glove.

They threw a big party for him downtown at Luchow's restaurant. All night, he sat there at a big table in the center of the room, having a ball. His doctor was there and he kept edging over to the table.

"You okay?" he asked Eubie.

"I'm fine." he said.

But George Liberman, the doctor, kept coming back and asking Eubie if he was all right and finally, Eubie reached up and pulled the doctor's ear down close.

"Listen" Eubie said, "you don't have to worry about me because I'm doing just fine."

He is a feisty, vibrant man, Eubie Blake is, and there is nothing that ever happened to him in his life that he does not remember. Nothing. He is as comfortable talking about 1889, when he wrote "Charleston Rag," as he is talking about something that happened last week.

"A fantastic memory," his doctor says. "And everything he says has got to be right because he tells those stories over and over, and they are always the same."

Eubie Blake comes out of Baltimore, the son of former slaves. Because of what he has done with the piano and ragtime music, most often now Eubie is referred to as a legend.

He has been writing and playing his music on the professional stage for 76 years. He has had five shows on Broadway, starting in 1921. His show, "Shuffle Along" was the first time Broadway ever had a show that was written, produced, directed and performed by Blacks.

Eubie is still on Broadway. He is not performing, but at the Ambassador Theater, his work is there. The marquee says "Eubie." Nothing more is needed.

But that show is only a sampling of the man's work. He has written more than 1,500 songs and yesterday, at 96, he was still going strong.

The secret? Always, Eubie Blake is asked what his secret is. He shrugs and laughs, and he says, "I wish I knew."

In New York City, more and more, the old people lock themselves up in their apartments. They sit there with television sets and empty lives.

Not Eubie. Early in the morning after the party at Luchow's, he was on a plane, flying off to Baltimore for the opening of "Eubie" in his hometown.

The other night, when everyone was asking him about retirement, he was busy talking with an Asian woman, telling her that he still had not given up on the idea of touring in Japan.

Eubie now lives out in Brooklyn, in the Bedford Stuyvesant district in a brownstone that is just across from the Bridge Street AME Church. He lives there with his second wife, Marion, who is also his business manager and agent.

The church across the street is much like Eubie. It is old and its history is rich. Today the congregation of the Bridge Street Church is celebrating its 213th anniversary.

The elders are proud to tell you that once the church was one of the most important stops on the underground railroad that runaway slaves used in the flight North to freedom.

In the church last week, they talked about their history and today's celebration. They talked also about Eubie.

It has been Eubie's neighborhood for nearly 35 years but Clifford Terry, a young man who grew up on Hancock St., which is just around the corner, has never met Eubie. He is 22 now and spends his mornings working as a mail clerk. But it is a life on the stage that he dreams of. He is an actor and singer and pianist and knows that Eubie could help. "But I never knew him," he said. "I never knew how big he was."

He was in senior high school when he found out. He had made the all-city high school choir and there was a concert at the Americana Hotel. Eubie was there and he was introduced. "I was shocked," Cliff Terry said the other day. "When I heard the applause, I knew he was somebody big. Imagine, there was a gold mine right around the corner from me and I didn't know it."

Art Blakey

IN THE WORLD OF MUSIC, jazz is the what this country put into the pot. A lot of the rhythm of this American music was supplied by Art Blakey. In the world of jazz music, he was about as big as it was possible to get. As a drummer and leader of his band, the Jazz Messengers, Blakey had 40 years at the top.

Go back in the lives of most of the jazz greats. The stories they tell are much the same as the one that comes from Art Blakey.

He was born in Pittsburgh. He came from a poor family and grew up in the hard times. As he was later to say, he never had a childhood where he came from. He had to go right into being a man.

From the beginning, in Oct. of 1919 in Pittsburgh, to the end, in St. Vincent's Hospital three days ago, Art Blakey cut a wide path. He had many interests and did many things. But what he accomplished as a musician elevated him to a place where he became known and respected virtually everywhere in the world.

The hard truth for jazz musicians, though, is that no matter how much they accomplish, no matter how high they rise, they often still wind up getting short shrift in their homeland. The American government beams jazz world wide, through Voice of America and the Armed Forces radio networks. As a result, most countries of the world are familiar with the jazz giants. But, in the U.S., there is a declining number of radio stations playing jazz. And many of these legends here are virtual unknowns.

Blakey told a story one afternoon not long ago when he was sitting on the steps of a building in midtown. His health was failing. Maybe he was tired; perhaps he had just sat for a moment to take in the sights of his city.

A journalist passing noticed the jazz great.

"Art Blakey," the journalist said. "What are you doing sitting out here?" The two joined in conversation. Soon, a security guard interrupted.

"You have to get off these steps," ordered the young Black man who was the guard.

"Don't you know who this is," the journalist said. "This is the great Art Blakey." The look on the guard's face said that he had no idea as to who Blakey was, or what made him great.

At that point, another passerby stopped. "Hey," he shouted, "aren't you Art Blakey?" As the man grabbed for Blakey's hand, the guard disappeared.

On the occasion of his 70th birthday, to honor Blakey, the decision at the WKCR, the Columbia jazz station, was to play all of Blakey's music. To do that took nine days. That's how much Art Blakey has contributed.

One of the best of New York's jazz clubs, Sweet Basil's , was Art Blakey's home base.

"He was here five or six times a year," Horst Liepolt, manager of the club,said yesterday as he remembered Art Blakey.

Just a week ago, Blakey's band was at Sweet Basil. "He (Art) wanted to come in; he was ready to play, but he was just too weak."

"What do you remember most about him?" Liepolt was asked.

"The kids," he said. "e always liked kids. He really did and the kids could feel it."

With his drumming, he became a different person; you could seeit in his face. It clearly was spiritual for him. When he played, he was like nobody else. And he swung like nobody else.

This year proved to be winter in the lives of so many jazz visionaries. Many have gone to seed. At 71, Art Blakey joins them.

Doc Cheatham

ALONG ABOUT 1 O'CLOCK in the morning they just up and forgot about the time. Doc Cheatham, a funny little grin on his face, jumped off the chair he had been using all night and started to sing about New Orleans. He put his horn under his right arm and, as the crowd encouraged him, be began to tap, and he stomped one foot.

When Ram Ramirez came through the door, and he saw what was happening, he started to holler.

"All right, good doctor," he yelled. "I said, all right."

Ramirez didn't even look for a seat. He headed straight for the bandstand. He was ready, but Keith Ingram was seated right down front, and he beat Ramirez to the piano. Al Hall, who was on bass, hollered and laughed. The handful of people who were there began to make real noise.

Doc Cheatham finished his song and then he took the trumpet from under his arm and from there on, in the little back room of The Ginger Man, at 1:30 in the morning, it was magical.

It could have gone on all night; it might have, too. But the waitresses wanted to go home.

"That's okay," Al Hall joked to Ram Ramirez. "We can catch you on Tuesday."

"At Carnegie Hall," someone else said.

"Carnegie Hall," Ramirez said.

This is the week that jazz comes to the forefront. In Carnegie Hall, in Avery Fisher Hall and in Town Hall, in all of the blue-chip places, the music this week is jazz. It's the one week of the year when it is jazz, the American music, back where it belongs. But it's only for a week.

In the afternoon yesterday, the jazz festival had its official opening. There were cameras and glitter. A big fuss was made. It was only a facade. Jazz is the American music, born and bred here, but still it has a hard time.

A year ago, I spent six weeks traveling in Africa. Each day I listened to broadcasts on American radio. The staple of those broadcasts was jazz. Jazz is the music that America sends abroad.

In New York, jazz isn't dead. On any weekend, there are at least 100 places in the city when jazz is played. But still, it is difficult for the jazz musician to survive.

"Yes, there might be 100 places that have jazz on the weekend," Al Hall concedes, "but the musician can't survive on part-time work. You're talking weekends and a lot of those places are lofts, and the musician isn't making any money. Not the kind of money that it takes to survive on. That's the thing."

In addition to his playing, Al Hall teaches. The jazz musician has to double up. It's a part of the economics of jazz.

"Look at Doc," Al Hall says of his friend Doc Cheatham. "He's legendary. He's truly great. And what is he now, 75, 76? And they're just discovering him. Only now."

It's a part of the way it is with jazz.

Ruth Brown

SHE SANG ONE SONG. When she finished with that, she took the microphone and moved closer to her audience. "I'm Ruth Brown," she said, and because it was her second introduction, she explained, "I want you to know exactly who Ruth Brown is." She used that as her way of getting around to telling her story.

In the mid-50s, her music was rhythm and blues. It was the rage then, and she was among the superstars who dominated at the top.

But that was nearly 30 years ago. Now -- an hour before midnight on Thanksgiving Eve as she stood in the spotlight at The Cookery --- Ruth Brown had no idea what the people seated around her knew. Being from the old school, she was taking no chances.

"Let me tell you who Ruth Brown is," she said. She mentioned her early records and the Atlantic label, and then she came forward to 1954. "That year, Ruth Brown held every title," she said. "It didn't matter, Ruth Brown was No. 1 on all of them...in Variety and Downbeat and Cashbox..she was No. 1 in all of them." Then she came back to now.

"They have me now in that category they call oldies but goodies," she said, and her audience laughed. "But tonight, when you leave here, I hope you say, she may be an oldie but she is still a goodie," and then she laughed.

Music. There is this something about music, the way it has of picking us up and carrying us through at various times in our lives. Music can do that. It is a powerful thing. Recall any good time and look back, and most often it's the music you remember first. If you came through the 50s, through the time that rhythm and blues ruled, then you know Ruth Brown.

When she looks back now, she calls that time "the most powerful music era that ever existed."

If you wonder where Ruth Brown has been since the 50s, listen to a part of her story. "I was just starting to believe that the time of Ruth Brown was over," she said. She was in Las Vegas. "I was doubling," she said, which meant she had two jobs. She was singing at one club and, at the same time, appearing at another in all-Black version of the show, "Guys and Dolls." While dashing from one job to another, she had a heart attack. "Take it easy," her doctor ordered after 17 days in the hospital. It was then that she joined a drama workshop, and that led her to taking a part in a show at a local playhouse in Las Vegas. The next thing that happened was that she got discovered by TV producer Norman Lear.

"You have potential for going comedy," Norman Lear said. Not long after that, Ruth Brown landed a part in one TV series, then another. Television brought her name back. "Is that the same Ruth Brown?" it was asked. She was coming back. Next she was invited to Japan to perform at a music festival in Tokyo.

After that she went to Sweden. It was more of the same. "They had a 17-piece orchestra for me and they had been rehearsing all of my songs. It was just incredible."

Everything is breaking right for Ruth Brown now. In California, she often works with her oldest son. Recently, she was reunited with her husband, Earl Swanson, a saxophonist. "We were married right at the high point of my career," she said. "We really didn't have a chance back then."

Rhythm and blues is music that means drums and horns. But at The Cookery, the backup group that Ruth Brown has is piano and bass and guitar. But she is a pro and understands how you make do. So yesterday, on Thanksgiving, she did not mind working. "My sister lives in Long Island, and on Sunday my people are driving up from Virginia and we'll have our Thanksgiving then," she said. Last night, she sang.

"...You made me leave my happy home, took my love and now you've gone...love brings such misery and pain, I guess I'll never be the same...

"Well it's too bad and it's too sad but I'm still in love with you..."

It was vintage Ruth Brown, a woman and her music.

Moms Mabley

AT THE END, SHE HAD some nice shots on television, but her best work was done in the theater. It is still that way with a lot of comedians because the theater gives them the room they need to let their imaginations run.

Her imagination was something special. Moms Mabley was the name she used and, in every way, she was an original. She had a style, a voice, and a way that was all her own.

Through a good many years, she was a star in what was called the chittlin' circuit. In segregated America, this was the string of theaters played by entertainers who were Black. One of the most famous of those places was the Apollo Theater in Harlem. Moms Mabley played there even in her later years, even after she was discovered by television.

The thing Moms Mabley could do best was make people laugh at themselves. She would take things people would say or do, and twist them in her special way to make the words or the deeds so outrageous that laughing was the only thing you could do. It was that way one night at the Apollo when she was getting on Black folks for talkin' about the good ol' days.

"Yes," she roared in that craggy old voice, "we got these people walkin' round here talkin' bout the good ol' days."

She put a hand on her hip and paused, which was her timing. "Now when you ever had it this good?" she said. "The good ol' days is now."

She looked back in history and remembered the way things were. "And you got these people runnin' round here talkin' bout the good ol' days."

She was beautiful, Moms Mabley was, and her style and wit come back now because yesterday, on the Tuesday in October that is special because it's World Series Day, the talk was of the good ol' days.

It was of the time when the baseball games were played in the gold of October sun and the pictures were mostly the ones that formed in the mind from the words of a Red Barber or a Mel Allen. Nostalgia? No doubt about it. The good ol' days? Well, it may be the way that Moms Mabley said, which is that these are the good ol' days.

There is no argument against the October sun. October is the best of times and, when the sun is right, these are afternoons made for the ballpark and baseball.

There is no problem with the radio either. The only complaint with radio now is that too much of it is just music which only scratches the surface. When used properly, radio makes us listen, which helps us learn, which is something we need more of nowadays.

In the good ol' days of now, we have television. No matter how perfect the words that Red Barber and Mel Allen used, they could not make pictures the way television does. When the cameras are pointed at a play on the ballfield and capture all of the action, it is magic. There is no other word to describe it, and that alone is enough to make now the good ol' days. The people who run television understand the importance of October sun. But they also understand ratings and, between the two, the sun loses even when it is October gold.

Yes, Moms Mabley had it right. The good ol' days are now.

Yesterday, in the mountains of Pennsylvania, a guy they call Joey C. came walking down the street and, on the October day the World Series begins, he had on red pants, a red shirt, a red jacket and a red baseball cap.

Joey C. is a Phillies man, and he said, "I'm not taking this off until the World Series is over." It was beautiful. It was right out of the good ol' days, which are now.

Eddie Murphy

HE'S FUNNY ALL RIGHT. Nobody says he's not funny. But funny is not the issue with Eddie Murphy.

It's just that with him, nothing is sacred. He'll take anything and use it for a laugh. He puts everything on the table. That's a part of what makes his humor so . . different?

It is definitely different.

Dangerous?

It depends upon the way you look at it. But yes, some say it is dangerous to start laughing at the wrong thing.

Touchy?

No question. At times, the humor of Eddie Murphy is definitely touchy. "I don't like a lot of things that he does," said a woman I know. "But he's so funny, I have to laugh in spite of myself."

She mentioned the "ho-de-doh" joke Murphy tells.

"What has eight legs, runs and makes the sound ho-de-doh, ho-de-doh?"

"What?"

"Four Black guys running for the subway."

Humor. It has always been a tricky thing to deal with. What makes some people laugh does not strike some others as being funny at all. It depends upon whom we're laughing at.

The woman who didn't like the "ho-de-doh" joke was a Black woman. She told me that one day she was sitting on the train. Just as it was about to leave the station, there was commotion and then she heard the shouts:

"Ho-de-doh, ho-de-doh!"

On Saturday night, Eddie Murphy, who has to be the hottest comic there is this side of Richard Pryor, was at the club called the Comic Strip. An hour before showtime, the place was packed.

Murphy came in an hour late. It didn't matter. He was still right on time. He was on stage better than an hour. In that time he dealt with everything. When he was done, big applause was raised. There was another crowd outside waiting to get in that was as big as the crowd that saw the first show.

It's not the old chittlin' circuit that Eddie Murphy plays, which is also a part of what makes his whole thing so . . . touchy?

Definitely touchy.

On the chittlin circuit, where Moms Mabley and Pigmeat Markham were stars, everything was Black. The clubs were Black, the performers were Black and the audiences were Black. Most of The Comic Strip audience was White.

Humor.

It's always risky. A part of it is because humor deals on the edge. Slide whatever it is that is funny just a bit in any direction, and you have tragedy, or sickness, or ignorance.

But we must laugh. The hardest part is laughing at ourselves.

On the East Side, Eddie Murphy did one of his takeoffs on Stevie Wonder. With it he did a bit about how "the brothers" lecture him on using Stevie in his humor. The piece was funny, and a part of the reason it was is that it had truth in it. I am certain that Eddie Murphy does catch a lot of hell about making Stevie Wonder the subject of his jokes.

In the club, laughter rose. There was laughter when he did jokes about homosexuals. But something of a quiet came into the room when AIDS, the deadly syndrome, was a part of the joke.

Of Eddie Murphy, it could be said that he offends without regard to race, color, creed or sexual preference.

The thing is, can we take it?

I've heard Blacks say they do not like Murphy using Black stereotypes before mixed audiences, which is what he always plays. "Because when the laughter dies, the image is still there," is the explanation.

Eddie Murphy is not another Richard Pryor. He is Eddie Murphy. There has never been another one quite like him. Not a Black comedian anyhow. He even does a bit on Elvis, and it gets over.

It's because he's not political. It's because he's everyman.

He came onto the stage at The Comic Strip wearing designer jeans, and a leather vest that was black and open to his navel.

"This is my homo suit," he said, and he was off and never looked back.

It is said he is at The Comic Strip on weekends now trying out material in preparation for a tour he has coming up next month. He also has another movie out, this one called "Trading Places." It is not as good as "48 Hrs." I thought Eddie Murphy should have gotten the Academy Award, at least a nomination, for his role in "48 Hrs." But he has time. He is just 22. It's a neat trick the way he goes about doing what he does, which is being funny. He breaks new ground while walking on a precipice. And, he's funny all right.

Richard Pryor

AT THE HOSPITAL out in Los Angeles, Gary Swaye couldn't get off the phone. "I don't know where this stuff gets started," he said. "All I can tell you is that it isn't true.'

By "this stuff," Swaye, who is a spokesman for the Sherman Oaks Community Hospital in Los Angeles, meant the reports circulating yesterday that comedian Richard Pryor was near death.

"Is he worse?" Swaye was asked.

"There has been no worsening of his condition," he replied.

"Is there any improvement?"

"There hasn't been any improvement either," he said.

"How is he then?"

"He's in good spirits. Right now, he's out taking his daily exercise. Does that sound like a man who is near death?"

"Exercise?"

"He exercises every day. That's what he's doing right now. But this exercise now is mostly just walking. He walks in the hall, whenever he's able."

"You said he was in good spirits. What does that mean?"

"Well, they've just put a special television hookup in his room so he can watch the Duran-Sugar Ray Leonard fight today. Marlon Brando made the arrangements to have it installed. Richard is looking forward to watching the fight. He's in good spirits today, and he'll be watching the fight."

It has been 12 days since Richard Pryor suffered burns over 50 percent of his body in an explosion at his home. Just how the explosion occurred is still a matter of debate. First it was said that he was preparing a mixture of cocaine and ether, known as freebase, and that the explosion occurred when he attempted to light the mixture.

The report that freebase was the cause came from the police. But later a spokesman for Pryor denied that and said that the comedian was injured when a rum drink caught fire when he was attempting to light a cigarette.

Whatever the cause, the one thing that is certain is that Pryor was critically injured. On the day after it happened, his doctors gave him one chance of three of recovery.

Yesterday, from the Sherman Oaks Community Hospital, Dr. Richard Grossman said Pryor was still in critical condition. "He is very, very ill," Dr. Grossman said. "I cannot over stress the seriousness of Mr. Pryor's injuries." Dr. Grossman said also that he was "very concerned" with complications that have developed, including pneumonia, which has created problems with Pryor's breathing. As a result of the complications, Dr. Grossman said that surgery that was planned for yesterday had been put off until Monday.

After word that Pryor was near death circulated yesterday, Swaye said that so many calls came into the hospital that the switchboard was backed up for hours.

"It was amazing," he said.

"And you know, ever since Richard has been here, he has been receiving something like a thousand pieces of mail every day."

At the hospital yesterday, Jim Brown, the former football player turned actor, was at Pryor's bedside. Every day since the accident, Brown has been with his friend Pryor at the hospital.

"Of course he's in good spirits today," Jim Brown said over the telephone. "He's really looking forward to the fight. He has been talking about it a lot, and it has him really excited. And a lot of friends are coming over. Brando's coming and Redd Foxx and Sammy (Davis). Andy (Young) called. The response has been fantastic. I read some telegrams to him this morning. He gets a kick out of it."

"How is he taking it?" Brown was asked.

"Richard is amazing. When he takes his walks, he's out there putting the nurses on. He comes up with some funny things. But other times he won't talk to you. It's a tough, painful ordeal. Every minute there is pain. That's the toughest part. There is always pain. It's just a day-to-day fight. It's not a matter of being close to death but there is always the danger of infection. Today, though, is no different than four days ago. But being close to death, that's not correct."

"Was his face badly burned?"

"His face to me looks good. He looks like himself. In my opinion he should come out of this thing. But, like I said, that's my opinion, but I see him every day and I keep in close contact with the doctors and his family. Yes, he's critical, but basically he's stable. It's just that his body has to work overtime, and consequently, there's danger in just about any kind of contact."

Richard Pryor is 39 now. It has been said that he is to comedy what Malcolm X was to social and political life. He has that certain quality that links him to the street, although he is recognized as a genius among the country's comedians.

He is part actor, part performer and part writer.

"I like him because he's so uncivilized," an admirer was saying yesterday. "His humor is so way out there. He is one of a kind."

Richard Pryor is an original. But his has been a troubled life. Six years ago, he was jailed and put on three years probation because of his failure to file federal income tax returns. Two years ago New Year's Day, he was involved in an altercation with two friends of his former wife. He pleaded guilty to misdemeanor charges and was fined $200.

But still Richard Pryor worked. Twice he won Emmy Awards. The brilliance of his writing was evident in the award-winning Mel Brooks film, "Blazing Saddles." He has starring roles in two new films, "Stir Crazy" and "Holy Moses."

"He's amazing," people who know say. It's because he is real. You listen to Richard Pryor and you come away amazed at the realness in all that he does. There is nothing phony, nothing contrived. He is a single copy, and yesterday when the word circulated that he was near death, well, had Richard Pryor heard it, he would have twisted his face the way he does and cocked his head to one side. As always, he would have known exactly what to say.

Sammy Davis, Jr.

MAYBE THE MOST DIFFICULT book to write is the autobiography. For Sammy Davis Jr., it was easy. He just pulled all the covers back and put it all down on paper, both the bitter and sweet.

The book was published in 1965. He called it, "Yes I Can." The name was perfect, for in his life, it seemed there was nothing that he couldn't do.

He was born in 1925. To understand how close to the bottom he was at the start, go back to the first page of his autobiography. He wrote:

"I was born in Harlem on Dec. 8, 1925. My father was the lead dancer in Will Mastin's Holiday in Dixieland, a vaudeville troupe in which my mother, Elvera "Baby" Sanchez, was a top chorus girl. Good jobs were scarce, so she remained in the line until two weeks before I was born. Then, as soon as she was able to dance, she boarded me with friends in Brooklyn, and continued on the road with my father and the show."

In a lot of lives, that would have been the end right there. In 1925, though, it was different. So many doors were closed to Blacks then; it was an altogether different America. Blacks did have strong families to lean on. They didn't have much money. They had to scrimp and use a ton of ingenuity just to get by. But so many of those families had standards and values. They were always striving especially to help the kids get to a higher place. So in the very paragraph, Sammy wrote:

"My grandmother, Rosa B. Davis, came out from Harlem to see me and wrote to my father, 'I never saw a dirtier child in my life. They leave Sammy alone all day so I've taken him with me. I'm going to make a home for that child.'"

That is what a ton of kids now don't have, that someone to take them at an early age when there is nobody else.

The way Sammy tells the story, his grandmother gave him the good early years he needed. After that, his father came back and got him and took him on the road. He was not yet 3 years old, but that was the start. By 4, he was on stage and from there, what he went on to accomplish, put him into a category by himself.

It wasn't that he was so great as a singer, a dancer or an actor, although he was very good at all those things. What made him great was that he was the consummate entertainer. Nobody who ever saw him perform came away disappointed. It had to do with his bringing up. He was on the road with his father, and on stage before he was old enough by law. He never had any formal schooling. But that didn't mean he didn't get an education. Early on, he got it drilled into him to be the best that he could be all of the time. He heard that, and he never forgot. "Even if there's just one person in the audience, you must be the best you can be," his uncle, Will Mastin, told him.

In those times, that's what Blacks told their kids; be the best that you can be. "Be twice as good," they would say. It was their way of preparing the young for the time they faced. Sammy went out to make it big in segregated America. In his book, he told of how many ways he got humiliated in the Army, merely because he was Black. He didn't get bitter though; he climbed above it. It was while Sammy was a soldier that, for the first time, he read a book. But once he started, he read everything he could lay his hands on, Shakespeare included.

Some people have a few years of being a public figure. Sammy had a lifetime in the bright light.

Everybody saw all sides in his life, the bitter and the sweet. they saw him go through bad marriages. They saw him fight gambling, booze and cigarettes. Everybody saw the love and compassion that was a central part of his life. He broke with Blacks to back Nixon in his 1968 campaign for the presidency. But, in the entertainment world, he was as much a trailblazer for Black America as Jackie Robinson. He broke the color line that kept Blacks out of casinos in Las Vegas. He forced clubs all over the country to integrate because, once he could demand it, he refused to perform to segregated audiences. He was an early and very big supporter of Martin Luther King Jr. and civil rights causes.

Sammy. He was one of kind: tiny in size, but huge in talent. "The Candy Man," he called himself.

James Brown

WHAT IS ABOUT TO HAPPEN to James Brown amounts to a humdinger of a Christmas story.

"Which James Brown?"

"The one who has standing as the Godfather of Soul."

For James Brown, the name is not a gimmick. It's a title that he got the old fashioned way -- he earned it.

This Christmas brings him a piece of recognition he rightly deserves. To put an award in the hands of James Brown and say that it is for a song or even an album could only mean so much. He already has what must be trunks bulging with that kind of recognition.

In the world of music, James Brown is a giant. In his field, he is up there on a place so high that only a special few reach those heights. So with James Brown, an award that means something has to take a broader stroke. And that is exactly what is about to happen.

The American Music Awards are the top of the line. Among those awards, the Award of Merit is special and next month, in recognition of his lifetime contributions to music, that is the honor to be bestowed on James Brown.

The inscription on his award -- in James Brown's words -- "say it loud" is what the man and his music have been about.

"When this unique artist exploded on the scene, his energy and originality captured the music public and inspired so many of his fellow artists. Now, over three decades later, the Godfather of Soul continues to excite the world with his vibrant performances."

On stage, James Brown did it all. He gave definition to the word, "entertainer." He had the whole package. He was moon walking before Michael Jackson was born. With his energy and excitement, he made a song explode.

"Pappa's got a brand new bag."

He could be political.

"Say it loud, I'm Black and I'm proud."

He could send women into tomorrow.

"Please, please, please, please...."

And he could send women into rage.

"It's a man's world."

When he was on his high cycle, he had it all. At a theater such as the Apollo in Harlem, which he played when the Apollo was the place, you did not need to see his name on the marquee to know that he was there with his band, the Famous Flames. When James Brown was the attraction, the lines of those waiting to get inside seemed to wrap around the block four times.

Sammy Davis Jr. had standing as being the hardest working entertainer. If Sammy was first, James Brown could not have been more than a whisper behind. He was constant motion, and not just jumping up and down. Imitators are still trying to figure out the dances he did. At the end of a show, he collapsed on stage. His aides would come out and wrap him in a cape, virtually carrying him away. While the crowd was still roaring, he would always throw off the cape, escape the grip, and return for an encore -- doing the dances that only James Brown could do.

Of him, it could truly be said that he was legend in his own time. He carried so much influence, especially among Blacks, that when riots erupted in the nation's capital after the King assassination, then Vice President Hubert Humphrey sought his help to cool an uprising that eventually required federal troops to put down.

In the words of the poet Langston Hughes, though, James Brown's, life recently, "ain't been no crystal stair."

James Brown had his private hell. He admits to getting hooked on drugs. He went so far out of control, he wound up in prison in South Carolina, where there is no easy prison time. A domestic dispute ended with Brown being accused of trying to run down and kill two cops with his car . When convicted, he was sentenced to do hard time.

He did it, and as soon as that was behind him, he was in New York and launched right back into his career. At times, it gets said that America no longer produces anything. That is not true; music is an American product sought after all over the world. And James Brown was among the originals who created the demand.

This Christmas brings word that he will now follow such giants as Bing Crosby, Ella Fitzgerald, Irving Berlin, Stevie Wonder and Elvis Presley as a recipient of the Award of Merit. For what he has done, James Brown is a perfect fit in that kind of company.

Sidney Poitier

THE REUNION COMES at a perfect time. It stands as a huge reminder of what was, and, in a way, points a direction towards what could be. It has to do with opportunity.

All this goes back to the 1960s and the days when riots swept through a lot of American cities and had a lot of people grappling with the "what do we do" side of the problem.

Included in that group was Sidney Poitier. He was not just the most visible Black actor in the country. He was moving into positions of influence in Hollywood that previously had been closed to minorities. In 1968, among other things, Poitier was a member of the board of trustees of the American Film Institute (AFI). That put him in a position to give meaning to some of his ideas.

Poitier was good with words, and a speech he made to the AFI trustees led to a breakthrough moment. Poitier told of the huge numbers of young people in the cities, in Appalachia, and in Native American communities in the country, who had loads of talent and no opportunities. He outlined to the AFI board the way it could use its clout and resources to open a big door. Poitier's idea was get young people of talent, give them training in all of the aspects of film making, and then organize a way to place those trainees in jobs.

Out of that came the existence of the Community Film Workshop Council (CFWC), and later, Third World Cinema Productions (TWC) and the Institute of New Cinema Artists (INCA). Through the next 18 years, what those groups were to accomplish changed the personnel complexion in a lot of television studios, on a lot of movie sets, and eventually the ownership of some media properties.

A part of the reason it happened had to do with the "yes we can" environment of the 1960s. Even the federal government then was a partner in many of the projects. Through the war on poverty, the government supplied stipends for trainees; not much money was involved, but enough to keep a young person alive while getting the training that led to a career.

What did all of it accomplish? Just the venture Poitier opened the door for led to some 1,500 young people getting started in a career. The three organizations started back in the 1960s have since merged into the International Communications Association (ICA), headed by Cliff Frazier. The ICA convenes what it calls Reunion 2000 starting today at the Sheraton Hotel in Manhattan. Frazier, now president of ICA, was the first executive director of the Community Film Workshop Council which came out of Poitier's speech to the AFI board.

"Through the years, we have planted seeds that have become strong solid oaks and flowers of great variety," he said. "We smile upon their immense beauty and celebrate their great accomplishments."

Some 150 former trainees have signed up for the conference that runs through the weekend. Where are they now? The list reads like this: James McIver, editor, ABC-TV, Washington; Philip Harris, photojournalist, WITI-TV, Milwaukee; Linda Yearwood, writer, Fox Television, Los Angeles; Carl Clay, executive producer, Black Spectrum Theater, New York; Lisa Calderon, camera operator, Unitel Video, New York; Mort Hill, program director, Double Helix Media Center, St. Louis.

That's only a small part of what happened and it did because of the will that was there in the 1960s to "do something" about the problems that were. This was not the only such project. In newspaper journalism, a similar venture was undertaken and the results are much the same. That effort was the brainchild of Columbia University professor Fred Friendly. His idea led to what was called The Summer Program for Minority Journalists.

Friendly was a former head of CBS News and he was spurred to action after the publication of the Kerner Commission Report.

After the 1960s riots, the Kerner Commission was appointed by then President Lyndon Johnson. The commission found the news media to be a part of the problem. It was accused of reporting the news mainly through the White man's eyes only. The reason was that most newspapers had no minorities on their staffs. Media executives talked of wanting to hire minorities, but said they could not find anybody qualified. Friendly picked up on that at Columbia, creating the summer program that trained young people through an 11-week summer program for careers in journalism. That program, which still exists, also has a list of graduates that reads much like the one from the program Poitier conceived.

The Reunion 2000 is not to be just a get together to talk of old times. Rather, it deals with the "where do we go from here" strategy in widening opportunity. But 1992 is not 1968. The environment that said yes to ideas in the '60s, does not exist anymore. Jobs are harder to come by, and the federal government has turned its back on building hope at the bottom. So the convention has a big agenda; it has to create a way for rekindling a "yes we can" environment which is sorely needed if good ideas are to mean anything.

Moses Gunn

WHAT A FACE HE HAD. What an actor he was. And that name. That was something else too, wasn't it?

Moses Gunn. On him, it was a perfect fit.

He was my man. I loved Moses Gunn. It wasn't just that he was a great actor. He was, but he was also much more.

So much of the time, when a person excels in one area, so many of the other pieces of that person's life seem to be in shambles.

Not Moses Gunn. He was a renaissance man. He could do it all.

On the movie screen, he was fabulous. On stage, he could be electric.

He was nominated for an Oscar for his role in the film, "Ragtime," and he won a number of Obie Awards for his work on the stage.

He appeared in classics; was on television in Alex Haley's "Roots." In his craft, he excelled. And there was more.

He raised a family. He was a founder of the Negro Ensemble Company. He taught at the college level.

As the picture fills in, what you see with Moses Gunn is an extraordinary man who made the most of the time he had.

He was born in St. Louis, the oldest of seven children. His mother died when he was 12. He had the kind of start a lot of people don't survive.

Then you get to the matter of race.

Moses Gunn was an African American. A half century ago, when he was striking out on his own, America was a much different place. The military was segregated; few Blacks could vote; and it would be another five years before Jackie Robinson would break in with the Dodgers.

When you look back, you ask: What got Moses Gunn through? What did he have going?

Maybe it was this: He had strong identification with Black colleges. He went to college at Tennessee State University in Nashville, where he majored in speech and drama. Later he did some teaching at Grambling College in Louisiana.

It doesn't get said much, but when you look closely, an astonishing amount of talent came through the Black college system.

Start that count with Martin Luther King Jr. Then add almost the entire leadership Blacks have had in the last 30 years. Moses Gunn was part of that, too.

He was also lucky. When his mother died, he went to live with a woman who was an English teacher. Maybe that was something his mother had put into place. Maybe she made it happen that way for him. But he wasn't alone, fending for himself as a kid too young to know the way.

What Moses Gunn did with his life did not go unnoticed.

As an actor, his work was widely acclaimed. What he did with the rest of his life was part of the reason the NAACP put one of its highest awards in his hands a decade ago. He was given an Image Award, and that is about the kind of person you are, and what you give back to those struggling to get through.

Just look at the Negro Ensemble Company. All that it has meant for so many through the years. The Negro Ensemble provided a good place for a lot of talent when just finding a place to practice your craft took some doing.

The death of Moses Gunn did not come entirely as a surprise. He had been in failing health for some time. Still, 64 years is not a lot. If he was waiting until he was 65 to file for Social Security, he wound up like a lot of Black men. He didn't live long enough.

You do not look at the life of Moses Gunn, though, and see it as a sad story. His was a life to be celebrated. He started from far back, and yet he rose to make himself a role model.

His is another story of what you can do when you are prepared, and ready to work.

So in this holiday season, say goodbye to Moses Gunn. See that face; remember what he did with the talent in his life. Then smile for this man.

He made himself great, and he did it against the odds.

Ben Vereen

HE NEVER LIKED THE IDEA of a sequel. When he was asked, right away, Ben Vereen said no, he did not want any part of "Roots 2."

At the time, it seemed odd because the original televised version of "Roots" brought special acclaim for Vereen, who played the role of Chicken George. Not only that, the eight-part series that was shown in January of 1977 was seen by more people than any other program in the history of television.

The sequel promised to bring the kind of exposure that every actor wants. But Ben Vereen had his reasons for walking away.

" 'Roots' " he explained, "is too important to saturate. It should be left alone. It's a classic, so therefore I have no desire to do Part 2."

They made the sequel without Ben Vereen. Every night now, the series comes across on television. The early ratings are good. They are not the sensational figures that "Roots" brought in the winter of 1977. When you watch "Roots" now, you notice early that something is different; that the story is not the same.

"It seems to be getting Whiter and Whiter," a friend said after Monday night's episode.

In the winter of 1977 during the original showing, there was a habit that developed among Blacks. It seemed that just about everybody, at the conclusion of the nightly episode, dashed to the phone to call a friend.

"What did you think?" was always the question.

Then the only problem was finding the word to describe an experience that was so overwhelming. Now the question is not so easily answered.

In 1977, in one of those telephone calls just after the show, a friend said that what made "Roots" so different for him was that it was the first time he had ever seen a major show on television where the Whites were in the background. It was the first time where a show focused so completely and thoroughly on the Black experience.

On Monday night it began to become clear how "Roots" has changed. Its focus is no longer solely on the saga of a family -- or the ancestors of Alex Haley. It seems now it's Henry Fonda's story. The story of an aging colonel who is White, and the problems that rise in his family. It's a good story. But it's not "Roots."

"It looked like scenes from 'Gone With the Wind,'" one caller said after watching Monday night's sequence.

"From what I've seen so far," another caller said, "it seems as though they don't think the story of Haley's ancestors can carry the show."

The shift of focus has not gone unnoticed. Alex Haley's family, and the story they have to tell, have become a background fill for high-powered actors. What is left is another story of Black people in the old South. The show's ratings decline in the second half of the nightly episodes.

"Roots," the book that was written by Alex Haley, was something different. When it was published, Haley says, it hit with a force that was beyond his wildest dreams. He said that it was as though it was shot out of a cannon. In the time that it takes the best of books to reach the best-seller list, "Roots" became a legend.

But television now seems to have forgotten what made "Roots" special. It was not just another story of slavery. It was Alex Haley's story. It was the story of his ancestors, down through seven generations. It was a story that bridged the gap, driving back from a small town in Tennessee to Black Africa. It was a story so compelling that it touched everyone it reached.

And it was the way that the story was told. It was given to us through the eyes of Haley's ancestors. The story had never been told that way. Not ever, and that was what television had in the winter of 1977. That was a part of what kept us glued to our television sets then. It seems as though the sequel is about something else, about stars, ratings and commercials that cost more than $200,000 a minute.

Yesterday, the thought was of Alex Haley, the man who gave "Roots" to us. Haley now says that he is finished as an author. Before "Roots," Haley wrote "The Autobiography of Malcolm X." It is seldom that any author can deliver, back to back, two books of that caliber. But Haley did.

The last time Haley was in New York was in the middle of December, when fall was still lingering here. How warm it was then. Haley enjoyed none of it. He was then locked in a lawsuit, having been accused of copyright infringement. The word is plagiarism. He was accused of lifting portions of his book, of "Roots," from another writer's work. Haley denied it. After agonizing consideration, finally, he settled out of court. There were some paragraphs that appeared in "Roots" that were too similar to those that appeared in an obscure novel call "The African." Haley paid off.

But "Roots" was his story. It belongs to him. It was not something that could be lifted.

What the argument in court was about was background. It had nothing to do with the central story. It was largely filler. The story that is "Roots" is the story of generations in one family, and that cannot be stolen. There is only one story. That is what the version of "Roots" we are seeing now on television misses. It forgets that it is Alex Haley's story.

James Van Der Zee

AT THE END, the final remarkable chapter in his life was no different. He had a magic moment in the sun. Then it turned the other way. It was always that way in his life, the bitter pushing in on the sweet.

In the afternoon on Saturday, he was in Washington at the graduation ceremonies at Howard University. He was awarded an honorary doctorate in humane letters. It had been a perfect day. In the afternoon, as the citation for him was being read, the big crowd that was there stood. Applause began to rise. The last words that came from the president of the university were lost.

He would have been 97 in June. Age had put him in a wheelchair. But on the campus of Howard University, he pulled himself to his feet. He stood to accept the acclaim and the degree. It was, perhaps, the finest hour in the remarkable life of James Van Der Zee.

He could not shake his destiny, though, so it did not end there. By night he was ill. By 1 o'clock in the morning he was hospitalized. At 2:30 a.m. he was dead.

He was perhaps the most famous Black photographer ever. He had in his collection over 125,000 prints, negatives, plates and transparencies. He did all of his work in Harlem.

He had by 1969 close to 69 years of pictures from Harlem. He had faces, funerals, rallies and buildings. He had Father Divine and Adam Clayton Powell Jr. There was Marcus Garvey and Bojangles Robinson. He had them all, rooms filled with pictures and negatives. He was 83 years old when he was discovered.

It happened quite by accident. The Metropolitan Museum of Art was putting together a show of Harlem. "Harlem on My Mind," it was called. That was how it happened that Reginald McGhee stumbled onto James Van Der Zee. McGhee was working for the museum, helping to put the show together. So he was scouring around in Harlem.

"When he hit my place, it seemed as if he hit a gold mine," Van Der Zee was to say later.

The show the museum put together never received much acclaim. It was an idea that didn't work. But for Van Der Zee, it changed his life. It took him out of the obscurity where he had worked, and made him a star. His pictures were shown at the finest galleries. Publishers wanted his work. Books were made. Suddenly, he was an overnight sensation.

The bitter, though, always followed the sweet for him. In 1969 it was that way too. He had a brownstone in Harlem where he lived with his wife. His studio was there too. At the moment his work was being acclaimed at the museum, he was evicted from his home and his treasure -- his photographs -- was carted away by a city marshal. He lost a dispute concerning his mortgage. It cost him his home. "It is the highest time and the lowest time," he said.

The newspapers had stories of what happened and an institute was created just for his work. It opened on E. 125th St. and it looked good for him again, but then the money ran out. His collection moved to the Metropolitan for a while. Then it was placed in one of the leading Black cultural institutions, the Studio Museum in Harlem. His collection was given to the Studio Museum but later, Van Der Zee, who had no sufficient income, wanted the collection returned. Again, the bitter followed the sweet, and he found himself bringing a lawsuit against the museum to regain possession of his collection.

By yesterday, when he died, the lawsuit was still unsettled. But Van Der Zee went out with the one thing that he could not lose, which was the acclaim that his life's work brought. He was born in Lenox, Mass., in 1886.

"My mother and father were maid and butler to General Grant," he once told a reporter. "I didn't think much of it when I was young. Now there are so many questions I wish I'd asked them about that."

In the interview, he spoke of his first wife. There was the tinge of the bitter and the sweet in his words.

"My first wife thought I was a pretty smart fellow when she married me, but then as she got herself some education, I started getting dumber and dumber to her. Once she said something about my parents. I told her, "They didn't pick them out for the general because they were the dumbest Negroes they could find."

He started out with photography at an early age.

"I got my first camera when I was 12 years old," he said. "I won it as a premium for selling perfume. I kept running to the express office to see whether the thing was coming in a box or a barrel. One day it came. My heart began pumping and beating and my eyes began popping, and I was astonished and amazed when I saw it. The camera was a little thing about 2 1/2 inches by 2 1/2 by 4 inches."

He had two children by his first wife but both died -- a daughter when she was 15, and a son who did not live to a year. His life was filled with twists and turns. But he worked. He always worked. When the acclaim finally came for him, he had given his collection away. When he died, he had needed public assistance to keep going.

"It's a hard job to get the camera to see it like you see it," he once said of his work. "Sometimes you have it just the way you want it, and then you look in the camera and you don't have the balance. The main thing is to get the camera to see it the way you see it."

The life that he saw though his camera is recorded in a huge collection that is in the Studio Museum. That is the legacy of James Van Der Zee, whose life was a mixture of the sweet and the bitter.

He was 96.

Spike Lee

NOT IN A LONG TIME -- in fact, rarely in the history of motion pictures -- has a film come to the screen with the kind of buildup that preceded the move, "Malcolm X."

Attention has been called to this film in a thousand ways. For a while, it seemed impossible for Spike Lee to come anywhere close to delivering on all that has been promised. But he does it.

It may not be a perfect movie, if there is such a thing. It is more than a bit too long. Critics will surely find more to quibble with in their reviews. But all that really doesn't matter. The film is a huge piece of compelling history that comes from the places where Hollywood never goes.

This is the sixth movie to come from the film maker Spike Lee. If he never does anything else, let it be said that with "Malcolm X," he did the right thing.

It is one thing to make a movie in the quiet atmosphere that film makers usually enjoy. That quiet never existed for Spike Lee. Even before he took over the project, controversy had swirled around the idea. The moment he entered the picture, it was heightened. There were so many questions, all of them legitimate. Would he capture the man, the time and the message? How would he deal with the Nation of Islam? The questions kept coming.

Spike Lee contributed to the climate of controversy. He took a lot of hits for that. As T-shirts, baseball caps, sweaters, jackets and even gowns with the prominent "X" began to surface, the charge was that Spike had crossed the line, and that Malcolm was being exploited. The arguments became a roar. In it was the potential to destroy a career. It also made for the kind of pressure that has potential to immobilize. That didn't happen to Spike Lee: In that charged environment, he rose to a high place. The proof is there in the film that opens in New York next week.

In a lot of ways, "Malcolm X" is four movies tied together in a blockbuster package. All of it was not just Spike Lee's doing. Denzel Washington, who plays Malcolm X, delivers a huge performance. In making the film, he said: "They key for me was spirit. I've told people, and I'll continue to say, that I can't be Malcolm X. I'm not Malcolm X; I'm Denzel. But I know that the same spirit, the same God that moved him, can move through me. That was my desire and my prayer -- to be moved by the same spirit he was moved by."

It worked. On screen, the spirit of Malcolm was there.

So much of the time, the stories that tell of the Black experience do not get told in the movies. That's especially true with the story as political as the life of Malcolm X. That is another fence that has been torn down. This movie probes deep into the guts, and dark places of what life in America has been for Black people. So much of it is there, stark and real, that by the time the film gets to the Audubon Ballroom where Malcolm was assassinated, you know the truth in Spike Lee's words. He said: "This is an incredible story, and I know that it will inspire people."

Malcolm X the man is probably best known through the book written by Alex Haley, "The Autobiography of Malcolm X." That book is the guide for the story Spike Lee has put on film. So much of it is there, and more. Before the credits roll, even South African leader Nelson Mandela steps into a compelling scene, helping to make Malcolm's vision come full circle.

Parts of the movie are entertaining, and those moments draw laughter. But the movie is not an entertainment package. This is a huge, powerful lesson in the history that is part of the struggle of Blacks to find their place in America. Part of what makes the film important is that it explains why so many African Americans walk around in a state of rage so much of the time. Which makes it something that all Americans need to know.

Euzhan Palcy

HER FIRST MOVIE came out in 1983. It's not so easy to make a movie that lasts but Euzhan Palcy did it the first time she tried. That movie was called, "Sugar Cane Alley."

Although it was a low budget film, it was so good it became something of a classic. It still gets shown on television and in schools. It has so much of a following that a lot of people have copies to show on a VCR in their homes. To start off with a movie like "Sugar Cane Alley" was a remarkable achievement. And while that film got a lot of critical acclaim, Palcy didn't get a lot of notice.

She was just 26 then and she lived in her native Martinique in the Caribbean. With low budget films, it happens that way a lot of the time. The film gets around, but the where-with-all that gets the director around, too, is missing. So in 1983, you didn't see Euzhan Palcy. She's the type of woman you don't forget; you see her once and you always remember. She's not just beautiful, she's stunning.

The second film that Palcy has made is in the theaters now. It's a movie that has Marlon Brando in it and making the film cost enough (about $9 million) that a public relations firm is on board to plug the movie.

So as a director, Palcy is getting attention. At first, those who see her say she's so beautiful that she ought to be an actress. But she works the other side of the camera. She's doing just fine, thank you.

Her new movie, "A Dry White Season" may not get the critical acclaim her first film got. But movies like this one don't get a lot of acclaim. It's a movie so powerful, it makes a lot of people uncomfortable. We have a ton of movies about South Africa, and the brutality of apartheid. But never have we had a film that tells such a compelling story of what apartheid does to people.

As a film-maker, Palcy has one quality that sets her work apart. She focuses on people. In "Sugar Cane Alley," which she calls a love story, the focus is on a woman's determination to see that her grandson gets a good education.

What the film-maker Palcy was able to do in telling the story was to make the people and their lives so real that anyone who saw the film could not let go.

In "A Dry White Season," which Palcy also had a hand in writing, she does not let the politics climb in front of the people. She shows what apartheid does on both the White and Black side of the line. The movie is drawn from nearly 15 years ago, from the time of the Soweto uprising. So much of that history from South Africa has been told again and again. On film, though, Palcy makes it stick in the mind.

She takes two families, one White and the other Black, and tells of the way the events from Soweto turned their lives around. You read stories and see clips on television. But a movie, when well done, can take you there. That's what "A Dry White Season" does.

Marlon Brando says that's the reason he dropped what he was doing to be a part of a motion picture for the first time in nearly a decade.

What happens in South Africa is no longer something happening in a far away place. The United States is right in the middle of it. So we need to know. That's what Euzhan Palcy's movie is all about. It's one of those pieces of work, information really, that makes certain that people cannot look at apartheid and say, "I didn't know."

In an interview, Euzhan Palcy was asked her reason for making the movie, "A Dry White Season."

"To change things," she said. "It doesn't help to be angry. If you want to change things, be a film-maker." To see her movies is to understand the wisdom of her point.

Alex Haley

LAST YEAR, THE SAD PART of Black History Month was the death of Alex Haley. This year, it has been the trashing of Haley's legacy. It wasn't supposed to happen this way. Not now. Not during Black History Month. Not to Alex Haley. He did too much.

In his life, Haley undertook two huge projects. The first was "The Autobiography of Malcolm X." The second was "Roots." They were two enormous pieces of work; what Haley did with them made him a legend. Now, in 1993, comes the dirty business of picking them apart.

The book on Malcolm X is not the main target, although Haley has been accused of not telling the whole story, of being unfaithful to what Malcolm X wanted, of having his own agenda. Of course, Haley is not around to answer those charges.

The current controversy centers on "Roots," which is being attacked in a way so fierce that the underlying intent cannot be mistaken. The effort is to destroy not just Haley's work, but his reputation.

What Haley himself once described as "nitpicking" has gone far beyond mere scholarly quibbling. He is being called a fraud. "Roots" is being taken apart, chapter by chapter. It is being called an invention. He is accused of making it all up. It is almost as though his critics are saying that Blacks did not come from Africa.

But what is the truth? The question was put to the esteemed African American historian Dr. John Henrik Clarke. Yesterday, all the controversy over Haley's accomplishments was at the front of his mind.

"This is indirectly an attack on Black intellectualism," Dr. Clarke said. "Haley is just a handy way of doing it."

Dr. Clarke knows the ground and understands the demands. He knows that in the story Haley told, all the pieces were not in their perfect place. "Haley," he says, "made some mistakes. He didn't have the time to check all the research as he should have. And some people around him ran some games. Instead of doing the research they were paid to do, they copied some things. So Alex got caught in an old trap. But I don't think Alex was a fraud. He overestimated some things, and, to some extent, overtold the story. But none of this makes him a fraud. We're talking about the lack of longer or more astute research. I think what is being done (to Haley and his work) is a hatchet job. And that is not accidental. It's part of an international thing."

Instead of being celebrated during Black History Month, the legacy of Alex Haley is under an attack so concerted that there is even a move afoot to withdraw the Pulitzer that was awarded to "Roots" in 1977.

In a way, Haley saw it all coming. It goes back to 1978, when he was supposed to be riding the high cycle. Instead, his days in that long-ago December were filled with pain. Most of it centered around a lawsuit in which he was charged with plagiarism. In the end, Haley settled out of court, handing to author Harold Courlander, a handsome settlement.

On the evening before the suit was settled, he came back to his Manhattan hotel suite from a long day in the courtroom. He was so down, so sick and tired, that he said he was ready to throw in the towel.

"I'm going to quit," he said. "I'm not going to write anymore."

He tried to explain how pieces of Courlander's work wound up in his manuscript. What happened had to be accidental, or, at worst, sloppy work from researchers. But none of that mattered. Even then, it was said that "Roots" was a fraud, that Haley had perpetrated a hoax. It was as though Blacks had not come here on slave ships, and that there was no African connection. Haley got questioned. Courlander got a free pass. The truth that got lost was that Haley had something real, and made something of it. His grandmother did whisper those words in his ear. He did make the connection. It was so tight that scholars had to dig hard for something to yell about.

Haley had the facts on his side. That he told the truth didn't matter. What he called the "nitpicking" was under way -- and it hasn't stopped.

Judging by the events of this year's Black History Month, it never will.

August Wilson & Lloyd Richards

LLOYD RICHARDS, THE DIRECTOR, has a lot of gray in his hair, and the relaxed manner of a man who has celebrated his 68th birthday.

August Wilson, the playwright, is 44, and a tightly wrapped bundle of energy. He chain smokes cigarettes, gulps coffee, and seldom seems at ease. But they are no odd couple; together they seem as comfortable as father and son.

August Wilson has roots in the Hill District of Pittsburgh, which is among the most widely known of the Black communities in America. Lloyd Richards was born in Canada, raised in Detroit. When he linked up with August Wilson, he was in New Haven in charge of the repertory theater at Yale University.

In theater, Broadway is the pinnacle. It's the big league, and the place every playwright and director strives to reach and excel. So Broadway has in its history many stories of dazzling achievement. Now comes the story of one of the most remarkable collaborations of all, of Wilson and Richards.

On Monday night, before a glittering, sold-out crowd in the famed old Walter Kerr Theater, Wilson and Richards had their fourth Broadway opening. No opening night is ordinary, but this one was more special than most. A lot of that had to do what with Wilson had accomplished. Four days before the play, "The Piano Lesson," was to open, it won the highest acclaim there is for a writer -- the Pulitzer Prize. For Wilson, it was not his first; he got that several years ago for "Fences," which was his second play to make it to Broadway. In all the long and storied history of Broadway, only a handful of playwrights have been able to claim the Pulitzer Prize twice.

There is a lot that makes Wilson and Richards different. A part of it is that their collaboration has stretched now through most of a decade. Another part is that both are African Americans. Perhaps most significant is the subject matter. The stories they bring to the Broadway stage deal with the Black experience.

In many places nowadays, stories from Black America are ones that hold little interest. They are too painful, too angry and often, they arouse too much guilt. So, a lot of stories from Black America don't get told. But on Broadway, Wilson and Richards have broken through in a big way.

"I don't think of us as breaking new ground," Richards says. "Breaking new ground is something someone else says to you; it's not something you set out to do. Then, we turn around, and said, 'Oh!'"

They came together in 1982. But 1984, they had their first effort, "Ma Rainey's Black Bottom." Then came "Fences;" after that, "Joe Turner's Come and Gone." Now on Broadway is "The Piano Lesson." It amounts to a huge body of work, and they're not finished yet.

"All my life I've been writing," says Wilson. "The one thing I want to do is write plays, and get them produced. I work sporadically, mostly in bars and restaurants. I take my pad, and go out and get a cup of coffee, and sit there. At some point in the day, a couple lines may pop into my head; a character may say something, and I just write that down. After three or four days, I have a pile of dialogue, and see what sense I can make. Characters begin to develop."

"I don't have an outline. I don't know what's going to happen. A lot of the things the character says just come out. It surprises me, and I don't know whether to make use of it or not. Writing is a process of discovery. As you go along, you discover things about your writing."

"When I met (Wilson)," Richards says, "he wasn't yet a full-fledged playwright. He didn't know the rules. He didn't know the things he shouldn't do, and so, he did them anyhow. He doesn't write many directions. He just says, 'A house in Pittsburgh,' and so,

I start from that. To create the place that can bring the play to life. I take the words -- make them come to life -- so you can feel them."

On Broadway now, they have "The Piano Lesson." But Wilson and Richards have a new play coming, "Two Trains Running," which is now in the works at Yale.

James de Jongh

THE NAME OF THE PLAY is "Do Lord Remember Me." It reopens Wednesday at the American Place Theater, and it couldn't happen at a better time because more than anything else, it is about now.

Not the play itself, but the words and where they come from.

"Do Lord Remember Me" is a story about slavery, and that makes it the most difficult kind of story to tell. But this play is different. Its story is now because the roots of the play -- the raw material -- come out of another difficult time. It goes back to the 1930s and to the Depression years and the WPA, and something called the Federal Writers' Project.

And what makes it all about now is that these, too, are depression times and although other names are used, the thinking is that WPA-type projects are appropriate again.

The WPA. The Works Projects Administration established in 1935 as an independent agency by executive order of President Franklin D. Roosevelt. It came out of another time of incredible unemployment. It involved putting people to work, building roads and improving airports. But it was more than just that.

The WPA had many activities. Among them were the Federal Art Project, the Federal Writers' Project, and the Federal Theater Project. In all, close to 10,000 drawings, paintings and sculptured works were produced through the WPA and many public buildings -- especially post offices -- were decorated with murals.

The experiments in theatrical productions were highly praised, and introduced many fresh ideas. The number of musical performances under the project averaged 4,000 a month. The writers involved produced a series of valuable guide books.

At its peak, the WPA had about 3.5 million people on its payrolls. It employed a total of 8.5 million people. Federal appropriations for the program amounted to $11 billion. In those dollars were funds that supported the Writers' Project. One of the projects, carried out in Virginia, was the interviewing of old men and old women -- people who had been slaves in their childhood. Their words were written down, and they were collected and filed in the Library of Congress. It was a part of American history that otherwise would have been lost. It comes back now, in the City of New York, in the play called "Do Lord Remember Me."

The writer, James de Jongh, is a professor of English at City College. He went back to the archives, and brought back the words that were put down by writers who had no jobs, but who were given work that made use of their talents in another difficult time.

"I was looking for background for a play about the Civil War period," de Jongh said in an interview that is now a part of a booklet on the play and its history. "I had heard about some slave narratives, interviews conducted during the 1930s, and knew some of them had been published. So I went to the Library of Congress where the transcriptions of those interviews are stored, and started reading. I shortly realized that the material was in itself intrinsically dramatic. So, instead of trying to find background, I decided to become in a sense a medium for the voices of these former slaves. They had in effect done their own playwriting.

"This is verbatim material," he says of "Do Lord." "None of the language is my language. The only parts that don't come from those interviews are the words of Nat Turner, which come from his writings, and the words of the spiritual and work songs, all authentic period material, which we have interpolated into the text. The dialogue is the language of real people who have a right to their memories, and the things they say. I felt there was no way for me to match the authority and eloquence of the way the real people who witnessed and participated in these events told about them."

His challenge was to make it work.

"Do Lord" is a memory play," he says, "the memory of slavery. The subject itself is problematic. People say. 'Oh God, slavery, a play about slavery. I need this like a hole in the head.' How do you deal with a memory like slavery? How do you face up to it and make it a productive memory that isn't degrading or humiliating or just unpleasant?"

That was his challenge, and he met it. And the proof is that "Do Lord" reopens Wednesday at the American Place Theater.

What makes it work? It has to do with de Jongh and his approach.

"I want people to leave the theater feeling good," he said. "Not feeling good about slavery, but good about themselves and what they have seen in the play. The challenge for me was to be truthful to the way things were and still allow the audiences to leave the theater in a positive frame of mind."

He was equal to the challenge. He took the words written down by unemployed writers in the Depression years. He brought them together in a way that makes for a powerful theater that has humor, joy, sadness and triumph.

Another time also was echoed at the start of Christmas week in Washington as Congress wrestled with the hard times of now. The challenge was not really different from what it was in the 1930s. It was the government trying to do something about unemployment. Only last week, in Washington, Congress did nothing.

It talked of a jobs bill, but at Christmastime the legislators went home having left the matter unresolved. But the issue will come back. This will happen because unemployment is great, and it keeps growing.

In Congress, the idea that is discussed is the appropriating of money to create jobs. The work that is discussed is repairing roads and bridges, a sort of rebuilding of infrastructures. All of that is important. But there is other important work . It involves writers and artists. Some proof of that importance is at the American Place Theater where the legacy of work done in another tough time comes back.

There is also a need for things that enrich our lives. There is a valuable culture and heritage that needs to be brought forward. It shouldn't stop because the WPA money ran out.

Ashton Springer

IT'S THE OTHER NEW YORK. It's the New York, where million-dollar deals are cut, where mink coats are everywhere in the wintertime and every day there are limousines.

It's the New York that still offers the chance for a kind of success that cannot be matched anywhere else in the world. It's the New York that draws tourists from everywhere for a look, and lures the aspiring young to take a shot at a dream.

A part of this New York is on the West Side, in mid-town Manhattan in what is known as the theater district. Yesterday, sitting there on top, was the unlikely figure of Ashton Springer.

He's Black and he comes out of the South Bronx. Today it's fair to say that he is the hottest producer on Broadway.

In a season in which hits have been rare, Springer has done well. He has "Eubie," a show that has drawn full houses and rave review. He has added "Whoopee," another show that is already a box office success.

If you ask him what the secret to success is, he cannot answer. There is no secret.

"I have a tremendous amount of confidence in myself," he says. "Perhaps I have more than anyone should have."

He looks at life as a contest, "I have a tremendous amount of energy," he says, "and I go as far as I can to win the contest."

But Broadway is supposed to be White, he's reminded. There is not supposed to be a place for Blacks, especially as producers.

"We've come a long way in the last five years," Springer says. "A lot of things have changed."

"Like what?"

"Well, when I came along, I never ever thought of a Black guy producing on Broadway. But now I'm here."

"And how have you been accepted?"

"The response has been very good. As far as I'm concerned, the acceptance has been total."

As an example, he tells about some of his dealings with the unions. "I would say, 'Are you trying to get at me because I'm Black?' And they would say, 'Get off it, Ash.' Their concerns were only with money. Race had nothing to do with it."

He is a familiar figure now in the theater district. One afternoon a few days ago, he went into Sardi's restaurant and was waved to a large table in the center of the room. "He's gotta have a big table," Vincent Sardi, the owner, joked, and Springer smiled.

He does not mind the jokes about his weight. He keeps going on and off diets but still carries about 300 pounds on his large frame. "What I'm doing now," he says, "is walking a lot. Diets don't work for me."

He is 48 years old and there is a patch of gray gathering in his hair on the right side of his head. But he says he is having the time of his life. Now he talks of next year's show, and doing what he can to change the complexion of Broadway.

"They used to say that there wasn't a Black audience out there, but we've shown that there is, that it only needed to be developed. And we're still just scratching the surface.

His aim now is to get Blacks, who go to the theater to the point at which they'll say, "Let's see a good play, not just a Black play."

But he would like also to see Broadway become more receptive to Black shows other than musicals. "Maybe even a comedy," he says, "but one that has something to say. I think Broadway could handle that. We've already shown that White people aren't afraid to go into a show just because the cast is Black."

Springer is one of a handful of producers who are Black. There is also Ken Harper, who has had one hit, "The Wiz," Woodie King Jr. of the New Federal Theater, Douglas Turner Ward of the New Ensemble Company, and Vinnette Carroll of the Urban Arts Ensemble.

King, Ward, and Carroll are on Broadway occasionally but mostly the success they enjoy is off Broadway.

The springboard for Springer's success was the play "No Place to Be Somebody," a drama written by Charles Gordone that won a Pulitzer Prize. But it was "Bubbling Brown Sugar" that got him to Broadway. Since then, he has been moving up and "Eubie" cemented his arrival as a major producer.

The biggest problem for any producer is raising the money that is needed to put on a show. "That's not a problem for me now," Springer says. "I've got a track record now and that makes the difference."

"But how do you make it from the South Bronx to Broadway?"

"My mother was a West Indian. My father came from Harlem but, when I was a kid, I always remember my mother talking about college. Nobody in our family had ever gone to college but she was always talking about it, and when I was finished with high school, there was no question that I would go on."

College for Ashton Springer was Ohio State. "I had a scholarship to Morgan State, a Black school, but my mother wanted me to go somewhere else, to a school that was not all Black. She wanted me to be in the competition that she knew I'd face later on."

It was his mother. "You know, when your parents are immigrants, I think that pushes you. You know, people who get up and move, looking for something better, they pass that on to their kids and that has an affect and I think that accounts for a lot of my success."

Yesterday, Ashton Springer was out there in the other New York, the New York that is so close and yet seems so distant from places as the South Bronx.

Oprah Winfrey

GO BACK TO THE MOVIE, "The Color Purple." That was the film Steven Spielberg made from the novel written by Alice Walker. The way it turned out, the move made a lot of Black men see red.

On film, Black men always seem to take it on the chin. The Black man is the classic bad guy, always portrayed in the worst kinds of ways. A lot of Black men sat through "The Color Purple" and squirmed.

The movie did not have much to offer that they wanted to see. The movie was a story told from the perspective of a Black woman. It was Alice Walker's story. It was a Black woman looking at her Black experience.

It was a Black woman saying, this was the world that came by me. A lot of Black men got angry at Alice Walker's film because they saw themselves being portrayed as less than human.

But the film that made so many Black men uncomfortable in theaters, and sparked so much anger in debates, had an altogether different impact on women -- especially Black women. Most embraced the film, Alice Walker, and the story she had to tell.

Black men hated the "put down" roles they saw themselves cast in. Black women reveled in what they saw -- strong women fighting abuse, and doing for themselves.

As it happened, an unlikely star to emerge from the film was Oprah Winfrey. Her syndicated television show was top-rated, but, "The Color Purple" was her coming out on film.

As she had on television, Oprah also got over on film. She was declared a hit. The story is told now that while on the set, Oprah spent the dead time reading a novel. It was called, "The Women of Brewster Place."

It was written by the New York City novelist Gloria Naylor. When it was published, Naylor's book got rave reviews and a National Book Award. Hers was another of those stories that got a lot of Black men angry. Naylor's novel revolved around a series of profiles of Black women and their relationships with men.

It was another look at a lot of the pain in the Black experience as seen through the eyes of a Black woman. It sparked anger in men. Black women, including Oprah Winfrey, mostly embraced the story.

Now, Oprah Winfrey is in the midst of a ride to the top that's been a rocket trip. Hers is a rags-to-riches story that says, you can do whatever you want to if you set your mind to it. Her roots are in a placed called Koscjusko, Mississippi. She was born there in 1954, a historic year for Black America.

In 1954, the Supreme court delivered its historic ruling in Brown vs. Board of Education, desegregating the schools. In 1954, education was seen as the key for Blacks. "Get yourself an education, and you can be anything you want to be," Black children were told.

Oprah Winfrey was to become the model. She did not have the blue chip home life; she tells of being an abused child. So hers is a story that begins with running away from home. But she kept her eye on the prize, and she worked.

As a student at all-Black Tennessee State University, she got a job in radio. From there, she got into television in Nashville. Her rocket ship had a stop in Baltimore, and then on to Chicago, where she became host of "AM Chicago." That led to her getting her own show. She became a big hit, outstripping everybody, starting with Phil Donahue. She got so big, she bought her show.

To own a successful show in television is close to having a license to print money. Oprah has that. So she established her own production company. She calls it Harpo, which is Oprah spelled backwards.

These past Sunday and Monday nights, Harpo's network opening shot was a made-for-TV movie based on "The Women of Brewster Place;" that same novel Oprah read between shots of her first movie gig.

Give Oprah Winfrey credit. She beat the odds to make it to the top. But what is it that each time the focus is on the Black experience, the Black man catches hell? As quiet as it's kept, there is another side.

William & Camille Cosby

BILL COSBY'S OTHER WIFE, the one he goes home to in the real world, is very much aware of the other woman -- the bright, witty, confident and stylish Claire Huxtable of television's top rated Cosby show.

Indeed, Camille Cosby sees in Claire Huxtable a lot of herself.

"Bill is projecting Claire to be a self-defining woman," she says. "I think that, perhaps, he did pull that from me, because I perceive myself to be a self-defining woman."

This year, the real life Cosbys -- Bill and Camille -- celebrate 25 years of marriage. A lot of Americans feel they know Bill Cosby. With his television show, he does come into their homes on a weekly basis. Camille says her husband has a way of bringing experiences of his real life family with him to the make believe world of entertainment television.

"There are many similarities," she says. "Sometimes I have to chuckle because I know that he's pulling from specifics -- you know, within our family."

But while millions feel they know Bill Cosby, it's been exactly the opposite with his real- life wife. Camille Cosby shunned the spotlight. While her husband is a creature of TV, she was never on the tube -- until two days ago. As part of the something special she wanted to do for Black History Month, she agreed to a television interview with Charlayne Hunter-Gault of the McNeil-Lehrer News Hour. The real life wife of Bill Cosby proved even more provocative than her television counterpart. And, indeed, a self-defining woman.

Camille Cosby talked of many things. She started with Black history.

"When I think about Black History Month, I think about the exclusion of African-Americans from history. Because of that exclusion, all of us are walking mountains of misinformation.

"I don't think our society is going to change and include our (Black) history in these history books. I do believe that it will continue to practice exclusion, because it behooves the powers that be to continue to do that, so they can manipulate and control people who do not know what their history is. And not only African-Americans, in terms of being ignorant about their history. White Americans as well are ignorant about their history."

The Cosbys are one of the best known African-American families. They are also one of the wealthiest. Last year, they gave $20 million to Spelman College in Atlanta, one of the largest gifts ever to a private school.

"We wanted to give a gift not only to Spelman, not only to the African-American community, but to the world. When you educate African-Americans and present them to the mainstream of society, you are giving a gift to the world."

That the gift was given a predominately Black college had special significance.

"The Black institutions are very important because, number one, they create an environment of belonging. I think that many of the African-American students on the predominately White campuses do not feel that they belong there."

Camille Cosby grew up in the south and studied at Black colleges during her graduate work. She knows what those campuses provide.

"They (Black students) are surrounded by professional role models. They see African-American historians and scientists and mathematicians and artists, etc. The propaganda has always been that whatever is Black or African is not right or isn't good or isn't capable. These students who graduate from these (Black) institutions matriculate at the graduate schools at prestigious institutions, and they do very well."

Camille Cosby has her own career line. She is involved in film making, and with a co-producer, she holds the rights to make the story of another self-defining woman married to a famous man, Winnie Mandela of South Africa.

While she calls herself an African-American, her roots are American.

"It's very important for African-Americans to think of themselves as being Americans. That they belong here, and their history, our history, is inter-connected with European history and Native American history. We must remember that we are Americans. This is our home. This is our country and we have contributed a lot to the history."

Chapter Eleven

IMAGES

Editor's Note

Throughout much of the last two decades, Earl Caldwell often has been a critic of the mass media in the U.S. -- whether it's news in television, radio, newspapers, or the entertainment industry. Caldwell has called to task an industry infamous for discriminatory practices in both its portrayals, as well as its employment practices.

In addition, Caldwell has been a tireless ombudsman of ethical practices in the news industry, as well as First Amendment issues affecting the right to know.

1981

AT FIRST IT WAS ONLY an occasional letter, one every now and then. Because those were not signed, it was easy to toss them into the garbage.

But lately it has been more than an occasional letter. They come all too frequently now.

"You're a Black racist," the writers say. "All you ever write about is race," is the complaint.

In one recent letter there was not only the accusation, but the mention of a motive. "Caldwell, you've got a sweetheart deal," the writer said. "You have really got it made. All you have to do is sit there at the Daily News and pick up a fat paycheck for writing stories running down White people."

Then there was this: "What you are trying to do is start trouble between the races, that's it. You are trying to start a race riot."

It is a foolish suggestion, the one that says if you do not write about the problems of race they will disappear. It does not happen that way. It is only a dream.

It is the other way around. The danger lies in ignoring the problem of race. Listen to the poet Langston Hughes:

What happens to a dream deferred?
Does it dry up like a raisin in the sun.
Or fester like a sore-
And then run?
Does it stink like rotten meat?
Or crust and sugar over-
Like a syrupy sweet?
Maybe it just sags
Like a heavy load
Or does it explode?

The dream is that we can overcome race; that even the legacy of slavery, as terrible as it is, can be put behind us. But that has not happened. Not yet, not in New York City, not anywhere in the United States. The truth is that racism interferes with the dream. We know that it does not just sag like a heavy load. In time, it does explode.

Race. It is always with us. Remember H. Rap Brown? He was one of the leaders in what was called the Black Power movement of the '60s. One of the things Rap always said, and people shouted when he said it, is that Black is Black is Black.

"Thurgood Marshall," Rap Brown said. "He sits on the Supreme Court, but he's just another Black man." The evidence? "Let him take off his black robes, and walk down the street," Rap Brown said, "and the police will whip his head the same way they will whip mine and yours. Black is Black is Black."

There is the argument that the problems now at the core are not racial. It is said that they are economic. That argument is widely advanced now because the economic problems have begun to touch everyone. Who is hurt the worse? It is those who are at the bottom. Examine the bottom, and it becomes clear that race is still a problem.

On a weekend early last May, all of the judges and many of the lawyers who practice in the Second Judicial Circuit (New York) gathered at an old resort just across the border in Pennsylvania, in the Poconos, for their annual meeting.

On the morning of the second day of that meeting, a Friday morning, the speaker at the annual judicial conference was Supreme Court Justice Thurgood Marshall. He is an old man now, and his health is not good. There is a question as to how long he will be able to continue on the court. When he came into the room that morning, he moved very slowly, and everyone who shook his hand was careful. It was swollen, and he winced even when the grip was light.

Marshall is the justice who presides over the Second Circuit. He went before the judicial conference to give his annual report. As he talked, he leaned heavily on the lectern.

The report that Justice Marshall gave had already been typed, copied and distributed to the judges and lawyers in the room. But for a while Justice Marshall read. Then suddenly he stopped, and he took the papers that were in front of him and tossed them aside.

"If you are interested, you can go through it," he said. He did not want to waste anymore time. He had other matters on his mind that he wanted to talk about. He praised the judges for their record. He complimented them on the workload they had been able to deal with. But before he sat down, Thurgood Marshall said that he was concerned about the Second Circuit's record in cases dealing with affirmative action. He was talking about race. He said to win an affirmative action case in the Second Circuit, "you have to beat the judges over the head." It was strong language. When he finished, the applause was only polite. But nobody called him a Black racist. He saw something that was wrong, and he felt compelled to talk about it. It was a matter of race. It is still with us.

1981

HE DIDN'T RESIGN. It was never his intention to quit. But getting fired, that was something else.

Max Robinson woke up yesterday knowing that getting fired was a distinct possibility. But by late afternoon it had not happened. He was still hanging on to his status as the only anchorman delivering the nightly news on network television who was not White.

It's an exclusive club that Max Robinson belongs to. He was the first Black man to get membership, making him the Jackie Robinson of his field, as he has been called. Anyone who has ever played that role has many stories to tell. A newspaperman who was the first Black hired at one of the big New York City dailies likes to tell about the time there was a problem, and his editor called him in.

"Now listen," his editor said, "you are the Jackie Robinson here, and you ought to know that if you mess up, there aren't going to be any more."

ABC-TV has a unique nightly news format. It uses three anchormen. Max Robinson handles the domestic news desk from Chicago.

Yesterday, he was in deep trouble with Roone Arledge, the president of ABC network news. The result was that on a day when he was supposed to be out in Chicago preparing his nightly broadcast, he was here in Manhattan at ABC news headquarters, where he had been summoned by his boss.

"Is getting fired a possibility?" Robinson was asked before the meeting with Arledge.

"It is," he said.

What Max Robinson did to get into this kind of trouble was to make a speech. He was up in Massachusetts, at Smith College, talking to students. One of the things he discussed was network television coverage of the inauguration and the release of the hostages.

He questioned why no Blacks were used in the coverage and suggested that some unconscious racism was operating. He did not single out ABC. He was talking about the industry.

As often happens when a distinguished figure goes to a campus in a small town to make a speech, a part-time reporter is usually somewhere in the back of the room. They call these reporters stringers. Sometimes they are students. They use this work to earn some extra money, to make good contacts, and, in a way, to launch their careers.

On this night there was a stringer present, and as Max Robinson spoke, the stringer wrote furiously in a notebook. As soon as Robinson was finished, the reporter phoned in the story. Then an editor took over. It was Max Robinson speaking -- an important name in American television. The story was sent out on the wires. Soon, it was in newsrooms all over the country. It was becoming a big story. Max Robinson was in the process of getting himself in trouble.

He has been at ABC since July 1978. ABC's network news was floundering then. It was ranked third, behind CBS and NBC. Then came Roone Arledge with his new format, and one of his key moves was bringing in Robinson to place him in the anchorman's chair in Chicago.

Max was ready. It was not one of those on-the-job-training deals. Max Robinson had been around in the mid '60s, in Washington, learning television news. He rose out of the pack to become a star. When he attracted the attention of ABC, he was anchoring the top-rated local news broadcast in the nation's capital.

Max Robinson was not the only journalist to notice that there were virtually no Blacks among the press corps that covered the release of the hostages.

"There must have been 1,000 reporters at West Point when the hostages arrived," a reporter from Detroit observed. "I counted just five who were Black," he said.

In the dispatches that came from his campus speech, Max Robinson was quoted as saying this:

"Certainly, racism should not be singled out at ABC any more than at NBC or CBS or any other major institution of this country. That's what I'm talking about, that it is pervasive, that ABC is no different, no better, no worse, than any other place in this country."

Another quote attributed to him said:

"I am prepared to leave where I am, and go to another place. I'm not prepared to stop doing what I believe; what I, as an individual, must do, and what all Americans must do -- and that is start and make this country whole."

In the early hours of the morning yesterday, Max Robinson was in his hotel room on the East Side of Manhattan. He spoke with a small group of friends, most of them journalists. He acknowledged the trouble he was in. He had climbed to a place where no Black man had ever gone before, and what he said was that if being honest meant that he had to lose everything, then he was prepared to be fired.

"Am I wrong?" he asked. "Am I wrong?"

Roone Arledge comes out of ABC Sports. He was a legend there. A genius, they called him. It is why he ought to be able to understand: Max Robinson is a hero.

1986

WHAT GOT LOST WAS THE QUESTION Al Campanis asked. He was half-way through "Nightline." Ted Koppel knew what terrible trouble Campanis had made for himself. So Koppel lobbed him up an easy one.

"I'd like to give you another chance to dig yourself out," Koppel said. And that's when Campanis asked his question: "How many executives do you have on a higher level or higher echelon in your business, in TV, I mean? How many Black anchormen do you have?"

Koppel told Campanis there are a few Black anchormen -- and dodged the first part of the question. But it didn't end there. ABC News has another broadcast called "Viewpoint." On that program, viewers have the chance to talk back to TV. On the "Viewpoint" broadcast of May 18, Les Csorba of Accuracy in Media told Koppel that Campanis had raised a legitimate question and asked it again. Koppel said he was sure the number of Blacks in the high echelon was infinitesimal. "I suspect that they (Blacks) are probably less than 5 percent. It may be considerably less than 5 percent."

As it turns out, even at 5 percent, Koppel's figure was fat. Apparently the accurate figure of Blacks in top management at ABC News is zero. Earlier this month, a group of Black employees met with senior management at ABC News. They said that of the four top programs at ABC News ("World News Tonight," "Nightline," "20/20," "This Week With David Brinkley"), not one has a senior producer who is Black. They said that of *all* the senior producers at ABC News, only one is Black -- and that he has only "minimal" editorial involvement.

A story in Sunday's newspaper accused New York Yankees' owner George Steinbrenner of putting a foot in his mouth. In a discussion about the paucity of Blacks in the front office baseball jobs, Steinbrenner made a point that it wasn't a problem peculiar to baseball. And he turned it around. He asked a question very similar to the one Al Campanis had asked.

Steinbrenner sees the writers who cover the Yankees. He noted that none from the major papers was Black. He could have gone a lot further. He could have asked: Where are the Black sports editors? And it's not just newspapers. The media are having a field day knocking the hiring practices of professional sports teams. But their own record is worse.

George Steinbrenner has it right. "This (hiring of minorities) isn't a problem peculiar to baseball," he said. "The problem is everywhere."

"What do you do about it," he was asked.

"Education," Steinbrenner said. "The problem starts with quality education. Everybody that wants a quality education and wants to work for it, ought to have it. That's the single most important thing. We've got to encourage young kids to get an education."

Steinbrenner also took a lot of heat for using the word "boy" when speaking of an employee in the Yankee organization. But the person he spoke of was the chief accountant in the Yankee organization. He was there. He had the job. And, as Steinbrenner said, the color of his skin had nothing to do with it.

Al Campanis lost his job and was widely ridiculed because of what he said on "Nightline." But the question he raised has made a lot of people aware that the problems of hiring minorities are not, as George Steinbrenner said, peculiar to baseball.

1987

IN ABOUT ANOTHER MONTH, Jesse Jackson will make it official: He'll be off and running again. This time, though, Jesse starts out with solid standing in the polls. And no matter what he does in Iowa and New Hampshire, the Super Tuesday presidential primaries in the South next March seem perfect for him.

As good as the prospects are for Jesse, and they do look good, it's Harold Washington who is the real symbol of Black political power.

In the United States, we have three cities that stand above the others; New York, Los Angeles and Chicago. No political leader who is Black has ever come close to winning a mayoral race in New York. Tom Bradley has won four terms in Los Angeles. The form of government in L.A., though, doesn't give the mayor much power. In Chicago, the mayor has power. The mayor of Chicago runs a big, thriving, important, and key American city. Harold Washington is in his second term as mayor of Chicago. He didn't slip into office. He ran with a strong, organized base. His support was solid and demanded that he reach for the kind of power Mayor Richard Daley, his legendary predecessor, had. Washington won, but as he reached for power he met opposition at every turn. Nobody gives power; it has to be taken and Washington fought for it, Chicago style. He was rough; a brawler. he didn't get the power he wanted at first try, but he won reelection with his efforts. Bit by bit, the power is coming. So in the bigger picture, Harold Washington has emerged as the symbol of the kind of political strength Blacks aspire to; that which the late Adam Clayton Powell Jr., once called audacious power.

In Miami last week, Harold Washington was the keynote speaker at the annual convention of the National Association of Black Journalists. He came on, Chicago style: tough, strong and demanding.

"You are the third wave," he told us. The way he explained it, once Blacks won self-determination, efforts were concentrated on politics. As advancement was made in that arena, the next front became business and Black economic development. From his insider position, he argued to us that the media now is the crucial area where gains must be made.

"We can't function if we can't speak with parity in the media," he said. "It's not enough to start your own newspaper. The institution called the media must be reformed.

"We (Blacks) have got to do whatever it takes to see that we have parity." Economic muscle has to be used, and also protest demonstrations, if necessary."

He described the media as "about as biased as any institution in the country. Every morning when I get up and read the newspaper, I see lies."

Twenty years ago, Blacks were just beginning to break into politics. In the late 1960s, mayoral races were won by Blacks in Cleveland, in Gary, Ind., and in Newark. While much was being made then of the breakthrough in politics, that was not all that was taking place. Black journalists were beginning to make their way into what Mayor Washington called the institution of the media.

In the late 1960s, the numbers of Blacks were small. The Kerner Commission in 1968 criticized the media, saying it saw America only through "the White man's eyes." The presidential commission also found that so few Blacks were employed in the media that the media were not even in a position to report accurately on Black America.

The convention in Miami was a reflection of progress made. There were enough journalists to fill two large hotels. For his speech, Mayor Washington had an audience close to 2,000. He came armed with figures that showed Blacks remain a small minority in the news media.

"Those who wield power can't do it," the mayor said, "unless they have the vehicles to explain to their constituencies what they are confronted with."

In a lot of big cities, Black mayors have newspapers that should have stayed open, close down. Journalists by nature are wary of politicians. But Harold Washington struck a chord.

"You are the third wave," he told us.

1981

WE CALLED IT A SUMMIT MEETING. We used those words because all of us are newspaper journalists, and it was our way of saying the meeting was important.

And it was. It was important because its purpose was to move forward with the business of fully desegregating every aspect of the American newspaper industry.

There are always stories written about the problems of dealing with discrimination in the police departments, the public schools, hospitals, labor unions and on down the line. But what we do not read much about is the problems that exist inside our newspaper. But it is happening.

In 1968, in all of the United States, there were only about 400 journalists on the major dailies who were not White and they worked for just 20 percent of the newspapers. Ten years later, the jump was to 1,700 non-Whites, and they worked on 32 percent of the newspapers.

There has been progress, the figures show that. But the shocking fact is that even now six of every 10 major daily newspapers in the U.S. do not have even one professional on the staff who is not White.

It is not one of those things that can be shrugged off with a "So what?" The newspapers are too important. Even more important than government itself, is what Thomas Jefferson said.

It is about information. The notion is that if people are given all of the information, given it straight and honestly, they will make the right decisions. That is where the newspaper come in; not the TV camera, the radio station, or the book publisher. Each of them plays a role, but it is the newspaper that is key.

But for the newspaper to be effective, to truly do its job, it cannot itself be a tool of just some of the people.

On Friday, we had our summit meeting: It began early in the morning in a conference room off a balcony that overlooked the news room in the journalism department at the University of Arizona.

On one side of the conference table sat Thomas Winship, one of the best known names in the newspaper industry. He is editor of the Boston Globe and serves now as president of the American Society of Newspaper Editors.

Across from him was John Quinn, the senior vice president and chief news executive of the Gannet Co. Other names are more familiar: Hearst and Newhouse and Scripps-Howard. But Gannett is by far the largest and most important of the group-owned newspaper organizations. Gannett now controls 82 papers, coast to coast.

Larry Allison also was at the table. He is publisher of a newspaper in Long Beach, but more important he is president of the Associated Press Managing Editors. And in between, there was Felix Gutierrez, who heads the Chicano News Media Association in California, and John L. Dotson Jr., a senior editor at Newsweek magazine, who also is chairman of the board of the Institute for Journalism Education.

The summit was five days business. On Saturday, the Institute for Journalism Education held its board meeting. The IJE is the board that I sit on, and the meetings that were held here for two days were special.

The IJE is new. It is a name that is becoming more familiar all the time, both inside and out of the newspaper industry.

The IJE's goal is simple: To eliminate segregation from every aspect of the newspaper industry. It is Washington-based, and operated by professional journalists. Aside from Washington, it also operates programs in Berkeley and in Tucson.

In Berkeley, it is the Summer Program for Minority Journalists. The Summer Program, it is called. Each year it finds talented young people who have been kept out of careers on newspapers because they are not White.

When it was started, and people were asked why, Robert Maynard knew the answer:

"So we can eliminate from the lexicon of journalism, the phrase 'can't find anyone qualified.'"

In Tucson, the IJE operates the Editing Program for Minority Journalists. In the '60s and the '70s, the major task was to open the door for journalists who were not White.

That job still is not complete. There has been progress. It is the battleground now and much of the discussion around the table at the summit on Friday dealt with the issue of involving non-White journalists in decision-making.

"Sixty-seven percent of minority journalists work as reporters," Nancy Hicks, a former New York Times correspondent who serves now as president of IJE, said. In other words, when reporters who are not White get jobs on newspapers, they stay at the bottom and have little influence on the shaping and delivery of news.

But it is changing now, and if you sit on the board of an organization such as IJE, you are in the forefront of seeing that change -- even have a hand in making it happen. You come away from the meeting with the idea that the leaders of the newspaper industry are wising up and understand that it is important enough to make it happen.

1984

IT WAS MORLEY SAFER'S piece. At the start of the broadcast, he said the story he was about to tell was "guaranteed to ignite debate." He had it wrong; what the story sparked was anger.

The story was aired Sunday evening as part of the weekly CBS "60 minutes" broadcast. As Morley Safer described it, the story dealt with the question: "Is there a case for South Africa?" That alone made it a very important broadcast. Finally, South Africa is on the agenda. Finally, the most racist government in the world is under scrutiny.

The 60 Minutes piece was especially important. The program is one of the most popular on television. It always has an enormous audience. It's a program that has the kind of influence that can change minds.

That counts because, for all the charges that have been made, there is still much about South Africa that is not known. The question that was posed: Is there a case of South Africa? In a way, it was saying that the issue was not cut and dried. It was saying that maybe the South Africans are not all wrong. Just the question was casting doubts. In the broadcast, 60 Minutes did more than just cloud the issue. It did something that was far worse. It gave a misleading picture of South Africa.

It took the power of its cameras and captured pictures of life in South Africa that made it appear as though the issue was one of integration and little more. It showed Blacks standing in line with Whites at bus stops. The pictures made it appear that because there was some integration, South Africa was moving forward. The broadcast had pictures of Blacks and Whites together in parks. The pictures were used to convey the impression that a kind of equality is being instituted in South Africa. And the piece went on that way. It had at its center an interview with Prime Minister P.W. Botha.

It wasn't really an interview. It was more a lobbing up of fat softball questions certain to give the Afrikaner a free ride on American television. In the whole discussion of "the case for South Africa," it never came out that Blacks, who are the big majority in the country, have no rights. The point was never made that no Black person, regardless of education, wealth or status, has any say whatsoever in government. It never came out that no Blacks have the right to vote.

The broadcast had Botha talking of democracy, boasting of the fairness of the South African courts, and the freedom the press has in the country. It was just never mentioned that none of that included Blacks. In South Africa, Blacks live under a system of unmatched oppression.

The law determines where they live. The law demands they always carry special identification cards. The law allows them to be picked up and detained at the whim of the police. For Blacks, due process does not exist, and the broadcast never dealt with any of that in what is called the examination of the case for South Africa.

It's crucial now the way the story of South Africa is told. Every piece is important, especially the ones that are on television, and seen by audiences that are counted in the millions.

The piece that CBS broadcast provoked so much anger that by Wednesday, pickets marched outside the network's broadcast center, and the words they shouted gave some hint of the anger the broadcast had aroused.

Yesterday, there was this: Word came from South Africa that officials had confiscated film from offices of ABC and the BBC. It was the kind of film the rulers in South Africa don't want the world to see, film that documents the oppression that exists in the country.

Every story is important now. The South Africans understand. It's the reason they sent the police to confiscate the film that documents the case against South Africa.

1988

IT HAD THE MAKINGS OF THE KIND of hearing that attracts attention and impacts policy. An impressive array of American journalists agreed to come before a committee of Congress and explain the meaning of the outrageous restrictions the government in South Africa has imposed on the news media.

But in Washington on Wednesday, a stunning thing happened. At the last minute, all of the journalists except one suddenly canceled their testimony.

In Congress, groundwork is being laid for possible enactment of new, more stringent sanctions against South Africa. Rep. Howard Wolpe (D-Mich.) heads the House Subcommittee on Africa. Just after 2 p.m., the committee convened its hearings. The purpose was to focus on what can or should be done about increasingly repressive actions against the press.

Even before the gavel sounded though, the bottom fell out. Walter Cronkite canceled. Hodding Carter, a prominent commentator and anchor of Public Broadcasting System programs, also canceled. Tom Winship, former editor of the Boston Globe, now with the Center for Foreign Journalists, cancelled too. Rick Manning, former head of the Newsweek bureau in Johannesburg, was also scheduled to testify, along with John McChesney of National Public Radio. They also canceled.

So before any testimony was taken, before any witness was sworn, Rep. Wolpe did some explaining. "These events are truly alarming," he said. "They suggest that South Africa's manipulation of the press penetrates well beyond its borders. It extends right into Capitol Hill."

Wolpe said the principal reason the journalists decided not to appear was "fear that if they testified publicly about the realities of working in South Africa, these individuals would put themselves and the media organizations at serious risk of retaliation."

So the way it turned out, only Kenneth Walker, formerly of ABC News, kept his commitment he made and appeared before the Wolpe committee.

"Let us not be misled," Walker said. "The true source of the problem of news coverage in South Africa rests not with press restrictions. I submit the U.S. News media have used those regulations to return to the indifference, almost hostility, that had long characterized their South African coverage prior to the mid-1980s.

"This historical reluctance to cover South Africa is evidenced in other ways," he said., "Newsweek's chief of correspondents, Bob Rivard, has acknowledged publicly what other news executives have conceded privately, and what Black American journalists have suspected for years; that the White minority regime has long exercised a veto over the race of U.S. journalists in South Africa. Allowing the South Africans to bar the stationing of Black American journalists there makes the U.S. companies accomplices in apartheid; and in my view, places them in violation of American law."

In 1981, Walker visited South Africa as a reporter for the now-defunct Washington Star. In 1985, he was the lead correspondent for an ABC-TV Nightline series from South Africa. He recently left ABC to become an anchor with the new USA Today television broadcast. On Capitol Hill, he told the committee, "Richard Cohen of CBS News is right when he says, 'if U.S. news organizations cannot operate inside South Africa in the way they have led the public to believe that American reporters operate, they should get out.'

"By maintaining their bureaus in South Africa, news organizations suggest that the public is getting all the relevant news in a normal and orthodox way," Walker said. "And that," he added, "is a fraud on the American people."

1990

THROUGH THE 1980s, with a call-in "talk radio" format, they took the station and across Black New York built both reputation and audience. In a very definable way, WLIB became the communications link that tied the various African American communities in the city together.

Historically, it was music that Black radio used to build audiences. WLIB, owned by Percy Sutton's Inner City Broadcasting, was in the forefront of changing that. WLIB was so successful that a move was afoot to create a national Black talk radio network.

In New York, Blacks have always had numbers. But no cohesive "community" existed because of the lack of communications. That led to years of "Harlem Blacks" moving in one direction, "Brooklyn Blacks" moving in another, and "Blacks in Queens" going in another way. WLIB became a sort of glue; through endless hours of debate, positions were arrived at and the numbers that were always there began to act in concert.

Recently, when the Haitian community staged a huge demonstration of perhaps as many as 100,000, the outpouring caught official New York by surprise. "How did that happen?" many asked. A part of the answer comes back to WLIB. The station has become an awesome tool for organizing. Jesse Jackson tapped into that with his presidential campaigns in 1984 and again in 1988. David Dinkins too, in his successful mayoral race, benefited from WLIB.

Whatever the issues confronting Blacks, they were always sure to be thrashed out over the microphones at WLIB. The station became so much a barometer of Black sentiment that a few years ago, at the height of Tawana Brawley controversy, a police intelligence unit was actually moved to monitor and record conversations.

But just as WLIB rose to gain standing as a powerful instrument in communications in New York, unexpected trouble has developed; so much so that Percy Sutton has threatened to close the station down. It has to do with the sharp attacks on Mayor Dinkins mounted by Blacks speaking over the WLIB airwaves.

"I will close down WLIB before I see it used by Blacks to attack Blacks," Sutton said.

The first "talk" broadcast over WLIB on Monday was "the Global Black Experience" hosted by Gary Bird. It was broadcast live from the Apollo Theater in Harlem; Sutton had anticipated more harsh attacks on Dinkins, and he came to the microphones in the theater to drop his bombshell.

He conceded that Dinkins had made mistakes. But he also said that certain mayoral advisors had not served Dinkins well in letting him say that the boycott of Korean stores was an action based on race. "But WLIB cannot be used for us to destroy each other," he said. "We have come too far as a people."

He compared Black attacks on the mayor to what is happening in Africa with Nelson Mandela. He said that because of violence among Blacks there, Mandela was being diminished in the eyes of the world. He mentioned attorney C. Vernon Mason who was sharp in his criticism of Dinkins. "My heart hurt," Sutton said, but he called Mason "a true leader," and attributed his remarks to frustration. He then pleaded, "Don't for Godsakes let us here in New York destroy this man (Dinkins). He's made a mistake. Don't destroy him; be restrained. Don't turn on him."

At the end though, he came back to his threat. He said that rather than see the station used for Black on Black attacks, he would shut it down, even though he had been in the forefront of attempting to create the national Black talk radio network.

The Rev. Herbert Daughtry of Brooklyn was also at the Apollo, and he voiced support for Sutton's position. "Let's don't destroy him (Dinkins) before we teach him," Daughtry said. On Monday, Daughtry, too, dropped something of a bombshell. He announced that he was stepping back from his longtime role as activist. Daughtry said that he intended to write, lecture, but said that he would be available on a more elder statesman basis for consultation.

Less than six months ago Dinkins came into office with a lot of goodwill, especially from Blacks who gave him more than 95 percent of their votes. But his handling of the Brooklyn boycott and his approach to dealing with racial tensions have gotten him into trouble. Just how much trouble the mayor has with his base is perhaps best reflected in Percy Sutton's stunning threat to close WLIB, the station that has become the communications link for Black New York.

1991

IT WASN'T SUPPOSED TO HAPPEN. At least in New York, Rupert Murdoch was supposed to be finished in the newspaper business. That is, unless he unloaded his Fox 5 television station, which he has no intention of doing.

But like a lot of laws and rules that are put in place because they are supposed to protect the public, the one that was supposed to bar Murdoch (or anybody else, for that matter) from owning both a newspaper and television station in the same market is about to get bent.

So today, Murdoch is back in control at the New York Post. That being the case, maybe more important than asking how did he get there, is the question of which Murdoch is it that New York is getting this time around?

Is this a rerun of 1976 when Murdoch bought The Post and promptly turned it into one of the most divisive, race-baiting newspapers in the country?

Or is this the Murdoch of television, the creator of the Fox Network, who introduced a line of programming so diverse it shook up the whole industry. Unlike his newspaper which shut Blacks and other minorities out, the Murdoch of television had more Blacks with their own shows than any other network. It wasn't just "playing it safe" programs either.

Murdoch's network airs the cutting edge comedy show, "In Living Color." His network also puts on "Roc," which stars Charles Dutton. The show, which is produced live, and has as its cast Dutton and other central players from August Wilson's Broadway hit, "Two Trains Running." While the show, "Roc" has standing as being a comedy, the humor spins off real stories that have a lot of social and sometimes political importance. More recently, it was the Fox Network that introduced "Martin," a series produced by Topper Carew, which features Martin Lawrence, who may be the hottest and most creative African-America talent to surface on the comedy front since Eddie Murphy. All that is just some of what happened at Murdoch's television network.

But his days as a newspaper publisher in New York make for an altogether different story. What accounts for the difference? Maybe Murdoch has changed. He hinted at as much in an interview published in the Post yesterday. For several years, a Black media watch organization known as CEMOTAP (Committee to Eliminate Media Offensive to African People) has been leading a boycott against the Post. A prime reason for the boycott was the Post record for hiring minorities. In the Murdoch era, when the paper went from a liberal to right wing editorial policy, the staff changed from diversity in the newsroom to Whites only.

On his first day back, though, Murdoch expressed surprise when told of the absence of minority in newsroom at the paper he ran. In an interview in the Post, Murdoch was quoted as saying, "I was shocked when I found out there were no Black reporters when Pete Hamill took over as editor." Speaking like the Murdoch of television, he said that would change. "Diversity is the key," he was quoted as saying.

In a way, though, if Murdoch wants the Post back, he has to offer a different front. He had enormous power and wealth. Politicians are falling over each other to get the Federal Communications Commission to grant him a waiver from complying with its cross ownership rule, which is designed to prevent wealthy people just like Murdoch from having too much influence by owning both a newspaper and television station in the same market. It is a rule that was adopted for good reason. Anybody can start a newspaper. To do that, you just go into business. But there are only so many channels for television, so, it is reasonable -- even right and proper -- to say that in the same market, one individual should not own both.

Now, Murdoch returns to New York. The truth, though, is that he does not yet have what he wants -- which is the waiver from the FCC that would allow him to operate the Post beyond the current wait and see period he's been granted. So it is important to know which Murdoch is coming back. If it is the Murdoch of television who made diversity the key, that will be one thing. If it is the old Murdoch, though, coming back for a rerun, he's got some difficult days ahead. A lot of people are ready to get on line to give that Murdoch a fight.

1980

IT HAD NOT YET GONE out over national television. There were still nearly five hours left, but Paul Brock knew that already it was too late. NBC was going ahead with the show.

"But I just heard that one of the prime sponsors pulled out," Brock said.

It was not a boast. He was just putting it on the record. It was in the middle of the afternoon now, and Paul Brock was at his desk at the national headquarters of the National Association for the Advancement of Colored People, on Broadway at 57th St. It had come to Paul Brock first.

"It was last November," he said. Brock was out in California then, in Hollywood on a mission for his boss, Benjamin Hooks, the executive director of the NAACP.

As he remembered it yesterday, he was with a friend, and had just walked out of a meeting when they bumped into two actors, Bernie Casey and George Sanford Brown. Both actors are Black.

"They were excited," Brock said. "They grabbed us and asked if we had heard about the series NBC was doing. We hadn't heard anything, and they told us about it. They said that something had to be done. That was the first that we heard anything about it."

That was how the series that began last night on national television, the one that is called "Beulah Land," first came to the attention of the NAACP.

"Ivan Dixon was there, too," Paul Brock said yesterday. "He said that they wanted him to direct it, but after he had seen the script, he said he didn't want anything to do with it."

That afternoon last November, Brock, who is the NAACP's director of information, asked only that a copy of the script be sent to him in New York. It was, and he took it to the executive director, and that was when the NAACP began to mount its fight against the television miniseries that it says is "insulting, degrading and dangerous" to Black people.

Yesterday, Paul Brock's desk was piled high with papers, documents and other literature that was used to build the NAACP's case against the "Beulah Land" series.

"You know, they're not even going to show it in Jackson, Miss., or in Baltimore," he said. And in San Francisco and in Portland, they're giving the NAACP branches 45 seconds each night to make their own statements about the show. There has been a strong reaction. I don't believe they (NBC) thought that Blacks would stand up so much."

On top of the papers that were on his desk, was a statement Brock had written that was issued by Benjamin Hooks.

"'Beulah Land' is not the real issue," the NAACP's executive director, said, "but only the vehicle that forcefully focuses on the real issue before us. We at the NAACP are concerned that there are no positive Black images on television for our children to see and emulate. We are concerned that negative portrayal of Black people cannot end because the nation's film production houses, the TV networks and stations, and the news media-both print and electronics -- have few, if any, Blacks in decision-making positions."

There were other words in the executive director's statement, but, in a sense, that was it. He put his finger squarely on the problem. It was about White people tampering with Black people's history. There was a time when there would have been no outcry. A series such as "Beulah Land" would have gone by without protest. But no more.

There was Hooks voicing his outrage. And Rep. Cardiss Collins (D-Ill), chairman of the Congressional Black Caucus, added her voice.

"Slavery was a debilitating, dehumanizing experience for Blacks just as the Nazi Holocaust was for Jewish people. Moreover, it should not be romanticized and sugar-coated with distortions of reality in order to seek HUTs (Households Using Television) for an insensitive sponsor."

Rep. Collins's words were included in a telegram to NBC. It said, "We believe this program to be a self-serving and inaccurate representation of the oppression against Blacks in the Civil War South."

There were other voices also raised in protest. And here in New York City yesterday, there was an effort under way to add to it with a demonstration against NBC in Rockefeller Center.

"It was designed as an entertainment program," Jay Rodriguez, NBC vice president for corporate information, said yesterday in defense of the "Beulah Land" series. "And we think it is entertaining," he said.

It was the perfect statement. It said something about NBC. It also made it easy to argue that is how the network feels about its Black audience.

1983

THE BEAUTY WAS IN THE WAY he took the story and put it on film. He just took his cameras and put them on Willie Mae Ford Smith and Thomas Dorsey and Sallie Martin and once he did that, he couldn't lose.

The whole history of the music and the people who made it was right there, getting old but still moving around. He came with his cameras at the perfect time. The names and the faces the cameras introduce -- Mother Smith, Professor Dorsey and Sallie Martin -- are not so familiar, but in the world of gospel music these are legendary figures.

The remarkable story of these three people and what they did with their lives is not so different from the remarkable story of the photographer, James Van der Zee, who died last week. Van der Zee was a man so accomplished in his work that in his time on the streets where his photographs were known, he was called a Michelangelo.

But James Van der Zee worked in Harlem and the pictures he took were of people and places in that community and because they were, it was not until he was an old man and his life's work was done that acclaim came to him. He was 82 years when his photographs were shown at the Metropolitan Museum of Arts, and that was when he was discovered.

It is that way with Mother Smith and Thomas Dorsey and Sallie Martin. The vehicle that pulled Van der Zee from obscurity was the show at the museum. For the three of them, pioneers in the building of a special kind of music that comes out of the Black church, it is through a film that the stories of their lives are discovered. The film is called "Say Amen, Somebody," and it is showing now at the 68th St. Playhouse.

The show at the Metropolitan where Van Der Zee was discovered was "Harlem On My Mind," produced by Thomas P. Hoving in the summer of 1969.

The documentary that tells the history of the people who were the pioneers in gospel music is the work of George T. Nierenberg, a young film maker who lives in Brooklyn. He is White, 31 years old, and he says himself that when he started out, he knew little about gospel music, and that is a part of what makes the film he came back with so remarkable.

"We started visiting churches and we were readily accepted by the church community wherever we went," he said, "just because we were interested enough to be there. It wasn't always churches. Sometimes it was a hall and even a large gathering at the Felt Forum at Madison Square Garden.

"We slowly began to realize the wide variety of performance styles of gospel. There are quartets, slow singers, gospel groups, choirs and choruses. Local groups and national groups, men's groups and women's groups and many more. I also learned to my surprise that gospel music is 20th century music and an expression of Black culture. It's only about 50 to 60 years old."

Gospel music. It makes a church rock. "The church was moving this morning." The words come off the sidewalk after service and they are words about gospel music.

"When I first started out, churches didn't want it," Willie Mae Ford Smith says in the film that George Nierenberg has made. "(They would say) don't you bring that ragtime in here," she said. Now everybody's doing it.

Gospel music is an outgrowth of the spiritual. The spiritual was a wail, "Oh Lord, I want to get to Heaven." The spiritual was a reflection of slavery and the toughest of times." "Steal away to Heaven" The spiritual was part music, Part anguish.

Gospel is the other side. Gospel is uplifting. "How I got over," is about a winner. "My Jesus can do anything." Gospel music comes with a beat, and in time this is the music that became the fountainhead for rhythm and blues. Aretha Franklin sang gospel.

Billy Preston, who played with the Beatles, had gospel music as his background. The same was true of the Staples Singers.

The camera is beautiful. Train it on these old people and let them tell their stories and it is magic. The film, "Say Amen, Somebody," does exactly that and it comes together a powerful and moving documentary.

The words, though, stick in the mind. The story that Professor Dorsey, whose face is dark and lined with age, tells of how he happened to write the song "Precious Lord" is an example.

He said that his wife and baby had just died. He was in shock and the hurt was deep. " I didn't know what to do," he said. He was a writer, though, and he took the words that came to the front of his mind and he put the words on paper. "Precious Lord, take my hand, lead me on, let me stand."

In the film, there is also the story that Mother Smith tells of the trouble she had with her husband. He did not approve of the music or of her traveling across the country singing it. "You ought to be ashamed of yourself," he said to her. She told how he was waiting at the train station in St. Louis one day when she returned home after a trip and how angry he was and the way he went stomping from one car to another, searching for her. Then she told how, in his anger, he accidentally fell into an elevator shaft and injured himself so badly that he was confined to a wheelchair. "He stayed that way for eight years," she said.

The film is built around the words and the faces of the people who were pioneers with their music. It makes the theater on Third Ave. move the way that churches do on Sunday morning, and when you hear it, you understand Willie Mae Ford Smith. "When I sing it," she says, "I feel I could just take off." You also understand the arguments she heard 60 years ago when she tried to bring the music into the church. "(They said) you're bringing the blues into the church. They said you must be Bessie Smith or one of those Smith sisters."

She sees it another way. She calls the ones who sing gospel "anointed singers." You watch her work and you understand why she also says, "You can't be a pretty mouth and sing."

Mother Smith, Thomas Dorsey and Sallie Martin are all old now, but in the film they still sing. "I won't be through with my work until God takes my voice," Mother Smith says. "I may have cracks in my voice as wide as the Mississippi River, but the old Mississippi keeps on rollin."

There is all of this history out there walking around getting old and being ignored. There are all of these important stories waiting to be told. It is beautiful the way George Nierenberg has put on film the story he discovered, the one about Mother Smith, Thomas Dorsey and Sallie Martin.

1984

THE FIGURES SAY A HUGE audience tuned in and that made the debate all the more important.

In the making of the President 1984, the debate stands as a very important moment. But that moment has passed, and now the focus is on the question, "Who won?" Reagan's people say he won. Mondale's people say he was the winner. The polls suggest it came out just about even.

But there was another side. It had to do with who lost the debate.

In Kansas City, the loser was the press. The reporters who asked the questions shaped the debate, and they blew it. The why of it is not so hard to figure out. The debate was to focus on foreign policy. That alone made it important. In the world, there are not a lot of very heavy problems. But only in one place is the situation so bleak and so dangerous that it's impossible to wake any morning and learn that a true pogrom has taken place. And that's not in the Middle East, Central America or even in Russia. It's South Africa.

The situation in South Africa is so bad now that the army there is being used on a daily basis to enforce the apartheid laws that oppress 22 million Blacks. The situation is so much on the edge that, in awarding the Nobel Peace Prize to Bishop Desmond Tutu, the committee said it was trying to focus attention on events unfolding inside the country. And it ties in with the electing of a President of the United States.

In receiving the prize, Bishop Tutu was critical of the Reagan administration's policy of "constructive engagement" with South Africa. He said South African Blacks did not accept administration arguments that it was encouraging reforms but, instead, saw the policy as supportive of "this racist regime."

But in the debate, not a single question regarding South Africa was raised. In the whole 90 minutes, Africa came up only when Reagan and Mondale mentioned it on their own. It is one thing for the media to give short shrift to the events unfolding in South Africa in their own news reports. It is something altogether different, though, for reporters to ignore such a pressing issue in a presidential debate. But, in Kansas City, that is exactly what happened, and it makes the press the loser.

But it shouldn't be allowed to end there. If candidates seeking the presidency choose to stand before the people and ignore issues as crucial as South Africa, they have that right. But the people will see and the people will act accordingly. But the way the debates are set up now, the reporters decide everything. Their questions frame the whole debate and, in Kansas City, the reporters just locked the issue of South Africa out. Never again should that be allowed to happen. That's not the kind of power the media ought to have, especially not in debates that are so crucial in the making of a President.

In the first Reagan-Mondale debate there was a big flap over which reporters would ask the questions. That prompted Jesse Jackson to suggest that all panels ought to include a mix of White and Black and Latino reporters. He was accused of raising the issue of race where it didn't belong. After what went down in Kansas City, it is possible to see exactly where Jesse was coming from.

1992

IT ALMOST IS GENIUS THE WAY the Republicans do it. They take what they know is a lie and then repeat it so much it begins to have the ring of truth. It has become that way with what they call "the liberal media."

In Houston, through the day of their convention, the Republicans had a grand old time engaging in media bashing. As far as coverage is concerned, it may be that they do have a complaint. Maybe they have not gotten a fair shake. But even that does not justify the lie; what they call "the liberal media" is only a myth. It is something that does not exist.

Of all the institutions, maybe none is more conservative at its core than the news media. And all that is an old story. Go back 25 years, to the summer of 1967. The piece of history that summer holds has to do with the riots that swept through more than 100 cities. At the end, a presidential commission was appointed to examine "the why" of the uprisings that grew out of Black discontent. In its report, which has become a document that still holds a lot of validity, the Kerner Commission in part blamed the "what went wrong" in America on the media. The commission concluded the media had not been telling the truth; its finding was the news was not a fair portrayal but rather a view of
America as seen only through the White man's eyes.

It was easy for the commission to reach such a conclusion. It found the media was comprised almost entirely of Whites. And what is stunning is that 25 years later, not a lot has changed. The media still remain one of the most segregated of American institutions.

Just before his death a few years ago, the late Harold Washington, who was Mayor of Chicago, went before a session of the National Association of Black Journalists and discussed the problem. He concluded that if Blacks did not gain parity in what is known as the institution of the media, "all the gains we are making in other areas will not mean nearly what we think they will mean." But since Washington's death, little has changed.

A part of the genius of the Republicans is that in decrying the "liberal media" they do not bother to explain what they mean. They just use the code words and what they have found is that just the accusation is enough. There is no need to explain.

To look at the facts would undercut the argument. At the GOP convention now and at the Democratic convention at Madison Square Garden in July, much of the media effort involved analyzing the politics. Virtually all of that analysis, though, was done by journalists who were White. And that's not all.

On television every Sunday, the networks give hours to shows that look back on news events. What those shows have in common is that the panels are almost always all White and the voices which express the views are dominated by conservatives.

The media have a way of contributing to the false image. That is seen even in the area of sports. "Where are the Black coaches?" writers ask the commissioner of the National Football League. "Where are the Black managers?" is a question repeatedly put to baseball executives. But there is another side. New York Yankee owner George Steinbrenner, when the question was put to him, turned it around.

"I don't see any Black sports editors," he said.

And Steinbrenner put a finger on an important truth. Baseball has no Black manager; professional football has but a single Black head coach. But the more than 1,500 daily newspapers have a record that is even worse. And this, as the Republicans tell it, is the record of the media that rightfully deserves to be categorized as liberal.

Of course the Republicans know better. Media is big business and if anything, it stands for the status quo. What the Republicans are after is an edge; they know a strategy of attack, attack, attack can have an impact. They also know that in winning politics, it is not wise to let the facts get in the way of good strategy.

So they pound away at what they call "the liberal media" and they say it so much, they have succeeded in giving it the ring of truth. They even have a lot of the media believing it. It is too bad it is but a myth. For a change, a liberal media is not a bad idea.

1983

HE STILL HAS ALL OF THE OLD ANGER in his voice.

"It's not just one film," he said. "It's a lifetime of these films that help convince white people of their superiority and our inferiority. And at the same time, it affects our own youth, many who internalize these negative self images. So for us, it's more than a movie. It's part of our struggle for survival, respect and justice."

Yesterday Richard Perez moved through the rain to a meeting to put in place one more piece of the strategy for the fight that is shaping up. The fight is not new. But it comes back now, and it does because the movie, "Fort Apache, the Bronx," is coming back.

In the winter of 1981 the movie was in the theaters. Then the fight was there. Now, NBC-TV has the rights to the movie, and it is scheduled for showing on the network in two weeks, and it brings the old fight back.

Yesterday, Richard Perez went back to the archives.

"When the movie came out," he said, "the New York State advisory committee to the U.S. Civil Rights Commission put out a statement about Fort Apache. "To uniformly portray the South Bronx community as being composed of pimps, prostitutes, thieves, transvestites and junkies, is to reinforce the stereotypes that nurture the growth of racial prejudice and bigotry."

Perez picked it up there. "And when you nurture the growth of prejudice and bigotry," he said, "you nurture the growth of the Ku Klux Klan and you nurture the ability of the government to treat people of the Third World as they would never treat the people of Europe."

It was early in 1980, before the movie was even made, and NBC was buying rights to the film. There was also at the same time a coming together of many pieces from different places and in time, these pieces would make a powerful protest against the film. NBC was confronted.

Officials at NBC released a letter defending the movie. "We are certain," the letter read," that the final result will be acceptable entertainment for all major segments of our audience. We ask you to wait and see . . ."

Despite the controversy, the film was produced. By the time it was ready for release, the pieces of the protest had also come together. It was called the Committee Against Fort Apache, and Richard Perez who grew up in the Bronx, taught in the public schools there and who now teaches Puerto Rican studies at the college level, became a voice for the committee.

"We're telling NBC this film has an impact on our lives in many ways, and we don't intend to remain silent while these ideological foundations are being laid to turn public opinion against blacks and Latins in this country and abroad," Perez said.

"Not only have social conditions of Blacks and Puerto Ricans worsened," Perez said, contending that films like "Fort Apache" encourage the public to support acts of war abroad against people of color. "The United States is waging war against Black and Latin people around the world," Perez said, referring to campaigns against Nicaragua and the invasion of Grenada.

"It must be stopped."

Chapter Twelve

TOWN MEETING

Editor's Note

Earl Caldwell has written extensively about international leaders and events, including many developments at the United Nations, where most global and regional conflicts wind up -- as attempts either to prevent or to end violent confrontations.

1979

WE NOW GO BACK TO the morning last month when the doctors at New York Hospital who are attending the Shah of Iran came to us with the news about his illness.

On that morning late in October, they told us that it was cancer. They talked about how serious it was, how it was spreading, and how important it was that the Shah remain here for treatment.

That day, out in the city, what struck me was how many people were saying that they didn't believe it. They didn't believe the Shah had cancer at all; that it was all a part of the trick to get the deposed monarch into the country.

This wasn't what we call informed opinion. It didn't come from people who supposedly are in the know. This was off the street from people just listening to what the doctors at the hospital had to say. They walked away certain that it was all a lie. Back then, it was a reaction that seemed a bit amusing. But October has turned to November. Now there is nothing amusing about it. It is a serious question: Why is the Shah here? Could it really be as simple a matter as we're being told: that the Shah is sick, that he does have cancer, and his presence in New York is simply a matter of treatment? When that story was floated the first time, people laughed at it. Right away, people felt they knew.

So it only figures that, If the explanation was not accepted here in New York, then certainly it would not be bought in Tehran. And it wasn't. The only surprise is that the Iranian students didn't storm the American Embassy sooner.

Of course what they are doing is not right. It is beyond the limits of protest to hold the Americans hostage. So now there is another crisis. There is talk of war, a clamor to go in with the Marines. Of putting the Ayatollah Khomeini in his place. How quickly the madness spreads.

What is certain now is that there is no easy way out. What is just as certain is that those who can least afford it are the ones who are going to pay. Is the price of oil going up? It will. Are the poor going to be cold this winter? If anyone freezes, who it will be? Of that, there is no doubt. The question is why? Why are we in this situation? Why have we allowed ourselves to be pushed to the brink? Certainly, it isn't just because the Shah has cancer, and the only doctors in the world who can treat him are in New York. The one thing about the Shah that everybody agrees is that he is not poor. The man has money.

So we are back where we started. We are back with what is called the credibility gap. What it's called, though, makes no difference. The point is, we still cannot believe what our government tells us.

I think about the news that came recently from South Africa, the news that the most racist regime in the world had exploded a nuclear device; how there was proof of this because our detection system had picked it up. These were systems that had always been reliable. Always.

Yet, as soon as the announcement was made, there was an about-face. Not long after that the government was saying no, it didn't happen. It became a matter of credibility. On the streets, people were saying they didn't believe what they were being told. It was the same as it was when they told us the Shah was here because he was sick with cancer.

1980

SUDDENLY, THE DEBATE HAS CHANGED. Now all of the words that rise in the hallways and in the lounges and conference roms have turned against the United States.

It had been so different last November, in the days just after the young Iranians stormed the American Embassy in Tehran, and took the Americans hostage.

Then, in the hallways here in the UN, where the tan carpet is worn thin, all of the words were against Iran. They said no, what you are doing is not only wrong but against international law.

It was that way too in December, when the debate moved from the hallways to the great chamber in the conference building where the Security Council sits. Representatives of nation after nation came forward, took their seats at the council table, and said in a variety of ways that the Iranians were wrong, and the message that went out said turn the hostages loose.

Those were only words, and words alone do not end a crisis. So the Iranians continued to occupy the embassy. The hostages were not released. December became January, and the months stacked up. But the words stayed on the American side. On Friday, that changed.

In the morning, when he came off the escalator and reporters stopped him, Zehdi Terzi was ready. "All I can say is that this was an act of war," he said. "It was a violation of the territorial integrity of Iran."

Terzi, a short and stocky man who represents the Palestine Liberation Organization at the United Nations, had trouble waiting for the questions to be framed. He came into the United Nations the way the representatives of many governments came. He was ready, even eager to say that the United States was wrong.

Kurt Waldheim, the secretary general, was more cautious. "I've always said that only negotiations can solve this problem," he said. "We have to negotiate a settlement."

"But what does the American attempt to rescue its people mean?" he was asked.
"It certainly has created a grave situation," the secretary general said.

Waldheim measured his words. He understands perhaps better than most the situation that exists in Iran. Waldheim went to Iran himself in an attempt to negotiate an end to the crisis. The pictures are still clear of the fright that showed on his face the day that Iranian militants surrounded his car, beat on it, and forced his retreat.

Waldheim stood in the hallway. "We have to talk to the Iranian government," he said. "We have to see how we can get the negotiation process revived."

Yesterday, the flags hung limp in the plaza at the United Nations. The parking lots were empty. There was nothing anywhere within the UN itself that said the world was in crisis.

It was so different from last November. Then, there were early morning and late night sessions of the Security Council. There were even Sunday meetings. When ambassadors crowded into the chamber, they spoke with urgency in their voices.

It is still a beautiful idea, the notion that the United Nations can work. That the problems of the world can be taken there, to the great windowed buildings on the East River, and that with words those problems can be solved. But bit by bit as international tensions rise, it is an idea that is slipping away.

Late in the afternoon on Friday Mansour Farhang, the Iranian ambassador at the UN, spoke to reporters.

He is a tall, bearded man. When he sat down in the second-floor conference room, first he chastised the government of the United States. He said that the American raid into Iran was not really an effort to rescue the hostages, but an attempt to destabilize the revolutionary process. When he began, his words were delivered so rapidly that the reporters who were there had trouble keeping up with him.

One of the things that ambassador Farhang kept saying was that it had to be understood that Iran was in the midst of the revolutionary process. "You have to go beyond the hostage-taking as immoral or illegal," he said. "This has to be solved in the context of Iranian realities," he said.

The question of the hostages' release came up again, and again Farhang said no.

What it means is that the United Nations is being dealt out. The beautiful idea is not working. All of the words are in the hallways and in the lounges.

There is a feeling now that the world is edging towards a war that nobody wants.

The beautiful idea was that in times like this, the United Nations would take charge. But the one body in the world that should have been able to take charge of this months ago was still groping, almost helplessly, unable to do anything.

1981

FINALLY, IN THE AFTERNOON, it was over. The hostages were back and when they came off the plane the miracle was that they were alive. After all that they had experienced, they did not look bad, either.

There was a time when all that happened yesterday did not seem possible. Each night, when the pictures came back from Iran, it seemed that the hostages would never get out -- certainly not alive. Back then, on most days, the question was, how would they die.

They came home yesterday. But when their plane landed at Stewart Airport, it became a day set apart.

There were yellow ribbons everywhere and flags. People cried and said prayers. As the reunions began, one of the things that was impossible to get around was the fact that the hostages had been lucky. They were lucky to be home, lucky to be alive. They were lucky that everything broke right for them. Lucky that Carter, a hesitant (or patient) man was President. Lucky the rescue effort he finally tried, failed.

They were lucky because these were people who were not in Iran by accident. They were on assignment. They were there conducting the business of the American government. They had worked in a dangerous area, and were carrying out their jobs. But they made it out, and yesterday, on a day of glorious winter sunshine, they came home.

Nobody doubts the wrongness of the Iranians taking the hostages. Nobody questions the brutality the captives endured. And there is no doubt that celebrations now are in order.

The ticker-tape parade that the mayor insists on may not be a bad idea. Especially if the hostages themselves are up for it. But, bit by bit, the families of many of the hostages seem to be saying thanks America, we appreciate your standing with us, but now you have to give us some time. You have to back off and let us alone for awhile.

The problem, though, is that, now, other people need the hostages.

Certainly the news media do. It is too good a story to walk away. It is an important story, too. The news media will stay with the story but, as always happens, something else will break and the reporters and the people with the cameras will be gone.

It is right to honor the hostages. They were out there on the point, and they took the heat for the whole country. But it is one thing to honor them, another to hide behind them. After 444 days, the hostages have earned their rest.

1993

BY MORNING, HE WAS GONE. He had been an important part of the government put in place by Jimmy Carter, but yesterday it was over. Yesterday the government changed hands.

Quietly, Donald McHenry's term as American ambassador to the United Nations ended. His office was cleaned, polished, and ready for its new occupant.

Just before noon Monday, McHenry said the final words to his staff. Afterward, he stood ready to fly off to Washington. Maybe he would accompany the President on a hastily arranged trip to West Germany. Maybe he might be needed to unravel the hostage crisis.

As he waited, he moved nervously in the hallways, but by 1 o'clock Monday he knew that there had been a snag in the negotiations, and that there would be no immediate presidential trip to Germany.

The transition at the U.S. mission took place without a hitch. It did not matter that Donald McHenry was a Black man, or that his politics are different from those of his successor, Jeane Kirkpatrick. She is a Democrat, but is known to be conservative who has admitted having little knowledge of politics of southern Africa, an area of concern to Blacks, and an area of expertise with McHenry.

One of the remarkable things about the American government is how smoothly it changes hands when the time comes.

"It's a good system you Americans have there," Eddison Zvogbo, one of the leaders in the new southern African nation of Zimbabwe, said last year. It was early March, and his country was changing from White-ruled Rhodesia to Black-governed Zimbabwe. In the first days of the changeover, there was mostly confusion.

"The problem," Zvogbo said one night while speaking to reporters in Salisbury, "is that we don't have a system for the orderly transfer of power. I understand now why the Americans have a definite system to handle the transition of governments. Here you are either in or you are out."

McHenry's departure was routine. Yesterday, he headed to Washington, where he has accepted a teaching position at Georgetown University. But McHenry's importance in the Carter administration should not go unnoticed. He was not just a symbol. Even more than former Ambassador Andrew Young, McHenry was proof of how Carter opened foreign affairs to groups who had traditionally been on the outside.

On his last day, when McHenry was asked what he felt his most important achievements were, right away he said it was the way the U.S. Mission was able to reach out and get more groups involved in foreign affairs, and sensitized to the United Nations.

"The thing we have to recognize," he said, "is that foreign affairs no longer is very much separate from domestic affairs. If a war breaks out in Vietnam, it will require the service and possibly the lives of our young people, without discrimination. It will also affect some of the programs -- social and economic programs -- which are vital to significant segments of society.

"So Blacks can't afford, or Hispanics can't afford, or women can't afford to leave foreign affairs to the Wasps of our society, or to any particular interest group. I would say you can't even afford to leave it to the experts, because there are times when the experts become so engrossed in details that they lose the political and social touch. And this is a democratic society in which everyone has to continue to maintain a broad interest in our affairs."

McHenry went to the UN as President Carter's choice to succeed Andrew Young. Although both men are Black, their styles are different as night and day. Young is the politician, a preacher, and civil rights leader. He is outgoing, quick to give his opinion and always controversial. McHenry is forever the diplomat. "A child of the State Department," he calls himself, and he always has played the part.

On the last day, he was no different. He wore a conservative dark business suit with stripes, and every word he uttered was measured. But twice he managed to raise eyebrows.

Once was when he was referring to the Senate testimony of Alexander Haig, Ronald Reagan's choice for Secretary of State. Haig had said South Africa has strategic and economic interests and concerns that the United States shares. McHenry called Haig's remarks appalling.

McHenry was pointed also in his remarks about Mayor Koch, and the way the mayor criticized the United Nations.

"The mayor is hardly one to talk. He judges the UN on the basis of one thing, one issue -- the Middle East. He is not objective on that issue and hasn't demonstrated any objectivity. Yet he wishes to toss out the whole organization in terms of his own bias."

One measure of the impact that McHenry, and Young before him, had in opening foreign affairs to Blacks came earlier this month. It was a going-away reception in honor of McHenry held at the big hall at the U.S. Mission. There was a tremendous crowd, some said one of the most impressive gatherings of Blacks ever seen in this city.

"I'll bet this building has never seen anything like this," one guest remarked.

"Yes," another agreed, "and I'll bet that it will be a long time before it ever happens again."

1981

IN THE MORNING, THEY KNEW. The reports that came first from the wire services, and later from radio television, all said that Anwar Sadat was dead. Still the diplomats waited.

"It would be wrong for us to say anything before there is an official announcement from the Egyptian government," Mehdi Zentar, the Moroccan ambassador, said.

"Remember, we don't know what the situation is inside Egypt," he said.

All through the morning, the diplomats kept hustling along on the soft carpet in the hallways, whispering furiously among themselves, but stopping cold and then running away when reporters appeared.

"Is it confirmed yet?" an Algerian delegate asked about the reports of Sadat's death.

"Not by the Egyptians," he was told. Quickly, he disappeared down the hallway. At the UN, where words are everything, that was the way it went yesterday on the morning when the news came that Anwar Sadat had been assassinated.

It was about protocol. The UN is a house of diplomats, and diplomats live by the dogma of protocol. Yesterday, in the morning, that protocol demanded that the Egyptians be given some time.

"Let them be the ones to decide when they want to make the announcement," Zentar said.

But in the afternoon, it was different. The Egyptians made their announcement, and once they did, the UN became what it always is, a house of words.

"I don't know what will happen," Mohain Alaini, the UN ambassador from Yemen, said, "but I hope this will be a lesson for the United States that relations between them and another country should never depend on one man, on one individual. You should build relations with a population and a government, not just one man."

The ambassador was asked about the Camp David accords.

"From an Arab point of view, we don't consider Camp David anymore," he said. "Even public opinion in Egypt is against it. That was why Sadat arrested over 1,500 last month."

"You cannot use my name, of course," an African said. He was a tall, balding man and his English was excellent.

"Who is going to take over in Egypt?" he asked. "What is going to happen? And by that I mean, what is the policy going to be? Nobody knows. But the thing is, nobody else can do what Sadat did. Who else can go to the Knesset? It would be very, very difficult to find another Sadat. And what will be the position of Israel now? And what about the territory that was supposed to be returned? It is a very dangerous situation."

"I'm very sad," said a woman who wore a long robe. "I'm from Nepal. In my country, he (Sadat) was very well liked. Our king just visited Sadat in Egypt about four or six weeks ago. I liked him. To me, he (Sadat) was a symbol of peace. It is a great loss for Nepal."

Now, Ambassador Zentar could use his words.

"It was an act of terrorism," he said. "It's unfortunate that terrorism is still going on."

"What will it mean for your country?" he was asked.

"We had no relations with Egypt," he said. "We have had no relations with Egypt since Camp David, but I don't think anyone is going to be happy to hear this. It was not a coup d'etat. This was an aggression against one man, an act of terrorism."

"No," he said, "this is terrorism, and it is no good."

The words reached out in every direction.

"There will be a new situation in the area now."

Ambassador Habid Shati, the secretary general of the Islamic League, said. "It depends on who succeeds Sadat. But I can't see anything now. I just know he is dead, but peace was not depending on Sadat. Sadat was an obstacle to peace because he wanted peace for himself and Israel. No, in my opinion he was not a loss for peace."

Yesterday was not a good day at the UN. Yesterday, the weakness came through. The protocol worked all right. It always does. No matter how much animosity there is among nations at the UN, they still sit together and observe the rules of protocol.

To deal with the heavy issues, there are only words. The words are always there. But yesterday, on the day that Anwar Sadat was assassinated, guns spoke louder than words.

1983

ON FRIDAY, SHE KNEW it was time to leave. "When I woke up and looked out the window, there must have been 40 to 50 Marines on the lawn in front of my house. It was 6 o'clock in the morning and they were setting up artillery. I went out and talked to them. They said there was sniper fire. That was when I told them I wanted to get out."

It was the two of them. Jean Wiley and her 8-year-old son. They had left New York Aug. 10. It was their plan to live in the Caribbean on the island of Grenada for a year. She is a reporter. She understood the interest there was in the government of Maurice Bishop. It was her plan to spend a year writing and reporting from Grenada. She had arranged to file pieces for a radio station in Washington, and she would sell articles as a free-lancer.

In New York, she had been working on a film. It was a huge project, a documentary history of the civil rights movement -- of which she had been a part -- and it had been going well. But as happens with projects of the kind she was involved in, the money ran out, and everything was put on hold.

One of the loves of her life is the Caribbean. She knew the islands and had enjoyed many previous visits. Now, with the film at a standstill, and time on her hands, she took her son. The two of them went off to live on the island of Grenada.

"An unbelievably beautiful place," she said.

"How bad was it?" she was asked.

"It was worst the first day. We had never heard the sounds of war before. It was very hard for everybody the first day. Before our eyes, things were being blown up. I didn't think the fighting would last that long because the army (of Grenada) was torn. People didn't want their sons fighting for this military junta.

"I had a nice house with a real wonderful view of the sea. It was on the main road going into town. You couldn't see the house because of a hill, but it was between Butler House and Grand Ans Beach. Butler House (a hotel) was bombed the first day (of the invasion).

"Butler House was on the hill, up from us. Grenada is built on hills. The buses don't run after dark, so you hitchhike or walk. You walk and walk and walk. I was trying to be a reporter."

"Didn't they put the press out?"

"Only those who came to cover that (the coup). I had already established residence."

"How is it now on the island?"

"It's a very confused state of affairs. An invasion is war. People are dying, being bombed out. There is no food, no water. They (Grenadians) didn't ask for that (war) and it didn't have to happen that way. The whole country is upset."

"After the coup, did you feel as though you were in danger?"

"I had never lived under a military junta. Nobody (Grenadians) wanted to live under those men (Deputy Prime Minister Coard and Gen. Austin). They were wild men."

"Before the coup, how was it in Grenada?"

"Things were going very well. They had just gotten an IMF loan. That was just before Bishop (slain Prime Minister Maurice Bishop) went to Czechoslovakia. It was a $40 million loan. the IMF gave to them.

"The invasion was early Tuesday morning. That Monday was the first day we were free from the unbelievable curfew. It was an awful feeling and then, not being able to call home (to the United States). It was the first day we were allowed to move out of the house. People were looking for the dead. Far more than 17 were killed. The people, they haven't even had time to mourn their dead."

"How did the trouble begin, did they (leader of the coup) say why they were arresting the prime minister, Maurice Bishop?"

"They never told the country that Bishop was under house arrest. By that night, everybody knew it but they never made any announcement. They didn't kill him fast enough and word got out that they were trying to kill him. He was too popular. The whole country turned out to free him with their bare hands. I knew if they retook him, he wouldn't live."

"Was there any indication the coup was coming?"

"Nothing. I asked everybody. Did you know? Did you know? Nobody outside the party (the ruling New Jewel Movement) knew."

"What was the reason for the coup?"

"Ostensibly, it was because the party wanted him (Bishop) to share power. He apparently accepted that in principle but how does the head of state share power?" The dream became a nightmare and by Friday, Jean Wiley woke to find marines on the lawn in front of the house she had rented, and the Marines were putting in place the weapons of war.

At 3:45 that afternoon, she and her son boarded a military flight. At 4:25 pm, the two of them were safe in Barbados.

"I left everything there (in Grenada)," she said. "We were only allowed one bag, I put clothes in that bag."

Jean Wiley now wonders what will become of Grenada. "They (the government) were beginning to solidify gains. . . free health care, universal schooling, things like that. It was a very cosmopolitan atmosphere. People from all over the world were coming there. There was no hint that something like this could happen. You never saw any guns. It was just a nice, quiet, idyllic island. People didn't even steal. Houses were left open."

"Did you know the Cubans were there?"

"Anytime you went near the airport, you saw (the Cubans) there working feverishly. There were about 600. They (Cubans) were very centrally located. The area where they lived on the island was wiped out in the invasion. If they start fighting in the mountains, it's going to be a helluva guerilla war. I've never seen mountains like the ones in Grenada.

"I knew Cubans were there. They didn't try to hide.

"I'm also told they (Bishop's killers) were opposed to his plan to hold elections."

"Did you know the invasion was coming?"

"We expected it, but we didn't know they were going to come in shooting and bombing. We thought they (U.S. Marines) were just going to establish a military presence."

1984

YESTERDAY, AT THE UN, it all came up perfect. Flags of the member nations waved in dazzling sunlight. Diplomats arrived in black limousines, and tourists gawked from behind the iron fences.

At the United Nations it came up perfect yesterday, and it all stood in sharp contrast to a year ago.

"This is still a very confused world," Jorge E. Illueca, the president of Panama, said. "It's a world full of problems."

In the morning yesterday the president of Panama was moving through the final hours of his term as president of the General Assembly of the UN. In the afternoon, there would be a new president, and a new session of the General Assembly would be convened. There would be bright speeches and predictions of great promise for the world. The opening of the general Assembly is the UN's brightest moment. It is almost always that way. But last year, it was different. "There were very gloomy circumstances," Jorge Illueca said. He went back and brought all of the gloom of a year ago into focus.

He mentioned first the shooting down of the Korean airliner, then the breakoff in arms talks. The atmosphere was so charged that Soviet Foreign Minister Gromyko did not even attend the meeting of the General Assembly. That was not all. Violence raged in the Middle East, in Lebanon, and on the heels of that came the invasion of Grenada. In the atmosphere of a year ago, hostility rose even against the UN itself. A member of the United States delegation suggested the world organization leave New York. "And we'll be down at the docks to wave goodbye," he said. It was in that climate that Jorge Illueca of Panama began his term as president of the General Assembly.

"But we played the kind of role the UN should play," he said yesterday. "There was a maintenance of dialogue."

At the end, it comes down to that. The UN, at its best, keeps the nations at odds with each other at the table and talking.

Yesterday, when he stepped away from the world spotlight, the president of Panama said the UN is not just the best chance the world has. He said, "There is no other out."

Jorge Ilueca is tall and has brown, curly hair that has begun to move away from his forehead. He has the soft voice of a diplomat. He spoke of the reward he saw in his time as head of the General Assembly -- the reward that came from bringing parties in conflict into harmony at the conference table. "The machinery doesn't always work," he said, "but when it doesn't, it's the fault of the member nations, not the UN. That's what has to be understood."

The 39th session of the UN came to order yesterday in a world that Illueca said was "full of problems." But the atmosphere was different and that, he said, was the UN's doing. He said it was because of the UN that both President Reagan and former Vice President Walter Mondale were about to meet with Gromyko.

In the afternoon yesterday the presidency of the General Assembly was passed from Jorge Illueca of Panama to Ambassador Paul Lusaka of Zambia. The UN stands on the verge of its 40th anniversary. Illueca counted a long list of the problems of now. "The African situation," he said. "Such a grave problem." There is on one end of the continent the threat of war and, spread across the middle, a drought that threatens to starve hundreds of thousands.

"The high interest rates of the United States," he said. He told of the squeeze that puts on the developing nations. "The tremendous amount of money spent on arms," he said. He mentioned the figure of $750 billion. He said that soon, a trillion dollars a year would be spent on arms, and that alone, he said, makes it a very large issue.

But yesterday, as the new session of the General Assembly came to order, there was none of the gloom that was there a year ago.

1984

AT NIGHT, HE CAME TO DON BOSCO Catholic Church. In all of Panama there is no church that is bigger. Don Bosco is huge, but for the Rev. Jesse Jackson it was still not large enough.

On the night Jesse came, all of the seats were filled. In the back of the church many stood and others found space in the wide aisles along the walls. This is the first stop in Jackson's four-nation trip. He calls this a "mission for peace," but for now, the moment in it that is special goes back to Don Bosco Catholic Church.

It did not figure to be that way because in the morning, after he had barely been in the country an hour, he was at the presidential palace. President Jorge Illueca delayed a trip to New York, to the United Nations, to meet with Jesse. He gave the Black American a warm welcome and embraced his mission for peace, and it was a good start for the trip.

In the evening, Jesse sat with Nicholas Barletta, the president-elect of Panama. The two are old friends, and in the meeting the feeling was so warm that, playfully, Jesse slapped Barletta on the back and said, "Imagine, from finance minister to a president." The two of them laughed, and the president-elect had even kinder words for Jesse.

"By coming here, he highlights the importance of the issue (peace)...It's important for us to achieve peace."

It went back and forth between the two of them, the Black man from the United States who has reached higher than any Black man before him for political position and power, and the dark-haired president-elect who holds his doctoral degree from the University of Chicago.

The two meetings were high points for Jesse. While his primary mission is to promote peace, his trip represents another part of the moving out into the area of foreign policy and foreign affairs by Black Americans. At an airport press conference on his arrival, Jesse detailed 10 reasons for his trip and the indication was that his will be an on-going role in Central American affairs.

"We must see stopping the war as one of our most critical moral tasks," he said, "and we must pursue that goal in every way we can."

Jesse is a Baptist preacher and speaks no Spanish. But from the moment he stepped to the front of the pulpit in Don Bosco, he connected with the people.

"All too often my country has responded in precisely the opposite manner that it should," he said, "sending more arms and bombs to make major criminals out of petty criminals, instead of insisting on economic aid and trade."

An interpreter stood alongside him in the pulpit, translating his words, and the people clapped. At the end, they stood, and the noise was loud, lasting a very long time. It encouraged Jesse to step back into the front of the pulpit. It was the same for him as it had been for him in churches all across the United States in his presidential campaign.

"I am somebody," he shouted and the people picked up the words, and the shouts came back. "Our time has come," he said, and again the words came back. Jesse raised his arms high with his thumbs up, and the moment became special.

It will not get him any votes in the campaign. The primaries are over. It's doubtful it will swing any delegates to his side in the Democratic convention to come. The nomination of Walter Mondale is certain. But Jesse Jackson is moving out on the world scene.

There were rumors that in Cuba, Castro would release prisoners to him as a good-will gesture. Yesterday afternoon, it was said that Jackson was making progress in an effort to engineer a cease-fire in El Salvador.

1984

HAVANA, CUBA -- OUTSIDE, in the evening light, Fidel Castro moved into position. He came to the foot of the steps to the plane, and then, above him, Jesse Jackson appeared in the doorway and the high moment began to unfold.

They are two players filled with style. All of it was there, as they came face to face for the first time.

They were both wearing the uniforms that have become identifying marks. For Castro, it was crisp, green battle fatigues, a symbol of the revolution that brought him to power. For Jesse, it was a tailored safari suit, the popular dress of Black Africa and much of the Third World.

Jesse came off the plane smiling, almost bouncing down the steps. Then the two of them stood little more than a foot apart. Jesse and Fidel, similar in so many ways and yet, very different. Both are rebels. Both are dynamic speakers. Both have people who move with them, and a part of it has to do with the way they can take words and use them to persuade. That may have been a part of the reason that at the moment they came together, the two of them just stood there. Fidel and Jesse.

It was a grand stage the two players had for themselves, and Fidel was giving to Jesse the kind of reception held for chiefs of state. The big observation balcony that sweeps across the main terminal building at Jose Marti Airport was jammed. Bodyguards stood in a cluster, and photographers, reporters and television crews together made an enormous press corps.

It was Castro's move. Jesse is a political leader, but one who moves about without portfolio. Castro is the dominant leader in this region of the world. Castro is an old hand. Jesse is moving up. When they came together at the plane, Castro did not hug Jesse. He knew of the political problems caused by the pictures of Jackson embracing PLO leader Yasser Arafat.

Fidel put his hand out, and Jesse extended his, and then Jesse put his other hand on Castro's arm.

Fidel Castro was the third president Jackson was to meet in two days of his Central American "mission for peace." He started off in Panama with a meeting with President Jorge Illueca. Then he met at the presidential palace in San Salvador with President Duarte. El Salvador is a country fighting a civil war and Jesse arrived in a setting of extraordinary security. His American Secret Service bodyguards even wore bulletproof vests beneath their white, tropical weight shirts. And in the motorcade from the airport, instead of a limousine, Jesse rode in a reinforced bullet-resistant van.

After he had met with Duarte, the two stood on the front steps of the striking white building and Duarte praised Jesse's proposal for a "moral offensive" to end the civil war. But Duarte said that Jesse's plan was not new, and Jesse left El Salvador without the cease-fire he had tried to make happen. Then, it was on to Cuba.

The American government has no relations with Castro's Cuba. The rhetoric between the two countries is often harsh. In the presidential race of 1984, it is often asked, "What has Jesse won?" A part of the answer was evident in the way Fidel Castro welcomed him to Cuba. Castro understands that Jesse Jackson has something going that is not likely to end in July at the Democratic Party's national nominating convention.

Jackson left his airport welcome in a dazzling motorcade of shiny black Mercedes sedans. He rode in the special car, the one that also carried the President, Fidel Castro. Later, at the national theater, there was "an artistic evening" in Jesse's honor. He arrived with Castro, but now, there was no hesitation on Jesse's part. Jesse had Castro by the arm, and took him to the area security guards had set, to introduce the Cuban to American journalists.

At night yesterday, the two were to sit down for lengthy talks but even before those began, Jesse said there were "good vibrations" between him and Fidel. He suggested it would be a good idea if President Reagan also met with Castro. Yesterday, Jesse also stopped off at the office the American government has here, an indication Castro was sure to arrange the release of at least some of the prisoners Jesse has asked him to free. The high point, though, is that Fidel and Jesse have linked up. With the style, and the way with words the two of them have, it could be the start of something big.

1984

THE LINK HE HAS MADE with Castro keeps getting stronger. In a light early evening rain, Jesse Jackson came back to Cuba, and Castro had waiting for him a tumultuous welcome.

At Jose Marti Field, the big observation deck was jammed, as it had been for his arrival here on Monday, but this time, thousands more stood below. As soon as he appeared in the doorway of his chartered jet, the noise began.

"Jackson, Jackson," they shouted. "Jesse, Jesse, Jesse Jackson."

At the foot of the ramp to the plane, Fidel Castro was again waiting. The two of them, in political style, moved over to the crowd. In the rain, they moved down the long line. Castro was in his green fatigues, and Jesse, in his safari suit.

Jesse has his own brand of shuttle diplomacy. The things he put into place yesterday were in Nicaragua, and then, he came back here to Cuba to see Castro again.

In Nicaragua, he came away with the Sandinista government agreeing to a summit meeting of government and "legitimate political forces" of Central America and the Caribbean.

The Rev. Jesse Jackson has turned a corner. His run for the presidency is over. He has not said it that way, and he has a lot of unfinished business with the Democratic Party. But the race he made for the nomination -- that's over. It has been said that he won no trophy, that he comes back to the Black community having nothing to hold up and say, "Look, this is what I won."

If nothing else, on the Central American "mission for peace," Jesse won his trophy. He has emerged as an even larger figure, and as he showed earlier in Syria, when he won the release of Lt. Robert Goodman, he can get movement on the world stage. This time it was Central America.

The promise of a summit his shuttle diplomacy won might very well materialize, and it could become the kind of vehicle it takes to bring changes in that region.

In the late afternoon yesterday, as he was about to leave the airport at Managua, the signs of war were all about for him to see. At one point, an army helicopter and then two smaller fighter planes took off. The indication was that a military operation of some sort was under way.

Jesse cut short his stay in Managua. It was to get back to Cuba. He had made a solid link with Fidel Castro. He could not persuade Castro to send the Cuban team to the Olympics in Los Angeles. Cuba still has no relations with the U.S., but Jesse, who is an advocate of a policy that says you talk, no matter what, comes away from Cuba with a victory. He won the release of two groups of prisoners. On his plane back to Washington, he had on board every American who had been held in Cuban jails. Later, another 26 Cuban prisoners were to be freed by Castro, and all that was Jesse's doing. He comes away with all of that. In time, it is the solid link that he has with Castro that could be very important.

1985

MAURICE BISHOP WAS AT THE CENTER of the group that met in the crowded room in the UN two years ago, and he was saying how important it was for his country to have good relations with the United States.

But he said the trouble was with the Reagan administration. "They expect everybody to fall in line," he said.

Bishop had come to New York from Washington and a meeting with high officials of the American government. "We want relations," he said. "We want your ambassador in our country. We want our ambassador here. It's the way to conduct business." He was just 39 then, and in Grenada, a revolution had brought him to power.

Bishop said the problem was, that despite its own history, the U.S. always took a hostile attitude toward governments that took power through revolution.

At the UN in the morning, two days ago, the pictures from the summer of 1983 and the words of Maurice Bishop came back. It had to do with Daniel Ortega, the young president of Nicaragua. You watched Ortega as he came into a room crowded with reporters. As he stood in the bright light, it was the youth in his face that was noticed. He is also just 39, and like Maurice Bishop, was swept to power by a revolution.

"We want peace," Ortega said. "We are extending our hand to the U.S." He said his UN ambassador had gone to the UN secretary general, trying to arrange a meeting for Ortega with President Reagan. But he said there had been no response -- and that was only part of the story. He said his country was being subjected to a policy of genocide by the U.S. When he was questioned, he said American aggression in his country had already taken 11,000 lives and resulted in a $1.5 billion loss to the economy.

On his trip to the U.S. in 1983, Maurice Bishop also made accusations against the American government. He said CIA activity in Grenada was an established fact. He accused the Reagan administration of carrying out a program of economic aggression against his country, putting out damaging propaganda, and actually planning military destabilization.

Bishop went away feeling there had been some progress. "We can return home now feeling that what we came here for has, by and large, been accomplished," he said.

It has not happened that way for Ortega. In the room on the fourth floor of the General Assembly at the UN, he saw no bright side. Only the mounting trouble between the two countries.

Bishop had said he believed Grenada was caught up in the explosive politics of Central America. And he used for proof a TV appearance Reagan had made in which he showed pictures of an airport being constructed in Grenada, supposedly for military use. Bishop disputed that. He said the island was trying to bid for tourism and that was the purpose of the new airport.

But there is another tie. The government that Bishop brought to Grenada was Marxist, and it is the same in Nicaragua now with Ortega.

1989

HIS NAME IS ROBERTO BRYAN. He's 43 years old, married, and the father of a son who is 21 and daughter who is 11. Bryan is a native of Panama. He was 23 when he moved with his family to New York and settled in Brooklyn. In his native Panama, Bryan had worked as a police officer. A year after he came to the United States, he enlisted in the Army. He has 19 years in the military, and in that time, he climbed to about as high a place as an enlisted man can go. Then came the American invasion of Panama. Since then, the life of 1st Sgt. Roberto Bryan has been turned upside down.

Some charge that Bryan has been made a scapegoat for alleged atrocities committed by American troops during the invasion.

U.S. Rep. Charles Rangel yesterday asked officials at the Pentagon to reopen the investigation into court martial charges lodged against Bryan.

At Fort Bragg, N.C., headquarters for the 82 Airborne Division of which Bryan is a member, outrage has been expressed from a lot of quarters for what has happened to the model soldier from New York.

Sgt. Bryan is charged with the premeditated murder of a Panamanian. The surprising part in the story, though, is that the killing occurred in a combat situation. Even more surprising is that in the original investigation, and twice in subsequent reviews, commissioned officers said that no charges should be lodged against Bryan. One colonel even announced his intentions of dismissing the charges, but he got overruled by a lieutenant general. So the case goes forward, and Bryan faces a late August court martial. If convicted, he could face life in prison, or even the death penalty.

"It is an outrage," said Sylvia Ash, Bryan's sister who lives in Brooklyn. "They are making him a scapegoat," said Francisco Bryan, a brother of the accused who also lives in Brooklyn.

Apparently Rep. Rangel agrees. In a letter to Defense Secretary Richard Chaney, Rangel wrote: "I am deeply concerned that in pursuing Sgt. Bryan's court martial without benefit of a thorough investigation of relevant information, the Department of the Army runs the risk of embarking on an unjustified prosecution of an innocent American soldier."

The charges against Bryan stem from an incident that took place last Dec. 23, three days after the invasion was launched. The Army in its court martial accused Bryan of the unlawful killing of a surviving attacker. Some of his fellow soldiers who were there said the shooting was the justified response of an alert sergeant. It happened at a roadblock. A car had been stopped, and when searched, said to contain passengers armed with knives and guns. According to reports, they were ordered out of the vehicle, but before they could be searched, one threw a hidden grenade resulting in several American soldiers being wounded, and one being killed. The incident that led to the murder charges against Bryan happened in the aftermath of that.

Helicopters were summoned to remove the injured. Other soldiers, unhurt, had taken cover. Those taken from the car were believed to be members of Panamanian defense forces, or the enemy for American soldiers. They had been ordered to lie down. The grenade was tossed as those being held were searched. In that moment of confusion, Bryan said he saw another of those on the ground move in a suspicious way. He believed another grenade was about to be tossed. He is fluent in Spanish, and ordered the man down. His order was ignored. Bryan opened fire. Another soldier, Specialist Robert J. Valley, said that he had "taken a bead" on the Panamanian, and said he kept moving after Bryan had order him down. But still, charges were lodged against Bryan.

Lt. Col. Lynn Moore, commander of the 3rd Battalion, investigated and recommended charges be dismissed. Then, Lt. Col. John Woloski was the Article 32 investigating officer looking into the case. He said the facts mitigated against prosecution. After that, Brigade

Commander Jack Nix reviewed the findings and he said there was not sufficient evidence to go to trial. He said he would dismiss all charges. But Col. Nix got overruled by Lt. Gen. James Johnson Jr. So the charges against Sgt. Bryan stand, and the question Rep. Rangel and a lot of others keep asking, is why? The Army doesn't answer.

1990

THE WAY THE VOTE TURNED OUT, the Africans says they got what they wanted. But did they really?

The Americans say they were also pleased with the vote in the Security Council. But who are they kidding?

As for the Soviets, they have so much trouble of their own nowadays that whatever happened in the vote for a new Secretary-General at the United Nations didn't seem to make much difference to them.

Last month, when the UN turned its full attention to the business of electing a successor to retiring Secretary-General Javier Perez de Cuellar, the African states rose up in a way they seldom do. For the top leadership post of the organization, the Africans proclaimed that it was "our turn" and they backed that up with the threat of the kind of fight the UN has never had in electing a Secretary-General.

Usually, the Security Council votes. Once it reaches a consensus, that is tantamount to election. The history is that the General Assembly goes along. But the Africans said, not this time, not if an African is not the choice. The Africans promised that if they were ignored, they would lead a fight in the General Assembly that would be a donnybrook.

The Africans had strong reasons in pushing their position of "it's our turn." They were right; the UN had given its highest office to every section of the world -- every section that is, except Africa. Because the office of Secretary-General is a powerful one, Africans knew what it would mean for their continent to have that office in the hands of one of their own.

The Africans put forth a list of six candidates. "Any one is acceptable to us," they said. But they did have a favorite. They wanted Zimbabwean Finance Minister Bernard Chidzero. There were four other candidates from Black Africa, including, surprisingly, Egyptian Deputy Prime Minister Butros Ghali.

The Africans had such a long list because they didn't want a repeat of what had happened to them the last time they tried to get one of their own elected Secretary-General. That was two terms back, when de Cuellar was elected. The Africans then were solid behind Salim A. Salim of Tanzania. They believed that he was a strong candidate. Almost from the start, he was nixed by the United States and Britain, and that was the end of that. Because the Africans had only one candidate, when Salim failed, they were out.

So this time they came with a list. Along with the "our turn" position, the intention was to prevent anyone from raising the "best qualified" argument. But there was a silent issue. What the Africans desperately wanted was a Secretary-General from Black Africa. And that's what they didn't get.

At the end, and just when it had begun to seem as though Chidzero had it made, Butros Ghali came from far back to win the vote in the Security Council. The Africans had to say they got what they wanted. But not really. They wanted Chidzero; they wanted a Black African. What they got was an Egyptian, but what they know is that Egypt is Africa too. So, they went away from the vote saying they had gotten what they wanted.

With the United States, it was a different story. The Americans were not hot on an African, and they were especially not hot on Chidzero. But the U.S. didn't really have a candidate. For various reasons, the ones they would have liked for the job, stepped away from the competition. The end of the Cold War also figured into it. The Americans were not trying to stop the Russians. That competition is over, and so, the U.S. was left in a "we can live with that" position, when the election fell to Butros Ghali. There is no more talk of a fight before the General Assembly.

The new Secretary-General is 69 years old. It is said the United States would have liked a younger man, someone who would be in more of a position to be looking at two five-year terms. Ghali has standing as being one of Egypt's most able diplomats. He was an important adviser to the late president Anwar Sadat, and now, to President Hosni Mubarak. Ghali had been a strong backer of the Camp David peace agreement. He is a Coptic Christian, not a Muslim, and his wife is Jewish.

Mostly, the edge Ghali has is that he doesn't have enemies. He was virtually nobody's first choice for the job. But after his election, everybody (from the Africans to the Americans) seems to be saying, we can live with that.

1991

EVEN WHEN THE POLICY was being implemented, it caused concern. But Ronald Reagan, who was president then, was riding a high wave of popularity. He did pretty much what he wanted to do and when he took to bashing the United Nations, he didn't get a lot of opposition.

Reagan made himself the point man for the conservatives on the right, angry at UN votes that went against American policy. The strategy agreed on was to get even. That was left for Reagan to do.

For awhile, he was satisfied with UN bashing. In time, though, just that wasn't enough. Reagan's right wing wanted more, and he gave it to them. The decision was made to wreck the organization.

The Republicans hit on a plan they believed would do exactly that. What they agreed to do (with Reagan leading the charge) was to put the UN into oblivion through bankruptcy. That, they believed, would be easy to accomplish.

The United States would simply quit paying. What they knew was that, without American money to support it, the UN soon would be in a bind it would likely find that it could not escape.

All the while he was leading the effort to put the UN out of business, Reagan still had the audacity to show up at every session of the General Assembly, and use the platform for propaganda.

The irony was that it used to be the Soviets who were set on busting the UN, because they didn't like the way it worked. Gorbachev turned his country around; he ordered back payments, and put the Soviet Union on a pay-your-share basis.

In the 1980s, there was a lot the UN could not do. That was because it had Ronald Reagan and Jeane Kirkpatrick, and a lot of others on the right as enemies.

It actually got to a point where American representatives to the UN were inviting the organization to leave the United States. "And we'll be down at the dock to wave goodbye," was the derisive, but official, American comment.

The Reagan policies didn't succeed in putting the UN out of business. Far from it. The UN has flourished. So much so that last week when President Bush spoke before a joint session of the Congress, he talked of the UN in the most flattering way.

"We're now in sight of a United Nations that performs as envisioned by its founders," he said. "We owe much to the outstanding leadership of Secretary General Javier Perez de Cuellar. The United Nations is backing up its words with action."

President Bush got specific. "The Security Council has imposed mandatory economic sanctions on Iraq to relinquish the spoils of its illegal conquest.

The Security Council has also taken the decisive step of authorizing the use of all means necessary to ensure compliance with these sanctions."

The UN has of late been at its best. But that's not because the organization has changed; it because the policies of governments has changed. The UN can only be as good as its members want it to be. When those members stand up to be the best they can be, it makes the UN the best that it can be.

What Reagan did at the UN was wrong. When he didn't get what he wanted, he tried to wreck the organization.

Without an effective UN, the United States might be sitting with its army, and little else, on the Saudi Arabian desert. A lot of the world is there on the American side because of what happened at the UN.

Our past policy, that from Reagan's years, has left the United States in an embarrassing place.

Last week, it had Secretary of State James A. Baker III appearing before the Senate Foreign Relations Committee, and admitting that "we're the biggest deadbeats in paying our dues to the UN." He said that Congress has to make this right, "no matter what it takes." Thanks to Reagan, it'll take close to a billion dollars.

1991

THERE IS ANOTHER PIECE of the Haitian story that has not been told. It goes back more than 200 years; back to the time when a strong and independent America was more a dream than a reality.

It was 1779, and America then was in the midst of the Revolutionary War. What took place that September was a battle that does not get much telling in the history books. This was known as the Siege of Savannah.

The importance of what happened then comes back now. It is a story of what a courageous legion of troops from Haiti did for America.

Little gets said about the battle in Georgia, because, instead of victory, it turned out to be defeat for the French and American forces so one-sided, it bordered on disaster.

Those troops were not just routed by the British; they were very nearly annihilated. And history says that would have happened, had it not been for the Black troops from Saint Domingo, which was what Haiti was called when it was a French colony.

When the battle was over, instead of the Siege of Savannah, the battle became known as "the day Haiti saved the retreating Patriot army."

All this is a part of the history not told. It means something, especially now, for even the government of the United States pretends it owes no debt to Haitians. American policy toward Haiti seems to say: "What have you ever done for us?"

The answer, if the history be told, is that Haitians saved the American army. That happened at a moment so crucial that it may also be said that Haitians played a large role in saving American's chance for victory in its war of independence.

Across America now, the cry from minorities, that is more and more a demand, is for a curriculum of inclusion in the schools. Critics of that idea say minorities want to rewrite history.

That is not the case. Inclusion means being counted in. That's the demand, that stories like what Haitians did for the Americans in 1779, also be given proper recognition in the history taught in public schools.

But largely because of the history not known, the government can make one-sided policies. When Cubans were fleeing the Castro regime, they were on boats on the high seas, as the Haitians are now, trying to make their way to America. For them, the government reached out. They were granted a safe place.

For Haitians, there is another set of rules. The administration ordered the Coast Guard to seek out Haitian boat people and return them to Haiti, knowing many of their lives would be in danger from the ruthless and violent regime that overthrew Haiti's elected democratic government.

Many Americans, though, have not been upset about the treatment accorded Haitians. So American policy was not changed.

Attitudes might be different, though, if Americans knew more of how history links the United States to Haiti. In 1779, when American troops were in full retreat, at the hands of the British in Savannah, the army was saved by what was described as one of the most brilliant and bravest feats ever performed by foreign troops in the American cause. Haitians did that.

These were freed Black people fighting for a country that was to allow the enslavement of Africans for most of another century.

The Haitians who came to America as auxiliary troops with the French were volunteers. What they did ought to be remembered now.

Even if the Bush administration does not want to recognize it, the truth is that we owe the Haitians. At a time of need, they saved the American army.

1992

THE UNITED NATIONS IS ABOUT to see some heated arguments before long, mainly because many UN members are not buying into a key piece of the Bush Administration's New World Order.

The still brewing dispute involves the makeup of the organization's most powerful body, the Security Council. As it now stands, the Security Council comprises 15 members. Among that group, all are not equal. Five countries (the U.S., Britain, France, Russia and China) hold permanent membership. The other 10 seats rotate, with those countries serving terms of two years. Each of the permanent members also holds veto power, enabling any one of them to block any action by the Security Council.

This setup reflects the world of more than 40 years ago. In the fledgling UN, the victors of World War II were accorded special standing, which came in the form of permanent seats on the council. The council's major task is the preservation of world peace. But the world has changed since World War II -- and a growing number of UN members think the Security Council needs to change with it.

The timing of this dissatisfaction has much to do with the end of the Cold War and the collapse of the Soviet Union. Some nations feel that Russia, economically weak, though still a nuclear power, has lost so much of its standing that it no longer merits permanent-member status. Japan, a major economic power, has been bidding for a permanent seat. Germany has openly followed Japan in that quest. In both cases, the Bush administration appears to agree.

But that's not the only thing at stake in the debate. A number of large but poorer countries are saying: What about us? Why shouldn't we have standing as permanent members? That's not quite what Bush had in mind when he dreamed up his New World Order.

The poorer countries are not sitting idle. They, too, are a part of the quiet debate. Brazil, for example, has put forward a plan that would give Germany and Japan permanent seats on the Security Council -- in return for similar status (though without veto power) for Brazil, Egypt and India.

Last October, Ibrahim A. Gambari, Nigeria's ambassador to the UN, said that the case for an African seat on the Security Council was "particularly strong." He pointed out that the UN operates on a regional basis, and that Africa is the only region not represented on the council. "Our case is pressing," Gambari said. "And we are going to make our position, very, very clear."

If Africa is to have representation, Nigeria is the obvious candidate for the seat. It is the most populous country on the continent, and the leading economic power, outside of South Africa. In aaaddition, Nigeria, at present, is involved in six UN peace-keeping operations.

Ambassador Gambari also heads the UN special committee against apartheid and the special committee on peace-keeping operations. So Nigeria hastrong arguments in its bid for a permanent seat.

In three years, the UN will celebrate 50 years of being there trying to make things better in the world. To be as effective as it needs to be in today's world, though, the UN has to undergo some change.

1992

THE LEADER OF THE NAACP has dropped a bombshell. Benjamin Hooks, who heads the largest organization of Blacks in the United States, is urging Black Americans to quit buying Japanese cars.

What Hooks says is important for the NAACP, more than any other Black organization, has the muscle to put meaning behind its words. In all, the organization has more than 1,800 chapters and affiliates and those groups are located not only in most towns and cities but also on campuses, military posts and even in some prisons. So when the leader of the NAACP talks, there is sound reason for listening.

What Hooks has said to the Japanese cannot be ignored.

He is not proposing a boycott. He says he is not engaging in any Japan bashing. In his mind, his "don't buy Japanese automobiles" has to do with jobs and money, more than anything else. Hooks says he has looked at what the Japanese do with regards to Blacks, and what America's Big Three car makers have done. He's decided that it is no contest. He said the Japanese have been reluctant to establish dealerships owned by Blacks. And he also says that the Japanese have shown almost no interest in establishing factories in areas where large numbers of Blacks live. So, his conclusion is that with the Japanese, Blacks do not get a piece of the action. That being the case, his advice to Blacks in the tough times , is quite simple. Hooks says support those who support you.

"The Big Three (Ford, Chrysler and General Motors) have over 140,000 Blacks working for them," Hooks said. "The Big Three are responsible for a tremendous amount of Black middle class employment."

In all of this there is something of a silent issue. That has to do with the attacks on Blacks that have come from those in leadership positions in Japan. A few years ago, Jesse Jackson journeyed to Japan to speak to leaders about what he considered their many anti-Black statements. Demonstrations have been conducted at the Japan embassy in Washington. But until now, no major Black organization has moved to take any significant action against the Japanese.

Hooks insists that is not the NAACP's aim now. He says his suggestion is positive, that in recommending Blacks don't buy Japanese cars, that it is not to get back at the Japanese but rather, to protect the American companies. "We have a stake in seeing to it that the Big Three survive," Hooks says. "For us (Blacks), they represent a lot of jobs."

In a way, the Hooks suggestions breaks a lot of new ground for Blacks. Never has a major Black organization urged Blacks to use their economic clout the way Hooks is doing now. However, in 1968, Martin Luther King Jr. was urged to initiate a boycott if the government failed to respond favorably to his campaign to guarantee an income or a job for all Americans.

But it wasn't King who favored the boycott. That was Jesse Jackson's idea, and it led to some bitter arguments within King's inner circle. All this happened in Atlanta just before King was murdered. He was on his way to Memphis to help some striking city garbage workers. Before he departed Atlanta for Memphis, he held a strategy session for his planned Poor People's Campaign. The issues that led to sharp words and bitter dispute erupted in that meeting.

"Suppose the government doesn't respond," Jesse Jackson argued. "Suppose they run us out of Washington. What is our fall back position going to be?"

King argued that his Poor People's Campaign could not be allowed to fail.

Jackson saw another side. He said that in the event King was ignored by government that Blacks should then use their economic clout. "What we ought to be prepared to do," he said, "is take one of the big car makers and bust them."

Jackson wanted to make Buick the target. "Blacks buy a lot of Buicks," he said. "We ought to make them the target of a boycott if we don't get what we want in Washington."

Back then, those arguments died when King was assassinated shortly after the Atlanta meeting. But now the NAACP brings back the idea of Blacks using their economic clout. And, as in 1968, it has to do with the same issue -- jobs. "To deny a man a job," King said, "is to say that man has no right to exist."

Order Form

Fax Orders: (202) 388-5532 Include Amex, Optima, Discover, Visa or MasterCard information with fax.

Postal Orders: Lioin House Publishing, 1119 Staples Street, N.E., Washington, D.C., 2002-3921

Please add my name to the Lion House mailing list for future books.

Company Name:____

Name:____

Address:____

City:__________________________State:_________Zip:________

Sales Tax:
Please add 5.4% for books shipped to District of Columbia address.

Shipping:
Book Rate: $2.00 for the first book and $1.00 for each additional book.
(Surface Shipping may take three to four weeks)
Air Mail: $3.50 per book.

Payment:
Check
Credit Card: Visa, Mastercard, Optima, Amex, Discover

Card Number:____

Name on card:__________________________Exp. Date______/______

Order Form

Fax Orders: (202) 388-5532 Include Amex, Optima, Discover, Visa or MasterCard information with fax.

Postal Orders: Lioin House Publishing, 1119 Staples Street, N.E., Washington, D.C., 2002-3921

Please add my name to the Lion House mailing list for future books.

Company Name:____

Name:____

Address:____

City:_____________________________State:__________Zip:________

Sales Tax:
Please add 5.4% for books shipped to District of Columbia address.

Shipping:
Book Rate: $2.00 for the first book and $1.00 for each additional book.
(Surface Shipping may take three to four weeks)
Air Mail: $3.50 per book.

Payment:
Check
Credit Card: Visa, Mastercard, Optima, Amex, Discover

Card Number:____

Name on card:_____________________________Exp. Date______/________

Order Form

Fax Orders: (202) 388-5532 Include Amex, Optima, Discover, Visa or MasterCard information with fax.

Postal Orders: Lioin House Publishing, 1119 Staples Street, N.E., Washington, D.C., 2002-3921

Please add my name to the Lion House mailing list for future books.

Company Name:____

Name:____

Address:____

City:_________________________State:________Zip:_______

Sales Tax:
Please add 5.4% for books shipped to District of Columbia address.

Shipping:
Book Rate: $2.00 for the first book and $1.00 for each additional book.
(Surface Shipping may take three to four weeks)
Air Mail: $3.50 per book.

Payment:
Check
Credit Card: Visa, Mastercard, Optima, Amex, Discover

Card Number:____

Name on card:_________________________Exp. Date______/______

Order Form

Fax Orders: (202) 388-5532 Include Amex, Optima, Discover, Visa or MasterCard information with fax.

Postal Orders: Lioin House Publishing, 1119 Staples Street, N.E., Washington, D.C., 2002-3921

Please add my name to the Lion House mailing list for future books.

Company Name:____

Name:____

Address:____

City:_________________________State:________Zip:_______

Sales Tax:
Please add 5.4% for books shipped to District of Columbia address.

Shipping:
Book Rate: $2.00 for the first book and $1.00 for each additional book.
(Surface Shipping may take three to four weeks)
Air Mail: $3.50 per book.

Payment:
Check
Credit Card: Visa, Mastercard, Optima, Amex, Discover

Card Number:____

Name on card:_________________________Exp. Date_____/______

Order Form

Fax Orders: (202) 388-5532 Include Amex, Optima, Discover, Visa or MasterCard information with fax.

Postal Orders: Lioin House Publishing, 1119 Staples Street, N.E., Washington, D.C., 2002-3921

Please add my name to the Lion House mailing list for future books.

Company Name:______________________________

Name:______________________________

Address:______________________________

City:__________________State:__________Zip:__________

Sales Tax:
Please add 5.4% for books shipped to District of Columbia address.

Shipping:
Book Rate: $2.00 for the first book and $1.00 for each additional book.
(Surface Shipping may take three to four weeks)
Air Mail: $3.50 per book.

Payment:
Check
Credit Card: Visa, Mastercard, Optima, Amex, Discover

Card Number:______________________________

Name on card:__________________Exp. Date_______/_______